Deviance, Crime, and Control
Beyond the Straight and Narrow

Deviance, Crime, and Control
Beyond the Straight and Narrow

Lorne Tepperman

OXFORD
UNIVERSITY PRESS

70 Wynford Drive, Don Mills, Ontario M3C 1J9
www.oup.com/ca

Oxford University Press is a department of the University of Oxford.
It furthers the University's objective of excellence in research, scholarship,
and education by publishing worldwide in

Oxford New York
Auckland Cape Town Dar es Salaam Hong Kong Karachi
Kuala Lumpur Madrid Melbourne Mexico City Nairobi
New Delhi Shanghai Taipei Toronto

With offices in
Argentina Austria Brazil Chile Czech Republic France Greece
Guatemala Hungary Italy Japan Poland Portugal Singapore
South Korea Switzerland Thailand Turkey Ukraine Vietnam

Oxford is a trade mark of Oxford University Press
in the UK and in certain other countries

Published in Canada
by Oxford University Press

Library and Archives Canada Cataloguing in Publication

Tepperman, Lorne, 1943–
Deviance, crime, and control : beyond the straight and narrow / Lorne Tepperman.

Includes bibliographical references and index.
ISBN-13: 978-0-19-542952-8. —
ISBN-10: 0-19-541952-9

1. Deviant behavior—Textbooks. I. Title.

HM811.T45 2005   302.5'42   C2005-905026-8

1 2 3 4 - 09 08 07 06

Cover Design: Joan Dempsey/Brett J. Miller
Cover Image: Photodisk Blue/Getty Images

This book is printed on permanent (acid-free) paper ∞.

Printed in Canada

Contents

Preface   xi
Acknowledgments   xvi

Part I Introduction   1

Chapter 1   Sociological Approaches to Deviance   2
                   Learning Objectives   2
                   Introduction   2
                   (1) Functionalism   4
                   (2) Conflict Theories   10
                   (3) The Symbolic Interactionist Approach   19
                   (4) The Feminist Approach   24
                   (5) The Postmodern Approach   30
                   Concluding Words   33
                   Questions for Critical Thought   34
                   Recommended Reading   35
                   Recommended Websites   35

Part II Deviant Activities   37

Chapter 2   Appearance Issues   38
                   Learning Objectives   38
                   Introduction   38
                   Appearance: Its Social Meaning   40
                   The History of Appearance Issues and Public Reaction to Them   42
                   Appearance Communities and Cultures   44
                   Unintended Deviance: Anorexia, Bulimia, and Obesity   47
                   Eating Issues and Appearance Norms   48
                   Theories about Appearance Issues   51
                   Health and Social Consequences of Appearance Issues   56
                   Social Consequences   58

The Role of Families   59

Policies and Theory Applications to Control Appearance Issues   60

Likely Scenarios for Change in Appearance Issues   60

Concluding Words   62

Questions for Critical Thought   64

Recommended Reading   64

Recommended Websites   65

Chapter 3   Mental Illness   66

Learning Objectives   66

Introduction   66

The History of Mental Illness and Public Reaction   67

The Characteristics of Mental Illness and Mentally Ill People   68

Communities and Subcultures of the Mentally Ill   76

Theories about Mental Illness   80

Families, Stress, and Mental Illness   84

Social and Health Consequences of Mental Illness   89

Social Consequences of Mental Illness   90

Policies and Theory Application   93

Likely Scenarios of Change   93

Concluding Words   96

Questions for Critical Thought   98

Recommended Reading   99

Recommended Websites   99

Chapter 4   Sexual Deviance   101

Learning Objectives   101

Introduction   101

Sexual Deviance in Constant Flux   101

Negative Consequences of Deviant Behaviour   102

History of Sexual Deviation and Consequent Public Reactions   105

Prostitution   106

Pornography   115

Other Forms of Sexual Deviation   117

Deviant Communities and Cultures   118

Theories about Sexual Deviance   119

Sociological Approaches   120

Social and Health Consequences of Sexual Deviance   126

Homophobia as a Form of Sexual Deviance   129

Policies and Theory Applications to Control Paraphilia   131

Concluding Words   133

Questions for Critical Thought   134

Recommended Reading   134

Recommended Websites   135

Chapter 5   Substance Abuse   136
             Learning Objectives   136
             Introduction   136
             Intoxication: Its Social Role   137
             The History of Drug and Alcohol Abuse, and Public Reaction   143
             The Activities and Characteristics of Substance Abusers   150
             Drug-using Communities and Cultures   152
             Theories of Drug and Alcohol Abuse   154
             Sociological Theories   154
             Social and Health Consequences of Drug Use   159
             Health Consequences of Alcohol Abuse   160
             Policy and Theory Applications   162
             Decriminalization and Legalization   165
             Concluding Words   167
             Questions for Critical Thought   167
             Recommended Reading   168
             Recommended Websites   169

Part III Delinquency and Crime   171

Chapter 6   Risky Behaviours   172
             Learning Objectives   172
             Introduction   172
             The Work Ethic and the Pleasure Ethic   177
             Adolescent Risk-taking   179
             The Rave Subculture: Tribalism and Risk   182
             The Influence of Family and Peers   183
             The History of Juvenile Delinquency, and Public Reactions to It   187
             The Activities of Juvenile Delinquents   189
             Delinquent Communities and Subcultures   191
             Theories about Juvenile Delinquency   194
             Health and Social Consequences   200
             Policies and Theory Applications   200
             Future Trends   202
             Concluding Words   203
             Questions for Critical Thought   204
             Recommended Reading   204
             Recommended Websites   205

Chapter 7   Violent Crimes   206
             Learning Objectives   206
             Introduction   206
             The History of Violent Crime and Public Reactions to It   208
             Defining Crimes of Violence   211

Social Characteristics of Violent Criminals   213
Violent Communities and Subcultures   215
Patterns of Victimization   217
Family Violence   219
Theories about Violent Crime   223
Sociological Theories   224
Social and Health Consequences of Violent Crime   228
Policies and Theory Applications   231
Concluding Words   232
Questions for Critical Thought   233
Recommended Reading   234
Recommended Websites   235

Chapter 8   Non-violent Crimes   236
Learning Objectives   236
Introduction   236
Internal and External Controls on Criminal Behaviour   237
The Historical Development of Non-violent Crime   239
Demographic and Social Characteristics of Criminals   243
Non-violent Criminal Cultures and Communities   246
Classical Sociological Studies   249
Theories about Non-violent Crime   250
Social and Health Consequences of Non-violent Crime   254
Fear of Crime and Its Consequences   255
Policies and Theory Applications   258
Concluding Words   262
Questions for Critical Thought   265
Recommended Reading   265
Recommended Websites   266

Chapter 9   Political Crimes   267
Learning Objectives   267
Introduction   267
Corruption   269
Resistance   272
Riots and Collective Protests   273
The History of War, Protest, and Public Reactions to It   275
Theories about Protest, Rebellion, and War   278
Sociological Approaches to Protest and War   279
Communities and Subcultures of Protest   284
Social Consequences of Wars and Political Crimes   288
Health Consequences of Terrorism and War   291
Concluding Words   292

Questions for Critical Thought   295
Recommended Reading   296
Recommended Websites   296

References   298
Index   327

I

Loving Shepherd, ever near,
Teach Thy lamb Thy voice to hear;
Suffer not my steps to stray
From the straight and narrow way.

J.E. Leeson,
Hymns & Scenes of Childhood (1842)

II

In his younger gallivantings about places of ill repute,
and his subsequent occasional variations from
the straight and narrow path, he had learned much of the
curious resources of immorality.

T. Dreiser,
Financier (1912)

III

It's only the fear of pregnancy which keeps girls
on the straight and narrow.

F. Weldon,
Praxis (1978)

Preface

Why another book on the sociology of deviance and control? This book uses Canadian examples and is written for a Canadian undergraduate audience by an author with a lot of experience in explaining complicated ideas in simple ways. It discusses a wide variety of topics in the area of deviance and pays particular attention to the health and social consequences of deviance and control. The book is short and can be used, with appropriate add-ons, in a one- or two-term course, in a university or community college.

Deviance, Crime, and Control: Beyond the Straight and Narrow proceeds from the assumption that both deviance and conformity are normal *and* socially constructed. Social order is an ongoing accomplishment. The mere existence of the idea of *deviance,* and the 'discovery' of deviance in our midst, tells us about a society's degree of cohesion, tolerance, and control over individuals. Thus, this book is ultimately about social organization and sociology's most central concerns—social structure, how it arises, and how it is preserved. In this respect, the book is a logical second introduction to the field of sociology.

Deviance and conformity are universal. Likely, people have always been different and they have always changed over time. These are (more or less) demonstrable facts about humanity that can be documented with historical and anthropological data. The struggle to achieve stable uniformity—an absence of deviance—is an unending effort that can never succeed and never has succeeded. The benchmarks for what constitutes deviance are constantly changing, as are the limits of tolerable difference. Moreover, they vary both over time and from one place to another.

Thus, deviance is the reciprocal of social order, or what sociologists usually call 'social structure'. It is the failure to make everyone behave the same way in a given situation, or to cause people to change in expected ways as they pass from one situation to another. 'Deviance' by this reckoning is less the breakdown or moral lapse of particular individuals than it is the failure of social controls to enforce an unattainable degree of conformity. From this standpoint, the making and enforcement of social norms and rules is a central problem of sociology. It dwells on questions such as: Why do we make the rules we do and enforce them more or less loosely? Equivalently, why do we make the laws we do and enforce them more or less loosely?

Viewed from a conflict perspective, the enforcement of laws and norms is merely the exercise of power by socially dominant groups. Thus, changes in norms, laws, and rule enforcement reflect changes in the interests of the dominant social groups and their need to control certain kinds of behaviour. What constitutes deviance and crime will differ from a feudal agricultural society to a corporate capitalist society because there are different ruling classes, different possibilities for deviance and crime, and different interests at stake.

Once we pass from the realm of norms to that of laws, and from informal control to formal control, we pass into the domain of criminology. Criminology is concerned with why people act in ways that are perceived to be criminal, and why society and its agents of control respond to 'crimes' as they do. In this way, criminology becomes a subtype of the sociology of deviance, and the sociology of deviance a subtype of general sociology, which asks: What maintains social order? How is a society (or community, or group) possible? What negotiations are needed between individuals and their communities to create and maintain a social structure?

However, this is *not* a criminology textbook. It is much more general than that and views crime as only one species of deviant behaviour among many. The reader is advised to consult a book more specifically focused on crime and delinquency for detailed facts and theories about these behaviours.

As for outcomes, we sociologists are bound to ask: What price do individual members of society pay—in terms of control and repression—to be accepted as members of society? What are the costs in health and happiness of conforming to the rules? What are the costs of breaking them? How do we get the kind of society we want to live in—where we are secure but respectful of differences—and are we moving in that general direction?

What, then, makes this book distinctive? First, *Deviance, Crime, and Control* examines a variety of forms of deviance and conformity against the backdrop of the questions: Why do some societies require some kinds of behaviour, while other societies do not? How do socially required behaviours change over time? What social changes produce what kinds of change in the behaviours we require and the strictness with which we enforce our rules? Thus, in this book we keep the historical context in mind as we look at contemporary notions of right and wrong, deviant and conforming behaviour. The types of deviance we examine include risky delinquent behaviours, deviant forms of appearance, substance abuse, sexual deviance, mental illness, violent crimes, non-violent crimes, and political crimes (some of which are violent, some non-violent).

Second, *Deviance, Crime, and Control* takes a broadly theoretical approach. It attempts to link theories and facts about deviance to broader sociological issues about social organization, social control, cultural change, and social inequality. In these respects, the book is a logical extension of what students learn in their Introduction to Sociology course. As in that course, theories of deviance and control are organized into five main paradigms or approaches—functionalist, conflict, social constructionist (symbolic interactionist), feminist, and postmodern. This book shows how each approach makes a valuable contribution to understanding varieties of deviance and control, and emphasizes that they are all useful. They serve, as needed, as the philosophical backdrop against which we examine 'middle-range' theories about deviance, crime, and control.

Finally, this book puts a premium on learning aids: boxes, chapter overviews and summaries, discussion questions, and recommended readings and websites. *Deviance, Crime, and Control* brings its knowledge to the reader in a way that is most effective, making its points clearly, concisely, and in ways that students can readily grasp.

Organization of the Book

Deviance, Crime, and Control comprises nine chapters. After a general chapter outling the five theoretical approaches or paradigms of sociology—functionalist, conflict, symbolic interactionist, feminist, and postmodern—chapters follow on common and general types of deviance (risky delinquent behaviours, appearance issues), on slightly less common and more specific types of deviance (sexual deviance, mental illness, substance abuse), and finally on crime (violent, non-violent, and political).

The chapters are loosely organized according to the 'seriousness' of the impact of a deviant act and its harmful impact on society. Thus, Chapters 2 through 5 are about deviant acts that do *not* break the law; Chapters 6 through 9 are about delinquent and criminal acts that do. Chapter 6 is about delinquent behaviours while Chapters 7 through 9 are about criminal behaviours. Chapters 6 and 7 are about crimes that arguably hurt the fewest people in the least hurtful way, and Chapters 8 and 9 are about (violent) crimes that hurt a few people most extremely or (political) crimes that hurt many people less extremely.

In these respects, the book is organized something along the lines of John Hagan's classic deviance book that begins with social diversions (what he calls 'disreputable pleasures') and moves on to social deviations and serious crimes. Although the first of these acts—social diversions—are least serious, they are also the most common. By contrast, the last of these acts are the most serious but, happily, also the least common.

Each chapter is organized in roughly the same way. First comes a discussion of the background of a problem: the nature of the activity or behaviour in question (e.g., drug abuse) and public reactions to it. This is followed by a brief history of the activity. The largest part of the chapter is taken up with a discussion of the current situation. This includes the demographic and social characteristics of people in this domain, theories about this activity (according to the five paradigms of sociology), social and health consequences of the activity, and policies and theory applications to control this activity. The chapter ends with a brief discussion of future prospects: likely scenarios for change in this activity domain, concluding comments, and a chapter summary. However, chapters vary somewhat in their organization and coverage of these issues. We allow the book to wander into interesting related issues, when warranted.

Sociological versus other explanations

The topics of deviance, crime, and control are not the exclusive domain of sociologists. In fact, both the natural and the social sciences have contributed their own unique understandings and perspectives to the study of deviance and control.

It is important for the student of sociology (and of any other academic field) to note that where truth finding is concerned, disciplines need not be in competition with each other. For example, the contributions made by psychologists are not 'right' and those by anthropologists 'wrong'; both are correct, according to their own designs and self-imposed limitations. Each approach can further our understanding of the problems we are considering. The study of deviance and control is best understood as a complementary, multilevelled co-operative action in which the findings of one field or discipline corroborate or elaborate upon the research and theories of the others. This is not to suggest an absence of conflicting data or results in areas of study. The contradictory findings likely signify a flaw in one or another theory, calling for closer scrutiny and further refinement of theory.

That said, in this book we focus on sociological explanations of deviance and crime. No biological explanations are presented and the treatment of psychological explanations is brief. We also introduce public (or population) health approaches that, we think, enhance the sociological approaches. Because the size of this book is small and the scope large, we maintain a clear focus on what concerns us most centrally, namely, the role of social factors in deviance and control. Psychological explanations are of interest since they often enter into sociological explanations, with a few significant differences.

Psychological perspectives centre on individuals. They are concerned mainly with cognitive and perceptual processes. Much of psychology's contribution to the understanding of deviance has come from social psychologists who study the ways in which social and mental forces determine action. Social psychologists distinguish themselves conceptually from sociologists by limiting their research to the thought processes and personality characteristics of individuals as they are influenced by and represented in a social context. For example, a social-psychological approach to the Holocaust might focus on how a charismatic authority can create unwavering obedience among subordinates as a way of explaining why Nazi soldiers would carry out the atrocities ordered by Adolf Hitler against the Jews in the concentration camps.

Notice how this perspective emphasizes the individual soldier and his cognitive processes rather than the entire National Socialist (Nazi) party as a social group or the political ideology of German society. In practice, however, social psychological and sociological approaches often overlap.

Population health perspectives

As noted earlier, this book pays particular attention to the health consequences of deviance and control. Increasingly, social scientists are noting that good health is one of our society's chief concerns. Additionally, health condition is a useful criterion for evaluating the success or failure of various social arrangements. This approach is new in the study of deviance (also, crime and control) and we believe it helps us to more clearly understand the social significance of deviance and its impact.

Increasingly, social scientists have noted that many social problems, including some forms of deviance (e.g., drug abuse) and crime, are associated with health consequences. From these observations has emerged the *population health perspective,* a broad approach to health whose goals are to improve the health of the entire population and to reduce health inequalities between social groups. According to this perspective, health includes not only the traditional genetic or biological foundations, but also socioeconomic, environmental, material, cultural, psychosocial, and health system characteristics (Starfield, 2001). As a Health Canada study states, 'These factors, referred to as "determinants of health", include income and social factors, social support networks, education, employment, working and living conditions, physical environments, social environments, biology and genetic endowment, personal health practices, coping skills, healthy child development, health services, gender and culture' (Health Canada, 2001c).

Ideally, they would also include factors such as 'mental and social well-being, quality of life, life satisfaction, income, employment and working conditions, education and other factors known to influence health' (Health Canada, 2001c).

Because of complex interactions among the determinants of health, the population health perspective employs a multidisciplinary approach to theory and research, combining insights from a variety of government divisions, such as health, justice, education, social services, finance, agriculture, and environment, along with input from academic fields such as medicine, social work, psychology, cultural anthropology, and sociology.

This book takes as the proper criteria for the study of deviance the effects that social conditions have on the overall physical and mental health of the population. The first is that health consequences can be more easily measured than some other criteria being used in the study of social problems.

Solutions to problems of deviance and crime

Each chapter in this book contains a section on solutions to the problems under discussion, solutions that have been tried with varying degrees of vigour and success in Canada. These are solutions that individuals, groups, and organizations are using to address the problems, or solutions that should be undertaken to address them. For the time being, let's be careful to attend to solutions of two broad types: *individual solutions* and *groups-based or organization-based solutions.* We will see examples of many of each of these types of solutions as we move through the chapters that follow.

C. Wright Mills's (1959) point in describing 'the sociological imagination' in the way he did was that 'knowledge can be power'—if individuals choose to act upon it. That is to say, when we know what is going on in society then act accordingly and in our best interests, we stand some chance of maximizing our opportunities. Under individual-level solutions, we can act to 'work the system' to our benefit.

The analyses to come will indicate that dominant groups often oppose certain solutions to certain social problems because they are not particularly in their interests. As Marx and Max Weber, along with other scholars, have emphasized, such groups will have considerable organizational and ideological power. However, political struggles can be won. In Canada and the United States alone, there are many examples of successful protest movements by subordinate groups: the civil rights movement in the United States, the Quiet Revolution in Quebec, and the women's movement in both countries, to name only three. Another important example is the success of the labour movement in Canada and the United States, fighting over many decades to secure better wages and job conditions for the working class.

We will have occasions to discuss many such group-based strategies for solving social problems, including many initiated by government agencies. Such developments should give us heart concerning the possibilities of political action to resolve social problems. Many problems are formidable, but there is room to effect change.

A book of ideas

For various reasons, this is not primarily a fact book or almanac about crime and deviance—it is a theory book, a book of ideas about deviance and control, and the reasons people conform or do not conform. This approach reflects the view that we need to examine the basic ideas before we can make good use of facts. Second, it is an attempt to distinguish social science from journalism, which is heavy with current facts and light on ideas. Third, it reflects the fact that this is a book; facts change quickly, while ideas (and books) do not.

Finally, and equally important, for reasons that will become amply clear in the course of this book, we do not have good estimates, let alone secure facts, about many—perhaps, most—of the deviant behaviours discussed in this book. For example, estimates would vary widely on how many homosexuals, sex workers, delinquents, mentally ill people, drug users, obese people, or anorexics there are in Canada. Our figures on criminals of various kinds would be somewhat more precise, but they would be incomplete and flawed too.

Typically, facts about deviant acts and actors come from sources that are each flawed and may not agree. These are self-reports of deviant behaviour, victimization reports, and institutional reports (e.g., reports by hospitals, police forces, courts, prisons, and so on). Self-reports suffer from falsification: people often lie about themselves to seem better or worse than they actually are, or because they cannot always remember what they have done. Victimization reports also suffer from exaggeration and forgetting. Beyond that, many kinds of deviance—for example, drug abuse, obesity, or unsafe sex—do not have 'victims' other than the actor him- or herself. Finally, institutional reports describe only the deviants who have been apprehended by the institution—arrested, tried, convicted, and so on. Often, this represents only a small fraction of the entire deviant population.

So, in most instances, we have a very incomplete and imperfect knowledge of the numbers and characteristics of deviant people and their actions, let alone the reasons for their actions. However, we do have a good set of sociological questions and debates, and interesting speculation about the answers. This book is about what we do have.

Acknowledgments

This book took about two years to write, and I have learned a lot from the exercise. Many people have helped to make this book what it is now.

Megan Mueller, then-editor at Oxford, encouraged me to write a longer version of this book. I started out in the summer of 2003 with the assistance of a bright undergraduate, Maria Karasyova, who—under my supervision—researched and drafted chunks of chapters. Unfortunately, for health reasons, Maria had to leave her work unfinished.

I worked on completing and revising a draft of the book during the 2003–4 academic year, with the able assistance of undergraduates Evan Kazolis, Erik Landriault, Weeda Mehran, Victrine Tseung, and Michelle Wong. They critiqued what I had written and drafted learning aids for the book. I wrote a shorter, tighter draft of the book and used chunks of it in my two summer courses—Introduction to Sociology and Families and Health—during the summer of 2004. Then, I asked students to critique the chapters and improve them. Their response was interesting and mostly useful.

Over the summer I continued to revise the book, with the help of valuable criticism from Bill O'Grady (Guelph), Vince Sacco (Queen's), and anonymous reviewers commissioned by Lisa Meschino at Oxford. Since the summer, I have further revised the manuscript, with the able help and criticism of this year's crew of undergraduates, consisting of Monica Beron, Maygan Jorge, Erik Landriault, Aileen Lin, Weeda Mehran, Ruxandra Popescu, Kara Serebrin, and Joseph Tesoro—perhaps the best group of undergraduates I have ever worked with. Undergraduates Federica Genovese and Pamela Osorio read through the book one more time to suggest final changes. Months later Wen Xiao painstakingly combed the page proofs, leading to even more changes.

I continued to use the book in my small, first-year seminar during 2004–5, even while continuing to revise it. Getting the reaction of students fresh out of high school has been helpful. I am grateful they find the book interesting and clearly written. Having such bright, energetic undergraduates around makes the University of Toronto a wonderful place to work in; so I thank my assistants and students for all their help and stimulation.

In December 2004 the book went into the able hands of developmental editor Marta Tomins. Phyllis Wilson, managing editor, and Jessica Coffey provided meticulous copyediting in the last stages of production. As always I have been tremendously gratified by the support and professionalism of the people at Oxford University Press. They have made writing and publishing this book almost easy. So, I share credit with my helpers and advisors for what is good about this book; but as usual, I take responsibility for what I have failed to do well or do at all. Perhaps these flaws can be remedied in a later edition. I will look forward to receiving advice from my readers.

PART I

INTRODUCTION

CHAPTER 1

Sociological Approaches to Deviance

LEARNING OBJECTIVES
- To identify the five major paradigms of sociology
- To examine the major approaches to deviance and control
- To trace variations of thinking within each paradigm
- To discuss the major concepts in the field of deviance
- To consider debates within and between the paradigms
- To describe key theorists in the field of deviance and control

---

Introduction

This book is about deviant behaviour—behaviour that breaks rules and/or violates people's expectations. The behaviour we discuss in this book violates appearance norms, abuses chemical substances, breaks laws, takes risks, disrupts social occasions, or otherwise violates the rules. The rules these behaviours violate may be formal—like laws—or informal, like social norms and social (role) expectations.

When sociologists study social behaviour, we take into account history, geography, economics, politics, and culture, among other things. Accordingly, we sociologists cannot understand crime and deviance without understanding the political system, the economy, family life, and so on. As you learned in your introductory course, sociologists also approach issues from varying viewpoints. In fact, when we analyze reality, sociologists use five different 'paradigms': functionalism, conflict theory, symbolic interactionism, the feminist approach, and the postmodern approach. Each contributes to

a fuller understanding of deviance, crime, control, and conformity. Our approach here is intended to help students connect new materials on deviance to familiar materials from their introductory sociology course, where the main 'five paradigms' were systematically examined. Table 1.1 outlines the key elements of the five sociological paradigms that we will be looking at.

Despite the variation between approaches, all sociological approaches to deviance are different from psychological approaches, as we will see repeatedly in chapters that follow. Key to understanding this difference is the role of the 'three C's'—career, community, and culture (or subculture)—in sociological approaches to deviance and control. These three C's are essential features of *social structure*—the central concern of sociology as a discipline. They offer sociologists a particular way of thinking about deviance and control. So, while psychologists of deviance are thinking about personalities and psychopathologies, sociologists are thinking about careers, communities, and cultures.

Table 1.1 Five Main Sociological Paradigms

Functionalism

- Elements in society are interconnected and interrelated
- Crime strengthens social cohesion
- Crime renews commitment to social boundaries

Conflict Theories

- Conflict and change are basic features of social life
- Crime is a response to conflict, changes, and inequality
- Holds criminals responsible for their own misfortunes
- Notions of 'deviance' and 'crime' created to impose and justify control exercised in the interest of the powerful

Symbolic Interactionist Approach

- Society is a product of continuous face-to-face interaction
- Deviance is a social accomplishment and rarely practised solo
- Socialization and labelling shape identities of offenders
- Socialization and labelling stabilize their criminal activities

Feminist Approach

- Focus on gendering and gender inequality
- Society has a history of androcentric sociological thinking
- Interaction of gender with other victimizing social characteristics produce particular combinations of disadvantage
- Emphasizes gendered nature of both deviance and control

Postmodern Approach

- Power is exercised through the use of knowledge
- Modern societies are under constant surveillance by those in authority
- Standards of normality are used to judge and coerce
- Every modern institution exercises power in this way

'Careers' are sequences of activities that characterize a person's life course. Most people have educational careers and occupational careers; and sociologists argue that some people also have deviant or criminal careers. Often, people who live in different communities develop their own 'cultures', or at least subcultures; and people leading deviant lives do so too. 'Cultures' are sets of ideas, beliefs, practices, and values that members of a group tend to share. Common activities and values form the basis for communities—shared sentiments and identities. Equally, communal inter-actions support the creation and maintenance of shared values—in this case, deviant values.

This book is organized in a unique but helpful way. In the chapters that follow, we will see that all five sociological paradigms address the issues of career, community, and culture in explaining deviance and control. In every chapter you will find discussions of deviant communities, careers, and cultures. However, these concepts will have different degrees of importance in different chapters. After all, it is easy to identify a career in organized crime, but harder to identify a career in treason; it's easy to identify a community (or culture) of lesbians, but hard to identify a community (or culture) of embezzlers.

This book also groups theories in a somewhat unorthodox way, so that the material links more easily to what you studied in introductory sociology. As a result, some of the groupings are unlike what you might find in other deviance textbooks. For example, the theory chapters in a highly respected textbook on deviance and crime by Liska and Messner (1999) are titled: (2) The structural/functional perspective, (3) Ecological perspectives: Social disorganization, control and learning processes, (4) The rational choice / deterrence perspective, (5) The labeling perspective, (6) The constructionist perspective, and (7) The conflict perspective. Our grouping, into five main paradigms of sociology, is different from this but also reasonable, as you may agree in the end.

Note, finally, that this book is about both deviance and crime. The study of non-criminal deviance helps us better understand criminal behaviour, by helping us see both deviance and crime as the products of social beliefs and institutional efforts to exercise control.

(1) Functionalism

The first approach we will discuss, functionalism, has a long history. Functionalism (sometimes called 'structural functionalism') began about two centuries ago in the writings of early social philosophers.

From the nineteenth century onward, social thinkers were interested in the way that various elements of a society are interconnected and interdependent. The result of this thinking is what we call functionalism. Functionalism in sociology was inspired by one of sociology's founders, Emile Durkheim (1938). He was fascinated by the effects of rapid social change on social integration and conflict. Social change poses a problem for functionalists, who look at society as a social system—a set of components or structures organized in an orderly way and integrated to form a whole. According to functionalism, each social system has certain basic needs that a society, community, or group of people must meet if it is going to continue to survive. The various interdependent structures in a social system exist to fulfill one or more of these needs. Why a system changes, then, is a mystery for functionalists from Durkheim onward.

Durkheim attacked this mystery head-on, both by studying the causes of change—such as the increasing division of labour—and the consequences of change—such as the suicide rate. He insisted that we can never fully understand behaviour if we concentrate on the psychology of isolated individuals. In his early classic work, *Suicide*, Durkheim argues that we learn nothing about the causes of suicide by studying individuals who may be ignorant of the causes of their own behaviour. Changes in the whole society explain the behaviour of individuals. We must learn the laws of societies, and of social life, to understand the behaviour of individuals, he believed.

Another early functionalist work was Emile Durkheim's essay on the 'normality of crime'. It is typical of functionalists, like Durkheim, to label universal features of social life (like crime) 'normal' and look for contributions they make to the social order. Other interesting examples of this tendency are the functional theory of social stratification by Kingsley Davis and Wilbert Moore (1945), and the functional theory of prostitution by Kingsley Davis (1937).

Durkheim argued that crime is 'normal' in several senses. First, it is universal and inevitable, no matter the society or its laws. As American sociologist Kai Erikson (1966) later showed in a clever study of seventeenth-century Massachusetts Puritans, even saintly, god-fearing people manage to find rule-breakers in their midst. Second, by transgressing social boundaries, crime—and deviance more generally—helps to renew commitment to those boundaries. These violations bring people together in outrage, and in this sense, crime strengthens social cohesion. Even more, the punishment of crime strengthens cohesion and reminds people of the need to obey social rules.

Thus, for functionalists, deviance and crime demonstrate the need for social order; punishment is the effort a society makes to protect that order. At the same time, every society changes and, often, what is considered deviant or criminal at one time is deemed acceptable later on. Therefore, crime and deviance are sometimes forms of dissent and harbingers of necessary social change.

Partly because of the early influence of anthropology, functionalist researchers from Durkheim onward have ignored historical evidence, and looked instead at the interconnection among social institutions. This ahistorical tendency gave rise to the study of 'social morphology'—the study of timeless social forms, and 'social ecology'—the spatial relationship of timeless social forms. The ecology of crime and deviance became very important in early twentieth-century American sociology. At the University of Chicago, for example, sociologists nearly a century ago applied functionalism to studying city life and, particularly, the ways city communities differ from one another. Something about the settlement of large cities produced different kinds of neighbourhoods with different risks of social problems, they argued. It may have been due to spatial location, population composition, the rapid turnover of inhabitants, or otherwise.

In addition, functionalism adopted ideas from the natural sciences that they hoped could be applied to the social world with as much success as the natural sciences enjoyed at that time. For instance, functionalists applied the model of an organism to society. They asserted that each institution has a function to perform in society, much as each body part has a function to perform in maintaining a healthy body. Working together like a body's organs, social institutions work together to achieve balance or equilibrium. Within this functionalist perspective, Durkheim explained how crime and deviance can be explained as either

evidence of poor functioning (e.g., when anomie results from social change) or good functioning (e.g., when crime strengthens social boundaries).

Chicago sociologists, for their part, spent the 1920s to the 1940s studying rates of crime and deviance in different Chicago neighbourhoods, trying to relate these rates to important 'features' of the neighbourhood. Some compared statistics from different neighbourhoods. Others developed ethnographic (observational) strategies for studying neighbourhoods, communities, and groups with interesting social patterns.

Throughout the 1950s and 1960s, functionalism remained the dominant approach in North American sociology. At Harvard University, sociologist Talcott Parsons (1951) formalized the ideas underlying functionalist theories of society, grappling with the notions of 'functional requirements' of society and the reasons for societal change. He argued that societies, to survive, must adapt to the material environment, establish social goals, resolve conflicts, and teach the dominant values. Value consensus is particularly important because social equilibrium rests on consensus. Failure to satisfy functional requirements, or achieve consensus, loosens people from their social and psychological moorings.

Usually, according to functionalists, people play their learned, necessary social roles in all of a society's key institutions. This reproduces social life and it keeps individuals socially stable and mentally healthy (the two go together, in Durkheim's theory). In turn, these social institutions—families, the economy, government, education, and others—each make a vital contribution to the survival of society. Family, for instance, functions to reproduce and nurture members of society, while the economy functions to regulate the production, distribution, and consumption of goods and services among the people.

Sudden social, cultural, political, or economic shifts disrupt traditional norms and values. Signs of alienation and social disorganization multiply. Often, such sudden change gives rise to deviant behaviours like suicide, mental illness, or drunkenness, among other things.

When social norms are weakened, cohesion diminishes and deviant behaviour increases. Durkheim's 'anomie theory' argues that when rapid changes make norms and values weak or unclear, the result is 'anomie'—or 'normlessness'. People are not tethered to the social order as securely as usual. By creating ambiguous social rules, anomie releases people from the normal controls on their behaviour. Durkheim uses this theory to explain the rise of suicide rates during periods of rapid social change in France, but later functionalists used it to explain other types of deviant, delinquent and criminal behaviour.

Sociologists drew a similar conclusion about immigrants to North American cities in the early-twentieth century, explaining the delinquency of immigrant children in terms of normative breakdown. Similar principles can be applied to understanding the problem of addictions among North America's Aboriginal people. Some functionalists believe that social and cultural disorganization—a result of conquest, colonization, neglect, and abuse—account for the problems of substance abuse among Aboriginal people.

However, macrosociological theories of deviance are inadequate by themselves. Disorganization theories may explain why rapid change predisposes *some* groups to deviance or crime, but they are largely silent on the reasons why only *some* members of those groups become criminals. Here a microsociological functionalist theory is helpful: Travis Hirschi's (1969) 'social bond theory'. Hirschi argues that strong social bonds keep most people from succumbing to the temptation to engage in criminal activities. These bonds, including a variety of involvements and attachments, keep most people from giving in to deviant urges most of the time. Durkheim, setting the stage for this theory, noted (for example) that married people are less likely to commit suicide than single people—presumably because their social bonds give life meaning and control urges.

Thus, from a functionalist perspective, the conditions for deviant behaviour include both social disorganization and inadequate attachment. However, functionalists also recognize that people react to anomie, disorganization, and detachment in a variety of ways. They wondered then: how many ways are there to respond, and how do (all of) these responses contribute to social stability? American sociologist Robert Merton's (1957 [1938]) 'anomie theory', sometimes called 'strain theory', is an attempt to answer these questions. It holds that crime increases—as do other forms of deviance—when the social structure prevents people from achieving culturally defined goals (e.g., getting money) through legitimate means (e.g., through a job). He called this gap between goals and means 'anomie', after Durkheim's concept.

Merton believed that it is not a sudden social change that causes deviance, as Durkheim believed, but rather the persisting social structural gap that pushes people to break rules. Few people are able to follow *both* the cultural rules and the social norms for achieving them: most people are caught in a permanent conflict. People adapt to this strain in different ways.

To explain why some people are deviant while others are not, Merton describes five processes an individual may follow when adapting to strain. These include: Conformity, Innovation, Ritualism, Retreatism, and Rebellion. An individual who conforms accepts both the goals and the means for achieving culturally acceptable goals. An individual who innovates accepts the goals but not the means for achieving these goals. For example, drug dealers may accept materialist values but not through conventional education. Ritualists reject the goals but accept the means. Retreatists reject both the goals and the means. Lastly, rebels not only reject both the goals and means, but substitute the rejected goals with another set of goals.

Merton's theory comes up repeatedly throughout this book in explanations of various deviant and criminal behaviours. The important part to remember is that, according to Merton: (1) strain is normal and inescapable, (2) the adaptations to strain are normal and inescapable, and (3) these adaptations make possible the persistence of an unequal, acquisitive society. Thus, crime and deviance are normal, even necessary.

Merton's theory has been criticized from many angles. For example, Featherstone and Deflem (2000) argue that Merton has presented two, not always clearly differentiated, theories in his seminal paper 'Social Structure and Anomie' (1938): a strain theory and an anomie theory. Although structural strain—owing to unequal social opportunities—is one way to explain why deviance occurs in the context of anomie, it is not the only way. There are other causes of crime and deviance. Additionally, anomie theory is compatible with several other theories of crime and delinquency. For example, Merton's deviance theory can be related to theories of rational choice and social conditioning, and we will discuss these in connection with conflict theories, in a later part of this chapter.

That said, Merton's anomie theory is the most commonly cited theory in the field of crime and deviance—perhaps, in all of sociology. It cleverly combines a great many social causes and effects in a tidy parcel. As a result, sociologists have made as many efforts to refine and improve this interesting functionalist theory as they have to discard it.

Agnew (2001), for example, is well known as a developer of strain theory. He claims that strains are most likely to result in crime when they (1) are seen as unjust, (2) are seen as high in magnitude, (3) are associated with low social control, and (4) create some pressure or incentive to engage in criminal coping.

Merton's theory has been particularly valuable in the study of delinquent behaviour. For example, sociologist Albert Cohen (1955) modified Merton's strain theory by combining it with the idea of 'status frustration', not unlike the notion of 'relative deprivation'. Soon after, Richard Cloward and Lloyd Ohlin (1960) extended Merton's theory by developing the idea of 'differential illegitimate opportunity'. They agreed with Merton that people are driven to deviance in circumstances where success goals are emphasized but the legitimate means of attaining these goals are severely restricted. However, Ohlin and Cloward also point out that many poor people not only lack access to socially legitimate ways of attaining the desired goals, they may also lack access to illegitimate ways of attaining these goals. Thus, in studying crime and deviance, we have to look at both kinds of opportunity structure: law-abiding and criminal.

Delinquent behaviours, according to Cloward and Ohlin, flourish among poor people when illegitimate opportunities for success are more readily available than legitimate opportunities for success. Often, these behaviours support criminal subcultures. In turn, the types of criminal subculture that flourish—in the form of gangs—depend on the area in which they develop. For example, 'criminal gangs' emerge in areas where unconventional values of behaviour are closely tied to business opportunities. This type of gang is more stable than other gangs: it has clear goals and is well integrated with the community. Another type of gang, 'the conflict or violent gang', is much less integrated into professional crime. Its lack of criminal organization results in instability. Members of these gangs are double failures and often retreat into a world of sex, drugs, and alcohol.

Networks and conformity

As we have seen, the notion of social (dis)organization, like (dis)equilibrium, is central to functionalist thinking. Villarreal (2002) provides a subtle conception of 'social disorganization' by focusing specifically on relationships of political and social patronage. He argues that in societies characterized by the presence of patronage networks, social and political changes that undermine the exchange relations between actors at different levels in the social hierarchy result in a loss of social control and an increase in crime.

This is because people conform to social rules as long as conformity provides the rewards they value. When these rewards stop, people re-evaluate conformity. People deviate because conforming to the old rules no longer benefits them. This style of explanation, while related to the rational choice model we will discuss later in this chapter, focuses attention on the *structure or network of informal relationships* that control people's behaviour. When the social structure becomes unbalanced or unpredictable, deviance increases.

Functionalists believe that people behave properly when they develop a 'stake in conformity', thinking they will benefit, or at least avoid punishment, by doing so. As people get older and establish long-term social relationships with friends, spouses, children, neighbours, and workmates, they find themselves locked into networks of reciprocal obligation. Their networks reward conformity and punish deviance with exclusion, shame, or contempt. People continue to conform because they want and need the rewards conformity brings, and fear or dislike the punishments for deviance. They feel secure and socially connected. If their social networks break down, so do their motives for conforming.

Generally, larger social networks are better than small ones, and open networks of 'weak ties' may be better than closed networks of 'strong ties' (Granovetter, 1975). Stable social bonds in large, open networks are beneficial to individuals, and to society as a whole, from this standpoint: they bring rewards for conformity to a larger number of people. And since social networks change slowly, tendencies to conformity and deviance also change slowly.

As a result, just as people can get locked into conformity, so other people can get locked into deviant or criminal 'careers'. The research of Sampson and Laub (2002) shows that a process of cumulative disadvantage causes long-term stability in deviant behaviour. Early involvement in crime weakens social bonds to significant others and conventional institutions. The failure, early in life, to build social networks outside crime keeps people stuck in a criminal lifestyle.

Morality and self-control

Functional theorists are also interested in the ways that people internalize morality and 'control themselves'—that is, keep themselves from breaking the rules. Swiss psychologist Jean Piaget (1932) was a pioneer in studying the development of morality in children. In an early publication he discussed the way children think about social norms by asking them to discuss a game of marbles. He studied their moral thinking by telling them stories and asking them for comments. What he found is that children are not born to obey rules—they develop this obedience gradually.

Among children aged about four to eight years old, Piaget found what he called heteronomous morality—a respect for adult authority. Behaviour is 'wrong' if the children have seen adults punish or threaten to punish it. Young children consider adult rules and moral values absolute and unchangeable. As a result, they favour punishing rule-breakers severely. Among older children, however, Piaget found that autonomous morality prevails. Older children have already begun to think about and follow their own rules of conduct. They see rules as products of group agreement that promote cooperation within the group.

Thus, as they age, people internalize moral rules—make them their own. What's more, internal moral controls are superior to external controls. People with internal controls behave more predictably and consistently. Accordingly, parents are well advised to discipline their children in ways that emphasize internal, not external controls. This is one (of several) reasons why physical punishment is a worse way of training children than by reasoning with the child. Physical punishments—for example, spanking—teach a child aggressive behaviour and injures his or her sense of self, instead of helping that sense of self to develop. It leads to an externalized understanding of rules and the reason for obeying them.

The role of attachment

Functionalists believe that attachment to others, as well as to society, is an important foundation for conforming behaviour. 'Good parents' provide their children with love and attachment, emotional stability, protection and control, and fair and moderate discipline. Research shows that the three strongest influences on feelings of attachment are supervision, identity support, and instrumental communication (Cernkovich and Giordano, 1987). The result is a sense of attachment and related-ness among members of a family, maintained and signified by shared activities, self-identification as a family member, and signs of familiarity and liking.

In this respect, family rituals are as important for family stability and cohesion as religious (or patriotic) rituals are for communities. Researchers report that children who live in families that have sit-down meals together at least three times a week are much less likely to become delinquents in their adolescence, or to turn to crime in adulthood. Family dinners are a sign of family cohesion and stability, which contribute to the healthy emotional development of children. Likewise, families that have recreational activities together are much less likely to produce delinquent children.

No less important than love and stability is parental control—how firmly, consistently, and fairly parents make and enforce rules for the child. Good rules guide and protect the child. They signify the parent's concern and attachment. As func-tionalists would predict, it is the quality of family relationships and family dynamics that counts in forming and socializing children. Youths who are supported at home develop identities conducive to success, while youths deprived of support at home, school, and community form identities that make school success much less likely.

Rule enforcement is another form of attach-ment between parents and their children—a way

that parents show concern for their children. A survey of adolescents in Scotland identified four parenting styles, distinguished by their degree of acceptance and control of adolescent behaviour. (By 'acceptance' the researchers mean that parents like and respect their children.) The 'authoritative' parenting style (high acceptance, high control) turns out children who achieve the highest levels of academic performance and mental well-being. Adolescents raised by authoritative parents are also more likely than other adolescents to have a strong community orientation, are less self-centred, and are less likely to engage in deviant behaviour (Radziszewska et al., 1996).

Often, marital conflict interferes with good parenting. Unhappy marriages often produce more troubled children and deviance, for two reasons. First, an unhappy marriage can cause children to feel unloved. Unhappily married people often spend too little time with their children. The parents are depressed, stressed-out, and self-absorbed. Second, marital conflict disrupts the normal practices of discipline, especially by mothers, who are typically the family disciplinarians in Canadian society. This, in turn, reduces the attachment between parent and child.

Some forms of parenting produce undesirable outcomes. For example, 'authoritarian' parenting (low acceptance, high control) hinders the devel-opment of expressiveness and independence. This parenting style also increases the risk of adolescent drug use. Children whose parents are highly controll-ing but not as caring are more likely to become delinquents (Man, 1996), to become depressed, and to fail in school (Radziszewska et al., 1996).

Unengaged parenting (low acceptance, low control) can also be harmful. A study of high school students in the San Francisco Bay area found that 'permissive' (high acceptance, low control) parenting produces poor grades (Vergun, Dornbusch, and Steinberg, 1996). Poor students are more likely to come from families with permissive parenting styles (Bronstein, Duncan, and D'Ari, 1996; Radziszewska et al., 1996). What is more, differences in adjustment accumulate over time, and the harmful effects of neglectful parenting continue to take their toll as behaviour problems, internal distress, and poor school performance (Steinberg et al., 1994).

The issue of discipline is related to control. A desire for control leads to the creation of rules, and discipline is the enforcement of these rules. Overzealous discipline may eliminate the benefits of control, as may inattentive discipline. Hoffman (1979) distinguishes between three basic types of disciplining techniques: power assertion, love withdrawal, and induction. In power assertions, a parent or other caregiver threatens a child with punishment for non-compliance. The child changes his or her behaviour to avoid punishment. However, they do not base this compliance on moral learning. The child's seemingly moral behaviour is externally, not internally, driven. Physical punishments, and power assertions more generally, appeal to parents who do not have the time, patience, or inclination to teach rules inductively.

Perhaps the most significant variant of functionalist theory today is Gottfredson and Hirschi's 'general theory of crime' (1990). This theory proposes that self-control is the general concept around which all of the known facts about crime can be organized. Low self-control is supposed to explain an individual's inclination to commit or refrain from committing crimes, just as high self-control explains an individual's likelihood of conforming to social norms and laws. The researchers argue that self-control, internalized early in life, determines who will be likely to commit crime. According to this theory, good parenting is the most important factor in determining a person's level of self-control.

Lack of self-control is neither a sufficient nor a necessary condition for crime to occur, since other characteristics of the individual or of the situation may also influence a person's chances of committing a deviant act. However Gottfredson and Hirschi identify parents as the main source of socialization

for children. Thus, by studying and comparing families across social groups, one can make predictions of crime and delinquency across social groups. As groups vary in the families and their socialization, they will vary in their criminality. This assumption allows sociologists to apply the general theory to a variety of crimes, peer groups, schools, and families, even including cross-cultural comparisons, white-collar crime, and organized crime. Equally, the theory argues that any social policies that strengthen family bonds, increase socialization, and create greater self-control in the child will reduce criminality by reducing the likelihood a child (or adult) will behave in a deviant manner.

Though studies generally support the theory's major conclusion that low self-control leads to criminal involvement, critics also note weaknesses in the self-control theory of crime. For example, some critics question the ways to best measure 'self-control' the key variable in this theory. Other critics question the relationship between self-control, crime, and other deviant behaviours. Nonetheless, no more comprehensive theory of crime and delinquency is currently in use.

To conclude, functionalists emphasize the importance of value consensus, value stability, social cohesion, social involvement, informal control, and the internalization of morality as factors determining deviant and conforming behaviours. These principles operate at every level of society—within families, communities, classrooms, businesses, and societies as a whole.

(2) Conflict Theories

Conflict theory, by contrast, is a paradigm that emphasizes conflict and change as basic features of social life. For conflict theorists, change is the only constant in society. However, unlike functional sociologists, conflict theorists not only describe change but also explain how changes occur. They argue conflict and change are inevitable because society is composed of groups that differ in their power, status, and influence. Conflict theorists reject the functionalist emphasis on the coherent social 'whole'. Conflict theorists explain that different groups in society conflict because the goods that people value highly and desire—wealth, prestige, and power—are scarce.

Conflict develops between groups whose goals differ or even oppose each other—for example, the rich and the poor, men and women, workers and management. These categories of opposing people differ in at least one social characteristic: respectively, their wealth, gender, or relationship to power at work. For a conflict theorist, there is one basic sociological question: Who benefits from the existing social order and who suffers? Like structural functionalists, conflict theorists pay attention to the consequences of behaviours or relationships. However, the conflict theorist does not suppose that any behaviour or relationship will benefit the whole society, and does not look for such a benefit. Instead, the conflict theorist looks for particular groups that will benefit most and have the power to seize this benefit.

Thus, a typical piece of research by conflict theorists will focus on a conflict, inequality, or disadvantage—for example, the reason some people favour affirmative action (or employment equity) for women and racial minorities while others oppose it. Conflict theorists do not consider conflict a destructive force; instead, they believe it focuses attention on social problems and brings people together to solve these problems. Conflict is the source of the women's movement, civil rights movements, and trade unionism, among others. As a result, conflict serves as the vehicle of positive social change.

Conflict theorists are also interested in the ways beliefs support the status quo. For example, many people in our society believe they are responsible for their own success or failure. This so-called liberal ideology affects the way people behave in many situations. Always, this ideology encourages people to 'blame the victim' and support the status quo.

In conflict theory, the *dominant ideology* is the ideology of the dominant group, justifying its power and wealth. Young people learn this ideology in the schools, churches, and media; we hear it repeated throughout life. Marxist theorists embrace a particular version of conflict theory. We see this when people blame the shortcomings of other people, and not the way society is organized, for causing widespread problems. This often translates into poverty for the less fortunate working and lower classes—a social problem, but also one associated with many other social problems as well, including crime, drug use, underemployment and unemployment, homelessness, environmental pollution, gender issues, racism, and physical and mental health problems.

In this context, crimes can be viewed as forms of resistance, protest, or rebellion against the people in power, however unconscious the perpetrators may be of this fact. The powerful members of society make laws (and enforce them) to their advantage; the less powerful members of society break laws, when it is to their advantage.

Sometimes, by this logic, rule-making and rule-breaking are instrumental—aimed at gaining material benefits (property, money, or power). Sometimes, however, rule-making and rule-breaking are symbolic—aimed at enhancing a group's or person's social status and respectability. From the conflict perspective, the sociology of crime and deviance is a subcategory of the sociology of law. Since deviance is rule-breaking, fewer rules (and laws) would mean less deviance (and crime), since there would be fewer rules to break. If we lived with fewer rules and less rule enforcement—if we adopted a live-and-let-live attitude—we would have less deviance to worry about.

This observation is particularly applicable in relation to 'crimes without victims', such as crimes involving the recreational use of drugs. Keeping marijuana illegal profits an enormous criminal drug industry that does more harm than the drug itself. According to conflict theorists, the mass media do their part by glamorizing crime and criminals.

Indeed, to the extent they 'advertise' and glamorize crime through mass media fictions, crime is associated with particularly noticeable individual characters—criminals. The media also induce moral panics—mass fears about supposedly rising crime rates, criminal gangs, and new types of criminality.

As the data in Figure 1.1 show, crime rates are relatively invariant over time, whether we are looking at young people (as in the following graph) or older people. They are particularly stable for violent crimes—the kind of crimes people fear most—and most variable for property crimes, which tend to reflect shifts in employment opportunities and the poverty level in society.

Conflict theories, at bottom, are about the unequal distribution of wealth and power, and the ways people respond to inequality by breaking rules. Any theory that ultimately relates rule-breaking to social inequality, and to the opportunities for rule-breaking, is ultimately within the conflict tradition. Within the context of conflict and social inequality, rule-breaking is rational, given most people's limited opportunities and a desire for success. From this standpoint, Merton's famous 'strain theory' has connections to the conflict approach, since it contends that criminal behaviour is a result of the lack of opportunities combined with a desire for conventional success.

The focus in conflict theories, however, is on 'external' stimuli to crime (e.g., criminal opportunities)—and the lack of external controls (e.g., the lack of policing or certain and costly punishment). Internal controls—owing to socialization, attachment, involvement, and the development of self-control—are much more characteristic of functionalist explanations of deviance, crime, and delinquency. In that sense, Merton's anomie theory—which is about the gap between learned cultural goals and societal means—is a functionalist theory, not a conflict theory.

Much of the current research in a conflict tradition is macro level, for several reasons. Primarily, it is about rule-breaking that responds to societal, communal, ecological, or situational opportunities. Examples we will study include routine activities theory and rational choice theory. (Arguably, both routine activities theory and rational choice theory could be included under the functional perspective, since they do not question the exercise of power as conflict theories normally do.)

For conflict theorists as for functionalists, neighbourhoods and communities are necessary objects of study. As we said, all sociological approaches to crime and deviance are ultimately about 'communities, cultures, and careers'. For conflict theorists, macrolevel indicators of 'concentrated disadvantage' are among the strongest predictors of crime. These indicators include racial heterogeneity, poverty, and family disruption. Inequality and related concepts, including poverty and unemployment, are regularly used to predict crime or delinquency within the conflict approach.

So, for example, research shows that inflation, cyclical unemployment, frictional unemployment, and technological unemployment all increase the rates of property crime reported to police (Ralston, 1999). Unemployment among young people without educational degrees increases rates of both theft and violent crime. The inability of adolescents to achieve financial success or middle-class status through legitimate channels predicts later involvement in delinquency. More generally, 'social exclusion'—the ways in which young people are connected to, or disconnected from, mainstream opportunities, lifestyles, and outlooks—affects both delinquent and criminal behaviour.

Familial, school, labor market, and street factors all play a part in the criminality of homeless male street youths in Edmonton, Alberta, for example (Baron and Hartnagel, 1997). However, familial and school factors have only a small influence on current criminal behaviour, according to this research. Instead, criminal behaviour is influenced by a lack of income, job experiences, and perceptions of a blocked opportunity structure. Lengthy unemployment, unsatisfactory job experiences, and

Figure 1.1 Crime Rates, Youths Aged 12 to 17, Canada, 1978–2002

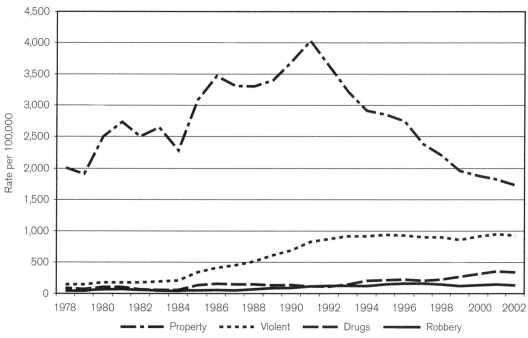

SOURCE: Statistics Canada, 'The State: Youth Crime', *Canada e-Book*. Catalogue 11-404-XIE, May 2003; available at <142.206.72.67/04 /04b/04b_graph/04b_graph_002b_1e.htm>.

a lack of income build a sense of anger and exclusion that fuels street youths' criminal activities. Homelessness, drug and alcohol use, and peers who engage in illegal activities also increase the likelihood of criminal activity.

In the United States, poor racial minorities are particularly likely to engage in crime, despite—or, as Merton would say, because of—their social values. African-American and Latino male gang members have basically conventional aspirations and values (Hagedorn, 1997). For them, the term 'crime' includes not only violence and lawlessness, but also any other survival strategies devised by people without access to legitimate means of opportunity. Limited social opportunities reduce school achievement and increase dropout rates, leading to more crime. Low-wage, service-sector concentration and unemployment increases the likelihood of both

fighting and drug use among adolescents (Bellair and Roscigno, 2000). In short, limited opportunity has a distinct effect on crime, even after we take into account other factors like family intactness.

In conflict theories, *opportunity* for crime is as important as *motivation*. Given social inequality, conflict theorists assume that people will act to improve their relative position, given the opportunity. However, community economic deprivation has two contrasting effects on property crime. In poor communities, there is more motivation to steal but less worth stealing. As a result, the relationship between levels of deprivation and property crime is curvilinear, with the deprivation having the strongest effects on property crime at relatively low levels of neighbourhood poverty.

For similar reasons, crime is least likely under the worst and best conditions of economic growth.

Box 1.1 PM High on Reviving Marijuana Bill: Martin Wants to Reduce Penalties for Simple Possession

Paul Martin said yesterday he will revive the Liberals' controversial legislation to reduce penalties for simple possession of marijuana when Parliament convenes in October.

'The legislation on the decriminalization of minor quantities of marijuana, that legislation will be reintroduced,' the Prime Minister said yesterday after meeting his new cabinet. It was his first comment on the matter since the June 28 election.

The earlier legislation, Bill C-10, died in the Commons when the federal election campaign was launched in May. The bill meant anyone caught with up to 15 grams of pot would face a ticket, not criminal charges. Fines would range from $100 to $400. Fifteen grams is enough to roll 15 or 20 joints. But anyone caught with more than 15 grams would receive harsher penalties. The legislation also included tougher penalties for those running marijuana grow operations.

Current law allows up to six months in jail or fines of up to $1,000 on summary conviction for possession. If the crown prosecutes under provisions for an indict-able offence, a conviction could mean up to seven years in jail.

The move to decriminalize pot had been introduced by prime minister Jean Chrétien's government as a way to keep thousands of young people from being saddled with criminal records for possession of pot.

But it had been fiercely debated, with critics saying it would encourage drug use and make it harder for police to curb serious drug crimes. The Bush administration suggested the legislation would force the US to tighten border controls.

Health Minister Ujjal Dosanjh, sworn into cabinet just one day earlier, questioned the suggestion that decriminalization would lead to greater use.

'I'm not so sure whether that argument has any validity. I don't know what the correlation is,' he said. 'My view is that, if you make something illegal, some people are more attracted to it. . . . If you allow people to possess it in small quantities for personal use, the allure kind of disappears for some people.'

SOURCE: Les Whittington, 'PM High on Reviving Marijuana Bill,' *Toronto Star*, 22 July 2004. © 2004 Toronto Star. All rights reserved. Reprinted with permission of Toronto Syndication Services.

Supporting this view, Beki and colleagues (1999) found that increased economic growth leads to: (1) slower growth in the number of thefts because prosperity reduces the incentive of potential criminals (motivation effect); (2) faster growth in the number of thefts because more goods are available (opportunity effect); and (3) faster growth in the number of violent offences because it leads to more outdoor activities (routine-activity effect). Table 1.2 shows the breakdown of crimes by offences across Canada.

Conflict theories of criminal victimization all emphasize the importance of criminal opportunities a location offers—the convergence of motivated offenders, suitable targets, and the absence of guardianship. The chances of victimization increase as proximity to motivated offenders, exposure to high-risk environments, target attractiveness, and ineffective guardianship increase. Therefore, victimization is likely where poor-to-medium-income young people—especially, young men—come together in public places. An example is public transportation (e.g., subways and buses), which brings together otherwise segregated social or ethnic groups.

Though youth engagement in risky behaviour is an important factor in victimization, other personal characteristics put youth at risk by making certain youth more 'congruent' with the needs and motives of potential offenders (Finkelhor and Asdigian, 1996). Three specific types of such characteristics are those that increase the potential victim's target vulnerability (e.g., physical weakness or psychological distress), target gratifiability (e.g., female gender for the crime of sexual assault), or target antagonism (e.g., behaviours or ethnic or group identities that may spark hostility or resentment).

The explanation of conventional crime by three factors—motivation, opportunity, and absence of a capable guardian—is even applicable to crime in cyberspace (Grabosky, 2001). As cyberspace grows, the variety and opportunity for crimes proliferates. Greater computer dependency and increases in the use of communications technologies to mediate traditional forms of interaction have resulted in a new class of criminal opportunities that both reduce the direct contact between criminals and their potential victims and facilitate criminal activities (Coffey, 2002). Criminals elicit the trust of potential victims by manipulating social roles, social scripts, and definitions of the situation. New criminal opportunities (e.g., Internet access, money laundering, political upheaval, etc.) even motivate individuals who formerly were not connected with criminal activity (Albanese, 2000).

Exposure to offenders largely explains victimization risks. Indeed, some criminal opportunities require close proximity to, and familiarity with,

victims. As one might guess from their frequently shared locations, criminal offenders and their victims often share many characteristics and behaviours (Mustaine and Tewksbury, 2000).

In general, predictable daily activities provide an increased opportunity for criminal activity: suitable targets for motivated offenders, in relation to a routine lifestyle. Police offer one good example of people whose routine work-activity exposes them to targeting by motivated offenders.

The role of rationality

Rational choice is a general theoretical perspective, or family of theories, that explains social outcomes by constructing models of individual action and social context. It fits well within the conflict approach. Like the conflict approach more generally, rational choice theory assumes that people are competing—indeed, in conflict—over desired social and economic resources. Unlike functionalists, rational choice theorists do not assume consensus and stability in a society—only, individuals pursuing their own goals as effectively as they can.

From the rational choice standpoint, illegal work (crime) and legal work are points on a continuum of income-generating activities. The links between crime and legal work involve trade-offs among crime returns, punishment costs, legal work opportunity costs, and tastes and preferences regarding both types of work. Often, quite ordinary people engage in illegal work because of the low wages and harsh conditions they find in legal work. Many criminal offenders participate in both legal work and crime, either at the same time or sequentially. This overlap suggests a fluid interaction between legal and illegal work.

Businesses as well as individuals behave rationally where crime is concerned, weighing the benefits and costs of criminal activity. Consider public bars and private non-profit social clubs, and ask: (1) What percentage of bars and clubs use video poker machines for illegal gambling? (2) How many video poker machines are currently used and how

Table 1.2 Crimes by Offences, Provinces, and Territories, 2004 (rate per 100,000 population)

	Canada	Nfld/Lab.	PEI	NS	NB	Ont.
All incidents	8834.9	6819.0	8962.5	9448.2	8185.2	6287.8
Criminal Code offences (excluding traffic offences)	8050.6	6320.2	8220.4	8764.1	7313.3	5702.3
Crimes of violence	946.1	917.2	798.6	1190.2	937.3	754.7
Homicide	2.0	0.4	0.0	1.4	0.9	1.5
Attempted murder	2.2	0.2	0.7	1.7	0.4	1.9
Assaults (level 1 to 3)[1]	731.8	766.5	681.8	973.5	758.6	566.9
Sexual assault	73.7	92.5	65.3	87.5	80.8	65.0
Other sexual offences	8.2	6.6	11.6	7.0	17.0	4.3
Robbery	86.0	24.4	18.9	78.9	33.7	74.7
Other crimes of violence[2]	42.3	26.7	20.3	40.2	45.9	40.4
Property crimes	3990.9	2738.0	3504.9	3893.7	3003.0	3013.3
Breaking and entering	859.9	861.3	589.0	831.1	712.0	597.7
Motor vehicle theft	530.7	190.9	187.9	357.8	243.0	337.5
Theft over $5,000	54.1	25.0	36.3	31.7	48.0	49.0
Theft $5,000 and under	2131.3	1358.5	2342.9	2126.6	1604.0	1645.1
Possession of stolen goods	110.8	52.2	58	213.1	76.0	105.6
Frauds	303.9	250.1	290.9	333.4	319.9	278.4
Other Criminal Code offences	3113.6	2665.0	3916.9	3680.2	3373.0	1934.3
Criminal Code offences (traffic offences)	372.1	237.9	472.2	325.3	366.7	262.3
Impaired driving	247.2	169.6	393.1	277.1	271.8	147.3
Other c.c. traffic offences[3]	124.9	68.3	79.1	94.5	48.2	115.0
Federal statutes	412.3	260.9	269.8	358.8	505.2	323.2
Drugs	304.1	157.4	199.5	266.7	356.1	229.7
Other federal statutes	108.2	103.5	70.4	92.1	149.1	93.5

1. 'Assault level 1' is the first level of assault. It constitutes the intentional application of force without consent, attempt or threat to apply force to another person, and openly wearing a weapon (or an imitation) and accosting or impeding another person. 'Assault with weapon or causing bodily harm' is the second level of assault. It constitutes assault with a weapon, threats to use a weapon (or an imitation), or assault causing bodily harm. 'Aggravated assault level 3' is the third level of assault. It applies to anyone who wounds, maims, disfigures or endangers the life of complainant.

much illegal revenue is being generated by these businesses? (3) To what extent are law enforcement officials enforcing the laws against the illegal use of video poker machines and are the laws being enforced equally between bars and clubs? (4) Are the current sanctions for the illegal use of these machines providing an effective deterrent for these establishments; and if not, what would provide an effective deterrent for these establishments?

O'Boyle (2002), who asked and answered these questions, finds the results solidly support a rational choice perspective of criminal behaviour. For public bars and private social clubs throughout Pennsylvania and specifically in Lehigh County, the chances of being caught using illegal video poker machines is extremely low, and the financial benefits obtained greatly outweigh the current State sanctions incurred if caught. Thus, these

Que.	Man.	Sask.	Alta	BC	YT	NWT	Nvt
7213.8	13667.6	16907.2	11207.3	13721.7	24983.2	45164.7	38493.5
6492.7	12752.8	15158.7	10389.8	12521.7	23124.7	42125.7	36685.3
725.5	1602.3	2005.8	1087.4	1195.2	3236.3	6865.2	7883.6
1.5	4.3	3.9	2.7	2.7	22.4	9.3	13.5
3.5	1.8	3.4	1.6	2.0	0.0	7.0	23.6
517.0	1251.0	1656.3	866.6	963.5	2842.1	6155.1	6628.7
58.6	127.7	128.9	76.5	79.2	182.6	418.1	941.2
13.5	8.6	12.1	5.4	9.4	57.7	25.7	40.5
90.2	149.3	119.6	86.7	107.7	67.3	44.4	10.1
41.1	59.7	81.7	47.8	30.7	64.1	205.6	226.0
3202.1	5698.9	6238.1	5064	6762.7	6341.1	7414.2	6959.3
857.6	1202.3	1701.7	971.2	1257.7	1762.3	2487.7	3548.8
519.0	1364.0	746.8	645.5	889.8	499.9	843.3	786.0
64.8	42.0	51.4	59.8	59.4	108.9	95.8	43.9
1476.9	2798.9	3039.1	2769.7	4015	3422.1	3464.1	2229.8
37.0	84.8	232.5	180.2	176.2	134.6	142.5	108.0
246.9	207.1	466.5	437.6	364.7	413.3	380.8	242.9
2565.1	5451.7	6914.8	4238.4	4563.9	13547.4	27846.3	21842.5
398.7	299.6	1002.3	481.3	440	1134.3	1562.7	735.4
240.8	245.3	560.9	378.3	353.3	1051	1371.2	580.2
157.9	54.3	441.4	102.9	86.7	83.3	191.6	155.2
322.4	615.2	746.2	336.3	759.9	724.2	1476.3	1072.7
273.3	236.7	326.3	260.3	634.2	480.6	925.0	914.2
49.1	378.5	419.9	76.0	125.7	243.5	551.3	158.6

2. Includes unlawfully causing bodily harm, discharging firearms with intent, abductions, assaults against police officers, assaults against other peace or public officers and other assaults.

3. Includes dangerous operation of motor vehicle, boat, vessel or aircraft, dangerous operation of motor vehicle, boat, vessel or aircraft causing bodily harm or death, driving motor vehicle while prohibited and failure to stop or remain.

SOURCE: Statistics Canada, CANSIM, Table 252-0013; available at <www.statcan.ca/english/Pgdb/legal04a.htm>, accesssed 26 July 2005.

small businesses rationally choose to violate the Pennsylvania gambling laws.

Corporate crime is similar to street crime in that sense. Though street crimes are a primary concern of most people (and criminologists), in recent years, crimes committed by corporations have increased greatly and gained a great deal more public attention. The factors encouraging corporate crime include the failure of government regulation, lack of corporate self-regulation, lack of public concern about corporate crime, corporate mechanistic structure, and the low self-control tendency of corporate managers (Mon, 2002).

Since immoral people are often controlled only by external sanctions—by the threat of detection, arrest, and punishment—a get-tough-with-offenders policy should work well to prevent crime. However, this is not always the case. Often, stricter

Box 1.2 Police Seek Greater Leeway to Open E-mail

VANCOUVER—Police want the federal government to give them greater access to Canadians' e-mail, the Internet, and other forms of electronic traffic to fight high-tech crime.

The Canadian Association of Chiefs of Police has been after Ottawa for Criminal Code amendments for some time and on Monday, the association's president reinforced that call.

Outdated legislation poses a significant threat to public safety, said Edgar McLeod, who is also chief of the Cape Breton Regional Police Service.

McLeod said police are losing the crime-fighting battle to legislation which was written in 1974, when the rotary-dial telephone was still in use.

'Since then the technology has advanced while the police ability to keep up has not,' Edgar said during a break at the association's annual conference.

Police organizations want more power, through warrants, to monitor e-mail, web surfing, instant messaging, mobile telephones and telephone services using Internet connections.

The police are especially concerned about child pornography, exploitation of children, and organized crime.

Support for the idea from the federal government seems to be growing.

In a speech to the Canadian Association of Police Boards last week, Public Safety Minister Anne McLellan described the issue as 'something my department is actively working on.'

But a Toronto-based national group known as Privateer says the police and the federal government must make the case to the public that cyber-crime is increasing and legal changes are needed.

'Those laws can apply to the existing medium quite well,' said Robert Guerra, managing director of Privateer, which describes itself as a coalition of computer professionals and human rights organizations.

'It doesn't mean that the old laws are bad,' he said. 'It means police and authorities have to go through just cause for them to prove to a judge that they can intercept communication.

'That is how it works now. Why do they need additional powers?'

Peter Barnes, president and CEO of Toronto-based Canadian Wireless Telecommunications Association, said there are huge cost implications to the police demands.

'We have to recover the costs associated with that,' he said. 'We don't think our customers should subsidize this enterprise that's carried out by law enforcement.'

Supt. Thomas Grue of the Edmonton Police Service said police were reluctant to discuss in detail the types of things they would like better access to for fear of alerting the criminals.

The association says other countries, including Britain, have laws aimed at modernizing their access statutes.

SOURCE: Greg Joyce, 'Police Seek Greater Leeway to Open E-mail,' *Edmonton Journal*, 24 August 2004.

enforcement and more vigilance simply increase the arrest rate without deterring the behaviour. Meisel (2002) notes, for example, that mandatory parole brings more youth under the umbrella of social control for long periods of time. The more time youth spend on parole, the greater the likelihood that these same youth are charged and convicted of new criminal offences while on parole. Thus, parole supervision imposes a 'hyperstructure' of responsibilities and obligations onto parolees that ultimately provides greater opportunities for parole failure.

However, rational choice theorists have a difficult time explaining the very aspect of crime that preoccupies the general public and academics most. Violent crimes such as homicide are often referred to as 'crimes of passion'. They are difficult to explain because even premeditated murders seem to lack rationality (whether judged by the objective reasonable person or subjective aggressor) and instead are fuelled by momentary emotions. In large part, crimes of violence are a product of particular situations and occasions. This could explain in part why women are more likely to be killed in the bedroom whereas men are more likely to be killed in the kitchen.

To conclude, conflict theorists emphasize the importance of value conflict, value change, social competition, social marginality, external or repressive control, and the imposition of 'ideology' as factors determining deviant and conforming behaviours. Underlying all this is social inequality and the endless battle for dominance and survival.

(3) The Symbolic Interactionist Approach

Symbolic Interactionism (SI) is a theoretical paradigm that views society as a product of continuous face-to-face interaction in different settings. It focuses on the processes by which people interpret and respond to the actions of others and studies the way social structures arise out of these processes.

When naming the approach 'Symbolic Interactionism' in 1937, Herbert Blumer described the basic elements of the paradigm in three propositions:

(1) 'human beings act toward things on the basis of the meanings that things have for them'; (2) these meanings 'arise out of social interaction'; and (3) social action results from a 'fitting together of person lines of action'.

Like the other paradigms we have discussed, symbolic interactionism has its own typical set of research interests and approaches. Often, symbolic interactionist research focuses on an interactional problem that results from a 'bad fit' between the ways that people see themselves, others, situations, or relationships. Two questions of interest to symbolic interactionists are: (1) How do people become the kind of people they are, that is, how does 'the self' (and self-control) develop? and (2) How do people reach new understandings about a situation and proper behaviour in that situation?

All sociologists view socialization as a social process, but symbolic interactionists are most concerned with understanding how socialization actually works. How specifically do people come to take on the norms, values, attitudes, beliefs, and behaviour patterns of the people around them? A related but more general question is: How do people come to be themselves? By 'self', we mean a person's experience and awareness of having a personal identity that is separate from that of other people. Sociologists believe that the process by which people develop this sense of self is the same as the process by which they internalize their culture.

As Piaget showed in his research, young children are egocentric; they have no sense of self as distinct from other people. Children only become aware of themselves as they become aware that other people (such as their parents or siblings) are distinct from them. This means that the self is a social product. It emerges as people interact with others, even with people they hate or admire from afar (such as movie stars or heroic ancestors). The person's experiences in life, the groups to which he or she belongs, and the sociohistorical setting of those groups all shape a person's sense of self. Because the self is a social product, it changes throughout life.

People's experiences and self-conceptions change throughout life, due to secondary socialization. We should not underestimate the role of adult experiences in continuing to change a person's values, norms and perceptions. Increasingly, we become what we do for a living and become like the people we work with.

Social theorists differ in their accounts of the emergence of the self, but they agree on one thing: social interaction is central to its growth. American sociologist Charles Cooley (1902) was the first to emphasize the importance of the self in the process of socialization. Cooley emphasized the role of the social environment in the development of a self-concept. According to Cooley, people form concepts of themselves as they see how other people react to them. The so-called labelling theory of deviance comes directly out of this principle.

A more complete approach to socialization can be found in the work of the American social theorist George Herbert Mead (1934). Mead suggests a child goes through a number of phases as he or she learns to internalize social expectations. We see a higher level of social behaviour in the *play phase*, when the child engages in solitary play. Both Mead and Piaget emphasize that, even if children are playing in each other's presence, play at this age is solitary because it involves no real interaction. The next phase, the *game phase*, involves an even higher level of social behaviour, for it means coordinating social roles. For symbolic interactionists, social life is like a game, and we learn how to play games—to take coordinated roles and anticipate the role-play of others—when we are children.

Mead and Cooley's symbolic interactionist theories continue to dominate the study of socialization. Structural functionalists have adopted Mead's theory to explain how people learn to accept the values, goals, and norms of the society around them. However, Mead's theory does not mesh well with structural functionalism, because it views people as active participants in their own socialization. Symbolic interactionism, much more than functionalism, views people as independent actors working together to build (and interpret) social reality.

Behaviour in situations

Symbolic interactionists want to understand how new meanings and new relationships arise as people interact with one another in a state of conflict or confusion. The meanings are social because, through interaction, people create them, share them, learn them, and often pass them down from one generation to the next. Sociologists capture the actor's point of view in another important idea, *definition of the situation*. We must understand an actor's definition of the situation, because people will act meaningfully in relation to their definition of reality, not ours.

Romantic comedies since Shakespeare have contained some element of mistaken identity, wrong expectations, or competing beliefs. Social life consists of forging and correcting our beliefs. In short, our beliefs and expectations shape our social interactions and individual behaviours. Social order emerges from two or even more different beliefs, expectations, and definitions of the same situation through negotiation.

According to symbolic interactionists, social arrangements require continuous negotiation, talk, bargaining, and compromise. Negotiation requires many social skills, and we all learn these skills in interaction, throughout our lives. Communication is often easiest if we can lead people to redefine the situation: to see the interaction in our way. Thus, the control and structuring of communication is critical: it sets the agenda for negotiation and interpretation.

In studying deviance, followers of this perspective analyze the ways that certain behaviours and conditions become defined as deviant acts and the ways some people become seen as, or see others as, deviant. Consistent with the basic premise of labelling theory, Herbert Blumer (1971) proposed that social problems develop in stages. The first stage is 'social recognition', the point at which a given condition or behaviour, say, drug use, is first identified as a potential social concern. Second, 'social legitimating' takes place—society and its various institutional elements formally recognize the social problem as a serious threat to social stability.

Compared to other theorists, symbolic interactionists are least interested in explaining 'primary deviance', that is, the reason people break society's rules—only the way society responds to rule-breaking. From their standpoint, it is the social response that 'creates' deviance and deviant communities.

The sociology of Georg Simmel (1906 [1902]), created nearly a century ago, offers important insights into the social construction of deviance and deviant communities. First, Simmel showed how our 'second' or constructed (often, secret) worlds— or deviant communities—build on, and build away from, the first 'real' world of our sense experience. There is the openly acknowledged world of socially acceptable activities in full view—that's our first world. At the same time, there is a second world of (slightly) hidden deviant activities—sexual affairs, drug addictions, treacherous plots, violent acts, acts of prostitution—ignored by most people most of the time, and in full view to people with the skill and desire to see them.

Second, Simmel gives us an understanding of the social role of strangers. Strangers occupy an interesting structural role in every group, community, or society. They are outsiders who, for some purposes, are allowed inside. When strangers interact with us, for self-protection, they control information flow (or practice 'impression management', as symbolic interactionists later called this). Because of their partial exclusion, strangers are free to do things that are forbidden to insiders. In that way, they are able to display and exemplify alternative ways of living.

Howard Becker (1963), a symbolic interactionist trained in the Chicago School, emphasizes that deviance is not to be explained by psychological or personality variables. Everyone is capable of deviance, and everyone practices deviance from time to time (just as everyone is a stranger in one setting or another). For Becker the important issue is the process by which a person discovers deviant behaviour, learns how to participate in deviance, and adjusts to the label of deviant. Becker's work, therefore, is mainly about the formation of deviant communities and identities.

In one classic work, Becker analyzed the ways that people progress into (and out of) the recreational use of marijuana. He emphasized that deviance is rarely practised solo; it is a social accomplishment. So, for example, people need others to help them recognize and enjoy the chemical effects of marijuana. Without such social assistance, they are unlikely to enjoy the experience and repeat it. Moreover, the activity of smoking marijuana often becomes a social activity in its own right, as enjoyable for its sociability as for its chemical effects.

However, those outside the deviant community are likely to view its members' activities with anger and fear. They spread rumours, gossip, and false tales. British sociologist Stanley Cohen has given us the notion of 'moral panic'. During a moral panic, certain groups periodically become the focus of attention. This process focuses on the role of the mass media in providing, maintaining, and 'policing' popular conceptions of deviance, which shape both public awareness of, and attitudes toward, social problems. According to Cohen, society is often subject to such instances of moral panic, characterized by stereotypical representations by the mass media and a tendency for those 'in power' to pronounce moral judgment.

Over time there have been a number of panics over a variety of issues, ranging from crime and the activities of youth, to drugs and sexual freedom, each considered a threat to the moral fibre of society at that particular time. Today, compared with 50 years ago, there is much less anxiety felt about, or anger directed toward, people who smoke marijuana, practice unmarried sex, watch pornographic films, or curse in public. Research finds that moral panics tend to occur when society has trouble adapting to dramatic changes and when such changes lead those concerned to express fear over what they see as a loss of control.

Labelling theory

The most important tool for understanding deviance that emerged out of the symbolic interactionist approach is labelling theory. Sociologists regard Edwin Lemert as a pioneer in the development of this approach, for his work on societal reaction theory, first published in his 1951 work, *Social Pathology: A Systemic Approach to the Theory of Sociopathic Behavior*. His work emphasizes 'secondary deviance'—rule-breaking acts that follow from, and react to, the imposition of a deviant label.

Lemert's theory holds that, contrary to what we might expect, people labelled as deviant become *more* likely to engage in deviant behaviour, because that fits in with their new self-image (and new, more restricted social opportunities). Labelling starts with a perception of difference. Some people attract attention through their deviant behaviour. The application of a label, whether formally or informally, may result in a changed self-image or social exclusion. As a result, labelling is the starting place for understanding deviant careers, identities, and communities.

Labelling theory turns our attention away from the deviant toward the person who is doing the labelling. What social forces or institutional goals increase the rate of labelling deviants? What factors influence the social construction of crimes, i.e., make certain acts deviant or criminal at some times, and not others? Such questions lead to the study of moral panics, moral entrepreneurs, and social intolerance. They lead away from questions about the reasons why people break rules or commit crimes in the first place. In other words, they lead away from psychological explanation toward sociological explanation.

However, there is no denying that psychological factors influence labelling practices. Research shows that certain social conditions produce people

Figure 1.2 Tattooing is gaining popularity among the general population and seen as a body art by many.

SOURCE: Every Tattoo Magazine; available at <www.everytattoo.com/heart11.jpg>

with views that are conducive to intolerance, hate, and fear. People play out patterns of social rejection every day at the neighbourhood level, as they apply their socialized understanding of the world to day-to-day interactions with others. They stigmatize—exclude, ridicule, and punish—people whom they view as socially and morally unworthy. We will discuss this at length in a later chapter, when we examine theories explaining homophobia.

Exclusion, in turn, often leads people labelled 'deviant' to form their own subcultures and communities. From the interactionist perspective, deviant subcultures are systems of beliefs, values, and norms shared by a substantial minority of people within a particular social context. Subcultures, like other cultures, are a result of collective creativity and are therefore subject to historical change and transformation.

Any large society divides into a dominant culture and various subcultures that flourish within the dominant framework. Deviant communities are the social mechanisms that promote and maintain deviant subcultures. They also give their members social support and facilities for remaining deviant. Deviant subcultures are the idea- and value-content of deviant communities: their ideological reason for existing. The two—communities and cultures—are analytically distinct but, in practice, there is no deviant subculture without a deviant community, and vice versa.

The sociological interest in deviant subcultures is closely related to an influential theory of crime and deviance first stated in the early twentieth century, 'Differential Association Theory'. This theory, first stated by Edwin Sutherland (1940) in 1939, states that deviance and criminality are behaviours learned through frequent and extended interaction with people who live an anti-social lifestyle.

Sutherland was not the first criminologist to argue that deviant and criminal behaviours have cultural, rather than individual (psychological or biological) roots. People imitate what they see other people doing. In communities where crime is common, accepted, and even highly organized— like the Neapolitan camorra about which Tarde was writing—otherwise normal people are likely to engage in crime too.

Living in a high-crime neighbourhood, and witnessing others benefit from a criminal lifestyle, increase the chances of engaging in illegitimate activities.

Symbolic interactionism is useful in studying the rise of new forms of deviance through imitation and acculturation. Take the growing acceptance of tattoos, discussed in the next chapter. Gradually, the spread of tattoos to normal, middle-class young people worked to overcome the negative meanings that prevailed when tattoos were associated with prisoners, sailors, and social outcasts (see Figure 1.2).

Symbolic interactionism also provides an insight into the ways that social issues (or 'social problems') arise. Take the rise of public concern over sex offending. During the 1990s, the media depicted, and policy-makers perceived, an increase in sex offending, particularly against children. Media accounts were dominated by images of sex offenders as compulsive recidivists whose behaviour often turned violent. However, law enforcement data indicate that sex crimes against children

remained stable over this period, and sex crimes against adults even declined. Sex offender legislation did not arise simply because of the growing objective harm of sex offending. Rather, it was the product of a socially constructed panic stimulated by media depictions and used by policy-makers to successfully promote sex offending as a menacing social problem worthy of costly and sweeping legislation.

In other words, social problems are socially created, or 'constructed'. The social construction approach—growing out of symbolic interactionism—examines how social problems come to be defined as problems. No problem, no matter how important, is self-sufficient in gaining widespread attention and concern without social construction. Even the most catastrophic social acts—genocidal mass murder—need a social explanation (Alexander, 2002). Legal interpretation and understandings of moral responsibility all have a social history. From the smallest issue in a single community to the biggest issue on the world-stage, social problems are rooted in a particular time and place, with a particular social meaning that someone has constructed.

What has been termed the victim rights movement has made great progress in promoting legislative changes regarding victim rights. This too has required social construction. Evans (2001) shows that the various devices used in the social construction of the problem include fear of crime, the use of victim imagery, construction of horror stories, use of the media in the dissemination of claims, the importance of framing victims needs as rights, the importance of support from public officials and private interest groups and finally, the networking that occurred among those groups.

Deviant communities and subcultures

Symbolic interactionists have always been interested in 'outsiders', minorities, deviants, rebels, and their communities and subcultures. Young people, for example, have always interested sociologists, whether organized in gangs, cliques, classrooms, or mass audiences. Likewise, immigrant communities and subcultures have always interested sociologists and influenced public perceptions of social problems.

Even people with unusual features interest sociologists, because they are more likely than others to develop deviant identities and lead somewhat deviant lives. For example, stuttering gives rise to a deviant identity and, sometimes, a deviant career (Hottle, 1996). Edwin Schur's (1971) concepts of labelling and role engulfment aptly describe how children's stutters quickly encompass their entire self-identity.

Symbolic interactionists argue that labelling and social reaction prolong the deviant behaviour, creating a career out of an attribute. People work out life strategies for dealing with their peculiarities and disabilities. The premise of labelling theory that links it with deviant careers is that initial delinquency increases the likelihood of being observed and negatively labelled. Socialization and labelling experiences shape the identities of offenders and stabilize their criminal activities. Social constraints and opportunities, socialization, and even biology may all influence, but never totally determine, the contingencies involved in criminal activity throughout the life course (Ulmer and Spencer, 1999).

To conclude, symbolic interactionists emphasize the importance of interaction, negotiation, symbolic meanings, stigmatization, and the effects of external labelling on sense of self, as factors determining deviant and conforming behaviours. Underlying all this is the human need to make sense of life, self, and society.

(4) The Feminist Approach

As the name implies, the feminist approach is about gendering and gender inequality—and most particularly, about the ways that women's lives differ from men's.

The feminist approach is not something new. The first wave of feminism occurred between the middle of the nineteenth century and the early twentieth century. It culminated in women gaining the right to vote in many Western countries.

Then two strands of feminism emerged: one concerned with the objective of gaining equal rights with men in the public sphere, and another with gaining recognition of women's difference from men and improving their position in the private sphere of the family. It is this wave that created the modern women's movement and has influenced sociology through a feminist critique of the male-dominated discipline.

Up to the late 1960s, feminism was concerned with understanding the oppression some believed that all women experience. More recent feminist scholarship has emphasized the diversity of women's experience as members of different countries, classes, and racial and ethnic groups. As a result, we have seen the growth of varied 'feminisms' that focus on one or another type of female experience. *Radical feminism*, for example, is characterized by a belief that patriarchy is the main and universal cause of women's oppression, owing to the superior power of men over women. This view has promoted the notion that women must organize separately from men to protect their own interests and foster a distinct women's culture.

Materialist feminism

Equally important in Canada and dominant outside North America, materialist feminism traces its roots to Marxism and views gender relations in a historical, economic context. It sees social class relations as determining the conditions women experience within capitalism. This approach calls for women to organize alongside men of the same social class to solve the problems women are suffering.

What the many types of feminism have in common is a belief that the subordination of women is not a result of biological determinism but is a result of socioeconomic and ideological factors. Though they differ in thinking about the ways they might achieve change, they are all committed to eliminating the continued social inequality of women. Feminism's general goal is equality between the sexes—to promote political, social, and psychological changes by calling attention to facts and issues many have neglected.

The application of feminism in sociology calls attention to the androcentric (or male-dominated) history of sociological thinking. To remedy this, feminist sociologists emphasize the experiences of women, because 'there can be no sociological generalizations about human beings as long as a large number of such beings are systematically excluded or ignored.' In practice, feminist research is a mixture of symbolic interactionist and conflict approaches. However, a unique set of assumptions about reality informs feminist research, namely:

- all personal life has a political dimension;
- the public and private spheres of life are both gendered (i.e., unequal for men and women);
- women's social experience routinely differs from men's;
- patriarchy—or male control—structures the way most societies work; and
- because of routinely different experiences and differences in power, women's and men's perceptions of reality differ.

So, for example, men and women typically have different views about divorce since each experiences divorce very differently. For men, it means a brief reduction in the standard of living, if any reduction at all, and a huge reduction in parenting responsibilities. For women, it usually means a dramatic, long-term loss in income and standard of living. Poverty is common among single mothers and their children. It also means an increase in parental responsibilities, since mothers usually retain custody of the children.

To be a woman in our society is to act out a role that others have defined. To be a woman is also to participate in a set of social relations that define one's status vis-à-vis others. This is true for males too, but with this difference: the 'feminine' role in our society places women in a subservient role to men, in which they are sometimes degraded or victimized. Along with children, women are less powerful than men and sometimes in danger of their lives. Men far more often kill women and children than women and children kill men, for example.

Thus, women's acceptance of the female role is far more costly—even dangerous—than men's acceptance of the male role. For example, consider the problem of witchcraft. Social science has long held that social concerns about witchcraft, sorcery, and magic reveal tensions in the society that need to be resolved. From a feminist perspective, the crackdown on witches in medieval Europe and colonial America was a gendered conflict. Men in authority may have aimed to reduce women's independence or, even, limit the spread of information about techniques of birth control. From this standpoint, it was patriarchal behaviour. Sydie (1964) points out that feminist sociology is political because 'it reveals the manner in which past sociologists have provided intellectual justifications for the persistence of gender inequalities.' So, for example, male sociologists were quick to defend gender inequalities in the family by creating the so-called functional theories that made gender inequality seem not only inevitable but also desirable.

Feminists emphasize that our notions of what it means to be male or female and our dealings with one another as male or female are a result of the social arrangements prevalent in our society. Feminism is also a form of political activism that attempts to change the circumstances within which men and women lead their lives.

Several features that come through in the literature on deviance and control, as we will see, have characterized feminist research. First, feminist research pays the greatest attention to gendered influences on social life, or *the gendering of experiences*. On the one side there is a 'splitting' tendency—showing that, contrary to prevailing views, some of women's experiences of the world are different from men's. Some experiences are specifically female or male, not automatically generalizeable to both sexes. Here, certain topics receive a great deal of attention, including violence against women, women's economic vulnerability, and women's vulnerability to male-dominated standards of attractiveness and social worth.

On the other side is the 'lumping' tendency—showing that, also contrary to prevailing views, some experiences of the world are the same. Here, the goal is to clear away historic misrepresentations of women and their supposed weaknesses or strengths—for example, the traditional male view of women as particularly emotional and irrational.

A second interest is in *the problem of victimization.* Since women have often been victimized, feminists have been particularly interested in victimization and the experiences of other victimized groups (e.g., the experiences of poor people, racial minorities, and people of alternative sexual orientations). Following from this, feminists have been particularly interested in 'intersectionality'—the interaction of gender with other victimizing social characteristics such as class and race, to produce particular combinations of disadvantage (e.g., the particular problems of black men, lesbians, or Muslim women).

Third, feminists are concerned with *the problem of truth-finding.* Since powerful men have often misrepresented women's lives and interests, feminists have tended to suspect theories and (supposed) facts promoted by people in power, and treated them as social constructions or ideologies instead. Feminists have also shown distrust for traditional views of science—including social science—and traditional methods of gathering and analyzing information. Related to this, they have distrusted generalization, preferring the study of individual cases and life histories—and have tended to emphasize not the average experience in a population but the varieties of experience in that same population.

Given these starting points, we are not surprised to find that feminists emphasize the gendered nature of both deviance and control: for example, the relationship between events in the private sphere (e.g., domestic violence) and events in the public sphere (e.g., the cultural and legal tolerance of domestic violence); the gendering of law enforcement practices (e.g., how the police treat prostitutes compared with how they treat prostitutes' customers); and the evidence of patriarchal values in the legal system (e.g., the centuries of failure to concede that husbands might be guilty of raping their wives). Here, as in other areas of sociology, the feminist approach combines macro sociological and micro sociological perspectives: fitting for an approach that emphasizes that personal lives and political issues are intertwined.

Kimerling and colleagues (2002), for example, examine gender differences in victim and crime characteristics in an effort to determine the extent to which sexual assault is a similar experience for men and for women. Researchers obtained data from medical charts of 842 women and 128 men seen at an urban hospital-based rape treatment centre. Men were more likely to report acute psychiatric symptoms, a history of psychiatric disorder, and a history of psychiatric hospitalization. Women were more likely to experience vaginal or anal penetration, to sustain injuries, and to make a police report.

Male and female victims of violent attacks also use different strategies for seeking help (Kaukinen, 2002). Victims who seek help from family and friends and the users of mental health, social services, and self-help groups tend to be female. In contrast, most male victims do not seek help at all. When men do seek help, they are more likely to call the police than to call on family and friends. Attacks by known offenders lead to help-seeking strategies that rely primarily on family and friends. Finally, help-seeking strategies are unique to particular gender/victim-offender relationship categories. Women victimized by known offenders rely on family and friends. Three mechanisms likely to

Box 1.3 Rape Myth

'The conduct of this investigation and the failure to warn, in particular, was motivated and informed by the adherence to rape myths as well as sexist stereotypical reasoning about rape, about women and about women who are raped.'
　　　　　－Justice Jean MacFarland

'The sexual victimization of women is one of the ways men create and perpetuate the power-imbalance of the male-dominated gender hierarchy that characterizes our society.'
　　　　　－Jane Doe

SOURCE: George Jonas, 'Police Acted as They Did Out of Arrogance, Not Misogyny', *Kingston Whig Standard*, July 1998.

Acceptance of rape myths has a strong influence over whether people report their rape experiences. The Illinois Rape Myth Acceptance Scale (Payne et al., 1999) is a 45-item scale created to assess the degree people adhere to rape myths. The following is the short form of the original scale. Users choose the extent of how much they agree with the statement ranging from Strongly Agree, Agree, Neutral, Disagree, and Strongly Disagree.

The Illinois Rape Myth Acceptance Scale
- A woman who is raped while she is drunk is at least somewhat responsible.
- Although most women wouldn't admit it, they generally like being physically forced to have sex.
- If a woman is willing to 'make out' with a guy, then it's no big deal if he goes a little further and has sex with her.
- Many women secretly desire to be raped.
- If a woman doesn't physically fight back, you can't really say that it was rape.
- Men from nice middle-class homes almost never rape.
- Rape accusations are often used as a way of getting back at men.
- Usually, only women who dress sexy are raped.
- If the rapist doesn't have a weapon, you really can't call it a rape.
- Rape is unlikely to happen in a woman's own neighborhood.
- Women tend to exaggerate how much rape affects them.
- A lot of women lead a man on and then they cry rape.
- A woman who 'teases' men deserves anything that might happen.
- When women are raped, it's often because the way they said 'no' was unclear.
- Men don't usually intend to force sex on a woman, but sometimes they get too sexually carried away.
- A woman who dresses in skimpy clothes should not be surprised if a man tries to force her to have sex.
- Rape happens when a man's sex drive gets out of control.
- Most rape and sexual assaults are committed by strangers.
- In Illinois, a 15-year-old can give consent to have sex.
- If someone came to me and claimed that they were raped, my first reaction would be to not believe them.

account for gender variance in responses to victimization are traditional feminine and masculine self-images; the internalization of certain moral beliefs; and relations with delinquent peers (Jensen, 2003). Likely, these affect the response to opportunities for delinquency, deviance, and crime as well.

The impact of 'strain' on criminal and delinquent activities is also gendered, and research suggests that males and females differ in their coping strategies as well as their emotional responses to strain (Oser, 2003). The anger females experience often shows itself in self-destructive behaviours such as drug use or eating disorders. By contrast, males respond to strain with other-directed criminal activity such as property or violent offences. In the face of stressful events, women also show more depression, men more criminal behaviour (Van Gundy, 2002). The assertion of autonomy—a traditionally masculine characteristic—reduces the risk of depression for both women and men; however, it increases the risk of crime among men and reduces it among women.

Desistance from criminality—staying away from criminal behaviour—is also gendered (Gunnison, 2002). Both male and female desisters are more likely to possess strong moral beliefs and exhibit attachment to religion than their persister counterparts. In addition, female and male desisters are less likely to have delinquent peer associations or use drugs and/or alcohol than female and male persisters. Females and males who are older, married, and have other family attachments are more likely to desist from general delinquency. Changing levels of delinquent peer associations have a more prominent effect on desistance from serious delinquency for males. Males who reduce their delinquent peer associations are more likely to desist from serious delinquency.

Classic theories ground female criminality in the social environment, which discounts and hides their illegal behaviour. These theories discount the apparent lower tendency of females to commit crime, arguing that because criminal codes and judges indulge women, some crimes go unrecorded, women act as instigators of or mediators in crime, and prostitution is really a crime against property (Bisi, 2002). Current theories expect a rise in female criminality as the social condition of women develops in Western society to allow greater autonomy, responsibility, and equality with males. Female crime rates remain low, and evidence supporting the notion of an increase is uneven. There is evidence of an increase in female property crime and youth crime, however.

As we see repeatedly in this book, risk-taking, delinquency, violence, and crime are largely male activities. The gender-delinquency relationship is one of the strongest relationships in delinquency research, and gender differences in both the experience of and response to family-related strain may account for the gender gap in delinquency (Hay, 2003).

Huebner and Betts (2002) have examined social control theory's 'attachment' and 'involvement' bonds as protective factors that affect gender differences in delinquency among 7th to 12th graders. 'Attachment bonds' include attachment to parents, to non-parent adults, and to peers; 'involvement bonds' include time spent in various school- and non-school-based activities. The researchers find that several of the involvement bond variables predict delinquency for both genders, but only the attachment bond variables provide an overall protective function for females.

Hagan, McCarthy, and Foster (2002) pay particular attention to gender-linked differences in delinquent aggression, as well as to the links between these forms of delinquent aggression, depression, and substance abuse. Their power-control theory of the gender-delinquency relationship draws attention to differences in familial control practices that are linked to gendered variations in the expression of delinquency and despair.

Even drug trafficking is gendered; women tend to occupy the high-risk, low-status role of courier (Harper et al., 2002). What's more, female couriers physically carry more drugs in terms of weight and value than male couriers. In addition, women are more likely to carry Class A drugs—like heroin or cocaine—rather than Class B drugs like marijuana.

Incarcerated women suffer many of the same problems as incarcerated men, but they also have some that are distinctive. Ferraro and Moe (2003), interviewing 30 women incarcerated in a south-western county jail, learned that the responsibilities of childcare, combined with the burdens of economic marginality and domestic violence, had led some women to choose economic crimes or drug dealing as an alternative to hunger and homelessness. Other women, arrested for drug- or alcohol-related crimes, related their offences to the psychological pain and despair resulting from loss of custody of their children. Many women were incarcerated for minor probation violations that often related to the conflict among work, childcare, and probation requirements.

Close to the direct concerns of feminism is the fear of potential violence (i.e., threat) that many women experience on a daily basis. Women's individual and legal responses to stalking are similar to the responses of women who have experienced other types of violent crime, specifically physical assault, sexual assault, and attempted rape. Through socialization processes, learned by women from their mothers, family members, friends, and through exposure to the mass media, women learn the social cues that mark danger.

In Western scholarly debate, there is nearly universal acceptance of rape as a male trait typical of all time periods and cultures. However, cross-cultural data provide insight into societies where rape is rare or unknown and can therefore help to develop strategies for prevention. Gendercide against women typically involves rape, which has come to be recognized as a war crime. Against men, war crimes generally involve the selective separation of young civilian men 'of military age' (i.e., 18 to 45) from old men, children, and women of all ages for punishment, torture, and execution (Watson-Franke, 2002).

Mother-blaming is another form of victimization women experience. Vander Ven and Vander Ven (2003) examine trends in mother-blaming over time, through a textual analysis of scholarly accounts of the etiology of anorexia nervosa. These expert accounts suggest that mother-blaming for child pathology is interconnected with changing ideas about proper social roles for women. Deficient mothering has often been linked to a woman's ambitiousness, willingness to abandon familial duties in favour of careers, or, conversely, her embrace of patriarchal proscriptions for what a woman should be. Poor maternal parenting was a consistent and dominant theme over a long period.

Another belief hostile to women is that teenage single-mothers form an important part of the culture of poverty, by which one generation of children after another are socialized into welfare dependency. Though teenage mothers are often faced with high barriers in their attempt to complete their education and enter into the workforce, they are not doomed to welfare dependency, poverty, crime, and unemployment, as the prevailing wisdom suggests (Durden-Findlay, 2002). Young mothers tend to continue their education, show a strong tendency toward marriage, consider themselves to be religious, do not use drugs, and express conservative views of the world around them.

Unwed pregnancy, however, violates patriarchal notions of femininity, motherhood, family, and sex. Moreover, the ascription of deviance in the case of illegitimate pregnancy is racially constructed: white unwed mothers are considered maladjusted and psychologically depraved, while black ones are considered deviant and biologically pathological. Both are seen as deviant and guilty of gender insurrection, but the black illegitimate mother is labelled hypersexual (Pietsch, 2002).

Resistance to gendered victimization comes in various forms. Certainly, the women's movement was one example. In short, feminist approaches to crime and deviance reflect women's historical experience of disadvantage and exclusion. Women's sociology sees social life from another angle, another side: perhaps, from the underside. This gives feminist approaches to crime and deviance a much more sensitive understanding of underdogs and outsiders than we find among, say, functionalists and even conflict theorists.

(5) The Postmodern Approach

According to postmodernists, propaganda often masquerades as truth and scientific knowledge merely reflects the needs and beliefs of a given society at a given time. In the eyes of postmodernists, value-freedom is impossible and 'truth' doesn't exist. They believe that every piece of research, every theory, every analysis is a text with an underlying belief system informed by power and social engagement.

At the bottom of the propaganda machine is a set of beliefs about normality. It is thought that the job of science is to determine what is normal. Normality is good and abnormality is bad; so the job of applied science is to turn abnormal people into normal people. From a postmodern perspective, this begs several questions: namely, is there any such thing as normality, and if there is, what makes it so good? Within our current context, is deviance abnormal or normal? In either event, should social control be used to eradicate abnormality and enforce normality?

What is 'normal'?

In his classic work *Normal Accidents: Living with High-Risk Technologies*, Charles Perrow (1999 [1984]) describes several highly complex organizations and attributes serious accidents to structural factors and combinations of problems. In the past, individual human operator errors or design flaws of individual components have been blamed. In recent years, dangerous technologies—such as nuclear power and weapons systems, chemical and other toxic substances, recombinant DNA, and other genetic modifications—have proliferated, increasing everyone's risk. Disasters have routinely occurred.

In short, complex organizations create technological systems that regularly cause ecosystem disasters. One need only mention Three-Mile Island, Chernobyl, and Bhopal to remember that seemingly flawless structures often—or as Perrow says, *normally*—fail. Thus, societies that promote high-risk technologies are doomed to failure and environmental disaster. The unexpected is to be expected. In a large, diverse world, the very concept of 'normality' is, therefore, simple-minded, and even from a purely mathematical standpoint, we must conclude that the concept is largely ideological. That is, the very notion of 'normality' masks a set of important beliefs underlain by power relations, and it lends itself to domination, regulation, and control.

The first point to note, then, is that technological complexity is not a guarantee of normal 'progress', safety, or well-being. It is full of normal risk and disaster. Thus, normality is not necessarily a good thing. In a high-risk society, normality may be a bad thing. Yet, we cling to notions of normality, because they imply safety and well-being.

As well, notions of normality promote a sense of inevitability. For example, Katz and Marshall (2004) note that, in areas like gerontology and sex therapy, norms are being established to assess the 'functionality' of people's health, where 'normality' and 'functionality' are taken as synonymous. In the former case 'functional health' is linked to successful aging represented by technical tests around activities of daily living (ADLs) and risk-assessment profiles. We assess people's well-being by seeing how they compare with the norms for a group of people the same age, for example.

In the realm of education, we assess a student's performance by comparing it with norms established within the grade. We assess her school's performance by comparing it with norms established in the province. We assess her province's performance by comparing it with other provinces, or nations. The more nebulous our understanding of what is expected—what is normal—the more we rely on behavioural norms to provide guidance. A prime example is the DSM-III-R, the *Diagnostic and Statistical Manual of Mental Disorders* published in 1987, which serves as a guidebook for psychiatric therapists to provide criteria for different mental disorders and, by implication, for normality.

What is evident from a study of social and statistical norms—whether we are discussing books of etiquette, instructions to schoolteachers, or the DSM-III-R—is that our conceptions of normality and abnormality change over time. Efforts to state timeless, absolute standards of normality are fruitless; efforts to enforce them are brutal. And this observation brings us to the single greatest postmodern commentator on normality, Michel Foucault. In his studies of prisons, mental hospitals, sexuality, and otherwise, Foucault questions our changing notions of normality and the brutal efforts people in authority made to enforce them.

Foucault on prisons

A particularly influential example of postmodern analysis is provided by Michel Foucault's analysis of prisons and imprisonment. Foucault's interest in prisons reflects his desire to formulate a more general understanding of power than Marxists and socialists had provided. Foucault's work *Discipline and Punish* (1975) thus aimed at uncovering a new dimension of domination in modern society, 'technologies of power'.

Unlike traditional political philosophy, which viewed power in relation to the State, and Marxist (1988 [1848]) analysis which viewed power in relation to class structure, Foucault examined the relationship of power to knowledge and how people think about things So, Foucault links the birth of the modern prison in the nineteenth century to a history of institutions. He argues that all modern institutions—including the army, the factory, and the school—discipline the bodies of their subjects through surveillance techniques. Thus, he notes the rise of a disciplinary society and its new means of enforcing power.

For Foucault, philosopher Jeremy Bentham's (1995 [1787–91]) 'Panopticon' illustrates how an architecture designed for surveillance epitomizes the modern operation of power. Bentham's prison allows for the invisible surveillance of a large number of prisoners by a small number of guards. The prison itself, more than the guards, is a tool of discipline precisely because it allows guards to have complete knowledge of the prison's inmates. Thus, power and knowledge are inextricably linked. Control is achieved more by the internal monitoring of those controlled than by heavy physical constraints. The principle of the Panopticon can be applied not only to prisons but to any system of disciplinary power (a factory, a hospital, a school). According to Foucault, it is the instrument through which modern discipline has replaced pre-modern sovereignty (kings, judges) as the fundamental power relation.

At the core of Foucault's picture of a modern 'disciplinary' society are three primary techniques of control: hierarchical observation, normalizing judgment, and the examination. To a great extent, control over people (power) can be achieved merely by watching them. A distinctive feature of modern power (disciplinary control) is its concern with what people have not done—for example, that person's failure to reach required standards. This concern illustrates the primary function of modern disciplinary systems: to correct deviant behaviour. The goal of discipline is not revenge but reform, where reform means coming to live by society's standards or norms.

Discipline and Punish is a study of the development of the 'gentler' modern way of imprisoning criminals rather than torturing or killing them. Techniques and institutions developed for different, and often quite harmless, purposes converge to create the modern system of disciplinary power. Take that most dreaded of student activities: the examination. In Foucault's view, the examination—whether of students in schools or patients in hospitals—is a form of control that combines observation with assessment. In Foucault's account, the goals of power and the goals of knowledge are united: in knowing we control and in controlling we know. The results of exams are recorded in documents that provide detailed information about the individuals examined and allow power systems to control them.

Using these records, people in control can calculate norms that are both a basis for knowledge and for control. The examination objectifies the individual, turning him into both a scientific example and an object of care. In the end, the study of prisons is the study of modern society and all its rational institutions, all of which objectify the subject.

In Foucault's *Discipline and Punish* (1975) the prison represents a structure of maximum surveillance, an image powerfully charged with negative meaning. However, Foucaultian analysis is applicable to any space—including workspaces—characterized by power differentials. For example Hopper and Macintosh (1998) use Foucault's model of discipline and control in an analysis of the financial-based control systems of the International Telephone and Telegraph (ITT) Company. Foucault's model consists of several principles, among which are the needs to enclose and partition space; create functional, serialized spaces; and rank spaces and types of knowledge. These principles arise from Foucault's notions of hierarchization, panopticons, normalizing sanctions, and examinations. The authors state that under the direction of Harold Geneen, chief executive officer for more than 20 years, ITT's financial-based control system demonstrated all of Foucault's disciplinary principles. Geneen produced a panoptic, disciplinary environment in which workers were continuously monitored and regulated. Thus, Geneen's accounting system represented a major apparatus of discipline and punishment in the ITT organization.

Most, however, note that Foucault's work influenced the study of prisons. Foucault challenged the traditional assumption that modern penal practice has reflected a progressive evolution in social consciousness. Such an effect has redirected later research in three ways, leading to: (1) a blending of historical subjects and ethnographic forms of analysis; (2) a view of the prison as a means of expressing power over individual bodies and groups; and (3) a change from the focus on the state as the key actor in the evolution of penality toward a recognition of the role of technologies of power developed in both state and non-state settings (Simon, 1996).

Alford (2000), who studied US maximum security prisons, contends that contemporary prisons *cannot* be conceptualized as panopticons. Rather, maintaining power in penal institutions is achieved by merely controlling the institutions' entrances and exits. Foucault's assertion that prisons are characterized by surveillance, strict timetables, total control of prisoners' bodies, and rejection of idleness is rejected in relation to US prisons. Rather, Foucault's characteristics of surveillance, regimentation, and classification have migrated from the margins (i.e., penal institutions) toward the centre of contemporary society.

That said, Foucaultian techniques of control intrude into parole hearings. Silverstein (2001) analyzed institutional discourse at parole hearings, examining the way parole board members, inmates, and inmates' family members participate collaboratively in the construction of inmate identities as either parolees who should be released to the community or as prisoners who should remain in prison. This typology includes caring inmate mothers, caring inmate fathers, caring female partners, uncaring inmate fathers, uncaring male partners, and uncaring female partners. Underlying conceptions of normality inform the proceedings.

Foucault's work is not without faults. In speaking of the prison as a generic institution, Foucault fails to recognize the gendered nature of social control in men's and women's prisons. For men, the goal of incarceration could be argued to be self-control and the fashioning of the productive laborer; women are 're-formed' in the model of the family, and the state pays only nominal attention to the exploitation of their labour (Britton, 1998).

In contrast to Foucault's discussion of the unverifiable character of penal surveillance mechanisms, McCorkel (2000) shows that an embodied surveillance—one in which the observer and the observed are known to one another—contributes to the distinct hybridization of therapeutic and punitive controls that characterize contemporary women's prisons.

In a later paper, McCorkel (2003) asks whether the enactment of a gender-neutral 'get tough' policy in a state prison for women means that women's prisons are no longer operating as 'gendered organizations'. She concludes that even when women's prisons attempt to mimic the disciplinary policies associated with men's facilities, they modify disciplinary practices in response to perceived differences in offending between men and women. A crucial modification is the use of an 'embodied surveillance' that sharply differs from Foucault's analysis of penal surveillance mechanisms.

In a paper that is particularly memorable for its title—'Foucault on the Prison: Torturing History to Punish Capitalism'—von Schriltz (1999) asserts that *Discipline and Punish: The Birth of the Prison* is merely a collection of (incorrect) leftist beliefs about capitalism. We will discuss postmodern insights into themes surrounding hidden social control over behaviour—even over the body—in the chapters that follow.

Concluding Words

Each paradigm has valuable insights to contribute at both levels of analysis. All five paradigms have explanations for order and change, consensus and conflict. In one situation, the functionalist or feminist explanation may provide valuable insights. In another, the conflict paradigm or symbolic interactionist paradigm may be better. On the contrary, many sociological researchers—especially sociologists working on applied questions with a practical

significance—use all five paradigms interchangeably. As the feminist and conflict paradigms make particularly clear, sociology is not only a science—it is also an instrument of social criticism.

We can only make the necessary changes to society if we understand the flaws in our current way of doing things, and sociology provides this understanding. This outlook has several characteristics, among them cosmopolitanism, a sense of irony, a disregard for disciplinary boundaries, a tendency to question the basic assumptions of daily life, and a desire to use our knowledge to improve the social world.

Most important, doing sociology means critically paying attention to the relationship between public issues and private troubles, and the relationship between macro-events and micro-events in people's social lives. When taken apart by a skilled analyst, they reveal the biased assumptions people (including sociologists) routinely make about science, truth, and society. Nowhere is this clearer than in the study of deviance, control, and conformity.

Summary

The study of deviance and control is wide-ranging. What's more, the topic is marked by a variety of different theories and approaches. Nowhere is this difference in outlooks more evident than in the study of deviance and control—the topic of this book.

The single most familiar theory in the study of deviance—a functionalist theory—is attributed to Robert Merton, who argued that we are encouraged, through the socialization process, to want certain things in life, for example, to desire the 'American Dream' of economic prosperity. Yet, social inequality makes some people less able than others to achieve the cultural goals; they adapt by devising different deviant strategies. Others view it as a conflict theory, because it emphasizes the inequality of social opportunities. The fact that this theory has influenced sociologists operating in different paradigms shows just how fertile Merton's insight really is.

As we have seen, for functionalists, consensus and cohesion are key concerns; for conflict theorists, change and inequality are key. Socialization and formal laws are necessary for social organization in the eyes of functionalists. However, conflict theorists would argue that because social constructs work to maintain the ruling class's perception of deviant and undesirable behaviours, formal laws work to oppress society rather improve it.

A more complete approach to socialization is found in the work of symbolic interactionists, starting with George Herbert Mead. In studying deviance, followers of this perspective analyze the ways that certain behaviours and conditions become defined as deviant acts and the ways some people become seen as, and see others, as deviant.

Thus, labelling and social construction are key in this approach.

The fourth approach we have discussed is feminism, which is interested in the gendered nature of deviance and control, and falls into two categories. Materialist feminism, which is equally important in Canada and dominant outside North America, traces its roots to Marxism and views gender relations in a historical, economic context.

In certain respects, the feminist approach is an amalgam of conflict and interactionist perspectives.

Finally and briefly, we introduced a fifth approach—postmodernism—and related it to the concerns of its most famous protagonist, Michel Foucault. Here, the central organizing concept is normality, which links knowledge and power in a structure that coerces us invisibly even as it persuades us to change.

Questions for Critical Thought

1. Why is adopting a sociological paradigm critical when considering social issues?
2. What are some likely problems that will occur if strict adherence to one paradigm is used when examining particular issues?
3. Which of the paradigms would identify greater numbers of marginalized groups?
4. How does Durkheim's theory of anomie fit into the functionalist perspective? Illustrate your point using any type of deviance.
5. Are criminals to be blamed for their acts? Does society play a role in their outcomes?
6. Explain how discipline is related to control, using children as an example.
7. Why would a conflict theorist be interested in cyber crime? Be sure to include motivation and opportunity in your discussion.
8. Identify how the play and game phases relate to an interactionist understanding of crime.
9. Are the five sociological frameworks all-encompassing in terms of examining crime and deviance? Are there other ways of analyzing crime and deviance that you can suggest?
10. What are ways that individuals labelled criminals can be reintegrated into society with the new identity of 'non-criminal'?

Recommended Reading

Ferracuti, Franco, and Marvin E. Wolfgang. (1967), *The Subculture of Violence: Towards an Integrated Theory in Criminology.* London: Tavistock Publications. This classic work in the subculture of violence is one of the most important studies on violent crime. Though focusing on violent subcultures, the study makes interesting points that can be extrapolated to various other non-violent groups.

Gottfredson, Michael R., and Travis Hirschi. (1990), *A General Theory of Crime.* Stanford: Stanford University Press. This book is central to the study of criminology because it explains how the cause of crime isn't necessarily any of the factors that we often think of, like poverty, but is instead poor parenting.

Merton, Robert. (1938), 'Social Structure and Anomie', *American Sociological Review*, 3: 672–82. This classic work by Merton defines anomie and the various reactions that people may have towards alienation. In Merton's framework he sees that there are five responses to anomie: conformity, innovation, ritualism, retreatism, and rebellion.

Recommended Websites

Canadian Social Research Links
www.canadiansocialresearch.net

This comprehensive website of Canadian social research links is maintained by a retired federal civil servant. It has government and non-governmental links as well as thousands of links sorted by social theme. It's an excellent gateway for any internet research.

Department of Justice
www.canada.justice.gc.ca

The Canadian Department of Justice website is a great starting point for deviation research. It contains up to date information on laws and policy. The website also provides various publications such as reports, working documents, and policy papers.

Statistics Canada
www.statscan.ca

The Statistics Canada website is a comprehensive site that releases various studies, surveys, and documents daily. It contains plenty of relevant information to help Canadians and policy-makers better understand Canada.

PART II

DEVIANT ACTIVITIES

CHAPTER 2

Appearance Issues

LEARNING OBJECTIVES

- To understand the historical emergence of different types of appearance deviants
- To identify the characteristics of people who have appearance issues
- To understand the sociological perspectives used to explain appearance deviance
- To see the role that societal reaction plays in shaping the deviant's behaviour
- To know how fashion communities project image standards
- To understand the social and health consequences of appearance deviance issues
- To examine policies proposed to control appearance issues
- To identify effective methods for dealing with appearance issues

---

Introduction

In this chapter, we discuss rule-breaking and unexpected behaviour that is associated with people's appearance. This includes non-normative ways of dressing and adorning the body and takes us into a discussion of punk culture and tattooing. We briefly discuss tattooing and piercing as means of showing deviance from conventional appearance norms. We also discuss a specific, well-known style of appearance—punk—to illustrate the effort that some people make intentionally to deviate from the usual standards of appearance and behaviour. The chapter also includes discussions of non-normative eating behaviour. This overeating or undereating produces bodies that are, on the one hand, drastically overweight or obese and on the other hand, drastically underweight, due to anorexia or bulimia.

As a result, this chapter tends to skip around between deviant appearances that *intentionally* convey cultural meanings—as high-fashion clothing and tattoos and punk dress do—and *unintentionally* convey cultural meanings—as severely overweight and underweight bodies do. In some instances, people harm their health by deviating from the appearance norms; in other cases, they harm it by conforming; while in other cases still, deviance and conformity have no health effect whatever. What all these behaviours have in common is that they violate social expectations and, in that sense, are deviant appearances.

Since appearance is about visibility—being seen—and being judged, the chapter draws its theoretical significance from a number of places: from Erving Goffman's (1963) symbolic interactionist theory about 'stigma', from Michel Foucault's (1975) postmodern work on surveillance, and from feminist theory's thoughts about 'the male gaze' (Schroeder, 1998). We begin with a discussion of appearance norms, focusing on what fashion defines as the accepted appearance norms at a given time.

Like it or not, people *do* judge books by their cover and strangers by their appearance. In judging appearance, people often look for points of similarity and familiarity that make them feel secure. Beyond that, they look for evidence of the cultural ideal. People admire others who look prosperous, healthy, and attractive, according to society's standards. Appearance features that approximate the ideal—not merely the familiar—are important, because individuals want to fit in and be accepted. Such ideal features constitute what we consider 'appearance norms'. Most people prefer others who meet their appearance expectations or at least try to obey the appearance norms of their own subculture.

Appearance norms are often measurable, in terms of body size and shape, dress, and other adornment. We all look at appearance features for signs of rebellion, carelessness, or ignorance. Violations of the appearance norms may lead to misunderstanding, mistrust, stigmatization, and exclusion.

For example, we hold norms about appropriate clothing. The way people dress is a central contributor to the initial impression they make. A person's dress is paramount when we form an opinion of the individual, and may affect that person's ability to get a needed job, form relationships, or even be treated with respect or dignity. Style of dress affects employers' perceptions of, expectations for, and responses to job applicants. To their disadvantage, most poor people lack the money needed to improve their outward appearance, and as a result, they look poor, needy, and unsuccessful. Some programs have recently been devised to help poor women obtain job-appropriate clothing, but these programs are limited in scope (Turner-Bowker, 2001).

Society's dependence on and need for social norms—even appearance norms—teaches us about deeper cultural ideals of beauty, propriety, and worth. Scarcity alone lends value to some physical attributes—for example, perfect facial features or flawless white teeth—but far from all. Our cultural ideals are illustrated by the abundant photos and media images that glorify ideal men and women. To judge from these images of 'beautiful people', our culture idealizes youth, a slender toned body, and symmetrical delicate facial features. Departures from

these norms suggest poor genes, poor grooming, or a lack of self-discipline and self-worth.

To verify this fact, Spitzer and colleagues (1999) compared the body standards of North Americans aged 18 to 24 years. Data were collected from 11 national health surveys, over the 1950s to 1990s, in Canada and the US. The researchers compared these data to *Playboy* centrefold models, Miss America Pageant winners, and *Playgirl* models, and found a growing discrepancy between real bodies and ideal bodies in North America.

Since the 1950s, the body sizes of Miss America Pageant winners have *decreased* appreciably, and those of *Playboy* centrefold models have remained below normal body weight. Over the same period, the body sizes of average young adult North American women and men have *increased* drastically. The increase in body size of young men and women is mainly due to an increase in body fat—the result of a spread of obesity in the general population.

Thus, since the 1950s, the body size and shape of average young adults became increasingly different from the ideal promoted by the media. Further, male and female body images change in opposite ways: ideal women became more petite, yet toned and physically fit, while ideal men bulked up (mainly through increased muscularity). The difference between real men and women in the general population remained small, since both men and women got bigger.

These discrepancies between fantasy (i.e., the media images) and reality may account for the increasing prevalence of body dissatisfaction reported by both women and men. The divergence of cultural norms from real-world possibilities can have at least two results, as we know from Merton's (1957 [1938]) classic study of anomie. One is *acceptance* of the norms and an effort to reproduce them—what Merton called conformity or ritualism. The other is *rejection*, sometimes accompanied by what Merton called *rebellion*. Rebellion, as we will see, may lead to the spread of deviant styles and trends (such as tattooing and piercings) that purposefully violate prevailing appearance norms.

Punk culture, over the past two decades, has exemplified a choice to reject society's ideals and rebel against them. However, excessive thinness, dieting, and eating disorders—prevalent over the same period—have reflected the acceptance of cultural ideals. Anorexia and bulimia are a result of women overconforming to norms of slenderness and sacrificing their health for unattainable cultural goals of perfect thinness.

Always, we are interested in the following questions: Why do people deviate in these ways? How does conventional society respond to such deviance, and how does society's response affect the deviant's behaviour and self-image?

Appearance: Its Social Meaning

In his classic sociological work *Asylums*, Erving Goffman (1958) notes that the first step taken by a total institution, such as a prison or mental hospital is to re-socialize an inmate, by separating the inmate from old identities and identifiers. Interestingly, this process begins by changing the inmate's appearance—for example, by forcing the inmate to wear an institutional uniform, while removing all individual identifiers such as jewellery or personal assets. Often, the inmate is forced to wear a generic hairstyle, which is another way of regimenting the body and eliminating individuality. The loss of one's own clothing signifies the loss of an old identity and social status. The adoption of an institutional uniform represents entry into a low-status community of identical inmates or subjects. In this real sense, the old maxim is true that 'clothes make the man' (or woman). Humble clothes make humble people.

Consider the humble uniforms worn by members of the Salvation Army—a religious organization devoted to urban good works, originally involving the moral uplift of fallen people. Winston (2002) notes that the popular image of Salvation Army women changed during the period 1880–1918, due in part to their adoption of plain, unfashion-able clothing, which enabled them to enter public places such as saloons and brothels to do their work without criticism. So dressed, Salvation Army women practised spiritual warfare on establishments that promoted sin and vice. Their uniform, dramatically severe, came to represent traditional service and old-fashioned virtue.

The connection between appearance, clothing, and self has been known and commented on for a long time. The nineteenth-century Scottish novelist and essayist Thomas Carlyle wrote about clothing metaphorically in his comic work *Sartor Resartus*. There he used clothing to stand in for all symbols of self. People use clothing and other items related to their appearance to construct, confirm, and modify their personal identities within the context of their daily lives. However, personal identities are linked to social identities. Clothes define our place, role, and position in the social order. Carlyle believed that 'clothes present us to ourselves and to the world' as we negotiate our freedom of dressed self-expression.

In turn, society affects both what we reveal and conceal of our bodies (Keenan, 2001). Social pressures constantly undermine our realm of choice and reduce the basic right of self-expression. As a result, clothes never reveal the whole self, since they may be imposed on us or we may use clothes to conceal ourselves. However, given some modicum of choice in how we dress, the choices we make tell the world who we think we are, and who we want to be.

Not surprisingly, appearance norms are gendered—like many other social norms. Not only are men and women judged by different appearance standards; they also wear different kinds of clothing, connoting their different social roles and statuses. Take pockets: historically, pockets on women's clothing have been smaller and fewer than pockets on men's clothing. For women, pockets have been decorative, for men practical. Even today, men and women use their pockets differently (that's why women carry purses), and pockets play a part in the construction of gender.

Underwear is also gendered, though usually unseen except by their wearers and intimate acquaintances. Men's underwear tends to be sturdy and plain. Women's underwear tends to be flimsy and decorative, as though it was on display as part of the mating game. When middle-class women began to wear underpants in the early 1800s, their 'drawers' were feminized by fabric, ornamentation, and an open crotch (Fields, 2002). Such open drawers on respectable, supposedly passionless women presented female sexuality as both erotic and modest. In the twentieth century, however, women demanded crotches in their drawers, to establish their sexual propriety. Women increasingly chose to wear closed drawers during a period of women's greater public presence and feminist activism. This change symbolically closed the gap between men and women.

Even today, the type of underwear known as 'lingerie' is particularly invested with meanings of femininity, sexuality, and pleasure (Storr, 2002). Mass-market lingerie, sex toys, and other 'personal' products are sold to women through the use of particular strategies and images. The processes of choosing and buying lingerie involve identifications of gender, sexuality, and sensuality, even though the garments themselves are rarely if ever worn in public. Moreover, they hold implications of class (and classiness). The class connotations of mass-market lingerie are used by working- and lower-middle-class women to distinguish themselves from higher-class women who are thereby defined as pretentious, boring, or tasteless.

Fashions, then, declare a person's gender and class, and they also declare ethnic origins. In multicultural urban areas, women's fashion choices are closely tied to issues of self-definition. For example, young Asian and white women living in urban, 'multicultural' areas in the United Kingdom express their differently sexualized and racialized female identities through styles of appearance and tastes in clothing, hairstyles, and cosmetics (Malson, Marshall, and Woollett, 2002). In doing so, they are making statements about who they are and how they differ from conventional United Kingdom style and culture.

As we saw with degradation ceremonies in total institutions, when people in authority want to control people, they try to control their modes of dress. This has been evident in the history of fashion in fascist countries, and it is true of dress codes for schoolchildren in our own society. Paulicelli (2002) notes that Italy under the fascist dictator Mussolini used fashion to discipline the social body—especially women's bodies—and to create an identifiable national style. The issue of school uniforms in our society—a practice of imposing dress codes to regiment people's self-expression—brings up a variety of issues that include safety, egalitarianism, social inclusion, and marketing that encourages students to dress competitively (Bodine, 2003).

Left on their own, and unless required to wear uniforms, young people develop clothing aspirations very early in life. Even before adolescence, at ages 8 to 12, children begin making product decisions and building knowledge about different products and brands (Meyer and Anderson, 2000). A desire to conform to appearance norms influences their shopping behaviour, especially with regard to clothing purchase criteria and shopping independence. As preadolescents age, they acquire more of the norms and information needed to make informed clothing decisions. Conformity concerns influence how children shop, whom they shop with, and what they purchase.

Clothing is an expression of both individual and collective identity even among 10 to 11 year olds (Swain, 2002). Relaxing the enforcement of school appearance norms (i.e., a dress code) allows pupils to use clothing to gain recognition, forge common bonds, and share interests within peer group cultures. It also, however, serves to distinguish and separate those who fit in with social expectations of dressing in popular fashions, and those who do not. Certain items and brand names—for example, Doc Martens—acquire a specific, symbolic value for purposes of conformity or rebellion. Pupils who conform to the school dress rules may satisfy the formal requirements of their institution but run a high risk of being stigmatized and excluded by their peers.

Our tendency to conform to appearance norms, learned from childhood onward, largely continues throughout life. This results in a widespread interest in 'fashion'.

The History of Appearance Issues and Public Reaction to Them

The earliest sociological work on clothing and fashion was by Thorstein Veblen (1979 [1899]) and Georg Simmel (1906 [1902]). In his classic work, *Theory of the Leisure Class,* Veblen emphasized that rich people use all fashions—whether fashionable new dances, vacation spots, or modes of dress—as means of 'conspicuous consumption', to distinguish themselves from their social inferiors. For this reason, fashions have to be costly, frivolous, and short-lived. It is precisely their conspicuous wastefulness that makes these fashions 'status-markers'— a means of distinguishing the rich from the thrifty middle-class or the abject poor.

Veblen claimed that fashion is an elite phenomenon that trickles down to lower classes, and new fashions are created as soon as the old fashion has diffused to a larger portion of (common) society. By the time a new appearance norm has been widely adopted in the middle class, it is no longer 'fashionable' to the wealthy. The rich will have long since moved on to a new fashion.

Imitation, however, is as central to fashion and fashionableness as is innovation, as we can see in all hierarchical societies. For example, in colonial societies, the natives often imitate the clothing of colonizers, to signify their identification with the colonial rulers. Friedman (1990) writes that all consumption—including modes of dress—reflects a system of social values and categories imposed from the outside. In the Congo, for example, the practice of *la sape* (meaning 'to dress elegantly') is

even considered a means of gaining power over the (European) life force, whose form is wealth, health, whiteness, and status. In short, *la sape*—a type of social imitation—is a means of accumulating what sociologists call social and cultural capital.

However, colonized peoples do not all imitate their colonizers to the same degree. Some resist the colonizers' norms. In Hong Kong over the past 150 years, both nationalism and colonialism have affected modes of dress, according to gender and social class. For example, Chinese men adopted Westernized dress earlier than women, while working-class Chinese women moved earlier than middle-class women away from the traditional *cheongsam* (Chan, 2000).

Veblen's approach to fashion should be understood in terms of the history of so-called 'sumptuary laws'. These laws, dating back to medieval European society, were used to regulate which types of people were permitted to wear which kinds of clothing and fabrics. Sumptuary laws were intended to prevent low-status people from representing themselves above their station, by means of dress or otherwise. People were expected to dress for the part they played in society—not the part to which they aspired. To keep the lower classes from emulating the clothing of the upper class, most European countries passed sumptuary laws to regulate dress (Giusberti and Belfonti, 2000). Foreign visitors to cities and courts devoted considerable attention to the appearance of the people they encountered. Such close observation was motivated by a serious purpose. Clothing was thought to offer a kind of window on individuals and societies alike. It told the observer about the general prosperity of the population, and its degree and extent of social differentiation (Allerston, 2000).

With the end of sumptuary laws but prior to industrialization, fashion was largely restricted to prosperous, educated people. In the middle and upper classes, a new form of fashion talk emerged. Fashion came to be seen as important and a sign of cultivation—not merely a form of conspicuous consumption by the rich (Rantanen, 2001). A self-conscious fashion cycle was noted first among the European aristocracy in the eighteenth and nineteenth centuries. There, the fashion system celebrated novelty over tradition, highlighting the individual aesthetic. People of 'taste' were increasingly celebrated.

In European societies before industrialization took hold, two related social processes—the imitation of social superiors and the effort to distinguish oneself from one's equals or inferiors—had been central to changing lifestyles, fashions, tastes, and consumption patterns. Then, as Pierre Bourdieu (1984) has shown in 'A Social Critique of the Judgement of Taste', to achieve the standard of good taste required the accumulation of 'cultural capital', an ability afforded only to the upper classes.

During the seventeenth and eighteenth centuries, both the French and English clothing industries expanded, largely because of increased demand by the working classes. Gradually, the influence of fashion filtered down to the middling and then even the labouring classes. In England, the dress of the common people changed considerably over the eighteenth century (Lemire, 2000). Efforts to prevent the lower classes from wearing fashionable-looking clothes—cheap knockoffs, then as now—generally failed. The fashion floodgates were opened even wider by the French Revolution, which encouraged every citizen to dress as he or she chose, in praise of individuality and against hierarchy.

With the continued mass production of clothing in the nineteenth and twentieth centuries, fashion trickled down from the richest to poorest classes. However, the imitation of social superiors was no longer the sole driving force. In modern societies, the idea that fashion arises only from the desire of the lower class to imitate the upper class is no longer valid. Some fashion trends continue to trickle-down from the elite; however, other fashion trends emerge from the 'streets' (Ragone, 1996).

Sociologist Georg Simmel (1906 [1902]), a far subtler thinker than Veblen (1979 [1899]), saw clothing, fashion, and other appearance issues as standing in a complex relationship to individuals and society. On the one hand, all items of appearance are individual—expressions of the self, as Carlyle had pointed out. On the other hand, all items of appearance are also social—a means of identifying with particular social groups or communities, as Veblen had pointed out.

Thus, fashion—whether in clothing, body shape, body adornment, or otherwise—must be viewed as a process of constant negotiation between these two levels of reality: between self and society. Simmel highlighted this phenomenon when he attempted to explain the rapid diffusion and decline of fashion. He hypothesized that the very instability of fashion results from the combined action of imitation (of higher status members) and distinction (from those belonging to lower statuses). This process—in earlier days, highly controlled and centralized—has been replaced by a system in which fashion designers around the world create designs for small publics in global markets. Often, these designers are in the 'fashion business' more generally, and not merely the clothing business; they make their profits from luxury products other than clothing (e.g., perfumes, jewellery, leather goods).

The designers of clothing and cosmetics are constantly producing new things for us to want and need. Consumerism drives the economy, and manufactured dissatisfaction with appearance drives consumerism. Thus, for the past hundred years at least, the spread of fashion has gone hand-in-hand with mass production and mass advertising. For example, Turbin (2002) writes that the Arrow Man, one of the most successful advertising images in early-twentieth-century America, was a visual representation of the 'New Man'. The Arrow Man was created to sell the Arrow collar, a new version of detachable collars, and a wardrobe staple for most American men and all but working-class men in Great Britain and Europe since the 1840s. Thus, to sell this new kind of shirt meant selling a desire to become this New Man.

The Arrow Man's story is part of the change in masculine ideals and physical appearance, heightened by a new visual and consumer culture. The Arrow Man carried messages of men's self-management of appearance and public performance. It created a new category of dress—office dress—that was appropriate to twentieth-century needs, and rejected any connection with European gentility. To sell this shirt meant telling the story of the new American white-collar man—the Arrow Man—and his place in the new occupational and social class formations of American society. It added a new character to American popular culture who was markedly different from any of the white-collar workers in nineteenth-century novels by, say, Dickens (e.g., Bob Cratchet).

Appearance Communities and Cultures

Appearance norms tend to homogenize the ways that people look. However, in the realm of appearance, self-presentation and behaviour, some people break the rules and violate expectations, forming deviant communities and subcultures. Like other deviant communities, appearance communities are supported by the powerful need to achieve social cohesion and inclusion. Often, appearance communities are also committed to the achievement of beauty and distinctiveness. One appearance community—the world of high-fashion modelling—sets the publicized (commercial) trends and, ultimately, the standards of beauty for all women.

Other deviant communities, such as the world of tattooing and body piercing, present alternative visions of dress and body adornment, through engagement in somewhat distinctive lifestyles and ideas.

Tattooing and body piercing

People decorate their bodies in all kinds of ways. Some rely on clothing, jewellery, hairstyles, and makeup, while others also use tattoos and body piercing as decorations. As we have said repeatedly, appearance is an indicator of who you think you are, and who you want other people to think you are.

Before the invention of the tattooing machine, tattoos were mainly seen in the higher echelons of European society, such as the aristocracy. Among high-class German men attending university, duelling scars served a similar purpose of designating class and manliness. Gradually, like other fashions, tattoos moved down the social hierarchy. The first professional tattoo artist in the United States—a man named Martin Hildebrandt—opened the first tattoo parlour in New York City in 1846.

Tattooing and piercing have always been connected to certain groups and their members. Group membership itself is an important part of self-identification—especially for members of marginalized groups; and tattoos make this identification easier (Jetten, 2001). In the past, tattoo wearers were particularly likely to have spent a lot of time in the presence of other men: in gangs, prisons, on ships, or on military bases. For gang members and prisoners, the layers of tattoos recorded personal experience. For people in prison, they expressed a convict's desire to remember his loved ones or his own identity (Kent, 1997). Tattoos, in this way, told the story of people's lives, aspirations, and group affiliations.

Today, male Chicano convicts still use body tattooing as part of a discourse of political resistance (Olguin, 1997). They use tattoos to speak their minds about the US war on crime and Chicano status in American society, for example. Given the high degree of surveillance in prisons that Foucault pointed out, and its relation to power, some convicts are able to 'regain' their bodies through illegal tattooing. Thus, by making a political statement through their tattoos, Chicanos are able to gain a small degree of power and freedom in their confinement, precisely because their tattoos are visible to people in authority.

Public views about tattooing have changed over the years. The increased presence and visibility of art-school trained, 'fine art', or 'custom' tattoo artists has contributed to a dramatically expanding range of images that many define as artistic products, not 'just tattoos' (Vail, 2000). Nor are tattoos limited to a small group of people, as in the past. Since the early 1990s, Canadian women have taken to tattoos in record numbers. Like men, these women are using tattoos to send a variety of personal and cultural messages, challenging the long-standing association between tattooing and masculinity. Women's tattoos reflect a desire to expose a feminine side to this masculine art.

Once considered low class or dangerous symbols, tattoos began to be defined as hip, trendy, and glamorous in the 1990s (Irwin, 2001). The shift in perceptions of tattooing illustrates some of the interpretive processes at work in the destigmatization of deviance. The process starts with individuals attempting to legitimate their tattoos—or other visible deviance—during interactions with others. First-time tattooees in the 1990s were 'agents of change' caught between multiple symbolic orders. Middle-class tattooees worked to overcome the negative meanings associated with tattoos by getting body art that conformed to core mainstream norms and values.

This decorative trend has a demographic aspect. Young people are far more likely than older people to practise tattooing and body piercing, and to experiment with a variety of other modes of dress, jewellery, and hairstyle. According to Health Canada (2001b), tattoos and ear/body piercings are especially popular today among people aged 18 to 22. An American university survey in 2001 found that 51 per cent of students had piercings and 23 per cent had tattoos. US studies show that the number of women with tattoos quadrupled between 1960 and 1980. In response to the new demand, the number of tattooing and piercing shops in Canada has also increased dramatically in the past few years.

Today, tattoos are more widespread than in the past. They are not restricted to men, or men who spend a lot of time in the company of other men. Yet, one thing has not changed: the tattooed body remains a distinctively communicative body. Body decoration has a great deal to say, not only about the identity of the wearer, but also about the culture in which the wearer lives (Kosut, 2000). Most tattoos still signify affection for families and loved ones. Among men, six images are the most common: an anchor, a woman, the crucifixion, a cross, a heart, and a mermaid. Like other forms of adornment, including clothing, tattoos are tools of individuality and affiliation. As we saw in the case of Chicano prisoners, they may also protest against oppression and exclusion from the larger social world (Phillips, 2001).

Wearing a tattoo may increase a person's acceptance in a deviant community but also increase the likelihood of rejection in a conventional community. According to the Health Canada (2001b) report on youth tattooing and piercing, body piercings and tattoos are visual cues suggesting that a teen wants to be associated with the experimental, risk-taking community. As a result, the tattooed and pierced teen emerges as significantly different from a mainstream teen. The tattooed teen (and to a lesser extent, the pierced teen) is an early style adopter, prone to risky behaviour and likely to use drugs and alcohol.

Punk Appearance

Another violation of the mainstream appearance norm is punk-oriented dress and behaviour; it too is associated with its own community and subculture. Punk culture in Canada and in the US emerged in the late 1970s with the appearance of punk bands in mainstream rock music. The influence of punk style peaked in the 1990s, and today it has a marginal but continued status in the youth culture, as part of a repertoire of (rapidly changing) clothing and behaviour styles.

Punk started in Britain. There, the punk subculture and its music helped change the way people talked about social stratification in Great Britain in the late-1970s. Punk music, and the musicians who made it popular, reintroduced working-class and youth values of rebellion into British culture, exposing the wider public to the privations of poverty during an era of economic recession. The punk songs had promoted punk values through the repeated use of words such as 'anarchy', 'pop', and 'violence' (Simonelli, 2002).

The punk style of dress is aggressively poor and openly opposed to conventional middle-class dress. It combines a variety of appearance traits: dress, makeup, hairstyle, body language, and body adornment (tattoos, piercing, and jewellery). These are as central to the punk persona as attitude, acting, speaking, or listening to punk music. In communities of young people, punk music is a central symbol around which punk socializing and organizing take place. Drug-taking is a central activity.

In Canada, punk culture serves mainly as a fashion that links young people with similar interests. Punk is a term usually applied to music. However, it is also used to describe the group of people who follow and produce the music. Besides direct contact with punk bands, some fans create shrines, set up concerts, and spend their free time in activities related to punk ideals. They adopt a lifestyle we can term 'punk'. Punk may be a way of thinking and acting that young people move through as they age, with a definite ending tied to age. Some psychological theorists also rely on early childhood trauma to explain punk culture, tattooing, and body piercing as deviant behaviours.

One researcher has proposed a developmental model for participation in the punk subculture, with three stages of progression: (1) rebellion against mainstream norms; (2) affiliation with the community/lifestyle; and (3) transcendence from the typical punk style resulting from serious commitment to the antiauthoritarian, individualistic punk ideology (Andes, 1998). Many—perhaps most—go through a fourth stage as they get older. They drop out of the punk subculture into a modified version of normal middle-class life.

Punk culture in Canada and the US emerged in the late 1970s and 1980s, with the appearance of punk bands in mainstream rock music. During the early 1980s, a separate faction of the punk rock movement emerged in the US and Canada. They called themselves 'straightedge youth' and took a militant and often violent stance against alcohol and drug use and casual sex. In doing so, this new subculture distinguished itself from the general North American punk rock youth phenomenon (Wood, 1998).

In short, the punk culture has always been a rebellious culture, or collection of related subcultures, each with its own language, style, and dress code. It offers people who appreciate those standards an attainable model of beauty or physical appeal, correlated with a shared value system. The codes of appearance enable members to find each other and form subcultures together on the outskirts of mainstream culture. It allows them to bypass the sometimes unattainable social appearance norms, and find acceptance more readily.

The reaction of most mainstream members of our society to punk style is shock and repulsion. Punkers intentionally choose styles of expression that will symbolically reverse or otherwise violate values and norms of the dominant culture. What the punk phenomenon shows is that cultural, social, and political ideas, expressed musically and in other ways (e.g., through drug use), can be associated with particular styles of dress and appearance.

There are loose connections between punk culture and the so-called rave culture. Like punk culture, rave culture developed in an urban environment, as part of the urban lifestyle. Drug use in the rave culture, as in the punk culture, focuses on music and dance as well as aesthetics (e.g., clothing and adornment). Decorative surroundings (e.g., lighting and trendy clothing) accentuate the participants appearance. Rave culture is not unified, however, and comprises many differing cultures, reflecting (in part) differences in the drugs used—whether psychedelic or stimulant. Psychedelic culture is an aspect of the rave culture where mainly psychedelic drugs such as LSD, mescaline, and Ecstasy are used, while smoking cannabis is viewed as a customary part of everyday life. This (rebellious) form of drug use is typically regarded as 'invisible rebellion': rebellion against parental authority and the rules of society.

Members of rave culture are very particular about which substances are used, where and how. Hard drug use is usually restricted to parties and on weekends. This is because, even though the culture appears to be founded on deviance, its members share some values held by conventional society, such as employment and success. Many similarities can be found between the rave culture and the cannabis culture of the 1960s, as both were part of a wide and profound societal change. However, rave culture also embodies those values that are prominent in Western capitalist societies, emphasizing individuality, a faith in technology, a desire for new experience, and a strong esthetic sense.

Fashion models

One might think that people who embody the cultural ideal were conformists, but in fact they are deviant—in the same sense that Mother Teresa—though saintly—is a deviant. The community of high-fashion models is deviant in its approximation to the ideal body. Thus, fashion models are to appearance norms as saints are to everyday morality.

'Fashion models': the very words cause people to conjure up images of runways, beautiful clothes, foreign travel, glamour, and fame. For many, models represent the ideal woman or man. Their rare and perfect beauty captures the attention of fashion-conscious people everywhere. Over time, the modelling industry has become more inclusive, by widening the range of qualifications that models may possess in different types of modelling (e.g., plus-size modelling, petite-size modelling, catalogue-modelling). Plus-size (i.e., large) models and petite-size models, as their names imply, are hired to sell products designed to meet the needs of larger-than-average and smaller-than-average individuals, respectively. And, as we noted earlier, most real people today are far closer to plus-size

models than they are to ordinary models, thanks to our common eating habits.

However, tall, slim, waiflike runway and high-fashion models continue to get the greatest media attention. Runway and high-fashion modelling has very specific expectations as for physical appearance. The requirements for high-fashion models include: a height of 5'9" to 6', a small dress size of 6 to 8, a 32" to 35" bust, 22" to 25" waist, and 33" to 36" hips. Additionally, top models are expected to display confidence, independence, discipline, intelligence, and stamina. There are only a few top models in the world, and they certainly are not representative of most women. Yet, in a society like ours that places enormous value on physical beauty, this elite group exerts great influence on the average woman. Some researchers suggest that this influence is a factor in the development of anorexia, especially among the female population.

Unintended Deviance: Anorexia, Bulimia, and Obesity

As with fashions in clothing and adornment, fashions in body size and shape change over time. For centuries, eating disorders among women have been the subject of discussion and debate. Anorexia has its roots as far back as the thirteenth century. People then canonized religious women as saints for their fasting practices. Scholars sometimes call these women 'holy anorexics'. Eating disorders have probably occurred in other societies too. However, the reasons may have been somewhat different. In other cultures, young women who denied themselves food may have valued spiritual health, fasting, and self-denial much as our own society values thinness, self-control, and athleticism (Eating Disorder Recovery Centre, 2005).

Seventy years ago, the woman for whom a King gave up his throne—Wallis Simpson—declared that you can't be too rich or too thin. Today, people might disagree with the second part of that statement. Increasingly, people consider thinness to the degree that bones show through skin—whatever its

**Table 2.1   Obesity by Household Income[a]
            Quintile, Canada and United
            States, 2002 to 2003[‡]**

Income Quintile	Canada	United States
1st (poorest)	17.6	27.3[*]
2nd	16.6[*]	23.4[*]
3rd	16.2	19.4
4th	14.4[*]	19.5[*]
5th (richest)	12.7	14.8

Notes:
i)   Household population aged 18 and over.
ii) Missing data ('I don't know', 'not stated', 'refusal')
     have been excluded from the analysis (except for
     income due to the high level of missing cases).
[a]   Household income adjusted for household size.
[‡]   Age-adjusted per cents calculated using the
     projected 2000 United States standard population.
[*]   Significant difference between Canada and United
     States (p < 0.05).

Source: Statistics Canada, Joint Canada/United States Survey
of Health, 2002 to 2003; available at <www.statcan.ca/english/
freepub/82M0022XIE/ 2003001/tables/tablea.9.htm>.

merits for fashion modelling or ballet—unhealthy
and unattractive. More than that, excessive thinness
is often linked to disordered eating. For centuries,
eating disorders resulting in too-little weight among
women have been the subject of casual discussion
and debate. In the 1970s and 1980s, eating disorders finally received media attention with the death
of singer Karen Carpenter from cardiac compli-
cations because of anorexia nervosa. This was the
first time the media focused attention on the life-
threatening consequences of eating disorders and
stopped viewing them as simply a group of 'benign'
psychiatric illnesses.

As for obesity, people increasingly recognize the
problems associated with too much weight. *Obesity
is excessive body weight*, given the person's age, sex,
and height, and the weight norms that prevail in
a given culture or subculture. There is a class and
status element to obesity that is opposite to that
of anorexia. Obesity and thinness, like clothing,

are status markers. Where thinness is often associated with highly educated middle- and upper-class
women, obesity is often associated with poorer
women. Less educated and rural people are also
more likely than average to be obese. Table 2.1 and
Figure 2.1 show obesity statistics based on household income in Canada.

Like excessive thinness, however, obesity often
diminishes the length and quality of life. It is associated with health problems such as diabetes, back
problems, smoking, and drinking. Typically, people
who are obese eat badly and abuse their bodies in
other ways as well—for example, by not getting
enough sleep, exercise, or fresh vegetables. Thus, like
thinness caused by anorexia, obesity is an indicator
of lifestyle and psychological state.

In earlier times, people thought obesity showed
a hearty, healthy appetite, a lust for living, and
good sense of humour (think of Santa Claus, for
example—round and jolly.) Today, increasing
numbers of people shun obesity, or even plumpness.
A huge industry devoted to dieting, exercise, and
'weight-watching' has developed to encourage
people to lose weight and keep it off. The majority
of consumers of this industry are women. They
continue to be more concerned about their
appearance than men, since they are more likely
than men to view their appearance as a major asset
in sociosexual exchange.

Eating Issues and Appearance Norms

Many different disorders involve food, eating, and
weight. However, in everyday conversation, the
term 'eating disorder' has come to mean anorexia
nervosa, bulimia, binge eating, and obesity. All these
disorders (except obesity) are more common among
women than among men. However, men are also
starting to come forward with problems of body
image, thinness concerns, and eating disorders. As
a result, young men are being encouraged to share
their concerns about body image and weight at an
earlier stage, since we now know that these issues are
common to both sexes (Eliot, 2001).

Figure 2.1   Obesity by Household Income Quintile, Canada and United States, 2002 to 2003

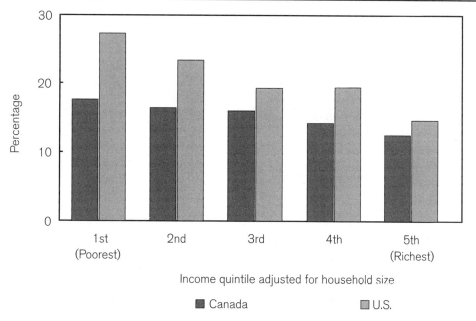

Income quintile adjusted for household size

■ Canada   ■ U.S.

SOURCE: Statistics Canada, Joint Canada/United States Survey of Health, 2002 to 2003; available at <www.statcan.ca/english/freepub/82M0022XIE/2003001/figures/fig9.htm>.

Anorexia nervosa is one of the most common eating disorders, characterized by a relentless pursuit of thinness and a refusal to maintain normal body weight, given the person's age and height. The characteristics of anorexia nervosa include a 15 per cent or more loss of body weight, the use of various strategies to lose weight, a weight phobia, body image disturbances, amenorrhea (i.e., the end of menstruation for at least three consecutive cycles), and a constant preoccupation with food (Polivy and Herman, 2002). Researchers are convinced that this eating disorder is part of a more general psychological disorder. For example, anorexia nervosa often includes symptoms of depression, irritability, and withdrawal. Eating becomes ritualized, as in other obsessive-compulsive disorders; the anorexic displays strange eating habits and a division of foods into good and bad categories. People suffering from anorexia often have a low tolerance for new situa-

tions, and dislike changes in their lives. Many fear growing up and assuming adult responsibilities or an adult lifestyle. For these people, dieting may represent an avoidance of, or ineffective attempts to cope with, the demands of a new life stage such as adolescence or adulthood.

About 95 per cent of anorexics are women. Though only 1 per cent of female adolescents have anorexia, certain attachment problems and anxiety disorders may put adolescents at risk of developing anorexia nervosa. Young females, who felt more anxious and concerned with their body image, shape, and size, preferred a more petite body ideal, and experienced more concern with their weight and physical appearance. Anxiety about weight and a negative body image were positively correlated to the development of eating disorders.

A related illness, bulimia nervosa, involves purging the food after consuming it: that is, vomiting after eating. Like an anorexic, a bulimic—a person suffering from bulimia—believes self-worth requires being thin. Bulimics consume large amounts of food in a short time. Their food-binges often occur in secret and typically involve high-calorie, high-carbohydrate foods they can eat quickly, such as ice cream, doughnuts, candy, popcorn, and cookies. Like anorexia, bulimia is lethal. About 50 per cent of people who have been anorexic develop bulimia or bulimic patterns. Research suggests that about four out of every hundred college-aged women have bulimia. However, because people with bulimia are secretive, it is hard to know how many older people are affected.

Obesity

Overall, our society deems a person obese if that person's weight is at least 20 per cent above the statistical norm for that person's sex, age, height, and skeletal frame. Given women's greater concern with thinness, it is no surprise that men are somewhat more likely than women to be obese.

Obese people—especially obese children—are often treated like deviants, ridiculed, and stigmatized. They are often the targets of teasing and exclusion, leading to increased psychological stress and lower self-esteem (Covington et al., 2001). Obese children are more likely to suffer rejection by others (Broadwater, 2002) and develop a fear of interacting with peers, leading to social isolation. They often experience hardships related to employment, intimacy, and familiar relations. This stereotyping and the resultant exclusion can lead to the development of a negative self-image that researchers have observed in children as young as five (Ebbeling et al., 2002). Many overweight individuals adopt methods of resisting the hurtfulness of exclusion; they include aggression, withdrawal, verbal reprimand of the abuser, and self acceptance and approval.

The abuse and exclusion is due, in part, because obesity is culturally assumed to connote laziness and lack of self-discipline, self-worth, or concern

Table 2.2 Diet and Nutrition: Proportion of Overweight and Obese Children and Adolescents Aged 2 to 19 Years by Sex, England, 1995–2000

	Percentage Overweight	Percentage Obese
Boys		
1995	18.6	3.7
1996	19.3	4.1
1997	17.7	4.0
1998	21.1	4.2
1999	23.0	5.9
2000	20.3	4.8
Girls		
1995	23.5	5.7
1996	22.7	5.9
1997	22.9	5.8
1998	25.5	7.0
1999	25.2	7.1
2000	26.6	6.8

SOURCE: Adapted from National Statistics Online; available at <www.statistics.gov.uk/cci/nugget_print.asp?ID=718>.

with one's personal appearance. And, indeed, there is some connection between obesity and behaviour. Activity patterns play a part in the development and avoidance of obesity. A study by Sarah Gable and Susan Lutz (2000) found that obese children spend fewer hours in active physical play, take part in fewer extracurricular activities and watch more television than other children. Not only do sedentary activities displace physical activity, but they also promote overeating. Children watching television tend to passively consume excess amounts of energy-dense foods, and often ignore satiety cues. Table 2.2 shows rising statistics for overweight children in England.

Yet, attributions of moral looseness are often unwarranted. Some obesity is beyond the control of the individuals concerned. For genetic and familial reasons, obesity often begins in childhood. In America, obesity is the most common nutritional disease, affecting one in five children (Broadwater, 2002). Obesity increases children's risk of chronic diseases such hypertension, dyslipidemia, impaired glucose homeostasis, steatohepatitis, and many others.

Several factors influence the development of childhood obesity. Alexander-Mott and Lumsden (1999) state that many countries are overnourished: that prosperity and abundance are at the root of the obesity problem. However, obesity is a result of environmental and genetic factors, and not simply the result of an excessive food intake (Wardle et al., 2001). Further, many obese people come from poor, not prosperous families. Children from low-income, ethnic minority families have experienced the greatest increase in child obesity over the past twenty years (Ebbeling et al., 2002; Strauss and Pollack, 2001).

Both family and genetic factors play a part in obesity. Researchers find that the children of an obese parent are five times more likely than children of normal-weight parents to become obese in adult life. The risk is even greater for children who come from families in which *both* parents are obese, compared to families in which only one parent is obese. To show the genetic connection between obese parents and obese children, Wardle and colleagues looked for and found a higher correlation between the children's weight and that of their natural parents, than with the weight of their adoptive parents.

The same researchers also compared children from obese and lean families, using parental obesity as a marker of the obesity-risk phenotype, to find a comparable difference between food and activity preferences. They found little difference between the food and activity preferences of children from obese and lean parents, further supporting a genetic (rather than social) explanation of childhood obesity. Supporting this, studies find a genetic component to the number of fat cells in a person's body.

However, other studies show that early childhood nutrition may also influence the number of adipose (fat-holding) cells. This implies a social component to obesity. A study conducted in February 2003 by the Weight Realities Division of the Society for Nutrition Education finds that, among children, eating attitudes, obesity, physical activity, and body image are all interrelated. Although genetic makeup is important, dietary and physical factors also play a key role. Fitness and leanness are far more common in the prosperous upper-middle class. So, we know that both social and economic factors are at work.

Certain types of behaviour are likely to increase the risk of obesity from childhood on. They include poor nutritional practices—for example, a tendency to eat junk foods, an absence of exercise, and a tendency to binge eating. They also include poor adaptations to mental stress. Females, young and old, are more likely than males to overeat in response to negative emotions, such as anger, anxiety, and depression. A comparison study between women who binge regularly and those who did not showed that in the former group, binge episodes were set off by troublesome or stressful events occurring on the binge days. Childhood sexual abuse can also affect a person's eating patterns. Presumably, sexual (and other) childhood abuse causes problems of self-worth that, in turn, cause self-damaging behaviours of various kinds.

Theories about Appearance Issues

Theories about people's conformity to appearance norms and the consequences of deviation—especially, theories about stigma, anorexia, and obesity—are plentiful.

Psychological theories

Psychological theories often argue that deviants are reacting against conformity itself or figures of authority; or that deviance shows self-hate and self-negation. All these may contribute to eating disorders. In addition, traumatic events may also lead to eating disorders: for example, forced sexual encounters early in life are reportedly associated with bulimic-type eating pathology (Kaltiala-Heino et al., 2001).

Further, because eating disorders are frequently associated with childhood conflicts or traumas, they are often connected to later incidents of depression, which are seen as the residue of childhood traumas. Even among adolescents, chronic depressive symptoms are highly correlated with symptoms of bulimia nervosa or binge-eating disorders (Zaider et al., 2002).

Typically, the same childhood conflicts or traumas appear to be responsible for the development of both depression and eating disorders. Other psychological symptoms are also associated with deviant eating patterns, such as the individual being a perfectionist, or the development of Obsessive Compulsive disorder. The rebellion against mainstream society, by means of extreme dress and body adornment, may reflect an extreme desire to reject and ridicule figures of authority.

So, we cannot ignore the possibility that some forms of appearance deviation have psychological as well as genetic bases.

Sociological theories

However, sociologists note that deviant appearance is not usually a solo accomplishment but often occurs in groups as part of communities and subcultures. We need sociological theories to explain the rise and survival of the social groups that encourage and support deviant appearance. With this in mind, sociologists have developed different perspectives on how appearance issues emerge.

Functionalist theories

The main functionalist approaches to understanding a deviant appearance are structural. Recall Merton's (1957 [1938]) theory of adaptations to anomie, in which certain deviant types of conduct arise out of the dissociation (or gap) between culturally prescribed aspirations and access to the socially accepted methods for attaining them. This approach applies to appearance norms too.

Bodily beauty as a cultural goal presents a strong risk of anomie, because beauty is largely an innate physical attribute. For example, evidence suggests an inborn preference for symmetrical (facial) features: babies smile when they see a symmetrical face and cry when they see an asymmetrical face. People born without such innate and accepted characteristics of beauty can do little to change this, as we are limited in the degree to which we can improve our appearance. Even with exercise and plastic surgery, we cannot all become gorgeous, or even as thin as the media urge us to be. Moreover, access to the means of acquiring beauty (e.g., the ability to pay for plastic surgery) is limited, like other consumer objects and services, by the money we have available.

The majority of individuals in society who are not thin or beautiful, or wealthy enough to afford a makeover, are caught in a dilemma. They may try to reject the beauty goals of our society, but this is hard to do in a society so immersed in media images of conventional beauty. Or, like the *rebels* in Merton's model of anomie, they can join a group that substitutes different, attainable norms of dress and appearance for the conventional ones. It is easy to understand punk culture within this 'rebel' framework. It offers group members a different way of being attractive, within the punk community. In this way, punk culture gives its members self-esteem and a social life outside the conventional norms of beauty and appearance.

However, the rebellious adaptation to anomie takes a lot of work. To maintain a rebellious community means recruiting new members. Such a community must grow or die. Learning and practising the punk appearance code is a means of initiation into the subculture. Piercings, tattoos, unnatural colors of hair (e.g., blue, green), and distinct manner of dress—all characteristics of the punk culture that many view as deviant—all serve social functions within the context of a deviant community. First, they give people membership in the deviant punk subculture. Being part of something is important to people, especially young people. In an atomized urban world, people sometimes find it hard to find an identity for themselves. Tattoos and body piercings

Box 2.1 Parent and Child Factors Associated with Youth Obesity

Having an obese parent greatly increased the odds of obesity among adolescent boys and girls, according to a new study.

Excess weight among parents was a major factor in excess weight for adolescent boys and girls. Among girls aged 12 to 19 who lived with an obese parent, 18 per cent were overweight and 10 per cent were obese. The situation was similar for boys: 22 per cent of boys with an obese parent were overweight, and 12 per cent were obese.

Aside from weight, other parental habits were associated with those of their children. These include physical activity, smoking, and eating habits—all factors that should be considered together in investigations of youth obesity.

Youth aged 12 to 19 with a reporting parent who was inactive during leisure time were more likely to be inactive themselves. And if the adolescents' parents smoked or ate fruits and vegetables relatively infrequently, the adolescents were likely to mirror these behaviours.

A subtle difference emerged between the sexes in adolescent activity during leisure time. The proportion of boys who reported being active was similar in households with an active or moderately active reporting parent. But this was not the case for girls, who were less active even when the reporting parent was moderately active. This raises the possibility that if parents' level of physical activity is mimicked by their children, then it is especially important that girls have an active role model.

SOURCE: Statistics Canada, *The Daily*, 3 November 2003.

give people an opportunity to identify themselves with certain groups and, at the same time, to distinguish themselves from the rest of society.

Second, deviant appearance (such as green hair) also serves as a boundary line to help people understand what is acceptable and what is not. Without such visible boundaries, it would be harder to enforce behavioural norms and rules that exist in a society. Thus, deviant items of appearance help strengthen social cohesion by drawing a clearer line between the people who violate the appearance norms and people who do not.

Conflict theories

Conflict theories propose that deviance is the result of a clash between competing value systems or lifestyles. These value systems or lifestyles are, in turn, produced by subcultures and transmitted by learning from one member to another. In this view, deviance is a normal, learned behaviour. Unequal power determines who has the right to declare what is normal and abnormal, proper or deviant. People with less power use deviant acts to challenge and rebel against the norms instituted by people in power.

Body image has become an enormous business enterprise in North America. Both men and women spend a lot of money on plastic surgery to achieve the appearance they are taught to desire by advertisers in the mass media. Nowhere is it more evident that our business-driven civilization is geared to making people hate themselves and feel discontented so that they can be sold a formula for happiness by some plastic surgeon, exercise clinic, diet planner, or other 'expert' in the area of appearance.

Interactionist theories

Interactionist theories, as we have seen, focus on the ways people interpret particular behaviours (whether deviant or not), and the ways such interpretations help to construct the social world and subsequent social problems.

We all learn our values from family, friends, co-workers, and others. Those values either oppose or support deviant behaviour. Differential association theory suggests that eating disorders, for example, are behaviours often learned directly from more powerful family members. Mothers with eating disorders, in particular, have the power to shape their children's eating habits, and are particularly likely to influence the development of eating disorders in daughters (Vander Ven and Vander Ven, 2003).

The onset of anorexia, bulimia, or other eating disorders is often a result of learned behaviour of preoccupation with food, especially the non-nutritional value of food, and dieting practices of parents, mainly of mothers. Many adolescents grow up with a distorted perception of food and the social value of food. For example, they may grow up associating food, food preparation, and eating with that part of the world dominated by women—especially, mothers. Thus, eating behaviour becomes a tacit acceptance or rejection of that world and the women who dominate it. To eat a lot is to give mother your love and approval; to eat little is to control her, reject her, or humiliate her.

The differential association theory can also be used to explain punk culture. Tattooing, piercing, and the other deviant behaviours associated with punk culture are learned from members of the punk subculture. People identify with the culture itself and with other members by 'marking' themselves so other people can also identify their membership. Additionally, as we have noted, the punk

culture declares itself to be anarchistic, or at least anti-middle class, in its dress, speech, and values. Its desire to deviate grows out of a deep-seated class (and age) conflict in Western societies.

Appearance and stigmatization

Sociologist Erving Goffman (1963) uses the theatrical metaphors of stage, actors, and audiences to examine the complexities of social interaction. Appearance issues are particularly well suited to this approach, because physical attractiveness—like theatre—relies so much on what we can see and can't see. Goffman notes that—like actors—we all bring social expectations to any situation and these serve as scripts we feel obliged to follow. We are motivated to give believable performances, but our performances and their credibility are put at risk by discrediting or discreditable features. Of these, a flawed or deviant appearance is the most immediately visible and therefore dangerous.

For example, a prominent black eye or facial scar invites staring, curiosity, and potentially unpleasant questions. These tend to undermine the actors' performances and impede social interaction. A person who has been physically deformed may even be excluded or targeted for his physical deformities (especially if the deformation is visible). He may be reduced in our minds from a whole and usual person to a tainted and discounted one.

Any attribute that has such a discrediting effect may be called a failing, a shortcoming, or a handicap. Goffman calls it a *stigma*—a brand or mark that brings disgrace. Such a mark reveals a discrepancy between virtual and actual social identity—between the person I am pretending to be and the person I actually am. In its most general meaning, a stigma is any characteristic, behaviour, or experience that may cause the 'branded' person to be rejected by others. The stigma spoils that person's social identity, and interferes with his or her social life.

Goffman specifically mentions two types of stigmatized people, the discredited and discreditable. The discredited are people who visibly vary from ideal humans. They are appearance deviants, as we are calling them in this chapter: the very fat or very thin, very tall or very short, and so on. They have to manage their social interactions in the face of their discredited, or visibly deviant, features. The discreditable, by contrast, vary from ideal humans secretly. They have secret deformities and 'scars'— for example, a history of sexual abuse, imprisonment, or expulsion from university. If their secrets were known, they would be discredited—that is, rejected by other people.

The discreditable have an interest in managing their social interactions to keep their stigmatizing qualities hidden. Discredited people may try to compensate for their status-losing deficiency, perhaps by developing a superior skill in another area. Discreditable persons try to hide their shame, and worry about their secret becoming known by critical people.

In the end, Goffman is talking about everyone. Everyone varies from the ideal human—both visibly and secretly—so everyone is both discredited and discreditable to some extent. The appearance of 'normality' is staged—a social accomplishment achieved only by people committed to sustaining an illusion of normality. People conform to appearance norms because they want to facilitate their social interactions. They recognize that their social life, social status, and social identity all rest on an appearance that is considered 'normal' and creditable.

From this standpoint, anorexia can be viewed as an attempt to perfectly satisfy the norms of a self-disciplined bodily appearance. Social norms have unintended consequences: the same norms that are meant to aid in maintaining social order also punish people who fall short. Their inability or refusal to follow social norms can have detrimental results (e.g., eating disorders, stigmatization, and deteriorating health). A prime example is the price women pay if they fall short of the society's beauty ideals. Women are judged by their appearance more consistently and more harshly than men.

Symbolic interactionists are interested in the learning of deviant values and behaviours. First, they are particularly interested in the means of transmission—in how people learn to conform and deviate. For example, *how* do people learn to identify and emulate a punk style of dress and speaking? How do they learn to dress 'well' or 'stylishly'? Second, symbolic interactionists are interested in secondary deviation: what happens to people *after* they have deviated, and how reactions to their deviance strengthen their deviant identity and group membership.

So, for example, where eating disorders are concerned, symbolic interactionists would be interested in knowing how people learn to binge and purge: what skills and drugs are used, and how people communicate this information. They would be interested in knowing whether excessively thin anorexic people feel a kinship with other anorexic people, and whether they express and enact this kinship through association and conversation. Likewise, they would be interested in knowing whether obese people feel a kinship with other obese people, a distance from people of normal weight, and any sense that they are violating weight norms of the society. Or, to take another example, they would be interested in knowing whether people with freckles, or gaps between their front teeth, or premature baldness, share a sense of ridicule or exclusion, and how they communicate about this.

Additionally, symbolic interactionists would be interested in knowing whether and how anorexic, obese, punk, or tattooed and pierced people are stigmatized for their deviant appearance. They might study the form this stigmatization takes: whether ridicule, exclusion, social distance, or job discrimination, for example. They would also be interested in knowing how people who suffer these reactions 'make sense' of their experience, and what effect it has, if any, on their social life, social behaviour, and self-esteem. McLorg (2001), for example, finds that, among women who strive for thinness by means of experimental starving and purging, stigmatization elevates a thin-body image to a self-concept or master status—a central feature of their identity.

Feminist approaches

A main concern of feminists studying appearance is focused on issues having to do with female beauty. Beauty is a tough standard to meet. Though women today enjoy a higher social status than they did in the past, some believe they still suffer from a continued effort by men to force them back into submission. Advertising (especially fashion and cosmetics) holds up perfection and an unattainable body image for women to emulate. By failing to meet this artificial standard, women feel as though they have failed in their role as women (whether as companions, lovers, or wives). This has the effect of strengthening the power of men over women.

A concept that has become widely used in social science is the notion of 'the gaze', a term that originates in film theory. As Jonathan Schroeder notes, 'Film has been called an instrument of the male gaze, producing representations of women, the good life, and sexual fantasy from a male point of view' (Schroeder, 1998). The concept derives from an article called 'Visual Pleasure and Narrative Cinema' by Laura Mulvey, a feminist film theorist. Published in 1975, this is one of the most widely cited and anthologized articles in all of contemporary film theory. No doubt it has gained wide currency because of this important concept, which, like Foucault's work, relates visibility (or surveillance) to domination.

Along similar lines, Duncan (1994) discusses how Michel Foucault's metaphor of the panopticon (1979), a prison structure that renders prisoners self-monitoring, offers a useful way of understanding the mechanisms that inculcate an unrealistic body ideal in contemporary women. A critical approach is used to show how textual mechanisms in two issues of *Shape* magazine—a women's fitness glossy— invite a continual self-conscious body monitoring in women. Two panoptic mechanisms, 'the efficacy

of initiative' and 'feeling good means looking good' are highlighted.

At the other end of the spectrum, Leblanc (1999) explored the participation of girls in the male-dominated subculture of punk, drawing on 1993–5 interviews with 40 punk girls in four North American cities. She found that girls use punk culture to resist the social expectations of femininity, which they perceive in terms of pressure from parents, peers, teachers, or a general political ideology. Punk gave them a better sense of self, helped them overcome feelings of isolation and depression, and provided resources to gain social skills. Moreover, they saw punk as an avenue toward greater self-expression and empowerment. On the other hand, participation in punk subculture exposed girls to a masculine subculture that heaped harassment and abuse on them. By distancing themselves from other girls, they lost the one connection that might provide them a basis for support.

Health and Social Consequences of Appearance Issues

Health consequences of eating disorders

Appearance issues continue to interest sociologists because they shed so much light on the boundaries between deviant and conforming behaviour and the measures people take to control other people. However, these deviant acts have a deeper significance, since they may be harmful to people's health and safety.

Anorexia is a prime example of a behaviour that is deviant because it exceeds, rather than falls short of, the appearance norms. Taken to extremes, the dieting and exercise associated with anorexia can be fatal. For more than a decade after getting psychiatric help for their anorexic eating habits, many women continue to struggle with low body weight and a variety of mental problems. As a result, anorexic individuals are more vulnerable to major depression, alcohol dependence, and anxiety disorders at the time of their illness and later in life.

Box 2.2   Media's Effect on Body Image

The popular media (television, movies, magazines, etc.) have, since World War II, increasingly held up a thinner and thinner body (and now ever more physically fit) image as the ideal for women. The ideal man is also presented as trim, but muscular.

- In a survey of girls 9 and 10 years old, 40 per cent have tried to lose weight, according to an ongoing study funded by the National Heart, Lung and Blood Institute (*USA Today*, 1996).
- A 1996 study found that the amount of time an adolescent watches soaps, movies, and music videos is associated with their degree of body dissatisfaction and desire to be thin (Tiggemann and Pickering, 1996).
- One author reports that at age thirteen, 53 per cent of American girls are 'unhappy with their bodies'. This grows to 78 per cent by the time girls reach seventeen (Brumberg, 1997).
- Teen-age girls who viewed commercials depicting women who modeled the unrealistically thin-ideal type of beauty caused adolescent girls to feel less confident, more angry, and more dissatisfied with their weight and appearance (Hargreaves, 2002).
- In a study on fifth graders, 10 year old girls and boys told researchers they were dissatisfied with their own bodies after watching a music video by Britney Spears or a clip from the TV show 'Friends' (Mundell, 2002).
- In another recent study on media's impact on adolescent body dissatisfaction, two researchers found that:
  1. Teens who watched soaps and TV shows that emphasized the ideal body type reported higher sense of body dissatisfaction. This was also true for girls who watched music videos.
  2. Reading magazines for teen girls or women also correlated with body dissatisfaction for girls.
  3. Identification with television stars (for girls and boys), and models (girls) or athletes (boys), positively correlated with body dissatisfaction (Hofschire and Greenberg, 2002).

Source: Duane A. Hargreaves and Marika Tiggemann, 'Female "thin ideal," media images and boys' attitudes towards girls', *Sex Roles: A Journal of Research*, November 2003, 9–10. With kind permission from Springer Science and Business Media.

Like anorexia, bulimia causes health problems for the sufferer. The physical and emotional weakness associated with eating disorders also affects social interactions with friends and a person's involvement in life overall. Ironically, people with an eating disorder often begin to diet in the belief that weight loss will lead to improved self-confidence, self-respect, and self-esteem—even popularity. However, persistent undereating, binge eating, and purging often have the opposite effect, contrary to what sufferers expect. Sufferers may also develop severe self-consciousness and think that other people are constantly watching and waiting to confront them or interfere in their lives. People with eating disorders often also harbour feelings of shame and guilt, preventing them from seeking help in a timely fashion.

Another problem commonly associated with eating disorders is compulsive behaviour. Rituals govern the everyday lives of many eating-disordered people—a result of feelings of helplessness. Eating disorders bring pain and suffering not only to the people who suffer them but also to their families, friends, and partners who struggle with guilt, worry, anxiety, and frustration. Such emotions have secondary health and social effects on families and their members.

Similarly, people who use plastic (cosmetic) surgery to improve their appearance also put their health at risk in order to exceed the appearance norms. Prime among these are women who use silicon implants to enlarge their breasts, in the belief that bigger is always better. Many harmful outcomes have been reported. Likewise, surgeries to reduce weight, eliminate fat, shape thighs, and generally 'improve' people's facial and body features have sometimes produced unexpected and unnecessary harm. Like steroids which body builders have used to 'bulk up' by enhancing muscle tissue, a variety of dieting and surgical strategies yield short-term satisfaction and longer-term harm.

Health consequences of tattooing and body piercing

As tattoos and piercings gain popularity, many people choose to get them despite the many risks of serious health consequences. The process may be dangerous if unhygienic. Many tattoos are applied with electronically powered vibrating instruments that inject tattoo ink into the skin. Some are still applied using pencils, pens, straight pins or needles to inject ink, carbon, mascara, or charcoal. Tattoos applied in this primitive, less-professional manner, usually to avoid the high costs of professional tattooing, increase the chance of acquiring a dangerous disease.

Body piercing also involves needles and can also infect the part of the body that is being pierced. Inadequate care of the area pierced or tattooed raises the risk of infection. The diseases acquired from unsanitary tattooing and body-piercing practices include hepatitis, tetanus, HIV, and skin infections (Health Canada, 2001b). People who get, or plan to get, tattoos and body piercings are often aware of the potential health risks associated with these practices. New risks are possible as people try to remove their tattoos.

Health consequences of punk culture

Punk culture is characterized by its own distinctive jargon, beliefs, clothing, and lifestyle, which all carry health consequences. As we have said, these behaviours include piercings, tattoos, and various other risky behaviours (alcohol, drugs, unprotected sex). Besides the direct health consequences of tattooing and piercing, there are indirect consequences associated with the higher rate of smoking and substance abuse among the members of this subculture. The lifestyle may also include sexual practices that increase the risk of sexually transmitted diseases for the participants.

Social Consequences

Social consequences of eating disorders

The societal impact of eating disorders extends far beyond the costs of the health care services for anorexic and bulimic people. Eating disorders tax the mental, social, and economic well being of people with the illness, family members, friends, and employers, the community, and the whole society. The costs include health services that are provided to the patients, family therapy, and prevention and educational programs as well as time lost from work and other socially useful activities. Rates of hospitalization for eating disorders are increasing among young women. This may signal an increase in the disorder or in the use of hospitals when treating the disorder, or both (Public Health Agency of Canada, 2002).

The costs of eating disorders are not as noticeable as the costs of other illnesses. Largely, these disorders are private matters that many families keep secret. Often, the stigma associated with eating disorders comes from a mistaken impression that others, especially parents, are to blame for the illness. Stigma also poses a problem for excessively thin people who are mistakenly thought to have an eating disorder. Many people, on seeing a thin woman, jump to the conclusion that she is anorexic or bulimic, though this may be incorrect.

Similarly, many people, on seeing an obese person, jump to the conclusion that he has a binge-eating disorder—again, not necessarily true. Some medical conditions cause people to be unusually thin or overweight, and there is nothing they can do about it. Nonetheless, people label them as though they had an eating disorder, creating conditions for the secondary deviation we discussed in the last chapter.

The Role of Families

As we will see throughout this book, families play a large part both in the initiation and control of deviant behaviour. The role of families in shaping us, for better or worse, has been commented on by social scientists since Freud (and by social thinkers since Plato). Families socialize us, teach us moral and social values, and give us the earliest preparation for school and work. In adulthood, families provide social integration and root us in our social lives as spouses, parents, neighbours, and of course, children to aging parents. We learn about appearance norms first in our childhood families. That is where we first learn to eat, dress, and adorn ourselves.

Family members often share many things: experiences, memories, resources, lifestyles, and even good and bad habits (Wickrama et al., 1999). The same holds true for eating patterns and the health benefits that follow. In part, this accounts for many health similarities between family members. Often, family members share good or bad health, and similar kinds of bad health in particular. Some family similarities (as between parents and children) are due to genetics. Some are due to a shared lifestyle—to the basis of all community life that

Max Weber called 'commensalism', meaning 'they eat together'. People are homogamous, typically marrying others who share the same interests and lifestyles. These can include an unhealthy diet, a preference for smoking and substance abuse, and too little physical exercise.

Family members can also share health-promoting habits (Weiss et al., 1996). Many studies show that spouses whose partners encourage and support their dieting efforts, for example, lose more weight and are better able to keep the weight off than dieters with spouses who are uncooperative and resistant (Brownell et al., 1978; Saccone and Israel, 1978). Open lines of communication are important if all family members are to stick to a common plan of healthy eating and, more generally, healthy living. Mealtime discussions of diet and nutrition make a lot of sense. The family meal is often a particularly good place for sociability, debate, bonding, and cohesion building (Kaplan, 2000; Lupton, 2000; Grieshaber, 1997). Further, talking about food while people are eating food makes sense. This practice has beneficial results for family members.

Families can play an important part by promoting a healthy diet and healthy eating practices. Healthy eating (or dietary) practices would mean the adoption and maintenance of eating patterns that include a variety of foods and sufficient nutrients and yet are not high in calories, fat, sodium, or sugar. Diet is important in preventing chronic diseases and reducing harmful eating behaviours in the population. In the long term, poor dietary habits can also combine with genetic, behavioural, or environmental factors to increase the overall risk of heart disease, osteoporosis, and certain cancers in later life.

The consequences of poor eating habits learned during childhood often also carry over into adulthood. Eating habits largely govern a person's fat and cholesterol levels, and high levels of these are associated with higher risks of cardiovascular disease. Major studies of heart disease have examined cardiovascular risk factors among children, all with similar results. All have found that cholesterol levels during childhood and adolescence predict cholesterol levels in adulthood (Ragone, 1996; Lauer et al., 1988; Freedman et al., 1985; Orchard et al., 1983; Laskarezewski et al., 1979).

Similarly, longitudinal studies recording patterns of obesity over a lifetime have found that overweight children tend to become overweight adults. Even more worrisome, children and adolescents with poor eating habits also tend to practice other health-damaging behaviours (Perry et al., 1997; Isralowitz and Trostler, 1996). We all make an early start on our later-life health problems, and poor eating practices play a major role from the outset.

Families can also be an important part of treatment for eating disorders. Traditional treatment approaches for child obesity focus on the child as the main agent of change, with parents acting as helpers. This seems logical since, in most families, parents buy the food, cook it, and put it on the table for their children (Golan et al., 1998). Research shows that an authoritarian parenting style, characterized by controlling, prohibitive, and anxiety-inducing strategies, hinders dieting. It can worsen parent-child relations and a child's self-esteem, if the child sees herself failing to meet parental expectations.

Social support, and especially family support, are key to solving children's problems. Some therapies encourage obese children to monitor their own behaviour and make use of social supports in dieting. Good therapies expose the child to positive eating environments, where the child is assured of having access to nutrient-dense meals and enough time to eat them—a minimum of 15 to 20 minutes. Setting goals for healthy eating that focus on dietary guidelines are also important.

Policies and Theory Applications to Control Appearance Issues

Some families have more difficulty providing the supports a child needs. In particular, challenges arise when attempting to treat low-income children (Broadwater, 2002). Parents in poor families typically work long hours that leave them little time to prepare home-cooked meals or promote physical activity. Often, they may be absent when the child is due to practice new eating patterns suggested by the therapist (Ebbeling et al., 2002). Health care workers need to develop new and better approaches for dealing with these vulnerable families (Chamberlin et al., 2002).

Schools are an ideal means of getting information into the family and the community, because schools can reach all parents through their children (and most adults in the community). Most children under the age of 16 are obliged to attend school, making them a captive audience for health promotion messages. Their parents are sometimes interested in hearing what children are learning at school. Most important, teachers and educational institutions enjoy a high degree of trust and respectability in our society. This is important because families also provide children with care and nourishment, and socialize them into young adults.

Likely Scenarios for Change in Appearance Issues

People in Western countries are flooded by media words and images. In those media presentations, happy and successful people are almost always represented by beautiful actors and models who are young, toned, and thin. In contrast, actors who are older, frumpy, messy, overweight, or perhaps physically challenged, portray evil, stupid, or unsuccessful people. Over the past decade, the body images portrayed by the media, and that of the average population has diverged immensely. The ideal images of males and females in the media is decreasing, becoming smaller and less achievable by the public. Conversely, the typical body weight of society for both males and females is increasing, due to a rise in body fat percentage.

Most people want to be happy and successful, states that require thought, personal development, and hard work. The media—especially commercials for appearance-related items—suggest that we can

Box 2.3 Female 'Thin Ideal' and Boys' Attitudes Towards Girls

The mass media have long been criticized for presenting unrealistic appearance ideals that contribute to the development of negative body image for many women and girls. A growing number of experimental studies have demonstrated a causal link between acute exposure to 'thin-ideal' images (i.e., images of impossibly thin and attractive female beauty) and increased body dissatisfaction. Overall, these studies consistently demonstrate a small, negative, immediate effect of exposure to such thin-ideal images (for a meta-analytic review, see Groesz, Levine, and Murnen, 2002).

A [more] likely outcome of repeated and ongoing exposure to thin, attractive women in the media, however, is the shaping of men's and boys' expectations and evaluations of women and girls. Yet this has largely gone unexamined. Certainly in the extreme case of pornographic material, increased exposure has been reliably associated with poorer evaluations of a sexual partner (Barak and Fisher, 1997; Jansma, Linz, Mulac, and Imrich, 1997) and increased sexually aggressive behaviour (Malamuth, Addison, and Koss, 2000). In an experimental study, Kenrick, Guiterres, and Goldberg (1989) found that men who were exposed to erotic images of women reported being less attracted to and loving their mates less than men who were exposed to abstract art images. Fortunately, exposure to such explicit materials is not common for most men (Goodson, McCormick, and Evans, 2001) and can be easily avoided. In contrast, the pervasiveness of female thin-ideal images in many male-oriented magazines, on television, and in other mainstream Western media makes exposure to the thin-ideal almost unavoidable. Cultivation theory (Gerbner, Gross, Morgan, and Signorielli, 1994) suggests that such ongoing exposure to a particular set of values, types of people, and themes (such as the thin-ideal for women) can powerfully influence viewers' conceptions of social reality. Thus the media's repeated presentation of thin and attractive women, frequently paired with beauty and success, may lead viewers to hold largely unrealistic expectations for women's appearance.

SOURCE: Duane A. Hargreaves and Marika Tiggemann, 'Female "thin ideal," media images and boys' attitudes towards girls', *Sex Roles: A Journal of Research*, November 2003, 9–10. With kind permission from Springer Science and Business Media.

avoid the hard character work by making our bodies copy the icons of success.

The visible differences between media images of happy, successful men and women are interesting. The women, with few exceptions, are young and thin. Thin is desirable, especially for women. A woman's success rests on her beauty, not on wealth or intelligence. A woman's body and physical beauty is the site of her power in the social world. For men in the media, power—not thinness—is desirable. Male media images are typically physically fit, tall, and visibly older, while emphasis is placed on monetary success and intelligence. Thin men are seen as skinny, and skinny men are often depicted as sick, weak, frail, or effeminate. Many people believe this media stereotyping helps explain why about 95 per cent of people with eating disorders are women and only 5 per cent are men.

Eating disorders are common among young women and are becoming increasingly prevalent among men, and they can be fatal. Existing data about eating disorders provide a limited profile of eating disorders in Canada. To improve our information base on eating disorders in Canada, we need to combine the available hospitalization data with other data. For example, we need better information about the incidence of each eating disorder, by sex, socioeconomic status, education, and ethnicity. What does the future hold for punk subculture and other subcultures that intend to subvert and ridicule middle-class propriety? Young people, it seems, will always be attracted to subversive subcultures and they will always make efforts to belong to them. However, the fraction of the youth population that favours subversive rather than conformist goals varies over time, as indicated by changes in stated educational and occupational aspirations. When punk fashion ceases to shock the parents' (and teachers') generation, it loses its value for young people, and a new subculture is invented.

Structural functionalist theorists, like Merton, recognize that modern capitalist societies have a considerable ability to tolerate, assimilate, and embrace every manner of deviant behaviour. Deviant behaviours that are symbolically *rebellious*, like punk subculture, reduce the likelihood of deviant behaviours that are actually politically rebellious. So long as young people think that attacking the status quo consists of wearing a tattoo or nose-stud, practising unsafe sex, and dropping out of school, capitalism and its masters will be safe for another hundred years.

The challenge of global multiculturalism

Increasingly, in multicultural societies like Canada's we are likely to encounter appearance issues—non-normative modes of dress or adornment—that violate our expectations. This has already become a problem in certain parts of Europe where multiculturalism is unfamiliar and traditional modes of dress are required. Throughout the world, school uniforms signify both regimentation and status—a leftover, perhaps, from the days of aristocratic academies, lycées, and gymnasia. Nowhere is the debate over school dress more active today than in France, in relation to the demands that children avoid wearing items of clothing—hijabs, large crosses, or yarmulkes (skullcaps)—that declare their religious affiliation.

In the Islamic tradition, both men and women are required to dress modestly. Women traditionally cover their hair with a hijab (Islamic scarf), and this practice seems to have created a controversy in France in recent years. The debate over religious symbolism in secular state schools stemmed from a 1989 incident involving the expulsion of three schoolgirls in France for wearing the traditional Muslim headscarf (Laborde, 2002). The headscarf debate became problematic because it challenged the traditional secularism of the French political system.

The image of the Muslim woman's veil is as a symbol of oppression and violence in Islam in the popular Western media. The forced covering of women in post-revolutionary Iran or under the Taliban in Afghanistan seems to confirm this image of the veil. The recovering movement challenges the reductive image of the veil as a symbol of Muslim women's oppression. Due to the ubiquitous image of the veil as a symbol of oppression or violence, Muslim women living in the West who cover often suffer discrimination, harassment, even assault. In France, wearing the Islamic headscarf in school has resulted in dress code and discipline problems, with its underlying symbolism causing widespread arguments about laicite, religious pluralism, and integration (Liederman, 2000).

Concluding Words

Sociological theories often focus not on the cause of deviance, but on its consequence. In fact, many sociological theories (especially, functionalist theories) assume the consequence to be the cause. People deviate, or are perceived to deviate, because of the outcomes. For example, people adopt a particular deviant appearance in order to gain acceptance by other people whose appearance they have adopted. Moreover, people commit deviant acts because society 'needs' such acts.

The social deviations discussed in this chapter have included styles of dress and self-presentation that are uncommon among the majority of the Canadian population. They include multiple earrings, nose studs, tongue rings, multiple tattoos, interesting coloured hair, and odd clothing. Such fashions are more common among young people, and older people consider them deviations from the established societal norms and values. One reason they give is that such dress codes and deviant appearances are associated—rightly or wrongly—with high-risk behaviours such as promiscuity, substance abuse, and even violence, or in the case of obesity, with low status and lack of self-discipline.

For some, the violation of appearance norms is one form of what Frenchmen used to call '*épater la bourgeoisie*', or bowling over the middle class: that is, holding up to ridicule the stark, thoughtless conformity of middle-class, middle-aged people. Young people and poor people love to do that, for they have nothing to lose. For them, projecting a deviant appearance is an 'innovative behaviour'. The unequal structure of opportunities and influences in our society makes such innovations almost inevitable.

In most aspects of life, people want to be accepted by their peers. Therefore, they typically dress and present themselves in ways that conform to current fashions. They try to obey the norms for successful, attractive people. Acceptance, in turn, increases the likelihood of getting a good job, a promotion, a desirable sex partner, better service at a restaurant, less interference from narrow-minded groups, and generally a more active social life.

Summary

Most of us get at least some of our ideas about appearance norms from the mass media. The appearance norms portrayed by the media are nowhere near the reality. As a result, some develop dangerous and sometimes life-threatening eating disorders. They engage in deviant behaviours such as starving themselves or purging the food they have eaten, in hopes of turning themselves into impossibly tall, thin sticks. Finally, others dress up in dangerous-looking outfits, bodies covered with studs and tattoos, personally illustrating the belief that having nothing to lose is equal to winning.

Often intentionally, behavioural innovations will seem threatening at first (in the case of punk culture) and members of the upstanding middle-aged middle-class will attempt to control and stigmatize these new behaviours. Some innovations (as in the case of eating disorders) will be truly harmful and call attention to the social pathologies of the age. Others will seem less harmful as time passes (as in the case of tattooing and piercing).

As we have seen in this chapter, understanding eating disorders, punk culture, and deviant appearance requires understanding how and why these behaviours emerge. Some may just provoke a negative public reaction, and some may have dangerous health and social consequences. All violate social norms and social expectations. In conclusion, we have seen that deviance has a great many aspects of diverse kinds. While some kinds of appearance deviation are behavioural, some are not. Likewise, some kinds of appearance deviation are voluntary and intentional, and some are not. Finally, some kinds of appearance deviation violate ideals, and some merely violate the commonplace. Though some kinds of appearance deviation are largely social in their origins, others are largely genetic or chemical.

Though appearance deviation is widely variable, a few common features tie them together. *All kinds of appearance deviation* vary over time and place, according to prevailing cultural standards;

are social in their consequences, if not their origins; are liable to provoke labelling, stigmatization and exclusion; have the potential to give rise to social forms—including deviant communities and subcultures—in reaction to exclusion and stigmatization.

We are now ready to discuss mental illness, another common form of deviance, in Chapter 3.

Questions for Critical Thought

1. In his classic work on anomie, Merton discusses various reactions to norms. Contrast a Goth and a *haute couture* purchaser's reaction to the norms.
2. Personal identities are linked to social identities. Illustrate this using any of the theorists discussed in the chapter.
3. Discuss Veblen's approach to fashion and how it has been applied to colonial discourse. How is this significant to the contemporary study of deviance?
4. Explain how a symbolic interactionist might view the rising mainstream popularity of tattoos.
5. Given the popularity of punk culture and music, is it still a form of rebellion? Discuss this issue using current media examples.
6. How can appearance-deviant communities provide positive spaces for their members?
7. Discuss the ways sociologists might see anorexia as an attempt to satisfy appearance norms.
8. Compare the effects that the fashion industry and advertising have on women and men using a feminist perspective.
9. What role do families have in mediating the health and social consequences of appearance deviance?
10. Highlight the media's role in constructing appearance issues. How may the stereotyping create different levels of risks for men?

Recommended Reading

Lee, Michelle. (2003), *Fashion Victim: Our Love-Hate Relationship With Dressing, Shopping, and the Cost of Style.* New York: Broadway Books. This book, by the former editor of *Glamour* and *Mademoiselle,* offers an insider's account of how the fashion industry is able to manipulate people. It follows how trends are created in *haute couture* lines all the way to their demise once they hit the low-end shelves of Wal-Mart and K-Mart.

Spitz, Marc. (2001), *We Got the Neutron Bomb: The Untold Story of L.A. Punk.* New York: Three Rivers Press. This is a study of various punk-rock bands on the American West Coast that catalogues the ups and downs of the punk movement. The book follows the rise of the punk scene in LA and explains through the use of first-hand accounts how punk-rock has enjoyed success.

Wolf, Naomi. (2002), *The Beauty Myth: How Images of Beauty are Used Against*

Women. New York: Perennial. In this classic feminist work, Naomi Wolf discusses how an ideal version of the modern woman has been constructed through marketing and extensive advertising. She looks at how women deal with an unhealthy obsession toward becoming the 'ideal'.

Recommended Websites

Campaign for Real Beauty

www.campaignforrealbeauty.com

This website is the centre for an international advertising campaign which was started by Dove soap to urge people to look at 'real' beauty, instead of what people find in magazines. The website catalogues the release of advertisements in which non-traditional models are used and gauges the press and public's reaction to the ads.

Canadian Broadcasting Corporation

www.cbc.ca/news/background/tattoo

This website is part of CBC's in-depth coverage, titled 'Body Art: The Story Behind Tattooing and Piercing in Canada'.

The CBC provides a brief historical account of tattooing and piercing in Canada, as well as describing many of the risks and trends. There are also numerous links to published articles on the subject and links to similar websites online.

National Eating Disorder Information Centre

www.nedic.ca

The National Eating Disorder Information Centre provides important resources for those seeking any information about eating disorders or weight issues. The website contains numerous links to various other organizations as well as hosting readings related to eating disorders.

CHAPTER 3

Mental Illness

LEARNING OBJECTIVES

- To understand the development of ideas about mental illness
- To identify the varieties of mental illness
- To understand the theories and perspectives that explain mental illness
- To identify the social and health consequences of mental illness
- To be familiar with the policies aimed at helping and controlling mental illness
- To understand the reasons for the de-institutionalization of mentally ill people

Introduction

In this chapter, we discuss rule-breaking or unexpected behaviour that is associated with mental illness. Mental illness is deviant in the sense that it is statistically unusual, feared, and stigmatized. Some behaviours associated with mental illness are 'deviant' in the sense of being unusual, unexpected, and disruptive. Conversely, some mental illness results from deviant behaviour: for example, from family violence or substance abuse.

What we call 'mental illnesses' are characterized by alterations in thinking, mood, or behaviour (or some combination of these) associated with significant distress and impaired functioning (CAMIMH, 1999). The symptoms of mental illness vary greatly, depending on the type of mental illness, the person, the family, and the socioeconomic environment. Typically, they result from conflicts people are experiencing, sometimes due to long-term feelings of shame, guilt, or fear.

Mental illness is considered deviant, not because it is rare but because it is a troublesome social problem with poorly understood causes and harmful consequences. It interrupts the normal functioning of groups, families, and other social institutions. It is a social problem because of the number of people it affects. According to Health Canada, 20 per cent of all Canadians will experience a mental illness during their lifetime (Public Health Agency of Canada, 2002). It is also a social problem because of the difficulty in defining, identifying, predicting, and controlling mental disorders. Finally, mental illness is a social problem because of the duration and uncertain outcome of treatments.

Mental illnesses are not limited to particular groups or classes of people in our society. No class or social group is free of mental illness. However, illnesses differ in type and prevalence in different social groups. Early research on this topic, for example, suggested that psychoses are more common among poorer people, while neuroses are more common among middle-class people. This finding may be outdated and was, in any event, far too simplistic. However, research continues to show that depression is more common among poor people, who typically suffer more stress due to poverty, inequality, and workplace control.

It remains unclear whether the mental illnesses found among poor people are because of poverty, or whether mentally ill people in the middle classes are more likely than healthy people to drift down into poverty. Lloyd (2000) notes that two competing explanations have been proposed: social selection and social causation. Using life history data, Lloyd finds that both processes of social causation and social selection operate over time. Most types of early-onset disorder hinder socioeconomic achievement. However, the extent of this hindrance varies from one type of disorder to another; in some cases the extent of hindrance also varies with class and gender.

Families can play an important role in causing mental illness, and they can also play a key role in helping the mentally ill person to recover from illness. As a result, sociologists who study mental illness have a lot to say about the family's role in producing, moderating, and helping to eliminate the deviant behaviours associated with mental illness. We will, as a result, discuss families in depth.

Sociologists since Durkheim have commented on the close connection between mental illness and family life. As Durkheim (1951 [1897]) showed in his early sociological study of suicide, close family ties can reduce the dangers of suicide and related mental distress. Families can provide a degree of security and personal meaning that no other social units can provide. However, no social unit is as likely as the family to cause or complicate mental illness, because of the stress, emotional demands, and even abuse that may be present. The paradox is that intimacy in general, and family life in particular, is both the best thing and the worst thing for people's state of mind.

Mental illness affects both the people who suffer from it and other members of society. The sufferer's family, community, and society experience consequences in the form of health care costs, crime due to victimization (of the mentally ill and also by

the mentally ill), and costly efforts needed to reduce stigma and the negative public reaction to mentally disabled persons.

The History of Mental Illness and Public Reaction

To understand mental illness today, we need to explore the social construction of mental illness throughout history, at least since the eighteenth century. Over centuries, there have been changing definitions of insanity as well as changing attitudes toward the mentally ill, and a development of institutional, medical, and cultural responses to the mentally ill.

Early explanations of mental illness involved the notion of 'evil spirits' and 'demons'. In pre-industrial societies, many believed that the strange, deviant behaviours associated with mental illness could only be due to the acts of the devil (or devils) as a punishment for wrongdoing. As a result, some communities tortured people suffering from mental illnesses (e.g., from delusions) in an attempt to drive out the demons.

Eventually, people realized that torture failed to return a person to sanity. Founded in London in 1247 by Simon Fitz Mary (Porter, 1997), Bedlam—originally called the Hospital of St Mary of Bethlehem and converted to a lunatic asylum—was an infamous institution where mentally ill people were chained to walls so the rest of the world could forget they existed. In time, the very name Bedlam came to be synonymous with the uproarious behaviour of the inmates. To say that a place was 'bedlam' was to say that it exhibited the utmost chaos and craziness.

As time passed, hospitals and asylums began to assume the care of the mentally ill. They began to treat mentally ill patients almost in the same way as other patients, providing cleaner surroundings, better care and nutrition, fresh air, and light. During the First World War medical caregivers discovered that emotional problems and shell shock incapacitated many soldiers returning from the front. Many evidently suffered from abnormal behaviour as a result. We see this same problem among returning soldiers today and call the illness 'post-traumatic stress disorder' or PTSD. Caregivers reasoned that if a trauma such as the war could cause such widespread symptoms, then lesser traumas, occurring often, might produce the same effect.

However, popular opinion about mental illness did not change very quickly. Most people continued to view shell shock as a disgrace rather than an illness, and as a demonstration of cowardice and moral weakness, for example. Many imagined that soldiers suffering from shell shock lacked the bravery and strength necessary to do combat (Bourke, 2000, 2002). In the 1940s and 1950s, researchers found medications that helped the severely mentally ill to cope with their illness. The public continued to define mental illness in much narrower and more extreme terms than the psychiatric community. Fearful and exclusionary attitudes toward people with mental illnesses were common.

Definitions of mental illness may have broadened, and the rejection and negative stereotyping of mentally ill people may have decreased since then. A comparison of 1950 and 1996 survey results shows that conceptions of mental illness today include more non-psychotic (i.e., non-delusional) disorders. There is a wider recognition that less dramatic, less visible, forms of mental illness—chiefly, neuroses—are common in the population. However, perceptions that mentally ill people are violent or frightening have substantially increased, rather than decreased (Phelan et al., 2000; Phelan and Link, 2004).

The Characteristics of Mental Illness and Mentally Ill People

Mental illnesses vary, but overall they are characterized by alterations in thinking, mood, or behaviour associated with major distress and impaired functioning over a long period of time. The symptoms of mental illness vary from mild to severe, depending on the type of illness, the person, the family, and the socioeconomic environment (Public Health Agency of Canada, 2002). No one is immune to mental illnesses. At some point, all Canadians are likely to be affected by the mental illness of a family member, friend, or colleague (see Table 3.1).

However, some mental illnesses are more prevalent in some population groups than others. For example, researchers note that structural characteristics affect the prevalence of mental disorders in particular neighbourhoods. As Silver and colleagues (2002) found, after controlling for person-level characteristics, neighbourhood disadvantage is associated with higher rates of major depression and substance abuse. For example, in low-income neighbourhoods, high residential mobility—the rate of people moving in and out of the neighbourhood—is associated with higher rates of schizophrenia, major depression, and substance abuse disorder. Hence, mentally healthy individuals increase their chances of becoming mentally ill when they move into neighbourhoods that are characterized by poverty and a transient population.

Mood Disorders

Mood disorders are among the most common mental illnesses in the general population. Canadian research has found that 7.9 to 8.6 per cent of adults over 18 years of age and living in the community met the criteria for a diagnosis of major depression at some time in their lives (Canadian Psychiatric Association, 2001) (see Table 3.2).

Most people experience a wide range of moods and have an equally large set of affective expressions; yet, generally, they feel in control of their moods and emotions. However, mood disorders reduce people's sense of control and they experience distress as a result. People with mania (i.e., elevated moods), for example, experience flights of ideas, decreased sleep, briefly heightened self-esteem, and increased imagination. People with depression (i.e., depressed moods) can lose their appetite, suffer decreased energy and interest, isolate themselves, express feelings of guilt, have difficulty concentrating, and think frequently

Table 3.1 Any Measured Disorder or Substance Dependence, by Age Group and Sex, Household Population Aged 15 and over, Canada Excluding Territories, 2002

	Total population	Had at least one measured disorder or substance dependence	Did not have any measured disorder or substance dependence	Any measured substance dependence, not stated
	Number	%	%	%
2002				
Total, 15 years and over	24,996,593	10.6	86.2	3.2
Men	12,286,109	9.9	86.8	3.3
Women	12,710,483	11.4	85.6	3.1
15–24 years	4,136,460	18.4	80.3	1.3
Men	2,111,183	17.3	81.5	1.2
Women	2,025,378	19.5	79.1	1.4
25–64 years	17,133,721	10.4	86.4	3.3
Men	8,543,283	9.4	87.1	3.5
Women	8,590,438	11.4	85.6	3.0
65 years and over	3,726,412	3.2	91.8	5.0
Men	1,631,644	2.9	82.0	5.1
Women	2,094,768	3.5	91.6	4.9

SOURCE: Adapted from Statistics Canada, Canadian Community Health Survey, Mental Health and Well-being, 2002 (updated Sept. 2004).

of death or suicide. Mood disorders include major (or clinical) depression, bipolar disorder (which alternates episodes of mania and depression), and dysthymia (being mildly depressed chronically).

Mood disorders affect people of all ages. The symptoms tend to appear in adolescence or young adulthood. Mood disorders are also more prevalent among women than men. Studies have consistently documented higher rates of depression among women than among men: the female-to-male ratio averages 2:1 (Kessler et al., 1994). Additionally, women are two to three times more likely than men to develop dysthymia (Public Health Agency of Canada, 2002). Though there are biochemical and psychological causes of depression, research repeatedly finds social causes as well. Poverty and poor living conditions, danger, subordination,

and conflict are some of the social conditions that increase the likelihood and duration of depression. It is not clear how much of the gender difference in mood disorders is due to differences in the life experiences of men and women.

Schizophrenia, an atypical disorder that causes people to have difficulty interpreting reality, is a form of psychosis. Schizophrenics develop a marked change in their thinking, perceptions, and behaviour, as evidenced by any or all of the following symptoms: hallucinations, delusions, disorganized speech, disorganized behaviour, apathy, and social withdrawal. By definition, therapists only diagnose schizophrenia if these symptoms last for at least six months and are associated with a significant decline in the person's ability to care for themselves or function in social and work situations.

Table 3.2 Major Depressive Episode, by Age Group and Sex, Household Population aged 15 and over, Canada Excluding Territories, 2002

	Total population	Major depressive episode, all measured criteria are met	Major depressive episode, measured criteria not met	Major depressive episode, not stated
	Number	%	%	%
2002				
Total, 15 years and over	24,996,593	4.8	94.8	0.4
Men	12,286,109	3.7	95.9	0.4
Women	12,710,483	5.9	93.7	0.5
15–24 years	4,136,460	6.4	93.4	0.3
Men	2,111,183	4.5	95.2	–
Women	2,025,278	8.3	91.5	–
25–64 years	17,133,721	5.0	94.6	0.4
Men	8,543,283	3.8	95.9	0.3
Women	8,590,438	6.3	93.4	0.4
65 years and over	3,726,412	1.9	97.1	1.0
Men	1,631,644	2.1	97.2	0.7
Women	2,094,768	1.8	96.9	1.2

SOURCE: Adapted from Statistics Canada, Canadian Community Health Survey, Mental Health and Well-being, 2002 (updated Sept. 2004).

Researchers believe schizophrenia results from a biochemical disturbance in the development of the brain. Gender differences have recently become more prevalent in this mental illness. According to *A Report on Mental Illnesses in Canada* (Health Canada, 2002), between 1987 and 1999, hospitalizations for schizophrenia increased among women (3 per cent), but they increased much more dramatically among men (28 per cent).

Anxiety disorders are mental illnesses that manifest themselves as phobias, panic attacks, or obsessive-compulsive disorders. These disorders are not only painful in themselves, but they are also likely to interfere with people's normal functioning at home, at work, and in the company of other people. According to the Anxiety Disorder Association of Canada (2002), 12.6 per cent of all Canadians over the age of 19 experienced an anxiety disorder in 2002. Of these, 9.2 per cent experienced mild disorders, 2.2 per cent chronic disorders, and 1.2 per cent serious disorders.

For various reasons, many people do not seek treatment for their anxiety disorder. They may think of their symptoms as mild or normal, and in some cases the symptoms themselves intervene with the individual's capacity to seek help. Moreover, anxiety disorders often arise during periods of intense stress, for example, during a terminal illness (Hayley, Breitbart, and Rosenfeld, 2002), and affect many aspects of life at this time. In this case, anxiety disorders impede the dying process for terminally ill patients and their families, causing even greater pain and suffering for everyone.

As with other mental illness, the genders differ when it comes to anxiety disorders. Women report, and are diagnosed with, anxiety disorders more

Box 3.1 Identical Quadruplets with the Same Mental Illness

The Genain quadruplets, a group of identical sisters who all developed schizophrenia of varying degrees and at varying ages, have been studied for decades to explore the influences of genetic and environmental factors in schizophrenia. This genetically identical group of four women with varying degrees of illness suggests that manifestation of schizophrenia may be determined in part by non-genetic factors such as, in this case, harsh punitive treatment, the prenatal environment (varying birthweights and early brain injury), and dietary factors. Both their father and his biological mother suffered from schizophrenia, and the girls' mother showed signs of schizophrenia although she was never diagnosed.

SOURCE: Excerpt, 'Understanding the Family Connection in Mental Illness', *The Pfizer Journal*; available at <www.thepfizerjournal. com>.

frequently than men. Of all the Canadians experiencing anxiety disorder, the majority are women. However, this may simply reflect the differences between men and women in their health-service-seeking behaviours rather than true differences in prevalence.

Suicide

Suicidal or self-destructive behaviour is a sign or outcome of mental illness, following from suicidal ideation—that is, thinking suicidal thoughts. There are strong connections between suicide and other mental illnesses. According to the World Health Organization, about 815,000 people died by suicide in the year 2000, and studies show that about 90 per cent of suicide victims have a diagnosable psychiatric illness. Not surprisingly, the same factors that predict and cause unhappiness and dissatisfaction with life—isolation, loneliness, lack of purpose—predict (and cause) suicide (Tepperman and Weerasinghe, 1995) (see Tables 3.3 and 3.4).

According to the Schizophrenia Society of Canada, 40 per cent of schizophrenia patients will try to commit a suicide and 10 per cent will succeed. Suicidal behaviour and ideation are, as one might expect, highly connected with depression. The *Diagnostic and Statistical Manual of Mental Disorders* states that 15 per cent of people diagnosed with depression commit suicide and between 10 and 15 per cent of people diagnosed with a bipolar disorder die by suicide (American Psychiatric Association, 1994).

Some might think that suicide, which is intensely personal, would not be subject to social influences. Yet Durkheim showed in his classic work *Le Suicide* (1951 [1897]) that suicide is indeed socially structured. For example, divorced people (especially men) without children are much more suicide-prone than married people (especially women) with children. Durkheim's research shows that marriage and divorce are social experiences—among many—that shape people's most important and personal actions. Moreover, focusing on the social element of suicide gives us more ability to predict rates of suicidal behaviour than does focusing on the personal, psychological aspect.

Suicide, like depression, is a highly gendered behaviour. Women are both more likely than men to get depressed and more likely to commit suicide when depressed. A study by Shaffer (1988) found that males diagnosed with depression are 8 times more likely to commit suicide than males not diagnosed with depression; depressed females are 49 times more likely to commit suicide than non-depressed

Table 3.3 Suicidal Thoughts, by Age Group and Sex, Household Population aged 15 and over, Canada Excluding Territories, 2002

	Total population	Suicidal thoughts in past 12 months	No suicidal thoughts in past 12 months	Suicidal thoughts, not stated
	Number	%	%	%
2002				
Total, 15 years and over	24,996,593	3.7	96.2	0.1
Men	12,286,109	3.6	96.2	0.2
Women	12,710,483	3.8	96.1	0.1
15–24 years	4,136,460	6.0	94.0	–
Men	2,111,183	4.7	95.2	–
Women	2,025,278	7.3	92.7	–
25–64 years	17,133,721	3.6	96.3	0.2
Men	8,543,283	3.7	96.0	0.2
Women	8,590,438	3.4	96.5	0.165
years and over	3,726,412	1.7	98.2	0.2
Men	1,631,644	1.3	98.5	–
Women	2,094,765	–	97.9	–

SOURCE: Adapted from Statistics Canada, Canadian Community Health Survey, Mental Health and Well-being, 2002 (updated Sept. 2004).

females. At the same time, women are more likely than men to attempt suicide without succeeding, which suggests that—for women—suicide attempts are often calls for help, not efforts to end life.

Differences in marital status, religious involvement, general community participation, depression/anxiety, anti-social behaviour problems, or alcohol abuse do not explain such suicide disparities between men and women. Instead, gender-based disparities in suicide result from differences in the ways men and women respond to the social relationships and mental health problems they experience (Lubell, 2001). Multiple risk factors are associated with suicidal behaviour. A history of previous suicide attempts drastically increases the chance that an adolescent will commit suicide (Pfeffer, 1989). In one longitudinal study, 1,508 high school students reported their history of suicide attempts before the study and then again one year later. Adolescents who reported having attempted suicide before the study

were 18 times more likely to try again during the year-long study than those who had not reported a previous suicide attempt (Lewinsohn, 1994).

So much is suicide a social illness that exposure to suicide through the media is associated with an increase in suicide rates (Phillips, 1974). Research finds that adolescent suicidal deaths increase shortly after media coverage of a prominent suicide or after television episodes featuring an adolescent suicide (Shaffer, 1988). This is called suicide contagion, also known as the 'Werther Effect'.

Substance abuse, personality disorders, stressful life events, and hopelessness are all secondary risk factors associated with adolescent suicide (Stoelb and Chiriboga, 1998). A troubled family history, poor family functioning, and conflictual parent-child relationships are also risk factors for youth suicide. Two aspects of family history are particularly relevant in this context: a history of psychopathology and a history of suicidal behaviours.

Table 3.4 Satisfaction with Life, by Age Group and Sex, Household Population Aged 15 and over, Canada Excluding Territories, 2002

	Total population	Very satisfied with life	Satisfied with life	Neither satisfied nor dissatisfied with life	Dissatisfied or very dissatisfied with life
	Number	%	%	%	%
2002					
Total 15 years and over	24,956,593	32.6	52.7	10.0	4.6
Men	12,286,109	32.6	53.3	9.6	4.5
Women	12,710,483	32.6	52.2	10.4	4.7
15–24 years	4,136,460	30.1	53.6	12.5	3.7
Men	2,111,183	32.1	53.2	11.3	3.3
Women	2,025,278	28.1	54.0	13.7	4.2
25–64 years	17,133,721	32.1	52.7	10.1	5.1
Men	8,543,283	31.6	53.6	9.8	5.0
Women	8,590,438	32.6	51.9	10.3	5.2
65 years and over	3,726,412	37.5	51.9	7.1	3.5
Men	1,631,644	38.3	51.7	6.5	3.4
Women	2,098,768	36.8	52.0	7.5	3.6

SOURCE: Adapted from Statistics Canada, Canadian Community Health Survey, Mental Health and Well-being, 2002 (updated Sept. 2004).

A family history of psychiatric disorders predicts youth suicidal behaviour, for example (Pfeffer, 2001). Parents of suicidal adolescents are found to be much more depressed, to drink more alcohol, to have lower self-esteem, and to be more anxious than parents of non-suicidal adolescents (Blumenthal, 1990). A mother's history of depression also predicts suicidal symptoms in young adolescents (Garber et al., 1998).

Depressed mothers often have dysfunctional parenting styles, characterized by hostility, criticism, and unresponsiveness. A family history of attempted or completed suicide also increases the risk of adolescent suicide (Kovacs et al., 1993; Brent and Kolko, 1990). Friedman and colleagues (1987) compared adolescent suicide attempters with depressed adolescents, adolescents thinking about suicide, and non-suicidal adolescents. They found that adolescent suicide attempters more often reported a history of other family members attempting or committing suicide.

Larsson and Ivarsson (1998) also found that the frequency of suicide attempts was related to whether a family member had attempted or committed suicide in the past. They note that 72 per cent of repeated suicide attempters report a family history of suicidal behaviour. Among first-time attempters, only 50 per cent report such a history. A family history of suicidal behaviours is therefore a risk factor for adolescent suicide. Adolescents may learn from their families that suicide is not only a problem-solving strategy for dealing with difficulties or stressful life events, but also that it is the only strategy.

Additionally, family structure affects suicide risk in adolescents. Brent (1995) found that a disruption in the family environment significantly increases the risk of repeat suicide attempts. A

Box 3.2 The Werther Effect: Is Suicide Contagious?

One theory about suicide prevention is that thoughtful media coverage about suicides might actually prevent future deaths.

The research, reported in the *American Journal of Epidemiology* in 2001, counters a traditional tenet of suicide prevention that can be traced back to *The Sorrows of Young Werther*, Goethe's 1774 novel about a sensitive, intelligent young man who shoots himself out of unrequited love for a married woman.

The book's romanticizing of suicide triggered numerous copycat deaths among young men who identified with the fictional Werther and it was banned in countries across Europe. More than two centuries later, many experts believe exposure to accounts of suicide, even fictional ones, can inflame suicide contagion, or the Werther Effect. It is believed especially harmful to impressionable teens.

Decades of study concludes news coverage of suicides, especially celebrity deaths, can push other suicidal people, many already ambivalent about life and death, to imitate the act. Suicides in the United States, for example, increased by 12 per cent in the month after the suicide of Marilyn Monroe in 1962.

Experts warn contagion can occur when the number of stories about individual suicides increases, or when a particular death becomes the focus of repeated and lengthy reporting, or when coverage is sensationalized and oversimplified—'Boy Kills Self Over Failed Exam.'

A famous episode of contagion began in Vienna in 1984, when media increased their coverage of people killing themselves by jumping in front of the city's subway trains. By 1987, the coverage had become extensive and often dramatic and the Austrian association for suicide prevention asked news organizations to curb their reporting, or to be more sensitive with the stories they still chose to run.

It argued contagion occurs when coverage includes details about the method of death, when motives are romanticized, when the victim is cast as heroic or desirable and 'having everything to live for' and, if the story is carried on the front page or at the top of a news broadcast. (Other experts complain the media almost always fail to mention most suicide victims suffer from mental illnesses for which there are often successful treatments.)

Some of Vienna's big media organizations agreed to reduce or tone down coverage. Within six months, suicides dropped by 75 per cent.

The Toronto Transit Commission, the coroner's office, and Toronto media have a similar, informal policy.

The most notable success in diminishing the Werther Effect followed the 1994 suicide of Seattle rock musician and cult figure Kurt Cobain, 27. Authorities and health workers braced for a rash of copycat deaths, especially after a 28-year-old fan took his life in the same way a week later.

But the phenomenon never materialized.

A study by US suicide expert Dr David Alan Jobes and colleagues credited thoughtful reporting that distinguished Mr Cobain's huge musical talent from his regrettable decision to take his life. It also commended the staging of a major public memorial service in Seattle and strong, repetitious anti-suicide messages from crisis workers and Mr Cobain's wife, singer and actress Courtney Love.

Surprising results

The *American Journal of Epidemiology* study concluded sensitive and considered media coverage may, in fact, prevent some suicides.

'What we found was surprising,' Dr James Mercy, of the National Center for Injury Prevention and Control, part of the US Centers for Disease Control and Prevention, told the Citizen. 'We found a modest protective effect in being exposed to the suicidal behaviour of a friend or acquaintance and a strong protective effect to being exposed to some form of media.'

The study involved interviews with 153 people, ages 13 to 34, in Houston, Texas, who had attempted suicide and were hospitalized. Their exposures to previous cases of suicide were compared to those of a random sample of 513 non-suicidal control subjects. It was the first effort linking individual suicide attempts to specific incidents of exposure, rather than simply comparing suicide news reports to changes in the overall number of suicides.

'If an event is glorified, if they see positive outcomes from the attention suicidal behaviour may get, or if people look up to that person in a certain way, they're more likely to imitate it,' Dr Mercy says.

But if they see the negative consequences, the impact on family and friends, the pain the individual suffered, they would be less likely to imitate it, he says.

'In the Kurt Cobain case, there was a very conscious effort not to create the context in which the behaviour would be imitated by not glorifying it, pointing out the drug abuse and the history of depression that Kurt Cobain had, so that people could see that.'

(The study was careful to note the apparent benefits of media exposure do not extend to the phenomenon of suicide 'clusters' in communities. The reason why remains unclear.)

'While at first glance, our findings seem to be counter to what people previously found, I actually think we need to look at this closer, it just may be two sides of the same coin,' Dr Mercy says. 'There's a potential opportunity here that we haven't fully exploited.

'We may be able to learn more about how to communicate more precisely. Instead of avoiding communicating about suicide altogether, there may be a possibility that we could find ways of communicating about suicide to have more benefit in terms of prevention.'

SOURCE: Excerpt, Ian MacLeod and Andrew Duffy, 'Into the Troubled Mind: Suicide Experts are Trying to Discover Why Canadian Are So Self-destructive', *Ottawa Citizen*, 10 October 2003.

disrupted family environment—because of separation, divorce, widowhood, absence of the father in the home, or separation of the adolescent from parents, for example—increases the likelihood of suicidal behaviours (Larsson and Ivarsson, 1998). Family dysfunction more generally is associated with continued suicidal ideation and continued re-attempts following a suicidal episode (Spirito et al., 2003). Adolescents who attempt suicide a second time describe their families as having poorer general functioning, ineffective communication skills, and limited problem-solving strategies, than adolescents who do not attempt suicide a second time.

This finding points to the importance of an adolescent's perception of his or her family and suggests that open, honest, and expressive communication between family members can positively influence this perception. Characteristics such as parental criticism, overprotection, low bonding, and low expressiveness have all been associated with an increased risk of suicidal behaviours (Toumbourou and Gregg, 2002).

Often, families have little understanding of the home conditions that are leading a family member to commit suicide. The day after a suicide attempt, families often report that 'it was a big mistake—nothing was wrong' (Rotheram-Borus et al., 1994). Besides denying the seriousness of a suicide attempt, family members often withdraw from mental health service organizations because they find treatment or therapy to be a painful reminder of a traumatic episode (Kerfoot et al., 1995).

However, family therapy can significantly reduce the risks of suicide. Compared to a control sample, adolescents whose parents were involved in the PACE program showed much lower levels of self-harm, delinquency, substance abuse, and increased family attachment—PACE, short for Parenting Adolescents: A Creative Experience, is a method of reducing risk factors for youth suicide. These positive behavioural changes were found even two years after the educational intervention (Toumbourou and Gregg, 2002).

Communities and Subcultures of the Mentally Ill

Though individuals suffer the effects, and there may be biochemical causes, mental illnesses are also social behaviours, with social causes and consequences. Not least, mentally ill people, like other deviant people, often end up as members of communities, with their own subculture.

Today, the communities of homeless people in our large cities contain particularly large proportions of mentally ill people. Often, these are de-institutionalized mental patients who have gone off medication; this will be addressed further in this chapter. Often, these are people who lack the money, kin, or social contacts that would keep them off the street. And, there is no doubt that, just as mental illness increases the likelihood that someone will end up homeless, so being homeless increases the likelihood a person will end up mentally ill.

Historically, mentally ill people were consigned to hospitals or asylums. Whatever the original motives for these institutions, in practice, they were warehouses for social outcasts. We learn a lot about social attitudes to the mentally ill from studying these institutions; and we also learn why de-institutionalization (discussed later in this chapter) was such an important change for this population. In his classic work *Asylums* (1961), sociologist Erving Goffman discussed the defining features of mental hospitals as social and cultural institutions. Goffman characterizes mental institutions as belonging to a larger category of organizations he calls 'total institutions'. Goffman writes: 'A total institution may be defined as a place of residence and work where a large number of like-situated individuals, cut off from the wider society for an appreciable period of time, together lead an enclosed, formally administered round of life.'

Mental hospitals, convents, prisons, and military installations have a lot in common as organizations. First, they are all organizations that exercise total control over their inmates—whether mental patients, nuns, convicts, or soldiers-in-training.

What Goffman (1961) tells us about mental institutions and prisons reminds us of what we have heard about life in totalitarian societies such as Nazi Germany and Soviet Russia. In fact, totalitarian societies are not only like total institutions, but they also make liberal use of total institutions to punish, brainwash, and re-socialize unco-operative citizens. The mechanisms for doing this are isolation, degradation, medication, and re-education.

In modern societies, free people usually sleep, play, and work in different places, with different people present, under the view of different eyes (and often, different authorities). The opposite is true of total institutions. All aspects of life in a mental hospital—or other total institution—are conducted in the same place and under the same single authority. Like Bentham's panopticon, discussed in Chapter 1 and used by Foucault to exemplify the use of surveillance for social control, the mental hospital puts inmates under continued view and supervision. Thus, the treatment of mentally ill people in institutions comes to signify low regard, an absence of trust, and a tendency to treat mentally ill people as dangerous or childlike. The result is often conflict and resentment, not rehabilitation.

Social support networks

In the world outside mental institutions, different types of community (and less surveillance) are available to mentally ill people. They include: informal networks of mentally ill, often homeless people; personal networks based on kin and friends; and support groups.

Of these, the support groups are seemingly the most directly related to solving problems related to mental illness. Given the relative unavailability of their doctors, many patients and their caregivers look for help from support groups. These groups vary widely in size, composition, and activity. Medical professionals lead some; social service professionals lead others; peers lead others still. They all share a desire to help patients and caregivers help themselves and one another (see Table 3.5).

However, people get far more of the information and support they need from their personal networks than from special-purpose support groups. Hundreds of empirical studies show that support from one's social network is a key factor explaining resilience in dealing with life stresses and adversity (Ganster and Victor, 1988). Social relationships give people a sense that they are receiving social support, and this perceived social support is important to their well-being (Gottlieb, 1985).

Beyond the emotional support they provide, social networks are also important for providing instrumental sustenance and social regulation or control (House, Umberson, and Landis, 1988). Strong social networks get people to address their medical needs and use the health care system regularly (Freidenberg and Hammer, 1998). They also increase compliance with treatment plans. Through personal and interorganizational networks, many people seek help with health problems (Pescosolido, 1996).

Network size and cohesiveness are particularly important: large, cohesive networks are best for people's health (Tennestedt and McKinlay, 1989). Among mental health patients, network size predicts hospitalization and service use. As the patient's network size increases, outpatient service use increases and hospitalization decreases (Becker et al., 1997). More resource-rich and diversified networks (of friends and neighbours) lead to more social support and, as a result, less activity limitation and better health (Litwin, 1998).

In fact, the greater a mental patient's social or family resources, the better his or her chances to avoid hospitalization, particularly from being committed to a state institution (Gove, 1980). Typically, large, cohesive networks are associated with higher levels of social participation. Social participation, in turn, leads to higher levels of well-being and life satisfaction. Personal characteristics also make a difference: they interact with network characteristics to produce positive health outcomes.

Table 3.5 Contact with Services and Support for Problems Concerning Emotions, Mental Health, or Use of Alcohol and Drugs, by Age Group and Sex, Household Population aged 15 and over, Canada Excluding Territories, 2002

	Total population	Contact with services and support	No contact with services and support	Contact with services and support not stated
	Number	%	%	%
2002				
Total, 15 years and over	24,996,593	9.5	89.9	0.5
Men	12,286,109	6.7	92.8	0.5
Women	12,710,483	12.3	87.2	0.5
15–24 years	4,136,460	9.2	90.5	0.4
Men	2,111,183	5.7	93.6	0.6
Women	2,025,278	12.7	87.2	–
25–64 years	17,133,721	10.7	88.8	0.5
Men	8,543,283	7.5	92.0	0.4
Women	8,590,438	13.9	85.5	0.6
65 years and over	3,726,412	4.5	94.8	0.7
Men	1,631,644	3.6	95.7	0.7
Women	2,094,768	5.2	94.1	0.7

SOURCE: Adapted from Statistics Canada, Canadian Community Health Survey, Mental Health and Well-being, 2002 (updated Sept. 2004).

Some people, however, do not have access to large or diverse social networks. For them, support groups are particularly useful. Increasingly, telephone- and computer-mediated support groups are coming into use. One study of caregivers to Alzheimer's disease victims compared two interventions. In one, four or five caregivers held supportive conversations with one another over the telephone. In the other, researchers provided taped informational lectures over the telephone. After three months, caregivers in both programs showed less psychological distress, more support satisfaction, and a greater perception of social support. After six months, the gains had levelled off or declined, however; caregiver burden and social conflict increased again (Goodman and Pynoos, 1990). As between the two programs, participants learned more by listening to the informational lectures.

Like telephone-mediated groups, computer-mediated support groups have the potential to serve clients who are unable or unwilling to participate in traditional face-to-face support groups. Computer-mediated groups offer advantages. They include the elimination of time and distance barriers, lack of group size restrictions, increased variety and diversity of support, anonymity, pre- and post-group support, opportunity for expression through written communication, and potential training experiences for group leaders (Finn, 1995).

As a result, health professionals have adapted computer technology to a variety of self-help/mutual aid groups, including computer-based, 12-Step groups for problems with alcohol, narcotics, eating, gambling, compulsive sexuality, relationships, smoking, and others. Where addiction problems are concerned, the benefits of going online, besides

Table 3.6 Barriers Accessing Mental Health Services Due to Accessibility Issues, By Aged Group and Sex, Household Population Aged 15 and Over, Canada Excluding Territories, 2002

	Total population	Barriers encountered due to accessibility issues	Barriers not encountered due to accessibility issues	Barriers not stated
	Number	%	%	%
2002				
Total, 15 years and over	24,996,593	0.6	99.0	0.4
Men	12,286,109	0.4	99.2	0.4
Women	12,710,483	0.7	98.8	0.5
15–24 years	4,136,460	0.8	98.9	0.3
Men	2,111,183	–	99.3	–
Women	2,025,278	1.3	98.6	–
25–64 years	17,133,721	0.6	98.9	0.5
Men	8,543,283	0.5	99.1	0.4
Women	8,590,438	0.7	98.7	0.6
65 years and over	3,726,412	–	99.5	0.4
Men	1,631,644	–	99.6	–
Women	2,094,768	–	99.5	0.4

SOURCE: Adapted from Statistics Canada, Canadian Community Health Survey, Mental Health and Well-being, 2002 (updated Sept. 2004).

those previously mentioned, include greater access to support, dispersal of dependency, meeting the needs of people with esoteric concerns, reduction of barriers related to social status cues, increased participation of reluctant members, improved relational communication, and better communication by people with interpersonal difficulties (see Table 3.6).

A new relationship-centred medicine that emphasizes communication skills can help improve patient compliance (Roter, 1998). Health professionals should understand how the doctor/patient relationship might reduce compliance. For example, they should avoid attitudes that imply stigmatization by diseases such as tuberculosis (Liefooghe et al., 1995), cholera (Nations and Monte, 1996), or HIV/AIDS (Demas et al., 1995).

Treatment and non-compliance

A problem therapists and mental health professionals face with many mentally ill patients is their refusal to take their medications—that is, to comply with their treatment program. In many cases patients reject or discontinue their medication treatment because they become disenchanted with the often-adverse physical side effects of the drugs (Karp, 1996).

Additionally, according to sociologist David Karp (1996), when a patient starts taking medication, he or she enters a process of new-identity building, in which the emotional malaise becomes a biochemical one. In a society where mental illness is highly stigmatized, the moment the patient initiates the medication treatment, he or she 'officially' enters the world of the mentally ill. Thus, rejecting medication treatment is a rejection of the label itself. In the course of a mental illness, taking 'medications involves a complex and emotionally charged interpretative process in which nothing less than one's view of self is at stake.'

Theories about Mental Illness

There is much professional agreement about the nature of *physical* illnesses that people experience. With *mental* illnesses, however, there is more professional controversy and less knowledge about causes and cures. This is partially due to the fact that neuropsychologists are not sure whether the psychoses are caused by chemical disturbances within the individual's brain or whether environmental stressors cause the chemical disturbance.

Psychological theories

Some psychologists believe mental illnesses do not even exist. 'Mental illness', in their view, is a myth—merely, a way of behaving and thinking that is rejected by society. The disorder, then, is society's disorder, not the person's. Along these lines, Horwitz (2002) challenges contemporary psychiatry's characterization of most mental illnesses as diseases, arguing that most of such disorders can be considered 'normal' reactions to stressful social circumstances or events, deviant behaviour, or cultural constructions, rather than disease entities. Mental illness, by this reckoning, is a cultural construct—not a medical reality. In the Western world, for example, hearing voices is generally considered pathological—a sign of mental disorder. In other cultures, hearing voices may be considered a form of dreaming, remembering, communicating with ancestors, or receiving a message from God or one's conscience. Such (latter) interpretations are much more benevolent.

There is much debate about the cultural construction and specificity of mental health notions. That said, the dominant approaches to mental illness in our culture are founded on psychological theories about personality, childhood development, and interpersonal conflict. Psychoanalytic theories originating with Freud and his disciples were once popular and have been substituted with more modern theories about childhood and parenting, and cognitive behavioural therapies that focus on changing individuals' negative thinking patterns, cognitive schema, beliefs, and behaviours. Currently there is a trend toward treating medical illness by many professionals, using a model that combines biological, psychological, and sociological elements.

Sociological theories

Sociological theories of mental illnesses focus on social factors that may be associated with certain mental illnesses. They are often critical of the psychiatric and medical models of mental illness and believe that mental illnesses are not like physical diseases. However, most sociologists agree that mental illness may be a result of combined biological, psychological, and sociological factors.

The functionalist perspective

Durkheim (1951 [1897]) was the first sociologist to study mental illness from a functional perspective. As we said earlier, he studied suicide as a highly personal act that responded to two social-structurally induced conditions. He viewed suicide as resulting, chiefly, from either insufficient moral regulation or insufficient social connectedness. These ideas gave rise to the social disorganization approach to mental illness, and the ecological approach, that dominated Chicago School studies of deviance in the first half of the twentieth century.

The thinking in Chicago was that modern urban life produces rapid change, disrupted relationships, and social isolation—all conditions that (by causing anomie and egoism) lead to deviance generally, and mental illness in particular. Because these conditions are most intense in cities, rates of mental illness would be highest in cities. However, we cannot be certain whether that is due to the stressfulness of city life or the tendency of mentally ill people to migrate to cities. Cities offer troubled people more opportunity, more professional support, and more anonymity than small communities.

Conflict theories

Conflict theorists would be inclined to view mental illnesses as reflecting the unequal distribution of social stresses, vulnerabilities, and class-based disadvantages in a society. They would expect to show higher than average rates of mental illness among the poorer, most vulnerable, members of society, because these people would suffer the greatest deprivation of supportive family relationships, living and work conditions, and good health services.

Health and health care have a great value in our society, and they are always scarce resources. Staying healthy requires having access to adequate food, housing, clothing, and health care. People with higher positions in the society are better able to obtain these scarce resources and therefore are in a position of advantage. That is why some conflict theorists believe that our health problems are rooted in capitalism. Through their reasoning, only when race, class, and gender-based inequalities are reduced will inequalities in health care be reduced.

If some group gains more benefits, another group must gain fewer (or lose some). In conflict theories, as in functionalist theories, neighbourhood characteristics play a role in mental health. However, conflict theorists focus on social deprivation. Conflict theorists show that socially deprived neighbourhoods experience a higher rate of mental illnesses. As a result of deprivation, mental illness—for example, depression—is more prevalent among the lower classes. Living in poor conditions and not having access to adequate health care contributes to the onset of mental illness.

Others note that, additionally, the statistics show higher levels of mental illness among poorer people because rich mentally ill people are less likely to show up in the official statistics. Wealthier people are more likely to receive early, often private, treatment for their illnesses, and are less likely to be counted and labelled than people who are institutionalized or receive treatment from public clinics. This exaggerates the class-based differences in rates of mental illness.

Symbolic interactionist theories

The symbolic interactionist approach emphasizes that people with mental or physical problems are cast into a social role, specifically, the sick role. As with other kinds of deviance, the topic of interest is not the original cause of the behaviour, but its labelling and stigmatization. The patient- or sick-role may temporarily free people of many social (and even occupational) responsibilities, but it also includes socially devalued and stigmatized elements. To receive a label means to become an outsider in the mainstream society. So, to be labelled mentally ill (or a drug addict, or developmentally handicapped) is to be freed of certain expectations and responsibilities, but it comes at a high cost. What's more, the labelling may itself complicate the disease and recovery from it, as the individual may refrain from seeking help in fear of rejection. Only two in every five individuals experiencing a mood, anxiety, or substance abuse disorder report seeking assistance in the initial year of the onset of the disease (WHO, 2001, 2004). This is an unfortunate fact, as an earlier diagnosis prevents people from having to endure the painful effects of a mental illness for a long period of time.

According to Thomas Scheff, a pioneer of the labelling theory, processes of societal reaction are a major component in the development of mental disorders. This is because mental hospitals are often managed in ways that override the more general concerns of patient welfare. They tend to weaken the inmate's sense of competence and self-esteem, and make him less fit to function in everyday life.

Considering the negative stereotypes evoked by the notion of mental illness, it is not surprising that many are opposed to the de-institutionalization of the mentally ill—to their release into the community and treatment as outpatients. Yet, in Canada during the first 20 years of de-institutionalization (roughly from 1965 to 1985), the number of beds in mental institutions was reduced by more than 60 per cent (Aubry, Tefft, and Currie, 1995).

One of the primary goals of de-institutionalization was to integrate the chronically mentally ill with other members of the community, to help them develop support systems and aid in 'normalizing' their lives. However, integrating de-institutionalized people into a neighbourhood is more easily said than done. 'Neighbouring' is based on the idea of well-disposed social interaction between people living in geographic nearness to one another. It is no surprise, given the negative attitudes surrounding mental illness, that the idea of placing community-based mental health services near neighbourhood residents has sometimes resulted in strong resistance (Aubry, Tefft, and Currie, 1995).

Neighbourhood residents often do not welcome facilities for the mentally ill, though few people mind outpatients coming into their community for treatment or day programs, so long as they leave again. A study by Arens (1993) found that 18 per cent of respondents believed that community group homes would endanger property values. Fortunately, people who oppose a residence in their neighbourhood are less politically active than people who support the location. Moreover, empirical research reveals that after a few years of living near a community mental health residence the majority of neighbours report no negative effects of the residence on property values. Community mental health facilities do not affect home sales activity (Taylor, Dear, and Hall, 1979). Comparing facility areas to control areas, researchers find that increases in the prices of homes in facility areas are comparable to the control homes.

Postmodern approaches

One of the great sociological works on mental illness is in the postmodern tradition. Michel Foucault's *Madness and Unreason: History of Madness in the Classical Age* (2005 [1961]) originated in Foucault's academic study of psychology and his work in a Parisian mental hospital. The book is an indictment of what he considers the moral hypocrisy of modern psychiatry.

Foucault studied the rise of the modern concept of 'mental illness' in Europe. Conventional histories depict the nineteenth-century medical treatment of madness as far more enlightened and generous than treatment in earlier periods. But Foucault claims that the new idea that the mad were merely sick ('mentally' ill) and in need of medical treatment was not at all a clear improvement on earlier thinking. He claims the supposed scientific neutrality of modern medical treatments of insanity disguise efforts to protect bourgeois morality against attack. In short, Foucault argues that the supposed scientific discovery that madness is mental illness is in fact a questionable social belief based on ideological assumptions and vested interests.

Foucault's approach reflected what he called 'the archaeology of knowledge'. This rests on the assumption that systems of thought and knowledge are governed by rules that operate beneath the consciousness of individual subjects. These hidden rules define a system of conceptual possibilities and determine how we think and what we think in a given period. So, the *History of Madness* is ultimately about the ways we came to think and talk about madness in the ways we do—ways that developed in the seventeenth to the nineteenth centuries, under the rubric of social progress.

Foucault's method, as a historian of thought, is to expose hidden, unconscious assumptions and beliefs. Doing so demonstrates that we think different ways at different times in history; that there are reasons for these differences and changes over time; and that one way of thinking may be as good as another, given the period. However, this 'archaeological analysis' could say nothing about the *causes* of a change from one way of thinking to another, so it could say nothing about the reasons why some positions were defended so vigorously and others were not.

This is a weakness in his formulation. Another related weakness is that Foucault fails to connect styles of thinking to material social conditions, and the ways that they change. The reason is that Foucault had explicitly rejected Marxian analysis, which made 'style of thinking'—otherwise known as ideology—secondary or superstructural to class relations based on ownership and production. So, having rejected Marxism, Foucault had nowhere to root his analysis of discourse. Nonetheless, his contribution is valuable. He warns us that everything we know that we think is universally valid must be tested and analyzed. We must avoid the easy belief that 'madness', 'delinquency', or 'criminality' are universals in that sense that they mean the same thing and behave the same ways in all historical periods.

On the contrary, we must investigate the ways that people in a given period make sense of reality—for example, recognize a subject as mentally ill. So the first rule of method in Foucaultian analysis is to avoid seeking universals; they do not exist, so we cannot examine them as historical constructs. Discourses about mental illness, delinquency, or sexuality exist only within a culturally specific set of rules. They set the stage within which meaningful interaction is possible between the subject (i.e., the viewer) and the object (i.e., the supposed madman), who are constantly modified in relation to each other.

That said, another principle of Foucault's method is to address 'practices' as a subject of study (e.g., of madness) from the angle of what 'was done': that is, the study of what is done to determine that a particular person is actually mad, and what was done with madmen (or delinquents or sick people). From this standpoint, the DSM-III-R—the handbook in universal use among psychotherapists to which we referred earlier—is not a fact book like the *Farmers' Almanac*, or even a set of scientific laws like Euclid's algebra. It is a compendium of cultural assumptions (considered 'findings') that masks the biased methodology used to 'discover' these 'findings'. In short it is a written system of beliefs, like *The Holy Bible* or *Mein Kampf*.

Mental illness: fact or fiction?

That said, there are visibly people who suffer depression or delusions; and there are visibly treatments administered that lessen their suffering. Can these observations be reconciled with Foucault's postmodern doubts?

Today, mental illness affects 400 million people worldwide (WHO, 2000). An estimated 22.1 per cent of Americans aged 18 and older—about 1 in 5 adults—suffer from a diagnosable mental disorder in a given year. When applied to the 1998 US census residential population estimate, this figure translates to 44.3 million people (NIMH, 2001).

The current prevalence of mental illness may be, at least in part, a result of medicalization and the constant redefinition of mental illness to include more people. Burr and Butt (2000) argue that the recent increase of mental disorders may indicate a pathologization of everyday life—a process that has relocated responsibility for mental disorders to the individual. Everyone today is more sensitive about their mental state, and the possibility of mental illness, than they might have been a century ago. Mental health professionals are also on the lookout for signs of mental ill health.

Some governments have used this awareness of mental health to their own advantage. A prime example was the use made of mental hospitals in the Soviet Union, to imprison and re-socialize political dissidents. In effect, psychiatric theories, language, and drugs were used to transform relations of domination and subordination. No wonder some have viewed modern psychiatric knowledge as an instrument of government oppression.

Symptoms of mental disorders, like language, fashion, or music, are tools in cultural interaction. Therefore, 'normal behaviours' can be judged only in relation to prevailing cultural norms. Horwitz (2002), for example, notes that 'symptoms' are not direct indicators of underlying dysfunction. They merely suggest underlying vulnerabilities, or risks, framed to match current cultural understandings about the forms and causes of mental illness. In short, they are nothing more than educated guesses about the boundary line between 'normality' and 'abnormality'.

The historical specificity of our knowledge is evident everywhere. So, for example, historical surveys of concepts of personality traits, manuals for kindergarten education, and psychiatric diagnosis in a children's hospital clinic show that the standards for the competent child have changed over time. Studies of child personalities and adjustment merely shed light on social techniques of defining and governing child behaviour. That is to say, our concepts of good behaviour, and even 'normality', for children change over time. As they change, we use new strategies to control 'abnormality'. The process of doing so starts with surveillance, assessment, classification, and streaming.

Policing too, as a profession, serves to enforce normality. Websdale (1991) notes that policing not only has a relationship with prisons, mental asylums, schools, reform schools, and other institutions that constitute disciplinary spaces, but it is also involved in the management of social life outside of these disciplinary spaces—for example, in public places of various kinds (shopping malls, streets, parks). Therefore, police deploy governmental power through the construction, elaboration, and implementation of disciplinary discourses.

The growing medicalization of deviance, and the normalization of vice as disease, is seen in a variety of situations. Collins (1996), for example, notes that today psychiatry and psychoanalysis offer a view of gambling, not simply as a bad habit or moral failing, but as a potentially addictive pursuit that can allow a judgment as to whether or not the individual's gambling is a form of mental disorder. Gambling in the nineteenth century was identified as a social problem, but at that time it was constructed in terms of threats to well-being, health, and happiness. Gambling today is seen as an addiction, a source of harm that justifies the scrutiny of populations and individuals to make mental abilities more governable.

Families, Stress, and Mental Illness

Stress is a major cause of mental illness—especially the more common forms related to anxiety, depression, and suicide. Families are not the only source of stress in our lives—often, the workplace is just as bad—but they are an extremely common source of stress. In the mass media, families are havens in a heartless world, but in reality, families can be danger zones—breeding places for mental illness. The research on family life is full of attempts to explain why domestic stress and violence are much more common than we would expect or hope. Consider the following studies:

- *Study number 1:* Freedman and Hemenway (2000) analyzed the social and family histories of 16 men sentenced to death in California prisons. Family violence was found in all 16 cases, including severe physical and/or sexual abuse in 14 cases. Other factors less directly related to family conditions included individual impairments in 16 cases: 14 with PTSD, 13 with severe depression, and 12 with histories of traumatic brain injury. Other conditions include: community isolation and violence in 12 cases; and institutional failure in 15, including 13 cases of severe physical and/or sexual abuse while in foster care or under state youth authority jurisdiction.
- *Study number 2:* A study of domestic violence in Korean-American families (Kim and Sung, 2000) concludes that male-dominance is a large part of the problem. In male-dominant immigrant Korean families, severe wife beating is four times more frequent than in egalitarian Korean immigrant families. The recency of immigration may affect the family stress level. The researchers report that husbands who experience higher levels of stress are more likely to assault their wives.
- *Study number 3:* Researchers (Klevens, Bayon, and Sierra, 2000) in Bogota, Colombia, interviewed males reported to authorities for

physical child abuse, and their female partners. Abuses are repetitive; occasionally, they involve alcohol abuse. The men who abuse their children are, usually, poorly educated stepfathers. They display, to varying degrees, signs of stress, substance abuse, mental illness, a history of childhood physical abuse, negative thinking, and unrealistic expectations of the child's behaviour. Typically, their female partners—the children's mothers—have no economic security, show a high degree of psychological dependency, and report histories of abuse (physical, sexual, and emotional) in both childhood and adulthood, including abuse by their current spouse.

Patterns of violence-producing stress and stress-producing violence tend to repeat themselves from one generation to the next. Additionally, cultural elements promote stress and violence. Male violence usually occurs in the context of patriarchal, male-dominant relationships. In this patriarchal context, stress and substance abuse often increase the risk of violence.

Sources of family stress contributing to violence are many. They include major family upheavals such as immigration, chronic stressors such as cultural dislocation, and recurrent stressors such as poverty, unemployment, and substance abuse. Dependent women in stressed, patriarchal relationships are additionally vulnerable due to their isolation from mainstream society (e.g., owing to a lack of English language skills, lack of job skills and income, or seclusion at home as caregivers) and lack of support groups based in friendship or kinship.

Family stress 'arises from an actual or perceived imbalance between a stressor (i.e., challenge, threat) and capability (i.e., resources, coping) in the family's functioning' (Huang, 1991). To explain the effect of stressor events on families, most current researchers employ a version of the 'ABCX family crisis model' first elaborated by Hill (1949). In this model, A, which represents the stressor event, interacts with B, the family's crisis-meeting resources, and with C, the interpretation a family makes of the event, to produce X, the crisis.

Researchers originally developed the model to study family adjustment to the crises of wartime separation and reunion (Hill, 1949). Sociologists have since used the model to examine differences in the ways families cope with a wide variety of difficult problems. One factor that always influences stress is the nature of the stressor event itself, as measured by its severity, intensity, duration, and timing. Typically, the longer a stressor event lasts, the more severe its effects. The more often it occurs, the more it strains a family's resources. Consequently, the harder it is for the family to cope successfully. How family members view and define that event determines the way they react to it. Their subjective evaluation of an event may not correspond to the researcher's objective evaluation. Like any self-fulfilling prophecy, a belief in their ability to cope increases the family's actual ability to cope.

Sociologists are interested in learning how stress changes the system of roles and relationships that make up a family. For example, they study how stress changes the ways that spouses relate to each other, parents relate to children, children relate to parents, or siblings relate to one another. They investigate the ways stress affects patterns of communication and interaction, marital satisfaction, or parental competence within the family. Finally, they investigate how stress changes a family's ability to socialize children, or provide a stable and healthy workforce.

Often, extreme stress reduces a family's ability to act well in these situations. For that reason, sociologists are interested in how family members cope and adjust to a long-term stressor. Some families and their members cope poorly by avoiding change as much as possible. Others cope better as individual members change their behaviours. Finally, others cope by changing their family relations. It is that change of family relations that interests sociologists most.

Ultimately, a family's success in coping with a stressor event will depend on the strength or quality of its crisis-meeting resources. As we will see, families that cope well with stresses are families that already had considerable resources—especially, cohesion and flexibility—before the stresses began. We will find systematic differences between the families that pull together and the families that fall apart under the strains of stressor events.

Common causes of family stress fall into at least four categories. First, they include major upheavals such as war and natural disasters (e.g., tornadoes, floods, and earthquakes) that affect many people simultaneously. Second, they include major life transitions—acute disruptions due to events that may affect some family members simultaneously, but not others—such as the birth of a child, the death of a parent, divorce, and retirement. Third, they include chronic stressors such as disability, chronic physical or mental illness, drug and alcohol abuse, occupational problems, unemployment, or imprisonment of a family member. For North American families, the Great Depression of the 1930s was a near-universal stressor causing widespread unemployment and poverty.

A classic study of family dynamics during the Depression (Cavan and Ranck, 1938) concluded that coping ability rests largely on a family's previous organization. Families reacted to the Depression in the same way they had reacted to earlier problems. All families showed increasing strain as the Depression continued; however, the degree to which this strain was felt differed from one family to another.

For many, the Second World War reduced family stress by providing jobs for people who had been unable to find work during the Depression. Simultaneously, however, the dramatically increased wages that many teenagers brought home weakened parental control and increased delinquent behaviour. Also, the loss of a father to military service, or a mother's change of roles from homemaker to workingwoman, required all members of the family to adjust.

Current research continues to examine the linkage between economic stress, poverty, and family dysfunction. Sociologists continue to find that economic pressure on a family increases parental unhappiness and marital conflict. It also increases parent-adolescent conflicts (Conger, Ge, and Elder, 1994). High levels of irritability, combined with arguments about money, lead parents to show greater hostility toward their children. In turn, these hostile exchanges increase the risk of adolescent emotional and behavioural problems.

Stress is known to increase the use of drugs, including cigarettes, alcohol, and illicit drugs (e.g., marijuana). This effect may be moderated by factors such as sex, income, family attachment, self-esteem, and mastery. Experiencing a high number of life events over time is related to a significant growth of drug use, even after controlling for such growth due to age or peer relations. High levels of family attachment significantly diminish this growth.

Alcohol and drug abuse are both causes and consequences of family stress. For example, Perreira and Sloan (2001) used four waves of the Health and Retirement Study to examine changes in alcohol consumption co-occurring and following stress associated with major health, family, and employment events over a six-year study period. Hospitalization and onset of a chronic condition were associated with decreased drinking levels. Widowhood was associated with increased drinking but only for a short time.

The care of ill or elderly relatives

Elderly people are an important subpopulation in the discussion of mental illness for several reasons. First, risks of some mental illnesses (e.g., dementia, Alzheimer's disease) increase as people age. Second, caring for elderly relatives often produces stress and stress-related mental health problems—such as depression and burnout. An aging, longer-living adult population leads to an increasing demand for care by families and increased family stress. Today, more than 20 per cent of Canadian seniors receive assistance because of long-term health problems (Perreira and Sloan, 2001). One result is the so-called sandwich generation: 42 per cent of Canadian women aged 40 to 44 balance parental care, child-care, and work outside the home.

Broader changes also include a shift from institutional to community-based care, a growing ideological commitment to elderly care by the state, and funding cuts by the federal government for such services (Rosenthal, 1997). Because of cuts to the health care system, Canada and other industrial nations with universal medical care appeared to slide back to the 'non-system' that exists in the United States (Chappell, 1997). Canadians value public health care, want good health and longevity, and view health as a public good, even while electing governments that carry out cost-reductions and ill-considered health care reforms (McDaniel and Chappell, 1999).

According to a joint study by the University of Alberta and Statistics Canada, the selfless people who take care of their elderly parents and grandparents save the national health care system $5 billion a year. If full-time paid workers replaced the roughly 2.1 million Canadians who care for elderly at home or in another unpaid situation, it would cost the health care system more than $5 billion annually. The study argues that better support for the elderly now—including more home care, more homes for the elderly, and more ways to help the unpaid caregivers—will save the taxpayers money in the future.

Evidence suggests that 75 to 85 per cent of seniors' total personal care comes from informal care arrangements (Chappell, 1996) and an equal proportion of Canadians report some type of self-care (Penning and Chappell, 1990). Family-enabling factors are the most important predictors of how much in-home service is used (Bass and Noelker, 1987).

Caregiver burden

Long-term care for elderly, disabled, or chronically ill kin can put great strains on a family's functioning. Often, the main caregiver has to add caring to other heavy responsibilities (Keating et al., 1999). As a result, caregivers frequently have to make changes in social activities, change sleep patterns, or give up holiday plans. Typically, caregiving creates a bigger burden for women than for men. At some time in their lives, a large fraction of women in their forties and fifties can expect to be sandwiched between responsibilities to old parents and their other commitments (Rosenthal, Matthews, and Marshall, 1989).

The 'caregiving family' in our North American culture contains people who provide assistance and people we perceive as having some obligation to provide assistance but who do not. An idealized view of family caregiving is used to put pressure on families to provide more care, but this is not justifiable in reality (Keating et al., 1994). Although caregivers often give elderly—and especially impaired elderly—parents many hours of personal care each day, caregivers vary widely in their incidence and severity of stress effects.

The extent, duration, and consequences of these family strains vary with the nature, severity, and duration of the illness. For example, informal caregivers for non-institutionalized parents with dementia report distress and heightened feelings of burden and depression because of the care recipient's aimlessness, aggressive behaviours, forgetfulness, and restlessness (Chappell and Penning, 1996). Strains also vary with the coping abilities and resources of the family, and with the disease-sufferer, whether a parent or child, old or young, male or female.

When caregiving responsibilities are added to an income-earning woman's 'double day', the dangers of caregiver burnout and family breakdown increases dramatically. The difficulty in balancing the demands of home and employment produces considerable stress which, taken to extremes, contributes to life-threatening health conditions (see, e.g., Ginn and Sandell, 1997; Scharlach and Fredriksen, 1994).

Coping with stress

Many families deal with stress successfully: family functioning returns to normal, though the stressor

Box 3.3   Could Marijuana Cause Schizophrenia?

Marijuana use is on the increase. Despite its reputation as a benign drug with medicinal properties, new Australian research is showing it may have a darker side after all—particularly for adolescent users. Links have been made between marijuana use and the onset of schizophrenia before but, as *Catalyst*'s Paul Willis reports, new research suggests something quite worrying for all young cannabis users.

Narration: Marijuana use is on the increase. Twenty years ago 1 in 5 young Australians had tried it, now it's up to 2 in 3. Research suggests some are starting as young as twelve.

Evidence suggests that in those people who are predisposed smoking cannabis can open the door to schizophrenia.

Dr Martin Cohen is trying to find out why. He's a psychologist at the Hunter Medical Research Institute, and he's comparing the functioning brain of young heavy dope smokers with the brains of schizophrenics. He had a hunch that smoking cannabis could be irreversibly changing the way an adolescent brain develops, to make it function more like the brain of a schizophrenic.

Dr Martin Cohen: During adolescence the brain's going through tremendous change. The neural networks and parts of the brain are changing the way that they're actually interconnecting to lead to development of the thinking capacities of an adult. Cannabis actually affects the way these processes occur and actually affects the way that the brain will be hard wired for later life.

Narration: Martin's research is suggesting something really worrying for ALL dope smokers; smoking cannabis is going to change the way your brain works.

Only some dope smokers will develop schizophrenia. But cannabis does seem to be changing the way a young adults brain develops so it functions more like a schizophrenic brain. And this is reflected in their behaviour.

Dr Martin Cohen: Clinically we see very similar deficits in their ability in terms of cognitive functioning, their thinking functions but also in terms of their planning, their organisation and their capacity to be motivated and exercise drive and be social.

Narration: Currently there is not enough evidence to say that marijuana causes schizophrenia and there's not enough to say it doesn't. But with two out of three young Australians trying marijuana, they do need to understand the risks.

may still be present. Families learn to cope by taking advantage of the resources they have available and by organizing their lives around handling their problems. Support from family, friends, and community agencies buffers the impact of caregiving, work, and family role strain. A supportive work environment also reduces physical and emotional strains (Lechner, 1993).

Two types of resources ease the burden for caregivers: assistance from other caregivers and support from people outside the caregiving situation. Caregivers with larger support networks—especially, networks of women and kin—report lower levels of stress. Close relationships with people who are both personal supporters and caregivers lighten the load of caregiving (Wright, 1994).

Two broad categories of resources—material and emotional/psychological—are key in deciding which families can withstand crises successfully. Stressor events always use up large amounts of all these resources. When a family member develops a chronic illness, families have to pay for costly medication (even in Canada if the person is not in hospital, which happens more and more with health care cutbacks) and family members have to take time off work to look after the ill person.

Psychological and emotional resources are more difficult to define. Family members commonly bring both resources to the family unit. Family members contribute to material resources, for example, by aiding in household chores or earning an additional income. Family members may build up the emotional resources of others by listening well and offering encouragement. It successfully predicts maternal coping 70 per cent of the time (Freidrich, 1979).

Dysfunctional families

Certain kinds of families are better than others at providing support. In cohesive families, members feel attached to the family, and to one another. In flexible families, members can change their ideas, roles, and relationships as the situation demands. Even families with adolescents (typically a predictor of diminished well-being) show high levels of well-being if they are cohesive and flexible.

Social and psychological disturbances characterize dysfunctional families. Poor family communication and lack of support within the family by one or both parents are indicators of the problem.

Dysfunctional families are notable for chronic conflict, child abuse or medical neglect, psychiatric pathology, or alcoholism (White, 1994). Families under the strain of chronic illness and treatment often reproduce and magnify their most troublesome characteristics. Families that were happy and healthy continue to be happy and healthy. However, in families with histories of drinking, marital strife, sibling rivalry, or financial instability, problems that begin as minor ones may explode into major ones.

Social and Health Consequences of Mental Illness

Health consequences

For many years, epidemiological studies have found that persons with serious mental illness have higher rates of premature death than the general population. Lifestyle has been an important factor, as so many persons with serious mental illness have had periods of homelessness and self-neglect.

Mood disorders

Depression and mania cause significant distress and impairment in all the important areas of functioning: social, occupational, educational, and other (Judd, 1996). Risk of suicide, loss of quality of life, and economic cost are the main health concerns for mood disorder patients. Among people with dysthymia, despite a high recovery rate, the risk of a relapse is great. People suffering from this disorder are also at high risk of experiencing episodes of major depression (Klein, 2000). Likewise, people who experience one episode of bipolar or major depressive disorder are more likely to experience future episodes of the disorder. In short, the experience of the first bout of depression increases the likelihood of a second one, which in turn increases the likelihood of the third one. Figure 3.1 shows the likelihood of bipolar 1 disorder recurring, based on the age of the first onset.

Mood disorders such as depression and mania often accompany other mental illnesses, such as anxiety disorders, personality disorders, substance abuse, and dependencies. The presence of another mental illness—or co-morbidity—increases the severity of the original illness and results in a poorer prognosis. People suffering from mood disorders are at high risk of suicide.

Schizophrenia is probably the most devastating mental illness when we consider how it affects the patients. The disease has a profound effect on people's ability to function effectively in all aspects of life. Functional impairment may occur in a person's family relationships, income, school, and employment—even, his ability to care for himself. As mentioned earlier, schizophrenia normally sets in during the early adult years, at a time when most people are forming families, establishing careers, and building their lives.

Early in the course of the disease, people with schizophrenia may lose their ability to relax, concentrate, or sleep. Performance at work or school often suffers. Though some are able to maintain healthy relationships, the majority of people with this mental illness (60 to 70 per cent) do not marry, and most have limited social contacts.

Another health risk arising from this mental illness is substance abuse. Up to 80 per cent of people with schizophrenia will abuse substances during their lifetime. Substance abuse is associated with poor functional recovery, suicidal behaviour, and violence. The level of mortality associated with schizophrenia is one of the most distressing consequences of the disorder. Roughly 40 to 60 per cent of people with schizophrenia attempt suicide, and schizophrenics are 15 to 25 times more likely than the general population to die of a suicide attempt. Approximately 10 per cent will die of suicide (Public Health Agency of Canada, 2002).

Anxiety disorders and their symptoms develop during adolescence. Most people suffering from this disorder have only a mild impairment. For those who are impaired more seriously, anxiety disorder can limit a person's education, work, recreation, and social participation. People with severe symptoms of anxiety disorder are also more likely to have other problems—for example, major depression or dysthymia, alcohol or substance abuse, or a personality disorder (Eaton, 1994). Anxiety disorders can also affect the sufferer's health if treatment is not received on time. Many people, as mentioned before, do not seek treatment soon enough. Others are afraid to seek treatment, fearing the stigma. Left untreated, anxiety disorder can affect the person's general health and quality of life.

Social Consequences of Mental Illness

Crime and victimization

A growing number of people who suffer from mental illness are running into trouble with the police and courts. In recent years, limited access to medical care and other services, deteriorating living conditions, and increasing resource limitations—repeated psychiatric emergency ward consultations, growing service demands on community resources—have made community care of the mentally ill more of an illusion than a reality.

Community living has been complicated by an increase in judicial processing (i.e., more policing, arrests, and convictions), resulting in multiple prison experiences for the mentally ill (Laberge et al., 2000). Mentally ill people are not only likely to involve themselves in some type of public altercation or minor offence, they are also at a higher risk of victimization than most other people.

Severely mentally ill people, particularly those experiencing delusional beliefs or hallucinations, often arouse negative responses in people around them who misunderstand the sometimes aggressive and impolite behaviours, which sometimes are consequences of the conditions, but that are not necessarily

Figure 3.1 Major Depressive Episode, By Age, Group, and Sex, Household Population Aged 15 and Over, Canada Excluding Territories, 2002

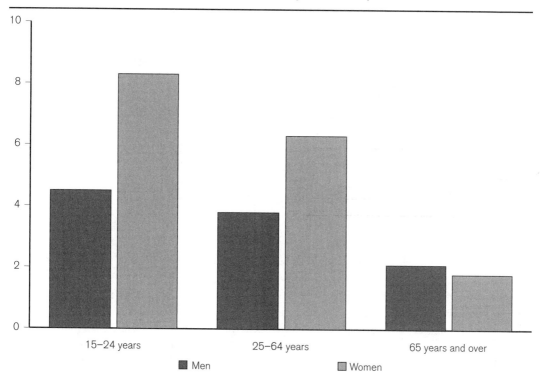

Note: Major depressive episode requires at least one episode of 2 weeks or more with persistent depressed mood and loss of interest or pleasure in normal activities, accompanied by problems such as decreased energy, changes in sleep and appetite, impaired concentration, and feelings of guilt, hopelessness, or suicidal thoughts.

SOURCE: Adapted from Statistics Canada, Canadian Community Health Survey: Mental Health and Well-being, 2002 (updated Sept. 2004).

personal characteristics. A study by Levinson and Ramsay discovered that ex-mental patients with high stress scores were more prone to verbal and physical conflicts (1987). The problem of violence against people with severe mental illness (SMI) has received little notice so far, despite several studies suggesting an exceptionally high prevalence of victimization in this population (Goodman et al., 2001).

Mental illness not only increases victimization, but victimization can also cause certain types of mental illnesses. Bullying experiences not only produce psychiatric consequences—stress reactions—but also predict future psychiatric symptoms

(Kumpulainen and Rasanen, 2000). The symptoms of post-traumatic stress disorder suffered by soldiers returning from war, or battered wives, illustrate this same point. Symptoms characteristic of PTSD include psychological numbing, increased states of arousal and anxiety, and a tendency to re-experience the trauma mentally. PTSD can be even more incapacitating than grief over the death of a loved one.

Stigma

The serious stigma attached to mental illnesses is among the most tragic realities facing people with mental illness in Canada and around the world.

Arising from superstition, lack of knowledge, old belief systems, and a tendency to fear and exclude people we perceive as different, stigma has existed throughout history.

In fact, Scheff finds that stereotypes delineating mental illness are learned quite early in childhood, and that such typecasting continues and is fortified through daily social interactions (Gove, 1980). Such stereotyping results in fear, embarrassment, anger, and avoidance behaviours. It forces people to remain quiet about their mental illnesses, often causing them to delay seeking health care, avoid following through with recommended treatment, and avoid sharing their concerns with family, friends, co-workers, employers, health service providers, and others in the community.

For instance, many women suffering from mental illnesses and addiction disorders are parents and caregivers and they fear that by seeking help they may lose their children or relatives to the authorities (Mowbray et al., 1995). This apprehension not only delays their recovery but it also puts their children in danger if the disorder is not under control. In the case of postpartum depression, or women experiencing distress from parenting difficulties, the WHO suggests that mental patients should be treated not in psychiatric hospitals, but in mother-baby units annexed to general maternity wards to reduce stigma (WHO, 1996). Under such conditions, women would be more inclined to seek professional help and maintain their roles as mothers, which is what they feared the most.

Public responses to depression affect patients' personal experiences of illness, the course and outcome of the illness, and their ability to obtain gainful employment. Mental-illness-related stigma reduction has become a priority, and to be effective, it requires innovative and effective public mental health interventions informed by a clear understanding of what stigma means (Weiss et al., 2001).

Attitudes toward people with mental illness vary among different groups in society. These attitudes affect the daily experiences of mental health service users. Our society makes it hard for these suffering people. Not only do they have to deal with the illness and the treatment, but they also have to overcome the stigma attached to their mental disorder. The ongoing process of recovery for individuals with severe mental illness means controlling symptoms, regaining a positive sense of self, dealing with stigma and discrimination, and trying to lead a productive and satisfying life (Markowitz, 2001).

Mental illnesses and work

Work is a central part of our society. Our occupational status is central to our assessment of our own and others social value: 'we are what we do' (Karp, 1996). A mental illness, however, can lead to unemployment, and this is highly disruptive to an individual's self-concept and self-worth. According to the Canadian Mental Health Association, 70 to 90 per cent of those suffering from mental illnesses are unemployed. One of the explanations is that, on the one hand, the stigma associated with mental illness keeps these individuals from getting or holding a job. On the other hand, the condition itself may lessen the person's trust in him- or herself. These feelings may prompt the individual to leave the job and discourage him or her from seeking future employment.

In several companies, permanent staff have a wide array of benefits that allow them to take time off in the case of mental illness and concentrate on recovering. Mood disorders and other psychiatric conditions translate into absenteeism, which becomes highly expensive for companies and limits productivity. In fact, for each employee who gets access to treatment, the employers will be saving between $1,000 and $5,000 a year.

Although many companies are making the move to a more comprehensive approach to mental illness, increasingly they are hiring temporary employees, who do not qualify for these benefits in most of the cases. Temporary or part-time employees often do not have access to paid vacation time or leaves of absence, and this is why they are a cost-effective solution for businesses. Thus, there is an increasingly large pool of individuals for whom taking time off to relieve the pressures and stresses that may lead to mental illnesses is not an option.

Economic costs

Much attention has recently been paid to both the prevalence and consequences of mental illness. In particular, public interest in the costs of mental illness has been limited to the direct costs of mental illness: to employment and earning losses (Marcotte and Wilcox-Gok, 2001). The World Health Organization predicts that by the year 2020, unipolar depression will be the second leading cause of global disability burden in the industrialized nations (WHO, 2001, 2004). Mental illnesses affect the Canadian society greatly in terms of health care costs and productivity losses, which translate into lost taxes. Measuring the economic cost of mental illness poses a problem, however. A 1993 study by Health Canada used several types of administrative and survey data—including physician-billing data, hospitalization data, and data on self-reported activity restriction—to estimate the cost of mental illnesses at $7.331 billion in 1993 dollars (Moore, 1993).

A later Canadian study drew upon the same data and also data from the 1996–7 National Population Health Survey questions regarding depression and distress and self-reported use of health services. The authors estimated from these data that the annual economic impact of mental health problems in Canada had risen to $14.4 billion (Stephens, 2001).

Policies and Theory Application

Education

It is likely that the stigmatization of mentally ill people will decline in the future, as people become more educated. Research generally shows that people with a higher education express more positive attitudes toward the mentally ill. For example, Rabkin (1974) finds that the less educated respondents are less tolerant than better-educated respondents. Other authors confirm education as an important variable and state that the more educated the person, the more accepting he or she usually is.

Another problem leading to stigmatization is unfamiliarity. Many people have negative attitudes toward the mentally ill because they do not know any better. It is the 'fear of the unknown' that provokes the stereotypes and stigma that many attach to the mentally ill. In future, governments will have to provide the public with more information about mental illnesses, their causes, and how people can help. Such measures will inform the public that these illnesses affect many people and no one can be sure of avoiding them. Public awareness programs, by reducing the social stigma that many attach to the mentally ill, will help to prevent an escalation of the symptoms and social isolation that many experience because of discrimination.

Poverty reduction

We have also mentioned in this chapter that there is a connection between mental illnesses and poorer, less socially integrated neighbourhoods. Governments should try to provide better services to the poor and ensure equal access to scarce resources poor people need to maintain health and a good quality of life. We also need more education in these poorer areas to ensure that people who experience mental health problems are not afraid to seek help. We can effectively treat most mental illnesses (or at least their symptoms) if people in need ask for help soon enough.

Likely Scenarios for Change

Diagnosis

Mental illness professionals assess the existence of disorders by observing symptoms. Ideally, patients with the same diagnoses will show similar symptoms and respond to similar treatments.

The unreliability of psychiatric diagnoses is a serious problem for our society. If mental health professionals cannot accurately detect and classify mental disorders, they are unlikely to be able to treat disorders effectively. Many people who need treatment are failing to receive it. However, some people who are diagnosed and treated for a certain mental health condition are not suffering from the disorder. They are merely experiencing some symptoms of the illness, but not the illness itself.

Some critics have concluded that the medical model of mental illness is not a useful way of understanding some mental disorders. In the future, new groundbreaking discoveries—including discoveries about the genetic bases of illness—may make it easier to detect and treat mental illnesses. However, for the time being we have to rely on existing tools. These include a variety of drugs, professional therapies, and family-based care strategies.

Family-based care in suicide prevention

Families play an important role in helping with a variety of mental illness problems. Consider the example of adolescent suicide prevention, as shown by the successes of three family-based treatments for suicide attempters: The Home-Based Intervention Program (HBI), the In-patient Specialized ER Care Treatment, and Successful Negotiation Acting Positively (SNAP) therapy.

Each of these treatments focuses on the suicide attempter in the context of their families and works to solve the problems within the context of the dynamics of the family. The HBI is set up to reduce the likelihood of further suicidal episodes. The aims of the program are to increase the family's acknowledgment and acceptance of the suicidal episode, to help the family improve its communication by focusing on expressiveness, appropriateness, and effectiveness, and finally, to help the development of problem-solving skills among family members (Kerfoot et al., 1995).

A second family-based treatment, designed specifically for in-patient treatment, is called

Specialized Emergency Room Care. The Specialized ER care includes staff training, a structured family therapy session, and the presentation of a videotape to the family that outlines both the harmful effects of ignoring suicide attempts and the benefits that come from treatment. The Specialized ER videotape and therapy sessions teach parents to define the suicide attempt as an ineffective way to solve problems, a serious event requiring immediate treatment, a roadblock to the positive feelings shared by the suicide attempter and their parents, and a problem that therapists can address through therapeutic intervention (Rotheram-Borus et al., 2000).

Rotheram-Borus and researchers evaluated the effectiveness of Specialized ER care immediately following a suicide attempt and again 18 months afterward, using a sample of 140 female adolescent suicide attempters and their mothers. Results of this study showed that after a suicide attempt, adolescents who receive the specialized care are much less depressed and report less suicidal ideation than adolescents receiving standard care. The researchers found more suicide re-attempts among adolescents who receive standard ER care than among those who receive the Specialized ER care. By contrast, the mothers who received standard ER care report deeper depression, more mental health problems, and less positive perceptions of their family over the next 18 months.

Compared to those receiving standard care, adolescents and their families who received specialized care were more likely to attend and complete their treatment, even completing their follow-up outpatient therapy. A third treatment program, called SNAP, is a six-session outpatient program for suicide attempters and their families. During these sessions, therapists establish a supportive family climate, help people air their feelings, solve family problems, and help family members plan and enjoy pleasant activities together.

Various exercises such as role-playing give family members the opportunity to work together and to enhance family cohesion (Miller et al., 1992). The suicide attempter, his or her family, and the therapist all evaluated the effectiveness of SNAP therapy after each session. Rotheram-Borus and colleagues (2000) found that ratings of the quality were high and rose slightly over time, suggesting increased satisfaction as the sessions went on. This therapy was found to have positive short-term effects on suicide attempters and their families.

Family functioning is a mediator of adolescent suicidal behaviour, which can act either as a buffer against suicide, or as a contributor to it. Given the family's role in producing, preventing, and treating adolescent suicide, parents are important targets of intervention. Therapists recognize the need to give family members new ways of understanding a suicidal episode, and not allow it to reinforce negative family patterns. Treatment must be family-focused to encourage protective factors such as family communication, cohesion, and effective problem-solving skills.

Community-based treatment: de-institutionalization

Increasingly since the 1950s, we have removed mentally ill people from institutional care. Researchers have been primarily concerned with the response of psychiatric patients to living in a 'normal' community environment, and particularly, with how well they can assume new social roles and identities after long periods of institutional care.

De-institutionalization has had an enormous impact on the mentally ill, the community, family members, and taxpayers. Some researchers find that, despite persistent mental illness, de-institutionalized patients develop new roles and new identities, a new sense of independence, new coping abilities, and a capacity to articulate future goals and desires (Newton, 2001). However, the exclusion of former mental patients continues. For example, some members of the public express concern that de-institutionalization and community-based programs increase the likelihood that women with serious mental disorders will be parents and will raise trou-

bled children (Firminger et al., 2001) Others are concerned about the safety of the community and others still about land values.

These concerns were anticipated, yet de-institutionalization has prevailed. It represents the convergence of many trends in social thought that reflect major changes in North American society. To an important degree, de-institutionalization reflects a belief in the human rights of mentally ill people, and skepticism about both the psychiatric profession and the therapeutic value of confinement.

Goffman and others writing in the 1940s and 1950s viewed total institutions, including mental hospitals, as anti-therapeutic and ineffective in helping the patients. Instead of making inmates healthy and better adjusted to life in the outside world, total institutions made inmates worse and less well-adjusted. This provided a first line of argument in favour of releasing patients from mental hospitals.

Social scientists and social workers provided a second support for de-institutionalization. They opposed a growing 'medicalization' of social problems. For sociology's labelling theorists, mental illness represented a problem of labelling and secondary deviation. They believed that if left alone, many 'mentally ill' people could function effectively in society. By labelling them and confining them, doctors (especially psychiatrists) worsened the problem. Social scientists and social workers, holding different views of 'mental illness' and professional goals of their own, challenged this medicalization process. Thus, in part, the fight against institutionalization was a fight over the right to define the boundaries of mental illness and ways of dealing with it.

A third support for de-institutionalization came from the legal community. Though a fight for civil liberties, lawyers' actions speaking for the mentally ill were also part of the war against the medicalization of social problems. From the 1960s onward, lawyers and doctors clashed often over people's rights, needs, and competencies.

A fourth support for de-institutionalization came from community mental health professionals. By 1960, traditional treatments of depression and schizophrenia such as electro-convulsive therapy (known as ECT or 'shock treatment') had acquired a bad name. Most people viewed them as harsh, excessive and—except for pacifying violent patients—ineffective. Increasingly, therapists substituted pharmaceutical drugs (especially tranquilizers, anti-depressants, and lithium for schizophrenia). Even more, citizens wanted lower taxes and less public spending, even if that meant fewer social services and more risk for vulnerable groups in society. Taxpayers wanted cheaper alternatives to institutional care for a variety of social deviants, including mentally ill people.

Supporters believed that de-institutionalization would, ideally, avoid the disruption of social ties and social roles that came with induction into 'total institutions'—whether mental hospitals, prisons, convents, or military camps. It would also permit patients to exercise initiative and learn skills associated with independent living. It would also allow mental patients to escape the dangers (like physical and sexual assault) associated with life in total institutions. So, outpatient care would be health-preserving and health-enhancing.

Regrettably, the fight to de-institutionalize mental patients had a negative goal—the virtual elimination of mental hospitals—but no positive goal. Though there was no standard plan for outpatient care, many felt that community-based professionals (in clinics and halfway houses) would provide better care than mental patients received in institutions.

In the end, the problems caused by de-institutionalization were largely economic. Unfortunately, the move to de-institutionalize mental patients coincided with major cuts in spending on health care and social services. The aim of these community-based mental health providers is also to detect and eliminate further sources of stress for the patient in the community, and to provide emotional support to mentally ill people and their family members.

Some critics are concerned that mentally ill people cannot function in the society.

Concluding Words

In the past 40 years, the number of people seeking help for psychological distress, either mild or severe, has increased more than four times. Some of this may be the result of increased stresses of family life and work life. This increase, however, does not just mean that more mental illness exists today. As well, people are more willing to accept help for psychological distress today because attitudes toward mental illness have changed and there is less shame attached to seeking mental health therapy.

This chapter has focused on theoretical approaches to explaining mental illness and the policies and programs that can help treat mental illnesses such as schizophrenia, anxiety disorders, mood disorders, and suicidal behaviours. We have come a long way from burning mentally ill people at the stake; today, we treat them in more humane ways. However, people still stigmatize and discriminate against the mentally ill. Mentally ill people are still viewed by many as deviant people and are treated accordingly.

Summary

What we call 'mental illnesses' are characterized by alterations in thinking, mood, or behaviour (or some combination of these) associated with significant distress and impaired functioning. The symptoms of mental illness vary greatly, depending on the type of mental illness, the person, the family, and the socioeconomic environment.

Mental illnesses, though personal, are socially structured. Because mental illness is socially structured, it is of interest to sociologists. Social supports for the mentally ill are key to recovery. Among the elderly, more resource-rich and diversified networks (of friends and neighbours) lead to more social support and, as a result, less activity limitation and better health (Litwin, 1998). However, as we have seen, providing support is stressful, increasing the risks of mental illness for the caregiver.

Box 3.4 FDA Issues Public Health Advisory on Cautions for Use of Antidepressants in Adults and Children

The Food and Drug Administration today issued a Public Health Advisory that provides further cautions to physicians, their patients, and families and caregivers of patients about the need to closely monitor both adults and children with depression, especially at the beginning of treatment, or when the doses are changed with either an increase or decrease in the dose.

FDA has been closely reviewing the results of antidepressant studies in children, since June 2003, after an initial report on studies with paroxetine (Paxil), and subsequent reports on studies of other drugs, appeared to suggest an increased risk of suicidal thoughts and actions in the children given antidepressants. There were no suicides in any of the trials. On close examination of the initial reports, it was unclear whether certain behaviors reported in these studies represented actual suicide attempts, or other self-injurious behavior that was not suicide-related.

FDA has initiated a full review of these reported behaviors by experts in such evaluation. However, it is not yet clear whether antidepressants contribute to the emergence of suicidal thinking and behavior. The agency is advising clinicians, patients, families and caregivers of adults and children that they should closely monitor all patients being placed on therapy with these drugs for worsening depression and suicidal thinking, which can occur during the early period of treatment. The agency is also advising that these patients be observed for certain behaviors that are known to be associated with these drugs, such as anxiety, agitation, panic attacks, insomnia, irritability, hostility, impulsivity, akathisia (severe restlessness), hypomania, and mania, and that physicians be particularly vigilant in patients who may have bipolar disorder.

FDA is asking manufacturers to change the labels of ten drugs to include stronger cautions and warnings about the need to monitor patients for the worsening of depression and the emergence of suicidal ideation, regardless of the cause of such worsening.

These interim actions follow recommendations made by FDA's Psychopharmacologic Drugs and Pediatric Subcommittee of the Anti-Infective Drugs Advisory Committees, which met on February 2, 2004. The advisory committee members advised FDA that the labeling should draw more attention to the need to monitor patients being treated with certain antidepressants.

SOURCE: Excerpt, FDA Talk Paper TO4-08, 22 March 2004; available at <www.medicinenet.com>.

Considering the negative stereotypes evoked by the notion of mental illness, it is not surprising that many people have been opposed to the de-institutionalization of the mentally ill and the idea of placing community-based mental health services near neighbourhood residents (Aubry, Tefft, and Currie, 1995).

People are more willing to accept help for psychological distress today because attitudes toward mental illness have changed; there is less shame attached to seeking mental health services. What remains is to create a society that is less stressful and more supportive, in this way preventing avoidable mental illnesses from developing.

Questions for Critical Thought

1. Describe the main social approaches to mental illness and explain which one you think best illustrates mental illness as a social deviance, and why?
2. Judging from the current state of de-institutionalization, what policy changes could ensure that de-institutionalization benefits those suffering from mental illness?
3. How do labelling theorists view the medicalization of deviance? Do you agree? Why and why not?
4. PACE (Parenting Adolescents: A Creative Experience), HBI (The Home-Based Intervention Program), the Specialized ER, and SNAP (Successful Negotiation Acting Positively) are all programs that aim to help the family understand the occurrence of a suicide attempt and therefore better prevent a re-occurrence. What possible prevention program could you design to target and reduce social causes of suicide?
5. Stigma and victimization of mental illness sufferers are still major problems in the community. As a policy-maker, what suggestions would you make to help the general population better empathize with mental illness patients?
6. What is mental illness? How would you define it? What might be some negative consequences of conceptualizing mental disorder from a statistical or 'norm' standpoint?
7. What factor do you think is more influential in causing mental illness: heredity or environment? Explain using examples.
8. Is mental illness found in all societies? Is it possible that our own definitions of mental illness are culturally bound?
9. Based on the information provided in this chapter, what effect do families have on an individual's mental health?
10. What model is predominantly used in our society to conceptualize mental illness: biological, psychological, or social? In your opinion, what is the best approach?

Recommended Reading

Foucault, Michel. (1965), *Madness and Civilization: A History of Insanity in the Age of Reason.* New York: Pantheon Books. One of the central works in the literature of mental health, this book traces the history and development of mental illness in European society. The author emphasizes rationality and civilization as a source of social control.

Karp, David. (1996), *Speaking of Sadness: Depression, Disconnection and the Meanings of Illness.* New York: Oxford University Press. This is one of the most eloquent and insightful books that explores the devastating capacity and unpredictability of depression. It is a personal account of the journey through the depths of depression analyzed from a scholarly sociological perspective. It's a definite must to understand depression.

Plath, Sylvia. (1971), *The Bell Jar.* New York: Harper & Row. This novel presents an intense fictional account that extensively captures an individual's journey through a nervous breakdown and treatment in North America during the early fifties.

Sontag, Susan. (1978), *Illness as a Metaphor,* New York: Farrar, Straus and Giroux. This provocative essay explores the notion of society's metaphoric thinking of illness. The book does not concentrate specifically on mental health but discusses it among many other types of illnesses, infectious diseases, cancer and other chronic illnesses.

Recommended Websites

Canadian Association for Suicide Prevention
www.suicideprevention.ca

On this site you can find resources and information about suicide prevention at a national and community basis.

Canadian Mental Health Association
www.cmha.ca

This section of the Canadian mental health association provides links to different entities that deal with specific concerns related to mental health, such as suicide prevention and terminal illnesses among other. Links to Canadian, American, and worldwide resources and information are also offered.

Canadian Psychiatric Association
www.cpa-apc.org

The official website of this association offers medical information and publications about the mental health profession and resources.

Centre for Addiction and Mental Health
www.camh.net

The Centre for Addiction and Mental Health (CAMH) is the leading Canadian addiction and mental health teaching hospital. CAMH provides information, assistance, and treatment as well as mental health promotion programs across Ontario through its 26 branches.

Mood Disorders Association of Canada
www.mooddisorderscanada.ca

This Canadian site offers a great deal of information about the different mood disorders, also providing statistics and surveys of the state of mental health of the population. It also provides information on resources in the community to help individuals with mental health concerns.

Public Health Agency of Canada
www.phac-aspc.gc.ca

This department of the Canadian Ministry of Health issued *A Report on Mental Illnesses in Canada*, an extensive report on the mental health of Canadians, that provides insight into current trends, needs, and situation of the mental health population.

World Health Organization–Mental Health Division
www.who.int/mental_health/en/

The WHO's comprehensive website provides up-to-date statistics and information on general mental health matters around the world. It provides a good picture of the mental health crisis and what is being done on a global basis.

CHAPTER 4

Sexual Deviance

LEARNING OBJECTIVES

- To understand norms about sexual deviation
- To identify the demographic and social characteristics of sexual deviants
- To understand the theories that explain sexual deviations
- To identify the social and health consequences of sexual deviance
- To be familiar with the policies that aim to control paraphilia
- To identify the scenarios for change in sexual deviation
- To understand homophobia as a form of sexual deviance

Introduction

How differently we would behave in a society that assumed the purpose of sexual activity is pleasure, and different people take pleasure from different kinds of sexual activities and sexual partners. Then, there would be no more reason for the idea of 'sexual deviation' than there would be in the case of sandwich preferences. (Obviously, some people like cheese sandwiches and others, peanut butter. People who like roast beef are not labelled 'sandwich deviants', except possibly in a vegan community.) Then, the traditional distinctions would make no sense and have no social acceptance. However, our society does make rigid, often needless distinctions of these kinds, with the result that many people are secretly, or publicly, sexual deviants.

In this chapter, we discuss rule-breaking and unexpected behaviour that is associated with sexuality, including homosexuality, fetishism, and pornography. We will explore the harmful consequences of prostitution for sex workers, sexual deviations that are deemed criminal (i.e., exhibitionism, necrophilia, bestiality, and incest), and sexual deviations that are not criminal (i.e., fetishism, voyeurism, and sadomasochism).

In short, this chapter discusses a variety of types of sexual deviation. *Paraphilias*, a name given to sexual deviations, are any sexual desires or activities that lie outside the cultural norm. Some are harmless; some risk harming the deviant him- or herself; others risk harming other people. We will provide theoretical frameworks for understanding these sexual deviations. The chapter will briefly consider psychological and sociological theories of sexual deviance to help us understand whether we consider sexual behaviours as deviant or not.

Sexual Deviance in Constant Flux

As with skin colour—on which societies often try to impose artificial labels and distinctions, calling some tones 'white' and other tones 'non-white'—societies also often try to impose artificial labels and distinctions on grades of sexual orientation. Societies designate some people as 'male' and others as 'female', when in fact any given person may have features—visible or not—that make them partly male and partly female. Our tendency to label reflects our notions of the hegemonic person.

For instance, a female who deviates from the notion of the hegemonic female is considered a deviant. Likewise, societies may designate heterosexuality the norm and homosexuality the deviation, married monogamy the norm and multiple partners the deviation, procreative sexual intercourse the norm and other types of sexual behaviour the deviations, and so on. Elements in the category 'sexual deviation' have no common feature except for social stigmatization. There are many varieties of sexual expression and, at one time or another, someone has condemned or labelled nearly all of them as deviant. Sexual behaviour has this effect on people. Perhaps it is because of the strong feelings that sex generates that people want to regulate sexual behaviour more than other types of behaviour.

Types of sexual behaviour deemed deviant may change over time, but what persists is the tendency to label certain behaviours as deviant because they are not conventional. Definitions are not static: they vary from one society to another. Today, violent homophobia—the aggressive and injurious rejection of homosexuals—is a new deviation of concern. Consensual sadomasochism, exhibitionism, voyeurism, and some forms of fetishism are increasingly becoming accepted forms of sexuality, though they are far from being widely practised or condoned.

Negative Consequences of Deviant Behaviour

Some sexual deviance is criminal. Often, crimes are committed by young men against young women with whom they are acquainted. Juristat, the chief supplier of criminal statistics in Canada, noted recently: 'Rates of victimization reported to the police were highest among female teenagers and young adults. Rates of sexual offending were highest among male teenagers. . . . Over 80 per cent

of victims in sexual offences . . . were female; males made up 29 per cent of child victims, 8 per cent of adult, and 12 per cent of youth victims.'

At the same time, official reports reveal that 'sexual offences are among the crimes least likely to be reported to the police. Persons charged with sexual offences are less likely than other violent offenders to be found guilty in adult court,' though 'sexual offenders found guilty in adult court are more likely than other violent offenders to receive a prison sentence' (Kong et al., 2003).

The first thing to note here is that sexuality, and responses to sexuality, are gendered. West and Zimmerman (1987) write about how males and females are subjected to gender-role expectations rooted in arbitrary labels—*male* and *female*. Sexual beliefs and practices, and deviations from them, are rooted in beliefs about men and women and the social roles that some people think men and women *should* occupy. It is this arbitrary set of distinctions that gives rise to what is called the 'double standard'.

The double standard and romantic love

The most common form of sexual deviance, in our and other societies, involves violating the so-called double standard: the rule that women are supposed to behave differently from men where sexual matters are concerned. Specifically, men are supposed to desire sex intensely—to be the sexual hunters—while women are supposed to be passive, almost asexual—the hunted sex-objects of men, their sexual prey.

Paradoxically, this long-lived double standard is at odds with another highly valued tradition: romantic love. Our society highly values romantic love. Yet, romantic love can serve as a basis for sex only in societies that allow both males and females to give (or withhold) sexual love freely. You can buy sex, but you can't buy passion. Since sexual attraction, and passion, are primary criteria of romantic love, there is a positive correlation between the importance of romantic love and social indicators of sexual equality. Drawing on data for 75 societies, De Munck and Korotayev (1999) show that societies that allow both men and women to enjoy (passionate) sex outside marriage rate romantic love much higher than societies with a double standard—that is, strong sanctions against female sexuality outside marriage, and a tolerance of male sexuality outside marriage. Stated another way, the traditional view that men are the sexual hunters and women prey—is profoundly wrong. The data suggest that no one gets good, romantic, passionate sex in that scenario.

Limits on female sexuality, but not male sexuality, indicate that a society does not really place much importance on romantic love or passion as a basis for intimacy. Sexual freedom and equality for men and women, homosexuals, bisexuals, heterosexuals, transsexuals, and other groups are fundamental to any society in which romance and sexual pleasure are fully possible. In a society that values romance, sex as pleasure becomes available equally to both sexes and all economic and social classes. No wonder, then, that around the world, people are re-examining the connections among sexual pleasure, romantic love, marriage, and childbearing. Increasingly, we have come to understand that these elements have many possible relations with one another.

Of these, sexual pleasure is the least negotiable: it is only possible for people who can freely choose it. For this, sex has to be freed from its economic constraints. For example, romantic love does not thrive where women are obliged to marry, or have sex, for financial reasons, or where sex is must always be tied to (potential) childbearing. Some would argue that the creation of the nuclear family seemingly based on the idea of romantic love is yet another economic negotiation occurring between husband and wife. In this conventional marriage, the male acts as the main breadwinner and the female services the male, sexually, and procreatively. Through all this, the female remains economically dependent. If so, given that prostitution is often defined as the exchange of money for sexual services, marriage is but another form of prostitution.

In democratic societies that value romance, sex as pleasure is increasingly becoming available equally to both sexes and all economic and social classes. People don't have to buy sex or marry for sex—in Canada, Sweden, or Japan, for example. Yet, in many societies around the world, this is far from the reality. Whatever lip service is paid to romantic love, the reality is a double standard that gives women much less sexual freedom than men.

Historically, the patriarchal gender order of Latin America, for example, has kept women in the home, reserving the public sphere for men; and it has imposed a double standard of female chastity/fidelity and male promiscuity (Rott, 1996). True, there has been progress in recent decades. All Latin American countries now recognize women's suffrage, and women's movements have strengthened from participating in democratization efforts. Domestic violence, reproductive rights, and other issues affecting women are receiving heightened attention as feminist groups redefine the private as political.

Such progress is evident around the world. Yet, even in egalitarian Scandinavia, a double standard persists in views of sexual behaviour. In Finnish sex-education literature aimed at young audiences, for example, there is a discrepancy between ideal and practical scenarios envisaged for sexual behaviour (Yesilova, 2001). This literature promotes the ideal of a steady relationship as a precondition for sexual activity, especially for women. It generally characterizes boys' sexual desires as instinctive and physical, without any connection to emotion or cognition, while girls' desires are subordinated to complexities of the heart and mind.

Sex education films aimed at North American adolescents also contain gendered messages. These contemporary sex education films contain different messages about male versus female sexuality. Overall, Hartley and Drew (2001) report that 63 per cent of individual scripts are gender differentiated, and

89 per cent of films contain at least some gender-differentiated scripts. The films reinforce a sexual double standard in which male erotic desire and sexual agency is legitimized, whereas female erotic desire and sexual agency is minimized. In addition, the films convey a 'sex as danger' message regarding female sexuality, thus creating a social context conducive to the suppression of female sexual desire, pleasure, and initiative.

Ungendered acceptance of sexual permissiveness—versus the traditional double standard—varies from one country to another. Despite the rise of a feminist movement in Korea, women are still beset by chastity ideology and the double standard of sexuality between men and women ordained by Confucianism (Shim, 2001). Despite evidence of the modernization of sexuality in Korea, traditional elements remain as the basis for the double standard.

In many important respects, there is little difference between sexual standards in the global North and South, the developed and developing worlds. In both parts of the world, boys still have more sexual freedom, while girls are controlled though labelling and rumours and are assigned responsibility for safer sex. Given the sexual double standard, an active desire for sex is positively regarded in men, and less so for women.

The sexual double standard is evident in both natural settings and experimental settings. For example, Hynie and Lydon (1995) conducted an experiment to examine the effect of the sexual double standard on impressions of a female 'target'. Female undergraduates read a fictitious woman's diary describing a sexual encounter under one of three conditions: in one condition the woman provided a condom, in another the man provided a condom, and in a third condition, the couple had unprotected intercourse. Participants made behavioural judgments and interpersonal judgments about the couple, and rated the female target on several personality traits. Female participants rated the target's behaviour more negatively, and as more

inappropriate, when she provided a condom, than when her partner provided a condom.

Medical and scientific experts—often, males—have often played a negative role in the battle for women's sexual freedom. Typically, experts have viewed female sexuality from a male perspective and labelled anything else deviant. From this standpoint, Alfred Kinsey's *Sexual Behavior in the Human Male* (1948) was liberating—one of the first books to publish basic factual information about people's sexual activities when most were refusing to discuss the topic (Allyn, 1996). However, Kinsey's effort to produce comprehensive classifications of sexual conduct excluded several forms of public sexuality, for example, voyeurism and exhibitionism, and ignored sexual expressions through pornography, homosexual activity, prostitution, and non-consensual sex.

The Myth of the Vaginal Orgasm by Anne Koedt (1970) also broke new ground in helping people to understand their own sexuality. First published in 1968, this book quickly became a feminist classic because it dealt with basic issues of female sexuality, including sexual freedom, the political meanings of sexual pleasure, and the psychological roots of male domination (Gerhard, 2000). Koedt challenged assumptions about heterosexuality that were generally accepted in psychoanalytic, medical, and popular discourse. Koedt's celebration of clitoral sexuality as a form of sexual expression—neither purely homosexual nor heterosexual—was a breakthrough for feminist sexual theories and American sexual thought. At least, it made clear that women did not need men to enjoy sexual pleasure. More important, it affirmed that the goal of sex was pleasure.

Yet even today, there are limited ideological avenues available for females to develop positive identities as sexually assertive women. Females are stigmatized when honest about their sexual explorations, while males are praised. Women who self-identify as 'sexually assertive' must struggle to create and maintain this identity (Moore, 2001). Many lack support systems to help maintain this positive perspective on being sexually assertive.

In short, the sexual double standard remains, despite liberalizing changes in the past 50 years and a virtual worldwide commitment to 'romantic' love and marriage. Sexual liberation—an inevitable consequence of access to secure birth control and the global industrial revolution—continues to spread. Gradually, the extent of the double standard in sexual behaviour of men and women is decreasing for younger generations, and the age of sexual initiation is decreasing as well (Anourin, 2000).

Cross-cultural analyses also find that the absence of a double standard concerning sex outside marriage—premarital and extramarital sex—is correlated to a variety of other variables indicating freedom and liberty. These include an absence of physical punishment of wives, an absence of beliefs that women are generally inferior to men, and the presence of such signifiers of female status as female leadership posts in kinship or extended family units, female ownership or control of dwellings, and a high value placed on female life (Artemova and Korotayev, 2003). Thus, the disappearing double standard is an important sign of wider gender equality.

History of Sexual Deviation and Consequent Public Reactions

Sexual variations have likely been part of human life as long as sex itself. Certainly, sexual variations have existed and been recorded for millennia in different parts of the world. For example, early Buddhist texts contain many references to sexually variant behaviours among monastic communities more than two thousand years ago. These behaviours included sexual activity with animals and sexual interest in corpses (De Silva, 1999). Behaviours that seem disgusting or incomprehensible to some are delectable to others, and this is nowhere more true than in the realm of sexuality. The point to remember is, people's views and tastes vary historically and from one culture to another.

Canadian public opinion about sexual topics has changed dramatically in the past generation. Consider attitudes regarding same-sex intimacy and marriage. Today, few Canadians view homosexuality as immoral or worthy of criminalization, as many did in the past. Yet, some people remain homophobic—that is, hostile to gay and lesbian people. Currently, homophobes are slowly becoming the deviants, rather than the homosexuals. Likewise, there is a greater recognition today that prostitution is a sex trade—an occupational category and type of work, not a form of immorality or wickedness.

Through the effects of organized Christian religion, people have long stigmatized homosexuality as sexual perversion, and some segments of the Western society continue to do so. Yet, with the passage of time and with secularization—the diminishing importance of institutional religion—homosexuality has become increasingly accepted. In time, the social and legal policies toward homosexuality have changed (as demonstrated by the legalization of same-sex marriage in Canada) and so have public attitudes. Homosexuality has not only captured increasing social acceptance, but it has also evolved into a subculture with its own norms, values, social networks, and support families. In fact, these two changes are related: in all areas of life, deviant groups rely on subcultures and communities to give them support while they are suffering exclusion and stigma. Sexually deviant (or variant) groups are no exception.

The term 'sexual deviation' has had a peculiar history. In earlier centuries, people used the term 'perversion' to refer to non-traditional sexual behaviour. However, that term came under considerable criticism for its negative connotation, and today people use terms such as 'sexual deviations' and 'paraphilias', referring to specific objects of arousal. Though less negatively connotative than perversions, they still imply criticism. Perhaps 'sexual variation' is the best term we can use to capture our idea that differences in sexual practice are natural though often disapproved.

Box 4.1 The Toronto Morality Department

Along with surveillance, police knowledge about sex between men generated through the discursive production and circulation by police statistics and other texts further facilitated the process by which 'gross indecency' was entered into public knowledge. The police also played a key role in transforming the knowledge gathered through surveillance into evidence. That was presented in court and often reported in the pages of the daily press. All of this was the process through which, by the early-twentieth century, police constables, reformers, lawyers, judges, and journalists discovered 'moral perverts' and their meeting places. It was, then, I would argue, both the activity of the men and the concrete/discursive manners of the police which forged and contributed to the growth in knowledge of the sexual underground.

The Toronto evidence is also interesting in the way it highlights the shifting modes used to regulate homosexual relations. For much of the nineteenth century, the regulation of sex between men took place (in addition to families and neighbourhoods) through the generalized legal control and sporadic use of the courts. By the turn of the century, these regulatory strategies were complemented by a more pervasive individual surveillance carried out by the disciplinary agencies such as the police: 'the technologies of surveillance used by the Toronto Morality Department to regulate homosexual activity represented relatively new forms of power that facilitated the extension of the local state into the realm of everyday life.'

SOURCE: Excerpt, Steven Maynard, 1994, 'Through a Hole in the Lavatory Wall: Homosexual Subcultures, Police Surveillance, and the Dialectics of Discovery, Toronto, 1890–1930', *Journal of the History of Sexuality*. 5 (2): 207–42. © 1994 University of Texas Press. All rights reserved. Reprinted by permission of the publisher.

Prostitution

According to Gagnon and Simon (1967), sexual deviance can be broken down into three general categories. First, there is behaviour that is socially disapproved yet has low visibility: for example, premarital sex and masturbation. Both of these behaviours are legal but neither is viewed favourably (at least in public) and neither is readily noticeable. The sheer invisibility of this behaviour complicates research. Even in the 1960s, Gagnon and Simon found that virtually all men and (at least) two-thirds of the female population engaged in masturbation, despite the stated taboos against it. This type of sexual deviance is so common it is referred to as 'normal' deviance.

A second category of sexual deviance is deemed pathological deviance, and includes pedophilia, voyeurism, incest, exhibitionism, and aggressive offences. This type of deviance, though relatively uncommon, receives the most attention because it is rare and violates both law and public mores. A third and final type of sexual deviance is reinforced by social structure and community norms. The best example is female prostitution—what has been called the 'world's oldest profession'. Whether there are laws against prostitution or not, community practice (including police practice) ensures this activity will continue.

Prostitution is an ancient activity, and is described in humanity's earliest written records. The topic of prostitution raises interesting questions about the deviance of the behaviour—how can it be deviant if it is so common and long-lived?—and about who should properly be considered deviant, the prostitute or her/his client (the 'john'). As we will also see, the topic raises important questions about choice and constraint in the performance of deviant activities. We are led to ask whether prostitution is a form of sexual deviance, a type of paid work, a response to childhood abuse, or a kind of modern slavery.

Though prostitution is found everywhere, it is more common under some circumstances than others. It is particularly common wherever certain groups of people are both impoverished—without financial means to live independently—and socioculturally vulnerable. In many parts of the world, women are viewed as worth less than men, and children are viewed as worth less than adults. Though personal experiences may incline a person toward prostitution, the practice of prostitution is more or less likely under specific cultural conditions. Typically, the sexual double standard, poverty, and an unequal labour market are factors that increase the frequency and likelihood of the activity. As a result, poor women and children, especially in societies without a social welfare net, are most likely to be engaged in prostitution.

In poor countries where old people dominate the traditional family, young people—male and female—may be virtually forced into the sex trade. The younger family members are expected to turn over virtually all of their earnings to the family elders. Most sex workers—male and female—still acknowledge and respond to these societal norms. Despite the greater choice of occupational opportunities for young men than young women, the need to meet their filial obligation may contribute to the choice of sex work.

However, women continue to practice prostitution more commonly than men, with predictable effects. In India, for example, women suffer from the double standard of morality that governs India's profitable sex trade. Despite the financial vulnerability that leads them to enter sex work and the health hazards they suffer, including physical abuse, Indian sex workers endure stigmatization because they must sell their bodies to live. In particular, 'floating' sex workers who return to their families after work suffer from the sense of leading a discreditable double life.

How the sex trade works

Throughout history, prostitutes have fallen into three classes. The lowest are the prostitutes of the streets. These women were originally slaves, and in later times came from the entrenched poor. The next class up is women who work in brothels or similar facilities; they typically came from working-class backgrounds. The upper classes of prostitutes are the courtesans.

Many communities are organized to recognize and segregate the practice of prostitution. As a result, many cities have a 'red-light' district where bordellos can be found and streetwalkers wait for a pickup. Changes in the location (and visibility) of prostitution in a city reflects a constant interplay between the ordering strategies enacted by the police, council, and community protestors and the resistive tactics adopted by sex workers. These strategies, in turn, depend on whether the society believes in the legalization or criminalization of prostitution. Many believe that prostitution ought to be regulated to improve working conditions for sex workers—that is, to reduce the potential harm associated with a sex trade. Then, prostitution would be a healthier and less dangerous occupation; often, when prostitution is regulated, the government can also gain revenue from the practice.

Especially when prostitution is decriminalized, distinctive red-light or brothel districts are created to segregate prostitution from other, more

Box 4.2 The Criminal Code Defines Bawdy-Houses, Procuring and Prostitution (Chapter C-46)

Bawdy-houses

Keeping common bawdy-house	210. (1)	Every one who keeps a common bawdy-house is guilty of an indictable offence and liable to imprisonment for a term not exceeding two years.
Landlord, inmate, etc.	(2)	Every one who

(a) is an inmate of a common bawdy-house,

(b) is found, without lawful excuse, in a common bawdy-house, or

Notice of conviction to be served on owner

(c) as owner, landlord, lessor, tenant, occupier, agent or otherwise having charge or control of any place, knowingly permits the place or any part thereof to be let or used for the purposes of a common bawdy-house,

is guilty of an offence punishable on summary conviction.

Procuring   212. (1) Every one who

(a) procures, attempts to procure or solicits a person to have illicit sexual intercourse with another person, whether in or out of Canada,

(b) inveigles or entices a person who is not a prostitute to a common bawdy-house for the purpose of illicit sexual intercourse or prostitution,

(c) knowingly conceals a person in a common bawdy-house,

(d) procures or attempts to procure a person to become, whether in or out of Canada, a prostitute,

(e) procures or attempts to procure a person to leave the usual place of abode of that person in Canada, if that place is not a common bawdy-house, with intent that the person may become an inmate or frequenter of a common bawdy-house, whether in or out of Canada,

(f) on the arrival of a person in Canada, directs or causes that person to be directed or takes or causes that person to be taken, to a common bawdy-house,

(g) procures a person to enter or leave Canada, for the purpose of prostitution,

(h) for the purposes of gain, exercises control, direction or influence over the movements of a person in such manner as to show that he is aiding, abetting or compelling that person to engage in or carry on prostitution with any person or generally,

(i) applies or administers to a person or causes that person to take any drug, intoxicating liquor, matter or thing with intent to stupefy or overpower that person in order thereby to enable any person to have illicit sexual intercourse with that person, or

	(j) lives wholly or in part on the avails of prostitution of another person, is guilty of an indictable offence and liable to imprisonment for a term not exceeding ten years.
Offence in Relation to Prostitution	213. (1) Every person who in a public place or in any place open to public view (a) stops or attempts to stop any motor vehicle, (b) impedes the free flow of pedestrian or vehicular traffic or ingress to or egress from premises adjacent to that place, or (c) stops or attempts to stop any person or in any manner communicates or attempts to communicate with any person for the purpose of engaging in prostitution or of obtaining the sexual services of a prostitute is guilty of an offence punishable on summary conviction.
Definition of 'public place'	(2) In this section, 'public place' includes any place to which the public have access as of right or by invitation, express or implied, and any motor vehicle located in a public place or in any place open to public view.

R.S., 1985, c. C-46, s. 213; R.S., 1985, c. 51 (1st Supp.), s. 1.

SOURCE: Department of Justice, Canada; available at <http://laws.justice.gc.ca/en/C-46/text.html>.

upstanding activities and people, and to keep women from walking the streets propositioning potential clients (Hubbard and Sanders, 2003). In Canada, prostitution itself is not illegal. However, one could be arrested for prostitution-related offences such as communicating offences, bawdy houses offences, or procuring offences. These offences tend to target those sex workers who are more visible to the public eye and thus easily targeted by authorities. As a result, the poorest paid, most socially vulnerable prostitutes—streetwalkers—are also the more liable to arrest.

In Figure 4.1, Lowman shows how recent changes in policies have led to less police attention on off-street prostitution and bawdy houses and more focus on the pimps involved in street prostitution in Vancouver (Lowman, 1998).

So, there has always been a geographic element to sexual activity, in the sense that certain cities or parts of cities—distinctive red-light districts—have always been known as places to find sex. Even in areas where prostitution is illegal, well-known places to find sex exist. On the street level, they are referred to as 'tracks'. The effects of such spatial concentration easily translate into the concentration of other vices, legal or not. For example, in Table 4.1 Lowman and Fraser (1996) look at how the media can trace a murdered prostitute to her corresponding tracks.

Prostitution is not the only sexual activity that is geographically concentrated. Some areas have also been particularly known for gay sexual activity. In Toronto, these places in the past have included Union Station, Sunnyside Beach, Albert Street Lane, and Queen's Park (Maynard, 1994). Today, the area around Church and Wellesley Streets is an important residential and commercial hub for Toronto homosexuals. Increasingly, as more gay and lesbian people come out, their spending power is catching the attention of business. New gay resorts are opening up throughout the developing world, for example. Gay travellers interpret these places as enclaves for sexual exploration, and overlook the poverty and social exclusion that such spaces reproduce.

Figure 4.1 Bawdy House and Procuring Charges in Canada: 1974 to 1995

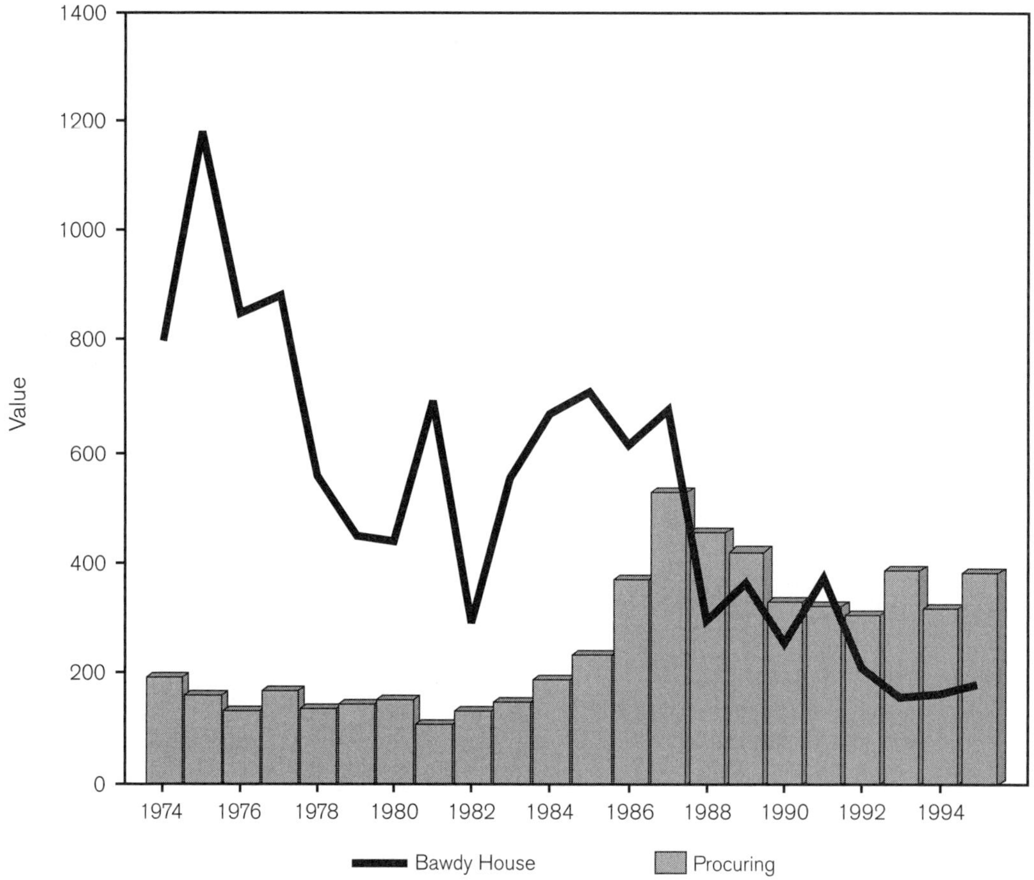

SOURCE: *Juristat,* Aggregate UCRs, (Ottawa: Canadian Centre for Justice Statistics); J. Lowman, 'Prostitution Law Reform in Canada', in *Toward Comparative Law in the 21st Century*, ed. Institute of Comparative Law in Japan (Tokyo: Chuo University Press, 1998).

Sex work, as a business, is about relations of production—relations between a prostitute, her client, and her pimp. Street-level prostitution includes both pimp-controlled prostitution and independent entrepreneurial prostitution. Pimp-related violence is common for women involved in pimp-controlled prostitution (Williamson and Cluse-Tolar, 2002). Female prostitutes are, in many senses, often at the mercy of their pimps. More will be said about this in connection with the global sex trade.

Even relatively protected sex workers are at risk. Guidroz (2001) examined two types of sex industry work—escorts and telephone-sex work—to explore sex workers' gendered work experiences in the sex industry. Both the escorts' and telephone-sex operators' personal lives are impacted by the work; several report experiencing isolation as a result of working in the sex industry. The work of escorts and telephone-sex operators involves emotional labour—a characteristically female activity. Sexuality is a core component of the work, and clients' patriarchal

Table 4.1 Types of Offences/Harassment Experienced by Prostitutes in Vancouver

	On-street (n=62)			Off-street (n=22)		
	Count	% of responses	% of cases	Count	% of responses	% of cases
General harassment	43	12.4	69.4	11	20.6	50.0
Threat/intimidation	41	11.8	66.1	9	15.7	40.5
Had/use knife	32	9.2	51.6	2	4.1	9.1
Dumped	27	7.8	43.5	1	2.0	4.5
Refused condom	26	7.5	41.9	7	14.7	31.8
Beating	24	6.9	38.7	3	6.1	13.6
Robbery	23	6.6	37.1	2	4.1	9.1
Sexual assault	23	6.6	37.1	2	4.1	9.1
Had/used gun	22	6.3	35.5	3	6.1	13.6
Unwanted acts	21	6.0	33.9	4	8.2	18.2
Kidnap/confine	20	5.7	32.3	1	2.0	4.5
Strangling	19	5.5	30.6	1	2.0	4.5
Other weapon	17	4.9	27.4	2	4.1	9.1
Attempt murder	6	1.7	9.7	0	0.0	0.0
Other	2	0.6	3.2	1	2.0	4.5
Total	**348**	**100.0**	**561.3**	**49**	**100.0**	**222.7**

Note: In the table above, '% of responses' refers to the number of respondents and '% of cases' refers to the number of incidents of violence experienced.

SOURCE: J. Lowman and L. Fraser, *Violence against Persons Who Prostitute: The Experience in British Columbia*, Technical Report TR1996-114e (Ottawa: Department of Justice, 1996), table 99.

notions of women's sexuality influence this aspect of the work. Thus, sex work is isolating and disempowering.

The imbalance of the relationship between a sex worker and a client is evident everywhere. In Third World countries, such as Uganda, some of the women work in the back-street bars, have no capital of their own, and are almost entirely dependent on selling sex for their livelihood. Another group of women, the more successful entrepreneurs, earn money from their own bars as well as from commercial sex. These women, so different in some ways, share similar disadvantaged backgrounds, and this explains their move into commercial sex. Due partly to their financial independence from men, women in the latter group have taken control of sexual relationships and can negotiate good sexual deals for themselves, both financially and in terms of safe sex. The poorer women are more vulnerable and

less able to negotiate safer sex (Gysels, Pool, and Nnalusiba, 2002).

As in Uganda, India, and Mexico City, female sex workers must switch between the distinct roles of mother and prostitute—they daily face society's double standard for women (Castaneda et al., 1996). Rationalizations of those who wish to legalize prostitution include justifying sex work as a better paying employment opportunity for women, a necessary evil, and a type of social service. Yet, female sex workers must often even hide their profession from their families, for fear they will be punished for their breach of expected female purity. As a result, they divide their lives between the mother/saint and prostitute/traitor roles.

Despite these difficulties, prostitutes have had difficulty mobilizing for their own protection and advancement. Some sex workers have tried to improve their health and social standing by forming social movements. In various locations, prostitutes are politically organizing and expressing their claims and grievances in the public debate about prostitution—a debate from which they are usually excluded (Mathieu, 2003). A crucial, but ambiguous, role is played by alliances between prostitutes and people from other parts of society (especially feminists).

Why people enter the sex trade

Many people have thought that prostitutes typically get their start through some kind of 'slave trade', or that someone at some point in their lives has forced them to sell their bodies for money. Although this does occur, most prostitutes have made a choice to earn money in that manner and nobody has forced them to do so—at least, not in the United States and Canada. Experts estimate that no more than 4 per cent are railroaded into the sex trade here (Thio, 1998). However, in saying this we immediately confront definitional difficulties. A high percentage of prostitutes have been physically or sexually abused in their youth. The consequent drop in their self-esteem may have contributed to their choice of occupation. In this sense, they were railroaded into prostitution by their (unchosen) childhood experiences.

Gaudette and colleagues state that the average age in which a sex worker enters the sex trade is 14. Usually, people enter the sex trade because they have no other choice. Either they are desperately poor or are fleeing something worse: for example, the Alberta Children's Services states that 85 per cent of sex workers were sexually abused as children before entering the trade.

To confirm this in a local setting, Nixon and colleagues (2002) studied women involved in prostitution from three Western Canadian provinces. The respondents described high rates of violence perpetrated against them, including considerable childhood sexual abuse, most often by a family member or by caretakers while they were living in foster care or group homes. The young women continued to experience violence as prostitutes so commonplace

that it almost seemed 'normal'. They were victimized by pimps, johns, other prostituted women, intimate partners, representatives from mainstream society, and members of the police. Their experiences of violence gave rise to health problems, attempts to protect themselves, and attempts to leave the streets.

Given the media's tendency to glamorize sex work in such well-known movies as *Pretty Woman*, with Julia Roberts, the unglamorous reality needs to be hammered home. Many prostitutes, here and elsewhere, grew up in harsh and even abusive families. Phoenix (Arizona) women engaging in prostitution, for example, have limited educational backgrounds and often have not completed high school. Survey results (Kramer and Berg, 2003) indicate that both white and minority women engaging in prostitution experienced high rates of physical and sexual abuse in childhood, as well as parental substance abuse. Familial environments of streetwalkers are characterized by parental alcoholism and drug abuse, domestic violence, parental absence and abandonment, and multiple forms of childhood abuse (Dalla, 2001).

To find out how young people got into the sex trade, Pedersen and Hegna (2003) studied all adolescents (ages 14 to 17) in the public and private school systems in Oslo, Norway. Of the adolescents who had sold sex (1.4 per cent of the total), boys had done so three times more often than girls. The researchers concluded that a small group in the general adolescent population sells sex, and many of the clients are assumed to be homosexual or bisexual men.

Nigeria has a large number of adolescents living and making a living on the streets. This has been attributed to economic factors and exposure to all forms of risks. The result is a spread of prostitution among the adolescents with its attendant problems (Bamgbose, 2002). The experiences of adolescent prostitutes vary: some are in brothels, some are streetwalkers, call girls, and casual, part-time, or floating prostitutes. The causes of adolescent prostitution in Nigeria are economic, sociological, and socioeconomic factors.

Among sex workers in Turkey, parental substance abuse, neglect, and emotional, physical, and sexual abuse are commonly observed in the lives of these girls. These girls run away from turbulent home lives and are trapped by the illegal world of underground prostitution. Their experiences must be understood in relation to the values and norms dominant in Turkish culture, especially those relating to childrearing practices. Some people just drift into selling sex, and the selling of sex can be casual or professional, implicit or explicit.

Wojcicki (2002) introduces the concept of *ukuphanda,* a Zulu verb that is used to describe the sex-for-money exchanges that take place outside of commercial sex work in some parts of South Africa. Women who exchange sex for money in taverns do not self-identify as commercial sex workers and experience less stigma from the community. Unlike commercial sex work, which is understood to be associated with short skirts and other revealing attire, sex-for-money exchange in the taverns is viewed as more private, ambiguous, and informal. Women who work as informal sex workers, or *phandela imali* ('try to get money'), are understood to be using sex-for-money exchange to survive financially.

Likewise, female garment factory workers in Cambodia also drift into paid sex on occasion (Nishigaya, 2002). Low socioeconomic status (low education, meagre factory wage, and high dependency rate at their rural households) and obligations as daughters to provide for the family mainly determine their entry into sex work. At the location of sex work, they are subjected to physical violence, alcohol and drug use, both self-taken and forced, and receive meagre wages. In a society where women are expected to be virtuous and obedient to parents and husbands, these workers are motivated to identify male sex partners in paid sex as 'sweethearts' rather than 'guests'. These factors contribute to low consistency of condom use—therefore, serious health risks from HIV and other sexually transmitted diseases.

Women in traditional societies are often financially (as well as socially and legally) dependent on men. They enjoy few opportunities for independence outside of sex work. As a result, it is as hard for them to leave sex work as it was easy for them to enter it—even when they run a serious risk of HIV/AIDS or other fatal diseases.

Manopaiboon and colleagues (2003) studied Thai women's ability to leave sex work, and the factors influencing their lives after leaving. All but 1 of the 42 current and former female sex workers had quit sex work at least once. Women's ability and decisions to leave sex work were determined primarily by four factors: economic situation, relationship with a steady partner, attitudes toward sex work, and HIV/AIDS experience. Most women perceived their risk for HIV infection to be lower after leaving sex work, but three of the 17 HIV-infected women acquired infection after having left, presumably from their steady partners.

To reiterate, the phenomenon of prostitution has the sexual double standard, poverty, and an unequal labour market as prerequisites. People typically drift into prostitution or 'sex work' because they are poor, addicted, or abused. Once in 'the life', they find it hard to leave. While in the life, they risk physical abuse and contracting deadly diseases. These facts make it hard to insist that prostitution is a profession, career, or form of work in the same sense as—say—secretarial work, school teaching, engineering, law, or sales work.

The traffic in sex

Everywhere in the prosperous West, prostitutes are appearing from Eastern Europe, Asia, and Latin America. The rapid expansion and diversification of the international sex trade can be attributed to the simultaneous rise in service occupations, temporary work, and corporate-fuelled consumption; to an increase in labour migrations, tourism, and business travel; to the close relationship between the information economy and the privatization of commercial consumption; and to new relationships of gender, sexuality, and kinship (Bernstein, 2002).

Throughout the world, girls suffer the assaults of war, and in addition face the escalating levels of sexual and domestic violence, poverty, and social dislocation that war brings. As well, they may be preyed on by international criminal rackets exploiting the invisibility of poor girls in war zones for illegal sexual, domestic, and industrial labour— the tragic underbelly of development that generates billions of dollars annually.

Part of the problem of regulating the sexual traffic lies in the complexity of the worldwide refugee issue. New programs for addressing the refugee problem have developed in the past 50 years, in response to a changing notion of 'refugee-ness' and the growth of a virtual 'refugee industry'. Refugee camps and passports have facilitated time-lier intervention, often in the face of genocidal civil wars. New government departments and multi-national organizations have developed to handle the problem, as have new forms of scholarship and research. That said, much difficulty remains in determining which kinds of refugees are legitimate and should be allowed to enter.

Words in current usage—like 'sex work'— promote the invisibility of prostitution's harm. The interconnectedness of racism, colonialism, and child sexual assault with prostitution is evident. Given the soaring demand for pornography, strip clubs, lap-dancing, escorts, telephone sex, and 'sex tours' in developing countries, it remains unclear how to control, much less prevent, the demand for sexual services and commodities.

Leaving sex work can be much more difficult than entering it. Some women do develop dangerous dependencies on abusive or potentially abusive men (Scott, London, and Myers, 2002). They end up relying on abusive men either for instrumental assistance or for more direct financial assistance as they struggle to move from welfare to work. Some extremely disadvantaged and vulnerable women

become enmeshed in even more dangerous depen-dencies as they hit time limits for welfare eligibility and fall through public and private safety nets into drug addiction and sex work.

Political, institutional, and cultural factors all determine state policy variation on sexuality, specifically, national laws on prostitution and homosexuality. For example, the changing notions of a prostitute coupled with new community-style policing have led to drastic changes in policies concerning the arrest of those suspected of pros-titution-related offences. Previously, women were unfairly targeted in prostitution-related offences, yet there has been a shift from the focus on prostitutes to the focus on 'johns' (Fischer et al., 2002). This reflects the changing notion from seeing a prostitute as deviant to seeing the prostitute as a victim. There has been a conscious effort as evident in a press release from the Vancouver police that stated: 'The root cause of Vancouver's street prostitution trade is the men who purchase or who recruit and control (pimp) juvenile or adult sex workers. Our limited resources are focused on pimps and "johns" and other abusers. . . . If we can reduce the demand, the supply will decrease' (Lowman, 1998).

From 1977 to 1985, two-thirds of all those arrested in the Vancouver sex trade were the prosti-tutes. By the mid-1990s the ratio of arrests changed to 50 per cent (Fischer et al., 2002). This era also marked the emergence of prostitution-offender programs and 'john schools'—for a fee, offenders can agree to go to such programs and subsequently have their charges dropped—or they can go through with the court procedure (Lowman, 1998). Fischer et al. (2002) see problems with this new change, such as an increase in the amount of discretion the police can exercise and the loss of due process.

Another example occurs in Britain, where the overriding logic consists in a state tradition of circumscribing sexual behaviour; in the Nether-lands, a more tolerant state attitude toward sexual policy is characteristic. Church-state relationships, political party systems, and political culture may enable or constrain sexual legislation. Additionally, nationalism plays a role in shaping state sexual policy, in which gender norms and appropriate sexual behaviour are tied to conceptions of a national ideal.

A significant reform in British criminal justice policy regarding prostitution is the change from viewing young female prostitutes as criminal offenders to seeing them as victims of a form of child sexual abuse (Phoenix, 2002). In its efforts to ensure that young prostitutes are neither criminalized nor punished for their activities, the law may actually be creating conditions for the perpetuation of their prostitution, by ignoring the material and social conditions keeping youth in poverty and forcing them into prostitution to survive economically. It may also be inadvertently punishing these young women through incarceration designed to 'protect' them.

Governments cannot, in good faith, just criminalize prostitution or other sexual 'deviants'. The sheer size of the deviant population is so great that the costs of imprisoning or treating more than a fraction of all deviants would be prohibitive. Harm reduction is a far better strategy, if we can bring ourselves to speak about the problem to be solved. A prime example is the discussion of sexually transmitted diseases: how to prevent them and how to cope with them, once contracted. Many families have particular difficulty discussing or even acknowledging the fact that a family member has contracted HIV/AIDS, probably through unprotected sex with someone of the same sex, and possibly as part of a secret or illicit relationship.

The emergence of social movements organized by the prostitutes themselves, is one of the major developments in the politics of prostitution. For the first time, prostitutes are engaging in a public discourse; a discourse in which they previously had no voice (Mathieu, 2003). But, as is the case for most stigmatized populations, this entry into the public debate is faced with many difficulties. Some of these are inherent to the world of prostitution, which is a largely hidden, competitive and violent world.

Pornography

Another common form of sexual deviance is the consumption of pornography. 'Pornography' is the explicit description or exhibition of sexual activity in literature, films, or otherwise, intended to stimulate erotic rather than aesthetic feelings. There is a lot of debate over whether pornography is healthy or pathological, and how it should be controlled. The issues are pressing: on the one hand, there are concerns about effects on children. On the other hand, a lot of money is changing hands.

Today, pornography is a multibillion-dollar worldwide business with alleged links to organized crime. So-called soft-porn magazines are available at a great many smoke shops and convenience stores. Pornography's popularity is seemingly exploding as the legal restrictions on the depiction of sex (in movies, television, and magazines) continue to weaken.

The essence of pornography is *easy sex*: sex without limits or commitments. Linda Williams (1989) suggests that heterosexual pornography creates utopias of sexual abundance—particularly, an abundance of attractive, naked, sexually obedient women for men who might otherwise have trouble (in reality) getting a date with one such woman, let alone several. No wonder the chief theme of pornography is abundance and gluttony—an unending, unquenchable desire for sex.

Pornography is nothing new. It emerged centuries ago with the growth of popular literacy (Toulalan, 2001). The increasing availability and development of a market for pornography went hand in hand with the expansion of print culture, as part of the private consumption of printed material for private pleasure. With the growth of photography, movies and television, the (visual) media have played a key role in the 'sexualization' of modern life (McNair, 2002). Since the late-nineteenth-century, pornography has relocated from elite society to mass culture and increasingly can be accessed on the Internet.

Although the media are credited with merely reflecting a society's sexual and behavioural norms, people partially learn their sexual roles and responsibilities through media outlets; therefore, the media are responsible for teaching understandings of sexuality. Some believe that this spread of sexual understanding should be viewed positively, arguing that it has benefited women's and gay rights movements, increased public awareness of certain health issues, challenged established notions of sexuality, and undermined patriarchal dominance in particular societies.

Perhaps this exaggerates the benefits of pornography. Putnam (2002) interviewed 64 pornography fans in the New York metropolitan area in an attempt to understand why pornography is meaningful to them. The findings show that pornography is not, as a rule, transformative. For some men, pornography ties into and solidifies pre-existing beliefs supporting sexism. Sexist men learn to solidify their misogyny with porn. Often at times, porn solidifies patriarchy by promoting the idea of women as commodities and playthings. Other non-patriarchal men—bisexual, gay, and straight—claim they get a lot from pornography that is positive for them and for their partners. Personality and individual differences predict different preferences for and choices of various forms of sexual materials (Bogaert, 2001). Personality (e.g., intelligence and aggression) and individual difference factors (e.g., prior sexual experience) both have an effect.

For example, men lower in intelligence and higher in aggressive/anti-social tendencies have a higher preference for violent sexual stimuli than men higher in intelligence and lower in aggressive/anti-social tendencies. Also, a study by Stack and researchers (2004) related the use of Internet pornography to social bonds. Among 531 Internet users taken from the General Social Survey based on a national random sample of the population for 2000, they found that strong conventional ties (i.e., religion and marriage) predicted a low likelihood of accessing cyberporn. Conversely, those who had earlier participated in forms of sexual deviance were more likely to make use of cyberporn.

So, pornographic availability interacts with personal predisposition to influence who will watch what kinds of pornography. When given a choice to view different media materials, men choose a broad range of media materials, although the 'female insatiability' films are more popular than the other sexual films (e.g., 'erotic' or violent).

Feminist scholars were among the first to see the body as a legitimate area of sociological inquiry. Accordingly, they have produced a vast literature that examines the link between mass media images of women's bodies and various personal troubles such as low self-esteem, eating disorders, and the increasing use of cosmetic surgery. Although groundbreaking, this work leaves two questions unanswered. First, are women really cultural dupes with little agency of their own and second, how do real women typically enact these images in everyday life? Reality is so much more complex than most theories would imagine.

An area of great concern today is the display and consumption of pornography depicting children. Many view this pornography to be a form of child abuse. Ost (2002) wonders whether there has been a moral panic regarding child pornography and the possession of such material, but also thinks there may be real reasons to consider that the possession of child pornography should remain illegal. More research is needed, however, to establish the existence of a causal link between possessing child pornography and the act of committing child sexual abuse, and to demonstrate that criminalizing the possession of child pornography reduces the market for such material.

Itzin (2001) argues that pornography may be only one point on a continuum of sexually abusive acts against children that include incest, pedophilia, and prostitution. To single out pornography is to neglect the crossover of victims and perpetrators and the overlap of intrafamilial and extrafamilial child sexual abuse and exploitation. Pedophile typologies and sex offender classifications obscure the role of normal, ordinary, heterosexual family men who sexually abuse their own and other people's children on a very substantial scale. Foucault notes that, at many times in the past, the sexuality of a child was recognized and promoted under a certain type of discourse. Today, we attempt to separate the child from sexuality, which reflects a different discourse.

An obvious fact about pornography is that it is gendered—mainly concocted so that heterosexual men can observe and vicariously consume naked women. However, from the beginning, women and homosexuals were also consumers of pornography (Toulalan, 2003). Much of the history of sexual titillation remains hidden from our view.

Other Forms of Sexual Deviation

Paraphilia is a general name for any kind of sexual deviation or departure from the norm. Some paraphilia violate the criminal laws and others do not. *Non-criminal paraphilia* are sexual attractions to objects or individuals not normally found attractive (Bhugra, 2000). Non-criminal paraphilia includes consensual fetishism, voyeurism, sexual sadism, and sexual masochism.

Psychoanalyst Sigmund Freud was among the first to describe sexual fetishism. It is a form of paraphilia or sexual deviance where the object of affection is a specific object or body part. Fetishism, like other forms of sexuality, can be extremely varied and take in almost any aspect of human behaviour—that is to say, almost anything can become a fetish, just as anything can become a compulsion, obsession, or addiction. And like other compulsions, obsessions, and addictions, sexual fetishism is generally considered a problem when it interferes with normal sexual or social functioning.

Voyeurism is another type of sexual deviance that is non-criminal if it is a consensual act. Voyeurism is an act in which individuals seek sexual pleasure by observing other people either in states of undress or having sex. Voyeurism is considered a deviant sexual act in most cultures, and is most frequently practised by males. Likely, male voyeurism is related to male dominance, the objectification of women in our society, and the sexual gaze that puts women under male scrutiny at all times.

Sadism is the taking of sexual pleasure by inflicting (physical) pain and suffering on another person. It takes its name from the Marquis de Sade, who wrote voluminously on sexual experimentation, pain, and pleasure in eighteenth-century France. In cataloguing sexual violence, Marquis de Sade noted that many engaged in non-consenting practices, which contrasts with what sadomasochism is today—now consent is a tenet of the behaviour (Moser and Madeson, 1996). The counterpart of sadism is masochism (named after the nineteenth-century Count von Masoch). Masochists take sexual pleasure from being beaten, humiliated, bound, tortured, or otherwise made to suffer. Together, sadomasochism (SM) describes the dominant (sadist) elements and the submissive (masochist) elements.

Criminal paraphilia

We have discussed paraphilia that is consensual and is not considered criminal. However, some paraphilia is criminal behaviour. For example, exhibitionism—the display of one's genitalia in a setting where this display is socially inappropriate or legally banned—if done without consent and in a public place—is considered a criminal activity. Other types of criminal paraphilia include necrophilia (sexual attraction to corpses); pedophilia (sexual attraction to young children who have not yet reached puberty); bestiality (sexual attraction to animals); and lust murder (taking sexual pleasure from the commission of a murder).

Pedophilia is probably one of the most common criminal paraphilias in our society today. Two-thirds of molested children are girls, usually between the ages of 8 and 11. Most pedophiles are men, but there are cases of women having repeated sexual contact with children (De Silva, 1999). Although uninformed people often cite pedophilia as a reason for excluding or mistreating homosexuals, pedophiles are rarely people who commonly practice homosexuality with other consenting adults.

Deviant Communities and Cultures

People who enjoy deviant sexual activities, like those who practise other deviant behaviours, often seek out familiar and supportive people similar to themselves, creating real or virtual communities. This is true of homosexuals, prostitutes, and sadomasochists.

Sadomasochistic communities and cultures

One of the reasons that sadomasochists are becoming more accepted in society is because they have organized themselves. In many urban centres in Canada and elsewhere, there exists a visible subculture of sadomasochists. Often, role-playing is involved and takes the form of master/slave or teacher/student (Madeson and Moser, 1996). Sadomasochism typically has an underlying element of sexual meaning. To obtain the greatest pleasure, in any sadomasochist behaviour, the partners share a common definition of the activity.

Sadomasochists are a varied group that includes people of different sexual orientations, religions, socioeconomic classes, races, and ages. Though open to any individuals, this community is usually composed of members over the age of 30. Estimates by Madeson and Moser based on the readership of different SM media and customers for SM businesses, suggest that about 10 per cent of the American population is involved in activities that are knowingly SM. Another 20 to 40 per cent of the population engages in SM behaviour, although they do not define it as such.

In studies of this community, some informants express a difficulty in joining the lifestyle. Most sadomasochists have to take two steps before they can fully engage: first, admitting to the self that he or she is interested in SM, and second, accepting

that SM is a natural part of sexuality. Once these two steps are taken, entry into the community is much easier. Then, the community serves as a support network that helps its members to overcome loneliness. SM communities exist because beyond the community, sadomasochists are often labelled as sexual perverts. The SM community provides structure and support through the formation of organizations and meeting places (Madeson and Moser, 1996). Structures include meeting places where members are introduced to each other and get support for what many label as their deviant behaviour.

Homosexual communities and cultures

Homosexuality is a sexual orientation characterized by a sexual or romantic attraction to people of the same sex. In males, we call same-sex orientation 'homosexuality' and in females, we call it 'lesbianism'. For a long time, homosexuality was considered a form of paraphilia, or sexual deviance.

So far as we know, people with homosexual desires constitute a minority of the population—probably less than 10 per cent, though the estimates are imprecise. In many communities, they are still stigmatized and may suffer discrimination at work, in school, and in the community. However, people are gradually becoming less tolerant of such exclusionary and discriminatory treatment. Many people believe, as Hulick (2003) does, that there is no excuse for letting ignorance and intolerance damage the self-esteem of another generation of gay, lesbian, bisexual, transgender, and questioning people.

Our culture as a whole does not completely approve of homosexual behaviour. In response, a subcultural world or community of homosexuals who support and befriend each other has developed. This subcultural world has a special 'language' that helps to distinguish its members from the outgroup. There are subcultural norms that define proper homosexual relations. Many communities have special meeting places where homosexuals can gather, usually at certain coffee shops, cafés, and clubs. The homosexual community provides a training ground for norms and values, a milieu in which people may live safely and comfortably, and social support with an information medium for its members.

Like many minority groups, homosexuals and lesbians have sought to educate, form organizations, change laws, and build their own communities with separate institutions in order to shed their castelike status. D'Emilio (1983) dates the beginning of the homosexual subculture, as we see it today, to the Second World War. That war separated the sexes somewhat and allowed homosexuals greater access to other homosexuals. Subsequently, cities like San Francisco and New York began to attract homosexuals to 'the gay life'. The growth of gay communities also coincided with reports by professionals that challenged the accepted definitions of sexuality.

The Kinsey reports, along with many professionals calling for a rethinking of the status of homosexuals, led to the open emergence of gay subculture. The Mattachines, for example, were a left-leaning group that called for the recognition of homosexuals as an oppressed minority. The Mattachines sought to promote the idea of a homosexual culture in which its members would be able to adopt positive values and be able to have pride concerning their sexuality (D'Emilio, 1983). The group helped to bring frightened men and women together and provide them with an organizational network by which they began to form their own distinctive culture.

Greater focus on homosexuality occurred in the late 1950s and 1960s, as newspapers and magazines helped to attract isolated individuals to the growing communities. Many more groups formed and gained professional allies such as Evelyn Hooker, who challenged the idea that homosexuality was an illness, and Wardell Pomeroy, a sex therapist who worked on and supported the Kinsey reports. By 1968, *The Gay World* was published, the first book dedicated to the study of gay communities (D'Emilio, 1983).

Beginning in San Francisco, the movement began to take an identity that was formed around sexual orientation and that could be recognized throughout the United States. The success of these communities meant that for the first time homosexuals had access to resources pertaining to their sexuality and could more freely engage in the gay subculture.

Today, sizeable gay and lesbian communities exist in various North American cities, including Toronto. Not only are these communities and their members increasingly visible—they are increasingly celebrated. Research by geographer Richard Florida, for example, has shown that cities with large homosexual populations typically have high levels of artistic and intellectual creativity. Resulting from this is a high degree of innovativeness and economic growth in the service sector, as well as a high quality of life for city residents. In this case, as in many others, we discover that human diversity pays off economically, as well as socially and culturally.

Theories about Sexual Deviance

The sexual deviates discussed in this chapter have nothing in common except their stigmatization on the grounds of sexual atypicality. Accordingly, we would need a variety of theories—and much more space than we can afford—to cover all these behaviours. Across all types of sexual deviance, the most useful of all are labelling theories, to be discussed shortly. What follows is a too-brief overview of a few forms of sexual deviance, starting with pedophilia.

Psychological theories

Any theory of pedophilia must be multifaceted and account for the wide range of behaviours, beliefs, and fantasies that may play a role in the development of this disorder. A comprehensive theory of pedophilia must refer to psychological, familial, environmental, social, genetic, hormonal, organic, and biological factors.

Psychological theories about pedophilia address only those aspects of the emotional congruence, sexual arousal, blockage, and disinhibition that are independent of organic causes. These theories include such diverse perspectives as psychoanalysis, social learning theory, and family systems. No single perspective can explain the complex phenomena of pedophilia.

Often, with respect to pedophilia, sexual abusers have been abused themselves in childhood. An unpredictable environment marked by parental inconsistence (i.e., the parent punishes the child for doing something, but later praises the child for doing the same thing) may cause masochism (Straus and Donnelly, 1994). Painful experiences in childhood that make people feel rejected or worthless may produce actions in adulthood that lead them to seek acceptance and validation in deviant ways. Therefore, they may enter into sadistic or masochistic sexual relationships because these more obviously link sexual pleasure with punishment and pain, or because they degrade one or both participants.

Straus and Donnelly (1994), in their book on corporal punishment *Beating the Devil Out of Them: Corporal Punishment in American Families*, provide a developmental explanation for sexual deviance, relating it to spanking in childhood. Historically, Jean-Jacques Rousseau spoke of his own sexual deviance and its links to childhood. As a child, he was regularly spanked, and he assumed that this was the reason he needed to be spanked to be sexually aroused because he learned to associate spanking with love (Straus and Donnelly, 1994).

Money (1986) explains this connection in terms of 'lovemaps', which are templates for sexual arousal in the human mind. He notes that adults can permanently alter the lovemap when the parent/guardian humiliates the child for sexual play or prematurely introduces the child to sexual play between the ages of four and nine. The parts of the brain associated with pain and sexual arousal are proximal to each other. It is proposed that when both are stimulated for a period of time, that the brain may lose its ability to distinguish between the two (Straus and Donnelly, 1994).

Sociological Approaches

The functionalist perspective

As we mentioned before, functionalists believe that the society works like an organism with each part having its own function. When it comes to sexual deviance, functionalists argue that, although many people view them negatively, some sexual deviations—for example, prostitution and pornography—play a valuable role in our society.

Like other deviant sexual behaviours, prostitution establishes the boundaries of acceptable morality within our society. By calling sexual deviance immoral and stigmatizing those who practice sexual deviance, our society is spelling out what is acceptable and unacceptable behaviour. This increases social cohesion, which from a functional standpoint is a valuable and desirable accomplishment.

Additionally, sexual deviance provides people with varied sexual outlets. Many people have fantasies they want to fulfill. Prostitution, for example, allows them the opportunity to fulfill these desires without putting undue pressure on spouses or other partners to engage in sex that they may consider distasteful or immoral. Depriving others of the sexual activities they wish might increase the likelihood of marital breakdown, infidelity, and affairs that end in divorce. Therefore, prostitution may help to keep families together and the family institution intact. By maintaining individual families and the institution of marriage and family, prostitution serves society as a whole.

This is, essentially, the argument that functionalist Kingsley Davis put forward in the 1940s. He notes that in societies where the family is strong, a well-defined system of prostitution is clearly marked off from family life. Prostitutes are members of a separate social caste and there is little movement between the family and prostitution sector. This very segregation enables the two opposite types of institutions to function side by side. They are each staffed by different personnel, and lead different lives. However, kinship systems and family controls are weak, and the system of prostitution tends to be poorly defined. More people satisfy their sexual desires outside the family, and it is easier to find respectable members of society to serve as partners.

As a result, both family life and the profession of prostitution decline together alongside a rise of sexual freedom. Women, freed from closed family supervision, can more readily seek gratification outside it. And as women have more freedom to enjoy sexual freedom, it becomes easier for men to enjoy intimate relations without recourse to prostitutes. Thus, the rise of sex-for-pleasure endangers not only the family but the profession of prostitution as well.

However, there is little likelihood that sexual freedom will ever displace prostitution. Reproductive institutions that govern marriage and parenting will continue to limit sexual liberty. There will always be a demand for the sexual favours of the most attractive, and a social hierarchy to motivate the selling of sexual favours. As we will see, poverty and other sources of vulnerability will drive people to sell sex and others to buy it—whether they are socially isolated, perverts, or physically repulsive.

A third function that prostitution plays in our society is providing sexual outlets for people who cannot engage in such behaviours otherwise. Many people with physical disabilities cannot readily satisfy their sexual desires anywhere else in the society, and prostitution provides sexual services for these people. The prostitute is, in these senses, maintaining the social order by reducing tensions and conflicts that might occur without such services.

Similar arguments might be made to support the use of pornography. The arguments concerning homosexuality are slightly different. A bulk of the early research on homosexuality was functionalist finding homosexuality to be a necessity since people need negative role models to help define the boundaries of acceptable behaviour (Murray, 1996). To boys, homosexuals provide an example of what not to become, whereas fathers (or more 'masculine') figures provide boys with positive role models. The ridicule and exclusion suffered by homosexuals reinforces traditional masculine norms operating both within and beyond sexual behaviour itself.

Albert Reiss's 1961 study of queers and peers illustrates functionalist views on homosexuality and shows how society at the time reinforced negative and positive stereotypes. Among homosexuals, 'peers' were the young, masculine men who engaged in sexual relations with effeminate 'queers'. As long as the peers 'never took it', then their sex with men was considered masculine and reinforced notions of masculinity. The position of the queers was degraded, not only because they played a submissive (feminine) role to the peers, but also because they were paid for sex. Sometimes the peers took the sex without paying, an act which among the peers was regarded as a show of masculinity and dominance over the queers. Reiss's study affirmed the dominant view that gender-deviant homosexuals were negative role models, because in this study they were the submissive queer prostitutes (Murray, 1996).

The conflict perspective

For conflict theorists, the basic question is: Who benefits from the existing social order and who suffers? If we apply conflict theory to sexual deviance, we see that people with more power are more able to label certain sexual expressions as deviant. Current debates about homosexuality—for example, same-sex marriage—could be viewed as nothing more than a result of conflicting beliefs about the purpose and meaning of marriage, as well as more or less understanding of homosexuality itself.

Many types of sexual deviance—for example, prostitution—relate to social inequality and the exercise of power. The dominant groups of our society control various kinds of sexual activities and determine whether they are legal or illegal. Consider the debates about the sex trade, which are certainly influenced by social inequality and the exercise of power. At one level, prostitution reflects gender inequality in a patriarchal society, because it mostly involves men gaining pleasure, or income, through the exploitation of women. Whether the men are the owners and managers of an escort service, for example, or the recipients of the sexual services it provides, they are the main benefactors of this industry.

At another level, prostitution concerns poverty. Typically, women (and occasionally men) who resort to prostitution lack access to legitimate means of earning enough money. This is evident by the enormous numbers of prostitutes in the developing countries where poverty marginalizes many people, especially women, and forces them to earn money by selling their bodies. In our own society, prostitution recruits its members from among less educated and socially disadvantaged women.

Interactionist approaches

Social scientists, anthropologists, and historians have argued that, where sexual deviance is concerned, everything depends on the structure of the society—its norms, values, concepts, scripts, and so on. The sociology of sexual deviance is a new area of research with promising potential for explaining sexual behaviour as our culture has shaped it. This sociological paradigm has considerably improved our understanding of homosexuality, for example, during the past few decades, and in the future it will no doubt give valuable contributions to other areas of sexual deviance as well.

According to this approach, sexual deviants are different, but only because we have repressed, labelled, and stigmatized them. The law does not sanction many types of sexual deviance, such as fetishism, homosexuality, and transvestism. Later, society labelled a group of people different, deviant, and immoral. As a result, we created a social problem, because these behaviours were not socially allowable and had to be controlled.

In the past 30 years, Canadian public opinion on sexual matters has become much more liberal. People are much more willing to view nudity in the media and to accept the marketing of magazines and films with pornographic content. Though popular norms remain strongly opposed to extramarital sex—sex after marriage with someone other than one's own partner—extramarital sex is apparently common. Sexual activity is only of concern to others when it harms other members of society. This is true for pedophilia, lust murder, sexual abuse, and other sexual deviations that are viewed as sexual offences against another person.

Norms and values change through time, because of the constant interaction between individuals, and between individuals and major social institutions. This explains why some kinds of sexual deviance—including homosexuality, sex changes, cross-dressing, and fetishism—are increasingly accepted sexual practices in the general population.

In the case of homosexuality, once people view behaviour as belonging to a category, they treat the individual behaving that way as though he or she is a member of that category. For homosexuals, this is classically viewed as boys playing with girls (behaviour) becoming viewed as sissy (category) and eventually being treated as though they were sissy. Through this type of social labelling, a boy learns what he is and thus defines himself this way (Murray, 1996).

This is not to say that every young boy who is labelled as effeminate grows up to be homosexual. Although there does seem to be a statistical relationship, homosexuality cannot be explained by childhood gender roles, since not enough study has been done on various gay groups such as hypermasculine gay men and their gender roles during childhood. It is also interesting to note that many gay individuals do not behave in a deviant manner before being labelled. Many homosexuals may engage in self-labelling, as when a homosexual joins a homosexual club before engaging in any homosexual acts (Murray, 1996).

The symbolic interactionist approach would also be useful in studying the socialization of prostitutes—their introduction to 'the life' and how they learn strategies for dealing with johns and pimps. Prostitution, as a type of work, is characterized by its own language, professional ethics, ways of exercising control and working around formal authority, and so on.

Feminist approach

Feminism, as we have seen, argues that society is patriarchal. Society is male-dominated, oppressive, and exploitative. The feminist approach argues that our society is sexist. For example, it provides an economic benefit to women who sell their bodies, and then labels them as deviant.

Sexual behaviour generally and sexual deviance more specifically are expressions or indications of the roles of men and women. A given sexual encounter between a man and a woman may mean different things to the two participants, have different consequences, or be interpreted in different ways by members of the society. As we have seen, people typically condemn a sexually active teenage girl, for example, more strongly than they do a teenage boy. This reminds us that the foundation of all deviance—the application of stigma or condemnation—depends on whom we are stigmatizing or condemning. In turn, this evaluation is based on the sex or gender of the enactor.

Likewise, many people regard the problems of teenage sex, pregnancy, and subsequent out-of-wedlock births as problems almost exclusively of the behaviour of girls. Boritch (1997) refers to the 'fallen woman' as one who as has shirked her gender role. A fallen women serves as an example of what can happen to a women, or in this case, a teenage girl who does not reflect a supposedly innate femininity. The finest example of a fallen woman is a prostitute. She becomes the symbol of immorality and crime. Women enact the vast majority of 'sex work' jobs for men. We view female sex workers typically as deviant women, whereas we see their customers as essentially normal men, thus the criminal justice system unfairly targets the prostitute and not the 'john' or 'trick'. For example, prostitutes were more

likely to be charged and convicted than johns.

Many phenomena that people might assume to be biological functions—such as the frequency of intercourse or experience of orgasm by a woman—are learned and not innate in the human organism. Cultural and historical factors affect our judgments concerning what constitutes normal sexuality and what constitutes sexual deviance. This applies clearly to issues of heterosexuality, homosexuality, bisexuality, and transgendering. Powerless, socially vulnerable people are more likely than others to suffer condemnation, stigma, punishment, or exclusion.

Queer theory grows out of the idea that people's identities are not fixed and do not determine who we are. For this reason, it is meaningless to talk about 'women', 'gays', or any other group 'in general'. Some would say that queer theory is based on the work of Judith Butler—in particular her 1990 book *Gender Trouble*—however, we can see the roots of this thinking in much earlier work, for example, the work of Alfred Korcybski, who argued for non-Aristotelian logic in the 1950s, insisting that everything is relative to the way we perceive and treat it.

In his General Semantics theory, Korcybski points out that the verb 'to be' hides a great many differences in point of view. Using the terms 'becomes', 'remains', and 'equals' is far more exact and places the observer more exactly in relation to the object viewed. Thus, a person is not 'a heterosexual' or 'homosexual'—he/she is only a person who, at a specific time and viewed from a specific perspective, displays features that the viewer associates with one or the other category. Similar comments can be made about all the 'types' of deviance we discuss in this book.

Sex work, and prostitution in particular, has long divided feminist thinking (Kesler, 2002). Much feminist thought condemns prostitution as a practice and wants to 'save' individual prostitute women. Should feminists support the legalization of prostitution and migration of foreign prostitutes? Coene (2001) states that, given the current circumstances and developments, feminists have very good reasons for criticizing the sex industry, but this claim should not necessarily prevent them from supporting more social rights for national and foreign sex workers.

However, the contemporary Euro-American feminist debate about prostitution on this topic may be far too limited. Davidson (2002) argues that to develop analyses relevant to the experience of more than just a small minority of 'First World' women, those who are concerned with prostitution as a form of work need to look beyond liberal discourse on property and contractual consent for ways of conceptualizing the rights and wrongs of 'sex work'.

Postmodern approaches

During the 1970s and 1980s Foucault wrote three volumes of *The History of Sexuality*, a project he would never finish. His history of sexuality was originally projected as a fairly straightforward extension of the genealogical approach taken in *Discipline and Punish* (1975) to the topic of sexuality. His goal was to compare ancient pagan and Christian ethics on the topic of sexuality and trace the development of Christian ideas about sex to the present day.

Foucault's idea is that modern thinking about sexuality has an intimate association with the power structures of modern society. Our Western understanding of ourselves as sexual beings, the relation of this understanding to our moral and ethical lives, evolved over a long period. Greeks' systems of rules were applied to sexual and other forms of social conduct, promoting self-control in all things, including sexual pleasure. Care for the self meant that excess was viewed as a danger. In this context, pleasure was gained from the play of power in social relations.

Only later, in Christianity, did sexual pleasure become linked to unlawful conduct and rule-breaking. In the Christian view, sexual acts were, on the whole, evil in themselves. By contrast, in the Greek view they were good, natural, and necessary, though open to abuse. Where the Christian moral code forbade or restricted most forms of sexual

activity, the ancient Greeks emphasized the proper pursuit of pleasures, including a full range of sexual activities. Heterosexual and homosexual activities, in marriage and out of marriage, were all acceptable if they were pursued with proper moderation.

Foucault seems to agree that pleasure comes from regulation and self-discipline, not wild or excessive behaviour. It is everyone's right and duty to pursue pleasure in this way, without impediment by the state, he believes. However, the state comes to intervene nonetheless. The modern (state) control of sexuality parallels modern control of criminality by making sex—like crime—an object of allegedly scientific disciplines, which at the same time offer knowledge and domination of their objects.

The supposed sciences of sexuality exercise control via their knowledge of individuals; they even attempt to control individuals' knowledge of themselves. Individuals internalize the norms laid down by the sciences of sexuality and try to conform to these norms. Thus, they are controlled not only as objects of disciplines but also as self-monitoring, self-forming subjects.

During the years Foucault wrote on this topic, he participated in political movements concerned with the reform of prisons and gay liberation. He continued to argue that 'truth' as we know it is not necessarily true. Discourse—how we talk about a topic such as sex, for example—constrains us because it trains us to look at sex in a certain way. By this reasoning, any changes in sexual practice, even including the increased acceptance of gay sexuality, is simply another form of constraint—not liberation. This brought him to a dead end, as least so far as the possibility of escape from domination was concerned.

According to Whitebook (2002), for Foucault as for Marcuse (1955) the goal is the liberation of bodies and pleasures from their imprisonment in conventional sexuality. This would seem to argue that what is needed is an escape from conventions, not a new set of conventions. Liberation, then, does not demand the rejection of civilization per se, as

Freud might have argued. Rather, awareness, resistance, and re-evaluation of sexuality are needed.

An example of needed resistance is given by Wojcicki and Malala (2001). Through interviews with 50 female sex workers in Johannesburg, these researchers explored sexual negotiations between men and women in the sex industry—specifically, the factors that affect sexual decision-making including safer sex practices. They show that sexual negotiations between men and women are complex, and women have some power to insist on safer practices. This focus on agency is important in trying to lessen the stigma and discrimination that sex workers face at the hands of clients, pimps/managers, police, and health care workers.

Women can also resist the media-driven expectations that they will be merely workers or merely mothers. Hyde (2000), along these lines, explores the ways in which the bodies and social roles of New Zealand women were constructed in the popular media prior to, during, and after the Second World War. During the war, women were primarily constructed in terms of their usefulness to the war effort. After the war, women were encouraged to regard their bodies and their social selves as the social currency by which they could attract and hold the scarce resource that men represented. They were also encouraged to construct their bodies as primarily suited to motherhood in the family-centred post-war social environment.

Sexuality, as a means of seeking pleasure, can be compared to consumption of many kinds, including the consumption of commodities. Orlie (2002) argues that, today, commodity consumption is central to the regime of political capitalism. With consumption coming to the centre of our current desires, understanding contemporary sexual tastes and desires means giving more attention to practices of commodity consumption and shifting our notion of desire from discourses of sexuality to erotics of appetite. In other words, we come to attach erotic levels of pleasure and desire to the consumption of material goods.

The postmodern study of power and sexuality has given strong support to the study of alternative sexualities, including homosexuality and homosexual practices. This has led to a growing recognition that multiple homosexual subcultures co-exist. Rosenfeld (1999) identifies two distinct homosexual 'identity cohorts'. One cohort is composed of those who were 'born' as homosexuals before the gay liberationist movements of the late 1960s, when homosexuality was stigmatized. The second cohort is composed of those who defined themselves as homosexual through the gay liberationist discourse, which defined homosexuality as a source of status. Members of each identity cohort developed different understandings of the meaning of homosexuality, the threat posed by the heterosexual world, and the appropriate response to that threat. Thus, for example, the actions that one identity cohort views as sensible are morally repugnant from the point of view of the other.

One central point of contention may be perceptions of anal sex. Gay men vary in how they talk about and experience anal intercourse as a relation of power between men. Some of the gay men's narratives believe that the anally insertive partner dominates the receptive partner. Others resist such an understanding by drawing upon the concepts of 'versatility', 'getting on top', 'sex is not about power', and 'active passivity'. Such resistant practices redistribute power from the insertor to the insertee, rather than eliminate power in sex (Kippax and Smith, 2001).

Hennen (2003) examines the various ways conventional masculinity norms are both subverted and reproduced in three subcultures within the larger queer community—the Radical Faeries (a community that promotes drag as a form of cultural expression), the Bears (a group seeking to normalize gay masculinity by striving toward 'regular guy' status via larger and hairier bodies), and the gay leathermen (a culture that celebrates extreme hypermasculinity). Each of the three communities shows evidence of innovativeness; however, conventional notions of masculinity continue to limit members in these communities, due to historical associations between male homosexuality and effeminacy.

Erotic pleasure extends far beyond the possibilities of an able-bodied, two-gender, two-sex society. Traditional conceptions leave the bodily impaired out of the sexual picture, for example. White (2003) explores the interaction between sexuality and blindness to illustrate how the history of sexuality, especially compulsory heterosexuality, has produced the need for a subject who is not merely seen but also sighted. All existing material on the sexuality of the blind has been developed by and for the sighted. This means that educational programs for the blind are used to suppress any 'abnormal' sexual heterogeneity; sex education only teaches the blind about the dominant mode of sexuality.

Similar comments can be made about the interaction between sexuality and other types of physical disability, since conventional notions of sexuality postulate conventionally able-bodied men and women. People who deviate from this physical norm—for example, who lack fully functional arms and legs or even conventional sex organs—must re-invent sexuality for themselves and negotiate their inventions with one another. In this respect, they are like Merton's (1957 [1938]) 'adapters to anomie'—unwilling to give up sex altogether and unable to conform, they have to innovate.

Social and Health Consequences of Sexual Deviance

Health consequences of prostitution

Many people disapprove of prostitution, for a variety of reasons. The health problems associated with the sex trade include violence, the risk of sexually transmitted diseases (STDs) such as HIV/AIDS, and the effects of drugs.

The relationship among social class, prostitution, and drug abuse is complex. Drugs aside, the poorest sex workers are usually unable to force their customers to use condoms, even though both their lives are at stake. In Cambodia, a very low propor-

tion of women sex workers are currently using a modern contraceptive method, except for condoms. Women sex workers report at least one previous induced abortion. These findings reveal the need for accessible contraception and safe abortion services among sex workers in Cambodia, and raise the issue of the reproductive rights and reproductive health needs of women sex workers in general (Delvaux et al., 2003).

The use and non-use of condoms in sex work is an international health problem of staggering proportions. Largely, the use or non-use depends on the balance of power between the sex worker and her client. When possible, female sex workers may employ condoms to maintain their emotional control over commercial sexual intercourse. Their use of contraceptives provides them the opportunity to construct working identities while preserving their emotional well-being (Sanders, 2002).

Sexually transmitted diseases aside, the mental health consequences of prostitution include stress, depression, anxiety, self-medication through alcohol and drug abuse, eating disorders, and even suicide. Recently, Farley (2004) discussed Post-traumatic Stress Disorder (PTSD) as a consequence of prostitution. PTSD sufferers experience fear and powerless. The severity of PTSD experienced by prostitutes is likened to that suffered by war veterans, rape survivors, and those seeking refuge from 'state-organized torture', and the severity would increase with the increase of time (and thus the increase of served customers) spent in the sex trade. Prostitution exacts a high emotional cost and perpetuates the view of women as sexual property.

Health consequences of homosexuality

Despite intensive efforts to educate homosexuals against the dangers of acquired immunodeficiency syndrome (AIDS) and other STDs, the incidence of unsafe sexual practices is on the rise. According to the Centers for Disease Control and Prevention (CDC), from 1994 to 1997 the proportion of homosexuals reporting having had anal sex increased from

57.6 per cent to 61.2 per cent, while the percentage of those reporting 'always' using condoms declined from 69.6 per cent to 60 per cent. Researchers believe that 95 per cent or more of the AIDS infections among gay men result from receptive anal intercourse. Some researchers report that AIDS is on the rise again in New York City because younger gay men have not watched an older generation die from AIDS and they feel it is a disease that can be managed well with drugs.

Health consequences of paraphilia

One reason some paraphilias are considered criminalized is because they cause harmful health or social consequences. Pedophilia for example, causes problems in the development of the child, because it affects self-image and how the child copes with difficult situations.

For example, young girls who are sexually abused are more likely to develop eating disorders as adolescents (Wonderlich, 2000). More generally, trauma in childhood increases the risk of developing an eating disorder. Abused girls may experience higher levels of emotional distress, possibly linked to their abuse, and have more trouble managing the stress. Food restriction and other eating-disorder behaviours may reflect their efforts to cope with such experiences.

Other criminal paraphilias may have harmful and even fatal health consequences for the victim. In lust murders, where an individual derives sexual pleasure by committing a murder, health consequences for the victim are self-evident. Criminal paraphilias may also harm the perpetrator. The compulsive sexual thoughts and behaviours that produce lust murders can also lead to increasingly severe depression, lower self-esteem, and increased shame, self-hatred, hopelessness, despair, helplessness, anxiety, loneliness, remorse, self-deception, moral conflict, and fear of abandonment.

Many behaviours considered deviant and labelled paraphilias are without any health consequences. If a person receives sexual arousal from feet or certain types of fabric (frotteurism), for example, there are no visible health consequences. One non-criminal type of paraphilia that has adverse health consequences is coprophilia—sexual attraction to feces.

Social consequences of prostitution

Throughout history, prostitution has aroused a wide range of social and moral reactions. However, no society has completely accepted prostitution as a valid and integral part of community life. This societal reaction is particularly true of child prostitution. Sometimes, children sell sex, and this is not always a choice, but a forced activity. A 1997 report by the Solicitor General of Canada concludes that migrant trafficking accounts for 8,000 to 16,000 illegal immigrants in Canada every year, many of them female youths and children who are forced to work in Canada's booming sex trade industry. The same report estimates that those profiting from the illegal trafficking of children and women in Canada earn as much as $400 million annually (Canadian Women's Health Network, 2002).

The traffic in vulnerable children and young people violates their rights to an education, leisure, good health, a family life, and safety from exploitation. This traffic in children is not new, though we are still inexperienced in combatting the traffic in children.

Social consequences of homosexuality

Although there is increased awareness and acceptance of homosexuality, most people still see heterosexuality as the ideal way of living. Because of this, we distinguish between people who do and do not satisfy this norm, between heterosexuals and homosexuals. We often do not know how to treat people or empathize with those having any other sexual preference. Parents of homosexual or bisexual children may have a particularly hard time accepting their children's sexual orientation. They may be disappointed because they have other expectations of their child, or because their child's behaviour embarrasses them. Their reactions can lead to

Box 4.3 Discrimination and HIV/AIDS

FREDERICTON (CP)—There has been an alarming increase in discrimination against New Brunswickers living with HIV and AIDS, a new survey suggests.

Claude Olivier, executive director of AIDS New Brunswick, said Wednesday the survey found two-thirds of respondents with HIV or AIDS experienced some form of discrimination.

That compares with only one-third in a 1992 survey.

'That is really quite a startling shift in terms of people actually experiencing discrimination,' Olivier said at a news conference.

'That is happening in the public sector around services, trying to get employment.'

The survey was funded by Health Canada and carried out by AIDS New Brunswick, which sent questionnaires to the estimated 300 persons living with HIV or AIDS in the province. Fifty people replied.

The responses didn't explain why discrimination was on the rise. However, Olivier said it is probably because new drug treatments are letting persons with HIV or AIDS try to return to the mainstream of society.

The *Human Rights Act* in New Brunswick makes it illegal to discriminate against someone with HIV or AIDS.

Rudi Sauracker of AIDS Moncton, who is living with HIV, said the law isn't being properly enforced.

'It is not legal but how are you going to prevent it?' he asked. 'You cannot go to a bank, you cannot go to an insurance company, you cannot go to a prospective employer, you cannot go to a health clinic, you cannot go to a hospital without experiencing some form of discrimination.'

Most people living with HIV or AIDS do not have the resources or the energy to fight the system or sue a major institution, he said.

'We may have the law but the law does not work,' said Sauracker. 'The enforcement is helter skelter.'

Not all the news in the survey was bad.

A large majority of persons with HIV or AIDS reported that their health care has been good or excellent.

Olivier also said statistics seem to show the infection level in New Brunswick has levelled off. However, he warned that AIDS and HIV among the intravenous drug community is under-reported.

SOURCE: Canadian Press Newswire, *Fredericton Gleaner* (accessed 8 October 2003).

depression, harsh words, aggression, and broken relationships.

Social consequences of pedophilia

Many of the children and teenagers that experience sexual harassment or sexual abuse suffer adult consequences, and some even become deviant adults. Pedophilia—though relatively uncommon—is much more dangerous than is often believed, because it introduces many girls to the world of 'non-romantic' sex. It is a form of sexual abuse, and as such, it lowers self-esteem and increases distrust.

Male victims of pedophilia often experience confusion about their sexual identity in adulthood and are more likely than average to become pedophiles themselves.

Pedophilia also contributes to the likelihood of juvenile delinquency and poor school performance. It interferes with the normal development of children and sets them apart from their peers. Often, the victims of pedophilia inhabit a world of secret guilt, fear, and regret. They find it harder to trust others—even friends, family members and adults in authority—and this hinders their ability to form close, stable relationships.

Homophobia as a Form of Sexual Deviance

In North America, gay men and lesbians are finally receiving legal rights and social acceptance. Yet, many people still fear and hate homosexuals. Such attitudes of fear and hate are called 'homophobia'. Homophobia creates conflict and occasionally violence. Increasingly it is becoming a form of sexual deviance.

However, the change from a focus on homosexual persons to homophobic persons as deviant is slow at best. In Canada, we continue to institutionalize homophobia as a norm, as shown by the homosexual panic defence. This defence can be used if the perpetrators of an attack on homosexuals allegedly suffer from homosexual panic. Not only does this defence legitimize violence against gay men and women, but it also tries to further distinguish between the normal (not gay) and the abnormal (gay) and steers attention away from the action of the defendant to the sexual orientation of the victim. Moreover, Ellen Faulkner's (2000) surveys have demonstrated, as shown in Table 4.2, that homosexual respondents in Toronto, Nova Scotia, New Brunswick, and Vancouver continue to commonly experience anti-gay or -lesbian violence.

Slow progress of the acceptance of homosexuals is also evident on examining Alberta's unwillingness to protect homosexuality under its human rights code. This reluctance stems from their historical Christian fundamentalist roots. It has been fuelled by the Social Credit Party's weekly magazine, *Alberta Report*, which provoked a homophobic discourse through the use of moral panics associated with homosexuality including 'sodomy, predictions of the demise of Western civilization and homosexual predators who prey on children' (Filax, 2003).

That said, progress in the acceptance of homosexuals has been rapid in the past few decades, and acceptance is particularly marked among certain kinds of people. The ruling principle is that more sexual experience reduces fearfulness about sex. For example, childhood sex play predicts earlier non-marital sexual activity in adolescence and young adulthood. In turn, premarital experiences reduce marital fearfulness about sex. People with first- or second-hand knowledge of premarital sex, extramarital sex, or homosexuality are less homophobic than people with more limited sexual knowledge and experience.

Another ruling principle is that familiarity breeds acceptance. People who know homosexuals personally are less often homophobic than people who do not. Personal contact with homosexual friends and relatives has more influence on attitudes toward gay men than any other social or demographic variable (Herek and Glunt, 1993).

Additionally, class and education correlate with homophobia. In part, these factors may operate through the principle of familiarity: people from larger communities, with more education and high class origins (therefore, larger, more varied social networks) are more likely to know homosexual people. Additionally, class and education may reduce homosexuality by increasing a sense of self-worth. People with low status have less self-worth and a less secure position in society; this gives them more reason to attack and oppose vulnerable groups like homosexuals.

Another social factor characterizing homophobes is their place of residence. Rural areas are particularly problematic for homosexuals, since

Table 4.2 Violence against Gays and Lesbians in Toronto, Nova Scotia, New Brunswick, and Vancouver, 1990–7

	Toronto	Nova Scotia	New Brunswick	Vancouver
Total sample	**368**	**294**	**176**	**420**
Females	181	133	51	122
Males	171	161	125	298
Percentage Reporting Each Type of Violence				
Verbal assault	76	72	82	85
Threatened with violence	51	42	35	54
Chased/Followed	38	33	34	41
Objects thrown	26	25	17	27
Spit at	17	9	10	–
Punched/Beaten	21	18	16	33
Assault with weapon	7	–	–	12
Harassed by police	21	19	23	18

SOURCE: Adapted from Department of Justice Canada, Research and Statistics Division, 1997, 'Anti-Gay/Lesbian Violence in Toronto: The Impact on Individuals and Communities'; Mary Ellen Faulkner, 2000, 'A Case Study of the Institutional Response to Anti-Gay/Lesbian Violence in Toronto', dissertation, *Abstracts International, A: The Humanities and Social Sciences*, 60 (10): 3630-A.

usually no 'gay' community exists there. This seriously restricts opportunities for help-seeking and help-giving. As well, rural attitudes and values often inhibit gays' use of available mental health services (D'Augelli and Hart, 1987). In contrast to rural people, urban people are more tolerant of homosexuals, and this tolerance includes a willingness to protect the civil liberties of homosexuals. Moreover, they are willing to allow free expression to people with non-conformist political views.

Homophobia is more often found among men than among women. Study after study confirms this gender difference. Kite (1983), reviewing 24 questionnaire studies with various sample sizes, found that men generally hold more negative attitudes than women towards homosexuals. Sex of the target is also important; typically, heterosexual men are more hostile to gay men than to lesbians. Gender-specific homophobia may be connected to male bonding. Research shows that homophobia is related to heterosexism—a belief in the moral superiority of heterosexual institutions and practices.

Learned attitudes also affect the probability of becoming a homophobe. Morin and Garfinkle (1978) report that the best single predictor of anti-gay sentiment is sex-role rigidity: a belief in the need to keep women 'in their place'. As well, sex-role confusion may explain why men are more prejudiced against gays than are women, why gay men elicit more negative reactions than do lesbians, and why effeminate gay men are less threatening to most non-gays than are their 'macho' counterparts (Siegel, 1979; for a contrary view, see Millham and Weinberger, 1977).

People committed to traditional sex roles show high levels of homophobia and low levels of openness to intimacy (Stark, 1991; Johnston, 1990). Likewise, male college students who endorse traditional sex roles are often homophobic, oppose self-disclosure to female (though not to male) friends, and favour unequal decision-making power in relations with their intimate partner (Thompson, Grisanti, and Pleck, 1985).

'Homosociality', a social preference for members of one's own gender (Britton, 1990) is also strongly correlated with homophobia. Since homosocial groups exclude both women and gays, homophobia and anti-femininity—though distinct—are highly correlated. Both are also correlated with the inability to form intimate non-sexual relationships. Typically, gay men are less opposed to emotional (non-sexual) closeness than heterosexual men who are homophobic and anti-feminine (McRoy, 1990).

Finally, the literature continues to report that religiosity and social conservatism, variously measured, contribute to homophobia. This pattern may be rooted in a larger syndrome of traits that Adorno and colleagues (1950) refer to as the 'authoritarian personality'. In this context, people who are homophobic tend to be conservative, anti-democratic, racist, superstitious, and opposed to the inspection of their own or other people's feeling.

Policies and Theory Applications to Control Paraphilia

Social policies concerning various types of sexual behaviour remain highly controversial. There is consensus on only a few things: in North America, people universally disapprove of sexual behaviour that involves the use of force or violence against an unwilling participant. Most people consider harmful paraphilias to be mental disorders. However, that's where the agreement ends; on most other issues, people disagree widely and often vigorously.

Criminalization of the sex business

Some believe that we should criminalize all forms of prostitution. However, other people believe the opposite. The latter believe that prostitution has no intrinsic social value and can be completely eradicated through vigorous and uncompromising enforcement of the criminal law (Reanda, 1991).

Canada today practices a hybrid form of criminalization. Although prostitution itself is theoretically legal in Canada, practising it is not. While the trend in other Western countries has been to move away from criminal sanctions for prostitution, Canada has done the reverse, legislating a tougher

anti-communication law in 1986. Various government committees and task forces have called for even tougher laws and more vigorous enforcement of the current legislation. In 1990, the Standing Committee on Justice recommended strengthening the laws, to include fingerprinting and photographing prostitutes and removing drivers' licences from those (customers) charged with communicating for the purpose of prostitution.

By contrast, prostitution is legal in many countries. In some, it is subject to government control, to reduce the health problems that may arise, such as the spread of disease or control by organized crime. The reason some people support decriminalizing prostitution in Canada is that no matter what policies we make, prostitution will still exist. Governments should, they reason, reduce harm by ensuring adequate health care services for sex workers, who are at risk of violence and sexually transmitted diseases.

As we have seen, poverty, inequality, and prostitution co-exist. Prostitution flourishes where economic inequality facilitates violation of the human rights of poor people, particularly poor children and women. Where people lack the basic rights to employment, a living wage, healthcare, housing and food, some people will be unable to survive without selling their bodies for sex. This is why governments cannot, in good faith, just criminalize prostitution. They must either ensure that poor people get enough health care, food, housing, and payment to survive without prostitution; or they have to make prostitution a safer, healthier line of legal work.

In some cases, people—usually women and children—are enslaved in the sex industry through physical and sexual violence, through forced or pre-existent addiction to drugs, or because of immigration and visa problems. People with money and power find it easy to own or rent the bodies of people who are refugees, homeless, unemployed, undocumented or unprotected immigrants, enslaved, abandoned children, or otherwise without economic rights and protection.

To deal with these human rights violations, governments have to set up policies that combat trafficking in people. Agreements will be needed at the international and national levels, to achieve cooperation among various governments and branches of government. Some progress has been made in this direction. The ILO Convention on the Worst of Forms of Child Labour (Convention 182) adopted in 1999 identifies the trafficking of children as a practice similar to slavery. The Convention calls for countries to take immediate action to secure the prohibition and elimination of all worst forms of child labour.

Incarceration

Many sexual deviants are put into prisons because of the outrage that they cause in the general population by their actions. Yet though their acts are considered crimes, some of these people are sick and need help: they are unable to act otherwise. All sex offenders should receive some form of treatment. However, not all sex offenders should receive the same intensity, duration, or type of treatment. Sex offenders are a diverse group. They differ in their personal and offence-related histories, the pattern of circumstances surrounding their offences, the age and sex preferences of their victims, the attitudes and beliefs that support their deviant behaviour.

Incarceration of sex offenders is important to prevent re-offending, and to provide citizens with peace of mind. However, little progress has been made in the direction of rehabilitating these offenders. Consequently, prevention and family and community support may have to play a larger part in solving the problem.

Family strategies for dealing with sexual issues

Just as they play a critical role in creating sexual problems, families can play a critical role in helping to solve them. However, families often have trouble discussing sexual issues. They tend to maintain secrecy about family issues towards outsiders, and sometimes they even avoid discussing these issues with one another. Prime examples are infidelity and homosexuality. Many families are unwilling to recognize that one of their members is gay or lesbian, that a family member is having an affair, or one family member is sexually abusing another. Another prime example is the discussion of sexually transmitted diseases: how to prevent them and how to cope with them, once contracted.

Thus, families have particular difficulty discussing or even acknowledging the fact that a family member has contracted HIV/AIDS, probably through unprotected sex with someone of the same sex, and possibly as part of a secret or illicit relationship. This fact is problematic because preventing the spread of a sexually transmitted disease requires disclosing the infection to others with whom one is sexually intimate, whatever the cost to the relationship. Seeking support and solace from family members also requires disclosing the infection to others with whom one is emotionally intimate, whatever the cost to the relationship. These disclosures are harder to accomplish than one might imagine.

HIV/AIDS and the problem of disclosure

Early disclosure of HIV infection could be a pivotal factor in reducing behaviours that continue the spread of HIV. However, within the context of intimate relations, the admission of being HIV-positive can lead to the revelation of one or more sexual partners, drug use, or bisexuality or homosexuality. So, revealing a diagnosis of HIV/AIDS can amount to revealing important and potentially discrediting secrets about one's life. Interestingly, despite the fears of stigma and rejection, HIV-positive people commonly reveal their condition to people close to them. One study found that 89 per cent of HIV-positive men revealed their status to their primary partner and 34 per cent revealed to a non-primary sex partner during the six months immediately following diagnosis (Wolitski et al., 1998). In fact, HIV-positives are twice as likely to disclose to all categories of persons than they had anticipated they would.

Nonetheless, they continue to conceal this information from many others. Reasons for concealing secret information about an HIV-positive diagnosis include concerns about personal risks, such as rejection and feared lack of understanding, or gossip, and desires to protect a partner or family member from being hurt (Derlega et al., 1998). Moreover, expectations about the reception of their disclosure are likely to vary widely, from one culture to another. Hispanic culture, for example, is particularly unforgiving (as we will see later).

Varieties of theories seek to account for the reasons people do and do not disclose their secrets to intimate partners. According to the communication boundary management theory, context and process are all-important. Some people try to protect themselves from being hurt by an unscrupulous person or by their own communication defects by relying on an indirect mode of disclosure. Given the uncertainty of how communications about HIV-positivity will be received, what Yep (2000) calls 'communication boundary coordination' is critical.

Much of the effort HIV-positive people spend on limiting knowledge of their infection is due to a fear of rejection. Over the course of time, they develop coping strategies that include all the essential processes through which individuals personalize the illness. Willingness to disclose varies from one HIV-positive person to another along social structural lines. An HIV-positive person with high structural embeddedness (i.e., where both partners inhabit the same social world) is more likely to disclose his HIV status to his partner than an individual with low structural embeddedness (i.e., where one or both partners inhabit two different worlds). So, for example, HIV-positive people are more likely to disclose if they have a high degree of knowledge about their partner's network, and vice versa—so that each knows many people in the partners' network on a first name basis.

Summary

Societies designate some people as 'male' and others as 'female', when in fact any given person may have features—visible or not—that make them partly male and partly female. In fact, sexuality and sex are extremely varied. The types of sexual behaviour that people deem deviant may change over time, but what persists is the tendency to label certain behaviours as deviant because they are not conventional. However, consensual sadomasochism, exhibitionism, voyeurism, and some forms of fetishism—though minority interests—are increasingly becoming culturally accepted forms of sexuality.

Concluding Words

One of the main concerns associated with sexual deviation today is the conduct of the sex trade, especially trafficking in virtually enslaved women and children. Other concerns include pornography—the commodification of sex, women, and children—and homophobia.

Much of the abuse associated with sexual deviation originates in childhood, with some women reporting severe degrees of emotional abuse, emotional neglect, or physical neglect before entering prostitution. Much debate concerns whether sexual activities associated with sadomasochism are likewise connected to earlier abuse. However, there is no evidence to support this view. On the contrary, much evidence shows that abuse in early life increases the likelihood of entry into the sex trade.

Gradually, throughout North America, gay men and lesbians are receiving legal rights and social acceptance that they have never enjoyed in modern times, including the rights to marry. Homophobia must be considered a form of sexual deviance today.

Questions for Critical Thought

1. Can you think of any other types of sexual deviance that are being normalized? If so, what do you think are the processes behind the normalization of these sexual activities?
2. Think about the double standard in regard to the expected behaviours of males and females. How has this double standard structured research on the topic of sexual deviance?
3. Why don't we see as many male prostitutes as female prostitutes? Discuss this from the interactionist and feminist viewpoints.
4. Identify the reasons why sexual deviance is often limited to distinct parts of cities. What purpose might this serve?
5. Why might women choose to enter the sex trade? Is it always a choice?
6. What is the main cause of street prostitution? Knowing this, what policy alternatives can be examined to reduce street prostitution?
7. Traditional heterosexual pornography is said to be gendered. How can homosexual pornography be just as gendered?
8. Between 20–40 per cent of the population is reportedly involved in some form of SM behaviour, but doesn't define it as such. How would a theorist then explain the fact that it is such a stigmatized activity?
9. Conservatives often argue for strong morality laws regarding sexual deviance. Why might a functionalist hold similar views?
10. How does the balance of power between deviant and non-deviant populations influence health outcomes?

Recommended Reading

Butler, Judith. (1990), *Gender Trouble: Feminism and the Subversion of Identity*. New York: Routledge. This book is a classic study of gender and sexual identity, which is paramount for any understanding of queer theory. Butler examines traditional conceptions of identity and explains how they are themselves produced and reproduced.

Califia, Pat. (1988), *Macho Sluts*. Los Angeles: Alyson Books. This book by Pat Califia, which contains SM lesbian stories, has garnered a lot of attention in the media because of its openness. Particularly because it contains SM lesbian porn, it has been censored extensively. The book provides an interesting (and graphic) look into the SM lesbian subculture.

Murray, Stephen O. (1996), *American Gay*. Chicago: University of Chicago Press. Comparative sociologist Stephen Murray examines the roots of gay identity in America. In his analysis he looks at media typifications, representations of men with HIV/AIDS, and how communities have been formed along gay identity.

Recommended Websites

Federal Initiative to Address HIV/AIDS in Canada

www.phac-aspc.gc.ca/aids-sida/hiv_aids/

> This website is an excellent resource portal for research and information on HIV/AIDS. It outlines government policy regarding HIV/AIDS and provides comparative information from other nations.

Prostitute Research and Education

www.prostitutionresearch.com

> Prostitute Research and Education is an NGO with the mandate to organize prostitutes and provide alternatives to the current forms of prostitution that exist in the United States. The website informs viewers as to laws, trafficking trends, and the latest research in prostitution.

Transgender Crossroads

www.tgcrossroads.org

> This is a portal website for transgender (TG) crossroads, which offers a myriad of information for transgendered people. It provides information on new books, civil liberties, laws, medical services, and some of the latest research concerning transgendered people.

CHAPTER 5

Substance Abuse

LEARNING OBJECTIVES

- To define drug use and abuse
- To recall the history of drug use and abuse
- To understand and analyze public reaction to substance abuse
- To learn the various sociological theories that explain abuse
- To examine the importance of women and drug use
- To judge the health consequences of drug abuse
- To think of possible solutions to the drug and alcohol abuse issue

Introduction

In this chapter, we discuss rule-breaking and unexpected behaviour that is associated with substance abuse—the inappropriate use of drugs and alcohol. We will discuss a variety of consciousness-altering drugs, including alcohol, marijuana, cocaine, and heroin. These substances all change a person's mental state and can sometimes—depending on the drug and its use—lead to serious health risks for the user and for others. There are close connections between drug use and important public safety issues that include crime and delinquency. That is why society has an interest in controlling excessive or deviant use of a number of these psychoactive substances.

In North America, most people use alcohol or drugs regularly, whether as a glass of wine with dinner or as a Tylenol to ease a headache. People use drugs because drugs make them feel good. We are a drug-using civilization.

More than that, we are a chemical-using civilization, always looking for ways to make life better through the use of chemical substances. We regularly use all manner of drugs to deal with the pains and tensions of normal, everyday life. Beyond that, most of us use drugs and chemicals every day, as part of striving for better health. This stems from the belief that health is not simply the absence of illness but something we must struggle (and spend) to gain. As a result, many of us use vitamins, lotions, teas, and many other products that promise us good health and longevity.

Also, in recent years many new disorders have been medicalized, creating a need for new drugs that have appeared, claiming to relieve stress, PMS, improve memory, or solve countless other problems. The billion-dollar weight-loss industry also offers a wide array of drugs, powders, and drinks that all promise to offer fast and easy ways to slim down.

Thus, ingesting chemicals generally, and drugs in particular, is a normal and common part of everyday life, even when people may not be ill. It is estimated that within a 20- to 36-hour period, 50 to 80 per cent of the adult population in the United

States and the United Kingdom ingests some type of legal drug. However, legal drugs are not always safe. Because of the push to launch ever newer and more revolutionary drugs, possible side effects are often insufficiently studied, although they are sometimes severe and even addictive.

Why, then, does society only punish some drug-using behaviours? Why do we treat drug-users in such an unequal manner?

Part of the answer has to do with the amount of drugs used. Problems arise when people use too many drugs at the same time, or use them too often. Additionally, once people are addicted to drugs or alcohol, they are at risk of committing acts— even criminal acts—that are potentially harmful. Addiction is always a potential problem too. People addicted to drugs may organize their entire lives around seeking gratification: around getting their next fix of heroin or cocaine, alcohol, nicotine, or even caffeine. This compulsion to find and consume drugs disrupts their work, family, and social lives. Their lives become a continuing search for the needed drugs, and an emotional roller-coaster ride: they are happy when they have ingested the drug, depressed and nervous when they lack it.

Nowhere is this truer than with caffeine—the most commonly used drug in Canadian society. Excess caffeine intake is not only addictive in the classic sense—that is, it creates a continuous need for more, and withdrawal leads to painful symptoms—but it also carries serious health and social consequences: sleep disturbance, edginess, mood swings. Yet many use coffee a lot, because it has social as well as biochemical and psychological value. Like alcohol and cigarettes, coffee helps people organize their time, deal with stress, and smooth social interactions. However, it is considered the least deviant of all drugs currently in use, hence the least sociologically interesting.

Both the law and the society have condemned 'hard' drugs, such as cocaine and heroin, but have condoned and regulated tobacco and alcohol. (There has been no effort made to regulate caffeine to date.)

This social ambivalence—condoning some drugs while condemning others—points to a central issue in the drug and alcohol 'problem', namely, we don't have a clear idea of what drugs we want to regulate, or why.

As a result, Canada's debate over legalizing or decriminalizing marijuana is back in the news. US legislators, worried about America's unmanageable drug problem, are watching the outcome carefully and indicating disapproval of potentially liberal laws. In Canada and elsewhere, the use of legal drugs, such as alcohol, tobacco, and prescription medicine, is much more common than the use of illegal drugs, such as heroin and cocaine. Yet, our society focuses on illegal drug use as a problem while ignoring the harm done by legal drugs.

Our ambivalent, 'irrational' behaviour where drugs are concerned reminds us that we socially construct all deviance—including our response to drug use. Nowhere is this more obvious than in our perception of 'drug addicts'. People addicted to hard drugs are seen as crazed, irrational, irresponsible, and unable to care for themselves. Therefore, we think they should be jailed, hospitalized, or at least kept out of sight.

This is nothing but a moral panic about 'addiction' at a particular point in human history. As Jacques Derrida (2003) wrote, in order to define addiction we need 'a history, a culture, conventions, evaluations, norms, [and] discourses . . . instituted on the basis of moral and political evaluations'. So, as sociologists we must beware that the negative ideas we associate with drug use, and our representation of addicts as crazed 'others' to be contained and punished are culturally specific, not scientific and universal. Often there is no logic to our acceptance of some drug-using activities and rejection of others.

Intoxication: Its Social Role

The age-old relationship between drugs and deviant behaviour has two distinct but related aspects: one is sociocultural and the other biochemical.

The biochemical effect of drugs is easily noticeable. Because of our body chemistry, drugs such as alcohol, cannabis, and opium have the power to alter our perception of the world, relax us, lower our inhibitions, and (occasionally) cause us to see visions or have other bodily experiences. Different drugs have different powers, but all commonly consumed drugs—including nicotine and caffeine—are psychoactive in one way or another.

At the same time, the social uses of and reactions to drugs vary historically (over time), and from one culture to another. For example, sixteenth- and seventeenth-century Jesuit missionaries to Peru reported that native South American peoples consumed alcoholic beverages during religious ceremonies and used hallucinogenic substances as a part of many social activities, such as the 'cult of the ancestors'. They also discovered that drug consumption was closely linked to local medicinal practices.

The ways that people behave after consuming a drug or drinking alcohol, for example, depend in part on the society in which people learned to drink the alcohol and the effects they expect alcohol to have. By comparing drinking in different societies, we find that the drug's 'effects' are partly biochemical and partly social. Intoxicated behaviours are social enactments of biochemical states, but they also result from our expectations—how we expect (and wish) the drug will affect us. Because intoxicated behaviours are enactments of both biochemical states and their expected effects, drugs and alcohol are often used to ritualize unusual, even rule-breaking behaviour.

So, for example, the Mardi Gras run in rural Louisiana is a rite of reversal in which a rowdy band of costumed merrymakers visits homes and businesses to collect 'charity' for a communal supper. Misbehaviour and violence in this context are often blamed on intoxication. However, the drinking that takes place is a form of ritualized inebriation that offers participants freedom owing to their anonymity. Although seemingly chaotic, Mardi Gras has mechanisms of control that allow for play, yet limit misbehaviour (Sexton, 2001).

As we have said, the same drug may be used differently in different societies, often with different effects. The Mediterranean pattern of drinking, characterized by frequent intake of small amounts of alcohol, produces a sense of serene well-being and permits continued functioning throughout the day. The Northern drinking pattern, instead, is characterized by an alternation between abstinence and binge drinking (i.e., drinking to excess) and gives rise to aggressive, even violent outbursts.

The latter practice stems from the stigmatization of alcohol by the eugenicist movement in the early-twentieth century and the prohibition of alcohol during the early years of independence. In Finland, for example, both drinking and alcohol are isolated from everyday life, with alcohol sold in separate spaces; thus, the state of drunkenness and the beverage are made 'sacred' (Keryell, 1997). Thus, Finnish attitudes are very different from the ones prevalent in France, where alcohol is far from 'sacred' and is a routine part of daily life.

The sacred and profane

Throughout history, people have known and used drugs. In every society, people have experienced intoxication—a word that means 'taking in poison'—as a departure from the usual. In that sense, drug use has always had something sacred about it. For most of recorded history, drugs have been used in sacred rituals—that is, as part of a respite from everyday life. Drugs are part of this shift out of the routine world.

As Durkheim pointed out, we lead most of our lives in a profane world of routine social objects: everyday clothes, food, ways of speaking, ways of behaving, and so on. On special occasions, we try to shift to another way of life, a sacred plane marked by special social objects: ritual clothing, symbolic foods, unusual ways of speaking and behaving, and so on. Drugs are part of this shift out of the routine world.

We associate different locations with these special activities, and accept certain behaviours as appropriate for these locations. As a result, people behave differently in churches and university lecture halls, for example. In the religious context of churches (also, synagogues, mosques, and temples), people have historically used drugs and alcohol to help them shift their consciousness from sober this-worldly concerns—thrift, efficiency, and profitability—to otherworldly concerns—ecstasy, reflectiveness, and a focus on the deeper meaning of life.

It is not accidental that, at a Catholic mass, the priest sips wine, representing Christ's blood. Wine plays a ritual part in the mass, standing in for holy blood. Cranberry juice, though the same colour, would not have the same meaning, because it does not have the same 'sacred' effect. So intoxication, the state associated with alcohol, is also associated with feelings and emotions and behaviours that are out of the ordinary. The very idea of collective 'intoxication' in Durkheim's time—the late-nineteenth and early-twentieth century—meant not alcoholic consumption, but rather, public delirium or mania (Cingolani, 1999). During the early years of social science, spontaneous social activity—the suggestibility of groups and the authority of leaders; the vitality, mobility, and impulsiveness of groups; and the ways crowds and groups formed and disbanded freely—fascinated Durkheim and others. Drug-induced intoxication was only one type of such lively activity. What was similar was the specialness and the intensity of such public behaviours.

The importance of place

Situational factors are an important part of the drug-using experience. Different situations—locations, settings, and occasions—can encourage or discourage the use of drugs. Most of us, for example, do not consume drugs or alcohol in the bathroom, at work, or in school. However, people do consume drugs or alcohol in bars and restaurants.

The strongest statement about the influence of situation on substance use and abuse is provided in a classic sociological work by Howard Becker (1953) that describes how people learn to smoke and

appreciate marijuana. Becker asserts that, contrary to then-prevailing theories, purely psychological theories about drug use, drug abuse, and intoxicated behaviour are insufficient. For example, though personalities are relatively stable, over the course of time people may drift in and out of marijuana use; and though some people may like marijuana, psychologically similar people may not.

The explanation for marijuana use—especially, continued use—requires a sociological explanation, says Becker. In short, to smoke and appreciate marijuana, the drug must first be made available; then, knowledgeable people must teach the newcomer how to smoke the drug and how to detect and appreciate its physical effects. Without these situational, subcultural conditions, people will not become users of the drug. Thus, drug use must be viewed in a social and cultural context. And though we may not think so, because drinking is so common, this is as true of alcohol use as it is of marijuana.

Moreover, variations in the drinking environment—in the particular bar or restaurant—influence the amount people drink, how they act afterwards, and even the likelihood of driving while intoxicated. Likewise, barrooms are more or less likely to promote violence, based on the situational characteristics of these establishments (Roberts, 2003). Noisier, smokier barrooms are likely to produce more excessive drinking and more aggressive behaviour. Obnoxious environmental stimuli (i.e., excessive heat, smoke, etc.), lack of bar staff, and bar staff or servers of alcohol who are themselves drinking alcoholic beverages also increase the likelihood of aggression in barrooms.

Most violence in or near drinking places is associated with high levels of intoxication and many patrons consider this to be exciting and enjoyable. For many, fighting after drinking is part of membership in a male subculture. Group drinking (and fighting) for many men symbolizes a rejection of middle-class values and social constraints. Sometimes, local authorities even provoke and condone such violence. The connection between drinking and violence is likely associated with the cultural construction of group drinking, masculine identity, and the rejection of social values, which has a long tradition stretching back to days on the frontier (Tomsen, 1997).

The ethic of masculinity—*macho*, in Spanish—has been part of the 'drinking and violence' problem, in the sense that men have always tended to act more aggressively masculine under the influence of alcohol. Part of this is the influence of the drinking place itself. The Midwestern saloon in the late-nineteenth century—like the contemporary barroom—both confirmed and challenged the manhood of its customers. While barrooms offered them a homosocial space to indulge in activities coded 'male', men who frequented them risked both becoming intoxicated and losing authority at home. Barroom attendance and all-male drinking early became an expression form of male independence.

Situational influences on drinking can be particularly important because people are often poor judges of their own behaviour. They don't realize that they have drunk too much, for example, or are behaving erratically. In judging their own drinking, people apply norms that are often erroneous. Wild (2002) found in Ontario, that frequent heavy drinkers are particularly likely to: (1) believe that heavy alcohol use is acceptable in their social reference groups; (2) overestimate the amount of alcohol that social and problem drinkers consume; and (3) rate several criteria (e.g., frequency of intoxication) as less definitive of problem drinking. Surprisingly, some studies reveal that some older heavy drinkers think that drinking moderately might actually have health benefits. In short, frequent heavy drinkers calibrate their beliefs about drinking in reference groups to view their own (heavy) drinking as normative and not so heavy, comparatively speaking.

Though some drinking situations lead to bad behaviour, others do not. Forsyth and Barnard (2000), for example, asked a sample of Scottish schoolchildren about their consumption of alcoholic beverages. Some drank a little, others quite

a bit more. However, the results also indicate a continuum of drinking styles between what might be regarded as low-risk and high-risk behaviour. At one extreme, much drinking tends to take place within the family home, usually under parental supervision. At the opposite extreme, alcohol consumption takes place in a variety of public or 'hidden' outdoor locations. Consumption in these latter locations more often results in intoxication. Also, more dangerous, high-alcohol, large-volume beverages (e.g., white cider) tend to be consumed in these locations.

Factors affecting alcohol abuse

Alcohol per se is not the problem, then. It interacts with culture and situation. It also interacts with personal variables such as gender, class, and race, to produce the deviant behaviour associated with it. Rojek and colleagues (2001), for example, find that black males have a homicide victimization rate that is 6 times higher than for black females, 7 times higher than for white males, and 25 times higher than for white females.

Homicide is often the act of an intoxicated or drug-abusing individual, and drug trafficking and drug abuse have become familiar aspects of lower socioeconomic neighborhoods, especially in the United States. The coupling of handguns and alcohol (or drugs) makes homicide an all-too-common response to problematic situations that escalate into lethal violence. Various forms of personal pathology in adulthood—including depression, mental illness, and homelessness—are associated with excessive alcohol use in adulthood, or childhood experiences involving alcohol.

Research suggests that adult substance abuse tends to follow from early traumatic experiences, chiefly suffered in family life. Stein and colleagues (2002), for example, explored the effects of early parental substance abuse on later chronic homelessness, depression, and substance-abuse problems in a sample of homeless women residing in shelters or sober living centres. The study found that parental

Table 5.1 Monitoring the Future Study: Trends in Prevalence of Various Drugs for 8th-Graders, 10th-Graders, and 12th-Graders, 2001–3

	8th-Graders			10th-Graders			12th-Graders		
	2001	2002	2003	2001	2002	2003	2001	2002	2003
Any Illicit Drug Use									
lifetime	26.8	24.5	22.8	45.6	44.6	41.4	53.9	53.0	51.1
annual	19.5	17.7	16.1	37.2	34.8	32.0	41.4	41.0	39.3
30-day	11.7	10.4	9.7	22.7	20.8	19.5	25.7	25.4	24.1
Marijuana/Hashish									
lifetime	20.4	19.2	17.5	40.1	38.7	36.4	49.0	47.8	46.1
annual	15.4	14.6	12.8	32.7	30.3	28.2	37.0	36.2	34.9
30-day	9.2	8.3	7.5	19.8	17.8	17.0	22.4	21.5	21.2
daily	1.3	1.2	1.0	4.5	3.9	3.6	5.8	6.0	6.0
Inhalants									
lifetime	17.1	15.2	15.8	15.2	13.5	12.7	13.0	11.7	11.2
annual	9.1	7.7	8.7	6.6	5.8	5.4	4.5	4.5	3.9
30-day	4.0	3.8	4.1	2.4	2.4	2.2	1.7	1.5	1.5
Hallucinogens									
lifetime	5.2	4.1	4.0	8.9	7.8	6.9	14.7	12.0	10.6
annual	3.4	2.6	2.6	6.2	4.7	4.1	9.1	6.6	5.9
30-day	1.6	1.2	1.2	2.1	1.6	1.5	3.3	2.3	1.8
Alcohol									
lifetime	50.5	7.0	45.6	70.1	66.9	66.0	79.7	78.4	76.6
annual	41.9	38.7	37.2	63.5	60.0	59.3	73.3	71.5	70.1
30-day	21.5	19.6	19.7	39.0	35.4	35.4	49.8	48.6	47.5
daily	0.9	0.7	0.8	1.9	1.8	1.5	3.6	3.5	3.2
Cigarettes (any use)									
lifetime	36.6	31.4	28.4	52.8	47.4	43.0	61.0	57.2	53.7
30-day	12.2	10.7	10.2	21.3	17.7	16.7	29.5	26.7	24.4
1/2 pack+/day	2.3	2.1	1.8	5.5	4.4	4.1	10.3	9.1	8.4
Smokeless Tobacco									
lifetime	11.7	11.2	11.3	19.5	16.9	14.6	19.7	18.3	17.0
30-day	4.0	3.3	4.1	6.9	6.1	5.3	7.8	6.5	6.7
daily	1.2	0.8	0.8	2.2	1.7	1.8	2.8	2.0	2.2

SOURCE: *Monitoring the Future Study*; available at <www.nida.nih.gov/Infofax/HSYouthtrends.html>. Reprinted by permission of Monitoring the Future, Institute for Social Research, University of Michigan.

substance abuse directly predicted later substance abuse by the women.

The importance of demographics

Studies have shown that the amount of drug, tobacco, and alcohol consumption varies by age. First of all, most people are likely to start using either one of these substances during their teen years under the influence along with their peers (see Table 5.1 and Figure 5.1). After age 26 the likeli-

Figure 5.1a   Past Month Drug Use by High School Seniors, by Drug Type, United States, 1975–2001

SOURCE: *Monitoring the Future Study*; available at <www.nida.nih.gov/Infofax/HSYouthtrends.html>. Reprinted by permission of Monitoring the Future, Institute for Social Research, University of Michigan.

hood of trying or experimenting with any substance for the first time or 'starting to smoke' decreases significantly. Also, during the teen years substance abuse seems to be more excessive, perhaps due to the increasing influence of the peer group as opposed to parents. In young adulthood, substance abuse decreases slowly, perhaps because of the assumption of new social roles such as parents, employees, and so on.

Overall excessive use or experimenting with legal and illegal drugs, though considered deviant, is usually seen as 'just a phase' of teenage development. However, when substance abuse continues into adulthood and affects employment or family well-being, it is seen as much more deviant. The irony lies in the fact that teen experimentation with drugs, though offering a sense of 'pseudo-adulthood', also socializes teenagers into deviant subcultures and roles. This increases the likelihood that they will continue to abuse substances and decreases their exposure to (learning of) mainstream norms. Thus, it delays their assumption of adult roles.

In short, then, deviant drug and alcohol use pose potential problems for society and its members. But deviance aside, there are cultural, historically specific reasons why—today—we consider drug

Figure 5.1b   Past Month Drug Use by 8th and 10th Graders, by Drug Type, United States,1975–2001

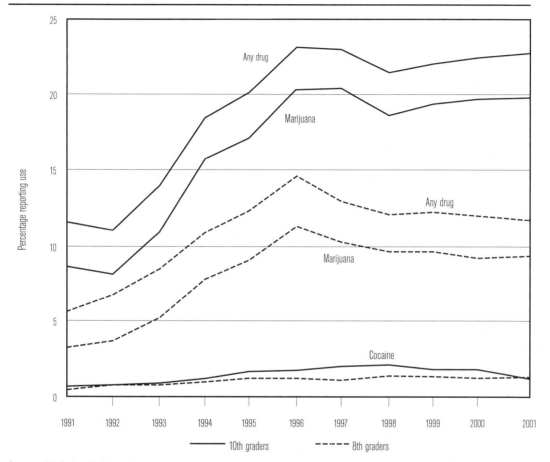

SOURCE: *Monitoring the Future Study*; available at <www.nida.nih.gov/Infofax/HSYouthtrends.html>. Reprinted by permission of Monitoring the Future, Institute for Social Research, University of Michigan.

and alcohol use problems, and deal with them the ways we do.

The History of Drug and Alcohol Abuse, and Public Reaction

Both social policy and popular attitudes towards drugs have changed over time, and they have influenced one another. Sometimes popular attitudes and behaviours have changed first, and sometimes they have followed policy changes. Because drugs and alcohol have cultural meanings, and not merely a biochemical influence, the use of drugs—who is permitted to use drugs and how they use them—changes over time.

Take the age restrictions on alcohol. In our society, alcohol consumption is formally restricted to adults, and many people view attaining the legal right to consume alcohol as a 'rite of passage' into adulthood. Some people even view getting drunk as a momentous activity, and they purposely set out to accomplish that goal. Young people drink beer and spirits at weekends, holidays, and during the period

Box 5.2 Alcohol and Drug Use in Early Adolescence

One major factor plays the biggest role in children's alcohol and drug use in early adolescence and the factor is the behaviour of friends, according to a new report. The report is based on data for 4,296 adolescents aged 12 to 15 who were part of the 1998/99 National Longitudinal Survey of Children and Youth. Two-thirds of adolescents who reported that all or most of their friends were using alcohol had, themselves, been drunk at least once. Only 8 per cent of those who reported having few or no friends who used alcohol had ever been drunk. Similarly, four-fifths (82 per cent) had smoked marijuana if most or all of their friends had done so, too. This compares with only 7 per cent who didn't have friends who used marijuana. The study adds to evidence that peer behaviour is related to an adolescent's own alcohol and drug use. However, it is not possible to determine a causal direction. For example, friendships may provide opportunities to learn through imitation and reinforce behaviour. It could also be that 'birds of a feather flock together', and adolescents

seek friends with similar attitudes toward alcohol and other drugs.

Early experimentation
Overall, 42 per cent of 12- to 15-year-olds reported that they had consumed at least one drink of alcohol—a bottle of beer or wine cooler, or a glass of wine—at some point in their life. By age 15, the proportion rose to 66 per cent. More than one-fifth (22 per cent) said they had been drunk at least once. Among those aged 15, this proportion was 44 per cent. In addition, about one-fifth (19 per cent) of 12- to 15-year-olds reported having smoked marijuana. Again, the proportion among adolescents aged 15 rose to 38 per cent. The average age at which adolescents reported having their first drink was 12.4 years, with only a slight difference between boys and girls. The average age of being drunk for the first time was about a year older, at just past 13 years. For other drugs, including marijuana and hallucinogens, the average age of first-time use was older, between 13.1 and 13.8.

SOURCE: Excerpt, Statistics Canada, *Health Reports*, Volume 15, Number 3. Catalogue 82-003-XIE.

of their final exams for intoxication, transition to a new phase of life, and celebration purposes within the peer group (Beccaria and Sande, 2003). In the modern youth culture, use of alcohol for intoxication purposes is a key symbol of transition from childhood.

However, public alcohol use was not always just an adult activity. In pre-industrial England, the same norms governed both adult and juvenile

(male) access to alcohol in the late-medieval period (Warner, 1998). Norms governing juvenile access to alcohol became their most restrictive when a shortage of jobs kept many males from entering adulthood—that is, from achieving financial independence—for extended periods.

Two other developments in the early modern period coincided with reductions in juvenile access to alcohol: (1) the gradual change of drinking into an essentially recreational activity carried on outside the home in groups consisting mainly of males; and (2) the introduction of new and potentially more intoxicating beverages, first in the form of beer and later in the form of cheap spirits distilled from grain.

Likewise, public alcohol use was not always mainly a male activity. Temperance only came to be viewed as an appropriate virtue for women in sixteenth- and seventeenth-century England (Warner, 1997). Attitudes shifted in respect to women who drank in public, as a result of economic and cultural changes. Up until the first decades of the sixteenth century, men and women both enjoyed considerable drinking freedom. It was only during the economic and social crises of the early modern period that two distinct drinking cultures started to emerge: one centred in the home and exclusive of men, the other centred outside the home and exclusive of women.

The emergence of temperance as a virtue specific to women occurred at a time when real wages were in sharp decline. Sanctions on female drinking had the effect of redistributing household income in favour of men, whose right to drink was never seriously challenged. Criticism of women who drank publicly (conveniently) coincided with the rediscovery of classical texts commending the supposed temperance of the women of early Rome.

As well, there has been a close relationship between religious change and the use of drugs throughout history. Historically, people have alternated between expressive and repressive religions, with consequences for drug use. Expressive religions develop elaborate rituals and artifacts to celebrate religious observance. Repressive religions tend to reject elaborate rituals and artifacts, calling instead for simplicity and modesty. Social and religious movements that aim to reform this world are usually repressive, relying as they do on the continuous, dedicated efforts of their members. This reliance makes sobriety—as well as thrift, industry, planning, and efficiency—central values of the subculture. Thus, for

example, the rise of Protestantism in Western Europe meant not only a shot in the arm for the spirit of capitalism, as Weber tells us, but it also meant a significant increase in sobriety.

Thus, culture change can promote a change in the use of drugs. Equally, sometimes the rejection of drugs and/or alcohol reflects a conflict between native born and immigrant cultures. Until the early 1900s, people commonly used opium as a painkiller. Cocaine, recently the object of a 'war on drugs' in the United States, was an active ingredient used in Coca-Cola until 1906 when caffeine replaced it. In fact, cocaine was also consumed as cocaine-wine and prescribed as a toothache medicine especially for small children. Eventually, people in authority started to deem both cocaine and opium dangerous. First, they subjected these drugs to strict regulation and then they banned the drugs completely. It was not medical research that proved these drugs caused social problems. For cocaine and marijuana, the attitude changes resulted from attitudes toward immigrants or racial minorities that were in some way connected to the drug.

A good example of this is the story of how marijuana got its name. Newspaper magnate William Randolph Hearst renamed marihuana 'marijuana'—with a Spanish *J* in it—to highlight the strong cultural connection he perceived between that drug and the resident Mexican minority. This racial minority, at the time, was blamed for seducing American youth into the drug culture and corrupting their morals. Overall, the spread of drugs to the American population, and allegedly drug-related crimes, were blamed on racial minorities that were represented in the popular media as crazed savages. (Take home the 1930s video *Reefer Madness* for a representation of the belief that marijuana produced craziness, sexual seduction, and death.) These changes in attitude had the effect of penalizing the most vulnerable, least powerful members of society.

The mass media have always boosted their circulation by raising fears about excessive drug use and its effects. Legislators and law enforcers

Box 5.3 Research May Aid in More Effective Drug Addiction Treatments

HAMILTON, ON–29 August 2002–New research by McMaster University researchers suggests that a learned compensatory response can trigger 'drug tolerance', a physiological process central to addiction.

Drug tolerance makes people need more and more drug to get the same effect, whether pain relief or a 'high'. It's newly discovered psychological aspect–in which a drug-predictive cue primes the body to react 'as if' the drug effect is imminent–might be used to treat addiction more effectively. In short, if drug tolerance can be learned, there's a chance it can be unlearned, reducing or eliminating the tolerance-related cravings and other withdrawal symptoms that can lead addicts to relapse.

Research by McMaster psychology Professor Shepard Siegel, graduate student Marta Sokolowska, and McMaster alumnus Joseph Kim (now a postdoctoral fellow at the University of California, San Francisco) demonstrated that there is a powerful 'internal cue' process that stimulates the body to react to the effect of a drug. The research results were recently published in the *Journal of Experimental Psychology: Animal Behavior Processes*.

'The effect of a drug depends not only on our response to the drug, but also our response to stimuli that in the past have been paired with the drug. We've known this for a long time in terms of external stimuli, such as where and when a drug is taken, but now it's also clear that internal stimuli also play an important role,' says Professor Siegel. Current drug addiction treatment programs often include a component that tries to remove the effects of the external cues (so-called cue exposure treatments), but they ignore the importance of internal cues.

Researchers had already shown that the drug tolerance of rats getting infusions of morphine depended on the presence of environmental cues (sights or sounds paired with drugs). These external cues have typically been used because they are easily controlled by the experimenter. The new findings are that there also are internal cues not controlled by the researchers– the early subjective effect surreptitiously provided by the drug itself.

The researchers first infused rats with morphine over several days, causing them to develop tolerance to the analgesic (pain-relieving) effect of the opiate. Following each infusion, it takes some minutes for the peak effect of a drug to occur; however, the early effects of the drug (termed 'drug onset cues') are experienced prior to the peak effect. The researchers hypothesized that every administration constituted a learning trial. The drug onset cues were inevitably paired with the peak effect of the drug, thus the rats associated the early effect of the drug with the later, larger effect.

After tolerance had occurred, the researchers gave the rats a small dose of morphine. This small dose usually has no effect, but, in rats that had prior experience with larger infusions of morphine, it replicated the drug onset cue–a cue that previously had occurred shortly before the peak effect of the drug occurred. These rats who had received larger hits of morphine compensated, in the presence of the small dose, by becoming more sensitive to pain. They flicked their tails more quickly out of a warm-water bath, a common way to test rats' pain sensitivity. The rats' bodies were demonstrating compensatory behaviour in response to an early-warning dose of the drug.

The results suggest why some 'cue-exposure' treatments for addiction have not worked as well as hoped; they do not wipe out the kinds of early drug-onset cues demonstrated in these experiments. The findings help explain why relapse is more likely when someone is exposed to a small dose. For example, recovering alcoholics can be extremely vulnerable to just one drink because their systems respond to this learned 'drug-onset cue' with full-blown tolerance-induced cravings, and they go on a binge.

In the example provided by Professor Siegel: 'You're a cigarette smoker and you're trying to quit. When do you crave cigarettes? It's the time of day when you usually smoke, or it's when you see other people smoking. These are external stimuli and there are treatment processes that are cue exposure treatments designed to present you with these stimuli, but not allow you to smoke. These treatments might be more effective if they included the most effective stimuli, which might be the early effects of nicotine. You would take one puff, but not be allowed to take more puffs.'

SOURCE: McMaster Univewrsity, News Release, 'Research may aid in more effective drug addiction treatments'; available at <www.mcmaster.ca/ua/opr/nms/newsreleases/2002/siegel.htm>, accessed 7 October 2003.

have likewise benefited by promoting the notion that drugs pose a public problem, which they are uniquely qualified to control. (For a discussion of the RCMP's sorry role in this in Canada, see *Panic and Indifference: The Politics of Canada's Drug Laws—A Study in the Sociology of Law* by P.J. Giffen and associates (1991), a comprehensive history published by the Canadian Centre on Substance Abuse.) As Giffen and colleagues have shown in their study of the history of narcotic legislation, though the focus of the original anti-opium statute may have been rooted in hatred towards a racial minority (i.e., Asians), the persistence and expansion of the narcotic laws were largely because of the central role of bureaucratic law-makers. It was in their occupational and professional interest to promote social concerns about narcotics that would justify further expenditure on the problem.

Likewise, the American government's continuing 'war on drugs' has benefited America's law enforcement personnel more than citizens by playing to hatred and anxiety about the urban black population. Drug use is heavily associated in the American public mind with urban blacks. Under the current punitive approach to dealing with drug use in the United States, the net result is a huge number of young black males in jail, and many more with criminal records.

Ample research shows that alcohol causes people more harm then all the other drugs put together. So why then is alcohol still legal? To answer this question we have to look at the failure of so-called Temperance movements to prohibit alcohol. They failed in their mission to prevent alcohol use and only succeeded, during a brief Prohibition period, in enriching black market gangsters. The Prohibition movements gave

Box 5.4 Canadian Tobacco Use Monitoring Survey

The prevalence of smoking in Canada has shown a slight decrease in 2002, according to the latest results from the Canadian Tobacco Use Monitoring Survey (CTUMS). Although the change is not statistically significant, the prevalence of smoking continues the downward trend that has been seen in recent years.

An estimated 5.4 million people, or 21 per cent of the population aged 15 years and older, were smokers in 2002, down from 22 per cent in 2001. Men outnumbered women by a small margin, with about 23 per cent of men aged 15 years and older smoking compared with 20 per cent of women.

Smoking rates for youth have not changed significantly since 2001. The proportion of smokers aged 15 to 19 years was 22 per cent in 2002, and 31 per cent for young adults aged 20 to 24.

In 2002, the vast majority of current smokers (82 per cent) smoked daily. In 1985, daily smokers consumed an average of 21 cigarettes per day. Since then, the number of cigarettes smoked has been gradually declining, falling to 16 cigarettes per day in 2002. Men continued to smoke more cigarettes than women: 18 compared with 15 cigarettes per day.

British Columbia once again had the lowest smoking prevalence rate, at 16 per cent. However, no province particularly stands out as having the highest prevalence. In three provinces, New Brunswick, Manitoba, and Saskatchewan the smoking prevalence rate went down to 21 per cent compared with 25 per cent (New Brunswick and Saskatchewan) or 26 per cent (Manitoba) in 2001.

Of women aged 20 to 44 who were pregnant in the five years prior to the survey, 11 per cent smoked regularly during their most recent pregnancy. However, this was down from the 19 per cent reported in the 1995 Survey on Smoking in Canada. As well, in 2002, 13 per cent had a spouse who smoked regularly at home during their most recent pregnancy.

The CTUMS, conducted since 1999 by Statistics Canada on behalf of Health Canada, provides timely, reliable and continuous data on tobacco use and related issues. The survey's primary objective is to track changes in smoking status and amount smoked, especially for 15- to 24-year-olds, who are most at risk for taking up smoking. Data cited from before 1999 have been derived from other surveys. This release is based on data obtained between February and December 2002 from about 23,300 respondents.

SOURCE: Health Canada, 2001a, 'Adult Smoking in Canada', CTUMS Annual, February–December 2000; available at <www.hc-sc.gc.ca/hecs-sesc/tobacco/research/ctums/2000-youth/youth.html>, accessed 23 September 2003.

gangsters super profits in the 1920s from an illegal traffic in bootlegged, often poisonous alcohol.

The social, political, and economic mechanism that drove restrictive legislation and enforcement during the Prohibition era—a combination of strong demand for the drugs with a status war between different segments of the population—were much the same as those driving today's drug epidemic. As sociologist Joseph Gusfield points out in his excellent history of Prohibition, the effort to limit alcohol use was much more symbolic than practical. When it failed, it failed both symbolically and in practice. People continued to drink, and small-town Protestant teetotalers lost their political influence. (That said, Prohibition may have reduced the incidence of liver cirrhosis to some degree.)

One reason for repealing Prohibition was the recognition that, when quality-controlled alcoholic beverages are unavailable, people drink just about anything. In the 1920s and 1930s, people died or went blind from drinking beverages that contained dangerous impurities or the wrong kind of alcohol (i.e., methanol instead of ethanol). More recently, some users have died of drug overdoses because they had no way of knowing the strength of the drug. Legalization could prevent this by regulating the strength and quality of the drugs.

Nicotine addiction

Cigarette smoking came into fashion during the twentieth century. Tobacco use seems to have originated in South America where the natives used it for religious, medicinal, or other purposes. North American explorers introduced it to Europe, where it became fashionable in the seventeenth century but was illegal and considered immoral at first.

During the World Wars, sending tobacco to those who were away fighting was promoted as a symbol of patriotism and love, and those at home were encouraged and praised for thinking of packing a carton of cigarettes. In Canada, for example, newspapers listed the names of donors to the tobacco fund. However, once the war was over

and new advancements in medicine led to several warnings about the very harmful effects of tobacco, attitudes toward tobacco use changed. Since the 1960s men have greatly reduced their consumption of cigarettes. Today, women are almost as likely to smoke as men, and an increasing number of teenagers also smoke cigarettes.

Prevalence rates for smoking among young people remain especially high, despite the proven health risks associated with smoking. Tobacco has long been the drug of choice for high school students—the substance that they use most commonly. In 2000, 25 per cent of Canadian teens aged 15 to 19 were smokers, down from the 28 per cent reported in the Canadian Tobacco Use Monitoring Survey (CTUMS) results from 1999 (Health Canada, 2001a). Unlike with alcohol and other drugs, the possible harms associated with cigarettes are not as imminent. Therefore, it's possible to fail school because of cocaine or heroin use or to crash a car while drunk—these effects are immediate; but getting cancer from smoking or suffering from receding gums takes years. Most youth believe that they will quit smoking before they ever begin to feel its negative effects. There is no 'war on drugs' aimed at cigarettes because for generations cigarette smoking has been a mainstream cultural habit, and it continues to support a billion-dollar industry. The largest Canadian tobacco company, Imperial Tobacco, earned about $900 million in 2000. If smoking were illegal, (legal) tobacco profits would fall. Smokers would use illegal means to get their cigarettes; organized crime would move into marketing cigarettes.

Attitudes to drug users

Despite a large volume of medical and social research showing that the use of illicit narcotics is far less costly in physical and social terms than nicotine or alcohol, the public continues to view illicit drugs—such as marijuana, cocaine, or heroin—as vastly more dangerous than these more common, legal substances. This popular perception of danger surrounding illegal drugs influences the way people view drug users; it affects the acceptability of drug users within the community—even of users who are in treatment or who have recovered. Ironically, many people can entertain both concepts of addiction—that it's immoral and that it's disease-based—at the same time.

On the whole, societal conceptions of drug addiction and drug addicts remain, as they were in previous eras, very negative. New to this era, however, is a wider public support for treatment programs—a direct consequence of the new medical discourse about drugs. Yet, while there is evidence of general support for the treatment of addicts, many members of the public are unwilling to see treatment facilities be constructed nearby.

People who hold conservative political attitudes or have authoritarian personalities are most likely to condemn recovering drug users and oppose treatment facilities in their neighbourhood. Other factors affecting the exclusion of recovering users—the so-called NIMBY (Not In My Back Yard) process—include a fear of declining property values, philosophical opposition to treatment methods, objections to a lack of involvement in the planning stage, a resentment of the profits of private hospitals, and political grandstanding by politicians who seize upon the issue to further their own interests.

The Activities and Characteristics of Substance Abusers

Tobacco

As we have said, tobacco is one of Canada's most popular legal drugs. Like alcohol, nicotine is a psychoactive substance that is to blame for many health problems. In 1999, according to Statistics Canada, 27 per cent of men and 23 per cent of women smoked in Canada. The active drug, nicotine, can enter the body in various ways. Nicotine is readily absorbed from tobacco smoke in the lungs, and it does not matter whether the tobacco smoke is from cigarettes, cigars, or pipes. People also readily

absorb nicotine when they chew tobacco, though chewing tobacco is much less popular than it was a century ago.

Risks associated with smoking cigarettes include a reduced sense of smell and taste, frequent colds, smoker's cough, gastric ulcers, chronic bronchitis, increase in heart rate and blood pressure, heart disease, stroke, and cancer. Research shows that cigarette smoking is the largest cause of preventable disease and premature death. Male and female smokers lose an average of 13.2 and 14.5 years of life respectively (NVSR, 2001). Researchers argue that smoking is most dangerous for teens, because their bodies are still developing and changing. The many chemicals in cigarette smoke can adversely affect this development process.

Increasingly, as people become aware of the health hazards associated with smoking and place bans on smoking in public places, smoking is regarded as a more deviant activity and smokers are more stigmatized. Today, people are more likely than in the past to form judgments about the social, psychological, or moral stability of smokers, who are visibly and intentionally acting against their own best interests. Further, society has started expressing disapproval of the fact that by inflicting dangerous second hand smoke on their family and friends, smokers are also thoughtlessly harming others.

Alcohol

Like most other drugs, alcohol is not bad when used moderately and responsibly. People of all nationalities and cultures have used it for millennia. Figure 5.2 provides statistics for Canadian alcohol consumption. People drink alcohol to achieve its chemical effects: to relax, smooth social events, reduce tension, and slow down perceptual, cognitive, and motor functioning. The goal of drinking then, is to escape from the speed, boredom, stress, or frustration of everyday life, and often, to do so in the company of others, as part of a shared, sociable haze. It becomes problematic only when drinking becomes excessive.

Figure 5.2 Absolute Alcohol Consumption per Capita, Canada, 1988–2001

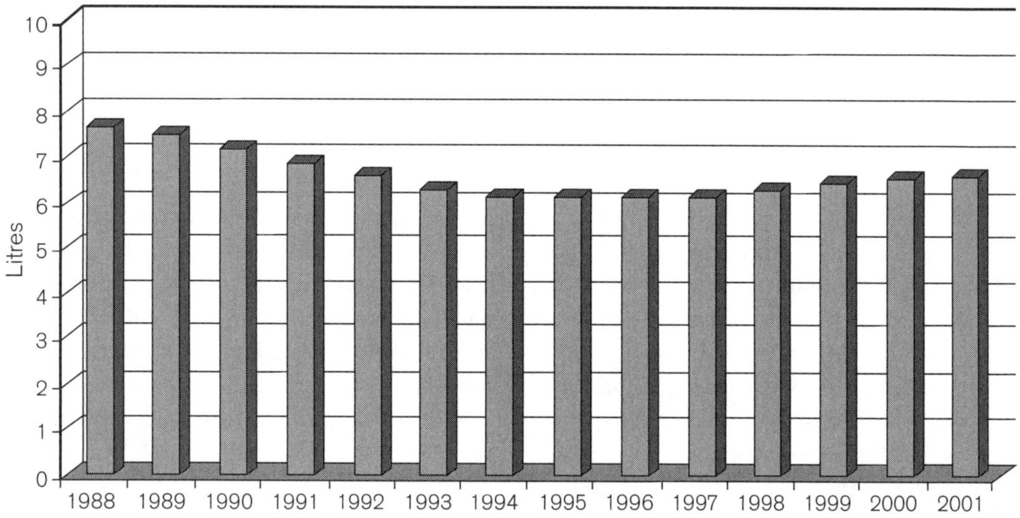

Note: The consumption figures are based on total population. Declared or undeclared alcohol brought across the border, and home or assisted production of beer (u-brews) and wine (u-vins) are not included.

SOURCE: Brewers Association of Canada, *Annual Statistical Bulletin 2001* (Ottawa: Brewers Association of Canada, 2002), 39.

Alcohol impairs judgment. It reduces sexual and other inhibitions. A combination of drinking and driving is the greatest challenge for our governments to solve. In 1999, researchers estimated that motor vehicle crashes killed 3,315 individuals in Canada. MADD Canada estimates that a minimum 1,247 of these fatalities involved impaired driving. Young men are the most extreme and the most variable in their drinking.

Marijuana

Marijuana is the most widely used illicit drug in North America, and likely the first illegal drug that teenagers will use. The short-term effects of using marijuana include sleepiness, difficulty keeping track of time, reduced short-term memory, a diminished ability to do tasks requiring concentration and coordination, increased heart rate paranoia, hallucinations, and decreased social inhibitions. The long-term effects may include enhanced cancer risk and a decrease in testosterone levels for men,

lower sperm counts and difficulty having children, an increased risk of infertility for women, and (for both men and women) diminished sexual pleasure and psychological dependence requiring more of the drug to get the same effect.

Juristat reported that in 2002 rates per 100,000 population for drug-related violations—mainly, cannabis possession—were highest for individuals between the ages of 18 and 24, followed by 12 to 17 year olds. The highest rates of drug offences were reported in British Columbia, Saskatchewan, and New Brunswick. Consequently, in 2001–2 drug offences represented 9 per cent of all adult criminal court cases (of which 5 per cent were for possession and 4 per cent for trafficking). In youth courts, drug offences accounted for 7 per cent of cases (of which 5 per cent were for possession and 2 per cent for trafficking) (Desjardins and Hotton, 2004).

Many critics worry about marijuana's role as a potential gateway drug—that is, as a drug that leads to the use of 'harder' drugs, such as cocaine or heroin. However, for social and psychological reasons, people who are willing to try one type of drug may already be likely to try another drug. So, it is not the drug itself that causes further drug use. This process of 'adverse selectivity' disappears when large numbers of people are using marijuana. Therefore, no particular gateway is needed.

Cocaine

Cocaine is an inhaled stimulant and has been used for centuries for religious, social, and medicinal purposes. Cocaine belongs to the class of drugs known as stimulants, which give the user a temporary illusion of limitless power and energy and leaves the user feeling depressed, edgy, and craving more. The substance called crack cocaine is a chemically altered form of cocaine that is smoked by users.

For some, cocaine is highly addictive and may come to control every aspect of the regular user's life. However, there is much debate whether cocaine is widely addictive. Cheung, Erickson, and Landau (1991) found that many have succeeded in using the drug only as an occasional recreation. While users do seek a quick and intense high from cocaine, most of them exercise caution, fearing addiction and the accompanying adverse consequences. Perceived risk of harm is the major factor that affects level of use.

Urban blacks were the first main users of crack cocaine in the United States. The demonization of cocaine in America coincided with a wave of repressive measures aimed at subordinating blacks during a period of urban protest (Giffen, Endicott, and Lambert, 1991). By contrast, cocaine use has been less widespread, contentious, or racially segregated in Canada. Less than 1 per cent of the population in Canada uses cocaine regularly. As with most other drugs, Canadian men are more likely than Canadian women to be users (Health Canada, 1999a).

Drugs—even powder and crack cocaine—are used differently according to socioeconomic background. In the Netherlands, for example, middle-class 'party youth' use the drugs in clubs and discotheques—occasionally, for recreational purposes. Deprived 'problem youth', from minority backgrounds, add the drugs to already troubled multiproblem behaviour in their marginalized lifestyles (Nabben and Korf, 1999). This shows that the problem to be solved is not drug use but deprivation.

Heroin

Heroin is the most commonly injected drug in Canada for recreational use, although, again, only a small fraction of the population reports using it. Heroin works fast, making it particularly addictive. Right after an injection, heroin enters the brain through the bloodstreatm. Once in the brain, it changes to morphine and binds rapidly to opioid receptors. As a result, users typically report feeling a surge of pleasure, commonly called a 'rush'. The intensity of this rush depends on how much of the drug is taken and how fast the drug enters the brain.

Tolerance to the drug develops with regular heroin use, meaning that the user must inject increasingly more of the substance to achieve the same intensity or effect. In time, physical dependence and addiction increase until a user can no longer control desire and need. Withdrawal symptoms will occur if the user reduces or stops using the drug. Sudden withdrawal by a heavily dependent user in poor health can be fatal.

Drug-using Communities and Cultures

As we have emphasized repeatedly, drugs can be a means of cultural or subcultural expression. For example, in the rave subculture the drug Ecstasy represents a way of bringing members of the subculture together through an understanding of shared symbols and coded messages related to the drug, as well as an expression of their philosophy of life.

Drugs are also part of our cultural consciousness because of the numerous references to them in the media. Drug references appear in movies that try to discourage drug use as well as in movies that celebrate drug culture. Even some children's movies and books contain references to intoxication. The abuse of substances by celebrities is constantly discussed and monitored in the media. Music videos contain endless drug references. Posters of 'drug heroes'— music idols, celebrities, or movie characters using drugs—are readily available. Numerous commercials contain drug references, symbols, or lingo associated with the drug culture since such lingo is associated by teens with 'being cool'. Magazines celebrating drug culture, such as *High Times*, are available in all corner stores. Hemp, from which marijuana derives, is celebrated for its medicinal benefits and it is used in clothing and numerous accessories.

In short, we are quite confused about whether to damn drugs or glorify them. Some drug paraphernalia (e.g., water pipes) are legally sold in stores on Main Street, but the drugs themselves cannot be. Teens form subcultures around these media symbols, just as they form them around designer clothing and other consumer items. For teens, drugs, cigarettes, and alcohol are just a few of the symbols of what it means to be 'cool'—a way of gaining acceptance in certain peer groups. They perceive smoking to be sociable, pleasurable, and empowering. This is why quitting drugs (or cigarettes or alcohol) means more than simply going through physical withdrawal. It means losing membership in a subculture, giving up its rituals (of smoking or drinking), and having to reject that subculture's norms and values.

Drug-using communities are particularly interesting to sociologists for a variety of reasons. First, community members may lead lives that are unusual, dangerous, and secretive, especially if they are committing criminal acts in order to get and use the drugs. They may also develop distinctive practices, customs, terminology, and safety and support systems. The more dangerous or hard-to-get the drug is, the more restrictive and mysterious the associated community is. As a result, the communities of heroin or cocaine users are somewhat more unusual and distinctive than those of marijuana users, which, in turn, are more unusual and distinc-

tive than those of alcohol or tobacco users.

Second, in the process of getting and using drugs, community members need to learn the skills for operating the relevant paraphernalia. Hard-drug users need to know where to get the drugs, drug pipes, needles, and other equipment. They need to know how to smoke, ingest, or inject the drug, to get a desired but non-lethal effect. Finally, they need to know how to appreciate and monitor the effects of the drug.

As we mentioned earlier, research by Howard Becker (1953) provided valuable insight into how new marijuana smokers learn to sense and enjoy the effects of the drug. Becker claimed that, without the appropriate knowledge, the effects of marijuana might pass unnoticed or cause feelings of fear and discomfort. Becker believed, then, that people have to learn to enjoy marijuana. Also, the careers of marijuana users—as opposed to the careers of those using harder drugs such as cocaine, heroin, and methamphetamine—suggest that marijuana is easier to integrate successfully into a lifestyle that can reasonably be described as normal or conventional. There are risks to its overuse, but they are not any more harmful than other substances our society considers acceptable.

Drug users, like other deviants, have a deviant lifestyle that may amount to a 'career' in deviance. Like any career, a drug-using career is made up of progressive stages of deeper involvement in the main (deviant) activity, the relevant community, and its subculture. The sociological notions of deviant career, community, and subculture are valuable additions to our understanding of drug use because they direct our attention away from individual behaviours and psychological explanations, towards collective behaviours and social explanations.

Where communities and cultures exist, they lend support to individual desires to use drugs or commit other deviant acts. Psychological or individual explanations of drug use become less useful when a full-fledged community and subculture are in existence. Some urban sociologists have also noted that there is a particular geography to drug use, and other deviant and criminal activities. Certain parts of a city are more likely than others to contain places and people who can supply drugs, paraphernalia, and expert knowledge. One researcher called these parts of a city 'deviant service centres', since a variety of deviant needs and tastes can typically be satisfied in these areas (including drugs, prostitution, gambling, and otherwise.).

Theories of Drug and Alcohol Abuse

Psychological theories attempt to explain drug use or addiction in terms of personality or social-psychological factors. They recognize that drugs and alcohol give people experiences they find pleasurable and necessary. For example, people who feel uncomfortable at parties may find that alcohol, marijuana, or a depressant relaxes them enough that they can talk, dance, and enjoy themselves.

Psychological theories focus on personality types that are most susceptible to this use of drugs as a stress reliever. For example, one psychological theory focuses on 'inadequate personalities', arguing that some people use drugs to help them cope with their emotional and physical defects. Drugs and alcohol are their means of escaping an everyday life that they find unbearable. This use of drugs, however, further weakens their ego strength, or personal ability to cope with crises. Each time a user relies on drugs to relieve tension and feel good about himself, he becomes a little less able to cope on his own. As a result, the user increases both the frequency of drug use and the variety of situations in which he uses drugs.

An alternative theory, *problem behaviour proneness*, argues that drug users and abusers are people who are typically rebellious, pleasure-seeking, and tolerant of deviance in others. These people, because of their risk-taking personalities, are most prone to becoming abusers of drugs and alcohol. Finally, a psychological *theory of euphoria-seekers* suggests that some people are motivated by the frequent need for intense pleasure.

The shortcoming of these theories, as with other psychological theories, is that they do not take social, cultural, or situational factors into account. Drug use, then, is not situational—it is portable. People abuse drugs precisely because they are likely to use drugs outside of socially acceptable situations, or use them to excess when possible. This is the point Howard Becker was making: though personalities don't change much over the lifespan, people's drug-using behaviour does change, as people pass through different groups, roles, and situations.

Sociological Theories

Sociological theories, accordingly, focus on the social and situational factors that increase people's likelihood to use drugs and alcohol, or to use them to excess. These theories proceed from the assumption that anyone could be a drug (or alcohol) user, or addict, under the right social circumstances.

Functionalist perspective

Functionalist theories argue that alcohol and drug abuse, like many social problems, stem from the way the social structure influences each individual. Functionalists theorize that drug and alcohol users are common because these substances fulfill an important social function: namely, they increase social cohesion.

Drinking and drug-using rituals give people in general—and particularly, members of deviant or excluded communities—a powerful sense of belonging. People use drugs to gain and retain membership in highly cohesive social groups. Even smoking cigarettes has this effect. Ashton (2003) suggests that because the results of smoking at first are unpleasant (dizziness and nausea), smoking must present an advantage to the smoker; socialization is one of the advantages. Ashton argues that as smoking continues, the effects of nicotine begin to overlap with social factors in reinforcing the behaviour. The smoker then learns to appreciate the rewarding effects of nicotine as he or she develops tolerance to its unpleasant effects.

Social disorganization theory, another functionalist approach, argues that drug and alcohol use increase when institutions that have traditionally acted to discourage deviant behaviours become less effective during times of rapid social change. Norms and values become unclear because of these rapid changes and people turn to deviant behaviour: here, alcohol and drugs. In short, people use and abuse drugs when norms prohibiting this break down and when the societal climate is filled with anxiety and uncertainty.

We can easily apply this perspective to the Canadian Aboriginal population and its problem with addictive substances, especially alcohol. For centuries after arriving in North America, Aboriginal peoples lived in many small communities or bands that varied widely but that had certain features in common. Despite differences in language and culture, the Native communities were all highly cohesive. A strong sense of community and the presence of moral custodians who stood guard over the group's traditions promoted the sharing of moral values.

With the arrival of European immigrants in the nineteenth and twentieth centuries, alcohol abuse and suicide spread among Aboriginal peoples. These problems were compounded by racism, poverty, and residential schooling. Few methods worked to stem this substance abuse problem, because they did not address the issue of social disorganization: the loss of traditional controls and values. In short, interaction with white society broke down traditional tribal societies, deprived Aboriginal peoples and individuals of a sense of meaning, and destroyed the ability of family, community, and religion to control people's actions.

According to this theory, alcohol abuse was a result of all these factors. Additionally, evidence suggests that Aboriginal people were less able than Europeans to metabolize alcohol effectively, leading to more drunkenness. The method of treatment that has worked best to control alcohol abuse has included addiction counselling by other Native people and the recovery of Native traditions. Sharing Aboriginal experiences, relearning the traditional culture, and practicing Aboriginal rituals all help Aboriginal addicts. With the reversal of social disorganization, alcohol abuse begins to subside.

A third functional theory of drug abuse focuses on the problematic gap between cultural goals and institutional means for satisfying these goals. According to Merton's (1957 [1938]) *theory of anomie*, the cause of excessive drinking and other substance abuse lies not in an absence of values and institutions but in the conflict between them. According to this theory, excessive drinking is driven by the gap between culturally defined goals and socially approved means for attaining those goals. Alcohol and drug abuse are adaptations to anomie.

The characteristics of capitalist society make excess drug use a necessary adaptation for some people. From society's standpoint, drug use is a functional adaptation. It allows social inequality under capitalism to persist, since instead of rebelling, many people dull the pain of disappointment with drugs or alcohol. People who retreat into drugs and alcohol are blamed for their own weakness and failure; this protects the social system from being blamed.

Merton's theory has strengths, but it has evident weaknesses as well. It explains why people drink too much in the United States or other capitalist societies, but not why they also drank too much in, say, Soviet Russia. Moreover, the use of drugs and alcohol is not merely an individual adaptation to anomie; it is socially organized. Alcohol and drug use vary widely by class and geography. For example, marijuana use by racial minority youth follows ecological patterns that are rooted in community, institutional, and personal networks (Brunswick, 1999).

Anomie theory is primarily useful in explaining drug abuse by the 'underclass' as an adaptation to impoverished community-level conditions—for example, poverty, unemployment, and other measures of social breakdown—among minority-group people. It cannot explain the drug-using behaviour of majority-group people who live in stable or affluent communities. To account for their drug use (and abuse), researchers often have to focus on household level explanations, such as family conflict (Covington, 1997).

Conflict theories

Alcohol and drug use affects different socioeconomic groups differently. For this and other reasons, conflict theorists focus on variations among drug and alcohol users, asking who is benefited and who is harmed by drug and alcohol usage. In particular, conflict theorists focus on the criminalization process. They note that in a capitalist economic system, the powerful members of society are in a position to define whether a substance is legal or illegal. The powerful are able to criminalize drug use by the powerless. Moreover, they are in a position to benefit from drug use at the same time as they may disavow it.

Moreover, some people benefit more from drug sales, and drug laws, than others. Alcohol and tobacco, for example, are drugs that are produced and sold by the wealthy and powerful. Both of these industries are regulated but are not considered illegal. Both profit the rich stockholders of alcohol and cigarette companies while harming the heavy users, who are often poor.

Enforcing the laws on alcohol cost Canadians $1.36 billion, while law enforcement activities to control illegal drugs cost only $400 million (Single et al., 1996). Canadian taxpayers indirectly finance the vacation homes of cigarette and alcohol magnates (such as the Bronfman family) while directly paying for lung cancer and heart treatments in working-class communities.

Some substances are banned not only because of their harmful pharmacological properties, but also for social and political reasons. Consider two examples: opium in Canada and marijuana in the United States. The Chinese brought opium to Canada, as well as their fondness for opium smoking to ease the pains of their meagre existence working

for low wages in dangerous jobs. The law offered no objections to either producing or possessing opium at that time. Subsequently, people came to feel that foreigners should be driven out of the country so that American-born labourers could take their jobs. At the time, the laws against opium and marijuana use were biased against racial minorities and poor people, and indirectly benefited prosperous white people.

Since the 1960s, when these laws threatened to penalize college-aged children of the white middle class, police and courts markedly weakened enforcement of the laws. Efforts have often been made to suppress the drinking and drug use of subordinate people. Schwartz (2000) notes that moral reformers in the nineteenth and twentieth centuries tried to fight urban poverty by instilling traditional values—such as hard work, sobriety, frugality, and family responsibility—in the poor population.

In the late-eighteenth and early-nineteenth century, Montreal's justices of the peace took a different and more direct approach: they designed police regulations regarding vagrancy to include licensed begging as a form of social welfare for the respectable poor (Poutanen, 2002). Vagrant men and women deemed unworthy of state-sanctioned begging were apprehended and punished in the House of Correction or Common Gaol.

Drug laws have often been forced on subject populations—whether teenagers, women, poor people, or conquered peoples. Foreign missionaries, for example, disapproved of the drug use (and other rituals) of many colonized peoples. Brown (2003) reports that the imposition of Western law in Hawaii extended new regulations and controls on the colonized Native Hawaiians. A primary focus was the control of drinking and the native intoxicant 'awa'. In general, efforts to attack drug use by colonized or subordinate peoples have focused on the wickedness, danger, or unhealthiness of drug use.

Symbolic interactionism

Issues of labelling and its consequences are very important to symbolic interactionists. They also focus on the social meanings people associate with alcohol and drug use and the labels they attach to others who use drugs.

Like conflict theorists, symbolic interactionists are interested in seeing which kind of people are labelled deviant, and why. Consider drinking as an example; almost everyone drinks alcohol at some time or another, and few are labelled 'problem drinkers'. Friendly social drinking is the code of the modern, advanced capitalist society. Often, we even link enjoyment and relaxation to drinking alcohol and getting drunk. Yet, we stigmatize and stereotype heavy drinkers in our society. We label some heavy drinkers 'alcoholics' and hold various beliefs about people labelled alcoholics. Likewise, many believe that heavy drinkers or alcoholics have a history of prior emotional difficulties—for example, an unhappy marriage—that explains their drinking pattern.

Symbolic interactionists, through a branch of study called 'social constructionism', are also interested in the processes by which moralistic conceptions attach themselves to social behaviours such as drinking. As mentioned earlier, sociologist Joseph Gusfield (1963) studied the 'symbolic crusade' that led to Prohibition in the United States. This study provides a good example of the social construction of deviant behaviour that benefits one group more than another. Prohibition consisted of a ban, from 1920 to 1933, on the sale and public use of alcohol in the United States.

The clash between drinkers and abstainers dramatized a deep conflict in American society. Between 1880 and 1920, the United States changed from a rural, small-town society to an urban, industrial power. During that time, huge numbers of immigrants poured into American cities. They shifted economic and political control of American society away from the native-born, white Protestant, small-town middle class, which had run the United States up through the nineteenth century. Symbolically, the attempt to impose temperance through Prohibition was a bid to turn the clock

back to a time when the United States was a uniform society dominated by middle-class Protestants. This historical episode suggests that societies seemingly plagued by deviance may actually suffer from too many rules.

In the social construction and transformation of views on substance abuse, we often find a transition from ignoring the behaviour, to considering it immoral, and then to considering it a medical or psychological problem. This last stage is usually called the 'medicalization of deviance'. In respect to the use of 'speed', Sato (1996) notes six 'medicalization of deviance' phases: (1) definition, characterized by alleged abuse of speed by those thought by the medical profession to be immoral; (2) prospecting, characterized by discovery and increasing interest among the medical community in the intoxication potential of speed; (3) claims making, characterized by increasing claims by different segments of the medical community that use of speed is a social problem and should be controlled or prohibited; (4) legitimacy, characterized by government definition of speed use as a medical problem and regulation of the traffic of speed; (5) institutionalization, characterized by the emergence of law prohibiting speed based largely on medical intoxication, and (6) designation, characterized by stricter legal prohibition of speed use and reform of mental health law to keep speed users off the streets.

As is evident, the medicalization of a social problem involving substances requires the collusion of media, public figures, law-makers, and medical experts.

Feminist approaches

For feminists, patriarchy—or male control—structures the way most societies work. This means, first of all, that women—like other less powerful members of society—will have more reason to drink and use drugs as a form of retreat in the face of anomie. Ironically, then, female alcoholics and drug abusers are less common than male alcoholics and drug abusers. When women do become alcoholics and drug abusers, they are likely to be more disturbed and more deviant than men who are using drugs as much. Likewise, they are more likely than men to encounter a hostile reception from their families and other members of society.

For women, the drugs of choice are more often prescribed tranquilizers. According to one researcher, women use over-the-counter (OTC) drugs more than men do and are twice as likely to be dependent on prescribed psychoactive medications. A survey done in Winnipeg showed that 70 to 90 per cent of all illnesses were not brought to a doctor's attention and were self-treated. Respondents reported that 95 per cent were currently using OTC medication, averaging three remedies in current use. Of these people, 94 per cent found the self-treatment to be effective. This is in part due to the increased medicalization of women's bodies and conditions, such as PMS, pregnancy and childbirth, and menopause, which encourage taking such medications to deal with mood swings caused by hormonal changes in the body.

Where smoking is concerned, women often have different reasons than men for smoking at all. Social factors play an important role in dictating who smokes and it is not merely the nicotine addiction that keeps women smoking. Since social status determines who smokes and who quits more than psychological or physiological makeup does, quitting smoking is far more difficult than merely battling nicotine addiction; it is as though women are being forced to give up a part of their social identity. Research shows that women smoke under different circumstances than men; for example, they are more likely to smoke when they are under emotional pressure, whereas men smoke in more relaxed or neutral circumstances. Women are also much more likely than men to depend on cigarettes to cope with their anger and frustration.

Social influence shapes people's smoking habits. Paradoxically, health care institutions like hospitals clearly illustrate this process. In hospitals, there is not only a division of people according to class and race but also sex. 'Being a women—nurse or otherwise—and working in an environment where all the key decisions are taken by men, can only exacerbate the frustrations and sense of dependence with which most women already grapple elsewhere. Smoking is merely a sign of anger at this subordination' (Jacobson, 1986).

Additionally, girls and women see smoking as a way of losing weight. However, smoking does not help them become slim. It does, however, increase the probability of a heart attack. Women who smoke are at an even greater risk of the disease if they are taking contraceptive pills. 'A woman who smokes and takes the pill is ten times more likely to die of a heart attack or stroke than a non-smoker not taking the pill . . . smoking does not simply add a little to the risk, it *multiplies* it' (Jacobson, 1986).

Greaves's studies (1992) of Canadian and Australian women lead to the following conclusions about the social role of tobacco for women:

- *Organizing social relationships.* Women report using smoking to equalize, bond, distance, defuse, or end relationships with others including partners, children, and workmates.
- *Creating an image.* Women report using smoking to feel independent, different, stylish, accepted and, in a few cases, to stay thin.
- *Controlling emotions.* Women report using smoking to suppress or reduce negative emotions, anesthetize certain feelings or, less frequently, to allow positive emotions to emerge.
- *Building a dependency.* On this theme, women report using smoking as a source of support, predictability, or controllability.
- *Finding an identity.* The women interviewed see their smoking as grounds for guilt, tension, contradiction, and a reason for self-castigation. As a result, the women

reflect on their identity in terms of their smoking.

Greaves sees the social circumstances at the root of women's smoking used in ads to sell cigarettes to women. During the Second World War, for example, smoking represented taking on a male activity for women just as they had with working. After the war, tobacco marketers could not afford to lose these new consumers. Therefore, especially in the 1950s, cigarettes were presented as symbols of sophistication in ads—essential accessories that enhanced a women's beauty while conferring on her a mysterious aura.

In the 1970s, 'a second wave of modern Western feminist movement' capitalized on 'the mood of rebelliousness which was cresting among White middle-class feminists at the time,' again targeting women in their ad campaigns. This time the most successful was Virginia Slims (Greaves, 1996): 'In 1968 Philip Morris launched Virginia Slims, the first ever "all-female" cigarette with the immortal slogan "You've come a long way, baby". . . [T]he beauty of the Virginia Slims woman is that she may have come a long way, baby, but she is still someone's baby.' The slogan refers to the fight for women's rights that was going on at that the time.

Social and Health Consequences of Drug Use

Social consequences
Social attitudes and policy responses depend on the context in which drugs are used. Put another way, drugs sometimes have harmful consequences and sometimes they do not—depending on the circumstances.

Crime and violence
Drug and alcohol abuse are important forms of deviance because they have an indirect link to other forms of deviance such as crime and violence. Most drugs, when used excessively, result in unpredictable and possibly deviant behaviour. Besides crimes associated with growing, processing, and trafficking illegal drugs, there are also crimes associated with drug use, committed by addicts to secure money. Entire deviant subcultures and underground economies survive and thrive on the ability to traffic illegal drugs. Addicts will often turn to crime to support their expensive habit. As tolerance to the drug increases and the addict requires larger and larger doses, the daily cost is more than most can afford. Crimes associated with securing money for drugs most often include theft, robbery, and prostitution.

Drunk driving is also a serious social problem, as we saw in an earlier chapter. Researchers estimate that drunk drivers are involved in more than one-third of the traffic-accident related deaths in North America. Drinking alcohol impairs a wide range of skills that are essential for carrying out these tasks. Moreover, young people are both inexperienced drinkers and drivers, which makes them particularly dangerous drunk drivers.

Juristat reports: '[A]fter a period of decline throughout the 1980s and early 1990s, the rate of police-reported drug offences increased by 42 per cent between 1992 and 2002. In 2002, three in four drug-related incidents involved cannabis offences, most of which were for simple possession.'

Other than for possession, the police report relatively few drug offences. Rates of drug import and production are relatively low, though they have more than doubled since the early 1990s. The rate of trafficking offences, which increased over the period 1977 to 1992, has since declined by 13 per cent. The same source reports: 'Estimates from the 1999 General Social Survey suggest that in half of physical (51 per cent) and sexual (48 per cent) assaults, the victim believes that the incident was related to the perpetrator's use of alcohol or drugs. Between 1992 and 2002, 684 (11 per cent) homicide incidents in Canada were reported to be drug-related.' Of these, 176 (26 per cent) were gang-related. 'Fully half of all homicide incidents in Canada involving heroin (52 per cent) and more than one-fifth (22 per cent) of cocaine-related homicides took place in Vancouver.'

Poverty

Alcohol and drugs give the user a temporary escape from reality. Sometimes substance abuse causes poverty, and at other times, poverty causes substance abuse. In any event, substance abuse worsens the abuser's financial situation. Established drug habits are costly, and many addicts—unless they are gainfully employed—have to resort to prostitution, theft, and robbery to satisfy their habit.

Addicts sometimes also affect the economic well-being of neighbourhoods. Consequences for the neighbourhood may include poverty, social disorganization, homelessness, gang activity, and invasive drug trafficking and distribution systems. The fear of recovering addicts in the community may hinder the process of constructing treatment facilities. This, in turn, slows down the process of providing effective methods of social control for drugs and alcohol and of minimizing their social and health consequences.

Violence

Alcohol abuse is associated with violence, especially domestic violence. Unchecked, domestic violence increases in frequency and severity. Some victims suffer all forms of abuse. Although alcohol and drugs do not cause domestic violence, alcohol abuse is unduly common among dysfunctional families in which violence occurs. According to the Health Canada (2005a) report on family violence and substance abuse, members of families in which one or both parents abuse substances are considered at high risk for physically abusing or neglecting their children. Alcohol acts as a catalyst that ignites violence in an already explosive domestic environment. This violence translates into the physical, emotional, and sexual abuse of spouses and children. Figure 5.3 shows the effects of alcohol abuse on rates of spousal violence. Such violence can lead to family disruption, jail sentences, divorce, and child custody battles.

Other social consequences

The high rate of alcohol and drug use, both legal and illegal, affects many aspects of our social life. Many days of work are lost each year because of excessive use of alcohol or drugs. Other economic costs of drug and alcohol abuse are associated with homelessness, educational and rehabilitation treatment programs, and the medical treatment of drug addicts and of substance-abuse-related injuries and fatalities.

Health Consequences of Alcohol Abuse

Many authorities regard alcohol abuse as one of the major health problems of our time because of its potentially harmful effects on an individual's health, welfare, and happiness.

The amount of alcohol considered excessive varies widely from person to person. For some people, two drinks a day can lead to problems; other people can consume the same amount without any harmful effects. Problems with health can begin when people consume more than two drinks per day, at which point alcohol can disrupt the normal body chemistry. Drinking too much alcohol increases the risk of cancer of the liver, pancreas, mouth, tongue, pharynx, larynx, and esophagus. These risks are even greater for people who also use tobacco products.

Other effects of alcohol may include gastritis (inflammation of the mucous membrane that lines the stomach), pancreatitis (inflammation of the pancreas), peptic ulcer (a raw area in the lining of the gastrointestinal tract), and an increase in blood sugar levels that causes diabetes. Diabetes, in turn, may lead to a variety of other medical problems and risks, including heart disease, kidney disease, circulation problems, injuries from falls, and other accidents.

Besides liver cancer, alcohol may cause fatty liver, hepatitis, cirrhosis, and other liver disease. By disrupting nerve function, alcohol can cause

Table 5.2 Alcohol, Drugs, or Intoxicants Consumed by the Accused in Spousal Homicides, 1979–1998

| Alcohol or substance consumption | Accused | | | | | |
| | Total | | Wife | | Husband | |
	No.	%	No.	%	No.	%
Total	1,732	100	394	100	1,338	100
No alcohol or drugs consumed	924	53	142	36	782	58
Alcohol only	569	33	217	55	352	26
Drugs only	28	2	5	1	23	2
Both alcohol and drugs	63	4	14	4	49	4
Other intoxicating substance	1	nil	1	nil	0	0
Unknown	147	8	15	4	132	10

Percentages may not total 100% due to rounding.

SOURCE: Statistics Canada, *Family Violence in Canada: A Statistical Profile*, Catalogue 85-224-XIE.

Wernicke's encephalopathy, which involves problems with eye movement, speech, and walking; in time, confusion and coma may result. Korsakoff's psychosis, a chronic condition causing short-term memory loss and affecting nerves in the brain and spinal cord, also results from excessive drinking.

Finally, drinking too much alcohol also may contribute to the incidence of high blood pressure (hypertension) and stroke. Alcohol is toxic to heart tissue and can lead to heart muscle disease (cardiomyopathy). Fetal Alcohol Syndrome affects women and their babies when alcohol is used to excess during pregnancy. Drinking may cause developmental disorders in the baby that show up after birth. Women who drink may also be at higher risk of having miscarriages, premature births, stillbirths, and low-birthweight babies. Finally, psychiatric and emotional problems associated with drinking can include anxiety, depression, confusion, and addiction.

Smoking

Tobacco has rightly been under heavy attack as a major contributor to a wide array of health difficulties. However, people rarely consider it one of our greatest drug problems. This failure to treat tobacco use as a drug problem is even more amazing when we survey the social and legal upheaval surrounding marijuana. Lifelong abstinence and avoidance of second-hand smoke are the only proven ways to avoid health risks from tobacco use. Cessation—even after many years of smoking—reduces risk and harm for many tobacco-related conditions, such as chronic breathing difficulties, cancer, and stroke.

Cigarette smoke contains hundreds of substances. Carbon monoxide and tars, as well as nicotine, are the prime producers of the harmful effects. The carbon monoxide combines with hemoglobin in the blood, displacing oxygen and making the blood less able to deliver needed oxygen to tissues throughout the body. The tars contain carcinogens, or cancer-producing substances. Nicotine, besides being the drug that causes addiction, also raises the LDL cholesterol (bad cholesterol) and lowers the HDL cholesterol (good cholesterol) levels, increasing the risk of atherosclerosis and cardiovascular disease.

Smoking is often considered an individual habit, an act of rebellion, personal indulgence, or addiction. Researchers know that young people are more likely to develop a smoking habit if at least one of their parents, siblings, or friends also smoke (Horn et al., 2000; Bewley and Bland, 1977). Conversely, parents who warn their children about the dangers of smoking help their children to avoid cigarettes in the future. Studies have shown that people whose parents actively discouraged them from smoking were less likely to experiment with tobacco products (Gittlesohn et al., 2001; Ary et al., 1999), even if the parents were smokers themselves (Henriksen and Jackson, 1998). Family conflict also increases the likelihood of adolescent cigarette experimentation (Horn et al., 2000).

Likewise, family members who smoke are less likely to quit if other people in the household continue to smoke, and if they do quit, are more liable to relapse (Mermelstein et al., 1986). In a study of how family members talk about health issues, Lloyd and her colleagues (1998) reported that even family members who smoke generally characterize the practice as a bad habit.

The non-smoker/smoker relationship can exist between parents/children or children/parents, suggesting that it is also common for children to try to influence their parents' health behaviours. Marijuana use also causes concern about adverse health effects, in part because so many marijuana users are young. Many of these harmful effects are similar to those associated with smoking, and include inflammation of the throat, sinuses, and airways, increased risk of lung cancer, decreased sperm count, heart pain, and suppressed immunity. Some researchers say that heavy, long-term use of marijuana produces a loss of motivation, including loss of energy, apathy, absence of ambition, inability to carry out long-term plans, and a marked decline in school performance.

Cocaine

Many health consequences of cocaine abuse are related to the means of administration. Smoking cocaine affects primarily the lungs, causing chronic cough, bronchitis, impaired lung function, and excessive fluid in the lungs.

Heroin

The two major health consequences of heroin abuse are infections and overdoses. Infections from heroin injection include cellulites, heart and vein infections, brain and lung abscesses, hepatitis B, and AIDS. Other effects of heroin use include a decreased sexual desire, amenorrhea, and chronic constipation. These symptoms disappear when heroin use stops.

Overall

Because drugs are psychoactive—they change people's consciousness—and they are at least potentially addictive, they are liable to harm people, especially people who are already unstable or socially vulnerable. Consider the effects on the children or families of addicts. Children who witness alcohol or drug use are more likely to use these drugs themselves. Also because their parents are intoxicated, they might not be able to properly socialize and educate their children. Children who live in households where drugs or alcohol are used are more likely to be victims of abuse. For the family, substance use by a member means loss of income, stress, and worrying about the well-being of this person; these factors can result in family breakup.

Studies also reveal that the use of drugs and alcohol can increase the likelihood of unplanned and unsafe intercourse among teens. For example, 68 per cent of males and 61.5 per cent of females reported engaging in unplanned sexual intercourse; 40.9 per cent of males and 32.1 per cent of females reported having more than one sexual partner; and 49.9 per cent of males and 64.1 per cent of females reported inconsistent condom use while intoxicated.

We will discuss the risky teen behaviours associated with alcohol and drug use in Chapter 6.

Policy and Theory Applications

Considerable disagreement surrounds different strategies for 'curing' substance abuse. Swora (2001) reports that Alcoholics Anonymous (AA) is the most successful of all addiction treatment processes, the paradigm for all other programs. AA views the alcoholic as a kind of person, or agent-in-society, and a member of a moral community. Conceptualizing alcoholism as a 'disease' works to create a sense of kinship among AA members. Sobriety is shown to be more than abstinence from the beverage alcohol, and abstinence is itself value-bearing, meaningful conduct. AA does not 'treat' the suffering alcoholic self, but rather the self-centred alcoholic person.

At AA, the common-sense understanding of 'alcoholics' changes to a disease model where they are no longer considered moral outcasts, but sick people. This resulted in the introduction of drug treatment courts such as the one that began in Canada in December 1998 and sentences addicts to rehabilitation treatment rather than incarceration. Both understandings of alcoholics may have detrimental effects: (1) the moral outcast model engenders a representation where alcoholics are unlikely to admit their condition; and (2) the disease model promotes the idea that alcoholics sober up only if they go to a treatment centre. Statistics on low recovery rates in Alcoholics Anonymous and treatment programs show that this is far from the case (Smyth, 1998).

Atkins (2000) notes that the founders of AA created a recovery program based on religious tenets and couched in the scientific ideology of addiction as disease. Today, virtually every treatment centre in the United States uses the AA 12-Step approach. In recent years, however, several alternative recovery movements have challenged this near-total institutionalization of the 12-Step Program in American addiction care. Challengers argue with the religious basis of the treatment and, in some instances, even dispute the concept of addiction as disease.

Therapists and policy-makers have taken many different approaches to reduce the impact and incidence of drug-related problems in our society. Some initiatives are directed at reducing the demand for dangerous substances. Strategies to reduce the demand include drug education, which primarily aims to reduce and delay initiation into drug use

and prevent the transition to regular use. They also include treatment programs directed at drug users.

Preventive strategies aim at delaying the onset of drug use and preventing the transition from initial use to regular use to abuse and dependence. Drug education, in its widest sense, aims to change beliefs, expectations, norms, values, and behaviours in ways that reduce drug use and drug-related harm. Spending money on drug education programs in schools is one of the most effective things a government can do to reduce drug use. After all, there is no other place in our society with such a large, well-organized captive audience. Many schools and local communities have also developed strategies to prevent or reduce alcohol, drug, and tobacco use among youth. Often, they design such strategies to strengthen existing positive (anti-drug) peer interactions and social networks (Vander Waal et al., 2003). As we will see in the next chapter, the teen years are high-risk years, so school programs for adolescents put the most intensive efforts into drug-education where we most urgently need them.

One approach to ending substance abuse is to limit the supply of drugs. Industrialization and development bring with them increased demands for attention and sobriety, for example, in motorized traffic and on the production line, which increased drinking may undermine. Decisions by international development agencies on investment in alcohol production and distribution should take account of both the positive and negative impacts on economic development as well as on public health.

A debate continues as to whether it is necessary to reduce the total amount of drug intake in society in order to target, control, and help the few who abuse drugs and alcohol. For this purpose, we need to be clearer on whether to target mainly moderate users in high-risk situations, or heavy users in normal situations.

Skog (1999) points out that the contribution of heavy and moderate drinkers, respectively, to the rate of alcohol problems in society must be evaluated for different types of risk functions. Mediterranean and

Table 5.3 Illegal Drug Use and Crime: A Complex Relationship Number of Police-Reported Incidents by Type of Drug Used, Canada, 1996–2000

	1996	1997	1998	1999	2000
Marijuana	47,234	47,933	50,917	60,011	66,171
Cocaine	11,478	11,468	12,183	11,963	12,812
Heroin	1,287	1,235	1,323	1,323	1,226
Other drugs*	5,730	5,957	6,509	6,845	7,736
Total	**65,729**	**66,593**	**70,922**	**80,142**	**87,945**

* 'Other drugs' include other illegal substances such as PCP, LSD, and Ecstasy as well as controlled substances such as barbiturates and anabolic steroids.

SOURCE: R. Logan, 'Crime Statistics in Canada, 2000', (2001), *Juristat*, Volume 21, Number 8, Catalogue 85-002-XIE (Ottawa: Canadian Centre for Justice Statistics), p. 11. Prepared for the Senate Special Committee on Illegal Drugs by Lyne Casavant and Chantal Collin, Political and Social Affairs Division.

Northern drinking styles produce different patterns of social and personal risk, for example. If the risk function is linear, moderate drinkers will be responsible for the bulk of the problems. When the risk function is curved upwards—that is, you must drink quite a lot on one occasion before you produce harm—the heavy drinkers contribute to a large share of the problem. Most accidents and aggressive outbursts seem to fulfill the latter qualification, because the causal mechanisms underlying such problems are connected to rates of acute intoxication, rather than to annual intake per se.

Legal restrictions on the sale and purchase of drugs, criminal sanctions, and law enforcement activities such as crop eradication and prohibition are designed to limit the availability of drugs. However, new techniques in chemistry and biology have created potential new drug problems at the same time as we are struggling to control old ones. With recent revolutionary developments in science, technology has made it possible to engineer recreational drugs. These advancements in technology make it hard to say that drug use and abuse will reduce in the future. With the elimination of some drugs, other ones will be engineered and used.

Likely, we will never be rid of recreational drugs. For this reason, it may be more prudent to adopt 'harm reduction' strategies that oversee and regulate

drug use—for example, providing quality and price control. Most arguments that support legalizing recreational drugs such as marijuana emphasize the practical benefits of legalization or the harm done by failing to legalize these drugs. They note that, to a large degree, current laws do not work. Laws aimed at preventing drug use have no effect and drug use is widespread. There is no sign that use is declining, or that stiff penalties control people's behaviour. No consensus exists among drug enforcement critics except that criminal sanctions do not affect drug use and attempts to control illegal drug use by law enforcement strategies regularly fail. Thus, a great deal of money spent on drug law enforcement is wasted.

Preventing people from starting a deviant career is usually easier than curing or rehabilitating them afterwards. Instead of spending money to arrest and convict drug users, we should work at learning how to reduce people's need or desire to use drugs. We should also educate people about the social, economic, and health costs of using recreational drugs. For the most part, recreational drugs are not a problem; crime is the problem to be solved. The public concern about drugs is really a concern about crime—the production, sale, purchase, and possession of illegal drugs, the commission of crimes to purchase illegal drugs, the commission of crimes while under the influence of drugs, and the violent and corrupt behaviour of drug traffickers. A related anxiety has to do with drug addiction. However, the most popular recreational drugs—marijuana and hashish—are not physically addictive and do not drive people to commit crimes.

Decriminalization and Legalization

In Canada, despite a long history of empirical research pointing away from aggressive criminalization, the most recent law (the *Controlled Drugs and Substances Act*, May 1997) affirms both the seriously deviant status of illicit drug users and the primacy of the criminal justice model over the public health and social justice alternatives (Erickson, 1998). Many Canadians believe it is time to change the law where soft drugs are concerned.

However, it is important to distinguish between two alternative ways of dealing with recreational drugs such as marijuana. One is decriminalization and the other is legalization. *Decriminalization* means taking laws against both marijuana possession and use off the *Criminal Code*: that is, eliminating all current penalties. *Legalization* means taking state control of the sale of these substances, as well as eliminating penalties for possession and use.

Legalization, which would allow the state to tax sales of the drug, would normally entail setting and enforcing quality standards, as the state does with other foods and drugs. While both strategies could be considered forms of harm reduction strategy, the most good would be done by the second approach because it would eliminate a criminal drug trade and ensure safe drugs for consumers. This is perhaps why the Canadian strategy of risk (or harm) reduction regarding marijuana is not very successful. Possessing marijuana is still illegal, although medical use of marijuana might have been decriminalized and thus illegal drug trafficking, with all the dangers involved, persists. Table 5.3 shows the number of drug-related crimes reported by police in Canada from 1996 to 2000.

All we know for certain is that wars on drugs—including Temperance and Prohibition movements—tend to fail, often with disastrous consequences. Alvarez (1995), writing about Latin America, argues that conservative policies against drug dealing have had negative effects on society. Drug dealing is an economic process with production, distribution, and consumption phases like any other commodity. Prohibition allows drug traffickers to create artificial monopolies, raising prices and creating the drug dealer-consumer as a fundamental element in assuring that millions of dollars in profit go to drug lords and intermediaries.

The long 'war on drugs' in the United States has failed: the availability and use of drugs has not decreased, incarceration rates have tripled since 1980, opportunities for corrupt government officials and local police departments to benefit have been opened up, and whole economies of certain countries have become drug-dependent. Additionally, the war on drugs undermines civil rights and appears to be a war on people of colour. Chambliss (1995) likewise notes that research from other countries experimenting with decriminalization shows that the legalization of possession of marijuana and small amounts of other drugs does not lead to increases in usage, and that drug usage can be reduced through education. The war on drugs persists because it provides political currency for conservative politicians, control of the 'dangerous' ghetto underclass, and work for police departments, lawyers, and the crime-control industry.

US drug enforcement programs have failed to control the trafficking, price, and consumption of illicit substances. Because multiple connections between drug trafficking and criminal behaviour exist, the decriminalization of some drug use would reduce not only criminal justice costs, but also reduce the incidence of violent drug-related criminal behaviour. While it may not be possible to determine whether legalization would increase drug use, and what the effects of that might be, some kind of reform is needed to ease the lives of inner-city residents (Reinarman and Levine, 1997).

The legalization of drugs is unlikely to decrease drug abuse and addiction in the current cultural context. Because risk factors (like poverty and discrimination) heavily outweigh protective factors in many countries, a decriminalization of drugs would probably result in increased social costs and more cases of addiction. Tretter (1995) concludes that the drug problem in many societies is unsolvable without a major social and cultural change. Some people oppose legalization for moral reasons: they believe that by legalizing drug use we conveniently ignore the plight of drug users—that is, the reasons why they use drugs.

Many look to the Netherlands as a source of evidence about the likely effects of decriminalization or legalization. Castro, Lehman, and Cannon (1996) note that the 1976 modification of the Netherlands' policy controlling the distribution, possession, and consumption of soft drugs (i.e., cannabis and derivatives) was intended to reduce the progression to hard drug use. In the years since this de facto legalization of drug use, an intricate set of relatively stable social structures have emerged to provide a stable supply of soft drugs.

There is no evidence that drug use has increased in the Netherlands as a result of this policy. However, in the past 30 years the increased cooperation between European Union member states in many policy areas has made it increasingly difficult for individual countries to pursue national policies on issues like drugs. The drug policies of the Netherlands, which centre squarely on harm reduction, have been under severe attack in recent years. Debates are also underway in many countries on drug policy reform. A wide variety of policies is under consideration, including everything from the decriminalization or legalization of cannabis to the legal prescription of heroin. This current wave of practicality throughout Europe has made the liberal Dutch approach less of an isolated case than it was when first implemented (Boekhout von Solinge, 1999).

Decriminalization of drug use currently has many supporters. There is little evidence that decriminalizing the use of 'soft drugs' (e.g., those containing THC—tetrahydrocannabinol) results in dramatic increases in substance abuse. Nor is there compelling evidence that they lead people to use addictive drugs like heroin or cocaine. Relaxation of police efforts to control marijuana use in the last decade has not led to epidemics of marijuana use. A regulated repeal of the prohibition on drugs would create a legal market in lower-priced drugs and would also reduce the revenues of organized crime. Many drug-related crimes would decrease if public health agencies provided free drugs or drug substitutes (like Methadone).

Decriminalization of the possession of marijuana since the early 1970s has, however, resulted in decreased costs of enforcement and prosecution of marijuana-related offences. Making drug use legal would also reduce many of the health risks associated with drug use today. While drug use remains illegal, we can do little to monitor the quality of drugs available to users, or the conditions under which people use these drugs. When drugs are illegal, users also take fewer health precautions. For example, needles shared among heroin users spread HIV/AIDs. By driving the drug-user culture underground, the law works against safety, good hygiene, and disease prevention. Programs in other countries have reduced the sharing of contaminated equipment without increasing drug use.

Likely scenarios for change: drugs in the twenty-first century

Drug abuse is a serious problem for which there is no quick or easy solution. Many experts would agree that harm reduction is a better approach to this problem than prevention, and that legalizing and controlling certain drugs are better strategies than prohibiting them outright. However, as Erickson points out, even if we relax punitive responses to drugs in the future and that policy approaches to all psychoactive substances converge, a major change will not occur without a concomitant shift in the social evaluation of the acceptability of losing self-control (Erickson, 1996).

Though people disagree about drug legalization, Canada is evidently moving toward harm-reduction policies more so than toward prevention policies. In May 2003, the government of Canada decided to invest $245 million over five years to reduce both the supply and demand for drugs. This involves a renewal of Canada's drug strategy, which adopts a focus on prevention, education, and treatment, with special emphasis on youth drug users (Health Canada, 2003). In addition, Canada has recently legalized the medical use of marijuana. With the medical use of marijuana, the Canadian government has effectively decriminalized marijuana. This does not mean that the possession of marijuana is now legal in Canada, but there is movement in that direction.

Concluding Words

Drugs are common in our society and people hold many opinions about their use. Drug use is not by itself a social problem. Drugs only become a problem when people abuse them and violate approved social practices. This then becomes costly to society in terms of accidents, crime, and family, work, and health problems.

Canadians consume many different kinds of drugs, both legal and illegal. It is important to note that legal drugs such as alcohol and tobacco are Canada's most severe drug problems, when they are used in excess. This chapter has provided various explanations of drug abuse. Psychological approaches to drug abuse suggest that addiction is a result of emotional or personality disorders. Sociological explanations focus on the role of culture, social structure, and social interaction in producing drug use and abuse.

Drug abuse is one of many costly public health problems in Canada. It will likely increase in severity over time unless users are treated. Evidence shows that many, or even most, drug addicts can be rehabilitated if they are given proper treatment such as counseling, methadone maintenance, and job training. Among adolescents at high risk of abusing drugs, school-based social support programs can reduce the likelihood of future involvement in drugs.

Summary

We regularly use all manner of drugs to deal with the pains and tensions of normal, everyday life. The ways that people behave after drinking alcohol depend in part on the society in which people learned to drink the alcohol and the effects they expect alcohol to have.

Ample research shows, however, that alcohol causes people more harm than all the other drugs put together. The social, political, and economic mechanisms that drove social pathologies during the Prohibition Era were much the same as those driving today's drug epidemic. In Canada, despite a long history of empirical research pointing away from aggressive criminalization, we continue to enforce laws against soft drugs. While we are tending away from an American-style War on Drugs in Canada, we are far from decriminalizing soft drugs and implementing a full harm reduction policy. Evidence from the Netherlands and elsewhere shows that such policies work well and alternative policies fail.

Questions for Critical Thought

1. Why do residents of an area express concern about having addicts in the neighbourhood?

2. According to conflict theory, what would the ruling class gain by criminalizing only certain drugs?

3. Discuss why some drugs are legal and others are illegal. Explain what factors play a role in the conception of drug problems

4. Compare and contrast alcohol regulation in Europe, Canada, and the United States from an interactionist perspective.

5. Howard Becker explains that one must learn how to use drugs. Evaluate his argument relating it to the social paradigm Becker follows.

6. Do you support the decriminalization of marijuana? Use sociological theories you have learned in this chapter to support your views on the issue.

7. How can drugs give people a sense of belonging? Discuss this in relation to anomie.

8. Do you think that the current Canadian policies regarding drug-use are good enough? What changes would you suggest to better deal with the problem?

9. Discuss changes in people's conception of drug-use in different historical periods and examine the stigmatization of drug users in a community.

10. Discuss the ways that drug regulation alters social and health consequences of use and abuse.

Recommended Reading

Becker, Howard. (1953), 'Becoming a Marijuana User', *American Journal of Sociology*, 59: 235–42. In this classic article, Howard Becker, shows how people who experiment with marijuana can become users. The process by which an experimenter becomes a user is quite complex. Becker outlines the social setting by which a marijuana user is formed, which still holds true today.

Frey, James. (2003), *A Million Little Pieces*. New York: Anchor Books. This national bestseller and work of fiction nicely illustrates the process by which a drug user can overcome circumstances to become a non-user. As an abuser of alcohol and drugs, Frey checks into a treatment facility and battles with AA's 12 steps.

Valentine, Douglas. (2004), *The Strength of the Wolf: The Secret History of America's War on Drugs*. New York: Verso. Douglas outlines the war on drugs and the various federal agencies that have been put in charge of monitoring various controlled substances. Though a dense work, it is a detailed examination of the American war on drugs.

Recommended Websites

Health Canada
www.hc-sc.gc.ca
> The Health Canada website brings together a range of reports and resources about the effects of various drugs. The website also outlines treatment and prevention options for various drugs.

Leave the Pack Behind
www.leavethepackbehind.org
> Leave the Pack Behind is a peer-to-peer initiative designed to reduce smoking rates among various groups of students.

> The website provides quitting information as well as research on smoking and its effects.

MADD: Mothers Against Drunk Driving
www.madd.org
> This Mothers Against Drunk Driving website provides great activism and education information for students. As one of the largest crime victim organizations in the world, MADD is able to generate quite a bit of attention toward research on alcohol use and abuse.

PART III

DELINQUENCY AND CRIME

CHAPTER 6

Risky Behaviours

LEARNING OBJECTIVES
- To identify youthful risky behaviours and the motivating factors behind them
- To understand that risky behaviour varies by gender
- To see that youth are the group most often negatively stereotyped
- To evaluate the influence of family and peers on risk-taking
- To trace the history of juvenile delinquency and public reactions to it
- To examine delinquent subcultures
- To discuss delinquency in terms of the four sociological paradigms
- To judge the health consequences that criminal youth experience
- To examine the outcomes of risk-taking behaviour and delinquency
- To describe the communities and cultures that support juvenile delinquency
- To examine policies that may prevent or reduce delinquent behaviours
- To learn about the *Youth Criminal Justice Act* and its implications

Introduction

This chapter is about rule-breaking by Canada's youth and the efforts sociologists have made to understand this behaviour. It gives a brief overview of the research currently available on delinquency and crime among young people. More than that, it is about risky behaviour—behaviour that endangers the actor and other people. Much delinquent behaviour is risky in this sense, although not all risky behaviour is delinquent.

Here, we understand a broad definition of the term 'delinquency' to include a variety of behaviours that often act as 'gateways' to more serious criminal acts. Moreover, we take a sociological approach to understanding these behaviours. As usual, we examine communities, cultures, and careers associated with delinquency.

Adults usually view adolescent risk-taking behaviours as hazardous and unhealthy. Many of these behaviours are anti-social, or seem so to adults. Often, these anti-social behaviours accompany a variety of health, learning, and legal problems. They may affect the well-being of the young people involved and also make heavy demands on health and social services. In this chapter, we explore a variety of common risky behaviours that include dangerous driving and unsafe sex. For adults, these behaviours are deviant—that is, they break rules and violate expectations. Some even break laws.

Teenage risk-taking and delinquency is commonplace and banal. What's more, perpetrators and victims are often the same people. So, for example, Paetsch and Bertrand (1999) examined survey data to examine the extent of victimization and delinquency among 962 high school students in Calgary, Alberta. In general, younger students reported higher rates of victimization at school than did older students. In addition, more than half of the students (males more than females) reported engaging in some form of delinquent behaviour within the past year. Most interesting of all, students who reported moderate/high levels of delinquency were more likely to report moderate/high levels of victimization, and students who reported no delinquency were more likely to report no victimization.

As sociologist David Matza (1964) wrote in his classic work *Delinquency and Drift*, a great many young people 'drift' into delinquency without a very strong motivation to do harm and armed with little more than 'techniques of neutralization'. These so-called techniques provide varied excuses or justifications for the rule-breaking and make the drift into delinquency easier morally, if not socially. Matza believes that delinquents share the same values and attitudes as non-delinquents, and need only the help of 'neutralizing' excuses to break rules. The drift into delinquency is common, and so is the tendency for young delinquents to leave delinquency as they become young adults with adult responsibilities.

That said, the drift in and out of delinquency is not without consequences, even if the period of delinquency is brief. Research shows that time spent in delinquent behaviour is time spent at the expense of activities—whether educational, occupational, or social—that contribute to eventual adult success. Moreover, social contacts made through delinquency are often at the expense of social contacts other young people make in the conforming world. Finally, skills that may benefit delinquent activity are often learned at the expense of skills useful in the conforming world. So, no behaviour is without the cost of foregone opportunities, and this is particularly true of delinquent behaviour.

As we will see, adolescents and young adults are particularly drawn to risky behaviour. Additionally, we will see that risky behaviour is often tied up with the search for independence, adulthood, and peer acceptance. Juvenile delinquency, like other rule-breaking, is highly gendered and mainly a male activity. Smoking may be one of the few exceptions to this rule: girls are smoking slightly more than boys in terms of both current and experimental smoking.

Canadian *Juristat* data report that, from early ages onward, girls are less likely than boys to report being involved in delinquent acts, including aggression. Most of the reported aggressive behaviours are relatively minor. However, many children involved in aggressive behaviours are also involved in delinquent acts involving property. For example, '47 per cent of the 12 and 13 year olds who reported high frequencies of delinquent acts involving property also reported high frequencies of aggressive behaviour.' As to causes, the research shows that children who report high frequencies of aggressive behaviour report being bullied a lot at school, higher levels of punitive parenting, and lower parental nurturance. A survey of 26,000 students released in 1999 by the McCreary Centre Society shows that youth are less likely to take risks when they feel that parents and teachers care about them and treat them fairly. Figure 6.1 shows the statistics for sexual risk-taking of youths in British Columbia.

Moods and behaviours change over the course of adolescence: though children who are not aggressive at an early age are unlikely to become aggressive, children who are aggressive are likely to become less aggressive with time. So, for example, 'of the children who were at the highest frequencies of aggressive behaviour at age 10 and 11, 45 per cent were not reporting any aggressive behaviour two years later at age 12 and 13.' Things change again at adolescence—a period of self-construction, even turbulence. It is a period when people's 'selves' are emerging. As we know from the work of Cooley (1909) and Mead, 'the self' is a social product. A person's experiences in life, the groups to which he or she belongs, and the socio-historical setting of those groups all shape a person's sense of self. Because the self is a social product, it changes throughout life. Adolescence, in particular, is a critical period for the development of self.

Figure 6.1 Sexual Risk-taking by Teens in British Columbia

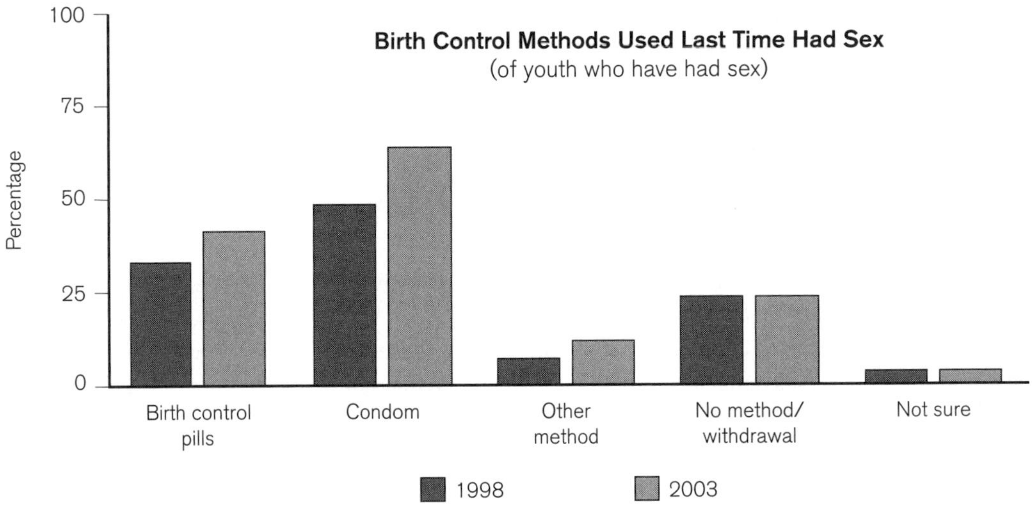

SOURCE: R. Tonkin, A. Murphy, M. Chittenden, and The McCreary Centre Society, 'Healthy Youth Development: Highlights from the 2003 Adolescent Health Survey III'; available at <www.mcs.bc.ca/pdf/AHS-3_provincial.pdf>, accessed 19 December 2004. Reprinted by permisssion.

Not all adolescents are delinquent or even dangerous risk-takers. In fact, some are militantly against such behaviour. So-called straightedge youth have galvanized largely around an opposition to drugs, alcohol, and perceived forms of promiscuous sexual activity. Moreover, in recent years, several distinct factions have emerged from the general straightedge youth subculture—some more severe than others. However, some adolescents do take big risks and break the rules. Some even become 'delinquents'.

The term 'delinquency' covers a variety of deviant behaviours—some of them violent crimes and some of them less dangerous or harmful acts. In criminology, the term 'juvenile delinquency' refers to deviant and, particularly, indictable acts committed by people between the ages of 12 and 20—that is, by teenagers. As we will see, both family and peers influence risk-taking and delinquency. Despite the importance of peers, families still play a part in the prevention of juvenile risk-taking. Despite the legal distinctiveness of delinquency, juvenile risk-taking is the seedbed of illegal behaviours.

Unlike psychological theories, which focus on personality problems, most sociological theories of juvenile delinquency try to explain these crimes in terms of societal precursors to deviant behaviour and their later social consequences, and in a more socially structured or communal sense. Typically, sociologists focus on the organization of urban gangs, delinquent subcultures, and limited opportunities for success in legitimate enterprises. They see delinquent behaviour as a 'normal'—that is, common and rational—social response to stresses and opportunities in the young person's environment. Sociologists direct our attention back to the social environment and how it can be improved.

Young people, for their part, see themselves as invincible, and these days—more than in the past—this is closer to being true. Their life expectancy is 79 years and many youth are perfectly healthy, never having experienced a serious childhood illness. Moreover, as we enter the twenty-first century, the youth literacy rate is the highest ever. In contrast to that, it is not an easy time for young people.

Box 6.1 Girls Nastier Than Boys in Dating

OTTAWA—Considerably more boys than girls say their dates yell at them, demean them, pinch them, slap them, and out-and-out attack them, according to preliminary findings in a study on dating violence.

Researchers caution they have not yet started analyzing the figures for the Teen Relationship Project, a collaborative project between York University in Toronto and Queen's University in Kingston, Ont.

Yet they were surprised to find slightly more than 20 per cent of boys reporting major abuse, compared to just under 20 per cent of girls. Roughly 30 per cent of boys experienced minor abuse, compared to just over 20 per cent of girls, and almost half of the boys reported verbal abuse, compared to roughly 45 per cent of girls.

The project surveyed an estimated 2,000 teenagers in 10-to-12 Quebec and Ontario high schools over three years, asking about their attitudes toward date aggression, how often it happened and in what context.

The study even examined what music the kids listened to and whether violent messages in the lyrics was linked to higher dating violence. (It did. The teens who loved the tough stuff were more likely to think dating abuse was OK.)

It will be at least two years before the study reaches its final conclusions. Still, the group put the results on its web site, remarking that 'contrary to popular belief, boys experience more incidents of all forms of aggression from their romantic partners.'

Jennifer Connolly, York University professor of psychology and one of the lead members of the study, said Friday: 'It's a very controversial and difficult finding to interpret. I'm really being cautious here because I do not want that finding displayed as if we can interpret it at face value.'

Connolly was particularly concerned that the figures might be interpreted to mean that women who suffered violence from men had somehow 'asked for it' by being aggressive themselves.

In fact, the study did look at immediate context and found that girls who admitted to aggression toward their boyfriends were usually reacting to some sort of conflict, whereas the boys were more likely to initiate the aggression. Having said that, Connolly acknowledged other studies have had similar findings.

'Girls are not only victims but they also perpetrate, and boys are not only perpetrators but victims. It is a consistent finding and something we need to think about.'

SOURCE: Excerpt, Jenny Jackson, *Times Colonist*, 5 December 2004, A3.

Many youth suffer from low self-esteem, stress, and depression. In 1996, more than 500 Canadian youth died by committing suicide. Table 6.1 shows the results of a survey of how Canadian students feel about themselves.

Partly because this is a period of transition and experimentation, young people often distance themselves from family and friends and experience loneliness as a result. In fact, loneliness is a bigger problem at this time of life than at any other.

Research by Rokach and Neto (2000a; 2000b) on the perceived causes of loneliness in adulthood surveyed 711 Canadian participants from all walks of life who answered a yes/no questionnaire reflecting on their loneliness experiences and causes. Four age groups were compared: youth (ages 13–18), young adults (ages 19–30), adults (ages 31–58), and seniors (ages 60–80). Results showed that young adults had the highest mean scores on all subscales, while seniors scored the lowest. Males and females differed significantly as well, with women scoring higher in loneliness than men.

The signs of mental turmoil are often hidden. Young men, in particular, often display a tough, active, unemotional masculine image. Delinquents may also display traits associated with the so-called culture of poverty: a belief in fate, danger, luck, and risk-taking. Activities can range in seriousness from vandalism, petty theft, breaking and entering, illegal alcohol and drug use, auto theft and dangerous driving, up through drug dealing, robbery, and gang fighting.

Some of these delinquent acts are aimed at making money, although most are intended to gain or defend status, protect gang territory, or prove the delinquent's manliness. Research in this area was hampered for a long time by the belief that delinquency is only lower-class behaviour. Self-report surveys measuring delinquent behaviour among young people have shown that delinquency occurs in all social classes, though the evidence of delinquency is clearest for poor youth in poor neighbourhoods. Children from low-income homes are most at risk of running into trouble with the law but, increasingly, more criminal offences are committed by middle-class youth.

No other social group receives as much negative attention as the young. Often, adults view young people as troubling and troubled, and as a frequent source of fear and worry. Media reports fuel these fears with stories of youth riots, violence in schools, and crack use. While the deviant motifs may vary over time—from bike gangs to punk—what remains

constant is a negative view of youth. Youth are often negatively stereotyped. This is evident through the media, politics, and the public in their reaction to youth and in their failure to acknowledge their positive contributions to society. It is almost as though young people take risks and break rules to live up to (down to?) the worst expectations of adults.

Sociologist Travis Hirschi (1969) has developed a comprehensive theory to explain why individuals choose to conform to conventional norms and, by implication, why they break them. He assumes that everyone has potential to become delinquent and criminal and social controls, not moral values, maintain law and order. Without controls, he argues, people are more likely to commit criminal acts. According to this theory, delinquents defy moral codes because their attachment to society is weak.

Four social bonds that routinely promote conformity are attachment, commitment, involvement, and belief. The first bond, *attachment*, refers to a person's interest in or attachment to others— especially parents, schools, and peers. The depth and quality of these attachments and the frequency of interaction (e.g., the amount of time child and parent spend together) are also important, leading to intimacy and identification. Hirschi states that a child's attachment to parents and school is more important than the bond formed with one's peers.

The second bond is that of *commitment*. Time, energy, and effort spent in conventional lines of social activity tie an individual to the moral code of society. People who invest their effort building a good reputation and acquiring property are less likely to engage in criminal acts that endanger their social position. The third bond is *involvement* in activities that support the conventional interests of society, since such activities don't leave time to engage in delinquent or criminal acts. Such activities—which include going to school or work, or participating in organized sport or volunteer work—insulate a juvenile from potential delinquent behaviour that may be a result of idleness. Even sports, extracurricular activities, and community involvement have

Table 6.1 How Canadian Students Feel About Themselves, 1998

	Males (%)			Females (%)		
	Yes	No	Don't Know	Yes	No	Don't Know
I have a happy home life	78	11	11	67	15	18
My parents trust me	74	13	14	71	12	18
I argue a lot with my parents	29	65	7	36	57	7
I like myself	85	4	11	70	9	20
I have confidence in myself	74	12	15	55	23	23
I often wish I was someone else	21	70	9	37	53	10
I would change how I look if I could	37	51	12	54	32	14

SOURCE: Statistics Canada, CANSIM II, Table 1100017, accessed 28 January 2004.

stabilizing effects on young people. In general, any engagement with the law-abiding world increases conformity and reduces delinquency among young people.

Finally, a *belief* in the laws of society—and in the people and institutions that enforce such laws—provides a fourth bond promoting conformity.

According to this theory, adolescents take risks and break the rules if their bonds to conventional society are weak and they feel they have less to lose than other people do. They lack the attachment, commitment, involvement, and belief that keep people law-abiding. They do not have a 'stake in conformity', no career, mortgage, or credit rating to jeopardize. As we will see, when young people do finally get jobs, mates, or good career prospects, their risk-taking, delinquency, and chances of getting into trouble reduce enormously.

The Work Ethic and the Pleasure Ethic

Juvenile delinquency, in its many forms, is a risky and anti-social behaviour; moreover, it is non-productive and sometimes even destructive. For this reason, we can view juvenile delinquency as a repudiation of North American society's dominant value, sometimes called (after Max Weber) the Protestant Work Ethic (1974). In saying this, we are attaching particular importance to Hirschi's 'control theory', which calls attention to a 'stake in conformity' as the motivation for rule-abiding behaviour.

In Weber's classic study of the Protestant Ethic, religious systems of interpretation are shown to have been important in transforming economic life. Weber argued that the economic behaviour we associate with modern life in the West would have been impossible without a major shift in religious values. In the medieval societies of Europe, people thought a concern with worldly activities, wealth, and making a profit through the investment of money at interest was immoral or base. For people to change their economic behaviour, Weber argued, they had to first change their ideas about money and morality—and work.

Later Protestants, called Calvinists, took this doctrine of Luther's, combined it with a belief in predestination, and unwittingly helped to create a new economic system: capitalism. Weber explained the change as follows: Calvinists believed that all people are predestined to go to either heaven or hell. Precisely who is going to heaven and who is going to hell is already decided. Nothing people do will change the outcome, neither church, nor priest, nor ritual. As a result, Calvinist groups strongly emphasized the freedom of the individual on earth, and reduced people's dependence on the Catholic Church, priesthood, and ritual. What one did in the marketplace could have no ultimate effect on one's likelihood of going to heaven, so one was free to profit and still think oneself blessed.

Because they believed salvation was predestined, Calvinists searched for a sign from God that they were among the elect. Since they believed they were working for God, it made sense to see success at work as a sign of their good standing with God and God's overall approval. Rather than seeing money as immoral, Calvinists thought it now became a measure of a person's moral status. The good were wealthy because the wealthy were good—that is, chosen by God.

Many centuries have passed since the Calvinists adopted these beliefs, and clearly our society is much more secular—less visibly committed to religious principles—than Calvinist or Puritan societies that Weber described. Yet these values continue to influence our own conception of proper middle-class behaviour. The so-called work ethic remains a widely held belief in the secular calling of work that emphasizes continued hard work in the pursuit of personal and family success.

Juvenile delinquency, with its emphasis on thrills and unproductive risk-taking, violates this norm of hard work. Most young people learn the work ethic and do not become delinquents. This happens because they are socialized to follow the rules. Early in life, we are most concerned about relations with our parents. Parents' efforts to implant a strong work ethic often begin when children are still very small. It invades every portion of some children's lives. Over the last generation, an institutionalized 'after-school' period has arisen, for example, marked by children's involvement in adult-organized and supervised activities (Adler and Adler, 1994). Even adults' organization of child's play helps to reproduce the existing social structure and socialize young people into the corporate work values of North American culture.

Of course, how parents talk about their work makes a difference too. Adolescents have more respect for their parents' work when they learn to view it as satisfying and personal (Galambos and Sears, 1998). When fathers hold more self-directed jobs and enjoy close supportive relationships with their sons, the sons are more likely to learn their fathers' work values (Ryu and Mortimer, 1994).

Such value transmission occurs largely because of direct parent-child communication about the value of work and the example parents set. As well, visible examples of work attachment influence young adults' perceptions of future economic self-sufficiency through hard work (Iverson and Farber, 1996). During early adulthood, young people's work values change and gradually become more realistic (Dunlap et al., 2002). They come to know more about the jobs that exist and the rewards—in money and prestige—attached to these jobs. Increasingly, young people come to equate work with social responsibility and inclusion. Increasingly, they value the sense of self-worth and economic freedom that work provides (Jeolas et al., 2002).

However, work is more than just earning money and gaining economic freedom. Even volunteer work develops commitments to a 'work ethic' in young people. Adolescents who become involved in volunteer activities develop higher educational plans and aspirations, higher grade point averages, more academic self-esteem, and a stronger motivation toward schoolwork (Johnson et al., 1998). Most important, volunteering strengthens intrinsic work values and teaches the importance of community involvement.

Work commitments continue to strengthen with age. As young people mature, they develop career values—ideals and ideas important to professionals over their entire careers, and not merely one specific job or work episode (Murphy, 2001). All the primary career values—including advancement, authority, autonomy, creativity, economic rewards, economic security, personal development, prestige, and social relations—intensify.

Along with age, formal education plays an important part in developing a strong work ethic. Johnson and Elder (2002) find that young people who continue their education beyond high school maintain their initial values—their career goals—more than young people who end their education after completing high school. Their work values lead them to invest in education and, in turn, formal education strengthens and revises their work values. Besides age and education, experience in the workforce also affects work ethic. The mere experience of job rewards reinforces the value young people attach to work (Johnson, 2000). Work values are also strengthened by other experiences related to 'growing up', such as marriage. Gorman (2002) writes that marriage brings a change in attitudes toward money. In turn, employers reward them with higher earnings.

So the Protestant work ethic, and experience with hard work, promotes three of Hirschi's bonds: commitment, involvement, and a belief in the dominant social values.

Juvenile delinquency, by contrast, is a repudiation of this work ethic, often because of a failure to learn it during childhood and early adulthood. The reasons can begin with early problems of child-parent attachment or poor parenting. These in turn may result in poor cognitive development and poor results in school. Increasingly, boys do more poorly than girls in formal education, with the result that more of them drop out of school and get into trouble through risky behaviour.

Adolescent Risk-taking

One place to start a discussion of risky adolescent behaviour is with alcohol and drug use since this connects so well with other kinds of risky and delinquent behaviours. Problems related to adolescent drinking include interpersonal aggression, accidents and injuries, trouble with the police, and problems at school or work (Hammer and Pape, 1997). Moreover, as explained later in the chapter, young people have the highest risk of automobile accidents.

As we have seen repeatedly, rule-breaking is gendered behaviour. Men report more problems due to drinking, in both alcohol consumption and general problem proneness, than women, for example. Early age at first intoxication seems to be a male-specific predictor of negative consequences of drinking. Typically, there is a substantial reduction in problems attributed to drinking between late adolescence and early adulthood. Even so, alcohol-related problems before ages 19–22 are the most powerful predictor of similar problems six years later.

Drinking and driving

Nowhere is the recklessness of youth more evident than in respect to motor vehicle accidents. Some kinds of situations and people are particularly likely to suffer accidents and their consequences. People at a high risk of automobile accidents have a particular demographic profile, drinking profile, and personality profile.

Young men, of all drivers, have the highest risk of automobile accidents. As a result, automobile accidents—along with homicides and suicides—are the most common causes of death for young men. The reasons are simple. Compared with old men, young men have less driving experience, drive more often at night, and are more likely to drive while intoxicated (or drive with someone else who is intoxicated) Young drivers are also more likely to take risks on the road, and they are more often absorbed in talking or listening to music while driving. According to American statistics (Newburn and Shiner, 2001), 60 per cent of drivers between the age of 15 and 19 drank before being involved in an accident. As a result, young people—especially young men—have more automobile accidents and suffer more driving-related fatalities than anyone else.

Alcohol and drugs are an indirect cause of many traffic accidents, fatalities, and associated property damage; and young men are the riskiest drinkers. Young, single men who drink often are more likely to drink and then drive than older, married men. In a study of students in grades 10–12, 13 per cent admitted to personally driving under the influence (DUI) of alcohol, and 31 per cent reported having driven in the last month with someone who was DUI. Males are also more likely than females to drink underage and ride with drunk drivers. Teen peers are more ready to forgive this male misbehaviour than similar female misbehaviour, it seems. Despite the double standard, they give males more approval than females for driving after drinking and the approval may encourage males to do this repeatedly. Boys often view dangerous driving as 'sporty', feeling personally involved with their car, and approve of other people's dangerous driving.

Binge-drinking male drivers are at particularly high risk of traffic fatalities. Environmental risks such as deep water, cliffs, and traffic also predict alcohol-related driving incidents (Newburn and Shiner, 2001). Rule-breaking even extends to minor infractions, like the use of parking spaces reserved for disabled people. Violators such as college students who, by their own report, have parked illegally in disabled people's parking spaces are more likely to be male, and to report smoking, drinking frequently, and driving after drinking.

Similarly, research also shows that high school boys who drive after drinking are more likely than average to take on such rebellious and/or unconventional habits as smoking cigarettes and marijuana, carrying a knife, and fighting. They are less likely than average to finish their homework, eat nutritious food, fasten their seat belts, get enough sleep, and brush after every meal. High school students who drive dangerously spend much of their time 'hanging out' in unstructured social activities and engaging in criminal behaviour, heavy drinking, and drug use. Young traffic offenders are more likely than non-offenders to have a history of criminal aggressiveness. In short, risky young drivers often engage in multiple health-risk behaviours—even including violence, casual and unprotected sex with multiple partners, and unintended pregnancy. In doing so, they conform to a rebellious social norm, rejecting conventional adult norms by seeking out danger. This is a result of the way we tend to socialize boys to externalize their fantasies in risky behaviours.

Table 6.2 Hashish or Marijuana Use of 15-year-old Students in Canada, 1998

	Male (%)	Female (%)
Never	56	59
Once or twice	13	12
Three times or more	32	29

SOURCE: Statistics Canada, CANSIM II, Table 1100003, accessed 1 February 2004.

Table 6.2 compares statistics for marijuana use for 15-year-old males and females.

Risky driving is part of a larger package of rule-breaking behaviours. Junger, West, and Timman (2001), for example, found that people who displayed risky traffic behaviour leading to an accident were two-and-a-half times more likely to have a police record for violent crime or for vandalism, one-and-a-half times more likely to have a record for property crime, and over five times as likely to have been involved in traffic crime.

These results are consistent with the idea of a common factor underlying risky behaviour in traffic and criminal behaviour. Pickett and colleagues (2002) examined the role of multiple-risk behaviours and other social factors leading to medically attended youth injury. Youth reporting the largest number (7) of risk behaviours experienced injury rates—especially, multiple injuries and severe injuries—that were more than four times higher than those reporting no high-risk behaviours. The analyses suggest that multiple-risk behaviours may play an important role in the social etiology of youth injury. Interestingly, the researchers found little evidence of a socioeconomic (or social class) variation in these risks.

Risky and anti-social behaviours rapidly decline in number as young males leave adolescence and develop a stake in conformity. Even young men in the ages 18–25 show a decline in risky driving and increased social conventionality after they enter

Figure 6.2 Reported Infectious Syphilis[1] Rates[2] in Canada, 1993–99[3]

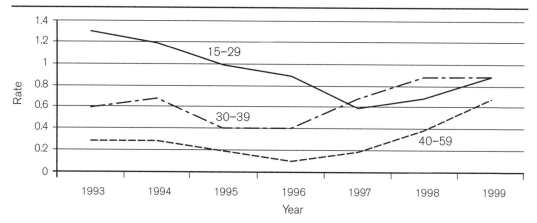

[1] Infectious syphilis includes early symptomatic and early latent syphilis.
[2] Rate per 100,000 population. Population estimates provided by Statistics Canada.
[3] 1999 numbers are preliminary.

SOURCE: Division of STD Prevention and Control, Bureau of HIV/AIDS, STD and TB, Centre for Infectious Disease Prevention, Health Canada (Oct. 2000), '1998/1999 Canadian Sexually Transmitted Diseases (STD) Surveillance Report'; available at <www.phac-aspc.gc.ca>, accessed 19 December 2004.

adult social roles. As young people assume adult roles and learn to conform to them, their risky driving starts to disappear. The same is true of risky drinking, violence, and sex.

Unsafe sex as risk behaviour

Along with smoking and drinking, unsafe sex (e.g., non-use of a condom) is another health risk behaviour often exhibited by teenagers. Kordoutis and researchers (2000), in a study of youth aged 18–25 found that inconsistent condom use was more frequent among partners whose ages differed by two or more years. In short, some unsafe sex is a result of mating between younger, naïve women and older, experienced, and possibly exploitive, men.

To assess the association between substance use, unplanned sexual intercourse and other sexual behaviours among adolescent students, Poulin and Graham (2001) studied a sample of just under 10,000 adolescent students in Nova Scotia, New Brunswick, Newfoundland and Labrador, and Prince Edward Island in 1998. Items on sexual intercourse,

unplanned sexual intercourse, number of sexual partners, condom use, alcohol use, episodes of binge drinking and drunkenness, cigarette smoking and cannabis use were analyzed. About 37.5 per cent of males and 39.7 per cent of females reported having engaged in sexual intercourse in the 12 months prior to the survey. Of those, 68 per cent of males and 61.5 per cent of females reported having engaged in unplanned sexual intercourse, 40.9 per cent of males and 32.1 per cent of females reported having more than one sexual partner, and 49.9 per cent of males and 64.1 per cent of females reported inconsistent condom use.

In short, unplanned sexual intercourse under the influence of alcohol or other drugs was found to be an independent risk factor for multiple sexual partners and inconsistent condom use. Men and women differ in their reasons for not using a condom. Women who fail to use condoms often say they feel there is little risk of pregnancy or of getting a sexually transmitted disease during sexual intercourse. Men who fail to use them are more likely to cite inconvenience or unavailability as their reason (Carter et al., 1999).

However, in the end, condom use comes down to the willingness of the male partner. Since heterosexual women do not usually wear a condom, they must negotiate condom use with their male partners. Williams and colleagues (2001) found three strategies that people often employ when engaging their partners in a discussion of safe sex practices: (1) taking the initiative in discussing condom use; (2) resolving conflicts with their partner about condom use; and (3) maintaining the intention to use a condom. Kordoutis and colleagues (2000) find that, in 80 per cent of the cases where condoms were not used, there was no negotiation about this between partners.

Typically, women play a more active role in the negotiation process, and men tend to play a more reactive role. Positive attitudes toward safe sex promote an open dialogue regarding condom use and condom use during intercourse (Troth and Peterson, 2000). However, often there is no open dialogue, largely because the woman is reluctant to risk her partner's anger by raising the issue. Figure 6.2 shows the infectious rates for syphilis by age in the 1990s.

The Rave Subculture: Tribalism and Risk

Nothing in the youth culture so clearly demonstrates the repudiation of the middle-class work ethic than the rave subculture.

The 'rave' subculture is a culture of middle-class youth renowned for their 'neo-hippie' perspectives, attendance at all-night 'rave' dance parties, use of amphetamine drugs, and interest in technology—especially, computer-generated music known as 'techno'. Wilson (1998; 2000) notes a relative lack of empirical research on the 'rave subculture' in Canada—a surprising absence considering the group's sizable membership and the notoriety the group has received in popular media, government-related health reports, and scholarly work on youth in other countries.

Rave emerged in the late 1980s and early 1990s in the UK as a new youth cultural phenomenon (Critcher, 2000). Later transformed into clubbing, it became a significant part of the leisure activities of young people well into their twenties. Raving resulted from the coming together of innovations in music, drugs, and dance and the largely negative social reaction from media, police, and government. According to Luckman (2000), the all-night dancing in this subculture is marked by a sense of carefree abandon. The rave, however, refers to a varied body of practices, people, and sites beyond mere dancing.

Raving is associated with recreational drug use—especially with the drug known as Ecstasy. Forsyth (1996) examined the use of drugs among participants (average age 24) active in the rave scene in Glasgow, Scotland. He found that 51 discrete drugs were used by the respondents. Alcohol and cannabis were the most widely used drugs during the past year, followed by Ecstasy, tobacco, LSD, and amphetamines. The setting in which drugs were used varied greatly, with amphetamine, nitrites, and Ecstasy most commonly used in dance settings. Tobacco, cannabis, and depressants were not used in dance settings.

Additionally, the techno-mix aspect of the music is important. Gaillot (2001) notes that techno-music associated with raving reflects the tendency of modern society to create by recycling pre-existing materials. Raves promote collective self-abandonment, along with the resulting emergence of a special sort of sociability. Dance itself plays an important part in this. Aaronson (1999) notes that in dancing to techno music, the body acts out the rhythm. The dancers' movements are intuitive and, by breaking down rational thought, the dances break down social, cultural, and gender barriers. In the huge warehouses where techno and rave dances are held, participants in the trancelike dance rituals can experience freedom from the class bonds of society. The individual personality disappears into the crowd.

Others have pointed to the tribal, almost sacred aspects of rave activity. Cova (1999) claims that this tribalism reflects the efforts of postmodern individuals to avoid isolation. Rave parties give the individual an alternative to isolation, by permitting the individual to participate in an imaginary community. Indeed, Takahashi and Olaveson (2003) claim that raving is a meaningful and spiritual experience for some participants. In effect, the rave phenomenon is a new religious or revitalization movement. The seven central themes of the rave experience are connectedness, embodiment, altered states of consciousness, spirituality, personal transformation, utopian models of society, and neo-tribalism.

There is some debate whether the rave culture is political or not. Lau (1995), evaluating the techno-music 'rave' scene in contemporary Germany as a subversive youth culture, finds it to be apolitical. He argues that the rave is a primarily cultural event characterized by specific dance styles and its own print media. It uses music from the past, but does so in a non- or de-historical way. The associated clothing is marked by pluralism, as is the rave scene itself, with all-night parties drawing a variety of youth, many members of other youth cultures or scenes. He contends that this social phenomenon is a leisure culture with no real history, voice, or autonomous social or political demands.

Nonetheless, some authorities have reacted against raving, often without success. Sean Hier (2002) examined the anxieties that crystallized in the summer of 2000 concerning the uses and abuses of Ecstasy at local raves in Toronto, Ontario. Despite the fact that concerted efforts were made on the part of a host of 'moral entrepreneurs' to extinguish raves held on city-owned property, Toronto's rave communities were able to subvert the moralizing discourse designed to characterize them 'at risk', escaping the near moral panic.

The Influence of Family and Peers

As we have said, in early adolescence, parents have a tremendous influence on their children's health attitudes and actions. Partly through modelling and partly because of access, adolescents often adopt the health-related lifestyles of their parents and guardians. For example, teenagers whose parents smoke are much more likely to smoke than teens whose parents do not (Rantakallio, 1983). Likewise, teenagers whose parents drink a lot of alcohol are more likely than other teens to start drinking at an earlier age and to drink more heavily than average (Colder et al., 1997).

Family processes, and parent-child relations in particular, have a key influence on risky behaviour. Where family relationships are tense and conflict-filled, adults have less control over teenagers' behaviour. Family conflict disrupts parental control over children by reducing family attachment, parental monitoring, and normative regulation. Reductions in attachment and monitoring are consistent predictors of adolescent drinking (Gilbreth, 2001). However, authoritative parenting—which is loving and firm but fair—is the best parenting strategy, not only to prevent adolescent drug and alcohol abuse, but more generally to raise happy, confident children (Simons-Morton et al., 2001).

Besides the influence of parents, friends and peers are the most important source of socialization among teenagers. Study after study has reported that children and teenagers who believe their peers are using illegal drugs are much more likely to use them too (e.g., Dunlap et al., 2002; Cardenal et al., 2000). Curiosity, peer pressure, a desire to fit in, and a shared positive attitude towards drugs are reasons older teenagers often give to explain why they use illicit drugs and alcohol. Figure 6.3 shows peer influence on risk-taking behaviour in Canadian youths.

Teenagers who drink are unlikely to seek out friends who do not drink (Sieving et al., 2000). As a result, data from the National Longitudinal Survey of Children and Youth reveal that two-thirds of adolescents who report that all or most of their friends are using alcohol have, themselves, been drunk at least once. By contrast, only 8 per cent

Figure 6.3 Peer Influence on Risk-taking Behaviour

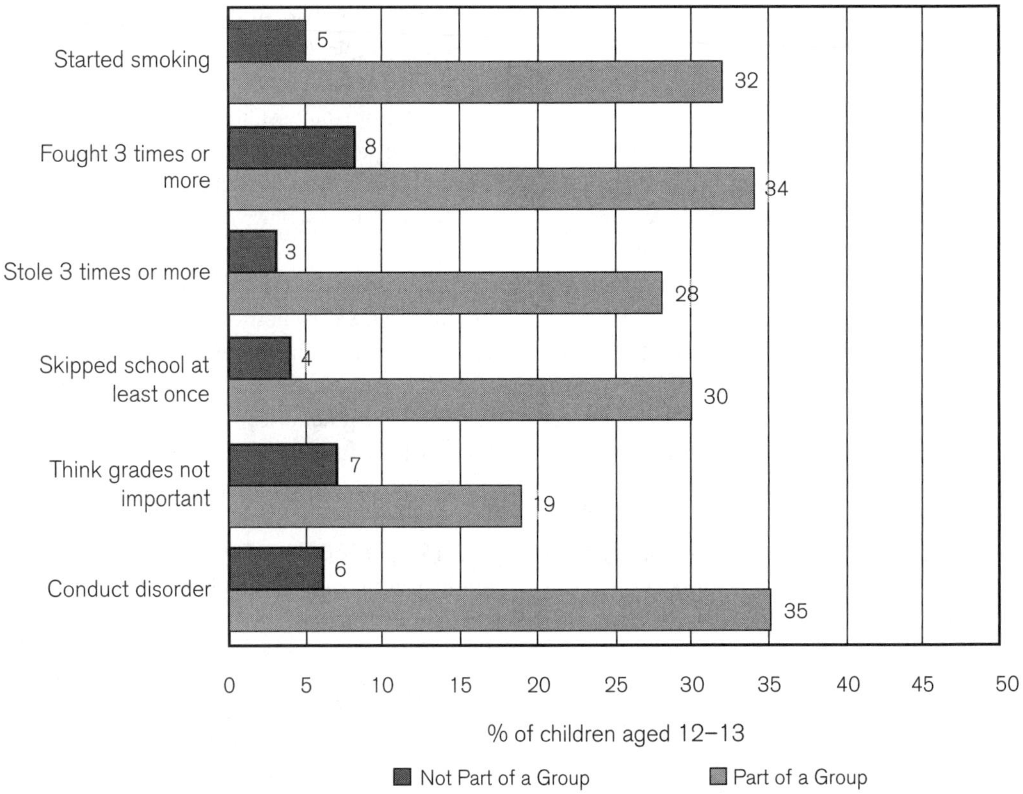

Started smoking: Not Part of a Group 5, Part of a Group 32

Fought 3 times or more: Not Part of a Group 8, Part of a Group 34

Stole 3 times or more: Not Part of a Group 3, Part of a Group 28

Skipped school at least once: Not Part of a Group 4, Part of a Group 30

Think grades not important: Not Part of a Group 7, Part of a Group 19

Conduct disorder: Not Part of a Group 6, Part of a Group 35

% of children aged 12–13

■ Not Part of a Group   ■ Part of a Group

SOURCE: Statistics Canada, Children and Youth in Canada Profile Series (Ottawa: Canadian Centre for Justice, Children and Youth in Canada); available at <www.statcan.ca>, accessed 19 December 2004; 1996 National Longitudinal Survey of Children and Youth, Cycle 2.

of those who report having few or no friends who use alcohol have ever been drunk. This research suggests, then, that friendships change teenagers' behaviours; however, the process appears to be indirect. Often the goal of adolescent risk-taking is as much to cement peer relations as it is to enjoy the outcome of the risk—whether alcohol, drugs, dangerous driving, or unsafe sex. Acceptance and status are key elements in the group equation. For this reason, we need to understand the relative strength of peer versus family influences on adolescents.

Thombs, Olds, and Ray-Tomasek (2001), examining public middle and high school students,

found that at all grade levels, perceived peer norms predicted tobacco and alcohol use more strongly than perceived parental norms. Said another way, adolescents were most likely to behave the ways they believed other young people were behaving. Beal et al. (2001), however, found results that are more mixed. In their research, parental attitudes and behaviours influence alcohol use; however, peer attitudes and behaviours influence other health-risk behaviours including tobacco, marijuana use, and sexual activity. In short, family control, support, and approval play a role, and so does peer approval, modelling, and support in predicting substance use among teens (Jones and Heaven, 1998).

Box 6.2 Nagging Teenagers to Drink

OTTAWA–Teenagers are more likely to get drunk and use drugs if they believe their parents are nagging them constantly, a new study says.

But Statistics Canada's first national study of alcohol and drug use among 12- to 15-year-olds also found peer group pressure is the strongest risk factor for substance abuse, with drinking and drug-taking more likely when their friends also drank or did drugs.

The survey of 4,296 young people, released Tuesday, found 4 in 10 had consumed one alcoholic drink at least once and more than one in five (22 per cent) had been drunk.

About one-fifth (or 19 per cent) also reported having smoked marijuana.

The younger adolescents were not asked about hallucinogens–including mushrooms, ecstasy, and LSD–but 11 per cent of teens aged 14 and 15 reported having tried them.

The average age which they reported they had their first drink was 12.4 years, and they first got drunk on average at 13.2 years of age. The average age for first-time marijuana use was slightly younger, at 13.1, and for experimenting with hallucinogens slightly older, at 13.8.

'Statistically, we wouldn't characterize it as common or an epidemic,' said co-author Dave Haans of Statistics Canada's Research Data Centre at the University of Toronto.

'Experimenting with alcohol and drugs in adolescence is fairly common. One of the other ways of looking at our figures is the majority of adolescents in our survey engaged in no substance use. It's a matter of seeing the glass half full or half empty.'

After asking the young teens several questions about their relationships with their parents, the researchers considered three aspects: hostile parenting, parental monitoring and parent–child cohesion.

Only young people whose parents had a negative or hostile parenting style were found to have significantly high odds of drinking to intoxication or drug use. The odds of being drunk and engaging in drug use increased by a factor of about 1.1 for every point increase in the hostile parenting scale.

But the study cautions against drawing any conclusions about cause and effect.

'The causal direction of the relationship between hostile parenting and substance use cannot be inferred, however. It is possible that the parents' way of dealing with the adolescent may have changed following problem behaviours such as alcohol or drug use,' the report states.

SOURCE: Excerpt, Sarah Schmidt, 'Nagging Teenagers to Drink', *Edmonton Journal*, 19 May 2004, A1.

Many factors influence this tug of war between family and peer influences. For example, adolescents cannot indulge in illegal drugs unless their social worlds offer them contact with dealers and knowledgeable individuals. At the same time, families characterized by strong adult-child relations and authoritative parenting practices tend to prevent their members from associating with potentially dangerous peers. A serious, addictive drug habit is unlikely to form without a breakdown in family relationships and the development of friendship with frequent and experienced drug users. Indeed, many studies have found that the combination of low parental supervision and an association with drug-using peers is a particularly potent recipe for teen substance use (e.g., Caldwell and Darling, 1999; Crowe et al., 1998; Reifman et al., 1998).

The success of community programs to promote good health practices and reduce risk-taking will depend largely on parental actions to inform their children. Families—especially, parents—are intermediaries between their children on the one hand and community institutions on the other. Often, parent-child dynamics influence whether teens are receptive to third-party health-related messages.

Though there are children who respect and listen to their parents concerning third-party health messages, there are also children who respect but reject their parents' advice. Moreover, youths who reject parental authority are likely to rebel against professional health advocates as well. Research bears this out—for example, adolescents are more likely to participate in smoking and alcohol prevention programs if they feel strongly attached to their parents (Ennett et al., 2001).

In recent years, there has been a lot of public debate about teenage sexuality and the use of school sex education, to curb, to inform, and to moderate sexual behaviour. Healthy family relationships can play a part in promoting the use of birth control and STD protection during adolescent intercourse. In an investigation of the risk factors for contracting HIV and other STDs, Boyer and fellow researchers (1999) found that school AIDS education and condom instruction predict safer behaviour and less AIDS risk. Supportive families with strong parent-child relationships also increase a teenager's protection against STD infection (Sionean et al., 2002).

However, this formal training in matters of sex is not certain to have the desired effect, namely, safe sex. It appears that formal sex education and parental sources of sexual information may increase *erotophobia*—or guilty and shameful feelings regarding sexuality. By contrast, peer sources of sex information appear to decrease erotophobic tendencies and therefore promote safer sex. It would seem, then, that to play a positive role, families and schools will have to provide information in a way that avoids inducing shame or guilt.

Among researchers who study the role of families, opinions are divided as to whether family *structure* or family *process* is the more dominant factor in determining adolescent risk behaviours. Upchurch and colleagues (2001) find evidence that emphasizes the importance of *structure* in their investigation of first sexual encounters among Hispanic teens living in Los Angeles. They note, for example, that teens living with both biological parents have a lower risk of sex, suggesting that family structure—specifically, the presence of a nuclear family organization—inhibits early sexual experimentation among young teenagers. Two parents at home, even if they are not particularly supportive or controlling, seem to play a significant role.

On the other hand, Miller and colleagues (1999a, 1999b) find that family *process* variables are strong predictors of risky sex. Family process variables include maternal monitoring, mother-adolescent general communication, mother-adolescent sexual communication, and mother's attitudes about adolescent sexual behaviour. Thomas and colleagues (2000), finally, found evidence that both structure and process influence adolescent sexual behaviour. On the one hand, children living in single-parent families are more likely to take sexual risks and misuse alcohol. On the other hand, a process variable—poor parental monitoring—increases the likelihood that children will have deviant peers and risky sexual habits, by leaving the children unwatched (Metzler et al., 1994).

This, of course, ignores the role of other factors influencing adolescent risk-taking, such as television and advertising. For example, it is evident that cigarette companies make strong efforts to recruit new smokers through their sponsorship of sports and other public events. Dewhirst and Sparks (2003) report that the tobacco industry has commissioned research on adolescent male smoking to help it identify those groups most likely to start smoking; then, it has sought to reach and influence these groups through sponsored activities that link the sponsoring cigarette brands to desirable peer-defined attributes and identities.

And, as we suggested in Chapter 5 on substance abuse, advertisers play on women's anxiety about their appearance to promote smoking as a means of weight control. Crisp and colleagues (1999) note that teenage girls often smoke cigarettes in the belief that it protects them from the impulse to binge eat, with its feared weight-gain consequences. An analysis of data on London (England) schoolgirls reveals links between smoking and body-weight/shape concerns. Girls who smoked were likely to be moderately overweight. Sensitivity to shape is largely and qualitatively prompted by the development of body fat in puberty, according to this research. Smoking was powerfully linked with vomiting undertaken as another defence against weight gain.

No wonder, then, that adolescents' perspectives on the need to smoke (Dunlap et al., 2002) are couched in terms of smoking being 'social, pleasurable, empowering, emotional, and full-fledged'—concepts that reek of commercial manipulation.

The History of Juvenile Delinquency, and Public Reactions to It

Juristat reports that in 2002–3 'youth courts in Canada processed 84,600 cases, involving 205,100 charges. Five offences accounted for just over half

of the total youth court caseload in 2002–3: theft (15 per cent), failure to comply with a disposition, *Young Offenders Act* (12 per cent), common assault (11 per cent), break and enter (9 per cent), and possession of stolen property (7 per cent). . . . Total cases processed in youth court have decreased 20 per cent between 1991–2 and 2002–3, primarily due to the steady decline in the number of crimes against property cases,' a drop of 47 per cent in this type of case alone (Robinson, 2004).

This decrease in property crimes over the 1990s probably reflects a number of changes, notably: (1) more people working at home for wages (i.e., telecommuting); (2) people fortifying their homes more thoroughly with electronic and other security devices; and (3) a smaller cohort of young people—the group most likely to perpetrate property crimes—owing to continuously declining fertility in the Canadian population.

A majority of the cases before the youth courts involved older youth, aged 16 and 17. Most cases were concluded within four months and resulted in a guilty finding. Probation was the most serious sentence in the majority of cases, while custody (secure or open) was the most serious offence just over one-quarter of the time.

What has changed most in recent centuries is the tendency to view delinquent acts as 'non-crimes' and young people as distinct from older people. We have all accepted the premise that young people are different from adults. In turn, adolescents have developed a distinctive culture and social identity, by which they differentiate themselves. Due to the emergence of 'adolescence' as a life stage, governments and policy-makers have had to take this group into consideration when forming new laws and policies.

With the extension of schooling, peer groups have also become more important, and peer pressures to conform to deviant norms have shaped delinquency over this period, pushing rebellious tendencies in the direction of norm-violation. We cannot understand juvenile delinquency without understanding peer groups as 'reference groups'—

Box 6.3 Pledge of Sexual Abstinence No Help against Venereal Disease

PHILADELPHIA (AP)—Teens who make a one-time pledge to remain virgins until marriage catch sexually transmitted diseases about as often as those who don't pledge abstinence, according to a study of the sex lives of 12,000 adolescents.

Those who make a public pledge to delay sex also wind up having fewer sex partners and get married earlier, the research shows. But the two groups' STD rates were statistically similar.

One of the problems, researchers found, is that virginity 'pledgers' are less likely to use condoms.

'It's difficult to simultaneously prepare for sex and say you're not going to have sex,' said Peter Bearman, chairman of Columbia University's sociology department, who co-authored the study with Hannah Bruckner of Yale University.

'The message is really simple: 'Just say no' may work in the short term but doesn't work in the long term'

Data from the study, presented yesterday at the National STD Prevention Conference, was taken from the National Longitudinal Study of Adolescent Health. That study was funded in part by the National Institute of Child Health and Human Development and the Centres for Disease Control and Prevention.

The analysis also found that in commu-nities where at least 20 per cent of adolescents pledged to remain virgins, the STD rates for everyone combined was 8.9 per cent. In communities with fewer than seven per cent pledgers, the STD rate was 5.5 per cent.

'It is the combination of hidden sex and unsafe sex that creates a world where people underestimate the risk of STDs,' Mr Bearman said.

Critics of abstinence-only education saw the findings as evidence that adolescents benefit from sex education.

'It's a tragedy if we withhold from these kids information about how not to get STDs or not to get pregnant,' said Dorothy Mann, executive director of the Family Planning Council, an organization dedicated to reproductive health services.

But Pat Fagan, who researches family and cultural issues at the Heritage Foundation, cautioned that one-time pledges were different from abstinence-only education, which he said takes years of support and education. He noted that the virginity pledges delayed sex and led to fewer partners.

'It shows the power of the pledges by themselves,' he said. 'It also shows that alone, a one-time pledge is not enough. Anyone connected with the abstinence movement would never say it's enough.'

groups of people to whom young people compare themselves, in forming their attitudes, beliefs, actions, and evaluations of themselves.

Thus reference groups can act like cliques, putting people under pressure to conform to delinquent standards of behaviour and take risks that are deemed cool, smart, or honourable. Failure to live up to the group norms can result in criticism, ridicule, exclusion, and isolation. Where virtual reference groups are involved, young people put pressure on themselves to conform to idealized group norms of appearance, dress, and behaviour. Failure to live up to their own idealized group norms can result in self-criticism and self-hate.

Delinquency is by definition criminal behaviour that is limited to younger people. In 1977, Greenberg pointed out that the age distribution of crime was shifting toward younger age brackets in the United States and Western Europe. With economic stagnation, and to save jobs for adults, juveniles were excluded from the paid labour market and forced to remain in school. This generated strains leading to delinquency. At the same time, the state—for financial reasons—reduced the penalties for juvenile offences, weakening formal methods of control and further increasing delinquency.

The frequency of delinquent behaviour—its high prevalence among young people—is to some important degree related to young people's precarious link to labour markets in early adulthood. Young people who drop out of school and have trouble gaining steady work have a lot of free time in which to commit delinquent acts.

For years, delinquency has been described as a group phenomenon or, at least, an activity that involves friendly co-offenders (Erickson and Jensen, 1977). When a person's friends or associates engage in delinquent behaviour, that person feels pressure—merely from being or wanting to be part of the group—to go along with the group and imitate their behaviour. Most young people do not want to be singled out and risk losing acceptance or status with the group (Reed and Rose, 1998).

Strategies for controlling delinquency have also changed in the past century. In Canada, institutions devoted to controlling young people existed in the late 1800s. However, it was not until 1908 that government passed the first federal legislation dealing with juvenile delinquency, a law subsequently revised in 1929. Under the *Juvenile Delinquents Act*, 'delinquency' was defined to include more than the adult crimes in the *Criminal Code*. It also included sexual immorality and cases of neglected, abused, or uncontrollable children. This Act established the state as a sympathetic guardian and treated the juvenile as a lost, misguided child needing care and supervision.

Two goals of the new legislation, enacted in 1984, were, first, to ensure that young offenders enjoyed more secure and comprehensive legal rights than they had under the old Act; and second, to prevent the stigmatization of young offenders by ensuring that their records of delinquency would not prevent them from reforming and entering adult life with a clean slate. On April 1, 2003, the *Youth Criminal Justice Act* (*YCJA*) replaced the *Young Offenders Act* of 1984. The Act introduces important changes to the Canadian youth justice system. We will discuss these changes in 'Policies and Theory Applications' later in this chapter.

The Activities of Juvenile Delinquents

Motor vehicle theft

Juristat reports that youths aged 12–17 account for 42 per cent of persons charged with motor vehicle theft. Overall, motor vehicle theft rates are 10 per cent higher than a decade ago. Canada ranks fifth highest of 17 countries for risk of car theft, with 1.6 per cent of the population reporting being victimized by car theft. Most vehicles are stolen from parking lots, streets, and homes (garages, driveways) (Wallace, 2003).

In general, the clearance rate for stolen vehicles is low: only 13 per cent of all vehicle thefts incidents were 'solved' by police—a rate of success comparable to that of other property crimes such as break-ins.

Substance abuse

Alcohol and drug abuse are other main areas of juvenile delinquency. Findings from the 1999 Ontario Student Survey on Drug Use (OSDUS) show that drug use levels are similar to those of the late 1970s—a time when drug use was at its peak (Adlaf, Paglia, and Ivis, 1999). Drug users are generally young people, and the number of young people who use drugs, at least occasionally, has increased in the last generation. In fact, every day an estimated three thousand children begin smoking cigarettes regularly.

The most alarming trend is the increasing use by youth of illegal drugs, tobacco, and alcohol. Young people who use these substances risk developing lifelong dependency problems and run other health risks. The longer the youth depends on alcohol and drug abuse, the harder it becomes for the individual to avoid horrible withdrawal symptoms.

Impaired driving and other traffic offences

According to *Juristat*, the rate of persons accused of impaired driving offences in 2002 was highest among young adults between the ages of 19 and 24 and lowest for those 65 and over. Almost three-quarters of court cases involving impaired driving resulted in a conviction, and of these, 14 per cent were sentenced to custody (Jahnevich, Gannon, and Morisset, 2003).

Generally, impaired driving offences have been declining over the past 20 years; the 2002 rate is 65 per cent lower than the peak in 1981. The single most likely explanation is the 'aging' of the Canadian population and the decline in the proportion of young people—those most likely to cause this offence (Jahnevich, Gannon, and Morisset, 2003).

Failure in school

Since most juveniles are required by law to be in school, delinquency can have an effect on school performance. Failure in school is an important factor in predicting juvenile crime and a predictor of future criminal behaviour. Adolescents who report doing poorly or very poorly in school are more than twice as likely to report getting drunk during the past year than those who report doing well.

Leaving school early reduces the chances that juveniles will develop the vocational and social skills we learn in school, such as learning to meet deadlines, follow instructions, and deal constructively with authority figures and peers. Research shows that, among Canadian 24 year olds, the dropout rate was 15 per cent in 1995 (Human Resources and Skills Development Canada, 2000). In turn, this means a large number of young Canadians are unqualified for well-paid jobs and, as a result, may resort to other, even illegal, means of earning money.

Sexual behaviour

Many researchers believe that health-risk behaviours shown during adolescence have their origins earlier in childhood. Most young people have views and beliefs about sexual behaviour long before they begin to express them.

Given the early age of first sexual intercourse, especially among urban, minority youth, the risk of sexually transmitted diseases is growing rapidly. Because of high-risk sex, these youths are putting themselves and others in danger of contracting venereal diseases. By 1997, nearly half of all surveyed American high school students had engaged in sexual intercourse (National Institute of Child Health and Human Development, 1999). Research reveals an alarming prevalence of risky behaviours already evident by seventh grade and the trend increases throughout high school (Kann et al., 1999).

Like other risky behaviours, juvenile sexual behaviour thrives on unsupervised time. Many youth spend long periods without adult supervision and may have limited opportunities to participate in after-school activities (Cohen et al., 2002). More than half of sexually active youths report that they have had sex at home after school. As youths get older, parents are more willing to leave them on their own. Many parents have no choice, needing to work for pay outside the home. This gives the young people many opportunities for sexual activity at home. Accordingly, sexual activity and substance abuse increases with the amount of unsupervised time youths spend at home.

Crime

The rate of youth crime in Canada has been decreasing since 1992. Despite the falling rate of occurrence, youth crime continues to need official attention. In 2001, 25 juvenile males and 5 females were accused of homicide, for example (Statistics Canada, 2005). According to Statistics Canada, the most common youth crimes of violence in 2001 were common assaults (8,708 cases), major assaults (4,948 cases), and uttering threats (1,103 cases). Among non-violent crimes, the most common were drug possession (4,058 cases) and drug trafficking (2,000 cases) (Statistics Canada, 2005).

Though it rarely results in arrest or conviction, violence is a common form of risky behaviour among male youths. During the 1990s, people also began to express concern about increasing violence among female youths. Over the last decade, the rate of adolescent girls charged with a violent crime has more than doubled, increasing three times as fast as the rate for males. Since 1992, the US national rate of violent crime among female youth has increased from 38 per 10,000 to 47 per 10,000 (Dell and Boe, 1998).

On the other hand, violent crime among youth was down 2 per cent in 2002. After increasing steadily throughout the 1980s, the rate of youths charged with violent crime continued to increase during the 1990s, but at a slower rate. Even with the most recent drop, the 2002 youth violent crime rate was still 7 per cent higher than a decade ago. The youth property crime rate fell 5 per cent in 2002 to its lowest level in over 25 years. So, juvenile crime remains a disturbing problem, but there is no evidence that it is an increasing problem.

Delinquent Communities and Subcultures

Delinquency is social behaviour, and we cannot understand individual delinquency unless we understand the gang context within which it is usually learned and practised.

We can trace the beginnings of the sociological understanding of gangs to classic works by Thrasher (1927), Whyte (1993 [1943]), and Cohen (1955). Frederick Thrasher believed that gangs originate in the playgroups of youth. He proposed that when group cohesion increases because of conflict with another group, the playgroup may evolve into a gang. Thrasher argued, 'Gangs represent the spontaneous effort of boys to create a society for themselves.' He also proposed a list of 'delinquency-directing factors' such as disintegration of the family, corruption and indifference in politics, academic inability, and lack of opportunity. (It is because of Thrasher's emphasis on gangs as resulting from social disorganization and promoting social cohesion that we can view him as a functionalist.)

The gang offers members something they are missing: relief from the oppression of adult norms and excitement that socially accepted routines fail to provide. The purpose of gangs, for Thrasher, is to create a better society for boys because their real society is inadequate, due to controlling institutions, limited education and opportunities, and deteriorating housing. For Thrasher, the gang fills in the gaps of what society can offer. Members form friendships within the gang.

Thrasher says that gangs grow out of the desire of boys to take part in a society to which they otherwise have little access. The group becomes a gang when it starts to form a clearer group consciousness, including a sense of rivals and enemies. It attains the status of gang when people in the neighbourhood want to break it up. Once the gang is threatened, its members come closer together and work to defend their membership. Thus, in Thrasher's conception, a gang is typically at odds with both society at large and the community within which the gang has formed.

By contrast, another classic work—*Street Corner Society*, published in 1943—tells a different story in which the gang has an organic relationship with the community in which it forms. William Foote Whyte, the author, studied a slum district in Boston known as Cornerville. Occupied mainly by Italian immigrants, Cornerville was crowded with low-income, working-class people and had a high rate of juvenile delinquency. Like Thrasher, Whyte says that gangs in Cornerville arise from the daily association of members over long periods of time. The stable composition of a gang, and a lack of social assurance that limits members' contacts with outsiders, leads to high rates of social interaction within the gang. In turn, the group interaction produces a system of mutual obligations that is essential to group cohesion. The gang members—'corner boys'—have a code that obliges them to help each other when they can and do each other no harm.

However, here Whyte parts company with Thrasher. Early sociologists believed that crime in poor neighbourhoods of the United States resulted from social disorganization: the more disorganization, the more crime. After roughly 1940, however, with the publication of *Street Corner Society*, sociologists changed their views. They came to recognize that crime—especially organized crime in poor neighbourhoods—was highly organized. It was also intimately connected with the social, political, and economic life of the people in the community. It was an intrinsic part of city life—indeed, of national, corporate, and political life.

Research likewise shows that modern organized crime operates at the intersection of legitimate and illegitimate business, family, and formal organization. It has as strong connections to white-collar crime as it does to vice crimes (such as drugs trafficking, pornography, and prostitution). Organized crime draws on the talents of professional, amateur, older, and younger criminals. What organized crime shows us dramatically is that crime is a learned, organized social activity with historical cultural roots. It is infused with traditional notions of kinship and friendship, honour and duty. This understanding that crime grows out of organization, not merely out of disorganization, is a discovery we owe to William Foote Whyte and his study of Cornerville delinquents.

Albert Cohen provides a third influential theory of gangs in his book *Delinquent Boys*, published in 1955. Cohen notes that gang members resist the pressures of home, school, and other agencies that attempt to regulate their activities, whether delinquent or not. He asserts that this resistance to authority is due to ineffective family supervision, the breakdown of parental authority, and hostility of children toward their parents. Given their community and family situation, delinquents of a lower-class origin create a counterculture to resist middle-class values.

In short, Thrasher, Whyte, and Cohen all point to a problematic relationship between delinquent gangs and the middle-class work ethic. Writers since Thrasher, Whyte, and Cohen have acknowledged that youth gangs can have a wide variety of origins, activities, and purposes, but none have much to do with attaining traditional middle-class success values. Gordon (1995), for example, finds five distinct types of 'young gangs': youth groups, youth movements, criminal groups, criminal business organizations, and street gangs. Youth groups are small clusters of friends who usually hang out in public places. Youth movements, on the other hand, are groups that dress distinctively and participate in specific activities.

The next three categories are criminally active, with criminal groups being groups of friends that get together with the motive of committing a crime (consists mainly of adults). Criminal business organizations are also groups of youth and adults that participate in criminal behaviours, and their sole motive is financial gain. Finally, street gangs are combined groups of youths and adults who form semi-organized groups for the purpose of profit. What distinguishes them is that the members of street gangs identify themselves through dress and by giving their gang a street name.

Researchers disagree about the level of organization and leadership of gangs and some argue that a variety of organizational structures exist in gangs. Youth become involved for a wide variety of reasons. Teevan and Dryburgh (2000), for example, interviewed high school boys and asked them to explain why they had engaged in five particular delinquencies. The most popular reason given by the boys was peer influence. Boredom and the shortfalls of their parents were also reasons given.

Other studies have found that adolescents get involved in gangs for psychological and interpersonal reasons. Gordon (1995) notes the push and pull of multiple forces: for example, the attraction of monetary rewards and psychological rewards such as friendship and a sense of belonging, and the thrust towards gang life delinquency by familial problems, academic failure, and physical and sexual abuse.

Research on jailed Canadian gang members studied the reasons for members' initial joining of gangs, leaving gangs, organization, composition, and activities of gangs. The files of 41 gang members held in British Columbia's provincial correctional centres were analyzed as part of a general census of youth and adult facilities, and interviews were conducted with 25 of these inmates. The majority of the jailed gang members were 25 years of age or younger, male, and members of 1 of 11 gangs. The findings reveal that, usually, the first contact with a gang occurred at a young age via a close relative or friend. All said that they had joined the gang gradually because of the rewards, material or psychological, that the gang offered. Speaking about joining the gang, members said things like, 'It made me feel proud,' 'I felt more powerful, I had nothing else to do and I had more friends if I joined,' and 'It felt good, I felt protected' (Gordon, 1994). Others joined because of boredom and because the gang offered some excitement.

In time, young people leave the gangs to which they have belonged, and some gangs even disband. West (1978) explains the processes of departure and disappearance of established gangs in terms of the low and unsatisfactory rewards, the high risks of arrest and imprisonment, and the new interrelations that develop and take precedence over criminal activity—for example, new relations with wives, girlfriends, and families.

Street youth

For many youths, home is not a place of refuge but instead a source of abuse, and a negatively charged emotional atmosphere. Some of the youths do not even choose to leave home but instead are throwaways; they mainly consist of gay, lesbian, and bisexual youths. Eighty per cent of street youth have not been employed since they have taken to the streets. For these young people, the three predominant methods of finding money for food and shelter are panhandling (75 per cent of street youths have panhandled), social assistance, and crime. In terms of crime, many street youths rely either on prostitution or survival sex (a trade of sex for food, shelter, or drugs) (Gordon, 1994).

Depression, disease, alcohol and substance abuse, as well as physical abuse pose continuous threats to young people on the street. For some, grouping together as a street family is a form of defence protecting the members against attacks, as well as increasing the chance of finding food and making money. Many times, street families are not sufficient to protect from all dangers. Many street youth succumb to the addictions of drugs and alcohol. HIV and other STDs are also a risk that street youths encounter because many of them are promiscuous. Depression is also a significant threat because many street youths become suicidal and self-destructive (Gordon, 1994).

Life on the street is extremely dangerous, largely because of the other people who live there. Baron (1997) studied 14 male street skinheads, ages 15 to 22 in Edmonton to examine their violent behaviour and the reasons behind it. He found that skinheads are drawn from homes characterized by extreme violence and oppression, experiences that left them likely to behave in violent ways. These tendencies are intensified by their school experiences, their homelessness, and the group and street norms that support aggressive behaviour.

Homeless youth, or street youth, show a variety of forms of delinquency. The classic work in this area is *Mean Streets: Youth, Crime and Homelessness* by Canadian sociologists John Hagan and Bill McCarthy. To research their book, Hagan and McCarthy collected survey and interview data from more than 800 homeless adolescents in Toronto and Vancouver. As well, they gathered data from 400 high school youth to compare the backgrounds of youth who live at home with those who live on the street.

They found that, compared to school youth, the majority of homeless youth come from dysfunctional families. These include families who are experiencing economic strain where that strain is translated into dysfunctional parenting styles. As well, a disproportionate number of street kids come from homes where there is family violence and sexual abuse. Once on the street, youth's lives are characterized by a daily search for food, shelter, income, and companionship. If you hold all background variables constant, including prior involvement in crime, one factor consistently increases involvement in crime: lack of the necessities of life (i.e., food, shelter, or source of income). Crime, for street youth, is a clear practical response to need. The influence of peers is another factor that increases street youth's involvement in crime.

Once they arrive on the street, youth become increasingly immersed in networks of other street youth and street adults, many of whom are heavily involved in crime. Employment is a turning point in the lives of street youth. In the same way that the street network encourages certain behaviours, the work network promotes employment issues. Employment comes to have an important effect on street youth's involvement in crime and other dangerous activities characteristic of street life. Most street youth are in and out of employment,

not chronically unemployed. Street youth who find stable, long-term employment are less involved in several types of crime and spend less time hanging out on the street.

Theories about Juvenile Delinquency

Psychological explanations

From a psychological point of view, crime and delinquency among juveniles are due to personality disorders often developing during childhood. These include learned tendencies toward anti-social (e.g., violent or abusive) behaviour, feelings of low self-esteem that result in aggression turned inward or against others, and problems of attachment that may make it impossible for young people to trust others. Many kinds of childhood experiences can produce these psychological outcomes. Child sexual abuse, for example, is thought to be an especially important factor in female delinquency and crime, as well as prostitution, drug abuse, and bad parenting. Evidence supporting such connections between early childhood experience and later delinquency and crime comes from research on personality defects and disorders among delinquents, mental disease in prisoners, and studies of psychopathic and sociopathic personalities.

By their nature, however, psychological theories are non-situational. They emphasize the portable, relatively unchanging characteristics that predispose people toward deviant and criminal acts. Their virtue is that they provide a deep understanding of the internal dynamics that underlie delinquent behaviour by 'troubled' youth. Their weakness is that psychological theories are largely unable to account for the fact that most delinquents mature out of delinquency: that delinquency proves to be a passing phase of their lives. As such, delinquency is profoundly situational and social.

Sociological explanations

By contrast with psychological explanations that focus on the individual, sociological explanations explain youthful crime and delinquency in terms of culture, social structure, and social interaction.

Functionalism

Recall that functional theories of behaviour focus on the universality of the behaviour, and explain the behaviour in terms of its supposed contribution to the social order. Thus, for functionalists, the 'normality of crime' suggests that crime may make a positive contribution to social well-being and cohesion. Durkheim noted that in large societies, the social bonds are weakened and deviant behaviours increase. Norms and values are the social glue that bind people together in groups through a combination of informal social controls, restricted geographic mobility, and sense of familiarity.

As societies develop and grow, however, the moral ties that bind people together weaken because they cannot be reinforced by close, personal, contact. As societies become larger and more complex in terms of the multitude of social relationships that exist, they need complex mechanisms to regulate these relationships. Without the 'rule of law', social disorganization prevails. In effect, crime provides a positive function because it stimulates social cohesion and promotes the development of more complex social arrangements—such as a specialized legal system that is differentiated from the religious or political systems of society.

Secondarily, according to some functionalists, crime and delinquency are a result of social disorganization and defective attachment to the social order. Juvenile delinquency occurs because social bonds are weakened and youths spend less and less time with people who reinforce positive behaviours. Unsupervised households and neighbourhoods that lack cohesion, for example, are sources of social disorganization that produce personal disorganization and delinquency. Disorganized neighbourhoods lack the informal controls that help to prevent delinquency, and they undermine the controlling functions of family, school, and peer group (Peterson, 2002).

However, other functionalists take a different position on social disorganization. As Whyte (1993 [1943]) showed in his sociological classic *Street Corner Society*, gang delinquency may be tightly integrated with—and contribute to—the integration of political, economic, and adult criminal activity in a slum community. Additionally, juvenile delinquency and crime have their own functions for the youths, providing them with an 'alternative world' that requires consensus and cohesion. Thus, delinquency may not always be functional for the adult world, but it is often functional for the adolescent world—in the sense of creating communal and subcultural boundaries around young people.

To understand why adolescents engage in potential risk behaviours, it is important to look at the functions of these behaviours for adolescents' social and personal functioning. Risky behaviours may provide young people with an opportunity to strengthen their contacts with peers or initiate new contacts that produce positive peer relations (Engels and ter Bogt, 2001). From this point of view, then, delinquent behaviours give youths an opportunity to prove themselves and establish themselves among their peers.

Conflict theory

By contrast, the essence of conflict theory is to focus on how particular social arrangements benefit one social group at the expense of others. Conflict theorists reject the idea that any behaviour or arrangement benefits the entire society. For this reason, they assume that society will continually experience conflict between groups, and continually change because of this conflict. Accordingly, conflict theorists find that juvenile delinquency is a result of class-based conflict between one or more groups.

Conflict can also result from a power struggle, or arise between the legal system (judges, police officers, etc.) and minority groups who feel oppressed by it. It can even reflect a conflict between young people (and their value systems) and older people, many of whom are their parents. From this perspective, juvenile delinquency can be viewed as young people acting out against advantaged members of society. Consider, for example, a juvenile who damages his or her abusive parent's car or other property. The juvenile is committing an illegal act by destroying property, but we can also understand the behaviour as an outcry against abusive treatment.

In part, this is because economic exploitation produces stunted personal relations, as well as poverty. Low-income, urban adolescents of colour living in distressed neighbourhoods are at high risk for not developing the relationships and skills they need to progress from adolescence to adulthood. Many young people are forced to use unique strengths and strategies to make their way through the violence, racial discrimination, and lack of economic opportunities that characterize their communities.

In a society marked by poverty and class conflict, high rates of juvenile delinquency may indicate a deteriorating social fabric under conditions of rapid social change. Criminological theories suggest, however, that such conditions do not per se produce delinquency: instead, they force youth into pro-delinquent leisure activities—risky behaviours— with peers. Drinking, drug use, or automobile theft support delinquent behaviour and offer the infrastructure for it. The extent to which adolescents engage in pro-delinquent peer activities depends more on the cultural context that adolescents live in than on their personal experience in the family and in public.

Conflict theorists also recognize that the definition of what is criminal and what is delinquent reflects the desires, values, and interests of the most powerful groups and that these definitions both change over time and conflict with the interests of less powerful groups—juveniles in this case. Greater conflict and change in society means that more rules are formulated and applied. As a result, criminal and delinquent activity may increase from one time period to another simply because of an increase in the number of rules. What is best for middle-class members of society may not always be best for young members of the dispossessed 'underclass'.

Symbolic interactionist theory

According to symbolic interactionists, people define themselves—including their identity, self-concept, values, and attitudes—through the process of social interaction. Through interaction and negotiation, participants work together to define and construct social reality. Within this context, several approaches help to explain juvenile delinquency.

As we saw earlier, labelling theory is concerned with the processes by which a deviant label is attached to specific people and their behaviour. Being labelled a 'delinquent', for example, depends largely on the reactions of others toward nonconforming behaviours. Thus, the creation of delinquency is a two-person activity; it requires an actor and an observer (or labeller). Labelling theorists are not particularly interested in the reasons why people commit deviant acts. Further, they are interested in the consequences of being labelled deviant.

Labelling theorists recognize that an important consequence of the labelling process is its effect on the individual's identity and self-esteem. This labelling process may have a particularly forceful effect on young people. Some teenagers may respond to other's labels, at least in part, by accepting their judgment and engaging in behaviours that live up to, or down to, the given label.

Another consequence of labelling is that if a person's behaviour becomes known and labelled as deviant, opportunities for legitimate activity may diminish. Moreover, the possibility of associating with delinquent peers may increase as a result of the lack of respectable friends. By being labelled deviant and inadvertently associating with fellow delinquents, the individual increases his or her chances of increased deviant behaviour.

Differential association theory, the product of twentieth-century criminologist Edwin H. Sutherland (1940), grows out of Sutherland's observation that peers influence delinquent behaviour.

Learning involves motives and drives, as well as the techniques to commit the crime. Moral learning takes place in the course of social interaction, and people learn criminal or delinquent behaviour in the same way as any other social behaviour. Thus, the early socialization of juveniles plays a big role in their later life.

People behave the ways they think their reference group behaves.

Feminist approaches

As we have said, feminist theories focus on important differences between male and female behaviour, and explain the differences in terms of differential opportunities and pressures in what has historically been a male-dominated society.

While recorded female crime has not increased much in certain areas—for example, homicides or serious assaults—it has increased in others, including delinquency and minor assaults. Two points of view contend about this increase in female criminality. One approach, represented by Adler (1975), argues that as women have become more involved in public life and the labour market particularly, their opportunities for crime have increased and, therefore, so have their crimes. Critics respond that the increased criminality is more likely to indicate a reduced tolerance for female rule-breakers and a greater willingness to treat them the same as male rule-breakers.

This is supported by English research. Box and Hale (1983) tested the hypothetical relationship between women's liberation and the female crime rate in England and Wales using statistics between 1951 and 1980. Their indicators of liberation were (reduced) fertility, increased number of females who were higher education students and graduates, female labour force participation, and number of unattached (i.e., single, divorced, and widowed) women. The researchers found no relation to rates of female criminality. However, changes in female unemployment rates and reforms in penal procedures were significant. A related study by the same authors (1984) used national-level statistical data

from England and Wales for 1951–80 to compare three explanations of rising female criminality. They found little support for Adler's emancipation/liberation theory. However, changes in social labelling appear to have had a significant impact on female conviction rates.

We have already noted the predominance of males in a variety of risky behaviours—excess drinking, dangerous driving, and so on—and emphasized that this is due to male socialization. Our culture's idea of 'masculinity' requires this kind of dangerous, anti-social behaviour. Is it due to faulty parenting or a rejection of the female role? Some feminist theorists believe that recorded deviance by women reflects their economic marginalization, dependency, and close supervision by men. Others believe that it shows a growing equality between men and women. During the 1990s, for example, the rate of 12- to 17-year-old girls charged with a violent crime more than doubled, increasing three times as fast as the same rate for males (Statistics Canada, 2005). However, beyond that, little empirical evidence shows increasing female criminality or growing gender similarity in crime.

The differential treatment of boys and girls by the juvenile justice system is well documented in the literature. Prior research has shown that police and courts often penalize girls for participating in behaviours that violate gender role expectations, and do not penalize boys the same way. Girls who exhibit behaviours typically found under the umbrella of 'public peace' or 'status offences'—including activities such as being sexually active, running away, staying out past curfew, staying out all night, being truant from school or being disrespectful to parents—have traditionally been treated differently than boys (Shook, 2001).

Of course, gendered treatment of males and females does not only occur in our legal system. Parents treat girls and boys differently too. Svensson (2003), for example, investigated gender differences in adolescent drug use, in terms of parental monitoring and peer deviance. He found that parents monitored their daughters more closely than they monitored their sons, and sons were more exposed to deviant peers than were daughters. This supports both feminist theories about gendering and the differential association theory discussed earlier.

Gangs have historically been recognized as androcentric (male-dominated). Females were usually viewed as the sexual objects or deviant tomboys who were no more than the affiliates of male gang members. Increasingly, however, female gang members are establishing themselves as equals to their male counterparts. Statistics Canada shows that between 1986 and 1990, there was a 29-per-cent increase in the number of females charged by police (the numbers increased from a count of 18,336 to 23,610). Despite this increase in female offenders, 77 per cent of crimes are still committed by male delinquents. The existence and development of female gangs is receiving more research by experts.

John Hagan and his associates have attempted, in the power-control theory, to explain the observed interaction between class (on the one hand) and gender (on the other hand) in producing delinquency and crime rates. More specifically, they have attempted to explain why working-class girls have lower rates of delinquency than their working-class brothers, while middle-class girls have the same rates of delinquency as their middle-class brothers, and both have higher rates of delinquency than working-class girls. The answer has to do with occupational and domestic inequalities.

In a two-parent (two-earner) middle-class family, the husband and wife have roughly equal work roles; this translates into roughly equal household power and shared childrearing. This, in turn, translates into roughly equal treatment of sons and daughters. For a variety of reasons—not least, the absence of both parents from the home during the day—both sons and daughters are supervised loosely. Because of the middle-class value system, both sons and daughters are socialized to value success and mobility. In the capitalist economic system, this means they are taught to value risk-taking (within the framework of legally permitted behaviours). This lack of supervision and training in risk-taking increases the likelihood of delinquent behaviour by both sons and daughters equally.

By contrast, in a two-parent working-class family—with a stay-at-home or part-time working mother—the husband and wife have unequal work roles; this translates into an unequal household dominated by the husband and unequal treatment of sons and daughters. The father focuses on his instrumental responsibilities, granting sons greater freedom to prepare them for the traditional male role of their fathers. The mother is left to closely supervise the children, especially the daughters, who are socialized into domesticity in preparation for a life like their mother's, focusing on domestic labour and consumption. In this context, sons are encouraged to experiment and take risks. Daughters, on the other hand, are closely watched to prevent their participation in deviant or delinquent activity. This differential supervision of sons and daughters means a differential likelihood of delinquent behaviour.

As a result, working-class daughters are the least likely of all to engage in delinquent or criminal acts; middle-class sons and daughters are more likely to engage in delinquent or criminal acts, and working-class sons may be equally likely to do so. In short, sociologist John Hagan argues that to understand crime rates we need to know about more than just class or poverty: we need also to understand the interaction between class experiences and gender experiences.

Hagan's theory can be criticized as a variant of the 'liberation hypothesis', saying that as females experience upward mobility and status change, their access to deviant and illicit behaviours expand. It can also be seen as a critique of the two-earner, loosely supervised middle-class family. Most important, debate has raged about the role of class versus attachment in the production of deviant behaviour. Specifically, given what many sociologists claim to be the declining importance of social class as an explanatory variable (e.g., Clark and Lipset, 1991),

Hagan's theory puts a great deal of emphasis on the relationships among social class and patriarchy, values, child supervision, and delinquency.

If valid, the theory—really, a theory about the effects of patriarchy on children—may in time help us to explain other male-female differences besides criminality. A recent paper by Hagan, McCarthy, and Foster (2003), for example, has explored the effects of patriarchal upbringing on the distribution of depression (or 'despair') between sons and daughters.

As McCubbin (2002) points out, pathways to population health and well-being are rooted in the social, economic, and political organization of society. Structures of power and control shape our lives at both the individual and collective levels. As a result, empowerment and self-efficacy—psychological concepts—should be seen in relation to social outcomes such as work stress, with different effects on men and women. Despite possible negative effects in the form of criminality, empowerment and self-efficacy are generally good for people's health.

Runaway youths

Homeless youth, or street youth, show a variety of forms of delinquency. We need contributions from all the major sociological and psychological theories to explain this range of behaviours. Reasons for fleeing the parental home are both social and psychological. Explanations of their drug and alcohol abuse, and their petty larcenies and prostitution on the street, also require both sociological and psychological insights. Armed with both types of theory, we can begin to understand the delinquent behaviour of runaways, addicts, petty criminals and prostitutes.

Many street youth are 'runaways', children who stray from their parental homes, rules, and expectations and, in these respects, violate the norms of society. A variety of interpersonal and family relationships, school difficulties, and problems with siblings shape adolescents' decisions to run away (Spillane-Grieco, 1984). Most street youth come from families that suffer serious emotional, mental, or substance abuse problems. Unlike street children in developing countries, these youth are rarely on the street for reasons of family poverty (Price, 1989), though family financial difficulties increase the likelihood of physical abuse and abuse increases the likelihood of running away.

Homeless youth are most likely to come from broken families that are financially unstable or reconstituted (families comprising formerly married partners and their children) families that are financially stable (McCormack, Burgess, and Gaccione, 1986). Abuse aside, the children often come from 'chaotic/aggressive families' and reveal a mixed pattern of youth aggression and parental skill deficiency (Teare, Authier, and Peterson, 1994).

Sexual abuse is a common element in the stories of homeless youth. Here again, poverty is only a minor element. Both runaway males and females are likely to have been sexually abused (Rotheram-Borus et al., 1996). Among adolescent runaways interviewed in a Toronto shelter, one in three males and three in four females report having been sexually abused. Many male victims of sexual abuse report a fear of adult men. Another Toronto study also reports high rates of substance use and abuse, attempted suicide (30 per cent of runaways report having attempted suicide in the past), loneliness, and depression among the street youth population (Adlaf, Zdanowicz, and Smart, 1996).

Running away is usually a response to neglect, abandonment, and physical or sexual violence (Cote, 1992). Janus and colleagues (1995) estimate that 74 per cent of runaway males and 90 per cent of the females had been physically abused at least once. Most of these adolescents have been victims of chronic, extreme abuse, experienced at a young age, often perpetrated by the biological parents and initiated before the first runaway episode.

Abused runaways are even more likely than those who were not abused to describe their parents in ways that suggest serious anti-social personality and drug problems (Stiffman, 1989a, 1989b).

Parents are often the villains in these stories. Powers, Eckenrode, and Jaklitsch (1990) report that, of New York runaways and homeless youth, 60 per cent had suffered physical abuse, 42 per cent emotional abuse, 48 per cent neglect, and 21 per cent sexual abuse.

Officially there were about 1 million substantiated cases of abuse in the US in 1996, which makes the number actually higher, since many cases of abuse go unreported (Jenson and Howard, 1999). Biological mothers were the most often cited perpetrators of maltreatment (63 per cent), followed by biological fathers (45 per cent). Parents had pushed more than one-third of the homeless youth out of their homes.

Many chronic runaways grow up to be homeless adults who display higher than average rates of criminal behaviour, substance abuse, and other forms of deviant behaviour (Simons and Whitbeck, 1991). In the United States, children from families that have an income below $15,000 per year were shown to be 20 times more likely to be abused than children in wealthier families (Jenson, 1989). A history of foster care, group home placement, and running away is particularly common among homeless adults (Susser et al., 1991). In short, the production of runaways and homeless children is the production of a new crop of adult rule-breakers and, often, criminals.

Health and Social Consequences

All the delinquent and criminal youth behaviours we have discussed so far have important health and social consequences. Because they are risky behaviours they often carry heavy costs.

Substance abuse is often costly to young people, for example. Youth who inject drugs suffer an increased risk of contracting hepatitis from used needles. They are also at risk of HIV and other sexually transmitted diseases because they are likelier to engage in high-risk behaviours, including the use of injected drugs and in activities resulting from poor judgment and impulse control while under the effects of mood-altering substances.

Violence, though scarcely confined to youth, is another consequential behaviour. For millions of youths and their families, a period of life that should be marked by good health and great promise, instead is marred by injuries, disability, and death (Cook and Laub, 1998). Violent acts, for example, can have many types of health consequences. Repetitive violence can have major harmful effects on psychological well-being. Victims of intimate partner or dating violence have a greater risk of depression and self-directed violence. Further consequences are lowered self-esteem, anxiety, alcohol, and drug abuse.

Risky sex is a continuing problem, because it causes unwanted pregnancies—with attendant problems of interrupted schooling, family conflict, and bad parenting—and spreads sexually transmitted diseases. Sex education in schools and programs like SHOP (School Health Opportunities and Progress) promoted by SIECUS (The Sexuality Information and Education Council of the United States) provide teenagers with important information about sex, sexual orientation, and substance use and abuse.

All three of these consequential problems—substance abuse, unsafe sex, and violence—are discussed at greater length in other chapters of this book.

Policies and Theory Applications

A great deal of public effort is aimed at preventing and correcting risky behaviour, especially in the form of juvenile delinquency. This is not only because it is often costly in its consequences but also because it directly rejects the dominant value system of society—the work ethic we discussed earlier in this chapter.

Strategies of arrest, probation, and incarceration do not seem to result in significantly improved juvenile behaviour. *Juristat* reports that in 1999–2000, three-fifths of the nearly 57,000 convicted offenders between 18 and 25 years of age had at least one previous conviction, either in adult criminal court or youth court. Property offenders were particularly likely to re-offend.

A majority of recidivists aged 18 to 25—64 per cent of males and 57 per cent of females—convicted in 1999–2000 had been convicted at least once for an offence committed before they had turned 18 years of age. The earlier in life they had been first convicted, the larger the total number of prior offences they would have ever committed. 'Longer criminal histories tended to correspond with higher incarceration rates. Recidivists with multiple adult convictions had an incarceration rate nearly twice as high (41 per cent) as recidivists with a single adult conviction (22 per cent). Incarceration rates were higher for repeat offenders with an early age of first conviction,' nearly twice as high for those first convicted at age 12 than for those first convicted at age 17.

Thus, punitive strategies do not seem to cure children of their delinquent tendencies. In fact, they may solidify these tendencies and lock people into criminal careers. We have argued in this chapter that juvenile delinquency is highly correlated with—and may be a subtype of—youth risk-taking behaviour. Rotheram-Borus (2000), reviewing the progress of recent initiatives, reports that current programs reduce risk not only by curbing sexual activity and substance use, but also by 'decreasing poverty; ensuring access to HIV testing, health-care, general social skills training, and employment opportunities; and requiring community service for students.'

Recreational programs help to deal with the problem of youth supervision. They are a valuable addition to educational programs that provide useful information and keep youths off the streets, away from possible violence, substance abuse, and other risky behaviours.

All of these recreational programs give youth an opportunity to socialize, use their energy in organized sports, and stay off the streets where they are more likely to get into trouble and engage in risky behaviours. As Kahne and colleagues (2001) suggest, structured, safe, and enjoyable contexts provide youth with more than just encouragement to 'say no' to risky behaviour; they provide something to which youth can 'say yes'.

As a society, we can respond to the complex problems of risky behaviour and delinquency in many different ways. Public interventions associated with delinquency may have their origins in child welfare, child protection, mental health, physical health, education, criminal law, or family law. Most countries, including Canada, hold young people of a certain age responsible and accountable for criminal behaviour. In recent decades, the juvenile justice systems of most Western nations have been under pressure to impose harsher penalties on juvenile offenders.

Most experts believe that harsh punishments do not deter delinquent activities, so we should not bring juveniles into the harsh adult courts and prisons. Many members of the public believe that the punishments for delinquency are not harsh enough, especially when it comes to serious crimes such as murder. They would favour a symbolic, punitive exercise of the law, even if a more punitive law fails to reform juveniles or deter delinquency. For those youth who face the formal youth justice system, the new *Youth Criminal Justice Act* (*YCJA*) includes sentencing principles that provide a clear, consistent, and coherent code for youth sentences. They are intended to reduce disparity and reflect a fundamentally fairer approach to sentencing.

The new legislation states that the purpose of sentencing is to hold a young person accountable for the offence committed by imposing meaningful consequences and promoting the rehabilitation and reintegration of the young person. The Act makes a new effort to ensure that similarly situated youth receive similar treatment for similar offences. Proportionality sets the framework or limits within which the needs of the young person committing the offence are to be addressed through the criminal justice system in order to achieve rehabilitation and reintegration.

The *YCJA* does away with the possibility of transferring a youth into the adult judicial system. A young person, even if charged with a serious offence, still receives age-appropriate due process protections, such as special access to independent counsel and privacy protections. The youth justice procedure for the most serious offences will be speedier, while retaining age-appropriate due process protections and maintaining respect for the presumption of innocence.

The purpose of sentencing, under this Act, is to hold young people accountable for their offence by imposing penalties that have meaningful consequences and promote the offender's rehabilitation and integration into society. Under the new legislation, the sentence a youth receives is proportional to the seriousness of the offence.

One of the new sentences available under the *YCJA* is the 'custody and supervision order'. This sentence is made up of two components: a period of custody and a period of supervision within the community, specifically, in the ratio of two-thirds custody to one-third supervision. This sentence is intended for a young person who is found guilty of a serious offence—that is, murder, attempted murder, manslaughter, sexual assault—for which a non-custodial sentence would be inconsistent with the purpose and principles of youth sentencing. This sentence requires a plan for the intensive treatment and supervision of the offender, to assist the young person in the transition from custody to successful reintegration into the community.

Another option, the Intensive Support and Supervision Program, is a community-based program that is intended to be an alternative to custody for young offenders who do not pose a threat to public safety and can be supervised within the community. To aid in the young offender's rehabilitation, this program provides closer monitoring and more support than conventional probation. Designed to address the particular needs and risks of particular youth, this sentence requires the young offender to attend non-residential programs at spec-ified times and on conditions set by the court.

The *YCJA* recognizes that many young people are brought into the formal justice system for minor offences that often could be effectively dealt with in the community in less formal ways. While reserving the formal court process for more serious offences, *YCJA* provides for a range of penalties and programs to deal with less serious crimes. These extrajudicial penalties, focusing on personal accountability and repairing the harm done, include verbal warnings from the police and informal police diversion programs such as family conferences that bring together the youth, his or her family, the victim, and others in addressing the young person's offence. Other formal programs require community service or compensation.

Many provisions of this Act are intended to correct flaws in earlier delinquency legislation. The *Young Offenders Act* of 1984, and public responses to it, illustrated a basic conflict in popular views on juvenile delinquency. The juvenile justice system has historically struggled to fulfill the conflicting goals of maintaining public safety while helping youthful offenders integrate back into society. Though the problem of juvenile crime has persisted through the years, the repertoire of interventions employed by juvenile justice officials has swung between punitive and rehabilitative policies, and may continue to do so (Meisel, 2002).

Future Trends

The most important single fact to note is that, due to steadily declining rates of childbearing since the mid-1960s, there are ever-fewer young people in Canadian society. The exceptions to this rule are found in high-fertility Aboriginal and immigrant communities. The result of continued low fertility, a decline in young people, means necessarily a reduction in the numbers of young people at risk of delinquency, dangerous driving, substance abuse, and the other problems we have discussed in this chapter. As their numbers decline, society as a whole 'ages' and fewer young people are at risk of breaking the rules.

Additionally, treatment options for delinquent youths have diversified over the past 20 years. However, the debate about the most effective treatment of young offenders continues. Sociology argues that we need to understand delinquency in its social context. Research has shown that family and neighbourhood characteristics affect juvenile delinquency and crime significantly. Some of the delinquency in high-crime areas occurs because juveniles never learned the conforming behaviour and skills necessary to avoid getting in trouble.

Often, delinquency results from social disadvantage. So, for example, *Juristat* reports: 'Aboriginal youth continue to be over-represented in the youth correctional system, accounting for 24 per cent of admissions to sentenced custody and 22 per cent of probation admissions, while representing only 5 per cent of the youth population [in 2000–1]' (Marinelli, 2002). Given the role of poverty and neighbourhood characteristics play in fostering juvenile delinquency and crime, it is likely that reducing poverty and the economic disparity between the affluent and the poor members of our society would help reduce some forms of crime and delinquency among youths.

Young people use alcohol and drugs for some of the same reasons that adults use them—to relieve stress and to escape emotional pain. At the same time, young people may use these substances for a variety of other reasons: to declare independence, signal membership in a peer group, or satisfy curiosity, among other reasons. For this reason, comprehensive programs, involving multiple components, are much more likely to be effective than single-focused activities in solving the problems associated with delinquency. Because many factors contribute to problems associated with risky and dangerous behaviours—including delinquency, crime, and violence—it is important that communities identify and address relevant factors with programs that are well coordinated.

Families and schools are critically important domains in the prevention of youth substance abuse, for example. Because family life and school life are part of the problem, they must be part of the solution. Additionally, the media, youth agencies, sports and arts groups, communities of faith, and municipal governments should augment efforts at the community level.

Concluding Words

As we have seen, juvenile delinquency is a continuing concern in Canadian society, and people disagree about the best way to understand the prevalence of delinquency. Competing approaches provide competing interpretations of delinquency and competing suggestions for control. We have taken the approach that delinquency is largely a result of several main factors: especially, learned adolescent risk-taking, peer pressures to conform, and the lack of a stake in conformity.

The learning of risky behaviour, especially by boys, is something our culture has to remedy. Peer pressures to conform—especially, to deviant gang norms—can be remedied only by offering youth competing activities that yield fulfillment and status. Finally, aging and maturation will, for most young people, bring a stake in conformity. In the meantime, we need to reduce the risk and harm associated with deviant and delinquent adolescent behaviours. This we can do by improved public education, more sensitive parenting, and fairer, less stigmatizing strategies of control.

Where it is evident that we cannot eliminate certain types of delinquent or high-risk behaviours, we have to do the next best thing, which is to reduce the degree of personal and social harm associated with that activity.

Summary

Adolescence is a time of increased risk-taking. Among peers, we paid particular attention to the role of gangs in supporting and promotion of risky and delinquent behaviour. Different theories of deviance were examined, including psychological and sociological theories. Functionalism and Durkheim, conflict theory, symbolic interactionism, labelling theory, differential association, and feminist theories were all explained.

The consequences of youth deviance were explored through the health consequences that present themselves to society because of various youth deviant acts, such as HIV and risky sexual behaviour. Educational and recreational programs alike were created to better deal with the consequences, education and prevention of deviant behaviour. We saw how the Young Offenders Act and the Youth Criminal Justice Act are reactions to adolescent deviant behaviour and try to ensure that young rule-breakers will be treated somewhat differently from older (adult) ones.

Questions for Critical Thought

1. The 'culture of poverty' explanation holds that delinquents display traits such as a belief in fate, danger, luck, and risk-taking. Is this true of all delinquent acts? What is the major criticism of this theory?
2. What aspects of adolescent life can lead to a deviant behaviour?
3. The media portrayal of adolescent youth is overwhelmingly negative. In what ways (if any) is the media image of the delinquent youth justifiable?
4. Some classic studies claim that gangs originate in youth playgroups. Explain how this is a functionalist approach.
5. How does a conflict theorist conceptualize juvenile delinquency?
6. Girls now smoke more than boys do. Describe how a feminist theorist would explain this fact.
7. Why might some Canadians oppose the YOA and YCJA? What is your opinion of these acts?
8. According to Durkheim, where would one be more likely to find a higher crime rate: in a large city where people are unknown or in a small town where everyone knows each other?
9. What evidence could one use to prove delinquency is the result of parental influence? How could one prove that it was due to peer pressure?
10. The feminist theory mentions that males may be more deviant than females because of cultural ideas of masculinity. What aspects of masculinity lend themselves to a deviant lifestyle?

Recommended Reading

Mannheim, Betty. (1957), 'An Investigation on the Interrelations of Reference Groups, Membership Groups, and the Self-Image: A Test of the Cooley-Mead Theory of the Self', PhD dissertation, University of Illinois, Urbana. Adolescence is a period of self-construction and Cooley and Mead described the self as a social product.

The self is social and, as such, it changes throughout life, adolescence is a particularly crucial time during self-development.

Whyte, William Foote. (1993), 'Revisiting *Street Corner Society*', *Sociological Forum*, 8 (2): 285–98. The author reflects on his classic study of the Chicago gang subculture. Whyte tells how he immersed himself in the gang life and produced a classic qualitative study of gangs in Chicago, and their relationship to the social and political environment.

Williams, L. Susan. (2001), 'City Kids and Country Cousins: Rural and Urban Youths, Deviance, and Labor Market Ties', in *Social Awakening: Adolescent Behavior as Adulthood Approaches*, ed. Robert T. Michael (New York: Russell Sage Foundation), pp. 379–41. This chapter uses the 1979 and 1997 National Longitudinal Survey of Youth to examine differences in self-reported youth deviance. The focus is on how place influences juvenile deviance, noting the neglect of rural youth in the literature on youth crime. The findings showed urban-rural convergence over time in rates of serious youth delinquency

Recommended Websites

Punk Planet
www.punkplanet.com

This website explores the 'punk' subculture, politics, music, and opinions and more. It has many forums that allow for the discussion of anything that is not mainstream.

RCMP
www.rcmp-grc.gc.ca

In November 2002 the *Gazette*, a RCMP publication, published an issue on biker gangs, including biker history in Canada, and what Canada is doing to stop them.

This issue provides an excellent overview of biker activity in Canada.

US Department of Health and Human Services
www.oas.samhsa.gov/nhsda/2k2nsduh/Results/2k2Results.htm

Every year the American Department of Health and Human Services releases a report on drug use based on a national survey. The survey provides a thorough look at drug use in America and includes many diagrams that show the correlations between youth and drug use.

CHAPTER 7

Violent Crimes

LEARNING OBJECTIVES

- To understand the nature of violent crimes and the public reaction to them
- To be familiar with the social characteristics of violent criminals
- To understand the characteristics of violent communities and subcultures
- To be familiar with the theories about violent crimes
- To understand the patterns of victimization
- To understand the nature of the various forms of family violence
- To understand the role of mass media in the portrayal of violent crimes
- To identify the policies aimed at reducing violent crimes

Introduction

'Crime' is a term used to describe many types of wrongdoing in our society. It is any violation of the criminal law and not merely a deviant behaviour—a mere matter of labelling: crime often has real consequences for people's safety, health, and general well-being. Victimization can even cause people to lose trust in the existing social institutions and reduce their participation in community life.

This chapter is about violent rule-breaking, and particularly about violent crimes. By 'violence', we mean any act marked by great force, passion, or fierceness. This chapter, then, is about the most serious and outrageous criminal acts: armed robbery, kidnapping, assault, sexual assault, and homicide. In this chapter, we will also discuss stalking, duelling, and especially domestic violence. As we will see in this chapter, violent crime is relatively rare in our society and is becoming rarer all the time; yet it continues to capture a disproportionate share of public attention. Violence is frightening, somewhat unusual, and (therefore) interesting. For these reasons, it makes eye-catching news. Public concern about this topic is enormous. Though Canadian police services reported in 2003 the lowest homicide rate since 1967 (*Juristat*, 2000; 2004a), murder receives extensive media coverage both as news and entertainment (see Figure 7.1). The 'life-threatening risk' that a homicide offender can pose always captures public interest.

Violent crimes are usually perceived as 'high consensus' crimes, meaning people universally agree that these violent crimes are dangerous and must be controlled or prevented. The concern with these crimes is both societal and personal. People want to protect their property against theft and their bodies against harm. This is why the chapter is not only about criminal acts but also about its victims. It is also about the offenders (violent criminals) and about their responsibility, socialization, and guilt. The chapter provides a theoretical framework for understanding why such crimes occur and what we and our governments can do to contribute to the solution of this social problem.

Figure 7.1 Homicide Rate, Canada, 1961–2003

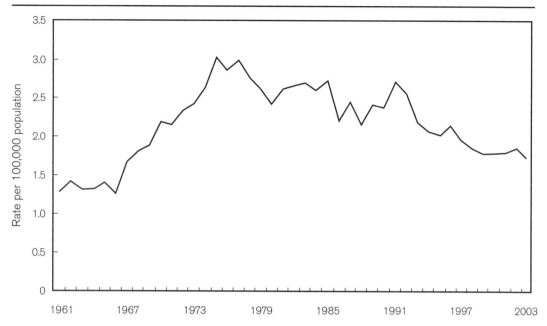

SOURCE: Statistics Canada, General Social Survey, 1999, Children and Youth in Canada Profile Series (Ottawa: Canadian Centre for Justice, Children and Youth in Canada); available at <www.statcan.ca>, accessed 19 December 2004.

There are many forms of violence—public versus private, intended versus spontaneous, and so on. As a result, we need to consider a variety of possible explanations. As we will see, sociological approaches to violence focus on social organization. These assume that violence occurs when the normal mechanisms of interaction—exchange, persuasion, altruism, or threat—do not achieve the desired purposes.

One sociological approach—a functionalist perspective—holds that violence is due to an organizational problem: the lack of peaceful strategies and mechanisms for resolving conflict. Another sociological approach—mainly a conflict perspective—focuses on the power imbalance between people. Sometimes the less powerful combatant is likely to use violence (e.g., terror) to redress the power balance, and other times the more powerful party uses violence with impunity. A third approach—symbolic interactionist—views violence in terms of faulty interaction: a breakdown in the normal communication process. We will examine all these sociological perspectives in this chapter to explore the reasons why, in some situations and for some people, violent behaviours seem appropriate or necessary.

Though we do not have reliable statistics over an extended period, it seems likely that violent crime is much less common today than it was a century ago. Since violence occurs when stable, accepted, non-violent means of achieving the desired result are lacking, violence declines alongside the growth of 'civility' that accompanies the rise of nation-states (on this see Elias, 1980). Nation-states bring about the 'rule of law' by creating written codes, courts, prisons, and law officers with a monopoly on the legitimate use of violence: primarily, police officers and soldiers.

However, when the legitimate use of violence by authority figures is extreme, it may be counter-productive. Then, instead of curbing the incidence of unlawful violent behaviour, the legitimate use of violence may exacerbate it. For instance, a study in California demonstrated that the increased use of death penalty increases the incidence of unlawful violence. This is referred to as the 'brutalization effect'. Between 1957 and 1967, there were executions every two months whereas between 1968 and 1991, there were no executions carried out. The homicide rate during the first period was twice as great as it was during the second time period, when no executions occurred (Center of Juvenile and Criminal Justice, 1995). Similarly, studies in New York demonstrate that homicide rates typically increase in the month following an execution, once again demonstrating the brutalization effect (Bowers and Pierce, 1980).

Violence occurs chiefly when these mechanisms for dispute resolution are absent or break down—for example, during a civil war. (More will be said about this in Chapter 9 on political violence.)

Fear is often a prime cause of violence in human relations. One person expects the worst of another and pre-emptively attacks before being attacked. This can often be avoided, however. Bornstein and Gilula (2003) show that communication between competing groups (or individuals) can be highly effective in bringing about a peaceful resolution when the conflict is caused by fear. Open communication can reduce conflict that is based on needless fear, though it cannot eliminate conflict based on other motives: for example, greed, or a desire for honour or status,

Often, interpersonal violence—including violent crime—is the outcome of a bargaining process between two people—the attacker and the victim—in which exchange, persuasion, appeals to altruism, and threat do not work; or, in which the attacker and/or victim are not behaving rationally—that is, assessing their own best interests. It may occur when people have no legitimate means of redressing their grievances, as happens between gangs. People often do not behave rationally when the stakes are high and especially when they are unclear and diffuse. Nowhere are conflicts less clear and more diffuse—hence, more irrational and violent—than in respect to issues of honour, pride, dignity, esteem, and 'saving face.' Moreover, there is little public visibility that prevents the outbreak of private violence in family or intimate relations.

Let's not forget the gendered aspect of violence. Men are far more likely than women to act out violently, and there are social (as well as cultural, psychological, and probably genetic) reasons for this. Proving masculinity is often a factor in violent crimes by males against other males. Proving masculinity may also be a factor in attacks by males on women. However, violent acts that grow out of male efforts to demonstrate masculinity and physical courage, and thereby to save face and seek honour, are not merely psychological responses to frustration. They are social and cultural, and have a long history, as we will see.

The History of Violent Crime and Public Reactions to It

To seek respect (or honour) and take revenge for disrespect (or dishonour) are both very old and established cultural practices in certain parts of the world, as is feuding to resolve a conflict. Though none of these is necessarily a crime, all remain important to our understanding of modern crimes of violence.

Duelling

The use of violence to settle interpersonal disputes appears to have been common in nearly all of Europe a few centuries ago. Gentlemen practised duelling as a way to settle disputes from the sixteenth century until the beginning of the twentieth century, though duelling was outlawed earlier (Magee, 2002). The spread of fencing and swordsmanship techniques grew originally from the Catholic Church's practice of judicial duelling in the early Middle Ages. These were based on the premise that God, in his mercy and wisdom, would not allow an innocent man to be harmed and as such he would win in combat against a well-trained court-appointed fighter. Noblemen for centuries fought duels over anything and everything, from revenge for violence against a friend, family member, or lover, to philosophical, religious, or scientific disagreements.

Governments, as their power grew, eventually took steps to provide alternative strategies for defending reputations and resolving conflicts. According to Shoemaker (2002), this resulted from a series of linked cultural changes, including a decreased tolerance of violence, new internalized understandings of elite honour, and the adoption of 'polite' and sentimental norms governing masculine conduct. The rise of courts, legal systems, and police forces was also important. Perhaps most important was the rise of a Protestant bourgeoisie more concerned with thrift and sobriety than honour and excitement.

In duels during the eighteenth and nineteenth centuries, pistols gradually replaced swords, seconds took on a new role as mediators, and new conventions of redressing grievance reduced the violence. Although duels continued to occur, growing opposition to the practice meant that the audience of people who supported duelling became increasingly limited and duels took place in places far from public view.

Outside Europe, duels continued, and even increased, over the same period of time. Piccato (1999) notes that in the early-twentieth century, duelling became increasingly common among Mexican elite men. Authorities refused to prosecute duellists. The translation and production of texts on duelling, as well as the influence of experienced duellists, taught men about the techniques and technology of honour. After the 1910 Mexican Revolution, as violence became widely associated with politics, duels became less frequent; but the concern among public men about honour and

virility expressed by violence remained visible in political life.

Honour

One cannot understand duelling without understanding the idea of 'honour'. Honour means respect, reputation, rank, or social position. In some societies, and some social classes, the accumulation and husbanding of honour is a matter of central importance; in our own society, they are much less so.

Changes in the struggles for honour, pride, and shame are linked to long-term transformations in society and the state (Inglis, 2001). In small and static communities, a good reputation was a critical social resource for the individual and his or her family. The pursuit of honour was part of the 'politics of reputation' in a community—the quest for social standing, acceptance, and respect. Marriage, business, and social opportunities all depended on a person's good reputation—his or her honour. Therefore, the acts of defending, losing, and regaining honour shaped a person's, and his family's, entire system of life chances. This was particularly critical for aristocrats and nobles.

The sixteenth- and seventeenth-century European code of honour surrounding the duel, therefore, was a form of communication between the individual and society. Culturally defined violence, such as duelling, was a clearly recognized way of claiming and defending social status in a status-conscious society of gentlemen and ladies. It was particularly common where the state (or monarch) was weak compared to the aristocracy, and aristocratic families competed with one another for power and reputation.

However, issues of honour have never been restricted to aristocrats. In societies where people have little material wealth, often all they have to keep, and fight about, is their intangible honour—the good name of their family, for example. In the east and south—for example, Turkey and the

Middle East—the concept of honour has also been represented by the blood feud. Both the duel and the blood feud fulfill a similar sociocultural function: in an insecure environment, they both provide the customary laws that regulate conflict. Paradoxically, although in some respects they stimulate violence, by regulating it they also reduce violence.

The duel and blood feud, though they serve similar functions (as mechanisms of regulating bloodshed), are different. The blood feud (or vendetta) is communal, involving the entire family or kin group, while the duel is individualistic, requiring only two individuals who may represent only themselves (or their families.) As a peculiarly 'collectivistic' form of institutionalized violence, feuding is found only in certain parts of the world where individualism is weak (far from where the Protestant Ethic and spirit of capitalism originated).

Feuding may also be a peculiarly chaotic form of violence, found where even rudimentary controls on interpersonal violence—signified by the duel—have ceased to function. As traditional duelling rules start to break down, there may be an increased reliance on blood feuds, in which no rules apply (Gronfors, 1986). Blood feuds cannot be settled through payments of compensation in any form; only by avoiding meetings between the feuding groups can a feud be stopped.

In societies founded on the honour principle, revenge is the necessary cure for dishonour. Often, revenge requires violent bloodletting. Note that revenge, like honour, is a learned social activity. It is socially structured, rather than a spontaneous emotional response. Learning the practice of bloody revenge is part of learning the culture and psychology of your group. It is persistently and globally linked to prevailing conceptions of masculinity (Errante, 2003).

As Brookman (2003) notes, 'confrontational' homicide and 'revenge' homicide are the two most common forms of male-on-male homicide. We will see that this is a recurrent theme in studying subcultures of violence too. For example, Klein (2003) notes that between 1996 and 2001, 14 boys from suburban and rural communities killed 39 people and wounded 92 in school shootings across the United States. Fatalities included 32 children, 14 boys, and 18 girls. Thus, even today, mass murder is typically carried out by males.

Feuding

As we have said, feuds, blood feuds, or vendettas are forms of intergroup violence that are intended to restore a group's honour and take revenge on another group for having dishonoured it.

Perhaps owing to the connection with masculinity, feuding often has a sexual content, when groups are revenging the dishonour of a female group member. Though focused on women and sex, this kind of behaviour is not to be confused with Western romantic or chivalric notions, in which a prized woman is sought, wooed, idealized, cherished, and wed. In traditional societies with a strong sexual double standard, where women are viewed as property, if someone rapes or seduces an unmarried woman, her bride price is lowered because she is 'damaged goods'. The goal then—depending on the society—may be to kill the seducer, kill the woman, or force the seducer (or someone else) to marry the woman, while taking revenge on the seducer's family.

In these societies, women have few personal rights; their feelings and experiences count for little. Since many men still consider women property, this poses problems for law enforcement on how to deal with sexual assault by spouses. In some parts of the world even today, women can suffer violent abuse if they 'dishonour' their spouse or their family by behaving too freely, in any of a number of ways. The results are called 'honour killings', and are practised in many Islamic societies. Akpinar (2003) notes that in Turkish society, for example, women are carriers and bearers of group identity. Women are physically abused when they violate the boundaries of their community's definition of acceptable femininity, by dressing, speaking, or acting in non-traditional ways.

In Palestine, despite the criminalization of abuses inflicted on women, the murder of girls or women for allegedly committing 'crimes of family honour' remains common (Shalhoub-Kevorkian, 2002). A silent masculine conspiracy keeps sexist and gender-biased legal policies in place here. Hasan (2002) argues that the entire matter of honour in such a society is a rationale for maintaining male control over women.

Lindner (2002) notes a long-term historical shift from 'honour' to 'human rights' as the basis for codes of human behaviour. From this evolutionary perspective, there are clear differences between societies founded on 'honour' versus societies founded on 'human rights', with respect to their codes of behaviour and use of humiliation. Violence—both political and personal—is more common in the former than in the latter type of society. Both women and men suffer under the 'honour' principle, though it is likely that women suffer more.

Canada is no stranger to the idea that a wife is the sexual property of her husband. Until it was amended in 1983, even Canada's *Criminal Code* limited the offence of rape to favour the rights of men over women. The offence of rape required proof that a man had had sexual intercourse with a woman *other than his wife*, without the woman's consent. This offence was punishable by up to life imprisonment. However, it was thought impossible for a man to rape his own wife; she was his sexual property, obliged to provide sex whether she consented to it or not on a particular occasion.

However, in 1983, Bill C-127 redefined the physical and sexual assault sections of the Canadian *Criminal Code*, abolishing the offence of rape and establishing three levels of assault. One level includes sexual touching or sexual intercourse without consent. A second includes incidents involving a weapon or resulting in bodily harm. A third, aggravated assault/sexual assault, is the level in which the victim is wounded or disfigured (*Juristat*, 1997). The

law has also abolished the distinction between men and women, no longer supposing that only men can commit rape; and has ended spousal immunity. Sexual conduct between intimates must now be consensual, whatever their marital status.

Perhaps it is because of a clear and abiding commitment to the principle of personal consent that reported sexual assaults have dropped another 5.2 per cent in Canada in the past year (*Juristat*, 2004a). It seems that the message 'No means no' is ever more widely understood by men, even where wives, girlfriends, acquaintances, and other women are in the vicinity.

Today, we pay more attention than in the past to the personal rights of individuals and the value of a human life. People understand that human lives should be valued more than property and that there are other means by which to solve disputes. Most people agree about the seriousness of crimes of violence and feel that we should not punish these with violence. However, we are still far from knowing how to prevent violence or to rehabilitate violent criminals.

Defining Crimes of Violence

When we think about crime, we often first think about violent crimes, such as murder, attempted murder, manslaughter, assault, sexual assault, and robbery. These types of offences have been given the term 'conventional crimes' by criminologists, precisely because they are the illegal behaviours that most people think of as crime (Koenig, 2000). They worry people and make them feel unsafe. Crime is on many Canadians' minds. Because they fear it, Canadians believe—largely without reason—that crime in general, and violent crime in particular, is on the rise (Federowycz, 1999).

Homicide

Homicide refers to the killing of one human being by another. Few would disagree that homicide is the most serious type of violent offence. It is also the least common offence, accounting for only 548 deaths in 2003, 34 fewer than the previous year (or 1.73 per 100,000 population), making this the lowest rate since 1967. In Canada, the rate of homicides is highest in Nunavut (at 10.21 per 100,000 in 2003). According to Statistics Canada, homicides continue to be committed primarily by people known to the victim. In 2003, 51.4 per cent of victims in solved homicide incidents were killed by an acquaintance, 19.2 per cent by a family member and 14 per cent by a stranger (*Juristat*, 2000; 2004a).

Typically, men are much more often involved in homicides than women, both as victims (two-thirds of all victims being men) and as perpetrators (88 per cent of those charged with homicide being men). Violent crimes are not the acts of strangers; people are significantly more likely to be attacked or killed by a family member or acquaintance than by a stranger.

Non-sexual assault is by far the most common violent crime, accounting for 82 per cent of all reported cases, an increase of 3 per cent since 2002 (Juristat, 2004a). The *Criminal Code* categorizes assault into three levels: common assault (level 1), assault with a weapon or causing bodily harm (level 2), and aggravated assault (level 3) in which the victim is wounded, maimed, and/or disfigured. Both men and women are equally likely to be victims of assault; however, men are more likely to be victims of assault in which a weapon is used.

Sexual assault

Like its non-sexual counterpart, sexual assault can be classified into three levels according to whether a weapon was used and whether the victim was wounded, maimed, or disfigured. We can also distinguish between (1) classic rape, which involves forcing sexual intercourse on a stranger against his or her will; (2) acquaintance rape, which involves sexual assault involving someone the victim knows casually; (3) statutory rape, in which the victim is under the legal age of consent (typically 18 years); (4) marital rape, which involves a spouse; and (5) incest, which involves a member of the family.

The penalties for committing these different types of sexual offences vary depending upon the severity of the offence. Social science and law enforcement experts agree that most sexual assault victims probably do not report their experience to the police, which is problematic for authorities because they cannot accurately calculate the extent of the problem and apply this information to reduce and prevent such crimes from happening. According to Statistics Canada, 61 per cent of all reported assaults involved young people, and 85 per cent of those attacked were young women.

Sexual assault, though not on the increase, remains a serious problem. In Canada, women experience sexual assault every day at home, at work, at school, and on the street. A 1993 Statistics Canada survey found that one-half of all Canadian women have experienced at least one incident of sexual or physical violence. Any woman, whatever age, race, sexual orientation, disability, socioeconomic status, or geographic location is at risk for sexual assault. That being said, some women are at greater risk than others. For example, 63 per cent of sexual assaults reported to the police involve girls and young women under the age of 18 (Russell, 1996).

Women outnumber men as victims of sexual assault by a margin of about 4 to 1, and generally, victims are young, averaging 17 years for females and 11 years for males (Federowycz, 1999). Male and female victims are most likely to be attacked by a casual acquaintance, a family member, or a stranger. When the victim is a very young female, the assailant is a family member in about half of the reported cases.

Robbery

Robbery is a form of theft that involves the use or threat of force. In 2003 in Canada, 28,332 robberies took place—a rise of 5.4 per cent since 2002 and about 10 per cent of all violent crimes. The robber is usually a young person, with the median age being 17 for female robbers and 21 for males. The victim is male in over 60 per cent of the cases (Kong, 1999).

Stalking

Stalking has emerged as a new form of criminal deviance in our society. This crime has gained a great deal of attention in recent years because it is common and is associated with gendered abuse and violence. Stalking is a type of relationship abuse that may evolve into violent physical, psychological, and sexual forms. In all stalking cases for the year 1997 stalkers made overt threats to about 45 per cent of victims; spied on or followed about 75 per cent of victims; vandalized the property of about 30 per cent of victims; and threatened to kill or killed the pets of about 10 per cent of victims.

Stalking often follows a relationship breakup or a rejection in a proposed relationship. In 1996, roughly 80 per cent of the 4,450 stalking victims in Canada were women and 88 per cent of the persons accused of stalking in these cases were male (Bunge and Levett, 1998). Most stalkers were former, rather than current, intimates. Usually, victims of stalking had to resort to help from the authorities and seek restraining orders to protect themselves from the emotional abuse and prevent the stalking from escalating into violence.

Social Characteristics of Violent Criminals

Canadian crime statistics for the period 1962–2002 show that rates of violent crime increased steadily (excluding murder, manslaughter, attempted murder, and robbery—which scarcely changed) until 1992, when they started to decline; they continued to decline until a slight increase in 2003. Specifically, this means that rates of assault and sexual assault rose over the period 1962–92 and, after 1992, began to decline.

This fluctuation mirrors the steady increase then decline of the proportion of men in the population ages 15–35. As we will see, they are the people most likely to commit these crimes. The number of young men in the population rose because birth rates 'boomed' in Canada between 1947 and 1967. The unusually large number of male babies, in due course,

became an unusually large number of young men. Thus, the short-lived violence explosion in Canada was because of a brief surplus of young men.

Among solved homicides in 2003, 88 per cent knew the killer. Half (51 per cent) of the victims were killed by an acquaintance, one-third (34 per cent) were killed by a family member, and the remaining 14 per cent were killed by strangers. In addition to 40 women who were killed by their husbands and 12 men who were killed by their wives, 87 other family-related homicides occurred, including 19 victims who were killed by their fathers and 11 by their mothers.

Interestingly, husbands are more likely to kill their wives in the bedroom, while wives are more likely to kill their husbands in the kitchen (Wolfgang, 1966). According to *Juristat*, 45 per cent of wives were killed in the bedroom compared to only 23 per cent of husbands. Conversely, 40 per cent of husbands were killed in the kitchen compared to only 19 per cent of wives. Wives who are pregnant, or were recently pregnant, are more likely to die of homicide than in any other fashion (Frye, 2001).

The use of violence, like other deviant behaviours, varies geographically. So, for example, homicide rates have continued to be higher in Western than Eastern Canada, with Saskatchewan reporting the highest provincial rate (4.12 homicides per 100,000 population) and PEI the lowest rate (0.73 homicides per 100,000 population). There has, however, been a decline in the homicide rates in British Columbia and Alberta since 2002 (see Table 7.1) (*Juristat*, 2000; 2004a).

Gender is the single most significant factor in any study of crime and delinquency, and this applies particularly to crimes of violence. In the United States, males account for 76 per cent of all murders and non-negligent manslaughters (Bureau of Justice Statistics Sourcebook, 2004). Men are 10 times more likely than women to commit murder, 78 times more likely to commit forcible rape, 10 times more likely to commit armed robbery, 6.5 times more likely to commit aggravated assault, and 7 times more likely

Box 7.1 More Stars Going to Police Over Stalking

NEW YORK (AP)–They're out there. Catherine Zeta-Jones, Sheryl Crow, and Mel Gibson recently faced theirs in court. Anna Kournikova's took a nude swim to find her. Andrea Evans feared hers for a decade.

They're celebrity stalkers, perpetrators of an emotional crime that's often–but not always–the result of mental illness.

Despite a recent rash of cases, experts say celebrity stalking isn't increasing but stars are more willing to go to police. And the media is more likely to cover subsequent arrests and trials. It has led to specialized police units aimed at dealing with a troubled few.

Evans was playing soap tart Tina Clayton on *One Life to Live* in the 1980s when her stalker showed up several times at her Manhattan set. He once slashed his wrists outside the studios.

'All of a sudden, I went from a nice, happy-go-lucky life to having regular conversations with the police,' says Evans, adding she was terrified.

After the murder of *My Sister Sam* actress Rebecca Schaeffer in 1989 and incidents like Evans,' celebrity stalking began to be recognized about 1990.

Stalking is hard to prove. Witness the love-struck Crow fan who was acquitted last year after pursuing the singer for 15 months, claiming he communicated with her telepathically.

'Stalking is much more nebulous, much more of a challenge,' said John Lane, a former Los Angeles Police Department detective. 'It is very difficult to investigate.'

Canadians became familiar with the phenomenon years ago as Saskatchewan farmer Charles Kieling stalked singer Anne Murray. He was jailed for a time and the subject of various restraining orders.

In recent years, the likes of Pamela Anderson, Madonna, Steven Spielberg, Nicole Kidman, David Letterman, and Gwyneth Paltrow have claimed stalkers. In the past two weeks alone, people were convicted or pleaded no contest to stalking Gibson and Zeta-Jones. And in the Kournikova case, a man was arrested Jan. 30 after swimming nude across a Florida bay toward Kournikova's $5 million US estate, then turning up on the pool deck at the wrong house and yelling, 'Anna! Save me!'

to commit arson (Wrangham and Peterson, 1997). The figures in Canada are comparable. For example, in 2003, the ratio of males to females charged with violent crimes in general was 5.3 to 1 (Canadian Centre for Justice Statistics, 2004). In Canada in 2003, 9 out of 10 of those accused of homicide were males (including murder, manslaughter, and infanticide).

Age is another factor that predicts violence: violent criminals tend to be younger than average people. Reasons for this were evident in the preceding chapter, on the risky behaviours of young

Table 7.1   Homicides by Province/Territory, Canada, 2002 and 2003

Province/territory	2003			2002		
	Population	Number of victims	Rate	Population	Number of victims	Rate
Newfoundland and Labrador	519,570	5	0.96	519,270	2	0.39
Prince Edward Island	137,781	1	0.73	136,998	1	0.73
Nova Scotia	936,025	8	0.85	934,392	9	0.96
New Brunswick	750,594	8	1.07	750,183	9	1.20
Quebec	7,487,169	100	1.34	744,3491	118	1.59
Ontario	12,238,300	176	1.45	12,096,627	178	1.47
Manitoba	1,162,776	43	3.70	1,155,492	36	3.12
Saskatchewan	994,843	41	4.12	995,490	27	2.71
Alberta	3,153,723	63	2.00	3,114,390	70	2.25
British Columbia	4,146,580	93	2.24	4,114,981	126	3.06
Yukon	31,060	1	3.22	30,123	0	0.00
Northwest Territories	41,872	4	9.55	41,434	4	9.65
Nunavut	29,384	3	10.21	28,740	2	6.96
Canada	**31,629,677**	**548**	**1.73**	**31,361,611**	**582**	**1.86**

SOURCE: Statistics Canada, General Social Survey, 1999, Children and Youth in Canada Profile Series (Ottawa: Canadian Centre for Justice, Children and Youth in Canada); available at <www.statcan.ca>, accessed 19 December 2004.

people. Generally, people who are going to break the law start getting into trouble when they are young. The vast majority stop after their first or second brush with the police and courts. A small group we might call *violent predators* continue to commit serious crimes—among them, robberies, assaults, and drug deals—often from childhood onward. Drug use is also common among violent predators (see Table 7.2). The explanation is more often sociological than not: their violence is often a response to the conditions in which they live.

Violent Communities and Subcultures

We started this chapter by asserting that, generally, violence reflects the absence of order and the failure of other mechanisms for resolving disputes. For this reason, violence (in the form of duels, feuds, and otherwise) declines with the development of a legal system. However, at the same time we recognized that communities vary in the importance they attach to honour and respect, and the willingness they show to use violence as a manly way of seeking

respect. Thus, sociologists explain violence both in terms of social disorganization—an absence of regulatory mechanisms—and subcultural variations in the value placed on violence.

The differential distribution of violence, within or between societies, then, is a function of differential cultural norms concerning violence (Gelles and Straus, 1988). Some societies hold values and beliefs that glorify aggression and violence. Cross-cultural research by Masamura (1979), for example, shows that wife-beating is associated with high rates of personal crime, theft, aggression, suicide, homicide, feuding, and warfare. Or, to take another example, compare the two contenders for dominance in the ancient Greek world. Sparta was a warlike state founded on discipline, hierarchy, and violence. Athens was a (relatively) peaceful state founded on discourse, democracy, and negotiation.

Sociologists have studied violent communities and subcultures to explain how values and belief systems contribute to violent criminal behaviour. Subculture theory is helpful in explaining why

Table 7.2   Drug Offences Reported to Police, Canada[1]

	2003		2002–3
	Number	Rate[1]	% change in rate
Total cannabis	60,670	192	−13.7
Possession	41,237	130	−17.6
Trafficking	10,300	33	−0.4
Cultivation	8,449	27	+3.3
Importation	684	2	−33.2
Cocaine	13,938	44	+8.5
Heroin	655	2	−17.4
Other drugs	10,690	34	+10.7
Total drugs	85,953	272	−8.1

[1] Rates are calculated per 100,000 population.

SOURCE: Statistics Canada, General Social Survey, 1999, Children and Youth in Canada Profile Series (Ottawa: Canadian Centre for Justice, Children and Youth in Canada); available at <www.statcan.ca>, accessed 19 December 2004.

arguments between young males, for example, are the most common precursor to homicide in our own society and elsewhere (Zahn and McCall, 1999). Largely, youths establish their identities and subcultures by opposing the middle-class social order and by challenging each other in quests for honour and respect (Le Moigne, 1998).

Inner-city youth often live according to a street code that justifies gaining respect from others through violence. Guns symbolize respect, power, identity, and manhood; they play a central role in initiating, sustaining, and escalating youth violence (Fagan and Wilkinson, 1998). Violence becomes appropriate behaviour for youth who are regularly exposed to violence, are gang members themselves, have family or friends who are gang members, and have peer support for violence (Krug et al., 1997; Katz and Marquette, 1996). In these subcultures, males who behave fearfully are likely to be threatened (Vander Ven, 1998).

In poor urban areas, as in peasant societies and tribal societies, all goods—including honour—are scarce. So honour is an appropriate metric for measuring social worth, and in this subculture, people can gain it by violence. People who live in neighbourhoods that are more prosperous can earn respect through their educational and career achievements. However, people who live in poorer areas, such as the inner city, may have to rely on strength, threats, or violent acts, and tough anti-social acts to gain their peers' respect. Viewed from the standpoint of law-abiding middle-class society, this is a chaotic, gang-dominated danger zone. Viewed from the standpoint of local residents, the same neighbourhood may seem more orderly. Gangs, after all, give minority youth an alternative community for achieving social status, friendship, and economic mobility (Gibbs, 2000).

In every gang-dominated neighbourhood, engaging in violence is part of the lifestyle of the 'subculture of violence' (Wolfgang and Ferracuti, 1967). Members of a violent community or gang internalize the norms of the subculture. Internalization of the norms and values of a violent subculture helps members to justify their actions and reduce feelings of guilt. Members of the subculture who refuse to engage in violence are deemed cowardly and may be expelled from the group.

Wolfgang and Ferracuti (1967) write, 'a subculture implies that there are value judgments or a social value system, which is apart from and a part of a larger central value system.' A subculture, when applied to violence, is simply a type of subculture in which there is a theme of violence in the values that are part of 'the lifestyle, the socialization process, [and] the interpersonal relationships of individuals living in similar conditions.' Wolfgang and Ferracuti's subculture of violence theory can be summarized as follows: when there is an overt use of violence by a group, it tends to be a representation of the values counter to those of the dominant culture of which the group is also a part.

Patterns of Victimization

Violent crime produces victims, and some people are more likely than others to become victims. Sometimes, this has to do with involvement in criminal activities: people who commit crimes are more likely to have crimes committed against them. More generally, victimization is a result of how and where people spend their time.

Routine activities theory predicts that victimization requires the convergence in space and time of likely offenders, suitable targets, and the absence of capable guardians. Generally, the growth of victimization by crime reflects the changing character of our routine activities—criminal and otherwise—and the increased opportunities for victimization in modern urban life.

Automobiles, vacations, college enrolment, female labour-force participation, and new consumer goods all improve our lives, but they also provide new occasions for criminal behaviour. *Hot spots* where the risks of crime are particularly great include downtown entertainment districts (Cochran, Bromley, and Branch, 2000) and tourist attractions abroad (Mawby, Brunt, and Hambly, 2000). In Toronto, and some other cities, the hot spots are clubs where young people gather to dance late at night.

Suitable targets are people who are routinely exposed to criminal activity or who for other reasons have heightened vulnerability. Generally,

people who are powerless or vulnerable run higher than average risks of crime and violence. Thus, tourists are highly likely to experience crime while on holiday in a strange place (Mawby, Brunt, and Hambly, 1999).

Three characteristics that put youth at risk of victimization probably apply to other types of people as well. They are the victim's target vulnerability (e.g., physical weakness or psychological distress), target gratifiability (e.g., female gender for the crime of sexual assault), and target antagonism (e.g., ethnic or group identities that may spark hostility or resentment) (Finkelhor and Asdigian, 1996).

Sociodemographic factors (such as age, race, and sex) and economic factors (such as income) predict victimization in a wide variety of situations, including homicide (Caywood, 1988). With some exceptions, poor and powerless people are more vulnerable than rich and powerful people, with one exception: people with more and better property—larger apartments, newer cars—are more likely to have their property stolen (Mesch, 1997).

As we have noted several times, women risk certain kinds of victimization more than men. People killed by a spouse are more likely to be women than men. Female homicide victims, generally, tend to be killed by a spouse, another family member, or an intimate partner because of domestic violence; men are more likely to be killed by a stranger in a public place (Pratt and Deosaransingh, 1997).

However, public places carry their own risks for women. Women run higher than usual risks, for example, when using public transportation, living near a park, or drinking alcohol. Women are 46 per cent more likely to be victims than men, especially if they eat out often and spend time socializing. Risk of victimization is, in these and other cases, due to increased exposure to offenders and lack of capable guardianship (Mustaine and Tewksbury, 1999).

Elderly people—though less at risk than young people—run higher risks than middle-aged people, especially for crimes of robbery, intimidation, vandalism, and forgery or fraud scams (McCabe and

Gregory, 1998). Robbery is the most serious offence committed against elderly victims of a violent incident, and men and women are equally likely to experience it (Bachman, Dillaway, and Lachs, 1998). Most such robberies take place outside the home during routine activities. Elderly people robbed in this way run higher risks of serious physical injury and even death than younger people who are robbed (Faggiani and Owens, 1999). Elderly people run a low overall risk due to their often-private lifestyles and routine activity patterns. However, their risk of theft-related homicide is relatively high. This risk increases with age, and is higher among socially distant (that is, unconnected) victims and offenders (Nelsen and Huff-Corzine, 1998).

At the other end of the age distribution, juveniles aged 12 to 17 are more likely than adults to be victims of violent crimes and to suffer from a crime-related injury. Juvenile victims are also more likely than adult victims to know their offenders (Hashima and Finkelhor, 1999). A Canadian study of high school students in Calgary found that, except for sexual victimization, males reported higher victimization rates than females. Younger students reported higher rates of victimization at school than older students. Finally, students who reported moderate to high levels of victimization were more likely to report moderate to high levels of delinquency (Paetsch and Bertrand, 1999), confirming the link between criminal activity and criminal victimization.

When potential targets are nearby and guardians are absent, the probability of a crime occurring is at its peak. Studies have identified several factors that are important in predicting the likelihood of violent crime. These factors are socioeconomic status, demographic characteristics, and lifestyle. Young, unmarried, and economically disadvantaged people are more likely than average to be in the proximity of motivated offenders and in the absence of guardians. Table 7.3 shows how youth feel about their safety from crime.

Immigrants and ethnic minorities are also at greater than average risk of victimization, especially with respect to crimes against persons. We often refer to these as *hate crimes*. In Sweden, immigrants with a non-European appearance are more often victims of personal crimes than are other immigrants (Martens, 2000). In North America, blacks are also the victims of hate crimes by whites, and there is some evidence that the number of hate crimes has risen in the past decade (Torres, 1999; but compare Steen and Cohen, 2004; Miller and Myers, 2000).

Gay men and lesbian women are sometimes also victims of hate crimes. Recent debates about the cultural and legal status of sexual-orientation minorities have increased the visibility and awareness of violence against gays and lesbians (Tewksbury et al., 1999). It is not clear whether this form of violence itself has increased. Our information about the extent of hate crimes against these groups is hindered by low rates at which gays and lesbians report violent crimes because of concerns about police homophobia (Peel, 1999).

Hot spots, as we have said, are places where targets of crime and violence are at greater risk in some places than others. For example, prisons are particularly dangerous places. In fact, all inmates of 'total institutions' risk victimization on a daily basis. Common offences against prisoners include assault, robbery, threats of violence, theft from cells, and verbal abuse (O'Donnell and Edgar, 1998). Prisoners are at particular risk of physical assaults by other inmates, as well as of theft of personal property (Wooldredge, 1998).

Public places increase the risk of rape for women, and highly mobile women (working women, students, and younger women in general) are at a much greater risk of rape than women who are less mobile (Ploughman and Stensrud, 1986). Situational context—the where and when of a sexually violent crime—is an even better predictor of the outcome of rape attempts than victim or offender characteristics (Clay-Warner, 2000).

Table 7.3 Feelings of Safety from Crime among Youth and Adult Populations, 1999[1]

	% of population	
	Youth population	Adult population
While waiting for/using public transportation alone after dark, how do you feel about your safety from crime?		
Not at all worried	54	54
Somewhat worried	41	38
Very worried	6	9
Don't know/Not stated	–	1*
How safe do you feel from crime when walking alone in your area after dark?		
Very safe	39	44
Reasonably safe	48	45
Somewhat or very unsafe	13	11
Don't know/Not stated	–	–
While alone in your home in the evening or at night, how do you feel about your safety from crime?		
Not at all worried	81	79
Somewhat worried	17	18
Very worried	2*	2
Don't know/Not stated	–	–
In general, how do you feel about your safety from crime?		
Very satisfied	49	44
Somewhat satisfied	45	47
Somewhat dissatisfied	3	4
Very dissatisfied	1*	2
Don't know/Not stated	2*	4

[1]   Includes only respondents who engaged in these activities.
–   Amount too small to be expressed.

Note: * Coefficient of variation between 16.6% and 33.3%. Figures may not add to 100% due to rounding.

SOURCE: Statistics Canada, General Social Survey, 1999, Children and Youth in Canada Profile Series (Ottawa: Canadian Centre for Justice, Children and Youth in Canada);available at <www.statcan.ca>, accessed 19 December 2004.

Family Violence

Families are common 'hot spots' for the experience of violence because they bring potential offenders into close, familiar proximity to suitable victims; often, the 'guardians' themselves—husbands or wives, fathers or mothers, brothers or sisters—perpetrate the violence.

Violence among family members is probably as old as the institution of the family itself. However, the systematic study of family violence is a new branch of academic research. It only emerged in the 1960s, launched by the publication of the first detailed case studies of seemingly inexplicable physical injuries that young children had suffered. Much of the difficulty in determining the extent or prevalence of family violence is methodological.

Family violence is an umbrella term covering a range of different kinds of violence, among different sets of family members. In addition to the obvious forms of physical violence, we need to include sexual violence, such as child sexual abuse, incest, and marital rape, which are likely to have a component of physical violence. As well, emotional abuse often accompanies violent acts. Often, emotional abuse is as painful or destructive of the self-esteem and healthy emotional development of its victims as physical violence.

Elder abuse

Children and spouses are not the only victims of domestic violence; so are elderly parents. Research shows that elder abuse cases fall into three categories, determined by the type of mistreatment (physical, psychological, financial, or neglect), the relationship between victim and perpetrator, and the sex and race of the victims and abusers. Profiles include: (1) physical and psychological abuse perpetrators, who are likely to be financially dependent on the victim; (2) neglect victims, who are likely to be dependent on the perpetrator; and (3) financial abuse victims, who are often lonely, with few social contacts (Wolf, 1996). Statistics Canada reports an estimated 7 per cent of elderly people are abused. In some cases of elder abuse, adult children abuse the parents who had abused them in childhood. Often, women abuse their mother-in-laws. This has particularly been the case in rural China, where very young women traditionally move in with their husband's family after marriage (Gallin, 1994). Young women who are treated poorly by their husband's mother often become abusive when they must look after these women in their old age (Kwan, 1995).

Unlike child abuse, elder abuse receives little attention in our society, partly because it is a less common form of abuse, and perhaps because we have less interest in our elders than in our children.

Child abuse

Child abuse has a long history in both our own and other cultures. In 2001, researcher Nico Trocme (Trocme et al., 2001) and his colleagues published a detailed examination of child abuse—the Canadian Incidence Study of Reported Child Abuse and Neglect. It was the first study of nationwide-reported child maltreatment. Trocme reported that, in 1998, more than 135,000 cases of maltreatment were investigated by child welfare services, and 45 per cent of these cases were substantiated. Of the reported maltreatment cases, 31 per cent were cases of physical abuse, 10 per cent were cases of sexual abuse, 40 per cent were cases of neglect, and 19 per cent were emotional maltreatment or abuse.

Often, child abuse is kept a family secret and even the child's non-abusive parent refuses to acknowledge the problem. In fact, Bolen and Lamb (2004) found that the most common response of non-abusive parents is ambivalence upon being told that their partner is sexually abusing their child. Other types of violence against children around the world are more culturally specific. Some Muslim cultures still practise female circumcision. The Jewish religion continues to require male circumcision, though few have viewed this activity as child abuse.

Where not condoned by culture and religion, a number of factors contribute to parental abuse of children. Parental substance abuse is a major factor contributing to child abuse and neglect, for example. Substance abuse occurs in a reported 40 to 80 per cent of families in which the children are victims of abuse. Children whose substance-abusing parents do not receive appropriate treatment are more likely to remain in foster care longer and to re-enter foster care once they have returned home.

Children whose parents abuse alcohol and other drugs are three times more likely to be abused and more than four times more likely to be neglected than children from non-abusing families. Parents' abuse of alcohol and other drugs can lead to a cycle of addiction, in which high rates of alcoholism and other substance abuse are reflected among children of addicts. Girls who suffer abuse as children are more likely to become victims of abuse in adulthood, whereas boys who suffer abuse as children are more likely to become abusers.

Not surprisingly, parent-child violence and exposure to interparental violence are significant causes of adolescent behaviour problems (O'Keefe, 1997). Witnessing violence between one's parents harms the emotional and behavioural development of children (Kolbo, Blakely, and Engleman, 1996). For example, exposure to family violence produces behavioural problems in girls and reduces self-worth in boys (Kolbo, 1996). Females usually internalize their emotions, reporting higher levels of shame and guilt. Among college undergraduates, witnessing marital violence is associated with other family mental health risks, childhood physical and sexual abuse, and adult physical assaults by strangers.

Partner violence

Juristat (2000b) reports: 'In 2003, there were 78 victims killed by their spouse (current or ex), 6 fewer than in 2002 resulting in a decline (8 per cent) in the spousal homicide rate for the second year in a row.' Contributors to the decline in spousal homicide include changes in intimate relationships, increases in gender equality, better training for enforcement personnel, and improvements in the support provided for victims.

As with rates of overall violent crime in Canada, rates of intimate partner homicide were highest in the Prairie Provinces (especially, Manitoba and Saskatchewan), and lowest in the Maritimes (especially, Newfoundland and Labrador, and Prince Edward Island.) A history of domestic violence was cited in two-thirds of all cases between 1991 and 2000.

Homicide is just the tip of the iceberg, where partner violence is concerned. Typically, homicide is preceded by a long history of abuse and assault. Increasing use is made of shelters for abused women and children, the most common victims of domestic violence. In 2002, Statistics Canada reported 'a total of 3,287 women and 2,999 children were residing in shelters in Canada.' A majority of women (73 per cent) and children (84 per cent) were there to escape. Many of the shelters are transition homes or emergency shelters. Many women and children were turned away because the shelter was full. Of women who left shelters on 15 April 2002, only 12 per cent returned to their spouse.

In spite of the continued difficulties in identifying family violence, sociologists have improved their techniques for estimating its prevalence. Most commonly used today in measuring the extent of domestic violence—especially, for purposes of criminal justice intervention—are Straus's Conflict Tactics Scales, developed in 1979. The first reliable and valid scales for measuring family violence, the Conflict Tactics Scales measure verbal aggression and physical violence on a continuum.

Research findings suggest that husband violence has occurred in up to one-third of couples that do not report distress with their marriage and one-half of maritally distressed couples. Studies of intimate violence and abuse examine a wide range of behaviours. Sociologists often use the term 'spousal violence', but unmarried couples also inflict violence on each other. In fact, research finds that severe violence is five times more likely among co-habiting couples than married couples (Yllo and Straus, 1981).

The strongest predictors of partner violence are interactional, that is, they arise from relationship processes such as marital conflict, customary modes of expressing aggression, and stresses induced by work. Accordingly, male violence in the home is a widespread and, in that sense, 'normal' element of marital interaction (Lupri, 1993). Spousal violence against women is most common when the wife has a job and the husband does not. Contrary to common belief, wife-to-husband violence is also common and, according to Lupri, Canadian couples are more likely to engage in domestic violence, both severe and minor, than are American couples.

Women use violence against their spouses for reasons that are different from men. Compared with male abusers, battered women who kill or seriously assault their partners are more likely to have believed that their lives were in danger. They were less likely to use violence against their partners and less likely to have a prior criminal record or to have served time previously than battered women jailed for other offences (O'Keefe, 1997).

Community violence increases the likelihood of family violence. Overstreet and Braun (2000) report that among African-American children ages 10 to 15 living in or close to an inner-city public housing development, exposure to community violence produced perceptions of decreased neighbourhood safety and increased family conflict, which, in turn, led to symptoms of PTSD in the children.

In short, we note a variety of 'causes of violence' in the family literature. The reason for so many causal candidates is, mainly, that we are confusing three different types of spousal violence. They include: (1) interpersonal conflict violence, which almost exclusively involves pushing, shoving, grabbing, and slapping; (2) non-systematic abuse, which involves a greater variety of violent acts, including threats, the throwing of objects, kicking, and hitting; and (3) systematic abuse, which involves a high risk of all types of violent acts, including life-threatening violence such as beating, choking, and attacks with knives or guns.

In their analysis of data from the *Canadian Violence Against Women Survey* (Statistics Canada, 1993), Macmillan and Gartner (1996) examine the effects of such proprietary or 'coercively controlling' attitudes on domestic violence. Often, psychologically and physically abusive men fear the loss of their partner, whom they consider sexual and emotional property. High levels of reported coercive control predict all three types of domestic violence and predict the most serious, systematic abuse most strongly.

In support of these observations, *Juristat* (2000b) reports: 'Women made up about 77 per cent of criminal harassment victims reported to police in 1999. Current or former husbands and boyfriends were offenders in about half these incidents.' Also: 'Women have a heightened risk of homicide after marital separation,' compared to women remaining

in a common-law or marital relationship. For men, the pattern is opposite: 'An average of 12 men per million couples were killed by a current common-law partner, 2 men per million couples by an ex-partner, and 1 man per million couples by a current marital partner.' Women, then, run the greatest risk from ex-partners, followed by current common-law partners; men run the greatest risk from current common-law partners, followed by ex-partners.

In general, women run a much higher risk of murder by their spouse or ex-spouse than do men: 'Men who killed an ex-partner were most often motivated by jealousy (44 per cent) while arguments or quarrels (41 per cent) most often motivated women.' Finally: '[E]stranged husbands were twice as likely as current husbands to have multiple victims. When marital relationships were still intact at the time of spousal homicides, children were the most likely victims other than the spouse. In estranged marriages, the victim's new partner was the most frequent third party victim.' A review of previous studies finds that assaultive husbands are likely to support a patriarchal ideology, including positive attitudes toward marital violence and negative attitudes toward gender equality. For their part, assaulted wives usually hold more liberal gender attitudes than non-assaulted wives (Sugarman and Frankel, 1996).

Partner violence may be just as prevalent in the gay and lesbian community as in the heterosexual community (Renzetti, 1997). This violence may take the form of lesbian battering, homophobic control, mutual battering, and violence associated with human immunodeficiency virus (HIV) status. In lesbian and gay male relationships, there may be additional fears of losing the relationship that confirms one's sexual orientation; fears of not being believed about the abuse, and fears of losing friends and support within the lesbian/gay communities. Data from 52 gay male couples show that psychological abuse is more frequent in egalitarian relationships than in those with power imbalances.

Consequences of family violence

Family violence has a deadening effect. Both perpetrators and victims of violence are less likely to reveal or explore their feelings than are non-violent people. Thus, for example, female victims are much less aware of their emotional states, and possess and express far fewer positive feelings than the average adult woman. Though some researchers may view this condition as a cause of domestic violence, we view it as an effect we spoke of earlier, called post-traumatic stress disorder (PTSD).

As physical abuse increases in severity, so does the victim's level of depression (Orava, McLeod, and Sharpe, 1996). Feelings of powerlessness, experiences of abuse, and insufficient social support all contribute to the persistence of her depression (Campbell, Sullivan, and Davidson, 1995). Our culture often encourages women to internalize and ignore this problem. As a result, many women remain with an abusive partner for extended periods. Partner violence often follows a cycle of violence consisting of three distinct phases. First, there is a build-up of tension, which some have likened to 'walking on eggshells'. This is followed by an explosion of spousal battery, set of by an often seemingly harmless event. Finally, there is the 'honeymoon' stage, filled with a significant amount of apology and remorse along with promises that it will never happen again (Government of Manitoba, 2000).

Feelings of commitment to an abusive partner are strongest among women who have limited economic alternatives and are more heavily invested in their relationships. Preoccupation with the relationship is associated with frequent previous separations from the relationship, continuing emotional involvement with the partner after separation, and more frequent sexual contact with the partner (Henderson, Bartholomew, and Dutton, 1997).

Juristat reports that spousal violence does not always end after marital separation. Forty per cent of women and 32 per cent of men with a former violent marriage or common-law relationship reported that violence occurred after the couple separated. Indeed, most who reported violence after separation state that the assaults became more severe, or even began after separation. Such assaults were more likely than pre-separation assaults to result in police contact, especially when women were the victims. Where violence occurred after separation, children were witnesses to at least one violent occurrence in half of all cases.

Theories about Violent Crime

Psychological Theories

Psychologists focus on how factors in the individual lead to a propensity to commit violent crimes. One historical line of research attempted to link intelligence to crime. Other social psychologists examine how otherwise 'normal' and mild-mannered citizens can change during wartime into soldiers capable of killing and injuring others, seemingly without hesitation or remorse. Philip Zimbardo (1971) suggests that assuming a role, such as 'soldier', is sufficient for someone to internalize that role's identity.

In his classic study, Zimbardo simulated a prison in the Stanford University psychology department, assigning student volunteers at random to play the role of guards and prisoners. To the 'guards', he gave uniforms, billy clubs, and whistles; to the 'prisoners', prison outfits and jail cells. After only one day, all the participants had become engrossed in their roles, with guards cruelly degrading prisoners, and prisoners suffering mental breakdowns or rebelling against their captors. The degree of social pathology that quickly emerged forced Zimbardo to end the experiment after only six days, though it had been scheduled to last two weeks.

In another classic experiment, Stanley Milgram (1974) enlisted Yale University students ostensibly to participate in a study on learning and memory, but in actuality to investigate the role of authority in maintaining obedience among subordinates. He showed that, in many instances, ordinary students could be induced by a white-coated person 'in authority'—the Experimenter—to administer what they believed were lethal and near-lethal doses of electrical shock to human subjects who were apparently failing to learn nonsense syllables at a fast enough rate. What this showed is that anyone—even students in the USA—can be led to behave inhumanly, like Nazi Gestapo torturers, under the right circumstances.

Sociological Theories

The functionalist perspective

Functionalist approaches to deviance converge on a few central tenets, namely, that crime is normal, universal, and inevitable, and that it is to be expected in any society. By implication, violent crime is also normal, universal, and in some sense necessary. This approach leads to a theory about the relationship between violence and social (and personal) disorganization.

As we saw earlier, Gottfredson and Hirschi's (1990) 'general theory of crime' usefully combines macro and micro perspectives in its emphasis on lack of self-control as a factor in criminal behaviour. Their theory, which applies to all criminal and deviant behaviours, stresses background or 'distant' factors that influence 'criminality'—the tendency to commit crime. At bottom, the origin of crime in their theory is low self-control, which results from inadequate, ineffective, and inconsistent socialization by parents early in childhood. Crime, in this sense, is aimed at pleasure. The drive for pleasure in a criminal is unconstrained by learned, internalized controls on behaviour.

According to this theory, people commit criminal acts because these acts provide easy gratification and/or they are exciting and pleasurable in themselves. People inclined to criminal acts, lacking self-control, are also likely to pursue other easy pleasures that are not criminal. Most criminals lack diligence and persistence; they tend to act impulsively. These criminal acts require little if any learning; criminals simply do what they feel like doing. Their behaviour does not reflect a rational orientation, merely lack of self-control.

Not all persons with low self-control commit crimes. However low self-control increases the likelihood someone will commit crime. These chances are increased if the motivated offender has access to a suitable target, for example, money that lacks a 'capable guardian'. The absence of adequate protection against crime, epitomized by social disorganization in the community, further intensifies the likelihood that a criminal will act out his impulses.

This theory adequately covers a great many situations—especially, impulsive acts of violent behaviour. Crimes of violence are often referred to 'crimes of passion' as they seem to adhere to no rational course of action. However, this theory fails to explain the aggressiveness and anger that some criminals show when committing their crimes, suggesting something more than an absence of self-control. Likewise, it fails to explain crimes—even crimes of violence—that are premeditated, goal-seeking, or demand skills (e.g., the use of guns) that take time to learn.

We can view the Gottfredson and Hirschi theory as an extension of social disorganization theory on the micro-sociological level. The theory points our attention to the socialization we receive in childhood and the relationships we establish with family members. Disorganized families hinder the formation of early attachments and commitments, and reduce the likelihood that young people will embrace conventional norms and values. As a result, children from conflictual families—families marked by neglect, abuse, violence, separation, or divorce—are at a higher than average risk of delinquent behaviour (on this, see, e.g., Ruchkin et al., 1998; Cox, 1996; Simons and Chao, 1996). Moreover, as we noted earlier, domestic violence is more common in conflictual families.

Conflict theory

Conflict theories of crime and violence point to inequalities in society as the cause of such deviant behaviour. Conflict theorists believe crime is inevitable whenever groups possess different levels of power and influence. One consequence is that as inequality increases in a society, criminal activity will also increase. Declining wages cause increased rates of 'quick cash' crimes, particularly in societies lacking a safety net of unemployment benefits, universal health insurance, and income security provisions (Gaylord and Lang, 1997). Violence may often be an unintended by-product of these acquisitive, hasty crimes.

As we noted earlier, people who are socially disadvantaged are more likely to embrace violent subcultures of honour and respect, leading to higher rates of crimes against persons. Deprived areas marked by poverty and inequality spawn social exclusion, alienation, and violence in pursuit of respect (Wilkinson, Kawachi, and Kennedy, 1998). Subcultures of violence emerge in poor neighbourhoods, not rich ones. That is because poverty and inequality are harmful to self-esteem; they are the results of the 'hidden injuries of social class', to use the words of historians Richard Sennett and Jonathan Cobb (1973). As a result, other things being equal, the homicide rates are highest in communities marked by low welfare-payment levels, a high percentage of female-headed families, and a high dropout rate from schools (Hannon, 1997).

Ralf Dahrendorf, in his classic work *Class and Class Conflict in Industrial Society,* notes that violence, as a means of conducting conflict, diminishes through the regulation of conflict. There is less violence when conflict is more regulated, even if the causes of conflict—for example, oppositions between authority holders and those subject to authority—continue to exist.

For conflict to be regulated, according to Dahrendorf, parties must recognize the conflict as inevitable outgrowth of conflicting interests, must be organized into groups, and must agree to rules under which the conflict will take place. Such rules protect the survival of both parties, reduce potential injury to each party, introduce some predictability into the actions of each party, and protect third parties from undue harm.

This suggests a framework for analyzing violent crimes and violent acts more generally. It assumes that violence is a means of conducting conflict in the absence of ground rules and shared assumptions. Conditions of trust and mutual understanding are needed for people to conduct social life—even, competitive or conflictual social life. Note that this theory contains elements of the conflict approach: most particularly, a recognition of the normality of conflict based on competing interests. However, in addition, this theory contains elements of the functionalist approach, with its emphasis on the way that agreed-on procedures can channel competition into peaceful, non-conflictual forms.

The conflict perspective also notes that people in privileged positions struggle to maintain their privileged status. They readily resort to criminal, even violent, acts if it will serve their purposes. Corporate crimes benefit the governing or upper class but harm the environment, place workers in danger (e.g., Westray Mines), and put the public at needless risk with dangerous products. Some might consider the negligence in Walkerton, Ontario, that resulted in multiple deaths from polluted water to be a crime of violence. It resulted from negligence on the part of those most directly charged with monitoring the water supply and the removal of environmental protections by a government willing to risk lives in order to cut taxes and, thereby, gain more votes.

Symbolic interactionism

Symbolic interactionism is typically less interested in the reasons why people commit violent acts than in the consequences of these acts for the actor. As usual, the emphasis would be on labels that are

Box 7.2 Police Chief Wants Federal Sentencing for Gun-Related Offences

TORONTO—The federal government should give anyone convicted of gun-related violence a minimum 10-year prison sentence, Toronto police Chief Julian Fantino said yesterday.

'The laws need to be changed,' Chief Fantino said at a news conference, where he asked the federal government to take some responsibility for a weekend of violence in Toronto that ended with two people dead and several others wounded.

'How many bloody weekends will it take? How many more people will have to die? And how many more assault rifles and armour-piercing rounds will have to be seized, taken off the streets of this city before we all say enough is enough?'

Toronto police made several arrests over the weekend in relation to separate incidents of gun violence, two of which involved men on conditional release for previous offences.

'Gun violence in the community doesn't appear to resonate with those in the strongest positions to take action against this scourge of violence,' said Chief Fantino. 'Criminals have no fear of the justice system, they hold it in undisguised contempt. It neither deters nor rehabilitates them.'

Chief Fantino characterized those responsible for weekend violence as 'hardcore, gun-crazed gangsters' and suggested many of the incidents were related to gang and drug activity.

Chief Fantino said there were also six armed robberies and numerous 911 calls reporting shots fired. He said 17 of 18 violent offences over the weekend involved guns.

Police will redeploy uniformed officers to 'problem areas' around the city, he said.

'We're doing our bit, but clearly when you have this revolving-door situation, hardened criminals are not getting the message,' he said. 'Other people have to step up to the plate.'

He praised former US attorney general John Ashcroft's decision to transfer the prosecution of gun violence to the federal court level.

Chief Fantino said this gave US judges broader latitude in their sentencing, and saw gun crime drop 32 per cent across the country as federal prosecutions rose 36 per cent.

Denise Rudnecki, director of communications for Justice Minister Irwin Cotler, said gun violence is a major concern of the department, but the Criminal Code already allows for appropriate sentences.

Ms Rudnecki said that in May 2004, the Department of Justice announced a series of amendments to the Criminal Code that would toughen the federal response to gun crime.

Six provisions were suggested, including stronger penalties for possession of loaded handguns in public places, increasing the minimum penalty for weapon trafficking, and ensuring judges give special consideration to domestic violence when deciding whether to prohibit someone's possession of firearms.

SOURCE: Siri Agrell, 'Use a gun, get 10 years, Fantino says "enough is enough"', *The National Post*, 15 February 2005, A6.

attached to violent criminals, and the consequences of such labelling.

Differential association theory, however, is relevant to violent crime because it describes the ways some people acquire both the skills and the rationalizations required for violent behaviour. To commit some kinds of violent acts—for example, assault with a weapon, or even simple physical assault—requires knowledge of fighting and weapons. The use of weapons in violent crime also requires access to and practice with weapons—especially guns. Finally, some subcultures provide the justifications (also, provocations) for such violent behaviour. Many people—lacking these skills, weapons, and rationalizations—are less likely to commit violent crimes.

Rationalizations for violence are important, and learned. Violent people interpret the situations in which they commit violent crimes as *requiring* violent actions. Athens (1997) states that an offender may use any of four types of interpretation:

1. The physically *defensive interpretation:* the offender believes that the victim will attack or has already begun to attack
2. The *frustrative interpretation:* supposedly, the victim is resisting a specific course of action, or the offender is expected to cooperate with an unwanted action
3. The *malefic interpretation:* the offender believes that he or she is being belittled, sees the victim as evil, and thinks violence is the best way to deal with this
4. The *frustrative-malefic interpretation:* a direct mixture of the frustrative and malefic approaches, with the proviso that the victim is not only an adversary, but loathsome as well.

Note that all these scenarios assume a set of beliefs about the situation, the adversary, and even the self. Athens (1997) distinguishes between a violent self-image, an incipiently violent self-image (those individuals seen as having a *willingness* to use violence instead of a *natural disposition* to use violence), and those with a non-violent image. To develop this typology, Athens interviewed violent offenders and asked them to attribute a type of self-image to themselves. Those who viewed themselves as non-violent interpreted the situations in which they committed the crime as physically defensive, whereas those that had a violent self-image interpreted their crimes in all four ways.

Feminist theory

Feminists emphasize the gendered nature of both deviance and control: for example, the relationship between events in the private sphere (e.g., domestic violence) and events in the public sphere (e.g., the cultural and legal tolerance of domestic violence, the gendering of law enforcement practices, and the evidence of patriarchal values in the legal system). We have already examined many feminist approaches to violent crime throughout this chapter.

Feminists have focused on sexual assault for many reasons. First, it is a terrifying, dangerous, and embarrassing experience that many women undergo and most women fear. Changing the laws related to rape, providing help and other services to women who have been raped, and finding ways to prevent rape are, therefore, important tasks facing society. While few men are rapists, most men benefit from the power over women that our society permits them. The rapist's power is analogous to that power—an extreme version of conventional patriarchy. Feminists argue that fear and dependence mark women's social relations with men at work, on dates, and in the home, and that women can never be equal to men if fear and dependence continue.

Sexual assault—a crime that most women would agree is of urgent and personal concern—has been a rallying issue for feminists. It has served to sensitize both women and men to the goals of the feminist movement. The media have helped by raising people's awareness of violent crimes against women. People are more aware of victimization and crime's victims today than they were a generation ago, largely because of the influence of the media and feminist researches.

At the same time, there is some evidence that female criminality is changing. Female homicide offenders are more numerous than in the past, for example. In only two categories of crime do females lead males, however: adolescent girls are slightly more frequently arrested for running away from home and women are twice as likely to be arrested for prostitution (Wrangham and Peterson, 1997). Some argue that biology is the answer, that men's higher levels of testosterone predispose them toward aggression and hostile actions. Others suggest that socialization is the culprit: that males are raised in a more violent culture and are taught to be less inhibited in using aggressive and violent behaviours.

Feminists have pointed out that women are often treated in a harsher manner than their male counterparts, in terms of sentencing. This is due to the sentiments of criminal justice officials who feel that the more 'masculine' the crime, the more flagrantly the female offender has violated gender-role expectations of society (Boritch, 1997). Because aggression and violence are seen as mainly male attributes, violent female offenders such as Cece and Taylor (recently convicted of Detective Bill Hancox's murder) are treated by the media as 'unfeminine'. However, some criminologists have disputed this position, asserting that women are actually treated in a more lenient manner than men (Spohn and Spears, 1997) and this is due to the criminal justice officials' 'chivalry' towards females (Pollak, 1950).

Social and Health Consequences of Violent Crime

Health consequences of violent crime

Crimes have consequences, and violent victimization harms people's health. Victimization is a risk factor for a variety of unhealthy outcomes. Not only does violent crime cause immediate physical injury and mental anguish, but it also increases the likelihood of future ill health. This is especially true for women who have experienced physical or sexual abuse. Researchers have linked violence to many serious health problems, both immediate and long-term. These include physical health problems, such as injury, chronic pain syndromes, and gastrointestinal disorders, and a range of mental health problems including anxiety and depression. Violence also undermines health by increasing a variety of negative behaviours, such as smoking and substance abuse.

Physical health outcomes

We can divide physical health consequences of violent crimes into two groups: fatal outcomes and non-fatal outcomes. The fatal outcomes of crime are usually a result of an immediate injury inflicted on the victim. In 2003, for example, 548 people died in Canada a result as a result of homicides: 161 victims were shot, 142 victims were stabbed, 120 victims were beaten, and 63 victims were strangled (*Juristat*, 2000; 2004a). There is also speculation that victims of violent crimes, especially victims of sexual abuse, are at a higher risk of committing suicide. Occasionally, hate crimes have ended in death—for example, the murder of a gay man.

There are long-term, lingering effects of such physical violence. Statistics show that rape victims are more than four times more likely than non-victims to have contemplated suicide and 13 times more likely to have attempted it. Another study showed that women who report having suffered sexual abuse in childhood have a history of suicide attempts. Suicide attempts among sexually abused males are from 14 to 15 times higher than among other males.

Another potentially fatal outcome of violent sexual assault is HIV/AIDS. If the disease weakens the person's immune system, AIDS eventually causes death. Victims of sexual assault who are penetrated orally, vaginally, or anally are at risk of contracting

Figure 7.2 Methods Used to Commit Homicide, Canada, 2003

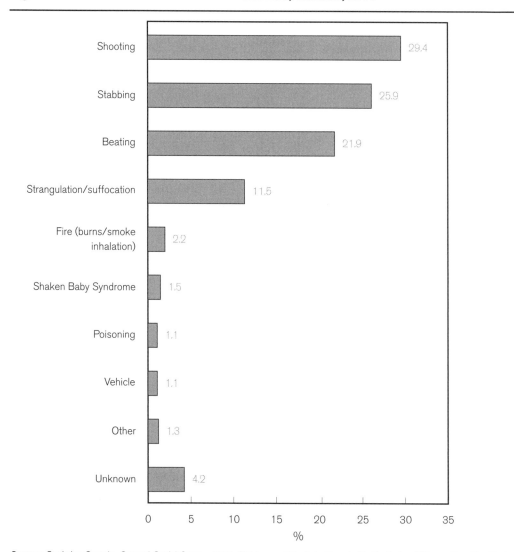

SOURCE: Statistics Canada, General Social Survey, 1999, Children and Youth in Canada Profile Series (Ottawa: Canadian Centre for Justice, Children and Youth in Canada);available at <www.statcan.ca>, accessed 19 December 2004.

the virus that leads to AIDS and eventually death. It is impossible, however, to calculate how many victims have become HIV-infected due to sexual assault.

The non-fatal outcomes of violent crimes are numerous. As mentioned before, victimization hurts people's health. Victims of crimes regularly report lower than average levels of well-being. Victims of violent crimes report lower levels of perceived health and younger victims report greater decrease in health than older victims. It is hard to pinpoint the precise long-term consequences of violent crimes because of the diversity of injuries that occur. The physical consequences of sexual assault are easier to discuss because of their common nature in many victims.

Box 7.3 'Unique' HIV Lawsuit

WINDSOR—A $10-million lawsuit filed by an alleged victim of accused HIV-assailant Carl Leone against the Windsor man, his family and local police is 'unique' and could set a legal precedent, Larry Wilson, University of Windsor professor of criminal and tort law, said Tuesday.

In the statement of claim filed Monday in Superior Court, the complainant referred to as 'Jane Roe' alleged she was a 16-year-old virgin when she met Leone, now 29, in an Internet chatroom. According to the statement, the woman, now 18, accused the Windsor Police Services Board, which oversees the force, of negligence. The suit also names Leone, his parents, and two siblings of failing to warn her that she might catch the AIDS virus from Leone.

Police 'failed to investigate . . . in a timely manner or at all,' a complaint lodged by Leone's fiance in 2000. Roe was infected sometime between July 2002 and June 2004.

Leone, who lives with his parents, was arrested last June 6 and initially charged with two counts of sexual assault for failing to tell two sexual partners he had HIV. The charges were later elevated to aggravated sexual assault. Since last June, at least 20 more women, including Roe, have come forward, bringing to 22 the number of charges he faces.

The lawsuit's outcome will be based on evidence that's presented in court, for example, the parents' knowledge of Leone's HIV status and the degree to which they facilitated the criminal conduct of their son, said Wilson. 'If they knew he was endangering people and actively encouraging it, there could be legal consequences.'

But knowledge, alone, isn't enough, he said, adding that 'it's extremely dangerous to impose on parents a life-long supervision of their children. If I have a 40-year-old son, how long do I have to keep track of him?'

SOURCE: Excerpt, Grace Macaluso, '"Unique" HIV Lawsuit', *The Windsor Star*, Windsor, 20 April 2005, A3.

Mental health outcomes

Victims of violent crimes suffer more distress symptoms and stressful life events than do non-victims and victims of non-violent crimes (Johnson, 1996). However, criminal victimization affects different people in different ways, even when the crime is identical. Resources such as social support, time, money, education, and the presence of other life stressors can affect one's resistance or vulnerability to stress (Gifford, 2001). As for both physical and emotional trauma, the health effect of a crime also depends on the social context of violence (Gilbert, 1996). For example, lesbians, gay men, and bisexuals who have been victimized by hate crimes report higher than average levels of depression, anxiety, anger, and symptoms of post-traumatic stress.

Victims of crimes are more likely than non-victims to suffer from PTSD, major depressive episodes, and a variety of phobias. The reaction depends largely on the crime. Though victims are affected most, a high risk of homicide or assault affects everyone in the community. Research on homeless adults finds a significant relationship between witnessing violence and reporting mental health symptoms (Fitzpatrick, LaGory, and Ritchey, 1999).

Victims of sexual assault often suffer from rape trauma syndrome, a type of PSTD. Sexual assault victims also suffer psychological reactions specifically related to sexual assault. Victims may feel terrified of the offender and fear for their lives. Victims may also feel humiliation, shame, and self-blame. If the attacker was an acquaintance, friend, or lover, violation of trust can be an issue for the victim. Many victims keep the rape a secret because of their shame and fear about how people will react.

Males are also harmed by sexual assault. Sexually abused boys report more high-risk sexual behaviour, including the use of prostitutes; unprotected anal intercourse; a larger number of sexual partners; a lower rate of condom use; higher rates of sexually transmitted diseases; and higher rates of partner pregnancy. Sexually abused boys were more than four times as likely to have forced sexual contact with another person, most often another boy (frequently an older brother).

Social and psychological consequences

Juristat reports, 'According to the 1999 General Social Survey, children heard or saw one parent assaulting the other in an estimated 461,000 households, which represents 37 per cent of all household with spousal violence in the five-year period preceding the survey' (Dauvergne and Johnson, 2001). Adult victims were more likely to seek help from the police or from social services when children had witnessed the violence. As a result of domestic violence, in 2002, an estimated 55,901 women and 45,347 children fled violence at home and were admitted to shelters across Canada. The majority of children were under 10 years of age.

Data from the National Longitudinal Survey of Children and Youth show that children who are exposed to physical violence in the home are less likely to have positive or effective interactions with their parents. Parental rates of depression are higher and parenting quality is low. Children, under these circumstances, are more likely to display physical aggression, emotional disorders, hyperactivity, poor school performance, and delinquent acts against property.

Other consequences of violent crime include the physical pain and suffering resulting from any injuries that the victim sustains, lowered self-esteem resulting from victimization, and the emotional loss experienced by the family and friends of victims of homicide. Fear of crime is not a problem only for individuals. It is also a social concern: 'If frightened citizens remain locked in their homes instead of enjoying public spaces, there is a loss of public and community life, and a loss of "social capital"—the family and neighbourhood channels that transmit positive social values from one generation to the next' (National Research Council, 1994).

Policies and Theory Applications

The criminal justice system

The Canadian criminal justice system is shaped like a funnel. Of the many crimes that are committed, few are reported to the police. Of all the crimes reported to police, only a fraction result in arrests and charges. Moreover, only a fraction of the crimes resulting in charges end with convictions. Finally, only a fraction of the crimes resulting in conviction end with incarceration. Thus, all of the people in jail for violent offences represent only a tiny fraction of all offenders, and they are disproportionately young, poor, and socially isolated.

The costs of our criminal justice system—of the police, courts, judges, prisons, and parole systems—are enormous; yet, many Canadians do not feel secure or well served by the system. They may not know precisely how few violent criminals are taken out of circulation for an extended period, but they sense that these numbers are small and large numbers of violent people are walking the streets.

Part of the crime problem we face is that, in Canada, as in most societies, many people feel dissatisfied with and distrustful of public institutions—politicians, police, judges, and lawyers. Though they dislike crime and criminals, they also dislike and distrust people in authority. This distrust may cause them to avoid reporting crimes or giving information to the police and courts. So, for example, in a recent shooting on a Toronto bus, a 10-year-old girl and her parent—innocent bystanders—were injured by gunfire. None of the 19 other passengers on the bus was willing to come forward with a description of the shooter.

In some countries, people may even use violence to take action into their own hands to settle disputes. In these countries there is no professional police force, or the police and military have historically been used by the government to oppress dissidents. When the existing order is disrupted—as in Haiti, or more recently in Iraq—there are no professional peacekeeping organizations to step in and enforce order and justice. The results are anarchy, crime, and sometimes a return to private revenge.

As we have seen, criminal behaviour is not fully rational. Yet, the criminal justice system is based on the principle of deterrence. This notion assumes that most crimes are rational acts in which the offender weighs the perceived benefits of committing the crime against the probability of being caught and the severity of the punishment. The 'get tough on crime' approach often discussed in recent years in North America calls for maximizing punishment to increase deterrent effects and thereby lower crime rates.

Finally, a deterrence-based approach to criminal justice fails to acknowledge and address the societal, economic, and political factors that encourage the existence of crime in the first place: unemployment, racial inequality, poverty, and the unequal distribution of resources and opportunities.

Moreover, biases intrude into the criminal justice system, even in Canada, where Aboriginal and black minorities are overrepresented in the prison population. Research has found discrimination against blacks in denying bail and in sentencing, especially for drugs, sexual assault, and bail violations. The discrimination against Aboriginal and black people is strongest at the policing point (Roberts and Doob, 1997).

In some communities, citizens have taken a more active role in keeping the peace. Some believe that the police are too weak, corrupt, or politically hampered to deal with crime effectively. Others feel that crime is a tenacious problem that cannot be solved without the help of the citizenry. Whatever their beliefs, citizen groups have tried in many places to help the police protect the community from crime. Often, community groups try to control crime through activities that make people aware of opportunities to join in crime prevention activities and develop support systems and role models.

Concluding Words

There is a widespread consensus in Canadian society and most other societies that violent behaviours are wrong and should be harshly punished. Despite biases in reporting, criminologists know enough about crime to venture several inferences. First, there is more fear about violent crime than the statistics warrant. The rates of homicide (also, robbery, manslaughter, and attempted murder) have changed little over the past 40 years, and rates of assault have fallen since 1992.

Second, crimes of violence often result from fights between spouses or friends. This is especially true when women are the victims. Men are more likely than women to be attacked by mere acquaintances, or even strangers.

Third, crimes of violence, as we have seen, are more characteristic of certain kinds of people—in particular, young, poor men. As we have suggested, the connection is probably a result of the interaction of economic and social variables. Often, criminals are more likely to be victimized than non-criminals, largely because of factors discussed in connection with routine activities theory.

To finish where we began, Canada is a relatively safe place where violent crimes are rare—rarer, perhaps, than at any time in the country's history, and rarer than most other countries in the world. Canadians, in this respect, are the beneficiaries of a stable government, reliable legal system, and established civil society. As a people, we are more oriented to human rights than to issues of honour; and we supply the poor with a social welfare net that increases their human rights and reduces the need for crime.

Yet, many Canadians are preoccupied with crime, even violent crime. That is rarely because they have been victimized by violent crime; likely, it is because they regularly view crime stories on television or in the newspaper. The media, not personal experience, shapes our fears about crime. However, if we are young men, the statistics show that we are right to fear our friends and acquaintances. If we are women (of any age), the statistics show that we are right to fear our intimates—our dates, lovers, husbands, and past partners. Unlike the movies, where psychopathic strangers kill and maim innocent people, in real life the people we know pose the greatest danger.

Summary

We have seen in this chapter that the list of illegal wrongs is enormous and yet the term 'crime' falls far short of covering all the damages done. Unlike much we discuss in this book, crime is not merely a deviant behaviour: it often has real consequences for people's safety, health, and general well-being. While violent crimes are responsible for 12 per cent of all crime and criminal homicide accounts for only 0.2 percent of all violent crimes reported in 2003 (*Juristat*, 2004a), homicidal violence receives extensive media coverage both as news and entertainment.

We have noted repeatedly that violent crime is gendered and age-graded; both the perpetrators and victims tend to be young males. Stalking has the potential of progressing to a more serious crime. There were nine stalking-related homicides in Canada from 1997 to 1999, each involving a female being stalked, and subsequently killed, by a recently separated husband, ex-husband, or ex-lover (Statistics Canada, 2000a). In 1996, 80 per cent of the stalking victims in Canada were women and 88 per cent of the persons accused of stalking in these cases were male. Most stalkers were former, rather than current, intimates. Likewise with domestic violence, usually the perpetrators are male and the victims are female. Women typically have different reasons from men for committing violent acts, if they commit them at all.

Three theories have been examined closely in this chapter. We have argued that violence results, first, from a breakdown of normal, reliable mechanisms for resolving conflict. Second, we have noted that violence often occurs in cultural settings where honour and respect are particularly important. Finally, we have observed that violence occurs where aggressors and victims routinely come together without the presence of protectors. Sometimes these occasions for violence bring together strangers on subways, and often they bring together spouses in suburban homes. That's what makes real life more interesting than fiction.

Questions for Critical Thought

1. What might account for the rising fear of crime? What social implications does this have for certain groups like the elderly?
2. Discuss the key differences between societies based on 'honour' and societies based on 'human rights'.

3. Since gender is the most significant factor in the study of any crime, does the feminist perspective provide the best lens of analysis? Argue for or against the feminist perspective.

4. Address how functionalist theory can account for impulsive acts of violent behaviour. Can any other sociological theories do the same?

5. Hypothesize why crime rates are relatively higher in remote regions such as Nunavut than in metropolitan regions.

6. Explain why families are hot spots of violence. Are families mirrors of what occurs on the streets?

7. Women use violence against men for different reasons than men use violence against women. Explain these reasons and the differences using a conflict perspective.

8. Develop a policy that aims to decrease crimes of violence committed by adolescents.

9. Choose a position and debate on the issue: Are strict gun regulations the answer to reducing crimes of violence?

10. Analyze why crimes create distrust in institutions. Why should this be such a large issue for policy-makers?

Recommended Reading

Dowler, K.G. (2003), 'Breaking News: The Portrayal of Crime, Justice and Victimization on Broadcast News', dissertation, *Abstracts International*, 64, 1086-A. This study analyzed four hundred news broadcasts across four television markets examining the relationships among story characteristics, type of crime, and demographic characteristics (race, gender, and age) of victims and suspects. The findings highlighted that newscasts provided less coverage for minority victims and male victims, crime stories that involved a proactive police response were more likely to involve a white victim, and stories that presented sympathy and outrage toward victimization were less likely to involve a minority victim.

Kaukinen, C. (2002), 'Adolescent Victimization and Problem Drinking', *Violence and Victims*, 17: 669–89. Victims of adolescent violence are more likely to engage in subsequent binge drinking and experience negative drinking consequences, particularly negative financial consequences. The findings are consistent with the adolescent development literature which highlights the importance of violent victimization in the transition to adult roles and responsibilities.

Lavoie, Francine, Line Robitaille, and Hébert, Martine. (2000), 'Teen Dating Relationships and Aggression: An Exploratory Study', *Violence Against Women*, 6 (1): 6–36. Qualitative data is included from discussion groups with 24 Canadian teenagers ages 14 to 19. The findings confirm that violence in dating relationships is present in numerous ways and that the teenagers' explanatory models still attribute part of the responsibility to victims. Results indicate that future research should study forms of abuse specific to teenagers, and prevention programs should address non-consensual as well as consensual use of violence in sexual relationships.

Miranda, D., and M. Claes. (2004), 'Rap Music Genres and Deviant Behaviors in French-Canadian Adolescents', *Journal of Youth and Adolescence*, 33: 113–22. This study investigated the links between genres of rap music and five types of deviant behaviours in adolescence (violence, theft, street gangs, mild drug use, and hard drug use). Results indicated that rap music as a whole was linked to deviant behaviours; however,

the nature of the relation differed according to genres

Pagani, Linda, Denis Larocque, Frank Vitaro, and Richard E. Tremblay. (2003), 'Verbal and Physical Abuse toward Mothers: The Role of Family Configuration, Environment, and Coping Strategies', *Journal of Youth and Adolescence*, 32 (3): 215–22. This article discusses the effects of violence within the family. The paper focuses on the rarely documented phenomenon of parental maltreatment by examining the factors that can increase the risk of abusive behaviour toward mothers. Findings revealed that parental divorce was associated with a greater risk of physical aggression directed toward mothers by adolescents. A positive family environment, reflecting a better parent-child relationship, partially diminished this risk.

Recommended Websites

Canadian Resource Centre for Victims of Crime
www.crcvc.ca

This website advocates for individual victims and their families in order to assist them in obtaining needed services and resources, and lobbies for victims' rights by presenting the interests and perspectives of victims of crime to government, at all levels.

Media Awareness Network
www.media-awareness.ca

This website discusses the possibility

that exposure to media violence causes children to behave more aggressively and affects them as adults years later.

National Crime Prevention Strategy
www.prevention.gc.ca

This is a government of Canada website that discusses public safety and preparedness.

Statistics Canada
www.statcan.ca/english/Pgdb/legal02.htm

This website provides a table of all 2003 crimes by type. It also gives the definitions of the various types of assault.

CHAPTER 8

Non-Violent Crimes

LEARNING OBJECTIVES

- To explain the development of non-violent crimes within a historical framework
- To understand how non-violent crime might be a normal reaction to social conditions
- To establish the characteristics of non-violent criminals
- To see how cultures and communities maintain non-violent crime practices
- To recall some of the classical sociological studies on non-violent crime
- To understand the diverse theories that can be applied to non-violent crime
- To describe the connection between crime and poverty within a sociological context
- To explain how non-violent crimes pose a threat to institutions
- To learn the effects that non-violent crime has on the perception of crime by citizens
- To form an argument about recidivism and penal reform
- To examine various policies that can reduce non-violent crime

Introduction

This chapter is about non-violent rule-breaking. The goal of most non-violent crimes is to obtain money or property. Violence is used rarely and only if needed to bring about that goal. Here, we focus on street crime, organized crime, and business crime. These crimes include: offences against property, such as breaking and entering for the purpose of committing an indictable offence (e.g., theft), automobile theft, and shoplifting; organized criminal activities, such as drug trafficking, prostitution, and bookmaking; and white-collar offences, such as embezzlement and fraud. Most people consider these offences wrong, but few wish to increase the severity of punishment, largely because they are not *violent* crimes. There is less consensus over the severity of less serious crimes than there is for violent crimes. Therefore, we distinguish the crimes

in this chapter chiefly by characterizing them as *non-violent* crimes. Though they are very different from one another, they have a non-violent element in common. They are also more repetitive than violent crimes. As we saw in the last chapter, violent crimes are often committed against friends, acquaintances, or family members. Non-violent crimes are more often committed against strangers or, at least, non-intimates of the criminal, and they represent a way of life. Moreover, they often constitute a source of income, a profession, line of work, or a carreer. As such, they are activities learned through observation, apprenticeship, and imitation.

In the late-nineteenth century, one of the first criminologists, Gabriel Tarde (1903), tried to explain the criminal behaviour of well-known groups such as the 'Black Hand' and the Camorra of Naples. Unlike Cesar Lombroso (1911), who reduced such crimes to biological depravity, Tarde offered a uniquely sociological explanation: imitation. People commit crimes in imitation of other people they see committing crimes, he said. There is no behaviour more social than imitation, and in this chapter we explore the ways this criminal imitation works—through communities, cultures, careers, and criminal organizations.

The crimes we discuss in this chapter are apparently based on a rational calculation of costs and benefits. Non-violent crimes are understandable as adaptations to *anomie*, as Merton described it: ways of dealing with the gap between success goals and legitimate means. Often, they are calculated, planned ways of making a living.

Internal and External Controls on Criminal Behaviour

To understand why people commit non-violent crimes, or give up committing them, we need to understand generally why people behave in the ways they do. One question has to do with the issue of internal versus external control over people's behaviour—the free will debate. The other has to do with people's rational, irrational, and non-rational assessment of risks and opportunities.

The behaviourist psychological approach to understanding why people act as they do grows out of work on reinforcement by psychologists John Watson (1913) and B.F. Skinner (1953). In sociology, George Homans (1974) built on this approach, establishing what is called 'exchange theory'. The essence of this approach is to recognize that people—indeed, all living organisms—seek gratification or rewards. They behave in ways that increase the likelihood of rewards.

Reinforcement patterns do not need to be regular and consistent to produce conforming behaviour. In fact, irregular or random reinforcement—as with gambling results—may be even more effective than regular reinforcement in producing long-term behaviour that is resistant to change. Additionally, not only the delivery of rewards shapes behaviour:

other influences include the withholding of rewards, the delivery of punishments, and the withholding of punishments.

Behaviourists assume that behaviour can be shaped from outside the organism. They expect that external influences—that is, rewards and punishments provided by others—will explain why people (or other organisms) conform to rules and expectations. Second, behaviourists assume that behaviour follows a kind of rational calculus. Organisms seem to behave in a way consistent with rationality when a reward is placed before them. They are instrumentally efficient; that is, they do the best they can to get the available reward as quickly and easily as they can, at the lowest possible 'cost'. In these two respects—responsiveness to external rewards/punishments and rational or efficient action—humans are no different from the pigeons and rats that Skinner studied, and conceivably no different from dogs, cats, pigs, and earthworms (etc.).

This said, many questions come to mind when we apply these assumptions to human beings. First, there is the question of *why* people value the rewards that they do. Rewards include money, love, sex, honour, acceptance, safety, and self-esteem. Our personal and cultural histories determine what we come to value. They also change over time. As we age, excitement and risk-taking—the rewards provided by sex, drugs, and rock 'n' roll—diminish in importance. This change is largely the result of learning and socialization. Note that members of different cultures and subcultures learn to value different things, and to age, mature, and change their values differently.

Thus, to understand people's conformity and deviance—their response to a *particular set of external stimuli*—we have to understand their external environment—their reference groups and competing reward systems—and what they have learned to value. Without knowing what people value, and how they perceive the probabilities of getting what they value, we are wholly unable to predict whether they will conform or deviate in any given situation. Pigeons are uncomplicated: whatever their personal history, they will swoop in for breadcrumbs 10 times out of 10. People, on the other hand, will rarely swoop for breadcrumbs. Some only swoop for love, some for respect, or security, or cash, or fancy cars, and so on.

What constitutes a reward is a perceptual matter, often a result of personal experience and social learning. Britt (2003) notes that crime is meant to satisfy a variety of basic human needs and desires including affection, status, stimulation, autonomy, security, money, and belief. People interpret these external stimuli internally. They do not respond, ratlike, to food pellets. They interpret their possibilities in terms of personal experiences, perceptions, and value systems. The external world, for many practical purposes, exists *only* as raw input to the internal processes that give experience meaning.

Moreover, people do not see the opportunity structure the same way. Humans have more information and more highly evolved brains than rats and pigeons. However, to be fair, for both rats and people, all rationality is bounded—that is, limited by the available information and the conditions under which we process that information. So, for example, information processed hastily or under stress will yield worse results than information processed gradually, whether a human or rat is doing the brainwork.

People—unlike rats—often make decisions through consultation with others. They seek wise counsel, sharing their information, and seeking input. That said, people are still subject to many kinds of irrationality. For example, consider the well-known 'gambler's fallacy': some people think their likelihood of achieving a desired reward increases each time they fail to achieve it. (The reasoning goes that, if the odds say a gambler will win once in a hundred trials, he is closer to winning after 98 losses than after 97 losses.) This erroneous belief, which keeps Las Vegas afloat, may be unique to humans; we cannot tell. It does, however, point to a defect in reasoning that is, however, pigeonlike.

So, for example, Pogarsky and Piquero (2003) note that, paradoxically, heavily punished individuals appear more likely to offend in the future, and believe that the certainty of punishment is lower than do their less punished (or unpunished) counterparts. One explanation the authors call 'resetting' invokes the 'gambler's fallacy'. Under this explanation, punished offenders reset their sanction certainty estimate, apparently thinking they would have to be exceedingly unlucky to be arrested again.

Other forms of irrationality and non-rationality enter human decision-making as well. De Haanm and Vos (2003), interviewing street robbers, conclude that rational choice theory fails adequately to understand some of the essential aspects of this behaviour: impulsiveness, expressivity, moral ambiguity, and shame. An adequate understanding of criminality requires taking more seriously the emotional aspects of criminal behaviour and the normative meanings that perpetrators attribute to their own behaviour before, during, and after the crime.

For example, thieves may misperceive the likelihood they will get caught and, if caught, the likelihood they will get arrested, convicted, and sent to jail. To answer this, we need to know how the thief views his own freedom, earning opportunities, experience with jail, and perceptions of the jail experience. Thieves rarely sit down with a pencil and paper and make detailed calculations before deciding to commit a crime. Beyond that, the severity of punishment—though it appears important in the Skinnerian scheme of reinforcements—appears to play little part in the lives of actual criminals.

A factor in deterring crime is the perceived certainty of arrest, conviction, and punishment. Criminals appear to commit crimes because, for the most part, they think they will not get caught. Doob and Webster (2003) note that literature reviews of sentence severity in the past 25 years have concluded that there is little or no consistent evidence that harsher sanctions reduce crime rates in Western populations. In short, sentence severity has no effect on the level of crime in society.

From this perspective, law-makers and law-enforcers cannot assume that rational punishments and the deprivation of external rewards—for example, the deprivation of freedom through imprisonment—will have the desired effect of preventing crime or recidivism (repeat crime), even where the motive is profit, as it is in most non-violent crimes.

So, our argument is the following: where acquisitive (non-violent) crime is concerned, humans—like pigeons and rats—want to maximize their rewards. However, there the similarity ends. Generally speaking, humans reason more effectively than pigeons and rats, have more information, are better able to organize with others, use more sophisticated technology, make plans, and—most important of all—put meanings on their actions. We cannot understand human crime unless we have a basic understanding of these meanings and the ways human criminals organize to achieve their meaningful goals.

The Historical Development of Non-violent Crime

Organized Crime

Compared with juvenile delinquency, violent crime, and amateur (street) crime, professional crime—for example, a career in automobile theft or embezzlement—is well organized. At the pinnacle of organized crime is what the media have come to call 'the Mafia'.

Organized crime, as in the Mafia, is sometimes violent. However, most of the violence of organized criminals is directed against other organized criminals. The most profitable business activities of organized crime are non-violent: they include prostitution, gambling, drugs, and pornography. Criminal Al Capone helped to 'organize' crime families and negotiate peaceful relations between them to ensure they could make as much money as possible, as peacefully as possible.

Despite the popular belief that organized crime, or 'Mafia' as many would refer to it, had somehow evolved from Italy; many separate historical investigations have found little evidence to support such a claim. Immigration from a variety of countries provided a fertile soil for the development of organized crime. As a result, there was organized crime in the United States long before the Italian immigrants took it over. Other immigrant groups—among them, the Irish, the Germans, and the Jews—controlled crime in the large American cities before the Italians took over.

Organized crime first became big business in the 1920s, when Prohibition diminished the legal supply of alcohol. Criminal organizations could monopolize the illegal manufacturing and delivery of alcohol for which the demand remained high. The discovery that providing illegal products and services could bring high profits at low risks led to more varied criminal activities that included gambling, drugs, prostitution, and money laundering.

As society changed, so did organized crime. In North America, it became a more diversified, less visible business. Besides its illegal activities, organized crime developed interests in legitimate business, such as real estate, trucking, and food, in part as ways of laundering the vast sums of money earned through illegal activities. Eventually, the problem of organized crime came to the attention of international organizations, state institutions, and the public of many countries that had not previously considered themselves affected by the problem.

Traditionally regarded as an issue that concerned only a few nations, today organized crime is a 'hot topic' of public discourse all over the world (Paoli, 2002). Increasingly, criminal organizations violate national sovereignty, undermine democratic institutions, threaten the processes of democratization and privatization of states in transition, and add a new dimension to problems such as nuclear proliferation and terrorism (Lloyd, 1999).

Business crime

There are, strictly speaking, two kinds of business crime (or 'suite' crime): corporate crimes—crimes committed by corporations in their own business interest, and white-collar crimes—crimes (such as fraud or embezzlement) committed by business-people or professionals, in their own interest and often at the expense of the larger corporate body within which they work. Within large business organizations, hidden from view by bureaucratic rules and corporate liability, individuals commit criminal acts that may not be easily observed, let alone be prosecuted.

Unlike amateur crime—for example, shoplifting—business crime victimizes millions of people; it robs businesses of billions of dollars annually; and it undermines the legitimacy of public institutions. Business crime has received ever more attention from investigators, because the number and influence of business organizations has increased dramatically (Shover and Hochstetler, 2002).

Frauds, such as insider trading and falsifying account books (e.g. Enron), is the perfect example of business crimes. Commonly, frauds misrepresent a product or service. This enables the criminal to sell something worthless for a large amount of money and make a huge profit. Fraud relies on the manipulation of information. The high-tech industry, for example, is a perfect place for fraudulent activity; rapid growth, high stakes, and a huge potential for profits characterize this realm of activity. In any 'wildcat' environment investigative protocols, internal controls, and good accounting practices are often lacking, and they are all essential weapons in the battle against corporate fraud (Hunt, 1995).

Since sociologist Edwin Sutherland (1940; 1949) carried out the first known research on the topic, business crime has evolved into a visible global problem. Governments around the world are putting more effort into fighting this social problem that affects the economy, government, and public. Offshore banking and bank secrecy, as historically practiced in Swiss bank accounts, are widely used to launder billions of dollars stolen from people throughout the world. US treasury officials believe that 99.9 per cent of foreign criminal and terrorist

money sent to the US is placed in secure accounts, making it safe from detection. Shell companies—also known as 'mailbox' companies, international business corporations (IBCs), or personal investment companies (PICs) marketed by banks and accounting firms—launder money and also hide profits from income taxes.

Some experts calculate that as much as half the world's capital flows are handled in offshore centres, and the International Monetary Fund (IMF) estimates that between $600 billion and $1.5 trillion of illicit money is laundered annually through secret bank accounts. In crimes of this sort, the line is blurred between corporate crime, organized crime, and political crime (which we discuss in Chapter 9).

The most recent and spectacular example of business crime was contained in allegations against Canadian-born magnate Conrad Black. He is alleged to have fraudulently misused millions of dollars from Hollinger Incorporated profit to maintain an extraordinarily lavish lifestyle. Critics said that Black had become unable to distinguish between the company's money and his own personal funds. This characteristic, which Max Weber called 'patrimonial rule', was common among kings and other aristocrats before the Industrial Revolution but has been largely eliminated in companies that are publicly traded on the stock exchange. There, an expert board of directors is expected to act forcefully in the interests of stockholders. In the case of Hollinger, they did not.

Street crime

Throughout history, people have cheated and stolen from one another. Today, we call these 'street crimes' because they often occur in public, in and around city streets.

Street crimes are common because, of all crimes, they require the least skill, experience, technology, organization, or capital. Anyone can commit a street crime; as a result, amateurs commit more street crimes than anyone else. Because amateurs commit

Box 8.1 Ring Around the White Collar: Why Is Stewart So Alone?

ORLANDO—Economic crime has been rampant in this country for a long time. Occasionally, its consequences pierce the public's consciousness—during the SandL crisis of the 1980s and the more recent Enron fiasco, for example—and a few very notorious prosecutions, like [Martha] Stewart's, result. But these crises are symptomatic of a much larger problem: people and their businesses routinely cheat on their taxes, defraud each other, steal from government programs, and lie about all this to regulators. So the critical issue is not why Martha, but why is Martha so alone?

The short answer is that, nationwide, a very small number of investigators and prosecutors are assigned to white-collar work. Police and local prosecutor's offices don't handle most economic crime; they have their hands full with other matters. State attorney general's take responsibility for some white-collar matters, but in most states they have only a token presence. The bulk of the responsibility for ferreting out financial crime rests with federal law enforcement. But it, too, has a lot on its plate, and only a small percentage of its resources are aimed in this direction. The result is that the annual number of white-collar prosecutions merely scratches the surface.

Flourishing under this surface is an astonishing amount of criminal activity. The National Health Care Anti-fraud Association estimates that $39 billion in health-care fraud is committed against private insurers and government programs every year. According to the IRS, the United States' underground economy—the amount of money earned by Americans on which they illegally pay no taxes—was $195 billion in 1998, a figure that many criticize as too conservative. The FTC reports that credit-card fraud totals hundreds of millions of dollars annually. More corrosive white-collar crime—such as official and law-enforcement corruption—is less commonplace, but still committed at an alarming rate.

Consider this: If the United States devoted as much prosecutorial resources to white-collar crime as it has devoted to drug offenses over the past two decades, our prisons would be filled with white, middle- and upper-income people—a very different population than the one behind bars today.

What's that tell us? Maybe too many tears have been shed for Martha because Americans identify with her not only as the icon of good taste, but as the person they aspire to be. Perhaps Stewart's dishonest reaction to the investigation of her stock trading hit too close to home. Every American should reflect on this the next time the boss offers a bonus 'under the table' or an insurance claim waits to be filled out. Realistically, law enforcement will never uncover most white-collar crime; prevention must come from within. But the few who are caught—famous or not—deserve punishment nonetheless.

SOURCE: Michael Seigel [Special to the *Sentinel*], 'Ring Around the White Collar: Why is Stewart So Alone?', *Orlando Sentinel*, Orlando, FL, 13 October 2004, A13.

Figure 8.1 Historical Perspectives on Crime in Canada

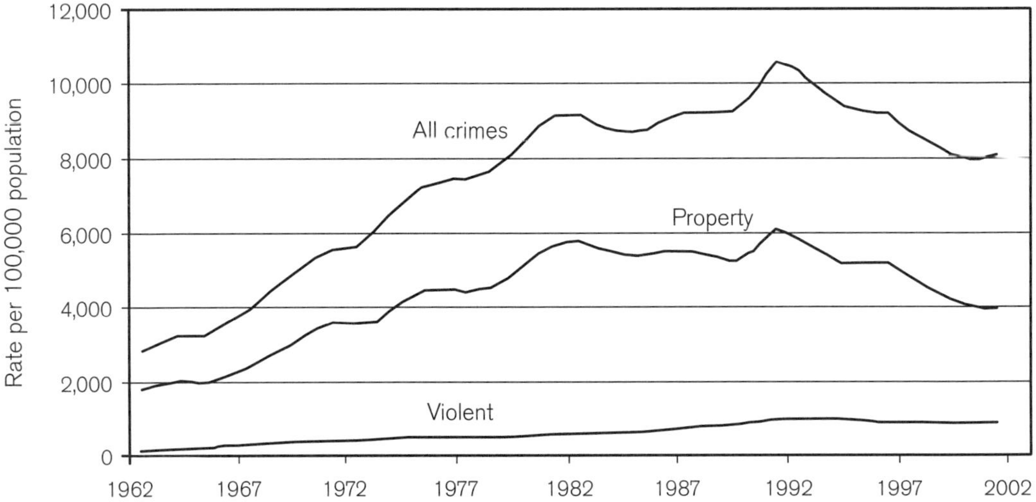

them, often in public places, street crimes are more likely to result in arrests than organized or business crimes. The result is that courts, jails, and prisons are filled with amateur, working-class criminals, most often people with little education, financial capital, or social capital. Street crime, unlike business crime, or even organized crime, is readily available to society's poorest people, yet it is a far from secure means of making a living.

The prevalence of street crime in Canada

According to *Juristat*, the rate of property crimes has been decreasing over the past decade. In 2002, the rate of break-ins dropped a further 3 per cent and vehicle thefts were down 5 per cent, though frauds increased by 4 per cent (Wallace, 2003a; 2003b). Fifty-two per cent of all 24 million *Criminal Code* offences (excluding traffic) reported to the police in 2002 were property crimes; another 35 per cent were 'other' incidents (such as mischief and disturbing the peace). By contrast, the violent crimes discussed in Chapter 7 accounted for only 13 per cent of the

total. Figure 8.1 shows the crime rate for Canada from 1962 to 2002.

Consider break and enter (B and E), a serious property crime often resulting in significant financial and psychological harm for victims. *Juristat* (Statistics Canada, 2000b) reports that the rate of breaking and entering in 1999—318,448 incidents reported, or 1,044 incidents per 100,000 population—was at a 25-year low. The rates were higher in the Western Provinces and lower in the East. Canada, with lower rates of violent crime, has higher rates of property crime than the United States. This includes 30 per cent higher rates of break-ins and motor vehicle thefts, for example. Otherwise, trends in crime between the two countries have been similar over the past 20 years (Gannon, 2001).

Compared with 12 other countries participating in the 2000 International Crime Victimization Survey, Canada is near the average (Besserer, 2001). That is to say, crime in Canada is quite representative of most industrial societies. The most common crimes reported are car vandalism and theft from a car. For the 11 crimes discussed in that report,

Figure 8.2 Community Perceptions of Crime, Canada, 1999
Response to the question: 'Do you think there is a serious crime problem in your neighbourhood?'

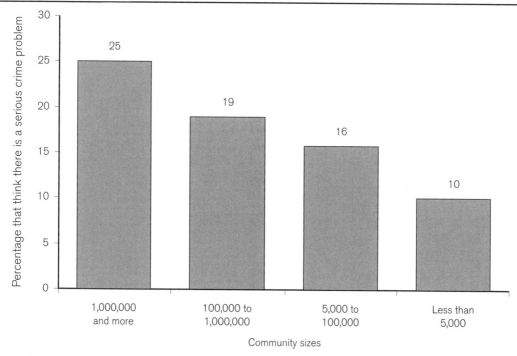

Community sizes

SOURCE: Department of Justice, Canada, 'Crime Trends, Demographics, and Public Perceptions of the Criminal Justice System', 26; available at <http://canada.justice.gc.ca>, accessed 1 November 2004.

about half of all incidents were reported to police (in Canada and internationally). Satisfaction with police performance is high in Canada (and the United States). In 2000, 89 per cent of Americans and 87 per cent of Canadians felt that the police were doing a very good or fairly good job at controlling crime in their area, the highest figures among the 13 countries. The public's perception of whether there is a crime problem in their neighbourhood is shown in Figure 8.2.

However, according to the 1999 General Social Survey (see Table 8.1), people's views of the criminal courts, prison, and parole systems are less favourable than their views of the local police, who most Canadians believe are doing a good job. *Juristat* reports, 'In most cases, people who have come into

contact with the police (as victim or perpetrator) or the criminal courts have less positive attitudes toward them' (Tufts, 2000).

Demographic and Social Characteristics of Criminals

Street crime

Most victims of street crime are men, and so are most of the perpetrators. As a result, any area with a high concentration of young men will likely have a high rate of street crime. A higher than average population density increases the rate of street crime because by definition, street crimes occur in public places, usually where the population density is greatest. For these reasons, there are more street

Table 8.1 Perceived Change in Crime

Population Aged 15 and Over by Perceived Change in Level of Crime in Neighbourhood During Past Five Years, by CMA, 1999

CMA	Total population	Increased	Decreased	Same	Don't know/ Not Stated
	'000s		%		
Canada	24,260	29	6	54	10
St John's	142	26	8	59	7
Halifax	286	36	6	48	10
Saint John	102	18	8	66	8
Québec	584	21	8	59	12
Montreal	2,721	25	8	56	11
Ottawa-Hull	841	27	8	53	13
Toronto	3,721	30	6	50	15
Hamilton	547	36	6	47	11
Winnipeg	533	38	4	48	10
Regina	154	38	–	48	10
Saskatoon	176	37	–	51	10
Calgary	744	31	7	47	16
Edmonton	738	30	4	54	12
Vancouver	1656	38	5	46	11
Victoria	264	31	–	50	15

SOURCE: Statistics Canada, General Social Survey, Cycle 13; available at <www.statcan.ca>, accessed 4 November 2003.

crimes than average in cities, in vacation spots during the peak season, on college campuses, and at other public gatherings.

As we have said, few people who commit street crimes are professional criminals. However, career (or professional) criminals learn their trade by committing street crimes. Imprisonment increases the chance that street criminals will become career criminals; prisons are good places to learn the criminal 'trades' and make criminal connections.

Graduating from amateur street crime to professional or career crime requires career skills, like any other career. The 'criminal career' is made up of social roles the offender plays, his self-identification with crime, self-concept, relationship with others, and the degree to which criminal behaviour has become a part of his everyday life. Career criminals are usually not connected with organized crime,

although highly specialized criminals (such as safe-crackers) may be. In comparison to other criminals, professional criminals develop common attitudes toward themselves, their crimes, and the police whom they see as the common enemy.

Organized crime

The term 'organized crime' has been used as a slogan to express the growing anxiety of national and supranational institutions over the expansion of illegal markets, the increasing mobility of criminals across national borders, and their growing ability to infiltrate the legal economy and undermine political institutions (Paoli, 2002). In recent decades, the scope and growth of organized crime has become globalized and out of control.

The people who participate in organized crime are typically professional, or career, criminals.

Table 8.2 Police vs Media Ranking of Problems Posed by Stated Criminal Activity

Criminal activities	Police managers	Media
Hard drugs production and trafficking	3.11	3.67
Drug import and export	3.44	4.06
Intimidation of justice officials	4.50	5.65
Money laundering	4.94	8.81
Intimidation/extortion of the public	5.28	5.35
Soft drugs production and trafficking	6.06	7.31
Economic crimes (telemarketing scams, securities fraud, etc.)	6.50	8.33
Weapons trafficking	7.44	8.24
Smuggling	7.89	9.35
Prostitution procurement	8.67	9.88
Migrant smuggling	9.11	7.83
Environmental crimes (illegal disposal of hazardous waste, etc.)	9.17	10.29
Auto theft (networks)	9.59	10.38
Counterfeiting	10.06	12.06
Gambling	12.22	12.63

Note: Order of importance: Most important = 1; least important = 15.

SOURCE: Judith Dubois, 'Media Coverage of Organized Crime–Police Managers Survey', (Ottawa: Research and Evaluation Branch: Community, Contract and Aboriginal Policing Services Directorate (RCMP), May 2003), 16; available by request at <www.rcmp-grc.gc.ca/ ccaps/media_coverage_e.htm>.

However, not all crimes—even professional crimes— are connected with what we call organized crime. Only some crimes require large-scale organization. For example, gambling and prostitution can bring huge profits to people who organize these activities. Other crimes, such as drug smuggling and trafficking involve substantial overhead costs and require organization to fund and carry out the activity. This leads to organized crime groups or syndicates—operations in which several criminal groups coordinate their illegal activity. Criminals take over and invest in businesses that customarily handle a high cash-transaction volume, mixing the illicit proceeds with those of the legitimate business. For example, criminals may purchase businesses that generate huge gross receipts from cash sales, such as restaurants, bars, nightclubs, hotels, currency exchange shops, vending machine companies, car washes, and other retail sales, for this purpose.

Organized crime poses a serious threat to Canada's institutions, economy, and quality of life— even more so than more common street crimes or more attention-catching crimes of violence. For example, drug traders and other organized criminals have made money-laundering the second largest global industry, with the circulation of 'dirty' money estimated at $3 trillion worldwide (see Table 8.2). Organized crime groups are well known for their use of sophisticated technology to commit crimes such as currency and credit card counterfeiting and fraud, as well as fraudulent investment and tele-marketing schemes. In May 2002 police closed a significant counterfeit credit card operation based in Quebec. Besides counterfeiting credit cards, this organization was involved in producing fraudulent identification papers.

Business crime

Organized crime is viewed as the shady activity of shady people. Business crime is quite different: respectable people of high social standing commit business crimes in the course of their normal work.

This type of crime occurs at many different levels. Business crime may be committed by employees against companies (e.g., through embezzlement), companies against employees (e.g., through violation of safety codes), companies against customers (e.g., by price fixing or fraudulent promises), or companies against the public (e.g., by dumping toxic wastes into the air, land, or water). For business crimes by people in high-status occupations, we often use the term 'white-collar crime'. White-collar crimes include insider-trading, restraint of trade such as monopoly, price fixing, illegal rebates, infringement of patents, trademarks, and copyrights, and misrepresentation in advertisements.

The range of business crimes is very wide. Business criminals may violate laws concerning food and drug quality and safety. Employers may violate laws regarding wages, hours, and public contracts. Politicians and government employees may gain illegal benefits by furnishing favours or confidential information to business firms. Embezzlement of trust funds is a common form of occupational crime as well for accountants and others with financial responsibility.

The examination of white-collar crime by sociologists has introduced an important balance to an otherwise distorted picture of crime that emphasizes the study of common (street) crime committed by poor people. However, despite the better balance in representation, perpetrators of white-collar crime, who are better educated, are less often sentenced to prison and are often not prosecuted formally by the criminal justice system. Instead, they may be disbarred from their profession or receive fines that they can pay more easily than conventional criminals.

White-collar crime costs the Canadian economy a huge amount of money. Fraud incurs significant costs and permeates all levels of Canadian society. One national organization estimates that insurance fraud alone costs policyholders $1.3 billion annually (Insurance Canada, 2003). Accordingly, Canada has devoted more attention to this crime problem in recent years. Ottawa has moved to crack down on corporate and securities crime by committing more resources to prosecuting white-collar offences and introducing tough penalties for illegal insider trading, with protection for whistle blowers (Laghi and Howlett, 2003).

Non-violent Criminal Cultures and Communities

Amateur criminals—typically, young men who commit occasional street crimes—belong to cultures and communities—gangs—similar to those we discussed in Chapter 6. Professional or career criminals, on the other hand, belong to cultures and communities that are more closely associated with organized crime.

Organized crime, therefore, offers a good example of how crime and deviance can give rise to normal, well-organized subcultural activities. Organized crime rings that currently exist in Canada include offshoots of the Chinese Triad, the Colombian Mafia, the Russian Mafia, and some motorcycle gangs. Law enforcement agencies have implicated these various groups in drug trafficking, prostitution, extortion, bribery, money laundering, assaults, and homicides. As a result, we know a fair amount about how these groups operate.

Sociology, as well, has helped to disenchant our thinking about organized crime, most particularly by dispelling the idea that it is an individualistic response to poverty. Early sociologists believed that crime resulted from poverty and that crime in poor neighbourhoods resulted from social disorganization: the more the disorganization, the more the crime. After roughly 1940, however, with the publication of William Whyte's (1981 [1943]) classic work, *Street Corner Society*, sociologists changed their views. They came to recognize that crime—especially, organized crime in poor neighbourhoods—can be highly organized. It is also connected with the social, political, and economic life of the people in the community. It is an intrinsic part of city, national, corporate, and political life.

We know now that modern organized crime operates at the intersection of legitimate and

Box 8.2 White-Collar Crime

White-collar and corporate crimes such as fraud rarely come to mind when addressing crime in Canada, yet they come in a surprising number of guises: cheque fraud, credit card fraud, forgery, unauthorized use of computers, mail and telemarketing fraud, and fraudulent manipulation of the stock exchange. As a result, fraud incurs significant costs and permeates all levels of Canadian society. One national organization estimates that insurance fraud alone costs policyholders $1.3 billion annually.

While the overall fraud rate fell in 1999 to its lowest point in 20 years, certain types of fraud have seen significant growth. Perpetrators of fraud have proven to be particularly deft at adapting to electronic commerce and information technology. As a result, fraud spans national borders and is a key element of organized crime.

The rate of fraud involving cheques has declined significantly since its peak in the 1980s, when it accounted for more than 60 per cent of all frauds. At that time, credit card fraud accounted for less than 12 per cent. By 1999, frauds involved cheques in 33 per cent of the cases and credit cards in 21 per cent. Other types of fraud offences, such as telemarketing fraud and forgery, remain the most prevalent, representing 46 per cent of all frauds in 1999.

About 80 per cent of fraud victims in 1996 were commercial establishments, banks or other financial institutions. Anyone can be victimized by fraud, however. According to a national task force, telemarketing fraud victimized 2,676 Canadians in 1996, averaging $2,600 per victim and totalling over $6.9 million in losses.

SOURCE: Excerpt, Statistics Canada, 'The State: Fraud' *Canada e-Book*. Catalogue 11-404-XIE. May 2003; available at <142.206.72.67/04/04b/04b_002d_e.htm>, accessed on 4 November 2003.

illegitimate business, family and formal organization (cf. Ianni, 1983). Often, it has as strong connections to white-collar crime as it does to vice crimes (such as drugs, pornography, and prostitution) that work through juvenile or amateur criminal associates. Organized crime often draws on the talents of professional and amateur, older and younger criminals. What organized crime shows dramatically is that crime can be a learned, organized, social activity with deep historical roots.

Organized crime is a social form, not the mere result of a biological genetic peculiarity, as early criminologists such as Cesar Lombroso (1911) believed. Organized crime is not a deviation from mainstream

society: it is fully a part of it, and plays a vital role in the world's economic and political activities. Our law-abiding society creates and maintains crime, because there are things that crime can do for 'legitimate society'—whether break union strikes, steal elections, or provide drugs and prostitutes—that legitimate society cannot do for itself. The traditional forms of organized crime suit nicely to the requirements of modern business and politics.

All secret organizations, such as those of organized crime, depend to an unusual degree on friendship and kinship relations, which facilitate the maintenance of order and conformity (on this, see Erickson [1985] and Simmel [1902] on secret

Box 8.3 Sense of Community in Saskatchewan: High Crime Rates

A dark reality underlies Saskatchewan's close sense of community—the highest murder rate among the provinces in 2003.

The number of victims—41—seems low when compared to the 178 murders in Ontario or 100 in Quebec last year. But with a small population of around 995,000, it's enough per-capita to give the province a 'No. 1' label it could well do without.

From murders to car thefts and break-ins, the province and its major cities like Regina and Saskatoon are used to high crime—even though Saskatchewan doesn't

feel unsafe. That's because the majority of crime victims continue to be First Nations people and those living in deprived inner-city neighbourhoods, far from the mainstream.

Making sure criminals pay dearly for their crimes goes without saying. But eliminating the fertile ground in which crime flourishes—poverty, addictions and alienation—also needs our urgent attention.

Our high crime rates indicate that not everyone feels part of the Saskatchewan community.

SOURCE: Editorial, *Leader Post*, Regina, 1 October 2004, B7.

societies). At the base of organized crime is an organizing principle that sociologists have variously called patronage or 'clientelism'. Originally, the word *client* meant a 'hearer' or 'person who listens to advice'. The client listened to the 'patron', or boss. The relationship between patron and client is personal and endures for life.

The organization of large-scale crime today is a particular mix of older and newer elements. The patron–client networks on which organized crime is based are a unique form of social organization. Unlike bureaucracies, patron–client networks are based on unwritten and particularistic rules. The conditions that support and spread clientelism in modern cities are high unemployment, low wages, low education, and low levels of labour participation (e.g., highly gendered work patterns). Because the state is largely organized by and for the most powerful members of society, organized crime constitutes—in some communities—an illegitimate state organized by and for the less powerful members of society.

Organized crime in Sicily, for example, has survived through all the political and economic changes that followed the Second World War. Keys to this survival are the ideas of trust and honour, and notions of crime and punishment, that we can still find among Sicilian peasants and Sardinian herdsmen. These ideas work well wherever people distrust the state, the police and other major institutions, and deprivation remains part of the historical memory (Cottino, 1999).

The Sicilian Mafia today is a complex subculture that combines ancient features and modern aspects with a great capacity to adapt to changing economic and political conditions. Key aspects of Mafioso culture continue to be the code of honour and instrumental friendship, secret power, and the underground economy (Catansaro, 1989). In recent times, the Mafia has discarded its control over the local agricultural sector for more profitable ventures in narcotics and public administration, penetrating the political structure of Italy's democratic state. The interests of the Mafia 'family' supplant those of the members' original family and prevent personal thought and autonomy. As in Roman times, patronage, respect, and reciprocity are highly valued—in the US Mafia as in Sicily's Mafia. Patronage continues to involve public shows of respect and power, in this way maintaining honour (Dixon, 1993).

The changing role of women offers one example of the organization's adaptability. In earlier times, women were excluded from the strictly masculine criminal organization. Today, increasingly often, women play a key role in maintaining the Mafia system.

In the former communist Eastern Europe and the former Soviet Union, crimes of all types have increased and police efficiency has fallen. Organized crime and fraud have flourished, because perpetrators can bribe the poorly paid police. Lack of trust in the Russian state has created a demand for protection at any price, evident from the reports of protection needed by small entrepreneurs (Varese, 1994). Governments have failed to regulate the new free market and fight fraud and tax evasion. Criminals throughout the region find it easy to make deals with leading executives, officials, and politicians. Moreover, black-marketeering is a large source of jobs and incomes (*The Economist*, 1995). As we have seen, these conditions support the rise of a Mafia-type system.

Tomaszewski (2003) has shown that compared to their better-off counterparts, poor neighbourhoods display much lower levels of informal social control and social cohesion. That's why they are a breeding ground for organized crime.

Organized crime prospers wherever a community meets four key conditions. First, organized crime is associated with conditions of scarcity and inequality. Second, it is common where poverty and prejudice keep people from moving easily to another community, to find work elsewhere. Third, organized crime provides protection in a society that lacks equal legal or human rights, or equal access to welfare, health care, and good quality education.

Finally, organized crime flourishes among people who lack human capital and cultural capital. North American capitalism is one type of economic and social system that produces these conditions, though it is not the only one. Russian capitalism is another, as is Sicilian feudalism.

Classical Sociological Studies

Clinard and Quinney (1973) were among the first to distinguish between occupational and corporate crime, whereas most sociologists simply referred to this type of crime as 'white collar'.

In their book, *Criminal Behavior Systems*, Clinard and Quinney defined occupational crime as 'violation of the criminal law in the course of activity in a legitimate occupation.' The first mention of white-collar crime has been attributed to E.A. Ross who coined the term 'criminaloids' and then in the 1930s, Albert Morris used the term 'criminals of the upperworld' (Clinard and Quinney, 1973).

At his presidential speech, Sutherland (1940) criticized academics for having a class bias, since little research was being done on criminality in the upper classes of society. From his research on white-collar crimes, Sutherland concluded, '[C]rime is in fact not closely correlated with poverty or with psychopathic and sociopathic conditions associated with poverty, and that an adequate explanation of criminal behaviour must proceed along quite different lines' (Shover and Wright, 2001).

Sutherland posits that white-collar crime should be regarded as a very important part of sociological and criminological research, since the financial cost of white-collar crime is likely to be a few times greater than all other crimes combined (Shover and Wright, 2001). More important, white-collar crime creates distrust in institutions and impedes social organization. Few crimes have such a far-reaching effect on every member of a society. Donald Cressey (1988), who worked with Edwin Sutherland on the classic book *Criminology*, points out in 'The Poverty of Theory in Corporate Crime Research' the problem of Sutherland failing to distinguish between people within a corporation and the corporation itself. Cressey goes on to argue that differential association may explain occupational crime, but it fails to explain corporate crime.

Organized crime

Two classic works on organized crime are by anthropologist Francis Ianni (1974; 1972), who has studied and understood the complex connections between criminal and legitimate activity. One, titled *A Family Business*, is a study of authority systems based on tradition versus expertise in a Mafia crime family; the other, titled *Black Mafia*, is a study of the role of crime in poor minority and immigrant communities.

Central to his studies are analyses of social cohesion: what holds criminal organizations together, aside from profit-making. Ianni's (1974) studies of organized crime in the black and Puerto Rican communities, for example, provide valuable information with regard to the two distinct types of networks that are found in these organizations: bonding relationships and criminal relationships. The bonding relationships maintain social cohesion and they are the foundation for criminal relationships.

Bonding relationships can form in any number of ways. They may form in childhood, originating in a gang or legitimate social connection. Sometimes, they form when an experienced criminal recruits a youth as an apprentice. This helps to reinforce criminal activity because it works as a type of role modelling. Prison acquaintanceship also helps to form bonds between men who are already in crime, bringing them together even if they were not working together before.

Ianni also notes that most blacks and Puerto Ricans view their criminal activity as part of the American business structure. That is to say, they feel that they are more into business than into crime. Ianni points out that often there is a blurry line between legitimate and illegitimate business in America. Additionally, the poverty and powerlessness these groups experience leads them to criminal activity, and the 'black mafia' is seen as a route to

success. Ianni explains that 'mafias' provide a social code of behaviour in societies that lack a strong social order.

Theories about Non-violent Crime

Psychological explanations

Many psychological approaches still receive strong support. Evidence for this connection comes from research on personality defects and disorders among delinquents, mental illness in prisoners, and studies of psychopathic and sociopathic criminals. Researchers have even argued that certain personality characteristics contribute to the commission of (seemingly rational) business or corporate crime. Piquero and colleagues (2002), for example, have explored the desire-for-control, which is related to several forms of corporate criminal activity. The results suggest that desire-for-control inhibits corporate criminal activity.

Sociological approaches

Although sociologists recognize the importance of personality and psychological processes, such explanations offer only a partial understanding of crime and delinquency. In many cases, people who commit crimes are free from the psychological disorders that we assume to cause crime, and people with personality disorders often do not commit crimes. Other factors leading to crime include a criminal lifestyle or membership in a criminal community, along with the stigma of a criminal arrest or conviction. Therefore, sociological approaches to crime emphasize the role of culture, social structure, and social interaction in bringing about criminal behaviour.

Functionalist perspectives

The main functionalist approaches to crime are structural. Functionalists attempt to show that social conditions are often structured in ways that unintentionally produce criminals, just as highways may be engineered in ways that unintentionally produce accidents or traffic jams.

Table 8.3 Low-income Cutoffs (LICOs), Canada, 2003

Size of family unit	Rural areas	Community Size Urban areas			
		Less than 30,000*	30,000 to 99,999	100,000 to 499,999	500,000 and over
2003					
1 person	13,680	15,690	16,862	16,979	19,795
2 persons	17,100	19,612	21,077	21,224	24,745
3 persons	21,268	24,390	26,213	26,396	30,774
4 persons	25,744	29,526	31,731	31,952	37,254
5 persons	38,778	33,004	35,469	35,718	41,642
6 persons	31,813	36,482	39,208	39,483	46,031
7 or more persons	34,847	39,960	42,947	43,429	50,421

* Includes cities with a population between 15,000 and 30,000 and small urban areas (under 15,000).

SOURCE: Statistics Canada, Income Statistics Division; available at <www.statcan.ca>, accessed 1 November 2004.

As we have said, the basic premise of functional theory is that the parts of society work together like parts of a living organism. From this point of view, high crime rates may indicate that the parts of society are not working properly, or not fitting together properly. It argues that crime is one adaptation to the gap between the cultural goals of society and the accepted means of achieving these goals. The theory would predict the highest crime rates among the poorest members of society, since they would be the least able to achieve the desired goals by prescribed means, and would thus have to resort to other (illegal) means of attaining those desired goals. For low-income statistics in Canada in 2003, see Table 8.3.

Not all people who are deprived of legitimate opportunities turn to a life of crime. Merton (1957 [1938]), in fact, identified four different ways in which people adapt to situations of anomie: innovation, ritualism, retreatism, and rebellion. Crime, which Merton characterizes as 'innovation', is only one of these four adaptations. Innovation, in turn, depends on the person's social environment, including his/her access to criminal culture and technology. However, not all deviant 'innovators' become street criminals. Some may pursue deviant academic achievement through cheating, deviant athletic achievement through steroids, or deviant economic success by joining the Mafia, Enron, or Arthur Andersen Co. As a result, some 'innovators' end up rich and honoured, while others spend their lives in and out of jail for small offences.

According to Merton, all criminal innovations, however lucrative or secure, help to preserve the workings of an unequal capitalist society, by allowing poor people to imagine that they or their children will someday be rich. This is what makes 'strain' theory a functionalist theory.

Some theorists also believe that the incidence of non-violent crimes has increased in post-industrial societies despite major improvements in the quality of life because of the relative deprivation certain individuals experience. For instance, a person who owns a house with three bedrooms may feel relatively deprived compared to his/her neighbour who has five bedrooms. Thus, the theory of relative deprivation centres on how individuals subjectively perceive themselves as victims of disadvantage (Stiles and Howard, 2000).

Routine activities theory (Cohen and Felson, 1979) is another aspect of the functionalist approach, in the sense that it emphasizes the 'normality' of crime as a part of routine everyday life. It proposes that the daily routine activities of a population have an effect on the availability of possible victims and the likelihood of a criminal occurrence. Though the theory is mostly used to explain predatory crimes, it can also be used as an explanation of non-violent crimes such as robbery, theft, and even white-collar crimes.

Today, the suburban home is not as well protected as residential homes in the past because of the lack of guardianship during workday hours (i.e., roughly, 9 am to 5 pm). Generally, homes in the suburbs are abandoned during the daylight hours when suburbanites are in the city centre at work. At these times, the suburban home becomes a suitable target for thieves. Motivated offenders aware of these social changes that have affected routine activities of suburbanites are now able to pinpoint when the homes are not protected and proceed to burglarize the home. This theory has affected methods used to prevent crime; Oscar Newman's (1972) book *Defensible Space: Crime Prevention Through Urban Design* advocates changing public space to semi-public space to ensure that people feel they have a stake in the area and thus are responsible for its protection.

The three components of the theory—presence of the offender, availability of the victim, and the absence of the guardian—can be applied to corporate crimes. The presence of an offending person in a business or corporation, lack of close supervision of the documents, and managerial corruption and ignorance can ease the way for committing crimes.

Regardless of the criminal's assumed motivation, functionalist theories make clear the importance of social control mechanisms. They assume that everyone is capable of delinquent or criminal behaviour and only external control will prevent it. Where conformity is needed to protect one's good name, this can be ensured only by tightening the controls on people's behaviour.

This seems to explain why daughters are controlled more strictly than sons in societies (like ours) that maintain a sexual double standard: girls simply have more to lose from non-conformity than boys do. Hagan (1985) notes that daughters are typically under more control by parents and under more pressure than sons to take their schooling and job responsibilities seriously. This both protects their good name and helps them get ahead. Early employment contacts increase their prospects of getting a job and advancing occupationally. According to this theory, boys (i.e., sons) commit more crimes than girls (i.e., daughters) because, at any level of class or income, boys are controlled less closely. The same theory would explain another evident fact, namely, that boys are more likely than girls to fall behind in school, or even drop out of school.

A final functionalist theory relates poverty to social disorganization. As signs of social disorganization become more visible, poor communities generate more crime. This theory is commonly known as the 'broken windows theory'—a theory best at explaining destructive property crime, in particular, vandalism.

Wilson and Keeling (1982) state: 'If a window in a building is broken and left unrepaired, all the rest of the windows will soon be broken . . . one unrepaired window is a signal that no one cares and so breaking more windows will cost nothing.' Similarly, if misconduct goes unaddressed, subsequent misconduct will follow. This theory has affected police tactics and even legislation. For instance, in May 2004 the City of Calgary imposed the 'Community Standards Bylaw' that outlines the citizens' responsibility to keep their property at or above minimum standards (City of Calgary, 2004).

Some believe that such tactics are successful in curbing more serious crime (Worrall, 2002). However, others believe that they simply produce an 'illusion of order' and while windows are being fixed, the actual window breaker is getting away (Harcourt, 2001; Sampson and Raudenbush, 1999).

The conflict perspective

Conflict theory proposes that competition and class conflict create deviance and crime. First of all, economic deprivation leads to offences, particularly property offences, among the poor. Conflict theorists argue that unequal access to scarce resources leads to crime. Crime is a normal, understandable response to conflict over scarce resources. From the conflict perspective, the legal and criminal justice system is organized to benefit the dominant groups in society.

Laws, by this reckoning, are mechanisms whereby the dominant social classes control and punish those below them. Thus authority figures are simply attempting to maintain the status quo. This effort is evident in a bias against working-class people observed in policing, arrest, bail-setting, conviction, and punishment patterns. Because of the way the laws are enforced, some people are more likely than others to get caught and punished for their rule-breaking. Other factors (such as offence seriousness) being equal, race—like class—has a strong effect on the chance of incarceration, with Aboriginals running the highest risk. Generally, the powerful members of society write the laws defining which activities will be considered criminal and what the penalties will be for those crimes. Thus, removing a television set from Future Shop in the middle of the night is viewed as criminal. Armed robbery can bring a 15-year prison sentence. Price fixing—for example, all gas stations agreeing to raise the price of gasoline the same amount—costs the public millions of dollars in excess expenditures, but rarely leads to arrests, charges, convictions, or prison terms.

We can see class-based efforts to use criminal actions to their advantage by studying changes in the law over time. For example, Chambliss (1964) linked the development of vagrancy laws to class-based conflict. Others have pointed out how vagrancy laws have targeted other marginalized populations, such as prostitutes (Lowman, 1997) and homosexuals (Maynard, 1994). As a consequence, conflict theorists blame crime on certain characteristics of capitalism—a system organized around the constant search for higher profits on invested capital. In short, the underlying cause of crime, for conflict theorists, is inequality and the competition to attain culturally prized material goals.

Symbolic interactionist perspectives

Symbolic interactionists do not dispute the sources of crime identified by functionalist and conflict theorists. However, interactionists see these approaches as incomplete because they do not explain the process by which a person becomes a criminal or the reasons why one poor person adapts to anomie through crime and another does not. Interactionist theories focus on the interpretations that people give to behaviour, and the ways their interpretations construct the social world, the identities of people, and, ultimately, how people behave.

Interactionist theories assume that crime, like every other social activity, is learned through interaction with others and involves the development of a criminal self-concept. The deviance is not a direct product of the social structure but of face-to-face interactions and personal interpretations. Therefore, understanding criminal behaviour over the life course is possible only if we consider interactional—particularly familial and neighbourhood—factors and their impact on early development. Adverse familial and neighbourhood contexts promote the socialization that results in anti-social behaviour (Piquero and Lawton, 2002).

This arrangement takes at least two forms: differential association theory and labelling theory. Criminologist Edwin Sutherland (1949) developed the most influential of these theories—differential association theory—in the 1920s and 1930s. Differential association theory states that crime is learned like any other social behaviour. There are several elements to this learning process. First, people may learn specific skills and techniques in order to help them engage in criminal behaviour. For example, by becoming a member of an organized crime unit a person might learn how to obtain necessary weapons and how to influence key individuals.

Second, some people learn to value criminality more highly than conventional behaviour. By associating with others who know how to commit crimes, people are more likely to learn to view these activities as desirable and think they are preferable to a conventional, law-abiding way of life. According to the differential association theory then, learning to be criminal or delinquent involves mechanisms of socialization similar to those associated with learning any values or behaviours—for example, learning to drive a car or become a Catholic.

That is not to say that those who learn delinquency is 'bad' will not take part in delinquent behaviour. In fact, Sykes and Matza (1957) note that some delinquents hold the same values regarding delinquency as any law-abiding citizen. However, they allow themselves to deviate by using techniques of 'neutralization' to justify their actions. Five techniques of neutralization they use are: Denial of Responsibility; Denial of Injury; Denial of Victim; Condemning the Condemners; and Appeal to Higher Loyalties. For instance, some thieves may feel that stealing from a public place (e.g., a school or library) is justifiable because in their opinion there is no particular victim.

Another theory that is useful in explaining crime is labelling theory, which shifts attention away from the transgressor and toward the way that others react to the deviant. This theory suggests that whether other people define or label a person as deviant is critical in the development of a pattern of deviant behaviour. Labelling perpetuates crime and delinquency because, once people have been labelled, they have fewer alternatives, and the deviant behaviour becomes a part of their social identity.

Feminist perspectives

All feminist research is guided by the notion that personal life always has a political dimension—much like sociology's central idea of the connection between private troubles and public issues. Feminists have made important contributions to the study of deviance and crime by de-romanticizing the image of the criminal that distinguishes the work of both functionalists and labelling theorists.

Three important points need to be made about the gendering of crimes discussed in this chapter. First, organized crime has always been strongly masculine. Organized crime 'families' have tended to mirror the gender patterns observed in traditional ethnic families from which they developed, so that women have been excluded except as partners, associates, and helpers—never as bosses or key actors. Likewise, street crime has always been strongly masculine. Violent street crime activities, such as assault and theft, remain disproportionately male criminal activities. Finally, white-collar or business crime has always been strongly masculine.

With the increased entry of women into professional and managerial roles, the possibility of female business crime has increased. This corresponds to a growth in women's opportunities to steal and embezzle as readily as men. Unfortunately, statistics on the extent of business crime are too incomplete to permit a clear indication of the degree to which this area of crime has become de-gendered.

Social and Health Consequences of Non-violent Crime

Organized crime

The Organized Crime Impact Study (Porteous, 1998) represents the first major attempt to examine key organized crime activities in Canada and to determine the costs of these activities for Canadian society. According to this study, with its combined social, economic, and violence-generating effects, the illicit drug trade has the greatest impact on Canada of all organized crime-related activities. Organized crime groups are also involved in the highly profitable area of counterfeit products. Governments and enforcement agencies are just beginning to assess the importance of this organized crime activity that may cost Canadians over $1 billion per year, according to the Solicitor General of Canada report (Porteous, 1998).

Social costs of organized crime

Organized crime has increased in such volume and scope that it now threatens national and international security. Laundered funds provide financial support for drug dealers, terrorism, arms' dealers, and other criminals to operate and expand their criminal empires. Investigations reveal that criminals manipulate financial systems in Canada and abroad to foster a wide range of illicit activities. When trying to control transnational organized crime, the problems are compounded by the capacity of criminal organizations to conceal their activities within a variety of legal transactions, to act rapidly in exploiting new opportunities, and to reconfigure organizational structures in response to law enforcement successes (Williams and Gobson, 2002).

Business crime

As discussed in Box 8.2, white-collar crimes such as fraud are not at the forefront of Canadians' crime concerns. However, due to the various forms in which fraud can occur, significant costs permeate all levels of society. For example, it is estimated that senior citizens comprise 40 per cent of all victims of telemarketing fraud in Canada (Solicitor General, 1997).

Social costs of business crime

Added to the enormous financial costs of white-collar crime, there are social costs as well. Exposure to repeated tales of corruption tends to breed distrust, cynicism, and ultimately undermines the integration of social institutions. People who think that all Members of Parliament are crooks refrain from voting. People who think that every police officer can be bought cease to respect the law. Thus, the costs of such crime go beyond the actual dollars involved in the crime itself.

According to Statistics Canada, more than $900 million was spent on the operation of courts in Canada in 1998–9, employing nearly 10,000 court staff and 2,000 judges. Adult corrections cost nearly

$2.3 billion. In 1998–9, the average daily cost of housing an inmate was $171 at the federal level and $123 at the provincial level. Legal aid expenditures increased substantially in 1998–9, following three years of consecutive decline. Nevertheless, spending on legal aid, which might help to keep people out of prison, remains 28 per cent lower than its peak of nearly $646 million in 1994–5. Tightened eligibility criteria and reductions in the types of cases covered have led to significant decreases in legal aid expenditures across Canada. Although there was a slight increase in the number of approved legal aid applications in 1998–9, the number remains 35 per cent lower than its high in 1992–3.

Fear of Crime and Its Consequences

The greatest cost to public health and social well-being because of non-violent crime results from the fear of crime. In poor neighbourhoods, some people resort to crime for financial reasons, such as selling drugs or theft to support themselves. Unintentionally, through their illegal actions, they destroy their own community. As street crime increases, businesses close early and citizens stay off the streets. This, in turn, allows criminals more opportunity to break the law with impunity.

Residents are very upset about the clustering of criminal and deviant activities in their midst. Every day, they see 'johns' in cars cruising for prostitutes, drug dealers waiting in coffee shops for buyers, used needles left behind in schoolyards by drug users, and a variety of vulnerable people—ex-convicts, mental outpatients, abused women, homeless people, and alcoholics—filling up the local shelters, community centres, and halfway houses. These activities feed a fear of crime, which is illustrated in Table 8.4.

In Chapter 7, we discussed the fear of crime and people's anxiety over possible victimization, with particular respect to violent crime. Street crimes and organized criminal activities, such as prostitution and drug selling, also contribute to a fear of crime in our communities. Street crime undermines people's sense of safety.

Table 8.4 Neighbourhood Fear, Canada, 1970–2000
Response to the question: 'Is there any area right around where you live, that is say within a couple of kilometres, where you would be afraid to walk at night?'

	Yes (%)	No (%)	Unsure (%)
2000	27	72	1
1999	26	73	1
1998	25	74	1
1997	30	69	1
1996	33	66	1
1995	33	66	1
1994	35	64	1
1992	36	63	1
1991	37	60	3
1990	34	63	4
1987	27	71	2
1979	31	67	2
1974	37	63	0
1970	29	66	5

SOURCE: Karin Stein, 'Public Perception of Crime and Justice in Canada: A Review of Opinion Polls RR2001-1e' (Nov. 2001), 4; available at <www.canada.justice.gc.ca>, accessed 1 November 2004.

Researchers have studied the characteristics of community members who are most fearful of crime. They find that gender is a consistent predictor of fear: women are more fearful than men. A study by Clemente and Kleiman (1977; see also Stanko, 1992) shows that women's fear of crime is three times higher than that of men, although young men are actually at greatest risk of being victimized. Belyea and Zingraff (1988) also find that women report a greater fear of crime. They suggest that the people most fearful of crime are those who are particularly vulnerable to it, in terms of potential harm. Women, though not the most likely victims, risk suffering the most grievous harm (e.g., sexual assault) if they are victimized. Accordingly, women express more fear of crime than men, because of their relative inability to fight off offenders (Donnelly, 1988). Age is also a consistent predictor of fear. Although elderly people are less likely to be victimized than young people, they are more likely to fear victimization. As with women, their fear may derive from their vulnerability and defenselessness against attack by (say) a young male.

Juristat reports that, according to the 1999 General Social Survey (GSS), 25 per cent of Canadians aged 15 and older were victims of at least one crime in the previous year. Compared with an earlier survey in 1993, increased rates were observed for theft of personal property and household property (Besserer et al., 2001). Of the 8.3 million victimization incidents reported to the GSS in 1999—of which only 4 in 10 were reported to police—one-third involved a household crime (break and enter, motor vehicle/parts theft, theft of household property, or vandalism). For the four household crimes, the rate of victimization was higher for urban residents. Households with higher income ($60,000+) had a higher rate than households with lower incomes. Rates were higher for people who rented rather than owned their home. One-half of the reported incidents involved a personal crime (sexual assault, robbery, assault, or theft of personal property). However, a large and growing percentage of the population are satisfied with their personal safety. Over 90 per cent report being very or somewhat satisfied with their personal safety in 1999, in a variety of situations that included being home alone, walking alone, or using public transportation alone after dark.

Sociodemographic correlates of fear reflect the actual risk of victimization, or 'vulnerability'. Donnelly (1988) suggests that there are two kinds of vulnerability. 'Physical vulnerability refers to a person's openness to attack and powerlessness to resist.' Women and the elderly tend to be more fearful because they are more physically vulnerable (i.e., less able to fend off attackers). 'Social vulnerability', on the other hand, refers to 'the daily threat of victimization and an inability to cope with the economic and physical consequences of victimization.' Overall, for the four personal crimes we discussed earlier in this chapter, rates of victimization for men and women are very similar. Higher rates of victimization are reported by young people (ages 15–24 years), urban dwellers, and people with household incomes under $15,000 (Besserer et al., 2001). Figure 8.3 shows self-reported rates of victimization based on age.

This explains the high fear levels among people of lower income and education. High-crime areas make them more susceptible to crime, causing them to fear it, even if they have not yet been victimized. Furthermore, if they are victimized, the costs of property or personal crime will be a larger burden to bear. A study by Clemente and Kleiman (1977) finds that poorer people are more fearful. People at higher-income levels have the lowest rates of victimization. They are better able to protect themselves (e.g., through the use of private security arrangements) and they live in safer neighbourhoods.

Researchers suggest three characteristics of lower-income neighbourhoods that may explain why residents express more fear of crime (Covington and Taylor, 1991). First, lower-income residents are more likely to see areas outside of their immediate block as foreign—outside their experience and control—and thus express fear of those areas. A second factor is that lower-income communities have more diverse populations than higher-income neighbourhoods. Because of the diversity, residents are more likely to live among people whose lifestyles are different from their own; thus, residents may be fearful. Third, Belyea and Zingraff (1988) report that less-educated and lower-income people are more fearful of crime because they are more vulnerable to the costs of victimization. They can less afford to be deprived of the little they own or deal easily with the costs of injury (e.g., missing days of paid work).

Social incivilities also contribute to a fear of crime, particularly among blacks because such incivilities are often more pronounced in black communities. These incivilities violate the rules of proper behaviour. When residents' 'desire for the observance of standards of right and seemly conduct in the public places in which one lives and moves' is not respected, fear results (Donnelly, 1988).

Baba and Austin (1989) relate this finding to earlier literature from the Chicago School of sociology on 'social organization'. Social organization means that people have ties to one another within the community. The longer people remain in the community, the stronger are the local social bonds and the larger is membership in neighbourhood organizations. As the average length of residence increases, so do the amounts of interpersonal communication and social integration. When people start moving in and out rapidly, social disorganization results. Often, social disorganization causes and is caused by crime and delinquency, and fear of crime.

Social integration (or organization) reduces fear in three ways. First, integration reduces the proportion of strangers (as opposed to acquaintances) in the area; said another way, it increases familiarity. Familiarity, as we have seen throughout this book, always reduces fear and ignorance. Second, integration makes available a larger number of networks with which people may associate themselves; this

Figure 8.3 Self-reported Rates of Victimization, By Age of Respondant, Canada, 1999

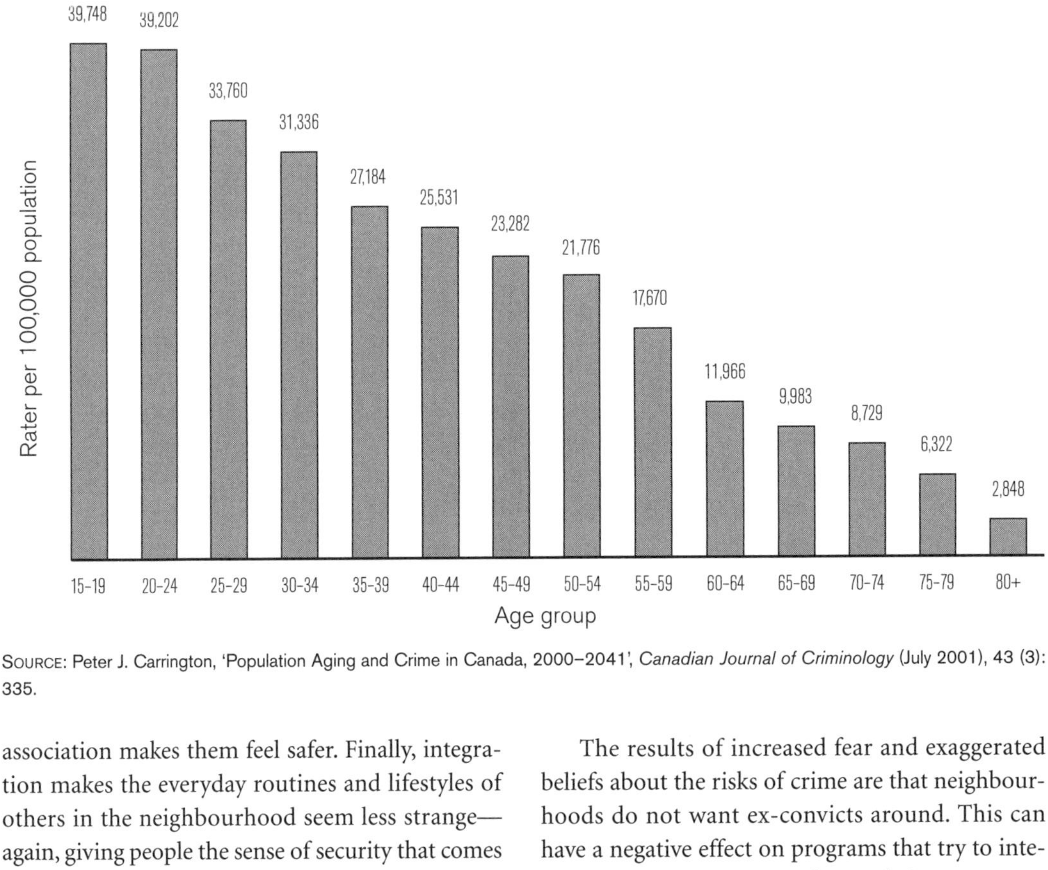

SOURCE: Peter J. Carrington, 'Population Aging and Crime in Canada, 2000–2041', *Canadian Journal of Criminology* (July 2001), 43 (3): 335.

association makes them feel safer. Finally, integration makes the everyday routines and lifestyles of others in the neighbourhood seem less strange—again, giving people the sense of security that comes with familiarity.

Most people learn about crime events through the mass media and, for many, the newspaper is the source to which respondents looked (Smith, 1984). Others rely on television for their crime news. By sensationalizing stories, the mass media create fears of crime that run counter to actual risks. Often, reports of property crime fuel fears of violent crime, or vice versa. However, it is not the total number of crime stories that affects fear of crime, but rather the proportion of crime stories in which the crimes are local, random, and sensational. If random and sensational crimes occur in a person's own locality, they induce fear. If they occur in other areas, people feel less fear and feel safe by comparison.

The results of increased fear and exaggerated beliefs about the risks of crime are that neighbourhoods do not want ex-convicts around. This can have a negative effect on programs that try to integrate people with criminal records into community life. Baker and colleagues (1983) suggest that a fear of crime elicits avoidance behaviour and can inhibit normal social interaction and alter everyday routines. In the end, this fear works against the rehabilitation and reintegration of convicted criminals, and against public safety. It may also produce a fearful punitive atmosphere, and calls for capital punishment, more policing, or fewer civil liberties.

Policies and Theory Applications

Given the role of poverty and economic inequality in fostering crime, it seems likely that reducing poverty and the gap between rich and poor would help reduce some forms of crime and delinquency.

If so, we need to create new jobs and provide job training to people without adequate job skills. The jobs people receive must pay a living wage, so that people can support their families. Further, there should be more investment in the institutions that prepare people for productive roles in society: at work, in families, and in schools. Failures in educational institutions and families have contributed to the inability of many young people to find and make use of legitimate job opportunities. However difficult, it is easier to prevent crime by improving families and schools than to rehabilitate criminals who know only a criminal lifestyle.

Arresting people who commit crimes at least temporarily reduces the likelihood that they will commit crimes again. While in custody, they cannot endanger the rest of society. Policing is important, and the police need resources and technology to do their job effectively. Increasingly, technology is playing an important role in the policing of crime. The growing international concern about electronic fraud and computer-related crime calls out for more education and technological development in this area.

At the same time, technology has made possible a host of new crimes, and has opened new avenues in which traditional crimes such as fraud can flourish. Electronic money laundering is one example. The illegal electronic transfer of funds challenges the legal system to develop new laws and adopt new strategies for coping with electronic crime.

Governments increasingly are working together to further the fight against e-crime. Its increasingly international scope and technological complexity has prompted several agencies to call for new resources and approaches to law enforcement. The Royal Canadian Mounted Police (RCMP) and the Canadian Security Intelligence Service (CSIS) are among them. However, Canada's police forces and security agencies may lack the essential skills, technology, and personnel to meet the growing threat posed by computer-related crime.

To assist and guide judges in the sentencing process, a number of changes have been made to Canadian law. Amendments to the *Criminal Code* in 1996, for example, promote the use of alternative measures, such as performing community service and attending education programs. In addition to providing judges with a wider range of sentences, alternative measures reduce the caseloads in Canadian courts.

Non-judicial, community-based initiatives are now used to divert those accused of less serious offences out of the formal court system. The 1996 reforms also include the creation of a new sanction designed to reduce the number of offenders sentenced to prison. Judges in Canada, as a result, may allow some offenders who would otherwise be imprisoned to serve a supervised conditional sentence in the community. The offender who receives such a sentence must abide by certain conditions, and may be sent to prison if the conditions are violated.

Yet some continue to believe punishment ought to be the basic response to crime. The threat of punishment is supposed to deter the population from committing crime (general deterrence) and accordingly the imposition of punishment is supposed to deter offenders (specific deterrence). Yet, there is no conclusive evidence that punishment does deter crime, a fact recognized long before empirical research threw doubts on its effectiveness. Measures such as penitence, work, education, and treatment have also been discredited as deterrents. Crime is now seen predominantly as a social and political problem. Anti-crime agencies—police, lawyers, courts, and prisons—cannot solve the problems of poverty and alienation we have discussed in this chapter.

Prisons are at the end of the criminal system's funnel. In effect, they handle the worst of society's unsolvable, unpreventable crime problems. In practice, most of the people who end up in prison are poor young men who were not skilled or smart enough to avoid arrest for stealing or drug use. (Some others will have committed violent crimes.) Every time we read a newspaper or watch a TV news program, stories and statistics about crime jump out at us. There seems to be a 'crime problem', but if so, what is the nature and extent of this problem, and most especially, will prisons solve this 'crime problem'?

The concept of prisons dates back over a century. Yet, only in the twentieth century did researchers begin to study prisons and prisoners systematically. One researcher, Donald Clemmer (1940), developed his 'prisonization' theory out of such careful work. Clemmer states that, by their nature, prisons degrade people, coerce them, and take away their rights. Without such treatment, prison officials cannot keep order in such large communities of (mainly) young men. Yet this tranquilizing effort has unintended and undesirable effects. It alienates prisoners and unites them against the prison administration.

Prison subcultures, growing out of everyday prison life, reflect and harden prisoner alienation. Prisoners learn the prison subculture and its anti-administration value system. As well, through contact with more experienced inmates, new prisoners acquire new criminal skills, often learning to behave in undesirable and violent ways. Prisons teach prisoners how *not* to adapt to life in the 'real world'. As their release from prison approaches, prisoners feel great stress. After release, they commit more crimes and many end up back in prison. This process is called recidivism or 'the revolving door'.

Goffman (1961) wrote that *all* residential facilities that try to shape inmate behaviour through continuous surveillance and control—including prisons, mental hospitals, concentration camps, military barracks, monasteries, convents, and even boarding schools—can be considered 'total institutions.' As such, they share many characteristics that Clemmer attributed to prisons alone. For example, they all degrade people, strip away old identities, impose uniformity on dress and behaviour, limit personal freedom, and in these ways create new identities. The process stamps inmates with the institution's character and makes them less prepared for the outside world. If this description of total institutions and inmate socialization is correct, we have to ask whether

prisons are really a solution to the crime problem or largely the cause of this problem.

Few harbour the illusion that prisons either deter crime or rehabilitate criminals. However, prisons at least get criminals off the streets for a while. If prisons don't solve 'the problem' in the long run, they buy time and a sense of greater safety for law-abiding citizens. Many prison administrators still claim that imprisonment's goal is rehabilitation: re-socialization into a new, orderly, law-abiding lifestyle. And prisons do provide order, rules, and rule enforcement. Unlike other agents of socialization (e.g., schools or the mass media), prisons can forcibly rehabilitate people, or at least appear to do so.

Some feel, however, that prisons do not fail the convicts. Prisons may fail to reform crime-prone people, but they are not to blame. Criminals are a 'different breed' of people. The kinds of people who are imprisoned fit easily into the prison subculture and upon release from prison commit more crimes because they are crime-prone to begin with. Said another way, a propensity to commit crime is established early in life and persists throughout the lifespan. This belief justifies using special, coercive treatment on prisoners. Anything less fails to keep order among poorly socialized people.

Some prisoners are what we might call 'rational calculators': they commit gainful crimes because the chance of big rewards outweighs the chance of even bigger punishments. Only by increasing the certainty and severity of punishment can we hope to deter these criminals from pursuing a profitable life in crime. To deter would-be burglars, for example, it is more important to increase the probability of imprisonment than the length of a prison sentence. Both the risk of being caught and the prospect of increased gain have a significant impact on burglars' decision-making. The threat of legal sanctions or fear of arrest, and conscience both inhibit the commission of illegal acts—especially where past accomplishments or future goals may be jeopardized by such an arrest. Where people have a stake in conformity—something to lose by deviance and something to gain by conformity—they are most likely to obey the law.

Even if they grant that prisons are unable to deter crime, rehabilitate convicts, or keep criminals off the street for long, advocates may still believe that prisons—public or private—are needed because we have no reliable alternative. They point out that other efforts to prevent criminal behaviour have failed. Community alternatives to custody—which we discuss shortly—do not necessarily guarantee better results. Some studies even find higher rates of recidivism with non-institutionalized offenders.

Moreover, even if it were possible to prevent crime through efforts of these kinds, many citizens would oppose them. They view crime as immoral behaviour. Accordingly, they believe that the criminal (and his family)—not society—should take responsibility and pay the cost. By this reasoning, we should prevent crimes by moral training at home, not by spending public money on costly remedies after the fact.

Some believe that privatizing prisons—putting their administration into private contractors' hands—increases efficiency and lowers the cost. This makes prisons affordable, despite a rising imprisonment rate. Issues that need further study include the use of deadly force by contractors, the effect of additional prisons on sentencing practices, and the problem of prison industries, for example, how to motivate unskilled, uneducated employees, and how to avoid competing with outside businesses. These issues aside, privatizing prisons does not improve prisoner rehabilitation. Research shows that in private facilities the treatment—food, living conditions, and skill training, for example—is actually worse, since the chief goal is to make a profit. Some have even pressed for the creation of 'mega-prisons'—prisons that house even larger numbers of prisoners under increasingly restricted conditions.

The other side of the argument

Other people—researchers and administrators—oppose using prisons to punish routine or non-violent offences. People holding this view believe that few criminals are dangerous or unchangeable. On the contrary, many people pass through periods of life, or circumstances, when criminal behaviour is likely.

Criminals are like everyone else, they argue. Most criminals are young—especially, young men. As they age, they become less likely to commit crimes. Likewise, as the general population ages a falling proportion of young men will lead to a decrease in the general crime rate. Crime and imprisonment rates will decline 'naturally'. Demographic factors aside, the view that criminals are just like everyone else is supported by labelling theories of deviance. They argue that, at one time or another, most people commit deviant or criminal acts. Few are caught and punished. Most give up their rule-breaking behaviour voluntarily, for a variety of reasons: maturation, a change of views or opportunities, or a stronger stake in conformity due to marriage and employment, for example.

However, because of the way laws are enforced, some people are more likely to get caught and punished for their rule-breaking. Gender also affects correctional practice, with women experiencing closer rule enforcement and more severe punishment in some prisons. Gender stereotypes also shape the nature of work and vocational training.

Conviction and imprisonment stigmatize people, giving them a deviant identity, reducing their legitimate opportunities and increasing their tendency to break rules. Sociologists have called this behaviour secondary deviation. Prison also costs society much more than probation, due to the combined costs of attempted rehabilitation and increased recidivism. Average North Americans want as many criminals as possible kept in prison for as long as possible. However, much of the support for imprisonment is based on ignorance of prison conditions and on short-term thinking—a desire for revenge rather than long-term safety.

The social benefits of imprisonment are only temporary. Movies and television programs show prisons to be unpleasant, but they do not dwell on the variety and seriousness of harms that prisons do. Consider this: prisons break up families. Family separation may produce a new generation of criminals. Imprisonment also contributes to child poverty—already a widely recognized social problem.

Prisons increase health risks too. Most American prisons are overcrowded, even by their own reckoning. As a result, prisoners are at greater risk of contracting communicable, often lethal diseases, than are non-imprisoned people. Violence—both mental and physical—is an ever-present feature of prison life (as in other 'total institutions'). This may result from drug use and drug trafficking, ineffective mechanisms of social control and dispute resolution, or new gang subcultures. The high risks of abuse and violence translate into stress reactions like sleeplessness, high blood pressure, respiratory problems, and high suicide rates. In many prisons, conditions are unconstitutionally awful. They represent a cruel and unusual punishment, whatever the crime a prisoner originally is labelled as having committed.

Alternatives to prison do work. For certain types of criminals community-based alternatives work better than prison: they are cheaper, more humane, and more effective. Some, like probation and parole, carry a low risk to public safety. Other alternatives include paying fines, making restitution, and performing community services. An additional alternative to prison is electronically monitored home detention or community service.

For three of every four accused people, jail or prison is unnecessary. A cheaper, healthier alternative—home detention—may in many cases work just as well, or better. Research suggests that socially integrated people with little or no previous record of criminal activity are good candidates for home detention. However, if the conditions are far too demanding and impractical, we can predict that the offender will 'reoffend', if only by breaching technical violations. This is often the case with

those offenders slammed with many conditions as is customary in the case of those under Intensive Probation Supervision (Petersilia and Turner, 1993). In fact, some criminologists argue that many of these supervisions are overintrusive, and the sentence is not proportional to crime committed (Von Hirsch, 1990).

Concluding Words

Crime is not increasing in Canada and, if anything, it is decreasing, but not because Canadians are becoming more virtuous, self-controlled or prosperous. Rather, it is because Canadians are getting older. According to criminologist Peter Carrington (2001), '[A]ll types of crime are forecast to decline, due to the continuing aging of the Canadian population. The overall recorded crime rate is forecast to fall to 85 per cent of its 1999 level by 2026 and to 81 per cent by 2041. . . . Recorded rates of crimes that are characteristic of teenagers and young adults such as robbery and break and enter, should fall slightly faster and farther; whereas crimes that are more characteristic of older adults, e.g., sexual assault and drunk driving, should be affected less by the aging of the population.'

As we increasingly become an 'information society', crime will increasingly focus on the theft and abuse of information. However, police agencies will increasingly use new technology to detect crime and pursue the offenders.

The growing use of Information Technology (IT) has already had a profound effect on society, and on crime. Information about ways to invade electronic systems—data systems, financial systems, or security systems, for example—is available more easily to more people. Besides providing more opportunities for crime involving technology, information communication technologies are providing better resources for law enforcers to fight crime.

Technology has made it possible to keep registries, re-organize law enforcement, and use high-tech gadgets that help to keep crime under control. Technologies are revolutionizing police work, just as they are revolutionizing crime. In short, modern IT is fundamental to the commission—but also, the detection, prevention, and control—of new forms of high-tech financial crime (McQuade, 2001). Again, it is hard to predict whether crime will increase—only that it will change and policing will change with it.

Globalization, too, is affecting technology, commerce, communication, and crime. Already, crimes on the Internet, drug dealing, and smuggling show the attraction of global crime, and the difficulty international crime poses for national law enforcement. People who commit global crimes often live outside the jurisdiction of nations where the crime occurs. This necessitates the integration of law enforcement agencies and the introduction of new technologies that enhance the global interconnectedness of police and other law enforcement bodies (Karstedt, 2001).

The reach of crime is farther than ever today. Once again, it is hard to tell whether globalization will increase crime, or simply change the nature, scope, and scale of criminal operations. Given all the above, it seems likely that fraud, impersonation, and extortion will increase in future, more crime will be committed outside national jurisdictions, and theft will increase—particularly, theft focused on electronic services. Margaret Beare (2002) writes, for example, that law enforcement and the judicial systems alone will not be sufficient to combat these forms of transnational crimes in our 'global community'. The example she uses is tobacco smuggling between Canada and the United States.

As crime detection improves through advances in forensic science, criminals will find new ways of covering their tracks. Some may find high-tech ways of leaving false tracks leading away from a crime scene, while others resort to more drastic ways of destroying the crime scene altogether, through arson or explosives. Fraud—on the Internet and otherwise—will become the most common offence, being used for financial gain or to obtain information; for example, a 'front' website might record credit card details for direct misuse or to seek personal/financial information to create a false identity.

The future of money, in its current physical (cash) form, will also have a major impact on crime. The criminal economy largely runs on cash—given its anonymity—and the larger the denomination of banknotes, the easier criminal transactions become. With the increasing use of virtual cash in the form of credit cards and smart cards, physical cash may eventually disappear, perhaps to be replaced by alternative anonymous forms of transactions. Crime may then concentrate even more on the electronic realm, where different, better detection methods will be necessary.

Snider (1997) reports that corporate crime—for example, salaries below minimum wage, dangerous working conditions, and defective merchandise—has serious economic, political, and even ideological consequences, which is why the state has traditionally intervened in private business. But in the past 15 years, responsibility and culpability for harmful practices have been redefined. As industries have been deregulated, risk management has taken the place of regulatory enforcement. Corporate crime has become normalized with the decline of the nation-state and the rise of global capitalism. This may continue.

Of all the changes that bear on the future of societies, and on the future of social problems, none is likely to have more impact than cyberspace and the information that resides there. One growing crime of the future is the theft of intellectual property. Today, the Internet shapes the relationship between consumers, producers, and knowledge, changing the whole way we view information and changing the relations of its production.

The result is a creation of worldwide virtual communities—communities of interest and shared viewpoints that are unhampered by distance or by many social factors (age, race, gender, class) that often keep otherwise similar people from meeting or interacting with one another. Community nets (or 'freenets') are developing in many towns and cities, often with terminals installed in public libraries, to give access to those who do not have computers at home or work.

Not only does the Internet ease information sharing, commerce, and social support, it also allows people to create and try out new identities. Such fantasy play enables unprecedented narcissism: new levels of social interaction that transgress old ways while providing a release from oppression. People are able to stalk others on the Internet, to enjoy Internet sex or cybersexual affairs, and to spread false information about themselves and others. Additionally, the Internet enables people to sell fraudulent selves, and products, more easily than if they had to persuade customers face-to-face.

Summary

In this chapter, we have focused on street crime, organized crime, and business crime. Canada has lower rates of violent crime, but higher rates of property crime than the United States. We have briefly discussed two kinds of business crime (or 'suite' crime): corporate crimes—crimes committed by corporations in their own business interest and white-collar crimes—crimes (such as fraud or embezzlement) committed by businesspeople or professionals, in their own interest and often at the expense of the larger corporate body within which they work.

Because amateurs commit them, often in public places, street crimes are more likely to result in arrests than organized crimes or business crimes. Even though amateur crime is the most visible of non-violent crimes, it ranks the lowest in terms of cost to society. Organized and business crimes rob society of more money than petty crimes do and they instil distrust in institutions—at a cost, which we cannot begin to measure. Street crime, unlike business crime or even organized crime, is readily available to society's poorest people, yet it is a far from secure means of making a living. Most victims of street crime are men, and so are most of the perpetrators.

What organized crime shows dramatically is that crime can be a learned, organized social activity with deep historical roots. As such, we can understand organized crime not as an individual response to poverty, but as a highly organized activity that operates in the boundaries between legitimate and illegitimate activity. Since non-violent crimes tend to be property crimes, common sense suggests a connection between unemployment (or poverty) and crime. However, many types of crime (e.g., embezzlement and other white-collar crimes) are not possible for poor people.

White-collar crime, though operating within a legitimate occupation, does violate the *Criminal Code* in some way. It provides an interesting case because respected organizations and individuals—those that reap the rewards of capitalism and live comfortable lives, commit these crimes. As mentioned by Sutherland, society is still myopic when it comes to studying and persecuting white-collar criminals.

White-collar, opportunistic crimes, and organized crime are all related. We now know that most criminals do not have psychological disorders and as such, we find a sociological explanation. The types of non-violent crimes discussed are mainly a result of disorganized communities: a structuralist finds that people are forced to react to anomie, a conflict theorist finds that deprivation leads to higher crime rates among the poor, and the symbolic interactionist finds that people learn these criminal behaviours in their communities.

As we have seen, crime affects a large part of society and touches the lives of everyone. This brings into question the judicial and penal systems that deal with criminals. Arresting people who commit crimes temporarily reduces the likelihood that those people will commit crimes again; however, once they are released, rates of recidivism are high. Few harbour the illusion that prisons either deter crime or rehabilitate criminals in the long run. Currently, there is a great deal of discourse regarding penal reform—the study of which is increasingly important as societies look toward different options.

Questions for Critical Thought

1. Do you think that prisons are an effective method of punishment when used to deter non-violent crimes? Provide examples to support your answer.
2. Brainstorm the different roles the mass media and the government can play in reducing the fear of crime among citizens.
3. According to symbolic interactionism, what is the process by which one becomes a criminal? Contrast this explanation with the explanation derived from another framework.
4. To what extent does poverty play in producing more crime? Discuss different methods that can be used to counter the effects poverty has on crime.
5. Capitalism is seen as the root of the crime problem by conflict theorists. Given this, discuss how the levels of non-violent crime may be diminished within a capitalist society.
6. Compare the type of anomie suffered by those who commit opportunistic crimes and those who commit white-collar crimes.
7. How would you rate the effectiveness of the penal system? Recommend changes that would make the system more effective.
8. Is it feasible to ask that the top executives be held personally accountable for crimes that the corporation commits? Apart from financially, is there any other way to hold corporations accountable for their crimes?
9. 'Non-violent crime is embedded in North American culture.' Argue for or against this statement.
10. Canada has lower rates of violent crime, but higher rates of property crime than the United States. What, if anything, does this tell us about the social organization of both nations?

Recommended Reading

Prus, Robert, and Irini Styllianoss. (1980), *Hookers, Rounders, and Desk Clerks: The Social Organization of the Hotel Community*. Toronto: Gage. This book contains a comprehensive ethnographic study on the urban hotel community. It investigates the everyday life of those who are a part of this particular community.

Reynolds, Marylee. (1995), *From Gangs to Gangsters: How American Sociology Organized Crime, 1918–1994*. New York: Harrow and Heston. The author provides a wealth of information that explains how sociologists of the Chicago School in the 1920s could describe lower-class crime and deviance in their city as social disorganization, when hindsight shows clearly that it was highly organized; and how over the next decades they came to acknowledge and study organized crime. A high point is unearthing John Landesco's 1929 classic *Organized Crime in Chicago* and considering why it was ignored at the time and had no influence on the field.

Simon, David R., and Frank E. Hagan. (1999), *White-Collar Deviance.* Boston: Allyn & Bacon. This book discusses a new conceptualization of the terms 'elite deviance', 'white-collar crime', and 'economic crime'. It includes both criminal and non-criminal deviance by individuals and organizations, as well as the conduct of the elite and non-elite.

Recommended Websites

Criminal Intelligence Service Canada
www.cisc.gc.ca

This website contains comprehensive information regarding organized crime in Canada. The agency has released the *2003 Annual Report on Organized Crime in Canada.* The report highlights how organized crime affects our daily lives and what actions are taken to reduce organized criminal activity.

National Crime Prevention Strategy
www.prevention.gc.ca

This website has a comprehensive list of documents and research data available in its research and evaluation section. The purpose of the website is part of a greater government initiative to curb reactive responses to crime in favour of early intervention to prevent crime and victimization.

International Association for the Study of Organized Crime
www.iasoc.net

This website provides a rather comprehensive bibliography of sources to begin any research about organized crime. It also offers quarterly trend reports, Internet links, and organized crime news.

Institute for Intergovernmental Research
www.iir.com/nwccc.htm

The IIR provides links to various websites for American data on white-collar crime and other types of non-violent crime. There are also several links to the National White Collar Crime Center.

CHAPTER 9

Political Crimes

LEARNING OBJECTIVES

- To understand political deviance and its different forms
- To examine how corruption is a social problem
- To study revolutionary groups and factors in the occurrence of revolutions
- To recall the violence perpetrated by governments in the twentieth century
- To evaluate political crimes from a sociological perspective
- To learn the ways that political crimes positively and negatively impact cohesion
- To see how some groups benefit from war
- To judge how the media alters perceptions of war
- To understand some of the causes and consequences of terrorism
- To understand the social, health, and psychological consequences of wars
- To examine how societies are able to reflect on war after the fact
- To understand the origins and outcomes of the political movements

---

Introduction

This chapter is about rule-breaking by people who are seeking political ends, or by people who are empowered to make the political rules. Within this context, we examine political crimes—the attachment of 'deviant' labels to people for their role in political conflicts.

Nothing shows the relativity of deviant labels more clearly than political events, especially wars. The side that wins has the ability to label some people 'heroes' and others 'villains', 'terrorists', or 'traitors'. Some non-participants even earn the label of 'deserter' or 'draft dodger' and suffer legal consequences and disgrace for their role in the conflict (or lack thereof).

Other types of political crime are less ambiguous and not always punished. Often these crimes are known as 'political corruption', and we will discuss them briefly here. At the extremes, governments may also practice political repression, terrorism, and genocide against their citizens. In these circumstances, resistance against the government, however illegal according to the laws of the state, can be viewed as conformity to a higher moral standard. We examine various forms of resistance, peaceful and otherwise, for they are types of deviance and they have a political impact. Usually, their impact is quieter, slower, and subtler than the impact of wars and revolutions.

This chapter largely focuses on macro sociological types of deviance—'terrorism', 'treason', and 'war crimes', for example. These deviations from normative behaviour are political activities that take place because certain individuals and groups

Table 9.1 Death by Government in the Twentieth Century

| Regimes | Years | Democode ('000s)[1] | | | Annual Rate%[2] |
		Total	Domestic	Genoicide	
Megamurderers[4]	1900–87	151,491	116,380	33,476	
Deka-Megamurderers[4]	1900–87	128,168	100,842	26,690	0.18
USSR	1917–87	61,911	54,769	10,000	0.42
China (PRC)	1949–87	35,236	35,236	375	0.12
Germany	1933–45	20,946	762	16,315	0.09
China (KMT)[5]	1928–49	10,075	10,075	Nil	0.07
Lesser Megamurderers[4]	1900–87	19,178	12,237	6,184	1.63
Japan	1936–45	5,964	Nil	Nil	Nil
China (Mao Soviets)[3, 5]	1923–49	3,466	3,466	Nil	0.05
Cambodia	1975–79	2,035	2,000	541	8.16
Turkey	1909–18	1,883	1,752	1,883	0.96
Vietnam	1945–87	1,670	944	Nil	0.10
Poland	1945–48	1,585	1,585	1,585	1.99
Pakistan	1958–87	1,503	1,503	1,500	0.06
Yugoslavia (Tito)	1944–87	1,072	987	675	0.12
Suspected Megamurderers[4]	1900–87	4,145	3,301	602	0.24
North Korea	1948–87	1,663	1,293	Nil	0.25
Mexico	1900–20	1,417	1,417	100	0.45
Russia	1900–17	1,066	591	502	0.02
Ceni-Kilomurderers[4]	1900–87	14,918	10,812	4,071	0.26
Top 5[4]	1900–87	4,074	2,192	1,078	0.89
China (Warlords)	1917–49	910	910	Nil	0.02
Turkey (Atatürk)	1919–23	878	703	878	2.64
United Kingdom	1900–87	816	Nil	Nil	Nil
Portugal (Dictatorship)	1926–82	741	Nil	Nil	Nil
Indonesia	1965–87	729	579	200	0.02
Lesser Murderers[4]	1900–87	2,792	2,355	1.019	0.1
World Total[6]	1900–87	169,202	129,547	38,566	0.1

[1] Includes genocide, politicide, and mass murder; excludes war-dead. These are most probable mid-estimates in low to high ranges. Figures may not sum due to round off.
[2] The per cent of a population killed in democide per year of the regime.
[3] Guerrilla period.
[4] Average.
[5] The rate is the average of that for three successive periods.
[6] The world annual rate is calculated for the 1944 global population.

SOURCE: R.J. Rummel, *Death by Government* (New Brunswick, NJ: Transaction Publishers, 1994). © 1994 by Transaction Publishers. Reprinted by permission of the publisher.

decide that they can improve society or the world at large. There are still many countries in which political conflict results in violence, deaths, and the overthrow of governments. Unlike Canada, many countries are still far from democracy and orderly political debate. So, it is important to understand how political conflict gives rise to deviant acts and deviant labels.

Many political crimes take place during wars, and for this reason we will have occasion to discuss war repeatedly. At no point in recorded history has there been a complete absence of war. As long as people are around, war will be too. Discussion, debate, protest, rebellion, and war are all varying means of conducting political conflict, along a spectrum from peaceful to violent. War between nations is the largest-scale, most-extreme version of civil conflict (see Table 9.1). Civil wars and acts of terrorism are smaller-scale versions of the same thing. So, by understanding war—its causes and consequences—we can understand more about protest, rebellion, and other forms of deviant political conflict.

However, the problem of politicized labelling involves more than wars. Governments themselves commit deviant, even criminal, acts. Most people would consider Hitler a war criminal, though he was the legal head of the German state when he committed his crimes against humanity. Some people would also consider Henry Kissinger and George W. Bush war criminals. Recently, Rwandan and Serbian leaders have been tried and convicted for war crimes. Some would view any use of state power to kill innocent civilians, whether at home or abroad, as a criminal act—perhaps a war crime—though one that is not always labelled as such by the World Court.

Corruption

This simplest form of political crime is 'corruption'. Corruption includes a wide variety of activities and especially, bribery, patronage, and fraud.

'Bribery' is the payment of money or favours to an official for special consideration in the application of formal rules. 'Patronage' is giving special consideration—including handing out contracts or jobs—to people on the basis of friendship, kinship, or the expectation of favours in return. 'Fraud' is any use of deception or false pretense for purposes of self-enrichment: for example, giving bank loans to non-existent people so the money is deposited in a secret account belonging to the bank officer.

Corruption is not supposed to happen in modern democratic societies, for several reasons. First, modern societies are bureaucratic, and bureaucracies are supposed to make efficient use of resources. Corruption, usually, is not efficient. In his classic analysis of bureaucracy as an ideal type, Max Weber distinguished between bureaucratic and pre-bureaucratic forms of organization, such as patrimony or clientelism. There are no written rules, job descriptions, regular payments, or career ladders. Weber argues that bureaucracy arises historically as an organizational form precisely because patrimony and other forms are inefficient. As a result, armies lose battles, businesses go bankrupt, and governments make wasteful or illegal decisions. Because bureaucracy is a superior organizational form, owing to its greater efficiency, it supplants earlier forms. From this standpoint, corruption is a step backward organizationally.

Second, along similar lines, modern societies are founded on scientific rationality, the rule of law, and democratic participation. This is what distinguishes modern societies from feudal societies. From this standpoint, corruption is a return to pre-modern practices. It favours a small number of interest groups or interested individuals—for example, financial contributors to the ruling political party—over everyone else.

Yet, in 2004, Canadian newspapers were full of information about scandals associated with corruption in the ruling Liberal Party under former Prime Minister Jean Chrétien. The news reports have alleged that Chrétien handed out plum jobs to close friends and supporters who were not necessarily qualified. Additionally, public funds were used to advance the financial interests of party supporters under the guise of promoting federalism in Quebec, via consulting and advertising initiatives.

Prime Minister Martin has attempted to distance himself from this corruption by claiming that he knew nothing about it and by firing key executives hired by Chrétien. Yet, many would argue that not only did Martin know about this, but also all political systems—even in democratic, modern societies—run on patronage and corruption. Such corruption is the essence of the party system: people group together to elect a government; doing so requires time and money; when elected, the government pays off its debts to its supporters. In Toronto, a city administrator was recently prosecuted for giving out untendered multimillion-dollar computer contracts to a man she had been sleeping with; testimony then revealed that she had been giving out contracts to lovers for quite some time.

Some might say that 'particularism' in government decision-making makes sense. At least people know who they are favouring, and why. At least people know that, if they work for a particular party, they will be rewarded. Political systems that run on friendship—that is, on patronage and corruption—work consistently. As sociologist Robert Merton (1957) showed in an early work on city politics, systems that run on supposed 'principles' usually fail to meet their stated goals. They are far less predictable because they cannot reward, and thereby hold, their supporters.

This seemingly cynical interpretation of politics helps to explain the recurrence—indeed, the universality—of political corruption in societies claiming to be modern, rational, efficient, and equitable. Russia is one of the most heinous offenders and the acceptance of corruption by the Russian people is having dire consequences for the working of the post-Communist government (Shlapentokh, 2003). The prevalence of corruption has reached a new

phase of normalization. According to a recent poll, two-thirds of the Russian people accept corruption as a normal part of economic and political life. President Putin has not only avoided taking serious action against corruption, but has even refused to discuss the subject. Corruption hurts small businesses and foreign investors, siphons money that is needed for growth outside the country, and destroys the state apparatus.

In Latin America, and elsewhere, corruption not only violates the basic democratic principles of equality, transparency, and fairness, but it may also foster a democratic breakdown by undermining the legitimacy of the democratic system in general, and people's trust in its core institutions in particular. When compared with consolidated democracies, both level of corruption and institutional distrust are significantly higher in almost all Latin American countries (Schneider, 2003). However, there is no evidence that the Latin American citizens' trust in the policy-implementing institutions (police, judiciary, public administration) is more negatively influenced by corruption than is the case for citizens in consolidated democracies.

Political corruption is worldwide and operates at the highest levels of society, infiltrating global politics and economics. However, the extent of corruption varies from one society to another. An organization called Transparency International makes annual ratings of the business climate in different countries to assess the level of political honesty versus corruption. Elshorst (2003) notes that the strategy of Transparency International (TI) in the global fight against corruption is based on the idea of making use of chances for change wherever they emerge, without being constrained by ideological premises or long-term action programs. In the last few years, TI was able to put corruption on the worldwide policy agenda and reach some concrete results at a national as well as international level. Today, Canada ranks 12th on the scale of corruption, and Scandinavian countries rank at the top—meaning, least corruption.

Box 9.1 Confidence in Politicians Grows Despite Scandals, Broken Promises

OTTAWA—In spite of the sponsorship scandal in Ottawa, a highly negative federal election campaign, and an Ontario government that has been nicknamed the 'fiberals' for backtracking on its promises, a new poll shows Canadians are becoming more confident in their politicians.

Once at an all-time low of 19 per cent in 1992, the 2004 Portraits of Canada survey shows 48 per cent of Canadians say they have a great deal or some confidence in their politicians.

Gina Bishop, who co-directed the survey, said the findings have caught some off guard.

'It wasn't what most people expect to see, that's certainly true. People seem surprised by this finding,' she said.

Bishop said a closer look at the historical data lead her to suspect that 'confidence' numbers are closely linked to how people feel about the state of the economy, noting that Canada is the only G-7 country to record consecutive budget surpluses over the past three years.

'It seems there might be an association with the economic performance of the country,' she said.

The results show confidence in politicians is at its highest recorded level since 1985 when an Environics survey pegged the level at 50 per cent.

But politicians shouldn't conclude that they have entirely shed their negative reputation for dirty deeds and self-interested behaviour.

Less than a quarter of Canadians—23 per cent—said politicians demonstrate honesty and ethics, lagging behind business leaders at 37 per cent and religious leaders who topped the list at 47 per cent.

'Canadians are making a distinction there on those two questions. Confidence doesn't really mean that people feel there political leaders have high honesty and ethical standards because that hasn't changed much since 2002 and that's very, very low compared to the other types of leaders that we asked about,' said Bishop.

For the first time, the annual survey also asked Canadians for their views on cronyism, asking if it was an avoidable or unavoidable part of Canada's political system for governments to give political appointments to party members or party donors. Fifty-six per cent said it was avoidable, but the results varied across the country.

'We found that a majority of Canadians felt that it's an avoidable part of the political system. They have expectations that this sort of thing doesn't necessarily have to be an inherent part of the way we do politics here in Canada. That's most true out West and in the North, but it's a little less clear when you go to Ontario, Quebec, and the Atlantic provinces,' said Bishop.

The Portraits of Canada survey is based on a combination of two surveys totalling 3,202 respondents, including a CROP survey of 1,000 in Quebec between Sept. 16 and Oct. 3, 2004, and an Environics Research Group survey of 2,202 people outside Quebec between Sept. 15 and Oct. 4, 2004. It has a margin of error of 1.7 percentage points, 19 times out of 20.

SOURCE: Bill Curry, *Kingston Whig-Standard*, 16 November 2004, 36.

Table 9.2   Percentage of Citizens Around the Globe Who Experienced Street-Level Corruption, and Explanatory Country Characteristics by Region

	New World[1]	Western Europe	Eastern Europe	Central Europe	South America	Asia	Africa
Corruption	0.3	0.7	10.2	14.6	20.3	20.6	9.3
Prosperity	4.3	4.2	3.8	3.8	3.6	3.3	3.3
Economic freedom	3.1	2.9	2.0	1.4	2.2	1.7	1.9
Democratic tradition	0.7	0.9	0.0	0.0	0.2	0.3	0.0
British legal culture	0.7	0.3	0.0	0.0	0.0	0.3	0.8
Government salaries	1.3	1.5	1.6	0.5	2.6	2.6	6.1
Politically stable	0.6	0.7	0.2	0.6	0.6	0.8	0.8
Non-federal structure	0.3	0.6	1.0	0.5	0.6	0.7	1.0
% Protestants	22.7	30.8	13.4	0.0	3.1	3.2	22.3
No. of countries	3	14	9	2	5	3	5
No. of respondents	2,185	6,177	7,733	1,953	4,163	2,416	2,829

[1] New World = Australia, Canada, and the USA.

SOURCE: Gerrit De Geest, Paul Nieuwbeerta, and Jacques Siegers, 'Street-Level Corruption in Industrialized and Developing Countries', *European Societies*, (2003) 5 (2): 156. Reprinted with permission.

Corruption occurs at the neighbourhood level too. Nieuwbeerta, De Geest, and Siegers (2003), comparing the levels of street-level corruption around the world, find that the least corruption is experienced by citizens living in countries with: (1) high levels of economic development, (2) high levels of economic freedom, (3) long exposure to democracy, (4) a non-federal structure, (5) Protestant traditions, and (6) a British legal culture (see Table 9.2).

Resistance

Given the evidence of corrupt misbehaviour by political leaders it is surprising that ordinary people challenge the government and the 'power elite' so rarely. Very few citizens resist the dictates of their government in a forceful way.

Instead, most people conform to their country's rules and social expectations, for many good reasons. Among the most important are beliefs about necessity, normality, and morality. Beliefs about *necessity* are beliefs that a person cannot act

otherwise than what is expected—for example, that young people cannot possibly understand what older people understand, that older people cannot possibly understand younger people, that workers cannot possibly understand what difficult decisions executives have to make, or that white people cannot possibly understand what it means to be black. Beliefs about *normality* are beliefs that people are not quite normal if they think or do certain things. For example, girls who violate the sexual double standard and show an interest in sex are not behaving normally, according to the traditional cultural script. As a result, people behave as they are expected to behave because they do not want to pay this penalty.

In general, many people who violate moral rules, social norms, or laws likewise will feel guilty and unsafe because they are breaking the rules.

States and ruling classes use a variety of methods to brainwash people, so they do not resist or oppose the current ways of doing things. Given the tendency for people to feel uncomfortable about violating the simplest social rules—for example, rules of etiquette—imagine how hard it would be to resist the demands of the state: for example, to march in protest against a government policy or side with an unpopular group of people. To protest the state's actions may feel impossible and useless. It may seem abnormal—crazy—to some, even to people we know and respect. In short, resisting and protesting institutions of power in our society requires courage and a sense of agency—the ability to overcome internal and external obstacles, and act on our beliefs. Those who do so are sometimes accused of treason.

Treason is the name of a crime the state gives to people who oppose state goals and take illegal actions to undermine them. In principle, criminalizing opposition to the state is a good thing; it maintains social and political stability. However, in the wrong hands, use of the label 'treason' can be an instrument of despotism and terror—especially when states are vulnerable to economic and political instability and rulers are willing to act despotically to secure order.

Discussions of treason are complex, as witnessed in discussions of 'war resisters' and 'conscientious objectors'—people who, on moral grounds, refuse to fight for their country and suffer penalties as a result. Sociologist John Hagan (2002) analyzed the lives of Americans who resisted the draft by 'dodging' and 'deserting' military service. In the largest political exodus from the US since the American Revolution, more than 50,000 young Americans migrated to Canada during the Vietnam War. Once in Canada, these selective service and military 'criminals' were converted by their adopted nation's immigration policy into 'New Canadians' and unexpected symbols of Canadian sovereignty. The latter more ambivalent war resisters who settled in Canada are still today less likely to participate politically by voting in Canadian federal elections.

Israel has had a continuing problem with its war resisters. The Israeli-Egyptian peace accord of 1979 caused two new forms of political culture

to emerge: a Jewish underground movement that appeared in Israeli-occupied territories, and a trend of conscientious objection that came about in 1982 as a reaction against the war in Lebanon (Reznik, 2002). The nearly simultaneous appearance of two groups—one that threatened violence and the other that refused to fight—is a result of both groups' desire to oppose the labour movement.

Riots and Collective Protests

Riots are another type of protest against authority. Emotional, violent, and localized collective behaviours that are mainly undirected, *riots* have outcomes that are unplanned. Generally, riots are a form of political protest that indicates grassroots dissatisfaction with the government.

In Canada, riots have been a relatively uncommon form of political expression, compared with Europe and Latin America. Part of the reason has to do with more control exercised over the police in Canada: riots require both aggressive protestors and even more aggressive police. Ericson and Doyle (1999) note that previous research shows a trend toward softer, more tolerant styles of policing protest in various Western democracies. Police behaviour at an international event—the 1997 Asia Pacific Economic Cooperation (APEC) summit, where Canada hosted rulers of less democratic regimes in a ritual celebration of economic globalization—was an exception to this rule. There, in the face of protests about undemocratic regimes elsewhere, the Canadian government and police used blatantly undemocratic tactics popularly believed to be more characteristic of those other regimes.

Riots have been far more common in the United States, particularly in connection with black-white relations and racial discrimination. During the 1960s, urban rioting in the United States was an enormous concern because it resulted in the destruction of much private and public property, looting, and civil disorder. Research on rioting during this period led to the conclusion that rioting expresses

Figure 9.1 The War at Home: US Anti-War Protests and Congressional Voting, 1965–73

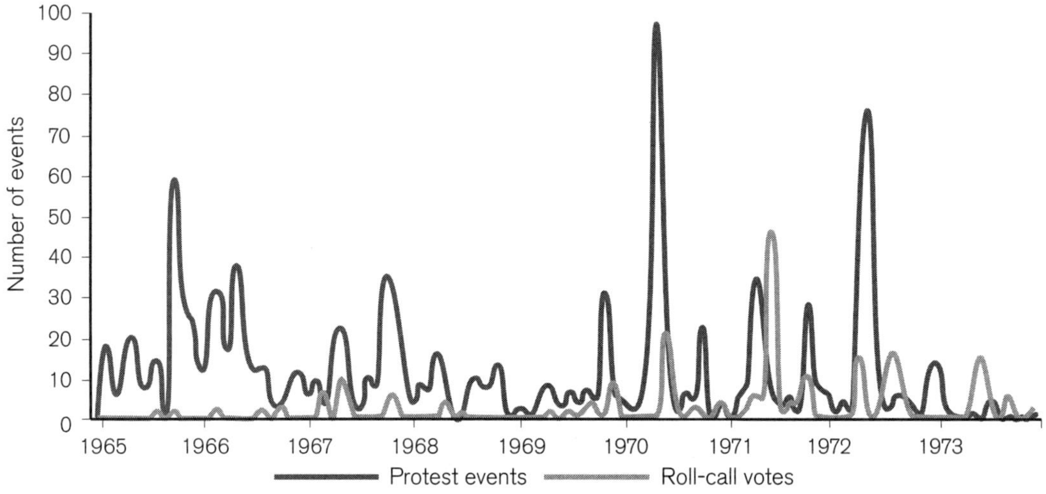

SOURCE: Doug McAdam and Yang Su, 'The War at Home: Antiwar Protests and Congressional Voting, 1965 to 1973', *American Sociological Review*, (Oct. 2002), 67 (5): 711. Reprinted by permission of the American Sociological Association.

social tensions and reflects weak or inadequate external control.

Because of widespread potentials for racial violence in many countries, the manner in which riots are handled and controlled deeply influences race relations and subsequent patterns of violence. Both local government and the local police are important in determining whether a riot will follow a precipitating incident. Research on American riots in the 1960s found that cities with fewer riots were typically cities with more racially integrated police forces, more representative forms of local government, and a larger percentage of blacks who were self-employed in retail trade, such as store, restaurant, or tavern owners; that is, they were cities with strong, independent black middle-class business groups.

Usually, rioting is set off by an incident involving the police in a minority neighbourhood, where some actual or believed violation of accepted police practice has taken place. Social control starts to break down and people see the opportunity for looting.

If, at this point, order is not restored, the riot moves into a third stage that includes arson, gunfire, and countermeasures by the police and militia. In short, the violence escalates on both sides.

There has been much debate in sociology about the degree of social structuring in riots. Generally, researchers conclude that some kinds of people are more likely than others to participate, and often the participants are linked to one another by social ties as well as shared motives. A large fraction—no fewer than 10 per cent and possibly as many as 20 per cent of the potential population—was involved in the American black urban riots of 1967. Often, people cannot say exactly why they are rioting, or express their motives in overly general terms of dissatisfaction. Often, the mass media play a role in riots, spreading the rationalizations and symbols of identification that rioters come to use. That said, researchers conclude that those who rioted in 1967 were typically less integrated into family life and more subject to informal street life than the average community dweller.

The History of War, Protest, and Public Reactions to It

Most people consider 'war' to be an armed conflict between two countries or two groups within a country. However, we can expand this definition of war to include undeclared battles, civil conflicts, guerrilla wars, covert operations, and even terrorism (Wright, 1964). In some countries, war even includes the use of military and police forces against the citizenry. Sociologists Francesca Cancian and James W. Gibson (1990) suggest that some countries can be said to possess a 'war system', in which key social institutions—economies, governments, and even cultural practices—promote warfare as a normal and comprehensive aspect of their lives.

Sullivan (1997) distinguishes the 'collective violence' of military conflict—organized violence used to promote an agenda or resist an oppressive other—from the localized 'interpersonal violence' that is characteristic of murders and domestic abuse we discussed in an earlier chapter. However, because violent acts at a local scale can be considered crimes, large-scale wars and terrorist attacks can also be considered crimes too—crimes against humanity.

Two centuries ago most wars were fought on a local scale between neighbouring groups. With advances in military technology, today's wars can be waged between parties thousands of miles apart, such that the killers and the killed may never even see one another face-to-face. No wonder then that the twentieth century has been called the bloodiest hundred years in human history.

Wars have changed in other ways. Between 1500 and 1950, most wars were fought in Europe. Since then, most of the world's wars have been fought in developing (low-income) nations, even when European or North American states have been involved. Today, there are an estimated 40 active military conflicts in the world, many of which are intranational. As well, with the growing popularity of terrorist tactics targeting civilian populations rather than military stations, war zones have shifted from secluded outposts and isolated bases to crowded urban centres.

Industrialization has allowed for the development of more destructive weapons of war. However, Cohen (1986: 265) also notes 'as societies become more industrialized, their proneness to war decreases.' According to Cohen's estimates, industrial nations averaged 2.7 wars per decade whereas pre-industrial states averaged 10.6. One possible reason for this trend is that industrialized countries have more to lose and less to gain from attacking other nations, and they resort to military confrontations only when provoked or threatened.

The causes of war are numerous and complex, and seldom is a conflict fought over a single reason. One of the most common causes of war is a dispute over natural resources, such as land and oil. Another reason that many parties go to war is over ideological beliefs. The Second World War was in many ways a global conflict between democracy and fascism. The Cold War between the United States and Russia, roughly between 1945 and 1989, was a war between Capitalism and Communism. As well, such conflicts are less likely than wars over resources or territory to be resolved through negotiation or the signing of a peace treaty, since they are fought over fundamental beliefs that cannot be compromised by the warriors involved.

Generally, countries with similar beliefs and values are less likely to wage war against one another than countries with divergent ones (Dixon, 1994). In particular, democratic societies are reluctant to go to war with one another, opting instead to resolve international conflicts with negotiation, compromise, and/or economic and trade sanctions (Doyle, 1986).

Like nation-states pursuing their national goals through violence, terrorists are often motivated by ideological beliefs to commit acts of violence against those they perceive to be the enemy. Followers of the Muslim fundamentalist leader Sheik Omar Abdel Rahman, who considers the US oppressive and immoral, perpetrated the 1993 bombing of the

World Trade Center in New York City. Followers of Osama bin Laden carried out the destruction of the World Trade Center in 2001 for similar reasons. Theodore Kaczynski, better known as the 'Unibomber', mailed out 16 letter bombs between 1978 and 1995 to business executives and university researchers; they killed 3 people and injured another 22.

Violent political protest

As societies industrialize and become democratic, movements of political protest tend to become less violent. Political protest continues in many forms, varying in terms of duration, reasons for initiation, scope of activities, degree of engagement in collective violence, motivations of the participants, and means for mobilization for action (Djoreya, 2001). Some protests become violent, but in countries like Canada, violent political protests are less common than in the past. In that respect, the violence of the FLQ in the 1970s was uncharacteristic.

Where protests arise, many worry that lines between criminal activities and political protest will be blurred by efforts to maintain order (Flyghed, 2003). In industrialized societies, non-violent tactics have often been used to reduce the likelihood of protests. Even urban planning plays a part in this process, by replacing public space (such as a sidewalk or a public square) with 'carceral' spaces—architecture that is more secure and easier to defend against attack (Davis, 1990, 1992).

Political protest reflects a bad fit between people's cultural goals and the means available to achieve them—what Merton called 'rebellion' in his typology of adaptations to anomie. Protest also typically accompanies frustrated hopes and expectations—indeed, expectations that may have been rising more rapidly than the means to satisfy them. Protest also requires resources and organization: typically, cash, weapons, information technology, and co-operation from influential individuals. Though some movements of protest are spontaneous, brief, and disorganized, most are planned, continuing, and rooted in both formal and informal networks of social contact. The most developed form of social protest is exemplified by a revolution.

Revolution

Zimmermann (1983: 298) defined revolution as 'the successful overthrow of the prevailing elite by a new elite who, after having taken over power, fundamentally change the social structure and therewith also the structure of authority.'

Revolutions are important events for individual countries and for the politics of the world as a whole. Though events of immense political and moral contradiction, and occasions for celebrating the heroic and the idealistic, revolutions rarely, however, achieve their original goals. Whatever their goals and high ideals, revolutions invariably substitute one form of restrictive power for another. They rarely replace despotism with a secure democracy and, often, they replace one form of despotism with another. That said, revolutions—even if they do not achieve their intended goals—affect other countries and the world as a whole. This is true of the French Revolution, the Russian Revolution, the Chinese Revolution, the Cuban Revolution, and many other smaller scale revolutions.

Observing the revolutions in France, Russia, and China, Skocpol notes that revolutionary crises developed there when the old aristocratic regimes failed to meet emerging challenges. What the imperial state and the landed aristocracy had in common in these countries was the exploitation of the people. Monarchs were interested in receiving increased resources from the society and channelling them into military or state-sponsored economic development (Skocpol, 1979). However, the economic interests of the landed classes placed obstacles in the way of implementing such plans of the state.

Skocpol defines pre-revolutionary France, Russia, and China as 'fully established imperial states'. Since these states were not fully bureaucratic or parliamentary, however, they could not offer representatives for the dominant class an opportunity to take part in political decisions making. As a result, the landed class developed a capacity for 'self-conscious collective organization'. It was in a position to 'obstruct monarchical undertakings that ran counter to their economic interests' (Skocpol, 1979). Their obstructions had the unintended consequence of destroying the military and administrative integrity of the imperial state. In effect, the landed aristocracy undermined its own traditional position in the society.

Historical research by Barrington Moore (1962) shows that the outcome of a revolution depends, to a great degree, on which social classes attack the monarch. When the attackers are primarily peasants, as in China, Vietnam, and Cuba, the result is a Communist regime that introduces land reform and social equality. When the attackers are primarily military—supported by a coalition of the landed aristocracy, Church, and large business interests—the result is Fascism, as in Germany, Italy, and Spain. Only when the revolutionaries are independent farmers, craftsmen, and other 'middle-class people' is the result likely to be parliamentary democracy, as in England, France, and the United States.

Rebellion, in common terms, is armed opposition by a portion of the citizenry to an established government or other authority. The difference between a *rebellion* and a *revolution* lies in the outcome. If the rebellion succeeds in overthrowing the government and making significant social and political changes, then it is considered a revolution. If, as with the so-called rebellions of 1837 in Upper and Lower Canada, the government is not overthrown, or few changes result then the act is considered a mere rebellion, or even *coup d'état*. Everyone who engages in rebellion against a government is liable to the criminal penalties of treason established by that government. If a rebellion becomes widespread, involving a considerable proportion

of the country, and the rebels receive the recognition of foreign nations, the government in charge treats captured rebels as belligerents. If the rebellion succeeds, and the rebels form a new government, the rebels are no longer criminals: they are heroes and rulers.

As mentioned, in 1837 Canada experienced a series of insurrections against the colonial rule of Great Britain, known as the Rebellions of 1837. These rebellions were driven by frustration over the oligarchic and politically irresponsible governments Britain had installed. Then, patronage and corruption were rife; the ruling families used wealth and power at their own convenience. The brief episodes of fighting in Upper Canada (present-day Ontario) and Lower Canada (present-day Quebec) were part of a single crisis where responsible government was at issue. By the time the crisis ended in 1838, hundreds had been killed and thousands more were refugees. Following Lord Durham's investigative report to the English Parliament, the road was clear for responsible government in Canada and, eventually, independence.

Both revolutions and rebellions are acts of deviance and crimes against the government of the day. To repeat, whether history views the rebels as heroes or villains depends on whether they succeed. Winners typically rewrite the history books to show themselves as heroes conforming to a higher standard of moral conduct. Louis Riel, a nineteenth-century Metis rebel in Western Canada, continues to be celebrated by Native people and Francophones, but ignored by most Canadians, for example. William Lyon Mackenzie, leader of the unsuccessful 1837 rebellion in Upper Canada is mostly just forgotten.

Yet, populist movements have always been common in Canada. By 'populist', we mean movements that aimed at moving power back to individual voters, rather than their representatives, elites, or backroom brokers. In this regard, the 'referendum' as a means of political decision-making is an example of populist politics. Some grassroots movements have resulted in the formation of new political parties in Western Canada (Social Credit, the CCF, and the NDP) and the Winnipeg General Strike. The early part of the twentieth century was a time of significant change within Canada while the country struggled to respond to a massive influx of immigrants, expansion in Western Canada, the impact of urbanization, two World Wars, a major drought, and economic depression. A variety of new populist initiatives emerged out of this national tragedy, especially in western Canada where waves of immigrants created a more heterogeneous population mix than in any other part of Canada (Guenther, 2000).

Political populism in Canada in the twentieth century comprised several important elements: a nostalgic view of society as expressing traditional Christian values associated with personal industriousness, thrift, and family attachment; criticism of industrial or big business capitalism as harmful to the interests of independent, small-scale commodity producers; and criticism of the political corruption resulting from control of political parties and institutions by large-scale finance, industrial, and manufacturing capitalists (McMenemy, 2001).

Populist movements in Canada have most often succeeded when led by charismatic individuals who could articulate regional grievances and exploit new techniques of communication such as radio and television. Populist sentiment in Canada continues among some members of the Conservative Party, especially the Western wing of Conservatism associated formerly with the Social Credit Party.

Increasingly, as Inglehart (1985) has said, movements of protest around the industrial world today are driven by non-class-based issues including environmentalism, civil rights, and feminism. Increasingly, they tend to recruit middle-class, highly educated young people—in Canada and elsewhere—who de-emphasize traditional working-class interests in wages and job security and may not be connected to any mainstream political party. This is a departure from past practice, and it suggests

considerable uncertainty and instability in political protests of the future. Michael Walzer (1965), in writing about the English revolution of 1640, referred to a similar phenomenon as a 'revolution of the saints'. This is protest that is driven by ideologies, not interests and free-forming social groups, not social classes; it recruits highly educated people with many ideas about building a better society.

Theories about Protest, Rebellion, and War

Psychological theories

Psychological theories of social protest have tended to focus on social conditions that promote alienation, rootlessness, or disengagement from the existing order. Originally, many psychological theories of 'mass' or 'collective behaviour' focused on the role of 'contagion'—the seemingly spontaneous spread of ideas and sentiments, a view popularized by the French theorist Gustav Le Bon (1896).

From a more modern version of the same perspective, social protest is the result of people with an insufficient stake in the existing society, owing to unmet needs and expectations. This then, raises the question of what drives people's hopes and expectations. Inglehart (1985), for example, has noted that people who grew up during a time of postwar prosperity and, therefore, are inclined to hold very high hopes and expectations, today drive many political protests.

A failing of the psychological approach is its tendency to view protestors and rebels as relatively unconnected, or 'atomized', individuals, each responding to a personal sense of grievance. However, research on the social networks of rebels, protestors, and dissidents—starting perhaps with work by Charles Tilly (1964) on the French Revolutionary period—suggests that, in fact, these people are rarely atomized. More often, they are highly interconnected and therefore easily mobilized. For this reason, we need to look at sociological theories of political behaviour.

Sociological Approaches to Protest and War

Functionalist perspectives

Functionalists believe that the way society is structured explains the development of political protest, rebellion, and war. Moreover, there is a belief that the 'laws' or central mechanisms of protest can be identified through a systematic comparison of different 'contentious movements'.

So, for example, McAdam, Tarrow, and Tilley (2001), in their book *The Dynamics of Contention*, assembled analytical narratives of 18 contentious episodes drawn from a variety of places and periods since 1800. They included the French Revolution of 1789–94, the US civil rights movement, the Italian protest cycle of the 1960s, plus four more Western European and American cases and 11 others from around the world. The result identified recurrent mechanisms and processes that help to explain critical features of those episodes and identify key structural features of civil wars, nationalist mobilizations, and transnational contention.

Merton (1957 [1938]), as we know, explains how social structural conditions produce anomie, which disconnects people from the existing institutional order. From this perspective, Merton would consider the politically motivated offender a rebel. The 'rebel' has an accepted role to play in modern societies, and for this reason (paradoxically) poses little danger to these societies. Thus, rebelliousness is functional to society because it helps to maintain the status quo. Presumably, war and terrorism are also 'functional' from this standpoint. Moreover, the consistency with which large numbers of people systematically try to kill one another suggests that war must have a social function, and that it may even be viewed as a social institution.

Paradoxically, any conflict increases social cohesion and group identity by creating a common cause for which people can fight. During a war, internal squabbles between political parties, ethnic communities, and special interest groups are put aside temporarily as the entire nation bands together to defeat a common enemy. Only when this larger antagonist is no longer a threat to national well-being do the intranational conflicts resume.

A second function of war is the economic benefit that comes from fuelling the war efforts. Canadian participation in the Second World War led to increased employment and production, helping to end the economic downturn of the Great Depression. Even after the war, Canadians rode the economic momentum through several more decades, experiencing prosperity and growth in all aspects of society. After the war, the gross national product doubled, industry developed exponentially, and consumer spending rose with the baby boom generation (*Canadian Global Almanac*, 2000). This was made possible only by the fact that the Allies won the war. The German and Japanese economies suffered significant setbacks in the years after the conflict.

Wars also lead to scientific and technological innovations that remain beneficial to society in peacetime. For example, the Internet was an invention of the US Pentagon as an emergency communications network in the event of a nuclear war. Other spinoffs of the Second World War were jet engines and atomic power.

In some cases, the solidarity between allies generated through the defence of shared interests lasts even after the war has ended. This cohesion between groups often translates into social reform, particularly for the poor: 'Only the promise of a better world can give meaning to a terrible conflict. Since the lower economic strata contribute more of their blood in battle than the wealthier classes, war often gives impetus to social welfare reforms' (Porter, 1994: 19).

There is typically a close connection between a society's propensity to make war, the development of its military institutions, and its strategic culture. *Strategic culture* is the collective belief or rationale about the use of force in international politics that has been based upon the experiences

Box 9.2   Two Sombre Warnings for Canada: Terrorists Will Exploit Open Society–Israeli Envoy

It is only a matter of time before terrorists exploit the openness and diversity of Canadian society and strike here, Israel's new ambassador to Canada warned yesterday.

Alan Baker said Canadians must realize additional restrictions on rights and freedoms are necessary to counter the relative ease with which terror groups can now infiltrate Canadian society and launch attacks here, against the United States or on Israeli and other foreign interests in Canada.

His comments to the Citizen's editorial board come as a parliamentary committee prepares to review a sweeping series of anti-terrorism laws enacted in the wake of the Sept. 11, 2001 attacks and which many legal and civil liberties experts believe already violate fundamental rules of law and democratic rights.

Mr Baker is a lawyer and expert on the legal aspects of the fight against terrorism.

Mr Baker said people must understand just how tempting Canada's open society is to terrorists.

'I very much fear that the openness of Canada might be interpreted by the various terrorist organizations as a sort of naïveté that can be utilized and abused,' he said.

'If I've become familiar with the psyche of the way terrorist organizations function, I suspect that it's a matter of time before they will abuse this Canadian openness.

'Canada, being confident of its diversity and openness, might be allowing itself to be misled and abused. It worries me. Canada should be very wary of this situation and should prepare itself. It's happened in Spain, it's happened in Turkey, it's happened in Moscow and I'm very fearful, about it happening in Canada.'

He suggested Canadians who believe in a society largely unfettered by new security restrictions and extraordinary legal powers do not realize the extent to which terrorists will exploit the vulnerabilities of an open society.

'The only advice that I can give on the face of things generally, is that I would hope that those responsible in Canada have their eyes fully open and won't allow themselves to be deceived by terrorist organizations which use the openness such as exists in Canada to further their own needs.

'The fact that I have to wander around everywhere with two RCMP (guards) . . . says something about the acknowledgment of the fact that there is a threat. This is important, this is good.'

Source: Excerpt, Ian MacLeod, *Ottawa Citizen*, 21 October 2004, A1.

of that group. A state's military behaviour is based upon its shared historical experiences in war and so each state will have its own unique strategic culture. As a result, some populations will be more accepting of the national use of violence. This predisposition may affect policy-making and a country's 'response and conduct in the international sphere' (Rummel, 1994). Basically, a nation's strategic culture may be determinant of its tendency toward a specific fighting stance or style. In this respect, Canada has acted consistently as a peacemaker and peace-keeper.

Conflict theorists

Conflict theorists argue that a war is merely a struggle between two opposing groups—over power, limited resources, or ideological domination—taken to its logical, violent conclusion. In much the same way that social classes battle one another for economic position within a society, nation-states and/or ethnic groups clash for similar reasons on a national or international stage. Protest, revolution, and terror occur where change can no longer be attained through discussion. Accordingly, groups or governments that try to prevent the expression of disagreement and conflict will often intensify them, and produce more violent forms of politicking, including protest, rebellion, and even civil war.

Conflict theory also emphasizes the ways in which war (and other conflict) benefits some groups—most notably, corporations, politicians, and the military—but not others. The government in power also benefits from war, since victory wins them admiration and gratitude, and therefore improves their chances of re-election. At a macro level, even the foreign aid intended to help Third World countries ultimately benefits First World nations. According to this perspective, wars are fought by nations seeking to increase their level of power and influence on the global level, or seeking to perpetuate the subordination of lesser nations. Wars are particularly beneficial for the military establishment. Historically, military forces and their

resulting communities were authoritarian, hierarchically stratified, and traditional in their values. Like other bureaucracies, military establishments fight to increase their power and resource base. At the same time, military forces derive their effectiveness from the fact that they are total institutions (which we discussed in connection with both mental hospitals and prisons). They must socialize recruits and turn them into killing machines. Military bureaucracies are well organized to achieve this kind of socialization.

Over time, with the growth of military spending, the activities of the military in many countries have become closely intertwined with general statecraft: with internal and external state policies. Likewise, the complexity of military technology, and the requirements for research, development, and technical maintenance, tend to blur the boundaries between military and non-military activities. In the United States and other countries where the military is large and prosperous, there is indeed a community and subculture of officers, enlisted soldiers, and veterans that is different from the general civilian culture. This difference is particularly marked in the elite military units—for example, the Marine Corps.

In a society with a highly developed military, such as the United States, military people often become involved in a variety of semi-public, semi-political activities that are not traditionally the responsibility or expertise of the military. For example, General Eisenhower, a hero of the Second World War, became US President Eisenhower. Colin Powell, a highly decorated military hero, became George W. Bush's secretary of state. Experiences in the military may have included planning and leading attacks, counterinsurgency, military assistance programs, paramilitary activities, and even nation-building. However, because military goals and means are different from political ones, military men often make poor statesmen and politicians. Often, military men end up criticizing the government, as was the case with Generals Macarthur and Patton in the United States, and more recently, General Romeo Dallaire in Canada.

The military is relatively unimportant in Canadian society, but the same cannot be said everywhere. In some societies, the military is a means of upward social mobility in the same way as a career in law, the Church, business, or academe may be in another society. As a result, underemployed military people—military men without wars to fight or other means of distinguishing themselves—are a potent threat to the social order. They may be counted on to foment rebellion and conflict. In this sense, they become a self-interested political class.

Civil wars, revolutions, and protests are even closer to the conflict perspective, since they cast light on the internal contradictions in a particular society. For Marx (1988 [1848]), the earliest conflict theorist, history is driven by class conflict and the replacement or overthrow of one ruling class by another. Marxist approaches to revolution emphasize the importance of the struggle between social classes or the contradiction within the mode of production between the force and the relations of productions. Contemporary Marxists who treat class conflict as the essential feature of Marxist analysis are likely to see revolution as the uncertain outcome of a complex combination of forces, mainly class consciousness, historical circumstance, political organization, and the repression of the working class.

We know today, however, that political conflict can also mean the alternation between military and civilian rule, or between successive military dictatorships, without any change in the means of production. Thus it could be argued from this perspective that because conflict will always exist between the opposed powerful and powerless groups, all crime and delinquency is a form of political protest. Crime, then, reflects on the one hand, an effort by powerless people to achieve wealth and power by 'innovative' means; and, on the other hand, an effort by powerful people to limit the access of others to wealth and power by any means.

Symbolic interactionism

This paradigm sees the society as a product of continuous face-to-face interactions among individuals in different societal settings. For example, symbolic interactionists examine the ways in which governments and media influence popular attitudes toward war and conflict.

The media, through cartoons and action shows, instill aggression and a habit of resolving conflicts with physical force as early as childhood, mostly in boys. GI Joe, Cowboys and Indians, those green plastic army men—these and other childhood toys and games implicitly teach young people that war is a noble and heroic adventure that the 'good guys' always win, and that national patriotism is crucial to victory. Kids are encouraged to join the Junior Canadian Rangers or other cadet programs as a sort of primer to life in the military, complete with ranks, drills, and patriotic zeal.

In times of war, people use a specific language to talk about and legitimize the combat and minimize the emotional impact of massive deaths that will ensue. Soldiers on both sides are not 'murder victims'; they are 'casualties'. The unavoidable killing of innocent civilians is referred to impersonally as 'collateral damage'. Nuclear missiles are not weapons of mass destruction; they are 'peacekeepers'. The stereotyping of enemies—focusing on ethnic, racial, and cultural differences—is a common way of dehumanizing the enemy, making him an easier victim and war more justifiable. The stereotyping may reflect current anxieties—for example, fears about Arab terrorism in the Middle East—but like all stereotypes, they are exaggerated.

The concept of war itself is given a positive spin in popular culture, as when the term is used in initiatives like the 'war on drugs', 'the war on poverty', and the 'war on cancer'. In recruitment materials, the military stresses honours, courage, and sacrifice for the greater good as defining characteristics of the ideal soldiers. Their well-groomed uniforms and combat decorations command respect and admiration from the public. The government often stresses the importance of military preparedness as vital to national prosperity. In reality, the military tends to recruit young, undereducated men and women from economically depressed areas, and subjects them to unrelenting discipline.

Even the subcultural value system that challenges authority, and in that way increases the likelihood of protests or riots, is also learned. Since inner-city children and immigrant children often live in close proximity to one another, immigrant children may learn to adopt the adversarial stance of inner-city children while shedding the hopes and aspirations of their immigrant parents (Zhou, 1999). As a result, assimilating or 'Americanizing' may lead to more protesting and rioting, not assimilation into the politically neutral middle class.

Feminist approaches

With few exceptions, men—not women—have historically fought wars. Men are also more often the leaders of a nation, and are therefore more likely to be in the position to declare wars against one another.

This socialization of masculinity and militarism begins in childhood. Stereotypically speaking, 'typical' or 'normal' boys wage make-believe wars with GI Joe figurines, while girls play with dolls and act out domestic routines like baking and childrearing. Ostensibly, Barbie is a military surgeon. When women have participated in military campaigns, they have usually performed stereotypically 'female' roles, such as nurses and clerical workers.

As the twentieth century progressed and feminist groups gained political and social clout, more diverse opportunities became available for women in the military. Women soldiers constituted 10 per cent of US combat troops in the first Gulf War. As warfare has become more technological and less reliant on individual, face-to-face armed combat, women have been able to enlist in any military position available to men. Currently, women are able to serve in most ranks and divisions of the Canadian military.

A gender issue related to war is the fate of innocent civilians of a war-torn region. During the Second World War, the Japanese military forced up to 200,000 young women into prostitution as 'comfort women' for military personnel, with many eventually dying from sexually transmitted diseases and torture. During the more recent conflicts in Bosnia-Herzegovina and Rwanda, and almost certainly in other hostile regions as well, women were raped, beaten, and killed by roving bands of soldiers (Amnesty International, 1995). Despite prohibitions outlined in the Geneva Conventions, rape, assault, and enforced prostitution of women continue to occur in armed conflicts today.

International feminist activists and women's organizations have played an important role in recent prosecutions of war crimes committed against women, especially rapes and sexual enslavement (Cooper, 2002). Feminists successfully pressured the UN to designate crimes against women as prosecutable human rights abuses and to include female prosecutors and judges in tribunals. So, for example, the Hague war crimes tribunal convicted three men for their role in the mass rape of Muslim women during the conflict in Bosnia-Herzegovina.

Buchanan (2002) notes particularly the problem of gendercide as a human rights violation. Gendercide against women typically involves rape, which has come to be recognized as a war crime. Against men, such crimes generally involve the selective separation of young civilian men 'of military age' (i.e., 18–45 years) from old men, children, and women of all ages for punishment, torture, and execution.

Many nations wish to forget the crimes they perpetrated against women during wartime. An example is Japan, which enslaved many Asian women for use as prostitutes for the Japanese military. In Japan, the production and consumption of television programs about this topic is linked with the exclusion of other historical memories from the public space (Ito, 2002). After all, the creation of public memories is related to social power.

Communities and Subcultures of Protest

Like other types of deviant behaviour, protest activity is socially structured. Typically, protestors—like other deviants—form communities and subcultures to provide one another with support. This is not true of rioters, since their actions are short-lived, but it is certainly true of bandits, revolutionaries, and terrorist bands.

Bandit communities

Historian Eric Hobsbawm (1959) defines banditry as a 'primitive' form of organized social protest—primitive in the sense of being small-scale, with few resources, occurring in pre-industrial (agricultural) societies, without any long-term political agenda. Banditry, from this standpoint, is a pre-class, pre-ideological formation.

In pre-industrial societies, the poor often protect the bandit, regard him as their hero, and turn him into a 'myth' (Hobsbawm, 1959). The most famous bandit protestor in our Anglo-dominant tradition is Robin Hood, who inhabited Sherwood Forest in England. Like other bandits, Robin Hood received support and protection from the ordinary people. In return, he tried to live up to his role as protector of the little people and defender of the wronged King Richard. As a social rebel, Robin Hood stole from the rich and gave to the poor, and he did not kill except in self-defence or to revenge wrongs. The victims of the Robin Hood bandit were enemies of the poor. Common people helped the bandit and hindered the Sheriff of Nottingham's efforts to arrest him.

According to Hobsbawm, a man becomes a bandit when he does something that is criminal by the state or local ruler's conventions but not illegal in the eyes of the local people. The bandit loses his local protection if he is seen to violate the local conventions. A bandit is very connected to his people and his birthplace: he may live near his village of birth, where he is supplied with food and other necessities. Typically, the peasant bandit is young, single, and unattached; it is harder to keep rebelling once he has family.

Many criminals adopt bandito strategies in order to succeed. An example is provided by Pablo Escobar, leader of one of Colombia's most notorious drug cartels. Although many Colombians disapproved of his involvement with drugs, Escobar enjoyed protection by living among the poorest Colombians outside of Medellin. The poor helped Escobar successfully evade the government for an extended period. Despite the large rewards offered and news of Escobar's use of violence, torture, and assassination to secure his goals, Escobar retained the support of the poor. This he did by enriching the poor with a small fraction of his own drug-based wealth. For example, he had built homes for more than two hundred poor families in a section named 'Barrio Pablo Escobar'. Escobar even told his brother he felt like a modern version of Robin Hood. When, eventually, he was gunned down by a Colombian elite squad, thousands of young, poor mourners gathered around Escobar's coffin while the rest of Colombia celebrated.

As Hobsbawm notes, banditry is a pre-political phenomenon in the sense that it does not lead to a stable political structure, nor does it contest power within stable political institutions (such as Parliament). Banditry is not about political parties and platforms. Once the bandit dies, his rebellion is over, unless followers maintain the effort.

Revolutionary communities

In modern times, political protest movements are more likely to orient themselves to forming parties and contesting power through institutionalized channels. However, in their early stages, political protest movements are often small, unstable, and cliquish.

Canadian sociologist Roger O'Toole (1977) wrote an important study of the subculture of a small revolutionary group or sect in Canada. In his book *The Precipitous Path* he discusses the characteristics of the League for Socialist Action (LSA). The LSA was, in the 1960s, a revolutionary organization that claimed leadership of the Canadian working class and the Canadian revolution it anticipated. It accepted the basic Trotskyite view of the need for world revolution. Group members viewed reformist social democrats and trade-union bureaucrats as enemies propping up a capitalist social system that Trotsky had diagnosed 30 years earlier as being in its death agony.

It promoted and strengthened these views by recruiting members and maintaining group cohesion. Besides its regular public forums, the LSA held meetings, showed films, and had social gatherings. The LSA youth also held gatherings, talks, parties, and poetry readings. In addition to other social activities the LSA members engaged in a very full social life. 'It is obvious . . . this social life is very deliberately placed in a definite contra cultural political context. Though the members are revolutionaries,

> debate is generally good-humored, little open hostility is manifested, and Robert's rules of Order prevail . . . the meeting is not unlike a meeting of a mainstream political party or voluntary association. . . . Nonetheless, even a cursory analysis reveals a high level of violent content in the speeches and discussions, a heavy conspiratorial style of political analysis which uncovers hidden meaning. . . . It reveals the insidious attempts of the capitalists to destroy their enemies by buying-off important people in the working-class movement and stresses the problem of apostasy and treason (O'Toole, 1977).

The group leadership invited members to work as a moral and intellectual elite operating in semi-secrecy. Recruitment was the bestowal of a high honour, and the individual decision to join was seen as a voluntary act of total commitment for life to the LSA cause and organization. LSA membership increased dramatically in the 1960s from the combination of Canadian youth radicalization and French-Canadian nationalism in Quebec, and the

lowering of barriers to membership. Moreover, the leadership involved its members in group activities to ensure that they remained 'uncontaminated' by capitalist propaganda.

It had what Raymond Breton (1964) has, in the context of ethnic communities, called 'institutional completeness'. Stable revolutionary communities or cells communities satisfy human needs for interaction and support. Second, they tend to produce new roles, rules, and cultural values. Third, through the establishment of a wide range of services and activities, they make it possible to live without having much, if any, contact with the 'outside world'.

Guerilla communities

Guerillas are soldiers in an irregular or undeclared war—usually a civil war. They too form communities for mutual support. Guerillas and terrorist groups share some perspectives, such as surprise tactics; both have the tendency to discredit the government through successful attacks. Often, terrorists have kept their numbers small to preserve secrecy, or have alienated large numbers of the public through indiscriminately violent means—for example, the bombing of subways in Madrid, which claimed nearly 200 civilian lives in 2004. Terrorist groups can work with fewer members and a smaller skill than the guerilla forces.

Guerilla groups try to maintain control and influence in the community. This means they have to work more openly than terrorists and use more focused methods of violence. They also use propaganda tactics and persuasion to hold control; only if that does not work do they use threats and terrorism. According to Mao, there are five components to a successful guerilla movement: mass support, party organization, military organization, favourable terrain, and economic strength.

The Khmer Rouge is a case in point. The Cambodian Khmer Rouge's main goal was to bring about an egalitarian society and a glorification of peasant life. This it did by mass deportations and mass murders in 'the killing fields'.

Box 9.3 The Killing Continues

WASHINGTON–Five weeks after Secretary of State Colin L. Powell described the killings in Sudan as 'genocide', the slaughter continues unabated. Sudan's government, which is responsible for these crimes in the vast western province of Darfur, still sends its soldiers to attack civilians and has not reined in its murderous allies in the Janjaweed militia. On Oct. 4 UN Secretary General Kofi Annan declared that Sudan had made no progress in halting the killing and no progress in prosecuting killers either. A week later a UN official reported that 220,000 people had been driven from their homes over the past month, swelling the number of displaced people to something near 2 million.

The displaced people of Darfur have lost crops, livestock and tens of thousands of loved ones. Some subsist on berries in the countryside; the rest huddle in dirty camps, where between 6,000 and 10,000 people die monthly for lack of food, medicine and sanitation. The camps are encircled by the militia death squads, making them prisons without walls. Men who venture out are sometimes killed; women risk rape on their daily search for firewood. Nobody knows how many people have died so far, but the commonly cited number of 50,000 is certainly too low. The World Health Organization reported on Friday that 70,000 have died since March in the camps to which aid workers have access. That leaves out most deaths from malnutrition outside those camps, as well as most violent deaths. Eric Reeves, an independent Sudan watcher who has analyzed family death rates reported by displaced people, puts the total death count at 300,000.

In Rwanda's genocide 10 years ago, the West pretended it could not see what was at stake until after 800,000 had been massacred. In Sudan's slow-motion catastrophe, involving death by starvation as much as death by violence, the West has acknowledged what is going on yet refuses to respond with any urgency. Food has been trucked and airlifted to the camps for displaced people, but roughly a third of those in need still go hungry. A series of diplomatic efforts to rein in the violence has progressed at a snail's pace. The United Nations has passed two resolutions calling upon Sudan's government to end the killing, but neither involved credible threats of sanctions. British Prime Minister Tony Blair visited Sudan this month, but it isn't yet clear that the fresh promises he extracted from the government are worth more than previous ones.

Terrorist communities

Terrorists are often motivated by a political or social cause, such as the promotion of an ideology, a struggle for the freedom of religious expression, or the desire to overthrow what is perceived to be an oppressive government or authoritative body. Terrorism is best viewed as a 'poor man's war', a war that is evidently fought by new rules. Most generally, *terrorism* can be defined as any act employing the unpredictable use of force by an individual or by a group that is intended to undermine the legitimate authority of a government or state.

The roots of terrorism can be found in the religious, ethnic, nationalist, political, economic, and social differences that prevent people from living together in peace. A rational cost-benefit analysis—not reckless impulse—leads them to this conclusion, often in view of various frustrating or limiting social, political, economic, and personal conditions. Hudson and den Boer (2001) report that terrorists are primarily men with a higher-than-average education from middle- to upper-class backgrounds, with specific skills and strong political motivation. Increasingly, terrorist organizations in the developing world recruit younger members. Often the only role models these young people have to identify with are terrorists and guerrillas.

Experts generally view terrorism as only a different form of soldiering, with the usual motives: to protect home and country. Jeffrey Simon writes, '[W]hat limited data we have on individual terrorists suggests that the outstanding common characteristic is normality' (2001: 338). As in the formation of social movements, the formation of terrorist groups relies on social networks to recruit members. Because terrorist activities are generally organized and carried out in secret, social networks are important as a source of social control over the recruits, in order to ensure their trustworthiness (see, e.g., Erickson [1983] on secret organizations).

State-sponsored terrorism is the state-sanctioned use of terrorist groups to facilitate foreign-policy objectives. In the eyes of the current US government, there are currently seven countries on the 'terrorism list': Cuba, Iran, Iraq, Libya, North Korea, Sudan, and Syria (US Department of State, 2001). Of the seven countries, five are Middle Eastern or other Islamic nations with mainly Muslim populations. Other governments might compile other lists. In the eyes of some, the United States itself might be viewed as a state that sponsors terrorism, to destabilize foreign governments and undermine progressive political movements.

In certain areas, state sponsorship remains an important driving force behind terrorism. The irony of state-sponsored terrorism is that while it can be a powerful form of terrorism—given the resources and expertise that governments pass on— it can be vulnerable to shifts in the international political arena. On various occasions, Third World rebel groups, like various governments, have found themselves suddenly deprived of support from the foreign sponsors that they had relied on. A variety of religious fundamentalists, including the Taliban and even Osama bin Laden, received support from the United States and its allies in an effort to undermine the Russians, only to be dropped and vilified later when they turned on the United States.

Because conventional wars are fought for territory, gains and losses are easily measured on a map. However, terrorism and wars against terrorism cover many domains other than the geographic. Issues of safety, security, and certainty are central, for example. Improved technologies help but they are not absolute guarantees against future terrorist attacks or criminal sabotage.

Terrorist tactics will continue to improve as long as detection techniques improve and as long as new weapons of destruction are perfected. But even low technology is sufficient for terrorist purposes. The suicide bombers are low technology: just one person and a homemade bomb. Also, note that on 11 September 2001, the terrorists used low-tech weapons to take over the planes, which they then used as high-tech weapons. It takes very little imagination to see how dedicated terrorists might easily and calamitously bring about mass death by infiltrating a city's water or subway system, the ventilation system in a skyscraper, or a country's food distribution system.

Without understanding terrorists' motives and winning over their supporters, no war against terrorism can succeed. Preventing future attacks will mean considering the historical, political, economic, and other factors that lead normal humans to see mass terror as legitimate and death by martyrdom as appealing.

Social Consequences of Wars and Political Crimes

Wars come at enormous economic costs, not least because of military spending. Currently, the US is spending $1 billion per day on military efforts. A very much larger sum is spent every day, if we add up all the spending by all the world's countries. The vast expenditures devoted to developing and maintaining the world's military forces take away from each nation's resources for other social programs. The (estimated) trillion dollars spent annually by the world's leaders on national defence could just as easily be spent instead on reforesting the planet, increasing energy efficiency, protecting croplands from soil erosion, feeding and educating the world's poor, and developing environmentally friendly, renewable sources of energy (Renner, 1993a; 1993b).

Beyond the dollars spent on strictly military needs, trillions more are wasted every year on repairing the physical damage to buildings and infrastructure (e.g., roads, bridges, public transit, hospitals, and waterways) and the environmental destruction caused by war and terrorism. Property damage incurred during the Second World War, for example, is estimated to be in the neighbourhood of $260 billion. The damage caused by the terrorist bombings of the World Trade Center in New York City and the Alfred P. Murrah Federal Building in Oklahoma City each cost the United States government and private companies $500 million to repair.

Wars can also destroy the cultural heritage of a nation or region. For example, during the civil war in Afghanistan, the Taliban destroyed a Kabul museum that was one of the richest and most famous in the world. In addition to the tremendous economic toll that war and conflict has on society, another consequence is purely human. For many people, morale is shattered by the effects of hostile combat. Although countries or groups that win the war may enjoy a general improvement in spirits, many people will experience the war as a gruelling and haunting experience.

For instance, many Vietnam veterans returned to the United States disillusioned, unable to understand their purpose in the conflict, and the lack of sympathy from fellow Americans upon their return. War affects not only those who fought in them, but also civilians—even those who are sheltered from the physical horrors of combat.

Social consequences of revolution

Use of the term 'revolution' seems appropriate when it refers to changes that have major and often unanticipated consequences. Most revolutions cause dramatic changes in the way people live, both for the better and the worse. Revolutions reveal internal cleavages between those who support and those who oppose the new order. There will always be people that oppose political change: not all people are revolutionaries and not everyone disagrees with the existing government. This cleavage can cause further conflict in the society.

After some revolutions, the general population suffers from a new government's lack of attention to domestic problems. Almost every revolution is followed by a period of famine, poverty, deprivation, class conflict, and even greater unrest among the general public. As American political activist Florence Kennedy once said, 'Oppressed people are frequently oppressive when first liberated. . . .

Somebody's foot on their neck or their foot on somebody's neck' (Peter, 1977).

Consequences of political violence

Political actions often involve a degree of violence. This is truer for rebellions and revolutions than for conventional political protest in the contemporary era.

Political violence differs from other kinds of violence, in that representatives of one political or national group inflict it to perpetuate or change the relative political status of another political or national group, or to prevent that group from achieving the changes its members desire (Kanaaneh and Netland, 1992). Rationalizations are commonly devised to explain away the extent of violence, its effects, or its lack of fairness. Rationalizations may even make the slaughtering of soldiers an acceptable cost of war but the slaughtering of civilians a criminal horror; these distinctions are socially and politically, if not morally, meaningful.

The process of rationalization begins by distinguishing between 'us' and 'them', the people and 'the other'. A group defined as outsiders or strangers is easily vilified and attacked—easily viewed as a means to an end, or fully expendable. The most horrific aspect of this process is *genocide*, the systematic and planned execution of an entire national, ethnic, racial, or political group. The most infamous case of genocide was the attempted extermination of Jews and Gypsies by Nazi Germany during World War II. Many others were also murdered at this time, because of their race and because of perceived physical and mental weaknesses. In all, 6 million Jews were killed, many in concentration camps like Auschwitz, where an estimated one million died.

Though many vowed after 1945 that this would never happen again, genocide has happened repeatedly since then, in the former Yugoslavia and in Rwanda, to name the most notorious cases. However, the world now has procedures for dealing with genocidal war criminals. Slobodan Milosevic, for example, was extradited to the War Crimes Tribunal in The Hague and formally indicted with charges of committing genocidal war crimes against ethnic Albanians. Milosevic is the first head of state in history to face international war crimes charges. (Hitler killed himself in Berlin before he could be tried.)

Issues involving war crimes fall into at least four categories: assigning responsibility for criminal acts; trying and punishing the criminals; bringing about national reconciliation; and ensuring that a nation remembers its criminal past and learns from it. Stefani (2002) notes that the International Criminal Court, which opened for business on 1 July 2002 upon the ratification of the Treaty of Rome, establishes a permanent, international, criminal court for the prosecution of war crimes and crimes against humanity.

However, the calls for international war crime tribunals are sporadic, due to tensions between selfishness and idealism within liberal states. Moreover, the war crimes tribunals are physically unable to process hundreds of thousands of trials. However, these tribunals are superior to acts of vengeance by the aggrieved parties. Right actions following wrongdoing, such as changing institutions, reparations, or giving apologies, may help to bring about healing and peace (Bass, 2002).

This is well and good at the level of grand principles. On the ground, it may be more difficult to reorganize people's lives after a genocidal episode. Babic (2002) discusses the return of war migrants to their homes in the former Yugoslavia, with an emphasis on the problem of social interaction between different ethnic, immigrant, and native groups in Brodsko-Posavska County. He studied 180 war migrants, including returnee Croats, returnee Serbs, and refugees-immigrants. He found that the co-existence of the antagonistic Croats and Serbs remains a problem, both for groups of war migrants in local communities and for the state of Croatia. The returnees are burdened with memories of the recent war conflicts, human and material losses, and issues of forgiveness and compromise. Ironically, all three groups confirm that, *before* the war, all three groups valued peaceful co-existence. The groups today differ in their perception of who is responsible for the war.

At a recent Toronto conference on war, Aersi Aafi from Somalia and Pradeepa Kandasamy from Sri Lanka spoke about the way war affects children and their later adjustment to life in Canada. Children who experience war first-hand continue to suffer psychological trauma even when the war is far away in time and space. For instance, Aafi is often afraid of authority figures—including his Canadian teachers— as a result of his past experiences with authority figures in Somalia. Because of PTSD symptoms like these, victims of war tend to further isolate themselves from normal Canadian life (Eglinton, 2005).

In Cambodia, another society racked by political violence, a series of public forums was organized in 1999 by the Center for Social Development to address the attitudes of the Cambodian people toward the prosecution of surviving Khmer Rouge leaders who were involved in the tyrannical 1975–9 regime (Vannath, 2003). Many who had suffered under the Khmer Rouge sought revenge while many former Khmer Rouge leaders believed they had participated in the just cause of liberating Cambodia's poor masses. A questionnaire completed by Cambodians indicated strong support for the trial of former Khmer Rouge leaders as war criminals, and 82 per cent felt a trial would help bring about national reconciliation.

National self-examination has been a continuing problem after wars and war crimes, but nations approach their history in different ways. The Federal Republic of Germany, for example, was slow to acknowledge its role in the Holocaust. While the interpretation remained basically the same throughout the existence of the German Democratic Republic (1949–90), the main focus in the Federal Republic of Germany changed several times. At first, textbooks to a certain extent maintained Nazi positions (in accordance with conservative nationalist policy) on many questions of national interest,

engagement, and expansion. Gradually, authors changed their underlying theories about National Socialism. The theory of 'totalitarianism', that is, of Communism and National Socialism as hostile twin brothers, was officially promoted in West Germany. There, the placing of the Nazi period (and crimes) in the continuity of German history and society was not seriously discussed before the 1980s.

For all victims and analysts of political violence, the Nazi Holocaust remains the benchmark against which all other crimes against humanity are judged. On the one hand, the Holocaust example likely speeded the development of a 'war crimes' concept, culminating in the International War Crimes court in The Hague.

Environmental destruction

War not only results in loss of human life, but causes extensive environmental damage—intentional and unintentional—as well. During the Gulf War, Saddam Hussein, for example, ordered the release of an estimated 11 million barrels of oil into Arabian Gulf, irreparably damaging the local marine life. The wanton pollution created by the Iraqi army was expected to affect crop yields in countries as far away as India (Sivard, 1991).

Military operations also harm the environment in peacetime. According to Calhoun (1996: 60), the United States military is the largest producer of hazardous materials of the country, and that 'decades of improper and unsafe handling, storage and disposal of hazardous materials while building and maintaining the world's most powerful fighting force have severely polluted America's air, water and soil.'

Landmines remain a serious cause of death and injury even long after wars have ended. According to the International Committee of the Red Cross, landmines kill or maim between 1,000 and 2,000 people in the world each month, with another 100 million landmines still lying undetected. Most of the victims are civilians in peacetime (cited in 'The Environmental Impacts of War', 1999).

Health Consequences of Terrorism and War

War invariably results in that most immediate and final of health consequences—death. Military conflicts in the twentieth century have resulted in the deaths of over 100 million soldiers and civilians—more than the total number of casualties in all previous wars in human history combined (Porter, 1994). Other approximations vary according to whether deaths stemming from war-related famine and disease are included.

Renner (1993b) calculates that 75 per cent of all military deaths since the reign of Julius Caesar have taken place in the 1900s. In part that is due to the large population today: 90 per cent of all the people who ever lived were alive in the twentieth century. However, one cannot deny the century's unique technological and organizational capabilities for war-making. The rapid rise in humanity's capacity for killing is clear from a comparison of the World Wars. The First World War claimed the lives of 8 million soldiers and 1 million civilians. Loss of life was far greater in the Second World War. The two atomic bombs dropped on Hiroshima and Nagasaki in the final stages of the war killed 250,000 Japanese civilians. In all, 17 million combatants and 35 million civilians were killed during the Second World War.

Technology is not to blame for the high death toll. People, not machines, make war. After all, in the civil war in Rwanda a decade ago, over 800,000 people died within a three-month period. Most were killed by machetes—broad swords—not guns (Gibbs, 1994). However, advanced military technology increases the likelihood that a high death toll will result, and here, we are far beyond what machetes could possibly accomplish. Currently, the nuclear weapons in major military arsenals are over 4,000 times as powerful as the atomic bombs dropped on Japan. Friedman and Friedman (1996) estimate that a nuclear war today would kill 160 million instantly. Exposure to war also increases the risk of health problems and lowers life expectancy.

One study of Second World War veterans who either remained in the United States or served overseas found that combat experience predicted physical decline or death in the 15 years after the war, even after self-reported physical health and birth cohort were controlled. Military rank and theatre of engagement with the enemy had no effect on the trend (Elder et al., 1997).

Just as death is an unavoidable consequence of war, so too are physical and psychological injuries. In general, the number of military personnel and civilians who are injured or maimed during a war exceeds the number of deaths. Part of common military strategy is to maim rather than kill the enemy, since it requires more resources for them to care for their wounded than to discard their bodies. Cambodia has been called the 'land of the one-legged men', referring to the more than 30,000 individuals—mostly rural citizen farmers—who have had limbs amputated as a result of accidentally detonating a concealed mine (Stover and McGrath, 1992).

Surviving a war physically unscathed does not guarantee complete well-being. Many veterans of war suffer the much slower torture of psychological disorders. Much of the mental health literature on the effects of war has focused on post-traumatic stress disorder (PTSD), which had previously been studied under names like 'shell shock', 'concentration camp syndrome', 'survivor syndrome', and 'war neurosis' (Summerfield, 2000). Although initially considered by military officers as an expression of cowardice, PTSD is now recognized as a legitimate form of psychological distress produced by a traumatic experience, be it crime victimization, sexual assault, or military combat.

Witteman (1991) estimates that 479,000 of the 3.5 million veterans of the Vietnam War suffer from severe PTSD, while another 350,000 have moderate symptoms. Andre Picard (1995) observed that many Canadian soldiers returning from Rwanda, Yugoslavia, and other war-torn regions were 'haunted by scenes of ethnic cleansing: fetuses cut from the womb, young girls who were gang-raped then set ablaze, entire churches full of people hacked to death with machetes' and most distressingly, by their inability as peacekeepers to intervene in the suffering around them (cited in Mooney, 2001: 505).

Civilians are also vulnerable to PTSD and other forms of war-related mental ill health. However, only within the past several decades have civilian responses to military conflict been the object of close scientific scrutiny. Examining the effects of the Lebanese war on citizens, Yaktin and Labban (1992) found that a traumatic war experience was a risk factor for the development of schizophrenia. During the 12 years of the war, schizophrenia diagnoses and admissions in the country increased substantially, particularly in the periods immediately following intense bouts of fighting. Another study of the conflict revealed that malingering and General Anxiety Disorder (GAD) decreased in the general population during the years of combat, but drug abuse, neuroses, and psychotic reactions such as anti-social personality disorders increased overall (Baddoura, 1990).

Not even children are safe from the brutal effects of political violence. Walton and colleagues (1997) found that children born into the Salvadoran civil war suffered psychological consequences, with those who experienced the highest personal-social impact of the conflict showing the poorest mental health. Higher socioeconomic status and parental education were associated with better psychological well-being. Intelligence, in turn, was directly linked to surviving with strong mental health.

Due to its unexpected, severe, and occasionally random nature, and because its targets are most often unsuspecting civilians who are sheltered from large-scale violence, terrorism is particularly likely to cause psychological trauma in its victims. The Oklahoma City bombing by domestic terrorist Timothy McVeigh was a shocking experience for all Americans, but particularly for survivors of the blast and for the family and friends of survivors

and victims. Risk factors for the development of psychological dysfunction include a prewar history of mental instability, as well as the effects of war on family, social, and economic statuses.

Even worse is political violence inflicted by the governmental authorities. 'When the police force of a governing political authority shoots randomly into a group of demonstrating opponents to warn dissidents and strike fear into potential demonstrators, that is political violence or terrorism' (Held, 1997). The rationale behind governmental violence is to show future activists that political protest will not be tolerated.

In Canada, such incidents are rare and officials are expected to maintain the safety of any political protests. Freedom of speech and expression allows people to demonstrate in front of Queen's Park as long as they do so in an organized and peaceful fashion.

Concluding Words

Criminalizing protest is one method that states use to keep the ruling class in power and control the extent of protest. Criminalizing excessive violence in warfare is one method that states use to reduce the number of civilian casualties. In neither case does criminalization work well to limit violence once warring passions are inflamed.

In this chapter we have discussed protests, rebellions, revolutions, and wars, and the crimes associated with them. In countries such as Canada and the United States, political conflict is seen in two forms: through institutionalized participation, which involves public polls and voting; and political protest, which involves demonstrations and rallies about numerous issues on the political agenda.

Canadians are fortunate in witnessing relatively little political violence—indeed, political crime. Many would argue that this is because of the fact that we have become democratic, and in democratic countries, political participation is typically non-violent. By contrast, there are still many countries in the world that are not democratic, where violent

Box 9.4 Seeing the Face of Evil

Anyone who has looked at a newspaper lately or watched the nightly news on TV will have seen some of the images of hostages in Beslan, Russia. Those images have been both heartbreaking and deeply disturbing. Which is precisely why the media had a duty to show them.

The Beslan video shows children, some with their hands clasped behind their heads, their eyes wide with fear. Masked terrorists fiddle with bombs and wires. There are streaks of blood on the wood floor. At least 335 of these hostages would later die, some shot in the back as they tried to run to freedom.

The video is certainly disturbing, as the terrorists intended it to be. But governments of all countries make decisions on behalf of their citizens about how to respond to terrorism. So citizens should have some idea of what terrorism looks like. They may decide to hide their eyes, or to steel themselves and watch, no matter how difficult it is to look evil in the face.

Terrorists are using the global media as a platform. But that doesn't mean all images of terrorism should be consigned to a vault where only news editors can see them. The truth, however unpleasant, belongs to everyone. Unfortunately, sadistic souvenirs have become part of modern terrorism. North American news outlets have not aired the most gruesome parts of hostage videos coming from Iraq, but they have shown excerpts from those videos. And anyone wanting to see more has been able to do that via the Internet.

That is why governments should not censor images. The US government's attempts to ban news coverage of the return of coffins carrying the remains of military personnel killed in Iraq was rightly condemned by supporters and opponents of the war alike. This wasn't because of some morbid delight in watching flag-draped coffins being unloaded from the belly of a transport plane, but because death is a fact of war, and no government should be allowed to censor facts.

News organizations will continue to use restraint when deciding whether to place the most gruesome images in full public view. But in the Internet age, it is pointless to suppress information. It would also be a disservice to the world's people, who have not only a right to know the truth, but a responsibility to face it.

SOURCE: Excerpt, *Ottawa Citizen*, Ottawa, 13 September 2004, A14.

political participation is ongoing and political crimes are common.

Summary

Protest, rebellion, and war are varying means of conducting political conflict, along a spectrum from peaceful to violent. Civil wars and acts of terrorism are smaller-scale versions of the same thing. So, by understanding war—its causes and consequences—we can understand more about protest, rebellion, and other forms of deviant, disorderly political conflict.

Table 9.3 Fifteen Most Lethal Regimes

Regimes[1]	Regime[2]			Annual rate[3] %	Domestic democide ('000)	Population[4] ('000)
	Years	Duration	Type			
Cambodia (Khmer Rouge)	1975-9	3.83	Communist	8.1605	2,000	6,399
Turkey (Ataturk)	1919-23	4.08	Authoritarian	2.6358	703	6,500
Yugoslavia (Croatia)	1941-5	4.17	Authoritarian	2.5132	655	6,250
Poland (Post War II)	1945-8	3.33	Authoritarian	1.9893	1,585	23,930
Turkey (Young Turks)	1909-18	9.17	Authoritarian	0.9553	1,752	20,000
Czechoslovakia (Post War II)	1945-8	2.83	Authoritarian	0.5390	197	12,913
Mexico	1900-20	21.00	Authoritarian	0.4497	1,417	15,000
USSR	1917-87	71.00	Communist	0.4224	54,789	184,750
Cambodia (Samrin)	1979-87	8.92	Communist	0.3976	230	6,478
Uganda (Amin)	1971-9	6.33	Authoritarian	0.3118	300	11,550
Angola	1975-87	12.17	Communist	0.3021	125	3,400
Rumania (Carol/Michael)	1938-48	10.08	Authoritarian	0.2949	484	16,271
Korea, North	1948-87	39.33	Communist	0.2502	1,293	13,140
Uganda (Post-Amin)	1979-87	8.75	Authoritarian	0.2038	255	14,300
Mongolia	1926-87	61.17	Communist	0.1873	100	873
World	**1900-87**	**17.46[5]**		**0.2350[5]**	**129,547[6]**	**2,325,000[7]**

1. For State regimes older than one-year and with a population of over 750,000.
2. Duration is in years.
3. Per cent of citizens killed in democide per year of the regime.
4. Mid-period population.
5. Average.
6. World total.
7. For 1944

SOURCE: R.J. Rummel, *Death by Government* (New Brunswick, NJ: Transaction Publishers, 1994). © 1994 by Transaction Publishers. Reprinted by permission of the publisher.

Protest, revolution, and terror occur where change can no longer be attained through discussion. Accordingly, groups or governments that try to prevent the expression of disagreement and conflict will often intensify them, and produce more violent forms of politicking, including protest, rebellion, and even civil war. This means they have to work more openly than terrorists and use more focused methods of violence. They also use propaganda tactics and persuasion to hold control; only if that does not work do they use threats and terrorism.

Protest, though often a response to conflict, can often cause further conflict in the society, as did the institution of the provisional government after the abdication of the Russian Tsar, following the Russian Revolution. Political violence differs from other kinds of violence, in that representatives of one political or national group inflict it to perpetuate or change the relative political status of another political or national group, or to prevent that group from achieving the changes its members desire.

Terrorism and war crimes against civilians are becoming more common. Distinctions that make the slaughtering of soldiers an acceptable cost of war but the slaughtering of civilians a crime are socially and politically, if not morally, meaningful. By universal standards, violent acts are no less reprehensible, deviant, or criminal when a state carries them out, even though states have the authority to label their acts as they wish.

Questions for Critical Thought

1. In principle, what are the checks and balances in democracies that prevent or limit corruption? Using a social paradigm of your choice, explain how corruption and democracy are related.

2. Define the notion of 'political crime' and discuss any political crime that has been perpetrated government.

3. In North America, riots and protests are not as popular forms of political expression as they are in Europe or Latin America. Brainstorm what sociological factors may influence this.

4. Merton speaks of anomie as a gap between cultural goals and the ability to achieve them. How would Merton have characterized war defectors from the United States to Canada?

5. Historically, military societies were authoritarian, hierarchically stratified, and traditional in their values. Explain why democracies such as the United States have been engaged in wars.

6. Think about the ways that the media helps to manufacture consent for war. What role, if any, has did media played in recent conflict?

7. Compare the ways that a functionalist and a feminist scholar would approach the study of war. What would they have in common?

8. How do sociologists account for the fact that many terrorists are middle- to upper-class men with a higher than average education?

9. Given the staggering social and economical costs of warfare, explain why these costs are sometimes considered legitimate and sometimes not.
10. No century has seen as much violence carried out in the name of governments as the twentieth century. In a democratizing world, with organizations like the United Nations, how can we make sense of such a century?

Recommended Reading

Chomsky, Noam. (2003), *Hegemony or Survival: America's Quest for Global Dominance*. New York: Metropolitan Books. Noam Chomsky's latest book is the first in a series that examines America's imperial tendencies. It provides an examination of how America has tried to maintain its hegemony through the use of its military.

Hobbs, Robert Carleton. (2003), *Mark Lombardi: Global Networks*. New York: Independent Curators International. When Mark Lombardi began to examine political and financial events, he was not aware of their connections. As he explored the events more deeply, he noticed that no event is independent, but that all events are connected to each other. In this book, the various networks that Mark Lombardi has drawn expose how corruption runs through networks.

Power, Samantha. (2002), *A Problem From Hell: America and the Age of Genocide*. New York: Basic Books. Samantha Power began working as a correspondent covering the Balkans in 1993. Soon thereafter, American forces withdrew as the conflict in Bosnia was labelled a civil war. At the same time, hundreds of thousands were being killed in Rwanda. Though the genocides in both nations were well documented in newspapers, Americans (and the world) failed to mobilize. Samantha Power examines America's record when it comes to preventing genocide.

Recommended Websites

Transparency International
www.transparency.org

This is the website of Transparency International, an NGO committed to providing information about global corruption. It provides links to research on corruption in business and government, as well as information on how to reduce corruption.

The World Bank
www.worldbank.org/wbi/governance/

The World Bank's governance and anti-corruption division provides information and research about global corruption. The main goal of this initiative is to alleviate poverty by eliminating corrupt practices and promoting good governance.

University of Hawaii
www.hawaii.edu/powerkills/welcome.html

This website, based at the University of Hawaii, provides resources about oppressive regimes, genocide, and democide. The website was created on the premise that democracy and peace are closely related, and promotes democracy as a means towards living in a less conflict-torn world.

References

Aaronson, Beatrice. 1999. 'Dancing Our Way Out of Class through Funk, Techno or Rave', *Peace Review*, 11 (2): 231–36.

Adams, Kimberly, Roger G. Sargent, Sharon H. Thompson, Donna Richter, Sara J. Corwin, and Thomas J. Rogan. 2000. 'A Study of Body Weight Concerns and Weight Control Practices of 4th and 7th Grade Adolescents', *Ethnicity and Health*, 5 (1): 79–94.

Adlaf, E.M., A. Paglia, and F. Ivis. 1999. 'Drug Use among Ontario Students, 1977–1999: Findings from the OSDUS', CAMH Research Document No. 5. Toronto: Centre for Addiction and Mental Health.

Adlaf, Edward M., Yola M. Zdanowicz, and Reginald G. Smart. 1996. 'Alcohol and Other Drug Use among Street-involved Youth in Toronto', *Addiction Research*, 4(1): 11–24.

Adler, Freda. 1975. *Sisters in Crime: The Rise of the New Female Criminal*. New York: McGraw-Hill.

Adler, Patricia A., and Peter Adler. 1994. 'Social Reproduction and the Corporate Other: The Institutionalization of Afterschool Activities', *Sociological Quarterly*, 35 (2): 309–28.

Adorno, T.W. et al. 1950. *The Authoritarian Personality*. New York: Harper & Brothers.

Adrian, Manuella, and Florence Kelner. 1996. 'The Need for a Woman-Centred Approach to Substance Abuse Issues', in *Women's Use of Alcohol Tobacco and Other Drugs in Canada*, ed. Manuella Adrian et al. Toronto: Addiction Research Foundation.

Agnew, Robert. 2001. 'Building on the Foundation of General Strain Theory: Specifying the Types of Strain Most Likely to Lead to Crime and Delinquency', *Journal of Research in Crime and Delinquency*, 38 (4): 319–61.

Aidoo, Magna, and Trudy Harpham. 2001. 'The Explanatory Models of Mental Health amongst Low-Income Women and Health Care Practitioners in Lusaka, Zambia', *Health Policy and Planning*, 16 (2): 206–13.

Ajzenstadt, Mimi, and Brian E. Burtch. 1990. 'Medicalization and Regulation of Alcohol and Alcoholism: The Professions and Disciplinary Measures', *International Journal of Law and Psychiatry*, 13 (1–2): 127–47.

Akpinar, Aylin. 2003. 'The Honour/Shame Complex Revisited: Violence against Women in the Migration Context', *Women's Studies International Forum*, 26 (5): 425–42.

Albanese, Jay S. 2000. 'The Causes of Organized Crime', *Journal of Contemporary Criminal Justice*, 16 (4): 409–23.

Alberta Children's Services. 2004. 'Protection of Children Involved in Prostitution (PCHIP) – Statistics'. www.child.gov.ab.ca.

Alexander, Bruce K., Gary A. Dawes, Govert F. Van de Wijngaart, Hans C. Ossebaard, and Michael D. Maraun. 1998. 'The "Temperance Mentality": A Comparison of University Students in Seven Countries', *Journal of Drug Issues*, 28 (2): 265–82.

Alexander, Jeffrey C. 2002. 'On the Social Construction of Moral Universals: The "Holocaust" from War Crime to Trauma Drama', *European Journal of Social Theory*, 5 (1): 5–85.

Alexander-Mott, L., and D.B. Lumsden. 1994. *Understanding Eating Disorders: Anorexia Nervosa, Bulimia Nervosa, and Obesity*. Washington, DC: Taylor & Francis.

Alford, C. Fred. 2000. 'What Would It Matter If Everything Foucault Said about Prison Were Wrong? Discipline and Punish after Twenty Years', *Theory and Society*, 29 (1): 125–46.

Allerston, Patricia. 2000. 'Clothing and Early Modern Venetian Society', *Continuity and Change*, 15 (3): 367–90.

Allyn, David. 1996. 'Private Acts/Public Policy: Alfred Kinsey, the American Law Institute and the Privatization of American Sexual Morality', *Journal of American Studies*, 30 (3): 405–28.

Alvarez, Gomez, and Ana Josefina. 1995. 'Antidrug Policies and the Neoliberal Project', *Estudios Latinoamericanos*, 2 (4): 71–87.

American Psychiatric Association. 1994. *Diagnostic and Statistical Manual of Mental Disorders DSM-IV-TR*, 4th edn. Washington, DC: American Psychiatric Association.

American Psychiatric Association, Work Group on Eating Disorders. 2000. 'Practice Guidelines for the Treatment of Patients with Eating Disorders', *American Journal of Psychiatry*, 157 (1 supp.): 1–9.

Amnesty International. 1995. *Human Rights are Women's Right*. New York: Amnesty International USA.

Andes, Linda. 1998. 'Growing Up Punk: Meaning and Commitment Careers in a Contemporary Youth Subculture', in *Youth Culture: Identity in a Postmodern World*, ed. Jonathon S. Epstein. Malden, MA: Blackwell.

Angenent, H., and A. de Man. 1996. *Background Factors of Juvenile Delinquency*. Pieterlen, Suisse: Peter Lang.

Anourin, Vladimir Fedorovich. 2000. 'Sexual Revolution and the Double Standard', *Sotsiologicheskie Issledovaniya*, 26 (9): 88–95.

Arens, Diana A. 1993. 'What Do the Neighbors Think Now? Community Residences on Long Island, New York', *Community Mental Health Journal*, 29 (3): 235–45.

Artemova, Olga, and Andrey V. Korotayev. 2003. 'Monopolization of Information and Female Status: A Cross-Cultural Test', *Cross-Cultural Research*, 37 (1): 81–6.

Ary, Dennis V., Lisa James, and Anthony Biglan. 1999. 'Parent-Daughter Discussions to Discourage Tobacco Use: Feasibility and Content', *Adolescence*, 34 (134): 275–82.

Ashton, C.H. 2003. 'Comparing Cannabis with Tobacco: Those Who Start Taking Cannabis Young Have the Greatest Problems', *BMJ. British Medical Journal, Clinical Research Ed.*, 19, 327(7407): 165.

Athens, Lonnie. 1992. *The Creation of Dangerous Violent Criminals*. Urbana: University of Illinois Press.

———. 1997. *Violent Criminal Acts and Actors* (Urbana: University of Illinois Press.

Atkins, Randolph Gilbert, Jr. 2000. '"No Outside Enterprises": Rational Recovery's Countermovement Challenge to the Institutionalization of the Twelve-Step Movement in American Addiction Care', dissertation, *Abstracts International, A: The Humanities and Social Sciences*, 60 (12): 4609-A.

Atkinson, Michael. 2002. 'Pretty in Ink: Conformity, Resistance, and Negotiation in Women's Tattooing', *Sex Roles*, 47 (5–6): 219–35.

Aubry, Tim D., Bruce Tefft, and Raymond F. Currie. 1995. 'Public Attitudes and Intentions Regarding Tenants of Community Mental Health Residences Who Are Neighbours', *Community Mental Health Journal, Special International Perspectives in the Care of the Severely Mentally Ill*, 31(1): 39–52.

Baba, Yoko, and D. Mark Austin. 1989. 'Neighborhood Environmental Satisfaction, Victimization, and Social Participation as Determinants of Perceived Neighborhood Safety', *Environment and Behavior*, 21 (6): 763–80.

Babic, Dragutin. 2002. 'Forgiveness and Reconciliation as a Prerequisite for Coexistence: A Process Which Has Already Begun or a Utopian Challenge? [The Case of Brodsko-Posavska County]', *Revija za Sociologiju*, 33 (3–4): 197–211.

Bachman, Jerald. 1997. *Smoking, Drinking and Drug Use in Young Adulthood*. Mahwah, NJ: Lawrence Erlbaum Associates.

Bachman, Ronet, Dillaway, Heather, and Lachs, Mark S. 1998. 'Violence against the Elderly: A Comparative Analysis of Robbery and Assault across Age and Gender Groups', *Research on Aging*, 20 (2): 183–98.

Baddoura, C. 1990. 'Mental Health and War in Lebanon', *Bulletin de l'Académie Nationale de Médecine*, 174 (5): 583–90.

Baker, Mary Holland, Barbara C. Nienstedt, Ronald S. Everett, and Richard McCleary. 1983. 'The Impact of a Crime Wave: Perceptions, Fear, and Confidence in the Police, Law and Society Review', 17 (2): 319–35.

Bamgbose, Oluyemisi. 2002. 'Teenage Prostitution and the Future of the Female Adolescent in Nigeria', *International Journal of Offender Therapy and Comparative Criminology*, 46 (5): 569–85.

Banks, Kathleen N. 1997. 'The "Homosexual Panic" Defence in Canadian Criminal Law', *Criminal Reports*, 5: 371–89.

Baron, Stephen W. 1997. 'Canadian Male Street Skinheads: Street Gang or Street Terrorists?' *La Revue Canadienne de Sociologie et d'Anthropologie/The Canadian Review of Sociology and Anthropology*, 34 (2): 125–54.

Baron, Stephen W., and Timothy Hartnagel. 1997. 'Attributions, Affect, and *Crime*: Street Youths' Reactions to Unemployment', *Criminology*, 35 (3): 409–34.

Barry, Kathleen. 1979. *Female Sexual Slavery*. Englewood Cliffs, NJ: Prentice-Hall.

Bass, David M., and Linda S. Noelker. 1987. 'The Influence of Family Caregivers on Elder's Use of In-Home Services: An Expanded Conceptual Framework', *Journal of Health and Social Behavior*, 28 (2): 184–96.

Bass, Gary Jonathon. 2002. *Stay the Hand of Vengeance: The Politics of War Crimes Tribunals*. Princeton: Princeton University Press.

Beal, Anne C., John Ausiello, and James M. Perrin. 2001. 'Social Influences on Health-Risk Behaviors among Minority Middle School Students', *Journal of Adolescent Health*, 28 (6): 474–80.

Beare, Margaret. 2002. 'Organized Corporate Criminality: Tobacco Smuggling between Canada and the US', *Crime, Law and Social Change*, 37 (3): 225–43.

Beccaria, Franca, and Allan Sande. 2003. 'Drinking Games and Rite of Life Projects: A Social Comparison of the Meaning and Functions of Young People's Use of Alcohol during the Rite of Passage to Adulthood in Italy and Norway', *Young*, 11 (2): 99–119.

Becker, Howard. 1953. 'Becoming a Marijuana User', *American Journal of Sociology*, 59: 235–42.

———. 1963. *Outsiders: Studies in the Sociology of Deviance*. New York: Free Press.

Becker, Thomas, Graham Thornicroft, Morven Leese, Paul McCrone, Sonia Johnson, Maya Albert, and David Turner. 1997. 'Social Networks and Service Use among

Representative Cases of Psychosis in South London', *British Journal of Psychiatry*, 171: 15–19.

Beedy, Dead. 2003. 'Health Canada Set to Release Users' Manual for Medical Marijuana', *Canadian Press*, 20 July.

Beitchman, Peter. 2002. 'Mental and Physical Health: The Vital Connection', NAMI-NYC. Accessed at www.naminyc-metro.org/board_vitalconnection.htm.

Beki, Cem, Kees Zeelenberg, and Kees Van Montfort. 1999. 'An Analysis of the Crime Rate in the Netherlands 1950–93', *British Journal of Criminology*, 39 (3): 401–15.

Belfanti, Carlo Marco, and Fabio Giusberti. 2000. 'Clothing and Social Inequality in Early Modern Europe: Introductory Remarks', *Continuity and Change*, 15 (3): 359–65.

Bellair, Paul. 2000. 'Informal Surveillance and Street Crime: A Complex Relationship', *Criminology*, 38 (1): 137–69.

Belyea, Michael J., and Matthew T. Zingraff. 1988. 'Fear of Crime and Residential Location', *Rural Sociology*, 53 (4): 473–86.

Bentham, Jeremy. 1995 [1787–91]. *The Panopticon Writings*, ed. Miran Bozovic. London: Verso.

Bernburg, Jon Gunnar. 2002. 'Anomie, Social Change and Crime: A Theoretical Examination of Institutional-Anomie Theory', *British Journal of Criminology*, 42 (4): 729–42.

Bernstein, Elizabeth. 2002. 'Economies of Desire: Sexual Commerce and Post-Industrial Culture', dissertation, *Abstracts International, A: The Humanities and Social Sciences*, 63 (2): 778-A.

Besserer, S., and C. Trainor. 2000. 'Criminal Victimization in Canada, 1999', Juristat, cat. no. 85-002-XIE. Ottawa: Canadian Centre for Justice Statistics.

Besserer, S., J.A. Brzozowski, D. Hendrick, S. Ogg, and C. Trainor. 2001. 'A Profile of Criminal Victimization: Results of the 1999 General Social Survey', Statistics Canada, cat. no. 85-553-XIE. Ottawa: Statistics Canada.

Bewley, B.R., and J.M. Bland. 1977. 'Academic Performance and Social Factors Related to Cigarette Smoking by Schoolchildren', *British Journal of Preventive and Social Medicine*, 31: 18–24.

Bhugra, Dinesh. 2000. 'Disturbances in Objects of Desire: Cross-Cultural Issues', *Sexual and Relationship Therapy*, 15 (1): 67–78.

———. 2002. 'Self-Concept: Psychosis and Attraction of New Religious Movements', *Mental Health, Religion and Culture*, 5 (3): 239–52.

Bisi, Simonette. 2002. 'Female Criminality and Gender Difference', *International Review of Sociology/Revue Internationale de Sociologie*, 12 (1): 23–43.

Blackman, Shane. 2004. *Chilling Out: The Cultural Politics of Substance Consumption, Youth and Drug Policy*. London: Open University Press.

Bland, R.C. 1997. 'Epidemiology of Affective Disorders: A Review', *Canadian Journal of Psychiatry*, 42: 367–77.

Blok, Anton. 1974. *The Mafia of a Sicilian Village, 1860–1960: A Study of Violent Peasant Entrepreneurs.* Oxford: Blackwell.

Blumenthal, Susan J. 1990. 'Youth Suicide: Risk factors, Assessment, and Treatment of Adolescent and Young Adult Suicidal Patients', *Psychiatric Clinics of North America*, 13 (3): 511–56.

Blumer, Herbert. 1937. *A Substantive Introduction to the Social Science.* New York: Prentice-Hall.

———. 1971. 'Social Problems as Collective Behavior', *Social Problems*, 18: 298–306.

Bodine, Ann. 2003. 'School Uniforms and Discourses on Childhood', *Childhood*, 10 (1): 43–63.

Boehnke, Klaus, and Dagmar Bergs-Winkels. 2002. 'Juvenile Delinquency under Conditions of Rapid Social Change', *Sociological Forum*, 17 (1): 57–79.

Boekhout von Solinge, Tim. 1999. 'Dutch Drug Policy in a European Context', *Journal of Drug Issues*, 29 (3): 511–28.

Bogaert, Anthony F. 2001. 'Personality, Individual Differences, and Preferences for the Sexual Media', *Archives of Sexual Behavior*, 30 (1): 29–53.

Bolen, Rebecca M., and Leah J. Lamb. 2004. 'Ambivalence in Non-Offending Guardians after Child Abuse Disclosure', *Journal of Interpersonal Violence*, 19 (2): 185–211.

Boonpala, Panudda, and June Kane. 2001. 'Child Trafficking and Action to Eliminate It', *International Labour Office International Programme on the Elimination of Child Labour (IPEC)*.

Booth, A., and W. Osgood. 1993. 'The Influence of Testosterone on Deviance', *Criminology*, 31: 93–117.

Boritch, H. 1997. 'Prostitution', in *Fallen Women: Female Crime and Criminal Justice in Canada*, ed. H. Boritch. Toronto, ON: Nelson.

Bornstein, Gary, and Zohar Gilula. 2003. 'Between-Group Communication and Conflict Resolution in Assurance and Chicken Games', *Journal of Conflict Resolution*, 47 (3): 326–39.

Bourdieu, Pierre. 1984. 'Distinction: A Social Critique of the Judgement of Taste', trans. Richard Nice. Cambridge, MA: Harvard University Press. *La distinction: Critique sociale du jugement.* Paris: Minuit, 1979.

Bourke, Joanna. 2000. 'Effeminacy, Ethnicity and the End of Trauma: The Sufferings of "Shell-Shocked" Men in Great Britain and Ireland, 1914–39', *Journal of Contemporary History*, 35 (1): 57–69.

———. 2002. 'Shell-Shock, Psychiatry and the Irish Soldier in the First World War', in *Ireland and the Great War*, ed. A. Gregory. Vancouver: UBC Press, 155–70.

Bower, Bruce. 1998. 'Women with Anorexia Face Ongoing Problems', *Science News* (18 July).

Bowers, William, and Glenn Pierce. 1980. 'Deterrence or Brutalization: What is the Effect of Executions?' *Crime and Delinquency*, 26: 453.

Box, Steven, and Chris Hale. 1983. 'Liberation and Female

Criminality in England and Wales', *British Journal of Criminology*, 23 (1): 35–49.

Boyer, Cherrie B., Jeannie M. Tschann, and Mary-Ann Shafer. 1999. 'Predictors of Risk for Sexually Transmitted Diseases in Ninth Grade Urban High School Students', *Journal of Adolescent Research*, 14 (4): 448–65.

Brener, N.D., T.R. Simon, E.G. Krug, and R. Lowry. 1999. 'Recent Trends in Violence-related Behaviors among High School Students in the United States', *Journal of the American Medical Association*, 282 (5): 440–6.

Brent, David A. 1995. 'Risk Factors for Adolescent Suicide and Suicidal Behavior: Mental and Substance Abuse Disorders, Family Environmental Factors, and Life Stress', *Suicide and Life-Threatening Behavior*, 25 (supp.): 52–63.

———, and David J. Kolko. 1990. 'The Assessment and Treatment of Children and Adolescents at Risk for Suicide' in *Suicide over the Life Cycle: Risk Factors, Assessment, and Treatment of Suicidal Patients*, ed. Susan J. Blumenthal and David J. Kupfer. Washington, DC: American Psychiatric Association.

———, Grace Moritz, Jeff Bridge, Joshua Perper, and Rebecca Canobbio. 1996. 'The Impact of Adolescent Suicide on Siblings and Parents: A Longitudinal Follow-Up', *Suicide and Life-Threatening Behavior*, 26 (3): 253–9.

Breton, Raymond. 1964. 'Institutional Completeness of Ethnic Communities and the Personal Relations of Immigrants', *American Journal of Sociology*, 70 (2): 193–205.

Britt, Chester L. 2003. 'Self-Control, Group Solidarity, and Crime: An Integrated Control Theory', in *Control Theories of Crime and Delinquency*, ed. Chester L. Britt and Michael R. Gottfredson. New Brunswick, NJ: Transaction, 161–78.

Britton, Dana M. 1990. 'Homophobia and Homosociality: An Analysis of Boundary Maintenance', *The Sociological Quarterly*, 31 (3): 423–39.

———. 1998. 'Workin' It: Women Living through Drugs and Crime'. Review of: Leon E. Pettiway. *Contemporary Sociology*, 27 (6): 647–8.

Broadwater, H. 2002. 'Reshaping the Future for Overweight Kids', *RN*, 65 (11): 36–41.

Bronstein, Phyllis, Paula Duncan, Adele D'Ari, Jean Pieniadz, Martha Fitzgerald, Craig L. Abrams, Barbara Franskowski, Oscare Franco, Connie Hunt, and Susan Y. Oh Cha. 1996. 'Family and Parenting Behaviors Predicting Middle School Adjustment: A Longitudinal Study', *Family Relations*, 45: 415–26.

Brookman, Fiona. 2003. 'Confrontational and Revenge Homicides among Men in England and Wales', *The Australian and New Zealand Journal of Criminology*, 36 (1): 34–59.

Brown, Marilyn. 2003. ''Aina under the Influence: The Criminalization of Alcohol in 19th-Century Hawai'i', *Theoretical Criminology*, 7 (1): 89–110.

Brownell, K.B., C.L. Heckerman, R.J. Westlake, S.C. Hayes, and P.M. Monti. 1978. 'The Effect of Couples Training and Partner Cooperativeness in the Behavioral Treatment of Obesity', *Behaviour Research and Therapy*, 16: 323–33.

Bruce, B., and Agras, S. 1992. 'Binge Eating in Females: A Population-based Investigation', *International Journal of Eating Disorders*, 12: 365–73.

Brunswick, Ann F. 1999. 'Structural Strain: An Ecological Paradigm for Studying African American Drug Use', *Drugs & Society*, 14 (1–2): 5–19.

Buchanan, David. 2002. 'Gendercide and Human Rights', *Journal of Genocide Research*, 4 (1): 95–108.

Bunge, V.P., and A. Levett. 1998. *Family Violence in Canada: A Statistical Profile*. Ottawa: Statistics Canada; Ministry of Industry.

Bureau of Justice Statistics. 2004. *Sourcebook of Criminal Justice Statistics*. Washington, DC: US Bureau of Justice Statistics Clearinghouse.

Burr, Vivien, and Trevor Butt. 2000. 'Psychological Distress and Postmodern Thought', in *Pathology and the Postmodern: Mental Illness as Discourse and Experience*, ed. Dwight Fee. London: Sage.

Buston, Katie, Daniel Wight, and Graham Hart. 2002. 'Inside the Sex Education Classroom: The Importance of Context in Engaging Pupils' Culture, Health, and Sexuality', 4 (3): 317–55.

Butler, Judith. 1990. *Gender Trouble: Feminism and the Subversion of Identity*. London: Routledge.

Caldwell, L.L., and N. Darling. 1999. 'Leisure Context, Parental Control, and Resistance to Peer Pressure as Predictors of Adolescent Partying and Substance Use: An Ecological Perspective', *Journal of Leisure Research*, 31: 57–77.

Calhoun, Martin L. 1996. 'Cleaning up the Military's Toxic Legacy', *USA Today*, 124: 60–4.

CAMIMH (Canadian Alliance for Mental Illness and Mental Health). 1999. 'Mental Illness in Canada'. www.cmha. ca/citizens/mental_illnessENG.pdf.

Campbell, J., C.M. Sullivan, W.D. Davidson. 1995. 'Women Who Use Domestic Violence Shelters: Changes in Depression Over Time', *Psychology of Women Quarterly*, 19: 237–55.

Canadian Global Almanac. 2000. Toronto: Wiley.

Canadian Psychiatric Association. 2001. 'Canadian Clinical Practice Guidelines for the Treatment of Depressive Disorders', *Canadian Journal of Psychiatry*, 46 (supp.).

Canadian Women's Health Network. 2002. *Child and Youth Trafficking and Prostitution in Canada*, by Kathleen O'Grady. www.cwhn.ca/resources/sex-trade.

Cancian, F.M., and J.W. Gibson. 1990. *Making War, Making Peace: The Social Foundations of Violent Conflict*. Belmont, CA: Wadsworth.

Cardenal, Carles Ariza, and Manel Nebot Adell. 2000. 'Factors Associated with Problematic Alcohol Consumption in Schoolchildren', *Journal of Adolescent Health*, 27 (6): 425–33.

Carrington, Peter J. 2001. 'Population Aging and Crime in Canada, 2000', *Canadian Journal of Criminology/Revue Canadienne de Criminologie*, 43 (3): 331–56.

Carter, J.A., L.D. McNair, W.R. Corbin, and M. Williams. 1999. 'Gender Differences Related to Heterosexual Condom Use: The Influence of Negotiation Styles', *Journal of Sex and Marital Therapy*, 25 (3): 217–25.

Castaneda, Xochitl, Victor Ortiz, Betania Allen, Cecilia Garcia, and Mauricio Hernandez-Avila. 1996. 'Sex Masks: The Double Life of Female Commercial Sex Workers in Mexico City', *Culture, Medicine and Psychiatry*, 20 (2): 229–47.

Castro, Russell A., Alan R. Lehman, and Kevin Cannon. 1996. 'Structurally Obscured Aspects of Normalization Policy in the Netherlands', Society for the Study of Social Problems.

Catansaro, Raimundo. 1989. 'Mafia', *Sotsiologicheskie Issledovaniya*, 16 (3): 99–104.

Cavan, Ruth Shonle, and Katherine H. Ranck. 1938. *The Family and the Depression: A Study of One Hundred Chicago Families*. Chicago: University of Chicago Press.

Caywood, Thomas E. 1988. 'Race, Public Assistance, and Homicides', *Sociological Imagination*, 35 (1): 5–21.

———. 1998. 'Routine Activities and Urban Homicides: A Tale of Two Cities', *Homicide Studies*, 2 (1): 64–82.

CBS News. 2003. 'Canada Will Legalize Gay Marriage'. www.cbsnews.com/stories/2003/06/18/world/main559147.shtml.

Center of Juvenile and Criminal Justice. 1995. 'How Have Homicide Rates Been Affected by California's Death Penalty', (April): 2–3.

Centers for Disease Control and Prevention. 1999. 'Increases in Unsafe Sex and Rectal Gonorrhea among Men Who Have Sex with Men–San Francisco, California, 1994–1997', *Mortality and Morbidity Weekly Report*, (29 Jan.): 45.

Cernokovich, Stephen A., and Peggy C. Giordano. 1987. 'Family Relations and Delinquency', *Criminology*, 25 (2): 295–322

Chamberlin, L.A., S.N. Sherman, A. Jain, S.W. Powers, and R.C. Whitaker. 2002. 'The Challenge of Preventing and Treating Obesity in Low-Income, Preschool Children: Perceptions of WIC Health Care Professionals', *Archives of Pediatrics and Adolescent Medicine*, 156 (7): 662–8.

Chambliss, William J. 1964. 'A Sociological Analysis of the Law of Vagrancy', *Social Problems*, 12: 67–77.

———. 1995. 'Another Lost War: The Costs and Consequences of Drug Prohibition', *Social Justice*, 22, 2 (60): 101–24.

Chan, Annie Hau-Nung. 2000. 'Fashioning Change: Nationalism, Colonialism, and Modernity in Hong Kong', *Postcolonial Studies*, 3 (3): 293–309.

Chappell, Neena L. (996. Editorial, *Canadian Journal on Aging/ La Revue Canadienne du Vieillissement*, 15 (3): 341–5.

———. 1997. 'Health Care Reform: Implications for Seniors – Introduction', *Journal of Aging Studies*, 11 (3): 171–5.

———, and Margaret Penning. 1996. 'Behavioural Problems and Distress among Caregivers of People with Dementia', *Ageing and Society*, 16 (1): 57–73.

Cheung, Yuet W., Patricia G. Erickson, and Tammy C. Landau. 1991. 'Experience of Crack Use: Findings from a Community-Based Sample in Toronto', *Journal of Drug Issues*, 21 (1): 121–40.

Chollat-Traquet, C., ed. 1992. *Women and Tobacco*. Geneva: World Health Organization.

Cingolani, Patrick. 1999. 'On Collective Intoxication in Social Thinking at the Beginning of the Century', *Raison Presente*, 132: 101–15.

City of Calgary. 2004. 'Community Standards Bylaw FAQ'. http://content.calgary.ca. Accessed 25 March 2005.

Clark, Terry Nichols, and Lipset, Seymour Martin. 1991. 'Are Social Classes Dying?' *International Sociology*, 6 (4): 397–410.

———, ———, eds. 2001. *The Breakdown of Class Politics: A Debate on Post-Industrial Stratification*. Washington, DC: Woodrow Wilson Center Press.

Clay-Warner, Jody. 2000. 'Situational Characteristics of Sexually Violent Crime'. Southern Sociological Society.

Clemente, Frank, and Michael B. Kleiman. 1977. 'Fear of Crime in the United States: A Multivariate Analysis', *Social Forces*, 56 (2): 519–31.

Clemmer, D. 1940. *The Prison Community*. Boston: Christopher Publishing.

Clinard, Marshall B., and Richard Quinney, eds. 1967. *Criminal Behavior Systems*. New York: Holt, Rinehart and Winston.

Cloward, R., and L. Ohlin. 1960. *Delinquency and Opportunity*. New York: Free Press.

Coccoli, Christine. 2003. 'Women Wasting Away: Body Image and the Media'. Southern Sociological Society.

Cochran, John K., Max L. Bromley, and Kathryn A. Branch. 2000. 'Victimization and Fear of Crime in an Entertainment District Crime "Hot Spot": A Test of Structural-Choice Theory', *American Journal of Criminal Justice*, 24 (2): 189–201.

Coene, Gily. 2001. 'An Analysis of Old and New Feminist Perspectives in the Contemporary Prostitution and Trafficking Debate', *Ethiek & Maatschappij*, 4 (2): 3–52.

Coffey, Amanda. 2002. 'The Self We Live By: Narrative Identity in a Postmodern World' (Review of: James A. Holstein and Jaber F. Gubrium. *Contemporary Sociology*, 31 (3): 294–5.

Cohen, Albert K. 1955. *Delinquent Boys: The Culture of the Gang*. Glencoe, IL: Free Press.

Cohen, D.A., T.A. Farley, S.N. Taylor, D.H. Martin, and M.A. Schuster. 2002. 'When and Where Do Youths Have Sex? The Potential Role of Adult Supervision', *Pediatrics*, 110 (6): 66.

Cohen, Lawrence E., and Marcus Felson. 1979. 'Social Change and Crime Rate Trends: A Routine Activity Approach',

American Sociological Review, 44 (4): 588–608.

———, ———. 1980. 'Human Ecology and Crime: A Routine Activity Approach', *Human Ecology*, 8 (4): 389–406.

Cohen, Ronald. 1986. 'War and War Proneness in Pre- and Postindustrial States', in *Peace and War: Cross-Cultural Perspectives*, ed. Mary LeCron Foster and Robert A. Rubinstein. New Brunswick, NJ: Transaction, 253–67.

Cohen, Stanley. 1972. *Folk Devils and Moral Panics: The Creation of the Mods and Rockers*. London: MacGibbon and Kee.

Colder, Craig R., Laurie Chassin, Eric M. Stice, and Patrick J. Curran. 1997. 'Alcohol Expectancies as Potential Mediators of Parent Alcoholism Effects on the Development of Adolescent Heavy Drinking', *Journal of Research on Adolescence*, 7 (4): 349–74.

Collins, Alan F. 1996. 'The Pathological Gambler and the Government of Gambling', *History of the Human Sciences*, 9 (3): 69–100.

Conger, Rand D., Xiaojia Ge, Glen H. Elder, Jr., Frederick O. Lorenz, and Ronald L. Simons. 1994. 'Economic Stress, Coercive Family Process, and Developmental Problems of Adolescents', *Child Development*, 65 (2): 541–61.

Cook, P.J., and J.H. Laub. 1998. 'The Unprecedented Epidemic in Youth Violence', in *Youth Violence: Crime and Justice—A Review of Research*, ed. M. Tonry and M.H. Moore, vol. 24. Chicago: University of Chicago Press, 27–64.

Cooley, Charles. 1902. *Human Nature and the Social Order*. New York: Scribner's.

———. 1909. *Social Organization: A Study of the Larger Mind*. New York: Charles Scribner's Sons.

Cooper, Sandi E. 2002. 'Peace as a Human Right: The Invasion of Women into the World of High International Politics', *Journal of Women's History*, 14 (2): 9–25.

Cote, Marguerite Michelle. 1992. 'A Painful Situation Still Crying Out for a Solution: Montreal's Street Youth', *Revue internationale d'action communautaire* 27 (67): 145–52.

Cottino, Amedeo. 1999. 'Sicilian Cultures of Violence: The Interconnections between Organized Crime and Local Society', *Crime, Law and Social Change*, 32 (2): 103–13.

Cova, Bernard. 1999. 'Tribalism: "Shared Emotion" or "Adjacent Emotion"?' *Sociétés*, 1 (63): 119–25.

Covington, C.Y., M.J. Cybulski, T.L. Davis, G.E. Duca, E.B. Farrell, M.L. Kasgorgis, C.L. Kator, and T.L. Sell. 2001. 'Kids on the Move: Preventing Obesity Among Urban Children', *The American Journal of Nursing*, 101 (3): 73–82.

Covington, Jeannette. 1997. 'The Social Construction of the Minority Drug Problem'. American Sociological Association.

———, and Ralph B. Taylor. 1991. 'Fear of Crime in Urban Residential Neighborhoods: Implications of Between- and Within-Neighborhood Sources for Current Models', *The Sociological Quarterly*, 32 (2): 231–49.

Cox, Ruth P. 1996. 'An Exploration of the Demographic and Social Correlates of Criminal Behavior among Adolescent Males', *Journal of Adolescent Health*, 19 (1): 17–24.

Cressey, Donald R. 1988. 'The Poverty of Theory in Corporate Crime Research', in *Advances in Criminological Theory*, vol. 1, ed. Michael B. Blankenship. New Brunswick, NJ: Transaction.

Criminal Intelligence Service Canada. 2002. 'Technology and Crime'. www.cisc.gc.ca.

Crisp, Arthur, Philip Sedgwick, Christine Halek, Neil Joughin, and Heather Humphrey. 1999. 'Why May Teenage Girls Persist in Smoking?' *Journal of Adolescence*, 22 (5): 657–72.

Critcher, Chas. 2000. '"Still Raving": Social Reaction to Ecstasy', *Leisure Studies*, 19 (3): 145–62.

Croll, Jillian, Dianne Neumark-Sztainer, Mary Story, and Marjorie Ireland. 2002. 'Prevalence and Risk and Protective Factors Related to Disordered Eating Behaviors among Adolescents: Relationship to Gender and Ethnicity', *Journal of Adolescent Health*, 31 (2): 166–75.

Crowe, Paul A., John Philbin, Maryse H. Richards, and Isiaah Crawford. 1998. 'Adolescent Alcohol Involvement and the Experience of Social Environments', *Journal of Research on Adolescence*, 8 (4): 403–22.

D'Augelli, Anthony R., and Mary M. Hart. 1987. 'Gay Women, Men, and Families in Rural Settings: Toward the Development of Helping Communities', *American Journal of Community Psychology*, 15 (1): 79–93.

D'Emilio, J. 1983. *Sexual Politics, Sexual Communities*. Chicago: University of Chicago Press.

Dahrendorf, Ralf. 1959. *Class and Class Conflict in Industrial Society*. Stanford, CA: Stanford University Press,.

Dalla, Rochelle L. 2001. 'Et Tú Brut? A Qualitative Analysis of Streetwalking Prostitutes' Interpersonal Support Networks', *Journal of Family Issues*, 22 (8): 1066–85.

Dauvergne, Mia, and Holly Johnson. 2001. 'Children Witnessing Family Violence', Juristat, vol. 21, no. 6. Ottawa: Canadian Centre for Justice Statistics.

Davidson, Julia O'Connell. 2002. 'The Rights and Wrongs of Prostitution', *Hypatia*, 17 (2): 84–98.

Davidson, Larry, Connie M. Nickou, Peter Lynch, Silvia Moscariello, Rajita Sinha, Jeanne Steiner, Selby Jacobs, and Michael A. Hoge. 2001. 'Beyond Babel: Establishing System-Wide Principles of Collaborative Care for Adults with Serious and Persistent Mental Illness', *Research in Social Problems and Public Policy*, 8: 17–41.

Davis, Kingsley. 1937. 'The Sociology of Prostitution', *American Sociological Review*, 2: 746–55.

———, and Wilbert Moore. 1945. 'Some Principles of Stratification', *American Sociological Review*, 10: 242–9.

Davis, Mike. 1990. *City of Quartz: Excavating the Future in Los Angeles*. New York: Verso.

———. 1992. 'Beyond *Blade Runner*: Urban Control, the Ecology of Fear', *Open Magazine*. Westfield, New Jersey.

Dawson, Deborah A. 2000. 'The Link between Family History

and Early Onset Alcoholism: Earlier Initiation of Drinking or More Rapid Development of Dependence?' *Journal of Studies on Alcohol*, 61 (5): 637–46.

De Haanm, Willem, and Jaco Vos. 2003. 'A Crying Shame: The Over-Rationalized Conception of Man in the Rational Choice Perspective', *Theoretical Criminology*, 7 (1): 29–54.

De Munck, Victor C., and Andrey Korotayev. 1999. 'Sexual Equality and Romantic Love: A Reanalysis of Rosenblatt's Study on the Function of Romantic Love', *Cross-Cultural Research*, 33 (3): 265–77.

De Silva, W.P. 1999. 'Sexual Variations', *British Medical Journal* (6 March).

De Weerd, Marga, and Bert Klandermans. 1999. 'Group Identification and Political Protest: Farmers' Protest in the Netherlands', *European Journal of Social Psychology*, 29: 1073–95.

Dell, Colleen Anne, and Roger Boe. 1998. *Female Young Offenders in Canada,* rev. edn. Correctional Service Canada, Research Branch.

Dellinger, Kirsten A., and Tracy Citeroni. 2003. 'Bodies at Work: "Doing Femininity" at a Feminist Magazine and at a Men's Pornographic Magazine'. Southern Sociological Society.

Delvaux, Therese, Francois Crabbe, Sopheap Seng, and Marie Laga. 2003. 'The Need for Family Planning and Safe Abortion Services among Women Sex Workers Seeking STI Care in Cambodia', *Reproductive Health Matters*, 11 (21): 88–95.

Demas, P., E.E. Schoenbaum, Q.A. Wills, L.S. Doll, and R.S. Klein. 1995. 'Stress, Coping, and Attitudes Toward HIV Treatment in Injecting Drug Users: A Qualitative Study', *AIDS Education and Prevention*, 7 (5): 429–42.

Department of Justice, Canada. 2004. 'PART VII DISORDERLY HOUSES, GAMING AND BETTING'. laws. justice.gc.ca/en/C-46/42271.html. Accessed 4 November 2004.

Derlega, V.J., D. Lovejoy, and B.A. Winstead. 1998. 'Personal Accounts on Disclosing and Concealing HIV-Positive Test Results: Weighing the Benefits and Risks', in *HIV and Social Interaction*, ed. V.J. Derlega and A.P. Barbee Thousand Oaks, CA: Sage, 147–64.

Derrida, Jacques. 2003. 'The Rhetoric of Drugs', in *High Culture: Reflections on Addiction and Modernity*, ed. Anna Alexander and Mark S. Roberts Albany, NY: State University of New York Press.

Dewhirst, Timothy, and Robert Sparks. 2003. 'Intertextuality, Tobacco Sponsorship of Sports, and Adolescent Male Smoking Culture', *Journal of Sport and Social Issues*, 27 (4): 372–98.

Dick, C.L., R.C. Bland, and S.C. Newman. 1994. 'Epidemiology of Psychiatric Disorder in Edmonton: Panic Disorder', *Acta Psychiatrica Scandinavica*, 376 (supp.): 45–53.

Dixon, Suzanne. 1993. '"Lousy Ingrate": Honour and Patronage

in the American Mafia and Ancient Rome', *International Journal of Moral and Social Studies*, 8 (1): 61–72.

Dixon, William J. 1994. 'Democracy and the Peaceful Settlement of International Conflict', *American Political Science Review*, 88 (March): 1–17.

Djoreva, Viara. 2001. 'Seeing beyond the Crowd. A Case Study of the Political Protests in Sofia in the Beginning of 1997', *Polish Sociological Review*, 1 (133): 99–122.

Doermann, David James. 2002. 'Sexual Perversions', *Gale Encyclopedia of Medicine*.

Donnelly, P.G. 1988. 'Individual and Neighborhood Influences on Fear of Crime', *Sociological Focus*, 22 (1): 69–85.

Doob, Anthony N., and Cheryl Marie Webster. 2003. 'Sentence Severity and Crime: Accepting the Null Hypothesis', *Crime and Justice*, 30: 143–95.

Doyle, Michael W. 1986. 'Liberalism and World Politics', *American Political Science Review*, 80: 1151–69.

Dudley, Leonard. 2000. 'The Rationality of Revolution?' *Economics of Governance* 1: 77–103.

Duhaime, Lloyd. 1996. 'Canada's Criminal Law: Stalking World Wide Legal Information Association'. Accessed 9 Nov. 2005 at http://wwlia.org/ca-stalk.htm.

Duncan, Margaret Carlisle. 1994. 'The Politics of Women's Body Images and Practices: Foucault, the Panopticon, and Shape Magazine', *Journal of Sport and Social Issues*, 18 (1): 48–65.

Dunlap, Eloise, Andrew Golub, Bruce D. Johnson, and Wesley Damaris. 2002. 'Intergenerational Transmission of Conduct Norms for Drugs, Sexual Exploitation and Violence: A Case Study', *British Journal of Criminology*, 42 (1): 1–20.

Durden-Findlay, and Sonya Rosetta. 2002. 'Teenage Mothers Becoming Sucessful Adults', dissertation, *Abstracts International, A: The Humanities and Social Sciences*, 63 (3): 1142-A.

Durkheim, Emile. 1938. *The Rules of Sociological Method*. Chicago: University of Chicago Press.

———. 1951 [1897]. *Suicide: A Study in Sociology*. Trans. J.A. Spaulding and G. Simpson. New York: Free Press.

———. 1964. *The Division of Labor in Society*. New York: Free Press.

Eating Disorder Recovery Centre. 2005. www.addictions.net/ info.htm.

Eaton, William W., Ronald C. Kessler, Hans Ulrich Wittchen, and William J. Magee. 1994. 'Panic and Panic Disorder in the United States', *American Journal of Psychiatry*, 151 (3): 413–20.

Ebbeling, C.B., D.B. Pawlak, and D.S. Ludwig. 2002. 'Childhood Obesity: Public-Health Crisis, Common Sense Cure', *The Lancet*, 360 (9331): 473–82.

Economist, The. 1995. 'A Real General Election', 23 Sept., p. 44.

Eglinton, Rick. 2005. 'Young War Refugees Face Difficulty Coping', *Metro,* 31 March, p. 3.

Elder, Glen H., Jr., Michael J. Shanahan, Elizabeth Colerick Clipp. 1997. 'Linking Combat and Physical Health: The Legacy of World War II in Men's Lives', *The American Journal of Psychiatry*, 154 (3): 330–6.

Elias, Norbert. 1980. *The Civilizing Process*, vol. 1: *The History of Manners*. New York: Pantheon.

———. 1982. *The Civilizing Process*, vol. 2: *Power and Civility*. New York: Pantheon.

Eliot, Alexandra O., and Christina Wood Baker. 2001. 'Eating-disordered Adolescent Males', *Adolescence*, 36 (143): 535–43.

Elshorst, Hansjorg. 2003. 'Transparency International: Successful without Lobbying?' *Forschungsjournal Neue Soziale Bewegungen*, 16 (3): 73–6.

Engels, Rutger C.M.E., and Tom ter Bogt. 2001. 'Influences of Risk Behaviors on the Quality of Peer Relations in Adolescence', *Journal of Youth and Adolescence*, 30 (6): 675–95.

Ennett, Susan T., Karl E. Bauman, Vangie A. Foshee, Michael Pemberton, and Katherine A. Hicks. 2001. 'Parent-Child Communication about Adolescent Tobacco and Alcohol Use: What Do Parents Say and Does It Affect Youth Behavior?' *Journal of Marriage and the Family*, 63 (1): 48–62.

'Environmental Impacts of War'. 1999. *Eco-Compass: The Internet Guide to Environmental Information*. www.islandpress.org/ecocompass/war/war.html, accessed 27 July 2001.

Epstein, Barbara. 1991. *Political Protest and Cultural Revolution: Nonviolent Direct Action in the 1970s and 1980s*. Berkeley, CA: University of California Press.

Erickson, Bonnie H. 1981. 'Secret Societies and Social Structure', *Social Forces*, 60 (1): 188–210.

Erickson, Maynard L., Jack P. Gibbs, and Gary F. Jensen. 1977. 'The Deterrence Doctrine and the Perceived Certainty of Legal Punishments', *American Sociological Review*, 42 (2): 305–17.

Erickson, Patricia G. 1992. 'Recent Trends in Canadian Drug Policy: The Decline and Resurgence of Prohibitionism', *Daedalus*, 121 (3): 239–67.

———. 1996. 'The Selective Control of Drugs' in *Social Control in Canada*, ed. B. Schissel and L. Mahood. Toronto: Oxford University Press, 59–77.

———. 1998. 'Neglected and Rejected: A Case Study of the Impact of Social Research on Canadian Drug Policy', *Canadian Journal of Sociology/Cahiers canadiens de sociologie*, 23 (2–3): 263–80.

Ericson, Richard, and Aaron Doyle. 1999. 'Globalization and the Policing of Protest: The Case of APEC 1997', *The British Journal of Sociology*, 50 (4): 589–608.

Erikson, Kai. 1966. *Wayward Puritans: A Study in the Sociology of Deviance*. New York: Macmillan.

Errante, Antoinette. 2003. 'Where in the World Do Children Learn "Bloody Revenge"?: Cults of Terror and Counter-Terror and Their Implications for Child Socialisation', *Globalisation, Societies and Education*, 1 (2): 131–52.

Evans, Angela Renee. 2001. 'The Victim Rights Movement: A Social Constructionist Examination', dissertation, *Abstracts International, A: The Humanities and Social Sciences*, 61 (8): 3359-A–3360-A.

Facy, François, Serge Brochu, and Françoise Simon. 1996. 'Therapeutic Injunction with Regard to Drug Addiction: Comparison of the French and Quebec Systems', *Criminologie*, 29 (2): 115–40.

Fagan, Jeffrey, and Deanna L. Wilkinson. 1998. 'Guns, Youth Violence, and Social Identity in Inner Cities', *Crime and Justice*, 24: 105–88.

Faggiani, Donald, and Myra G. Owens. 1999. 'Robbery of Older Adults: A Descriptive Analysis Using the National Incident-Based Reporting System', *Justice Research and Policy*, 1 (1): 97–117.

Farley, Melissa. 2004. 'Prostitution Is Sexual Violence', *Psychiatric Times: Special Edition* (Oct.).

Faulkner, Mary Ellen. 2000. 'A Case Study of the Institutional Response to Anti-Gay/Lesbian Violence in Toronto', dissertation, *Abstracts International, A: The Humanities and Social Sciences*, 60 (10): 3630-A.

Featherstone, Richard, and Mathieu Deflem. 2000. 'Anomie and Strain: Merton's Two Theories'. Presented at the annual meeting of the American Sociological Association.

Fedorowycz, Orest. 1999. 'Homicide in Canada—1998', *Juristat*, vol. 19, no. 10. Ottawa: Canadian Centre for Justice Statistics.

Ferraro, Kathleen J., and Angela M. Moe. 2003. 'Mothering, Crime, and Incarceration', *Journal of Contemporary Ethnography*, 32 (1): 9–40.

Fethers, Katherine, Caron Marks, Adrian Mindel, and Claudia S. Estcourt. 2000. 'Sexually Transmitted Infections and Risk Behaviors in Women Who Have Sex with Women', *Sexually Transmitted Infections*: 345.

Fields, Jill. 2002. 'Erotic Modesty: (Ad)dressing Female Sexuality and Propriety in Open and Closed Drawers, USA, 1800–1930', *Gender & History*, 14 (3): 492–515.

Filax, Gloria. 2003. 'Producing Homophobia in Alberta, Canada in the 1990s', *Sciences Sociales et Santé*, 21 (3): 87–120.

Finkelhor, David, and Nancy L. Asdigian. 1996. 'Risk Factors for Youth Victimization: Beyond a Lifestyles/Routine Activities Theory Approach', *Violence and Victims*, 11 (1): 3–19.

Finlay, W.M.L., S. Dinos, and E. Lyons. 2001. 'Stigma and Multiple Social Comparisons in People with Schizophrenia', *European Journal of Social Psychology*, 31 (5): 579–92.

Finn, Jerry. 1995. 'Computer-based Self-Help Groups: A New Resource to Supplement Support Groups', *Social Work with Groups. Special Support Groups: Current Perspectives on Theory and Practice*, 18 (1): 109–17.

Firminger, Kirsten B., Daphna Oyserman, Carol T. Mowbray, and Paula Allen Meares. 2000. 'Parenting among Mothers with a Serious Mental Illness', *American Journal of Orthopsychiatry*, 70 (3): 296–315.

Fischer, Benedikt, Scot Wortley, Cheryl Webster, and Maritt Kirst. 2002. 'The Socio-Legal Dynamics and Implications of "Diversion": The Case Study of the Toronto "John School" Diversion Programme for Prostitution Offenders', *Criminal Justice*, 2 (4): 385–410.

Fitzgerald, John. 2003. 'The Drug Addict in Absentia: Hidden Populations of Illicit Drug Users and the Gaze of Power', in *High Culture: Reflections on Addiction and Modernity*, ed. Anna Alexander and Mark S. Roberts. Albany, NY: State University of New York Press.

Fitzpatrick, Kevin M., Mark E. LaGory, and Ferris J. Ritchey. 1999. 'Dangerous Places: Exposure to Violence and Its Mental Health Consequences for the Homeless', *American Journal of Orthopsychiatry*, 69 (4): 438–47.

Flyghed, Janne. 2003. 'Normalising the Exceptional: The Case of Political Violence', *Policing & Society*, 13 (1): 23–41.

Forsyth, Alasdair J.M. 1996. 'Places and Patterns of Drug Use in the Scottish Dance Scene', *Addiction*, 91 (4): 511–21.

———, and Marina Barnard. 2000. 'Preferred Drinking Locations of Scottish Adolescents', *Health & Place*, 6 (2): 105–15.

Fosket, Jenifer. 2004. 'Biomedicalization: Theorizing Technoscientific Transformations of Health and Illness', in *The Sociology of Health and Illness: Critical Perspectives*, 7th edn., ed. Peter Conrad. New York: Worth.

Foucault, Michel. 1975. *Discipline and Punish: The Birth of the Prison*, trans. Alan Sheridan, 1977. New York: Pantheon Books.

———. 2005 [1961]. *Madness and Unreason: History of Madness in the Classical Age*. London: Taylor & Francis.

Freedman, D.S., G.L. Burke, D.W. Harsha, S.R. Srinivasan, J.L. Cresanta, L.S. Webber, and G.S. Berenson. 1985. 'Relationship of Changes in Obesity to Serum Lipid and Lipoprotein Changes in Childhood and Adolescence', *Journal of the American Medical Association*, 254 (4).

Freedman, David, and David Hemenway. 2000. 'Precursors of Lethal Violence: A Death Row Sample', *Social Science and Medicine*, 50 (12): 1757–70.

Freidenberg, Judith, and Muriel Hammer. 1998. 'Social Networks and Health Care: The Case of Elderly Latinos in East Harlem', *Urban Anthropology*, 27 (1): 49–85.

Friedman, George, and Meredith Friedman. 1996. *The Future of War: Power, Technology, and American World Dominance in the 21st Century*. New York: St Martin's Press.

———, Jill, M. Harkavy, Gregory M. Asnis, Marjorie Boeck, and Justine DiFiore. 1987. 'Prevalence of Specific Suicidal Behaviors in a High School Sample', *American Journal of Psychiatry*, 144 (9): 1203–6.

Friedman, Jonathan. 1990. 'The Political Economy of Elegance', *Culture & History*, 7: 101–25.

Friedrich, William N. 1979. 'Predictors of the Coping Behavior of Mothers of Handicapped Children', *Journal of Consulting & Clinical Psychology*, 47 (6): 1140–1.

Frigon, Sylvie. 2001. 'Women and Imprisonment: The Mark of the Body and Self-Mutilation', *Criminologie*, 34 (2): 31–56.

Frye V. 2001. 'Examining Homicide's Contribution to Pregnancy-Associated Deaths', *Journal of the American Medical Association*, 285 (11): 1510–11.

Fumento, Michael. 1987. 'AIDS: Are Heterosexuals at Risk?' *Commentary*, 84: 22–3.

Gable, Sarah, and Lutz, Susan. 2000. 'Nutrition Socialization Experiences of Children in the Head Start Program', *Journal of the American Dietetic Association*, 101 (5): 72–7.

Gagnon, J.H., and W. Simon, eds. 1967. *Sexual Deviance*. New York: Harper and Row.

Gaillot, Michel. 2001. 'Raves, a "Cursed Part" of Contemporary Societies', *Sociétés*, 2 (72): 45–55.

Galambos, Nancy L., and Heather A. Sears. 1998. 'Adolescents' Perceptions of Parents' Work and Adolescents' Work Values in Two-Earner Families', *Journal of Early Adolescence*, 18 (4): 397–420.

Gallin, Rita S. 1994. 'The Intersection of Class and Age: Mother-in-Law/Daughter-in-Law Relations in Rural Taiwan', *Journal of Cross-Cultural Gerontology*, 9 (2): 127–40.

Gannon, Maire. 2001. 'Comparison of Crime Rates between Canada and the United States', *Juristat*, vol. 21, no. 11, cat. no. 85-002-XPE. Ottawa: Canadian Centre for Justice Statistics.

Ganster, Daniel C., and Bart Victor. 1988. 'The Impact of Social Support on Mental and Physical Health', *The British Journal of Medical Psychology*, 61 (1): 17–36.

Garber, Judy, Stephanie Little, Ruth Hilsman, and Kristen R. Weaver. 1998. 'Family Predictors of Suicidal Symptoms in Young Adolescents', *Journal of Adolescence. Special Adolescent Suicide: Risk, Assessment, and Treatment*, 21 (4): 445–57.

Gaudette, Pamela, Bob Alexander, and Chris Branch. 1996. 'Children, Sex and Violence: Calgary's Response to Child Prostitution', *Child & Family Canada*. www.cfc-efc.ca/docs/cwlc/00000826.htm. Accessed 29 October 2004.

Gaylord, Mark S., and Graeme Lang. 1997. 'Robbery, Recession and Real Wages in Hong Kong', *Crime, Law and Social Change*, 27 (1): 49–71.

Gelles, R.J., and M.A. Straus. 1988. *Intimate Violence: The Causes and Consequences of Abuse in the American Family*. New York: Touchstone Books.

General Social Survey on Spousal Violence: A Fact Sheet. 1999. www.harbour.sfu.ca/freda/reports/gss02.htm.

Gerhard, Jane. 2000. 'Revisiting "The Myth of the Vaginal Orgasm": The Female Orgasm in American Sexual

Thought and Second Wave Feminism', *Feminist Studies*, 26 (2): 449–76.

Gibbs, J.T., and T. Bankhead. 2000. 'Joblessness and Hopelessness: The Case of African American Youth in South Central Los Angeles', *Journal of Ethnic and Cultural Diversity in Social Work*, 9: 1–20.

Gibbs, Nancy. 1994. 'Cry the Forsaken Country', *Time* (Aug.), 27–37.

Giffen, P. James, Shirley Endicott, and Sylvia Lambert. 1991. *Panic and Indifference: The Politics of Canada's Drug Laws*. Ottawa: Canadian Centre on Substance Abuse.

Gifford, Diane M. 2001. 'A Model for Analyzing the Effects of Neighborhood Characteristics on Adolescent Depression', Southern Sociological Society.

Gilbert, Leah. 1996. 'Urban Violence and Health–South Africa 1995', *Social Science and Medicine*, 43 (5): 873–86.

Gilbreth, Joan Gettert. 2001. 'Family Structure and Interparental Conflict: Effects on Adolescent Drinking', dissertation, *Abstracts International, A: The Humanities and Social Sciences*, 61 (7): 2936-A–2937-A.

Ginn, Jay, and Jane Sandell. 1997. 'Balancing Home and Employment: Stress Reported by Social Services Staff', *Work, Employment and Society*, 11 (3): 413–34.

Gittelsohn, J., K.M. Roche, C.S. Alexander, and P. Tassler. 2001. 'The Social Context of Smoking among African-American and White Adolescents in Baltimore City', *Ethnicity and Health*, 6 (3–4): 211–25.

Goffman, Erving. 1959. *The Presentation of Self in Everyday Life*. Garden City, NY: Doubleday Anchor.

———. 1961. *Asylums: Essays on the Social Situation of Mental Patients and Other Inmates*. Garden City, NY: Doubleday Anchor.

———. 1963. *Stigma: Notes on the Management of Spoiled Identity*. New York: Prentice-Hall.

Golan, M., A. Weizman, A. Apter, and M. Fainaru. 1998. 'Parents as the Exclusive Agents of Change in the Treatment of Childhood Obesity', *American Journal of Clinical Nutrition*, 67: 1130–5.

Goldstein, Joshua S. 2001. *War and Gender: How Gender Shapes the War System and Vice Versa*. New York: Cambridge University Press.

Gonzales, V., K.M. Washienko, M.R. Krone, L.I. Chapman, E.M. Arredondo, H.J. Huckeba, and A. Downer. 1999. 'Sexual and Drug-Use Risk Factors for HIV and STDs: A Comparison of Women with and without Bisexual Experiences', *American Journal of Public Health*, 89: 1846.

Goodman, C.C., and J. Pynoos. 1990. 'A Model Telephone Information and Support Program for Caregivers of Alzheimer's Victims', *The Gerontologist*, 30 (3): 399–404.

Goodman, Lisa A., Michelle P. Salyers, Kim T. Mueser, Stanley D. Rosenberg, Marvin Swartz, Susan M. Essock, Fred C. Osher, Marian I. Butterfield, and Jeffrey Swanson (Five Site Health and Risk Study Research Committee). 2001.

'Recent Victimization in Women and Men with Severe Mental Illness: Prevalence and Correlates', *Journal of Traumatic Stress*, 14 (4): 615–32.

Gordon, Robert M. 1994. 'Incarcerated Gang Members in British Columbia: A Preliminary Study', dissertation, Research and Statistics Directorate, Department of Justice, Ottawa.

———. 1995. 'Street Gangs in Vancouver', in *Canadian Delinquency*, ed. J. Creechan and R. Silverman. Toronto: Prentice-Hall.

Gorman, Elizabeth H. 2002. 'Marriage and Change in Work Attitudes and Effort'. Southern Sociological Society.

Gottfredson, Michael R., and Travis Hirschi. 1990. *A General Theory of Crime*. Stanford, CA: Stanford University Press.

Gottlieb, Benjamin H. 1985. 'Social Networks and Social Support: An Overview of Research, Practice, and Policy Implications', *Health Education Quarterly*, 12 (1): 5–22.

Gove, Walter R. 1980. 'Mental Illness and Psychiatric Treatment among Women', *Psychology of Women Quarterly*, 4 (3): 345–62.

Government of Manitoba, 2000. 'Domestic Violence and Stalking: The Cycle of Violence and How You Can Break It'. www.gov.mb.ca/justice/domestic/cycle_of_violence/.

Grabosky, Peter N. 2001. 'Virtual Criminality: Old Wine in New Bottles?' *Social & Legal Studies*, 10 (2): 243–9.

Granovetter, Mark S. 1975. 'The Strength of Weak Ties', *American Journal of Sociology*, 78 (6): 1360–80.

Grant, B.F., and D.A. Dawson. 1997. 'Age of Onset of Alcohol Use and its Association with DSM-IV Alcohol Abuse and Dependence: Results from the National Longitudinal Alcohol Epidemiological Survey', *Journal of Substance Abuse*, 9.

Gray, Alison J. 2001. 'Attitudes of the Public to Mental Health: A Church Congregation', *Mental Health, Religion and Culture*, 4 (1): 71–9.

Greaves, Lorraine. 1996. *Smoke Screen: Women's Smoking and Social Control*. Halifax: Fernwood.

———. 2003. 'Smoke Screen: The Cultural Meaning of Women's Smoking', in *High Culture: Reflections on Addiction and Modernity*, ed. Anna Alexander and Mark S. Roberts. Albany, NY: State University of New York Press.

Greenberg, David F. 1977. 'Delinquency and the Age Structure of Society', *Contemporary Crises*, 1 (2): 189–223.

Grieshaber, Susan. 1997. 'Mealtime Rituals: Power and Resistance in the Construction of Mealtime Rules', *British Journal of Sociology*, 48 (4): 649–66.

Gronfors, Martti. 1986. 'Social Control and Law in the Finnish Gypsy Community: Blood Feuding as a System of Justice', *Journal of Legal Pluralism and Unofficial Law*, 24: 101–25.

Guenther, Bruce L. 2000. 'Populism, Politics and Christianity in Western Canada', *Historical Papers: Canadian Society of*

Church History, 93–112.

Guidroz, Kathleen. 2001. 'Gender, Labor, and Sexuality in Escort and Telephone Sex Work', dissertation, *Abstracts International, A: The Humanities and Social Sciences*, 62 (6): 2252-A.

Gunnison, Elaine Kristin. 2002. 'Understanding Female Desistance from Crime: Exploring Theoretical and Empirical Relationships', dissertation, *Abstracts International, A: The Humanities and Social Sciences*, 62 (10): 3579-A–3580-A.

Guo, Jie, Ick-Joong Chung, Karl G. Hill, J. David Hawkins, Richard F. Catalano, and Robert D. Abbott. 2002. 'Developmental Relationships between Adolescent Substance Use and Risky Sexual Behavior in Young Adulthood', *Journal of Adolescent Health*, 31 (4): 354–62.

Gusfield, Joseph. 1963. *Symbolic Crusade: Status Politics and the American Temperance Movement*. Urbana: University of Illinois Press.

Gysels, Marjolein, Robert Pool, and Betty Nnalusiba. 2002. 'Women Who Sell Sex in a Ugandan Trading Town: Life Histories, Survival Strategies and Risk', *Social Science and Medicine*, 54 (2): 179–92.

Hagan, John. 2001. *Northern Passage: American Vietnam War Resistors in Canada*. Cambridge, MA: Harvard University Press.

———. 2002. 'Class and Crime in War-Time: Lessons of the American Vietnam War Resistance in Canada', *Law and Social Change*, 37 (2): 137–62.

———, and Holly Foster. 2003. 'S/He's a Rebel: Toward a Sequential Stress Theory of Delinquency and Gendered Pathways to Disadvantage in Emerging Adulthood', *Social Forces*, 82 (1): 53–86.

———, and Bill McCarthy, in collaboration with Patricia Parker and Jo-Ann Climenhage. 1997. *Mean Streets: Youth Crime and Homelessness*. New York: Cambridge University Press.

———, A.R. Gillis, and John Simpson. 1985. 'The Class Structure of Gender and Delinquency: Toward a Power-Control Theory of Common Delinquent Behavior', *American Journal of Sociology*, 90 (6): 1151–78.

———, Bill McCarthy, and Holly Foster. 2002. 'A Gendered Theory of Delinquency and Despair in the Life Course', *Acta Sociologica*, 45 (1): 37–46.

———, John Simpson, and A.R. Gillis. 1987. 'Class in the Household: A Power-Control Theory of Gender and Delinquency', *American Journal of Sociology*, 92 (4): 788–816.

Hagedorn, John M. 1997. 'Homeboys, New Jacks, and Anomie', *Journal of African American Men*, 3 (1): 7–28.

Halliday, Fred. 1999. *Revolution and World Politics: The Rise and Fall of the Sixth Great Power*. Basingstoke, UK: Macmillan.

Hammer, T., and H. Pape. 1997. 'Alcohol-related Problems in Young People: How are Such Problems Linked to Gender, Drinking Levels and Cannabis Use?' *Journal of Drug Issues*, 27 (4): 713–32.

Hannon, Lance. 1997. 'AFDC and Homicide', *Journal of Sociology and Social Welfare*, 24 (4): 125–36.

Harcourt, Bernard E. 2001. *Illusion of Order: The False Promise of Broken Windows Policing*. Cambridge, MA: Harvard University Press.

Harmann-Mahmud, Lori. 2002. 'War as Metaphor', *Peace Review*, 14 (4): 427–32.

Harper, Charles L., and Kevin T. Leicht. 2002. *Exploring Social Change: America and the World*. Upper Saddle River, NJ: Prentice Hall.

Hartley, Heather, and Tricia Drew. 2001. 'Gendered Messages in Sex Ed Films: Trends and Implications for Female Sexual Problems', *Women & Therapy*, 24 (1–2): 133–46.

Hasan, Manar. 2002. 'The Politics of Honor: Patriarchy, the State and the Murder of Women in the Name of Family Honor', *The Journal of Israeli History*, 21 (1–2) (Part 2): 1–37.

Hashima, Patricia Y., and David Finkelhor. 1999. 'Violent Victimization of Youth versus Adults in the National Crime Victimization Survey', *Journal of Interpersonal Violence*, 14 (8): 799–820.

Hathaway, Andrew D., and Patricia G. Erickson. 2003. 'Drug Reform Principles and Policy Debates: Harm Reduction, Prospects for Cannabis in Canada', *Journal of Drug Issues*, 33 (2): 465–96.

Hay, Carter. 2003. 'Family Strain, Gender, and Delinquency', *Sociological Perspectives*, 46 (1): 107–35.

Haynie, Denise L., Kenneth H. Beck, Aria Davis Crump, Teresa Shattuck, and Bruce Simons-Morton. 1999. 'Parenting Strategies Regarding Teen Behavior: Parent and Teen Perceptions', *American Journal of Health Behavior*, 23 (6): 403–14.

Health Canada. 1995. *The Effects of Tobacco Smoke and Second-Hand Smoke in the Prenatal & Postpartum Periods: A Summary of the Literature*. Booklet 3 of the Tobacco Free Booklets for Prenatal and Postpartum Providers. Ottawa: Health Canada.

———. 1999a. *Smoking Behaviour of Canadians Cycle 2, 1996/97* (Jan., No. 1). Centre for Chronic Disease Prevention and Control, Public Health Agency of Canada. www.phac-aspc.gc.ca.

———. 1999b. *Risk Behaviours Among Injection Drug Users in Canada*, Bureau of HIV/AIDS, STD and TB Update Series, Laboratory Centre for Disease Control. Ottawa: Health Canada.

———. 1999c. *HIV/AIDS Among Injection Drug Users in Canada*, Bureau of HIV/AIDS, STD and TB Update Series, Laboratory Centre for Disease Control. Ottawa: Health Canada.

———. 2001a. 'Adult Smoking in Canada', CTUMS. Canadian Tobacco Use Monitoring Survey. Annual, Feb.–Dec. 2000. www.hc-sc.gc.ca/hecs-sesc/tobacco/research/ctums/2000-

youth/youth.html.

———. 2001b. *Special Report on Youth, Piercing, Tattooing and Hepatitis C.* Toronto: Youth Culture Inc.

———. 2001c. 'Population Health.' www.hc-sc.gc.ca/english/socialmarketing/review99/pop_health.html.

———. 2002. *A Report on Mental Illnesses in Canada.* www.hc-sc.gc.ca/pphb-dgspsp/publicat/miic-mmac/.

———. 2003. 'Canada's Drug Strategy'. www.hc-sc.gc.ca/english/media/releases/2003/2003_34bk1.htm.

———. 2005a. 'Family Violence and Substance Abuse'. Information from the National Clearinghouse on Family Violence. www.hc-sc.gc.ca/hppb/familyviolence/pdfs/fvsubab.pdf.

———. 2005b. 'The Social Determinants of Health: An Overview of the Implications for Policy and the Role of the Health Sector'. www.phac-aspc.gc.ca/ph-sp/phdd/overview_implications/01_overview.html. Accessed 11 April 2005.

Held, Virginia. 1997. 'The Media and Political Violence', *Journal of Ethics*, 1 (2): 187–202.

Henderson, A., K. Bartholomew, and D.G. Dutton. 1997. 'He Loves Me; He Loves Me Not: Attachment and Separation Resolution of Abused Women', *Journal of Family Violence*, 12: 169–91.

Hennen, Peter Michael. 2003. 'Gendered Sexuality in the Age of AIDS', dissertation, *Abstracts International, A: The Humanities and Social Sciences*, 63 (8): 3009-A.

Herek, Gregory M., and Eric K. Glunt. 1993. 'Interpersonal Contact and Heterosexuals' Attitudes toward Gay Men: Results from a National Survey', *Journal of Sex Research*, 30 (3): 239–44.

Hier, Sean P. 2002. 'Raves, Risks and the Ecstacy Panic: A Case Study in the Subversive Nature of Moral Regulation', *Canadian Journal of Sociology/Cahiers canadiens de sociologie*, 27 (1): 33–57.

Higham, Philip A., and D. William Carment. 1992. 'The Rise and Fall of Politicians: The Judged Heights of Broadbent, Mulroney and Turner Before and after the 1988 Canadian Federal Election', *Canadian Journal of Behavioural Science/Revue canadienne des sciences du comportement*, 24 (3): 404–9.

Hill, Reuben. 1949. *Families: Under Stress.* New York: Harper & Row.

Hirschi, Travis. 1969. *Causes of Delinquency.* Berkeley, CA: University of California Press.

Hobsbawm, Eric J. 1959. *Primitive Rebels: Studies in Archaic Forms of Social Movement in the 19th and 20th Centuries.* New York: W.W. Norton.

Hoffman, Martin L. 1979. 'Development of Moral Thought, Feeling, and Behavior', *American Psychologist*, 34 (10): 958–66.

Hogg, R.S., S.A. Strathdee, K.J. Craib, M.V. O'Shaughnessy, J.S. Montaner, and M.T. Schechter. 1997. 'Modelling the Impact of HIV Disease on Mortality in Gay and Bisexual Men', *International Journal of Epidemiology*, 26: 657–61.

Homans, George C. 1974. *Social Behavior: Its Elementary Forms,* 2nd edn. New York: Harcourt Brace Jovanovich.

Hood-Brown, Marcia. 1998. 'Trading for a Place: Poor Women and Prostitution', *Journal of Poverty*, 2 (3): 13–33.

Hopper, Trevor, and Norman Macintosh. 1998. 'Management Accounting Numbers: Freedom or Prison-Geneen versus Foucault', in *Foucault, Management and Organization Theory: From Panopticon to Technologies of Self*, ed. Alan McKinlay and Ken Starkey. London: Sage, 126–50.

Horn, Kimberly A., Xin Gao, Geri A. Dino, and Sachin Kamal-Bahl. 2000. 'Determinants of Youth Tobacco Use in West Virginia: A Comparison of Smoking and Smokeless Tobacco Use', *American Journal of Drug and Alcohol Abuse*, 26 (1): 125–38.

Horne, John. 2002. 'Civilian Populations and Wartime Violence: Towards an Historical Analysis', *International Social Science Journal*, 54, 4 (174): 483–90.

Horwitz, Allan V. 2002. *Creating Mental Illness.* Chicago: University of Chicago Press.

Hottle, Elizabeth. 1996. 'Making Myself Understood: The Labeling Theory of Deviance Applied to Stuttering', *Virginia Social Science Journal*, 31: 78–85.

Hotton, Tina. 2001. 'Spousal Violence After Marital Separation', *Juristat*, vol. 21, no. 7. Ottawa: Canadian Centre for Justice Statistics.

House, James S., Debra Umberson, and Karl Richard Landis. 1988. 'Structures and Processes of Social Support', *Annual Review of Sociology*, 14: 293–318.

Huang, I-Chiao. 1991. 'Family Stress and Coping', in *Family Research: A Sixty-Year Review, 1930–1990*, vol. 1, ed. Stephen J. Bahr. New York: Lexington Books/Macmillan, 289–334.

Hubbard, Phil, and Teela Sanders. 2003. 'Making Space for Sex Work: Female Street Prostitution and the Production of Urban Space', *International Journal of Urban and Regional Research*, 27 (1): 75–89.

Hudak, Brian Keith. 2003. 'A Historical Analysis of Gender and Homicide'. Southern Sociological Society.

Hudson, Valerie M., and Andrea M den Boer. 2002. 'A Surplus of Men, A Deficit of Peace: Security and Sex Ratios in Asia's Largest States', *International Security*, 26 (4): 5–38.

———. 2004. *Bare Branches: Security Implications of Asias Surplus Male Population.* Cambridge, MA: MIT Press.

Huebner, Angela J., and Sherry C. Betts. 2002. 'Exploring the Utility of Social Control Theory for Youth Development: Issues of Attachment, Involvement, and Gender', *Youth and Society*, 34 (2): 123–45.

Hulick, Jessica Lee. 2003. 'A Queer Problem: Issues Facing GLBTQ Youth'. Southern Sociological Society.

Human Resources and Skills Development Canada. 2000. 'Dropping Out of High School: Definitions and Costs—October 2000'. www.hrdc-drhc.gc.ca.

Hunt, James B. 1995. 'Corporate Crime and the High-Tech

Industry: A Dangerous Brew', *Red Herring*. (Aug.) www. herring.com.

Hwang, Sunghyun. 2001. 'Substance Use in a Sample of South Korean Adolescents: A Test of Alternative Theories', dissertation, *Abstracts International, A: The Humanities and Social Sciences*, 61 (8): 3361-A.

Hyde, Pamela. 2000. 'Managing Bodies–Managing Relationships: The Popular Media and the Social Construction of Women's Bodies and Social Roles from the 1930s to the 1950s', *Journal of Sociology*, 36 (2): 157–71.

Hynie, Michaela, and John E. Lydon. 1995. 'Women's Perceptions of Female Contraceptive Behavior: Experimental Evidence of the Sexual Double Standard', *Psychology of Women Quarterly*, 19 (4): 563–81.

Ianni, Francis. 1972. *A Family Business: Kinship and Social Control in Organized Crime*. New York: Mentor Books.

———. 1974. *Black Mafia: Ethnic Succession in Organized Crime*. New York: Simon and Schuster.

Inglehart, R. 1985. *The Silent Revolution*. Princeton, NJ: Princeton University Press.

Inglis, Tom. 2001. 'Honour, Pride and Shame in Rural Ireland', *Amsterdams Sociologisch Tijdschrift*, 28 (4): 495–512.

Insurance Canada. 2003. 'IBC Releases Top Ten Canadian Insurance Frauds of 2003', newsletter. (Dec.) www.insur-ance-canada.ca/newsletter/issue2003-51.php.

Irwin, Katherine. 2001. 'Legitimating the First Tattoo: Moral Passage through Informal Interaction', *Symbolic Interaction*, 24 (1): 49–73.

Isralowitz, Richard E., and Naomi Trostler. 1996. 'Substance Use: Toward an Understanding of Its Relation to Nutrition-Related Attitudes and Behavior among Israeli High School Youth', *Journal of Adolescent Health*, 19 (3): 184–9.

Itzin, Catherine. 2001. 'Incest, Paedophilia, Pornography and Prostitution: Making Familial Males More Visible as the Abusers', *Child Abuse Review*, 10 (1): 35–48.

Iversen, Roberta Rehner, and Naomi B. Farber. 1996. 'Transmission of Family Values, Work, and Welfare among Poor Urban Black Women', *Work and Occupations*, 23 (4): 437–60.

Jacobs, P.A., M. Brunton, M.M. Melville, R.P. Brittain, and W.F. McClermont. 1965. 'Aggressive Behaviour, Mental Subnormality and the XYY Male', *Nature*, 208: 1351–2.

Jacobson, Bobbie. 1981. *The Ladykillers: Why Smoking Is a Feminist Issue*. London: Pluto.

———. 1986. *Beating the Ladykillers*. London: Pluto.

Jamieson, Alison. 2001. 'Transnational Organized Crime: A European Perspective', *Studies in Conflict and Terrorism*, 24 (5): 377–87.

Janhevich, D., M.Gannon, and N. Morisset. 2003. 'La conduite avec facultés affaiblies et autres délits de la route', *Juristat*, vol. 23, no. 9. Ottawa: Canadian Centre for Justice Statistics.

Janus, Mark David, Francis X. Archambault, Scott W. Brown, and Lesley A. Welsh. 1995. 'Physical Abuse in Canadian Runaway Adolescents', *Child Abuse and Neglect*, 19 (4): 433–47.

Jasper, James M. 1998. 'The Emotions of Protest: Affective and Reactive Emotions In and Around Social Movements', *Sociological Forum*, 13 (3).

Jensen, Gary F. 2003. 'Gender Variation in Delinquency: Self-Images, Beliefs, and Peers as Mediating Mechanisms', in *Social Learning Theory and the Explanantion of Crime: A Guide for the New Century*, ed. Ronald L. Akers and Gary F. Jensen. New Brunswick, NJ: Transaction, 151–77.

Jenson, Jeffrey M., and Matthew O. Howard, eds. 1999. *Youth Violence: Current Research and Recent Practice Innovation*. Washington DC: NASW Press.

Jeolas, Leila Sollberger, and Maria Elena Melchiades Salvadego de Souza Lima. 2002. 'Youth and Work: Between "Doing What You Like" and "Liking What You Do"', *Revista Mediacoes*, 7 (2): 35–62.

Jetten, Jolanda, Nyla R.Branscombe, Michael T. Schmitt, and Russell Spears. 2001. 'Rebels with a Cause: Group Identification as a Response to Perceived Discrimination from the Mainstream', *Personality and Social Psychology Bulletin*, 27 (9): 1204–13.

Joanisse, Leanne, and Anthony Synnott. 1999. 'Fighting Back: Reactions and Resistance to the Stigma of Obesity', in *Interpreting Weight: The Social Management of Fatness and Thinness*, ed. Jeffery Sobal and Donna Maurer. New York: Aldine de Gruyter, 49–70.

Johnson, Holly. 1996. 'Violent Crime In Canada', *Juristat*, vol. 16, no. 6. Ottawa: Canadian Centre for Justice Statistics.

Johnson, Joy L., Joan L. Bottorff, Barbara Moffat, Pamela A. Ratner, Jean A. Shoveller, Chris Y. Lovato. 2003. 'Tobacco Dependence: Adolescents' Perspectives on the Need to Smoke', *Social Science and Medicine*, 56 (7): 1481–92.

Johnson, Kevin R. 2002. 'U.S. Border Enforcement: Drugs, Migrants, and the Rule of Law', *Villanova Law Review*, 47 (4): 851–95.

Johnson, Monica Kirkpatrick. 2000. 'Job Values in the Young Adult Transition: Change and Stability with Age'. American Sociological Association.

———. 2002. 'Social Origins, Adolescent Experiences, and Work Value Trajectories during the Transition to Adulthood', *Social Forces*, 80 (4): 1307–41.

———, and Glen H. Elder, Jr. 2002. 'Educational Pathways and Work Value Trajectories', *Sociological Perspectives*, 45 (2): 113–38.

———, Timothy Beebe, Jeylan T. Mortimer, and Mark Snyder. 1998. 'Volunteerism in Adolescence: A Process Perspective', *Journal of Research on Adolescence*, 8 (3): 309–30.

Johnson, Stuart D., Lorne Gibson, and Rick Linden. 1978. 'Alcohol and Rape in Winnipeg, 1966–1975', *Journal of Studies on Alcohol*, 39 (11): 1887–94.

Johnston, George D. 1990. 'An Examination of the Psychological and Sociocultural Deterrents to Intimacy between Male Friends', dissertation, *Abstracts International*, 51(4-B): 2103.

Jones, Suzanne P., and Patrick C.L. Heaven. 1998. 'Psychosocial Correlates of Adolescent Drug-Taking Behaviour', *Journal of Adolescence*, 21 (2): 127–34.

Judd, L.L., M.P. Paulus, K.B. Wells, and M.H. Rapaport. 1996. 'Socioeconomic Burden of Subsyndromal Depressive Symptoms and Major Depression in a Sample of the General Population', *American Journal of Psychiatry*, 153: 1411–17.

Junger, Marianne, Robert West, and Reinier Timman. 2001. 'Crime and Risky Behavior in Traffic: An Example of Cross-Situational Consistency', *Journal of Research in Crime and Delinquency*, 38 (4): 439–59.

Juristat. 1997. 'Street Prostitution in Canada', Uniform Crime Reporting Survey, vol. 17, no. 2, cat. no. 85-002. Ottawa: Canadian Centre for Justice Statistics.

———. 2000. 'Homicide in Canada—2000', vol. 21 no. 9, cat. no. 85-002-XIE. Ottawa: Canadian Centre for Justice Statistics.

———. 2002. *Trends in Drug Offences and the Role of Alcohol and Drugs in Crime*, vol. 24, no. 1. Ottawa: Canadian Centre for Justice Statistics.

———. 2004a. 'Crime Statistics in Canada, 2003', vol. 24, no. 6. Ottawa: Canadian Centre for Justice Statistics.

———. 2004b. 'Les services aux victimes au Canada, 2002–2004', vol. 24, no. 11. Ottawa: Canadian Centre for Justice Statistics.

Kahne, Joseph, Jenny Nagaoka, Andrea Brown, James O'Brien, Therese Quinn, and Keith Thiede. 2001. 'Assessing After-School Programs as Contexts for Youth Development', *Youth and Society*, 32 (4): 421–46.

Kaltiala-Heino, Riittakerttu, Matti Rimpela, Aila Rissanen, and Paivi Rantanen. 2001. 'Early Puberty and Early Sexual Activity Are Associated with Bulimic-Type Eating Pathology in Middle Adolescence', *Journal of Adolescent Health*, 28 (4): 346–52.

Kanaaneh, M., and M. Netland. 1992. *Children and Political Violence: Psychological Reactions and National Identity Formation Among the Children of the Intifada*. Jerusalem: Early Childhood Resource Center.

Kann L., S.A. Kinchen, B.I. Williams, J.G. Ross, R. Lowry, J.A. Grunbaum, L.J. Kolbe, State and Local YRBSS Coodinators. 1999. 'Youth Risk Behavior Surveillance System, MMWR Surveillance Summaries'. www.cdc.gov/mmwr/preview/mmwrhtml/ss4905a1.htm.

Kaplan, Elaine Bell. 2000. 'Using Food as a Metaphor for Care: Middle-School Kids Talk about Family, School, and Class Relationships'. *Journal of Contemporary Ethnography*, 29 (4): 474–509.

Kaplan, Howard B., and Liu Xiaoru. 2000. 'Social Protest and Self-Enhancement: A Conditional Relationship', *Sociological Forum*, 15 (4).

Karp, David Allen. 1996. *Speaking of Sadness: Depression, Disconnection, and the Meanings of Illness*. London: Oxford University Press.

Karstedt, Susanne. 2001. 'Comparing Cultures, Comparing Crime: Challenges, Prospects and Problems for a Global Criminology', *Crime, Law and Social Change*, 36 (3): 285–308.

Katz, Roger C., and Joe Marquette. 1996. 'Psychosocial Characteristics of Young Violent Offenders: A Comparative Study', *Criminal Behaviour and Mental Health*, 6 (4): 339–48.

Katz, Stephen, and Barbara L. Marshall. 2004. 'Is the Functional "Normal"? Aging, Sexuality and the Bio-Marking of Successful Living', *History of the Human Sciences*, 17 (1): 53–75.

Kaukinen, Catherine. 2002. 'The Help-Seeking Decisions of Violent Crime Victims: An Examination of the Direct and Conditional Effects of Gender and the Victim-Offender Relationship', *Journal of Interpersonal Violence*, 17 (4): 432–56.

Keating, N.C., J.E. Fast, J.A. Frederick, K. Cranswick, and C. Perrier. 1999. *Eldercare in Canada: Context, Content and Consequences*. Ottawa: Statistics Canada.

———, Karen Kerr, Sharon Warren, and Michael Grace. 1994. 'Who's the Family in Family Caregiving?' *Canadian Journal on Aging*, 13 (2): 268–87.

Keenan, William J.R., ed. 2001. *Dressed to Impress: Looking the Part*. Oxford: Berg.

Keks, N., Mazumdar, P., and Shield, R. 2000. 'New Developments in Schizophrenia', *Australian Family Physician*, 29: 129–31, 135–6.

Kent, David. 1997. 'Title Decorative Bodies: The Significance of Convicts' Tattoos', *Journal of Australian Studies*, 53: 78–88.

Kerfoot, Michael, Richard Harrington, and Elizabeth Dyer. 1995. 'Brief Home-based Intervention with Young Suicide Attempters and Their Families', *Journal of Adolescence*, 18 (5): 557–68.

Keryell, Gaela. 1997. 'Finnish Drunkenness as a National Institution', *Alkoholipolitiikka*, 62 (3): 167–85.

Kesler, Kari. 2002. 'Is a Feminist Stance in Support of Prostitution Possible? An Exploration of Current Trends', *Sexualities*, 5 (2): 219–35.

Kessler, R.C., K.A. McGonagle, S. Zhao, C.B. Nelson, M. Hughes, S. Eshleman, et al. 1994. 'Lifetime and 12-Month Prevalence of DSM-III-R Psychiatric Disorders in the United States', *Archives of General Psychiatry*, 51: 8–19.

Khatapoush, Shereen Judith. 2002. 'Medical Marijuana Policy in California: Is it an Environmental Risk Factor for Youth/Young Adult Substance Use?' dissertation, *Abstracts International A: The Humanities and Social Sciences*, 63 (5): 2017-A.

Kim, Jae Yop, and Kyu-taik Sung. 2000. 'Conjugal Violence in Korean American Families: A Residue of the Cultural

Tradition', *Journal of Family Violence*, 15 (4): 331–45.

Kimerling, Rachel, Alessandra Rellini, Vanessa Kelly, Patricia L. Judson, and Lee A. Learman. 2002. 'Gender Differences in Victim and Crime Characteristics of Sexual Assaults', *Journal of Interpersonal Violence*, 17 (5): 526–32.

Kinsey, Alfred C., W.B. Pomeroy, and C.E. Martin. 1948. *Sexual Behavior in the Human Male*. Bloomington: Indiana University Press.

Kippax, Susan, and Gary Smith. 2001. 'Anal Intercourse and Power in Sex between Men', *Sexualities*, 4 (4): 413–34.

Kite, M.E., and B.E. Whitley, Jr. 1996. 'Sex Differences in Attitudes Toward Homosexual Persons, Behaviors, and Civil Rights: A Meta-analysis', *Personality and Social Psychology Bulletin*, 22: 336–53.

Klein, D.N., J.E. Schwartz, S. Rose, and J.B. Leader. 2000. 'Five-Year Course and Outcome of Dysthymic Disorder: A Prospective, Naturalistic Follow-Up Study', *American Journal of Psychiatry*, 157: 931–9.

Klein, Jessica Sharon. 2003. 'High-Profile School Shootings: How Violence Is Hidden in Masculinity Expectations', dissertation, *Abstracts International, A: The Humanities and Social Sciences*, 63 (9): 3362-A.

Klevens, Joanne, Maria Clara Bayon, and Margarita Sierra. 2000. 'Risk Factors and Context of Men Who Physically Abuse in Bogota', *Colombia Child Abuse and Neglect*, 24 (3): 323–32.

Koedt, Anne. 1970. *'The Myth of the Vaginal Orgasm', Notes from the Second Year: Women's Liberation*. New York: The New York Radical Women.

———. 1973. 'Lesbianism and Feminism', in *Radical Feminism*, ed. A. Koedt, E. Levine, and A. Rapone. New York: Quadrangle.

Koenig, Daniel J. 2000. 'Conventional Crime', in *Criminology: A Canadian Perspective*, 4th edn, ed. Rick Linden. Toronto: Harcourt Brace, 396–428.

Kolbo, Jerome R., Eleanor H. Blakely, and David Engleman. 1996. 'Children Who Witness Domestic Violence: A Review of Empirical Literature', *Journal of Interpersonal Violence*, 11 (2): 281–93.

Kong, Rebecca. 1996. 'Criminal Harassment', Juristat, vol. 16, no. 12. Ottawa: Canadian Centre for Justice Statistics.

———, Johnson, H., S. Beattie, and A. Cardillo. 2003. 'Sexual Offences in Canada, 2002', Juristat, vol. 23, no. 6, cat. no. 85-002-XPE. Ottawa: Canadian Centre for Justice Statistics.

Kordoutis, Panos S., M. Loumakou, and J.O. Sarafidou. 2000. 'Heterosexual Relationship Characteristics, Condom Use and Safe Sex Practices', *AIDS Care*, 12 (6): 767–82.

Korzybski, Alfred. 1933 [1994]. *Science and Sanity: An Introduction to Non-Aristotelian Systems and General Semantics*. Englewood Cliffs, NJ: International Non-Aristotelian Library/Institute of General Semantics.

Kosut, Mary. 2000. 'Tattoo Narratives: The Intersection of the Body, Self-Identity and Society', *Visual Sociology*, 15:

79–100.

Kovacs, Maria, David Goldston, and Constantine Gatsonis. 1993. 'Suicidal Behaviors and Childhood-Onset Depressive Disorders: A Longitudinal Investigation', *Journal of the American Academy of Child & Adolescent Psychiatry*, 32 (1): 8–20.

Kramer, Lisa A., and Ellen C. Berg. 2003. 'A Survival Analysis of Timing of Entry into Prostitution: The Differential Impact of Race, Educational Level, and Childhood/Adolescent Risk Factors', *Sociological Inquiry*, 73 (4): 511–28.

Krieg, Randall G. 2001. 'An Interdisciplinary Look at the Deinstitutionalization of the Mentally Ill', *The Social Science Journal*, 38 (3): 367–80.

Krug, E.G., N.D. Brener, L.L. Dahlberg, G.W. Ryan, and K.E. Powell. 1997. 'The Impact of an Elementary School-based Violence Prevention Program on Visits to the School Nurse', *American Journal of Preventive Medicine*, 13 (6): 459–63.

Kumpulainen, Kirsti, and Eila Rasanen. 2000. 'Children Involved in Bullying at Elementary School Age: Their Psychiatric Symptoms and Deviance in Adolescence. An Epidemiological Sample', *Child Abuse and Neglect*, 24 (12): 1567–77.

Kunz, Jean Lock, and Kathryn Graham. 1996. 'Life Course Changes in Alcohol Consumption in Leisure Activities of Men and Women', *Journal of Drug Issues*, 26 (4): 805–29.

Kwan, Alex Yui-huen. 1995. 'Elder Abuse in Hong Kong: A New Family Problem for the Old East?' *Journal of Elder Abuse and Neglect*, 6 (3–4): 65–80.

La Prairie, Carol, Louis Gliksman, Patricia G. Erickson, Ronald Wall, and Brenda Newton-Taylor. 2002. 'Drug Treatment Courts: A Viable Option for Canada? Sentencing Issues and Preliminary Findings from the Toronto Court', *Substance Use & Misuse*, 37 (12–13): 1529–66.

Laberge, Danielle, Pierre Landreville, and Daphne Morin. 2000. 'Judicial Diversion Practices for Mental Illness: The Urgence Psychosocial-Justice Model', *Criminologie*, 33 (2): 81–107.

Laborde, Cecile. 2002. 'On Republican Toleration', *Constellations*, 9 (2): 167–83.

Laghi, Brian, and Karen Howlett. 2003. 'Ottawa Cracks Down on Corporate Crime', *Globe and Mail*, 13 June.

Larsson, B., and T. Ivarsson. 1998. 'Clinical Characteristics of Adolescent Psychiatric Inpatients Who Have Attempted Suicide', *European Child & Adolescent Psychiatry*, 7 (4): 201–8.

Laskarzewski, P., J.A. Morrison, I. deGroot, K.A. Kelly, M.J. Mellies, P. Khoury, and C.J. Glueck. 1979. 'Lipid and Lipoprotein Tracking in Children', *Pediatric Research*, 13: 1082–4.

Lau, Thomas. 1995. 'Raving Society: Remarks on the Techno Scene', *Forschungsjournal Neue Soziale Bewegungen*, 8 (2): 67–75.

Lauer R.M., J. Lee, and W.R. Clarke. 1988. Factors Affecting the

Relationship between Childhood and Adult Cholesterol Levels: The Muscatine Study', *Pediatrics*, 82: 577–82.

Lavoie, Francine, Line Robitaille, and Martine Hébert. 2000. 'Teen Dating Relationships and Aggression: An Exploratory Study', *Violence Against Women*, 6 (1): 6–36.

Le Bon, Gustave. 1896. *The Crowd: A Study of the Popular Mind*. New York: The Macmillan Co.

Le Moigne, Philippe. 1998. 'Sanction, Individuation and Deviance: The Social Organization of Recidivism among the Young', *Schweizerische Zeitschrift fur Soziologie/Revue Suisse de sociologie*, 24 (3): 405–29.

Leavitt, G.C. 1992. 'General Evolution and Durkheim's Hypothesis of Crime Frequency: A Cross-Cultural Test', *Sociological Quarterly*, 33: 241–63.

Leblanc, Lauraine. 1999. *Pretty in Punk: Girls' Gender Resistance in a Boys' Subculture*. New Brunswick, NJ: Rutgers University Press.

Lechner, Viola M. 1993. 'Racial Group Responses to Work and Parent Care', *Families in Society*, 74 (2): 93–103.

Lemert, Edwin. 1951. *Social Pathology: a Systematic Approach to the Theory of Sociopathic Behavior*. New York: McGraw-Hill.

Lemire, Beverly. 2000. 'Second-Hand Beaux and "Red-Armed Belles": Conflict and the Creation of Fashions in England, c. 1660–1800', *Continuity and Change*, 15 (3): 391–417.

Levinson, Richard M., and Georgeann Ramsay. 1987. 'Dangerousness, Stress, and Mental Health Evaluations', *Journal of Health and Social Behavior*, 20 (2): 178–87.

Lewinsohn, Peter M., Gregory N. Clarke, and Paul Rohde. 1994. 'Psychological Approaches to the Treatment of Depression in Adolescents', in *Handbook of Depression in Children and Adolescents: Issues in Clinical Child Psychology*, ed. William M. Reynolds and Hugh F. Johnston. New York: Plenum Press.

———, R.H. Striegel-Moore, and J.R. Seeley. 2000. 'Epidemiology and Natural Course of Eating Disorders in Young Women from Adolescence to Young Adulthood', *Journal of the American Academy of Child & Adolescent Psychiatry*, 39: 1284–92.

Liederman, Lina Molokotos. 2000. 'Religious Diversity in Schools: The Muslim Headscarf Controversy and Beyond', *Social Compass*, 47 (3): 367–81.

Liefooghe, R., N. Michiels, S. Habib, M.B. Moran, and A. DeMuynck. 1995. 'Perception and Social Consequences of Tuberculosis: A Focus Group Study of Tuberculosis Patients in Sialkot, Pakistan', *Social Science and Medicine*, 41 (12): 1685–92.

Lindner, Evelin Gerda. 2002. 'Gendercide and Humiliation in Honor and Human Rights Societies', *Journal of Genocide Research*, 4 (1): 137–55.

Liska, Allen E., and Steven F. Messner. 1999. *Perspectives on Crime and Deviance*, 3rd edn. Upper Saddle River, NJ: Prentice-Hall.

Litwin, Howard. 1998. 'Social Network Type and Health Status

in a National Sample of Elderly Israelis', *Social Science and Medicine*, 46 (4–5): 599–609.

Lloyd, Barbara Bloom, Kevin Lucas, Janet Holland, Sheena McGrellis, and Sean Arnold. 1998. *Smoking in Adolescence: Images and Identities*. New York: Routledge.

Lloyd, Donald Arthur. 2000. 'Socioeconomic Consequences of Early-Onset Psychiatric Disorders: Mental Illness and Stress in a Life Course Perspective', dissertation, *Abstracts International, A: The Humanities and Social Sciences*, 61 (6): 2474-A–2475-A.

Lloyd, John. 1999. 'The Godfathers Go Global', *New Statesman*, 20 Dec.

Lombroso, Cesar, with Gina Lombroso-Ferrero. 1972 [1911]. *Criminal Man, According to the Classification of Cesare Lombroso*. New York: Putnam.

Lopez, Yanez Aina D. 2001. 'Theoretical Approximation of Sociological Studies of Anorexia and Bulimia', *Revista Espanola de Investigaciones Sociologicas*, 96: 185.

Lovejoy, Meg. 2001. 'Disturbances in the Social Body: Differences in Body Image and Eating Problems among African American and White Women', *Gender and Society*, 15 (2): 239–61.

Lowman, J. 1997. Prostitution Law Reform in Canada, Federal/provincial/territorial Working Group on Prostitution, 'Report and Recommendations in respect of Legislation, Policy and Practices Concerning Prostitution-Related Activities'. www.walnet.org/csis/reports/consult.rtf. Ottawa: Government of Canada.

———. 1998. 'Prostitution Law Reform in Canada', in *Toward Comparative Law in the 21st Century*, ed. Institute of Comparative Law in Japan. Tokyo: Chuo University Press.

———, and L. Fraser. 1996. *Violence against Persons Who Prostitute: The Experience in British Columbia*, Technical Report TR1996-14e, Department of Justice, Canada. http://users.uniserve.com/%7Elowman/violence/title.htm. Accessed 27 July 2003.

Lubell, Keri M. 2001. 'Gender, Social Isolation, and Psychopathology: Making Sense of Male-Female Differences in Suicide Mortality', dissertation, *Abstracts International, A: The Humanities and Social Sciences*, 62 (2): 799-A.

Luckman, Susan. 2000. 'Mapping the Regulation of Dance Parties', *Journal of Australian Studies*, 64: 217–23.

Lupri, Eugen. 1993. 'Spousal Violence: Wife Abuse across the Life Course', *Zeitschrift fur Sozialisationsforschung und Erziehungssoziologie*, 13 (3): 232–57.

Lupton, Deborah. 2000. '"Where's Me Dinner?": Food Preparation Arrangements in Rural Australian Families', *Journal of Sociology*, 36 (2): 172–88.

McAdam, Douglas, Sidney Tarrow, and Charles Tilley. 2001. *Dynamics of Contention*. Cambridge: Cambridge University Press.

McCaig, L. 1995. *Preliminary Estimates From the Drug*

Abuse Warning Network: 1994 Preliminary Estimates of Drug-Related Emergency Department Episodes (Nov.) Washington, DC: U.S. Department of Health and Human Services, Substance Abuse and Mental Health Services Administration.

McCorkel, Jill A. 2000. 'Embodied Surveillance and the Gendering of Punishment: Domination and Resistance in Women's Prisons', American Sociological Association.

———. 2003. 'Embodied Surveillance and the Gendering of Punishment', *Journal of Contemporary Ethnography*, 32 (1): 41–76.

McCormack, Arlene, Ann Wolbert Burgess, and Peter Gaccione. 1986. 'Influence of Family Structure and Financial Stability on Physical and Sexual Abuse among a Rrunaway Population', *International Journal of Sociology of the Family*, 16 (2): 251–62.

McCubbin, Michael, and Ronald Labonte. 2002. 'Toward Psychosocial Theory for an Integrated Understanding of the Health and Well-Being of Populations', *Ethical Human Sciences and Services*, 4 (1): 47–61.

McDaniel, Susan A., and Neena L. Chappell. 1999. 'Health Care in Regression: Contradictions, Tensions and Implications for Canadian Seniors', *Canadian Public Policy/Analyse de Politiques*, 25 (1): 123–32.

Macdonald, John, and Meda Chesney Lind. 2001. 'Gender Bias and Juvenile Justice Revisited: A Multiyear Analysis', *Crime and Delinquency*, 47 (2).

McGilloway, Sinead, and Michael Donnelly. 2001. 'Service Needs of the Homeless Mentally Ill in Belfast', *International Journal of Mental Health*, 30 (3): 50–6.

McKee, Peter. 2002. 'Re-Education, Adolescence and Conflict Resolution: Lessons from Northern Ireland', *Development*, 43 (1): 83–8.

McLorg, Penelope, and Diane Taub. 1996. 'Anorexia Nervosa and Bulimia: The Development of Deviant Identities', in *Deviant Behavior*, ed. Delos H. Kelly. New York: St Martin's Press.

McMenemy, John. 2001. *The Language of Canadian Politics: A Guide to Important Terms, and Concepts*, 3rd edn. Waterloo, ON: Wilfrid Laurier University Press.

Macmillan, Ross, and Rosemary Gartner. 1996. 'When She Brings Home the Bacon: Labor-Force Participation and the Risk of Spousal Violence against Women', *Journal of Marriage and the Family*, 61 (4): 947–58.

McNair, Brian. 2002. *Striptease Culture: Sex, Media and the Democratization of Desire*. London: Routledge.

McQuade, Samuel C., III. 2001. 'Cops versus Crooks: Technological Competition and Complexity in the Co-Evolution of Information Technologies and Money Laundering', dissertation, *Abstracts International, A: The Humanities and Social Sciences*, 62 (4): 1589-A.

McQueen, Carolyn, and Karen Henwood. 2002. 'Young Men in "Crisis": Attending to the Language of Teenage Boys' Distress', *Social Science and Medicine*, 55 (9): 1493–509.

McRoy, D.T. 1990. 'Gay and Heterosexual Men's Friendships: The Relationships between Homophobia, Antifeminity and Intimacy (Friendships)', dissertation, California School of Professional Psychology, Los Angeles.

McVeigh, Rory, and Christian Smith. 1999. 'Who Protests in America: An Analysis of Three Political Alternatives—Inaction, Institutionalized Politics, or Protest', *Sociological Forum*, 14 (4): 685–702.

MADD. 1999. *Estimating the Presence of Alcohol and Drug Impairment in Traffic Crashes and Their Costs to Canadians*. http://madd.ca/library/magnitudememo.htm.

Magee, R. 2000. 'Duels, Doctors and Death', *Australian and New Zealand Journal of Surgery*, 70 (8): 616–20.

Malson, Helen, Harriette Marshall, and Anne Woollett. 2002. 'Talking of Taste: A Discourse Analytic Exploration of Young Women's Gendered and Racialized Subjectivities in British Urban, Multicultural Contexts', *Feminism & Psychology*, 12 (4): 469–90.

Manopaiboon, C., R.E. Bunnell, P.H. Kilmarx, S. Chaikummao, K. Limpakarnjanarat, S. Supawitkul, M.E. St Louis, and T.D. Mastro. 2003. 'Leaving Sex Work: Barriers, Facilitating Factors and Consequences for Female Sex Workers in Northern Thailand', *AIDS Care*, 15 (1): 39–52.

Marcotte, Dave E., and Virginia Wilcox-Gok. 2001. 'Estimating the Employment and Earnings Costs of Mental Illness: Recent Developments in the United States', *Social Science and Medicine*, 53 (1): 21–7.

Marcuse, Herbert. 1955. *Eros and Civilization: A Philosophical Inquiry into Freud*. Boston: Beacon Press.

Marinelli, Julie. 2002. 'Youth Custody and Community Services in Canada, 2000/01', *Juristat*, vol. 22, no. 8, cat. no. 85-002. Ottawa: Canadian Centre for Justice Statistics.

Markowitz, Fred E. 2001. 'Modeling Processes in Recovery from Mental Illness: Relationships between Symptoms, Life Satisfaction, and Self-Concept', *Journal of Health and Social Behavior*, 42 (1): 64–79.

Martens, Peter L. 2000. 'Immigrants as Victims of Crime', *International Review of Victimology*, 8 (2): 199–216.

Martinelli, Alberto. 2003. 'Global Order or Divided World? Introduction', *Current Sociology/La Sociologie Contemporaine*, 51 (2): 95–100.

Marx, Karl, and Friedrich Engels. 1988 [1848]. *Manifesto of the Communist Party/The Communist Manifesto*. ed. Frederic L. Bender. New York: Norton.

Masamura, W.T. 1979. 'Wife Abuse and Other Forms of Aggression', *Victimology: An International Journal*, 4 (1): 46–59.

Mathieu, Lilian. 2003. 'The Emergence and Uncertain Outcomes of Prostitutes' Social Movements', *European Journal of Women's Studies*, 10 (1): 29–50.

Matza, David. 1964. *Delinquency and Drift*. New York; John Wiley & Sons.

Mawby, R.I., P. Brunt, and Z. Hambly. 1999. 'Victimisation on Holiday: A British Survey', *International Review of*

Victimology, 6 (3): 201–11.

——, ——, ——. 2000. 'Fear of Crime among British Holidaymakers', *British Journal of Criminology*, 40 (3): 468–79.

Maynard, Steven. 1994. 'Through a Hole in the Lavatory Wall: Homosexual Subcultures, Police Surveillance, and the Dialectics of Discovery, Toronto, 1890–1930', *Journal of the History of Sexuality*. 5 (2): 207–42.

Mead, George Herbert. 1934. *Mind, Self and Society*, ed. Charles W. Morris. Chicago: University of Chicago Press.

Mednick, S.A., T.E. Moffitt, and S.A. Stack. 1987. *The Causes of Crime: New Biological Approaches*. Cambridge: Cambridge University Press.

Meisel, Joshua Sager. 2002. 'Juvenile Parole and the Rehabilitative Ideal: A Study of the Relationship between Parole Length of Stay and Recidivism', dissertation, *Abstracts International, A: The Humanities and Social Sciences*, 62 (11): 3943-A.

Mercola, Joseph. 1997. *Psychosomatic Medicine*, 59. (Sept.– Oct.) www.mercola.com/1997/archive/violent_women.htm.

Mermelstein, Robin, and Tobacco Control Network Writing Group. 1999. 'Explanations of Ethnic and Gender Differences in Youth Smoking: A Multi-Site, Qualitative Investigation', *Nicotine and Tobacco Research*, 1 (supp.): S91–S98.

Merton, R.K. 1957 [1938]. 'Social Structure and Anomie', in *Social Theory and Social Structure*, 2nd edn. New York: Free Press.

——. 1957. 'Manifest and Latent Functions', in *Social Theory and Social Structure*, rev. edn. New York: Free Press.

Mesch, Gustavo S. 1997. 'Victims and Property Victimization in Israel', *Journal of Quantitative Criminology*, 13 (1): 57–71.

Metzler, Carol W., John Noell, Anthony Biglan, Dennis Ary, and Keith Smolkowski. 1994. 'The Social Context for Risky Sexual Behavior among Adolescents', *Journal of Behavioral Medicine*, 17 (4): 419–38.

Meyer, Deborah J.C., and Heather C. Anderson. 2000. 'Preadolescents and Apparel Purchasing: Conformity to Parents and Peers in the Consumer Socialization Process', *Journal of Social Behavior and Personality*, 15 (2): 243–57.

Milgram, Stanley. 1974. *Obedience to Authority*. New York: Harper & Row.

Miller, J. Kirk, and Kristen A. Myers. 2000. 'Are All Hate Crimes Created Equal?' Southern Sociological Society.

Miller, Kathleen E., Donald F. Sabo, Michael P. Farrell, Grace M. Barnes, and Merrill J. Melnick. 1999a. 'Athletic Participation and Adolescent Sexual Behavior: Where Race and Gender Intersect', Society for the Study of Social Problems.

——, ——, ——, ——, ——. 1999b. 'Sports, Sexual Behavior, Contraceptive Use, and Pregnancy among Female and Male High School Students: Testing Cultural Resource Theory', *Sociology of Sport Journal*, 16 (4): 366–87.

Miller, Kenneth E., Cheryl A. King, Benjamin N. Shain, and Michael W. Naylor. 1992. 'Suicidal Adolescents' Perceptions of Their Family Environment', *Suicide and Life-Threatening Behavior*, 22 (2): 226–39.

Millham, Jim, and Linda E. Weinberger. 1977. 'Sexual Preference, Sex Role Appropriateness, and Restriction of Social Access', *Journal of Homosexuality*, 2 (4): 343–57.

Mills, C. Wright. 1959. *The Sociological Imagination*. New York: Oxford University.

Mon, Wei-The. 2002. 'Causal Factors of Corporate Crime in Taiwan: Qualitative and Quantitative Findings', *International Journal of Offender Therapy and Comparative Criminology*, 46 (2): 183–205.

Money, John. 1986. *Lovemaps: Clinical Concepts of Sexual/Erotic Health and Pathology, Paraphilia, and Gender Transposition in Childhood, Adolescence, and Maturity*. New York: Irvington.

Moore, Barrington. 1966. *Social Origins of Dictatorship and Democracy: Lord and Peasant in the Making of the Modern World*. Boston: Beacon.

Moore, Laura M. 2001. 'Sexually Assertive Women: Their Identity Construction and Maintenance'. Southern Sociological Society.

Moore, R., Y. Mao, J. Zhang, and K. Clarke. 1997. *Economic Burden of Illness in Canada, 1993*. Ottawa: Health Canada.

Morin, Stephen F., and Ellen M. Garfinkle. 1978. 'Male Homophobia', *Journal of Social Issues*, 34 (1): 29–47.

Moser, Charles, and J.J. Madeson. 1996. *Bound to be Free: The SM Experience*. New York: Continuum.

Mowbray, Carol T., Daphna Oyserman, and Scott Ross. 1995. 'Parenting and the Significance of Children for Women with a Serious Mental Illness', *Journal of Mental Health Administration*, 22 (2): 189–200.

Mulvey, Laura. 1975. 'Visual Pleasure and Narrative Cinema', in Laura Mulvey, Visual and Other Pleasures. Basingstoke, UK: Macmillan, 1989 [originally published in *Screen* (Autum) 16 (3): 6–18].

Murphy, Susan Applegarth. 2001. 'A Study of Career Values by Generation and Gender', dissertation, *Abstracts International, A: The Humanities and Social Sciences*, 61 (9): 3781-A–3782-A.

Murray, C.J.L., and A.D. Lopez, eds. 1996. *Summary: The Global Burden of Disease: A Comprehensive Assessment of Mortality and Disability from Diseases, Injuries, and Risk Factors in 1990 and Projected to 2020*. Cambridge, MA: Harvard School of Public Health on behalf of the World Health Organization and the World Bank, Harvard University Press. www.who.int/msa/mnh/ems/dalys/into.htm.

Murray, Stephen O. 1996. *American Gay*. Chicago: University of Chicago Press.

Mustaine, Elizabeth Ehrhardt, and Richard Tewksbury. 1999. 'A Routine Activity Theory Explanation for Women's Stalking Victimizations', *Violence Against Women*, 5 (1): 43–62.

———, ———. 2000. 'Comparing the Lifestyles of Victims, Offenders, and Victim-Offenders: A Routine Activity Theory Assessment of Similarities and Differences for Criminal Incident Participants', *Sociological Focus*, 33 (3): 339–62.

Mysterud, Iver, and Dag Viljen Poleszynski. 2003. 'Expanding Evolutionary Psychology: Toward a Better Understanding of Violence and Aggression', *Social Science Information/ Information sur les Sciences Sociales*, 42 (1): 5–50.

Nabben, Ton, and Dirk J. Korf. 1999. 'Cocaine and Crack in Amsterdam: Diverging Subcultures', *Journal of Drug Issues*, 29 (3): 627–51.

National Forum on Youth Gangs. 1999. Solicitor General Canada; Department of Justice Canada; National Crime Prevention Centre. www.sgc.gc.ca/Publications/ Policing/199912_e.pdf. Accessed 17 May 2004.

National Institute of Child Health and Human Development. 1999. 'Research on Today's Issues', issue no. 10 (Dec.). www.nichd.nih.gov/cpr/dbs/pubs/ti10.pdf.

———, Office of AIDS Research. 1999. *Prevention of Health Risk Behaviors in Middle Childhood*, Release date: 2 Sept., RFA: HD-99-014. Bethesda, MD: National Institute of Mental Health.

National Institute of Justice. 1997. 'The Crime of Stalking: How Big Is the Problem?' www.ojp.usdoj.gov/ovc/ncvrw/1999/ stalk.htm. Accessed 15 August 2000.

National Research Council. 1994. *Understanding and Preventing Violence*, vol. 3: *Social Influences*, ed. Albert J. Reiss, Jr. and Jeffrey A. Roth, Panel on the Understanding and Control of Violent Behavior. Washington, DC: The National Academies Press.

Nations, M.K., C.M.G. Monte. 1996. 'I'm not dog, no!': Cries of Resistance Against Cholera Control Campaigns', *Social Science and Medicine*, 43 (6): 1007–24.

Nelsen, Candice, and Lin Huff-Corzine. 1998. 'Strangers in the Night: An Application of the Lifestyle-Routine Activities Approach to Elderly Homicide Victimization', *Homicide Studies*, 2 (2): 130–59.

Netland, Marit. 2001. 'Assessment of Exposure to Political Violence and Other Potentially Traumatizing Events: A Critical Review', *Journal of Traumatic Stress*, 14 (2): 311–26.

Newburn, T., and M. Shiner. 2001. *Teenage Kicks? Young People and Alcohol: A Review of the Literature*. York, UK: Joseph Rowntree Foundation.

Newman, O. 1972. *Defensible Space*. New York: Macmillan.

Newton, Liz. 2001. 'Self and Illness: Changing Relationships in Response to Life in the Community following Prolonged Institutionalisation', *Australian Journal of Anthropology*,

12 (2): 166–81.

Nieuwbeerta, Paul, Gerrit De Geest, and Jacques Siegers. 2003. 'Street-Level Corruption in Industrialized and Developing Countries', *European Societies*, 5 (2): 139–65.

Nijhof, Gerhard. 2002. 'Heterogeneity in the Legitimation of Hearing Voices', *Amsterdams Sociologisch Tijdschrift*, 29 (1): 117–35.

Nikelly, Arthur G. 2001. 'The Role of Environment in Mental Health: Individual Empowerment through Social Restructuring', *Journal of Applied Behavioral Science*, 37 (3): 305–23.

NIMH 2001. 'The Numbers Count: Mental Disorders in America: A Summary of Statistics Describing the Prevalence of Mental Disorders in America'. www.nimh. nih.gov/publicat/numbers.cfm.

Nishigaya, Kasumi. 2002. 'Female Garment Factory Workers in Cambodia: Migration, Sex Work and HIV/AIDS', *Women and Health*, 35 (4): 27–42.

Nixon, Kendra, Leslie Tutty, Pamela Downe, Kelly Gorkoff, and Jane Ursel. 2002. 'The Everyday Occurrence: Violence in the Lives of Girls Exploited through Prostitution', *Violence Against Women*, 8 (9): 1016–43.

NVSR (National Vital Statistics Report). 2001. 49, no. 3, US Centers for Disease Control (6-26-2001).

O'Boyle, Timothy J. 2002. 'Gambling and Small Business Crime Deterrence: The Illegal Use of Video Poker Machines by Public Bars and Private Social Clubs in Pennsylvania', dissertation, *Abstracts International, A: The Humanities and Social Sciences*, 62 (9): 3196-A.

O'Donnell, Ian, and Kimmett Edgar. 1998. 'Routine Victimisation in Prisons', *Howard Journal of Criminal Justice*, 37 (3): 266–79.

O'Keefe, Maura. 1997. 'Incarcerated Battered Women: A Comparison of Battered Women Who Killed Their Abusers and Those Incarcerated for Other Offenses', *Journal of Family Violence*, 12 (1): 1–19.

O'Toole, Roger. 1977. *The Precipitous Path: Studies in Political Sects*. Toronto: Peter Martin.

Ogborne, Alan C., and Reginald G. Smart. 2001. 'Public Opinion on the Health Benefits of Moderate Drinking: Results from a Canadian National Population Health Survey', *Addiction*, 96 (4): 641–9.

Olguin, B.V. 1997. 'Tattoos, Abjection, and the Political Unconscious: Toward a Semiotics of the Pinto Visual Vernacular', *Cultural Critique*, 37: 159–213.

Ontario Women's Directorate. 1995. *Facts to Consider About Sexual Assault*. Toronto: Ontario Women's Directorate.

Orava, T.A., P.J. McLeod, and D. Sharpe. 1996. 'Perceptions of Control, Depressive Symptomatology, and Self-Esteem of Women in Transition from Abusive Relationships', *Journal of Family Violence*, 1 (1): 167–86.

Orchard, T.J., R.P. Donahue, L.H. Kuller, P.N. Hodge, and A.L. Drash. 1983. 'Cholesterol Screening in Childhood: Does It Predict Adult Hypercholesterolemia? The Beaver County

Experience', *Journal of Pediatrics*, 103: 687–91.

Orlie, Melissa A. 2002. 'The Desire for Freedom and the Consumption of Politics', *Philosophy and Social Criticism*, 28 (4): 395–417.

Oser, Carrie B. 2003. 'Strain, Depression, and Criminal Offending across Male and Female Adolescents: Examining General Strain Theory'. Southern Sociological Society.

Ost, Suzanne. 2002. 'Children at Risk: Legal and Societal Perceptions of the Potential Threat That the Possession of Child Pornography Poses to Society', *Journal of Law and Society*, 29 (3): 436–60.

Ouimet, Marc. 2002. 'Explaining the American and Canadian Crime "Drop" in the 1990's', *Canadian Journal of Criminology/Revue Canadienne de Criminologie*, 44 (1): 33–50.

Overstreet, Stacy, and Shawnee Braun. 2000. 'Exposure to Community Violence and Post-Traumatic Stress Symptoms: Mediating Factors', *American Journal of Orthopsychiatry*, 70 (2): 263–71.

Paetsch, Joanne J., and Lorne D. Bertrand. 1999. 'Victimization and Delinquency among Canadian Youth', *Adolescence*, 34 (134): 351–67.

Pagani, Linda, Denis Larocque, Frank Vitaro, and Richard E. Tremblay. 2003. 'Verbal and Physical Abuse toward Mothers: The Role of Family Configuration, Environment, and Coping Strategies', *Journal of Youth and Adolescence*, 32 (3): 215–22.

Paoli, Letizia. 2002. 'The Paradoxes of Organized Crime', *Crime, Law and Social Change*, 37: 51–97.

Parsons, Talcott. 1951. *The Social System*. New York: Free Press.

Paulicelli, Eugenia. 2002. 'Fashion, the Politics of Style and National Identity in Pre-Fascist and Fascist Italy', *Gender & History*, 14 (3): 537–59.

Payne, D.L., K.A. Lonsway, and L.F. Fitzgerald. 1999. 'Rape Myth Acceptance: Exploration of Its Structure and Its Measurement Using the Illinois Rape Myth Acceptance Scale', *Journal of Research in Personality*, 33: 27–68.

Pearce, Frank, and Laureen Snider, eds. 1995. *Corporate Crime: Contemporary Debates*. Toronto: University of Toronto Press.

Pedersen, Willy, and Kristinn Hegna. 2003. 'Children and Adolescents Who Sell Sex: A Community Study', *Social Science and Medicine*, 56 (1): 135–47.

Peel, Elizabeth. 1999. 'Violence against Lesbians and Gay Men: Decision-Making in Reporting and Not Reporting Crime', *Feminism & Psychology*, 9 (2): 161–7.

Penning, Margaret J., and Neena L. Chappell. 1990. 'Self-Care in Relation to Informal and Formal Care', *Ageing and Society*, 10 (1): 41–59.

Perreira, Krista M., and Frank A. Sloan. 2001. 'Life Events and Alcohol Consumption among Mature Adults: A Longitudinal Analysis', *Journal of Studies on Alcohol*, 62

(4): 501–8.

Perrow, Charles. 1999. 'Organizing to Reduce the Vulnerabilities of Complexity', *Journal of Contingencies and Crisis Management*, 7 (3): 150–5.

Pescosolido, Bernice A. 1996. 'Bringing the "Community" into Utilization Models: How Social Networks Link Individuals to Changing Systems of Care', *Research in the Sociology of Health Care*, 13 (Part A): 171–97.

———, Figert, E. Anne, and Keri M. Lubell. 1996. 'Professional Work in Public and Private Settings: The Use and Evaluation of the DSM in Psychiatric Units', *Current Research on Occupations and Professions*, 9: 31–51.

Pessin, Hayley, Barry Rosenfeld, and William Breitbart. 2002. 'Assessing Psychological Distress Near the End of Life', *American Behavioral Scientist*, 46 (3): 357–72.

Peter, Laurence J. 1977. *Peter's Quotations: Ideas for Our Time*. New York: Quill/William Morrow.

Petersilia, Joan, and Susan Turner. 1993. 'Intensive Probation and Parole', *Crime and Justice*, 17: 281–335.

Peterson, Dana. 2002. '"Don't Forget the Women": A Multi-Level Analysis of Individual and Contextual Effects on Girls' and Boys' Delinquency', dissertation, *Abstracts International, A: The Humanities and Social Sciences*, 63 (3): 1139-A–1140-A.

Pfahlert, Jeanine Ann. 1999. 'Displaying the Dialectic: Punk as Fashion and Youth Culture'. Society for the Study of Social Problems.

Pfeffer, Cynthia R. 1989. 'Studies of Suicidal Preadolescent and Adolescent Inpatients: A Critique of Research Methods', *Suicide and Life-Threatening Behavior*, 19 (1): 58–77.

———. 2001. 'Diagnosis of Childhood and Adolescent Suicidal Behavior: Unmet Needs for Suicide Prevention', *Biological Psychiatry*, 49 (12): 1055–61.

Phelan J.C., and B.G. Link. 2004. 'Fear of People with Mental Illnesses: The Role of Personal and Impersonal Contact and Exposure to Threat or Harm', *Journal of Health and Social Behavior*, 45 (1): 68–80.

———, ———, Ann Stueve, and Bernice Pescosolido. 2000. 'A Public Conception of Mental Illness in 1950 and 1996: What Is Mental Illness and Is It to Be Feared?' *Journal of Health and Social Behavior*, 41 (2): 188–207.

Phillips, Susan A. 2001. 'Gallo's Body: Decoration and Damnation in the Life of a Chicano Gang Member', *Ethnography*, 2 (3): 357–88.

Phoenix, Joanna. 2002. 'In the Name of Protection: Youth Prostitution Policy Reforms in England and Wales', *Critical Social Policy*, 22, 2 (71): 353–75.

Piaget, J. 1932. *The Moral Judgment of the Child*. New York: Harcourt, Brace.

Picard, Andre. 1995. 'After Johnny Comes Marching Home', *Globe and Mail*, 8 April.

Piccato, Pablo. 1999. 'Politics and the Technology of Honor: Dueling in Turn-of-the-Century Mexico', *Journal of Social History*, 33 (2): 331–54.

Pickett, William, Michael J. Garner, William F. Boyce, and Matthew A. King. 2002. 'Gradients in Risk for Youth Injury Associated with Multiple-Risk Behaviours: A Study of 11,329 Canadian Adolescents', *Social Science and Medicine*, 55 (6): 1055–68.

Pietsch, Nicole. 2002. 'Un/titled: Constructions of Illegitimate Motherhood as Gender Insurrection', *Journal of the Association for Research on Mothering*, 4 (1): 88–100.

Piquero, Alex R., and Brian Lawton. 2002. 'Individual Risk for Crime Is Exacerbated in Poor Familial and Neighborhood Contexts: The Contribution of Low Birth Weight, Family Adversity, and Neighborhood Disadvantage to Life Course-Persistent Offending', *Advances in Life Course Research*, 7: 263–95.

Piquero, Nicole L., Alex Piquero, Lyn Exum, and Sally Simpson. 2002. 'Exploring the Relationship between Desire-for-Control and Corporate Offending'. Southern Sociological Society.

Plomin, Robert, and Kathryn Asbury. 'Nature and Nurture in the Family', *Marriage & Family Review*, 33 (2–3): 273–81.

Ploughman, Penelope, and John Stensrud. 1986. 'The Ecology of Rape Victimization: A Case Study of Buffalo, New York', *Genetic, Social, and General Psychology Monographs*, 112 (3): 303–24.

Pogarsky, Greg, and Alex Piquero. 2003. 'Why May Punishment Encourage Offending and Lower Perceived Sanction Threats? Investigating the Resetting and Selection Explanations', *Journal of Research in Crime and Delinquency*, 40: 95–120.

Polivy, Janet, and C. Peter Herman. 2002. 'Sociocultural Idealization of Thin Female Body Shapes: An Introduction to the Special Issue on Body Image and Eating Disorders', *Journal of Social and Clinical Psychology*, 23 (1): 1–6.

Pollak, O. 1961. *The Criminality of Women*. New York: A.S. Barnes.

Porteous, Sam. 1998. *Organized Crime Impact Study Highlights*. Ottawa: Public Works and the Solicitor General.

Porter, Bruce D. 1994. *War and the Rise of the State: The Military Foundations of Modern Politics*. New York: Free Press.

Porter, Roy. 1997. 'Bethlem/Bedlam: Methods of Madness?' *History Today*. www.findarticles.com.

Poulin, Christiane, and Linda Graham. 2001. 'The Association between Substance Use, Unplanned Sexual Intercourse and Other Sexual Behaviours among Adolescent Students', *Addiction*, 96 (4): 607–21.

Poutanen, M.A. 2002. 'Regulating Public Space in Early Nineteenth-Century Montreal: Vagrancy Laws and Gender in a Colonial Context', *Histoire sociale/Social History*, 35 (69): 35–58.

Powers, Jane Levine, John Eckenrode, and Barbara Jaklitsch. 1990. 'Maltreatment among Runaway and Homeless Youth', *Child Abuse and Neglect*, 14 (1): 87–98.

Pratt, Carter, and Kamala Deosaransingh. 1997. 'Gender Differences in Homicide in Contra Costa County, California: 1982–1993', *American Journal of Preventive Medicine*, 13 (supp.): 19–24.

Price, Virginia Ann. 1989. 'Characteristics and Needs of Boston Street Youth: One Agency's Response', *Children and Youth Services Review*, 11 (1): 75–90.

Public Health Agency of Canada. 1994. *Suicide in Canada: Update of the Report of the Task Force on Suicide in Canada*. www.phac-aspc.gc.ca/mh-sm/mentalhealth/problems. htm.

———. 2002. *A Report on Mental Illnesses in Canada*. www. phac-aspc.gc.ca/publicat/miic-mmac/. Accessed 12 April 2005.

Putnam, Michael Charles. 2002. 'Private "I's": Investigating Men's Experiences with Pornographies', dissertation, *Abstracts International, A: The Humanities and Social Sciences*, 62 (9): 3202-A.

Rabkin J. 1974. 'Public Attitudes Towards Mental Illness: A review of the Literature', *Schizophrenia Bulletin 1974*, 1 (Experimental Issue No.10): 9–33.

Radziszewska, Barbara, Jean L. Richardson, Clyde W. Dent, and Brian R. Flay. 1996. 'Parenting Style and Adolescent Depressive Symptoms, Smoking, and Academic Achievement: Ethnic, Gender, and SES Differences', *Journal of Behavioral Medicine*, 19 (3): 289–305.

Ragone, Gerardo. 1996. 'Consumption Diffusion: Elite Phenomena and Mass Processes', *International Sociology*, 11 (3): 309–15.

Raitakari, O.T., S. Taimela, K.V. Porkka, R. Telama, I. Valimaki, H.K. Akerblom, and J.S.Viikari. 'Associations between Physical Activity and Risk Factors for Coronary Heart Disease: The Cardiovascular Risk in Young Finns Study', *Medicine and Science in Sports and Exercise*, 29 (8): 1055–61.

Ralston, Roy W. 1999. 'Economy and Race: Interactive Determinants of Property Crime in the United States, 1958–1995: Reflections on the Supply of Property Crime', *The American Journal of Economics and Sociology*, 58 (3): 405–34.

Rantakallio, Paula. 1983. 'Social Background of Mothers Who Smoke during Pregnancy and Influence of These Factors on the Offspring', *Social Science and Medicine*, 13A (4): 423–9.

Rantanen, Pekka. 2001. 'Class Society and Finnish Nationalism in the Fashion Talk of Newspapers in the Late 19th Century', *Sosiologia*, 38 (2): 93–103.

Reanda, L. 1991. 'Prostitution as a Human Rights Question: Problems and Prospects of United Nations Action', *Human Rights Quarterly*, 13: 203.

Reed, Mark D., and Dina R. Rose. 1998. 'Doing What Simple Simon Says? Estimating the Underlying Causal Structures of Delinquent Associations, Attitudes, and Serious Theft', *Criminal Justice and Behavior*, 25 (2): 240–74.

Regnerus, Mark D. 2002. '"Friends" Influence on Adolescent

Theft and Minor Delinquency: A Developmental Test of Peer-Reported Effects', *Social Science Research*, 31 (4): 681–705.

Reguillo, Rossana. 2002. 'The Social Construction of Fear: Urban Narratives and Practices', in *Citizens of Fear: Urban Violence in Latin America*, ed. Susana Rotker. New Brunswick, NJ: Rutgers University Press, 187–206.

Reid, Lesley Williams. 2002. 'Crime and the Labor Market: The Effect of Perceived Economic Returns to Crime'. Southern Sociological Society.

Reifman, Alan, Grace M. Barnes, Barbara A. Dintcheff, Michael P. Farrell, and Lois Uhteg. 1998. 'Parental and Peer Influences on the Onset of Heavier Drinking among Adolescents', *Journal of Studies on Alcohol*, 59 (3): 311–17.

Reinarman, Craig, and Harry G. Levine. 1997. 'Crack in Context: America's Latest Demon Drug', *Crack in America: Demon Drugs and Social Justice*, eds. Craig Reinarman and Harry G. Levine. Berkeley: University of California Press, 1–17.

Reiss, Albert. 1961. 'The Social Integration of Queers and Peers', *Social Problems*, 9: 102–20.

Renner, Michael. 1993a. 'Environmental Dimensions of Disarmament and Conversion', in *Real Security: Converting the Defense Economy and Building Peace*, ed. Kevin J. Cassidy and Gregory A. Bischak, eds. Albany, NY: State University of New York Press, 88–132.

———. 1993b. 'Preparing for Peace', in *State of the World 1993*, ed. L. Starke. New York: W.W. Norton, 139–57.

Renzetti, Claire M. 1997. 'Violence and Abuse among Same-Sex Couples', in *Violence Between Intimate Partners: Patterns, Causes, and Effects*, ed. A.P. Cardarelli. Boston: Allyn & Bacon, 70–89.

Reynolds, Ariel Catherine. 2003. 'Religiosity as a Predictor of Attitudes toward Homosexuality'. Southern Sociological Society.

Reznik, Shlomo. 2002. 'Political Culture in Israel in the Era of Peace: The Jewish Underground and the Conscientious Objection Movement, 1979–1984', *Peace & Change*, 27 (3): 357–84.

Roberts, James Christopher. 2003. 'Serving Up Trouble in the Barroom Environment', dissertation, *Abstracts International, A: The Humanities and Social Sciences*, 63 (9): 3367-A.

Roberts, Julian V., and Anthony N. Doob. 1997. 'Race, Ethnicity, and Criminal Justice in Canada', in *Ethnicity, Crime, and Immigration: Comparative and Cross-National Perspectives*, ed. Michael Tonry. Chicago: University of Chicago Press, 469–522.

Robinson, Paul. 2004. 'Youth Court Statistics, 2002/03', *Juristat*, cat. no. 85-002-XIF2004002, 2004-03-12. Ottawa: Canadian Centre for Justice Statistics.

Rojek, Dean G., Tanja C. Link, and Michelle Neal. 2001. 'Black Homicide: Theory, Trends, and Correlates'. Southern Sociological Society.

Rokach, Ami, and Felix Neto. 2000a. 'Causes of Loneliness in Adolescence: A Cross-Cultural Study', *International Journal of Adolescence and Youth*, 8 (1): 65–80.

———, ———. 2000b. 'Coping with Loneliness in Adolescence: A Cross-Cultural Study', *Social Behavior and Personality*, 28 (4): 329–42.

Roscigno, Vincent J. 2000. 'Family/School Inequality and African-American/Hispanic Achievement', *Social Problems*, 47 (2): 266–90.

Rosenfeld, Dana. 1999. 'Identity Work among the Homosexual Elderly', dissertation, *Abstracts International, A: The Humanities and Social Sciences*, 60 (4): 1348-A.

Rosenthal, Carolyn J. 1997. 'The Changing Contexts of Family Care in Canada', *Ageing International*, 24 (1): 13–31.

———, Sarah H. Matthews, and Victor W. Marshall. 1989. 'Is Parent Care Normative? The Experiences of a Sample of Middle-Aged Women', *Research on Aging*, 11 (2): 244–60.

Ross, Laurie B. 2002. 'Rebuilding Communities, Shaping Identities: The Impact of a Participatory Neighborhood Planning Process on Young, Low-Income Urban Adolescents of Color in Worcester, Massachusetts', dissertation *Abstracts International, A: The Humanities and Social Sciences*, 63 (3): 1146-A.

Roter, D.L., 1998. 'Effectiveness of Interventions to Improve Patient Compliance: A Meta-analysis', *Medical Care*, 36 (8): 1138–61.

Rotheram-Borus, Mary Jane. 2000. 'Expanding the Range of Interventions to Reduce HIV among Adolescents', *AIDS*, 14 (supp. 1): S33–S40.

———, Joyce Hunter, and Margaret Rosario. 1994. 'Suicidal Behavior and Gay-Related Stress among Gay and Bisexual Male Adolescents', *Journal of Adolescent Research*, 9 (4): 498–508.

———, Karen A. Mahler, Cheryl Koopman, and Kris Langabeer. 1996. Sexual Abuse History and Associated Multiple Risk Behavior in Adolescent Runaways', *American Journal of Orthopsychiatry*, 3(July): 390–400.

———, John Piacentini, Ronan Van Rossem, Flemming Graae, Coleen Cantwell, David Castro-Blanco, and Julie Feldman. 2000. 'Treatment Adherence among Latina Female Adolescent Attempters', *Suicide and Life-Threatening Behavior*, 29 (4): 319–31.

Rott, Renate. 1996. 'Gender Constructions in Latin America', *Asien afrika lateinamerika*, 24 (3): 219–30.

Rousseau, Jean-Jacques. 2002 [1782]. *The Confessions of Jean-Jacques Rousseau*, trans. and with an Introduction by J.M. Cohen. London: Penguin Classics.

Rowe, David C., D. Wayne Osgood, and Alan W. Nicewander. 1990. 'A Latent Trait Approach to Unifying Criminal Careers', *Criminology*, 31(1): 93–117.

Royal College of Psychiatrists. 1998. 'Tattooing'. www.rcpsych.ac.uk/info/help/anor/.

Ruchkin, Vladislav V., Martin Eisemann, Bruno Hagglof, and C. Robert Cloninger. 1998. 'Aggression in Delinquent Adolescents vs Controls in Northern Russia: Relations with Hereditary and Environmental Factors', *Criminal Behaviour and Mental Health*, 8 (2): 115–26.

Rummel, R.J. 1992. 'Megamurders', *Society*, 29 (6): 47–52.

———. 1994. *Death by Government*. New Brunswick, NJ: Transaction.

Russell, S., and the Canadian Federation of University Women. 1996. *Take Action for Equality, Development and Peace: A Canadian Follow-up Guide to Beijing '95*. Ottawa: CRIAW, Canadian Beijing Facilitating Committee.

Ryu, Seongryeol, and Jeylan T. Mortimer. 1994. 'Further Assessment of the "Occupational Linkage Hypothesis": The Intergenerational Transmission of Work Values', American Sociological Association.

Saccone, A.J., and A.C. Israel. 1978. 'Effects of Experimenter Versus Significant Other-Controlled Reinforcement and Choice of Target Behavior on Weight Loss', *Behavior Therapy*, 9 (2): 271–8.

Sachs-Ericsson, Natalie, and James A. Ciarlo. 2000. 'Gender, Social Roles, and Mental Health: An Epidemiological Perspective', *Sex Roles*, 43 (9–10): 605–28.

Sagarin, Edward. 1975. *Deviants and Deviance*. New York: Praeger.

Saito, Tomonori. 2002. 'Association with Delinquent Peers, Social Bonding and Delinquent Behavior: Testing the Differential Reinforcement Hypothesis and Social Control Theory', *Kyoiku-shakaigaku Kenkyu/The Journal of Educational Sociology*, 71: 131–50.

Sampson, Robert J., and John H. Laub. 2002. 'Life-Course Desisters? Trajectories of *Crime* among Delinquent Boys Followed to Age 70', *Criminology*, 41 (3): 555–92.

———, and Stephen W. Raudenbush. 1999. 'Systematic Social Observation of Public Spaces: A New Look at Disorder in Urban Neighbourhoods', *American Journal of Sociology*, 105 (3): 603–51.

Sanders, Teela. 2002. 'The Condom as Psychological Barrier: Female Sex Workers and Emotional Management', *Feminism & Psychology*, 12 (4): 561–6.

Sato, Akihiko. 1996. 'On the Creation of Philopon-Crime in Japan from the Perspective of the Medicalization of Deviance', *Soshioroji*, 40 (3): 57–76.

Scharlach, Andrew E., and Karen I. Fredriksen. 1994. 'Elder Care versus Adult Care: Does Care Recipient Age Make a Difference?' *Research on Aging. Special Work and Eldercare*, 16 (1): 43–68.

Schneider, Carsten. 2003. 'Prospects for the Consolidation of Latin American Democracies: Rethinking the Role of Corruption and Institutional Trust', *Sociologia – Problemas e Praticas*, 42 (May–Aug.): 65–90.

Schroeder, Jonathan E. 1998. 'Consuming Representation: A Visual Approach to Consumer Research', in *Representing Consumers: Voices, Views and Visions*, ed. Barbara B. Stern.

London: Routledge.

Schulze, Beate, and Matthias C. Angermeyer. 2003. 'Subjective Experiences of Stigma: A Focus Group Study of Schizophrenic Patients, their Relatives and Mental Health Professionals', *Social Science and Medicine*, 56 (2): 299–312.

Schur, Edwin. 1971. *Labeling Deviant Behavior*. New York: Harper and Row.

Schwartz, Joel. 2000. *Fighting Poverty with Virtue: Moral Reform and America's Urban Poor, 1825–2000*. Bloomington: Indiana University Press.

Scott, Ellen K., Andrew S. London, and Nancy Myers. 2002. 'Living With Violence: Women's Reliance on Abusive Men in their Transitions from Welfare to Work', in *Families At Work: Expanding the Bounds*, ed. Naomi Gerstel, Dan Clawson, and Robert Zussman. Nashville, TN: Vanderbilt University Press, 302–16.

Scully, Angus, John Bebbington, Rosemary Evans, and Carol Wilson. 1993. *Canada Through Time*. Toronto: Prentice-Hall.

Sennett, R., and J. Cobb. 1972. *The Hidden Injuries of Class*. New York: Vintage Books.

Sexton, Rocky L. 2001. 'Mardi Gras: Ritualized Inebriation, Violence, and Social Control in Cajun Mardi Gras', *Anthropological Quarterly*, 74 (1): 28–38.

Shackelford, Monisa, and Michael G. Bisciglia. 2003. 'Public Perception of Mental Illness: Intimate Knowledge and Social Distance'. Southern Sociological Society.

Shaffer, David 1988. 'The Epidemiology of Teen Suicide: An Examination of Risk Factors', *The Journal of Clinical Psychiatry*, 49 (supp.): 36–41.

Shalhoub-Kevorkian, Nadera. 2002. 'Femicide and the Palestinian Criminal Justice System: Seeds of Change in the Context of State Building?' *Law and Society Review*, 36 (3): 577–605.

Shim, Young-Hee. 2001. 'Feminism and the Discourse of Sexuality in Korea: Continuities and Changes', *Human Studies*, 24 (1–2): 133–48.

Shipley, Martin, Stephen Stansfeld, Carol Emslie, Rebecca Fuhrer, Kate Hunt, and Sally Macintyre. 2002. 'Gender Differences in Mental Health: Evidence from Three Organizations', *Social Science and Medicine*, 54 (4): 621–4.

Shlapentokh, V. 2003. 'Russia's Acquiescence to Corruption Makes the State Machine Inept', *Communist and Post-Communist Studies*, 36 (2): 151–61.

Shoemaker, Robert B. 2002. 'The Taming of the Duel: Masculinity, Honour and Ritual Violence in London, 1660–1800', *Historical Journal*, 45 (3): 525–45.

Shook, Scott (Rocky) Lee. 2001. 'Probation Officers' Perceptions of the Seriousness of Behaviors Engaged in by Boys and Girls', dissertation, *Abstracts International, A: The Humanities and Social Sciences*, 62 (6): 2245-A.

Shover, Neal, and Andy Hochstetler. 2002. 'Cultural

Explanation and Organizational Crime', *Crime, Law and Social Change*, 37 (1): 1–18.

———, and John Paul Wright. 2001. *Crimes of Privilege: Readings in White-Collar Crime*. New York: Oxford University Press.

Siegel, Jane A., and Linda M. Williams. 2003. 'The Relationship between Child Sexual Abuse and Female Delinquency and Crime: A Prospective Study', *Journal of Research in Crime and Delinquency*, 40 (1): 71–94.

Siegel, Paul. 1979. 'Homophobia: Types, Origins, Remedies', *Christianity and Crisis*, 39 (17): 280–4.

Sieving, Renee E., Geoffrey Maruyama, Carolyn L. Williams, and Cheryl L. Perry. 2000. 'Pathways to Adolescent Alcohol Use: Potential Mechanisms of Parent Influence', *Journal of Research on Adolescence*, 10 (4): 489–514.

———, Cheryl L. Perry, and Carolyn L. Williams. 2000. 'Do Friendships Change Behaviors, or Do Behaviors Change Friendships? Examining Paths of Influence in Young Adolescents' Alcohol', *Use Journal of Adolescent Health*, 26 (1): 27–35.

Silver, Eric, Edward P., Mulvey, and Jeffrey W. Swanson. 2002. 'Neighborhood Structural Characteristics and Mental Disorder: Faris and Dunham Revisited', *Social Science and Medicine*, 55 (8): 1457–70.

Silverstein, Martin. 2001. 'The Ties That Bind: Family Surveillance of Canadian Parolees', *The Sociological Quarterly*, 42 (3): 395–420.

Simmel, Georg. 1906 [1902]. 'The Sociology of Secrecy and of Secret Societies', *American Journal of Sociology*, 11 (4): 441–98.

———. 1990 [1907]. *The Philosophy of Money*, 2nd edn. New York: Routledge.

———. 1991 [1908]. 'The Problem of Style', *Theory, Culture & Society*, 8 (3): 63–71.

Simon, Jeffrey D. 2001. *Terrorist Trap: America's Experience with Terrorism*, 2nd edn. Bloomington: Indiana University Press.

Simon, Jonathan. 1996. 'Discipline and Punish: The Birth of a Middle-Range Research Strategy', *Contemporary Sociology*, 25 (3): 316–19.

Simonelli, David. 2002. 'Anarchy, Pop and Violence: Punk Rock Subculture and the Rhetoric of Class, 1976–78', *Contemporary British History*, 16 (2): 121–44.

Simons, Ronald L., and Wei Chao. 1996. 'Conduct Problems', in *Understanding Differences between Divorced and Intact Families: Stress, Interaction, and Child Outcome*, ed. Ronald L. Simons and Associates. Thousand Oaks, CA: Sage, 125–43.

———, and Les Whitbeck. 1991. 'Running Away during Adolescence as a Precursor to Adult Homelessness', *Social Science Review*, 65 (2): 224–47.

Simons-Morton, B., D.L. Haynie, A.D. Crump, S.P. Eitel, and K.E. Saylor. 2001. 'Peer and Parent Influences on Smoking and Drinking among Early Adolescents', *Health Education & Behavior: The Official Publication of the Society for Public Health Education*, 28 (1): 95–107.

Single, Eric W., Joan M. Brewster, Patricia MacNeil, Jeffrey Hatcher, and Catherine Trainor. 1995. 'Alcohol and Drug Use', Results from the 1993 General Social Survey Report prepared for the Studies Unit, Health Promotion Directorate, Health Canada.

———, L. Robson, X. Xie, and J. Rehm. 1996. *The Costs of Substance Abuse in Canada*. Ottawa: Canadian Centre on Substance Abuse and the Centre for Addiction and Mental Health.

Sionean, Catlainn, Ralph J. Gina M. Wingood DiClemente, Richard Crosby, Brenda K. Cobb, Kathy Harrington, Susan L. Davies, Edward W. Hook, III, and M. Kim Oh. 2002. 'Psychosocial and Behavioral Correlates of Refusing Unwanted Sex among African-American Adolescent Females', *Journal of Adolescent Health*, 30 (1): 55–63.

Sivard, R.L., 1991. *World Military and Social Expenditures – 1991*. Washington, DC: World Priorities.

Skinner, B.F. 1953. *Science and Human Behavior*. New York: Macmillan Free Press.

Skocpol, Theda. 1979. *States and Social Revolutions: A Comparative Analysis of France, Russia, and China*. Cambridge: Cambridge University Press.

Skog, Ole-Jorgen. 1999. 'The Prevention Paradox Revisited', *Addiction*, 94 (5): 751–7.

Smith, Russell G. 1999. 'Organizations as Victims of Fraud', *Trends and Issues in Crime and Criminal Justice* (Sept.).

Smith, Susan J. 1984. 'Crime in the News', *British Journal of Criminology*, 24 (3): 289–95.

Smyth, Deirdre M. 1998. 'Common Sense Understanding of the Female Alcoholic'. Society for the Study of Social Problems.

Snider, Laureen. 1997. 'New Legislative Data and Causes of "Corporative" Criminality', *Criminologie*, 30 (1): 9–34.

Snyder, H.N., and M. Sickmund. 1995. *Juvenile Offenders and Victims: A Focus on Violence–Statistics Summary* (prepared by National Center for Juvenile Justice) (May). Washington, DC: Office of Juvenile Justice and Delinquency Prevention.

Solicitor General of Canada. 1997. 'Federal Solicitor General Andy Scott Presents Contribution to Telemarketing Fraud Prevention', 11 Dec. www.sgc.gc.ca/publications/news/19971211-e.asp.

———. 1998. 'Major Study on Organized Crime Confirms Need for National Strategy Solicitor General Andy Scott Tells Chiefs of Police', www.psepc-sppcc.gc.ca/publications/news/19980824_e.asp. Accessed on 24 August.

Spillane-Grieco, E. 1984. 'Characteristics of a Helpful Relationship: A Study of Empathic Understanding and Positive Regard between Runaways and Their Parents', *Adolescence*, 19 (73): 63–75.

Spirito, Anthony, and James Overholser. 2003. 'Child

and Adolescent Psychiatric Eemergencies: Family Psychodynamic Issues', *Child & Adolescent Psychiatric Clinics of North America*, 12 (4): 649–65.

————, Sylvia Valeri, Julie Boergers, and Deidre Donaldson. 2003. 'Predictors of Continued Suicidal Behavior in Adolescents Following a Suicide Attempt', *Journal of Clinical Child & Adolescent Psychology*, 32 (2): 284–9.

Spitzer, Brenda L., Katherine A. Henderson, and Marilyn T. Zivian. 1999. 'Gender Differences in Population versus Media Body Sizes: A Comparison over Four Decades', *Sex Roles*, 40 (7–8): 545–65.

Spohn, Cassia C., and Jeffrey W. Spears. 1997. 'Gender and Case Processing Decisions: A Comparison of Case Outcomes for Male and Female Defendants Charged with Violent Felonies', *Women and Criminal Justice*, 8 (3): 29–59.

Stack, Steven, Ira Wasserman, and Roger Kern. 2004. 'Adult Social Bonds and Use of Internet Pornography', *Social Science Quarterly*, 85 (1): 75–88.

Stanko, Elizabeth A. 1992. 'The Case of Fearful Women: Gender, Personal Safety and Fear of Crime', *Women and Criminal Justice*, 4 (1): 117–35.

Starfield, B. 2001. 'Basic Concepts in Population Health and Health Care', *Journal of Epidemiology and Community Health*, 55 (7): 452–4.

Stark, Leonard P. 1991. 'Traditional Gender Role Beliefs and Individual Outcomes: An Exploratory Analysis', *Sex Roles*, 24 (9–10): 639–50.

Statistics Canada. n.d. 'On Fraud'. www.statcan.ca.

————. 1993. 'The Daily: The Violence Against Women Survey', 18 Nov.

————. 1997. 'A Graphical Overview of Crime and the Administration of Justice in Canada', cat. no. 85F0018XIE.

————. 2000a. 'The Daily: Homicide Statistics', 18 Oct.

————. 2000b. 'The Daily: Break and Enter', 19 Dec.

————. 2001. 'The Daily: Crime Comparisons between Canada and the United States', 18 Dec.

————. 2004a. 'The Daily: Alcohol and Drug Use in Early Adolescence', 15 (3): 18 May.

————. 2004b. 'The Daily: Canadian Community Health Survey: A First Look', 15 June.

————. 2004c. 'The Daily: Health Reports', 15 (4): 21 July.

————. 2005. 'Cases in Youth Criminal Court, 1998–2002' cat. no. 63-002, table no. 252-0003. www.statcan.ca/english/Pgdb/legal25a.htm. Accessed April 2005.

Steen, Sara, and Mark A. Cohen. 2004. 'Assessing the Public's Demand for Hate Crime Penalties', *Justice Quarterly*, 21 (1): 91–124.

Stefani, Paolo de. 2002. 'The International Criminal Court: Toward the "Globalization" of Justice', *Aggiornamenti Sociali*, 53 (6): 490–500.

Stein, Judith A., Michelle Burden Leslie, and Adeline Nyamathi. 2002. 'Relative Contributions of Parent Substance Use and Childhood Maltreatment to Chronic Homelessness, Depression, and Substance Abuse Problems among Homeless Women: Mediating Roles of Self-Esteem and Abuse in Adulthood', *Child Abuse and Neglect*, 26 (10): 1011–27.

Steinberg, Laurence, Susie D. Lamborn, Nancy Darling, Nina S. Mounts, and Sanford M. Dornbusch. 1994. 'Over-Time Changes in Adjustment and Competence among Adolescents from Authoritative, Authoritarian, Indulgent, and Neglectful Families', *Child Development*, 65 (3): 754–70.

Stephens, T., and N. Joubert. 2001. 'The Economic Burden of Mental Health Problems in Canada', *Chronic Diseases in Canada*, 22 (1): 18–23.

Stiffman, Arlene Rubin. 1989a. 'Physical and Sexual Abuse in Runaway Youths', *Child Abuse and Neglect*, 13 (3): 417–26.

————. 1989b. 'Suicide Attempts in Runaway Youths', *Suicide and Life Threatening Behavior*, 19 (2): 147–59.

Stiles, Beverly L., Xiaoru Liu, and Howard B. Kaplan. 2000. 'Relative Deprivation and Deviant Adaptations: The Mediating Effects of Negative Self-Feelings', *Journal of Research in Crime and Delinquency*, 37 (1): 64–90.

Stoelb, Matt, and Jennifer Chiriboga. 1998. 'A Process Model for Assessing Adolescent Risk for Suicide', *Journal of Adolescence. Special Adolescent suicide: Risk, Assessment, and Treatment*, 21 (4): 359–70.

Storr, Merl. 2002. 'Classy Lingerie', *Feminist Review*, 71: 18–36.

Stover, E., and R. McGrath. 1991. *Landmines in Cambodia: The Coward's War* (New York: Asia Watch/Human Rights Watch and Physicians for Human Rights.

————, ————. 1992. 'Calling for an International Ban on a Crippling Scourge: Land Mines', *Human Rights Watch*, 10 (2): 6–7.

Straus, Murray A. 2004. 'Cross-Cultural Reliability and Validity of the Revised Conflict Tactics Scales: A Study of University Student Dating Couples in 17 Nations', *Cross-Cultural Research*, 38 (4): 407–32.

————, and Denise A. Donnelly. 1994. *Beating the Devil Out of Them: Corporal Punishment in American Families*. New York: Lexington Books/Macmillan.

Strauss, R.S., and H.A. Pollack. 2001. 'Epidemic Increase in Childhood Overweight, 1986–1998', *Journal of the American Medical Association*, 286 (22): 2845–8.

Substance Abuse and Mental Health Services Administration. 1995. 'National Household Survey on Drug Abuse', unpublished data. Rockville, MD: Center for Mental Health.

Sugarman, David B., and Susan L. Frankel. 1996. 'Patriarchal Ideology and Wife-Assault: A Meta-Analytic Review', *Journal of Family Violence*, 11 (1): 13–40.

Sullivan, Thomas J. 1997. *Introduction to Social Problems*, 4th edn. Boston: Allyn & Bacon.

Summerfield, Derek. 2000. 'War and Mental Health: A Brief

Overview', *British Medical Journal*, 321: 232–5.

Susser, Ezra S., Shang P. Lin, Sarah A, Conover, and Elmer L. Struening. 1991. 'Childhood Antecedents of Homelessness in Psychiatric Patients', *American Journal of Psychiatry*, 148 (8): 1026–30.

Sutherland, Edwin. 1940. 'White Collar Criminality', *American Sociological Review*, 5: 1.

——. 1949. *White Collar Crime*. New York: Dryden Press.

Svensson, Robert. 2002. 'Strategic Offences in the Criminal Career Context', *British Journal of Criminology*, 42 (2): 395–411.

——. 2003. 'Gender Differences in Adolescent Drug Use: The Impact of Parental Monitoring and Peer Deviance', *Youth and Society*, 34 (3): 300–29.

Swain, Jon. 2002. 'The Right Stuff: Fashioning an Identity through Clothing in a Junior School', *Gender and Education*, 14 (1): 53–69.

Swora, Maria Gabrielle. 2001. 'Personhood and Disease in Alcoholics Anonymous: A Perspective from the Anthropology of Religious Healing', *Mental Health, Religion & Culture*, 4 (1): 1–21.

Sydie, R.A. 1994. 'Sex and the Sociological Fathers', *La Revue Canadienne de Sociologie et d'Anthropologie/The Canadian Review of Sociology and Anthropology*, 31 (2): 117–38.

Sykes, Gresham M., and David Matza. 1957. 'Techniques of Neutralization: A Theory of Delinquency,'' *American Sociological Review*, 22 (6): 664–70.

Takahashi, Melanie, and Tim Olaveson. 2003. 'Music, Dance and Raving Bodies: Raving as Spirituality in the Central Canadian Rave Scene', *Journal of Ritual Studies*, 17 (2): 72–96.

Tarde, Gabriel. 1903. *The Laws of Imitation*, trans. E.C. Parsons, with an Introduction by F. Giddings. New York: Henry, Holt and Co.

Taub, Diane E., and Penelope A. McLorg. 2001. 'Anorexia Nervosa', in *Extraordinary Behavior: A Case Study Approach to Understanding Social Problems*, ed. Dennis L. Peck and Norman A. Dolch. Westport, CT: Praeger.

Taylor, S. Martin, M.J. Dear, and G.B Hall. 1979. 'Attitudes Toward the Mentally Ill and Reactions to Mental Health Facilities', *Social Science and Medicine*, 13D (4): 281–90.

Teare, John F., Karen Authier, and Roger Peterson. 1994. 'Differential Patterns of Post-shelter Placement as a Function of Problem Type and Severity', *Journal of Child and Family Studies*, 3 (1): 7–22.

Teevan, James J., and Heather B. Dryburgh. 2000. 'First Person Accounts and Sociological Explanations of Delinquency', *La Revue Canadienne de Sociologie et d'Anthropologie/The Canadian Review of Sociology and Anthropology*, 37 (1): 77–93.

Tennestedt, S., and J. McKinlay. 1989. 'Informal Care for Frail Older Persons', in *Aging and Health Care*, ed. M. Ory and K. Bond. London: Routledge.

Tenore, Josie L. 2001. 'Challenges in Eating Disorders: Past and Present', *American Family Physician* (1 Aug.).

Tewksbury, Richard, Elizabeth L. Grossi, Geetha Suresh, and Jeff Helms. 1999. 'Hate Crimes against Gay Men and Lesbian Women: A Routine Activity Approach for Predicting Victimization Risk', *Humanity & Society*, 23 (2): 125–42.

Thio, Alex. 1998. *Deviant Behavior*, 5th edn. New York: Addison Wesley Longman.

Thomas, Charles W., and John R. Hepburn. 1986. *Crime, Criminal Law, and Criminology*. Dubuque, IA: W.C. Brown.

Thomas, George, Alan Reifman, Grace M. Barnes, and Michael P. Farrell. 2000. 'Delayed Onset of Drunkenness as a Protective Factor for Adolescent Alcohol Misuse and Sexual Risk Taking: A Longitudinal Study', *Deviant Behavior*, 21 (2): 181–210.

Thombs, Dennis L., Scott Olds, and Jennifer Ray-Tomasek. 2001. 'Adolescent Perceptions of College Student Drinking', *American Journal of Health Behavior*, 25 (5): 492–501.

Thompson, Angela M., and Karen E. Chad. 2002. 'The Relationship of Social Physique Anxiety to Risk for Developing an Eating Disorder in Young Females', *Journal of Adolescent Health*, 31: 183–9.

Thompson, Edward H., Jr., Christopher Grisanti, and Joseph H. Pleck. 1985. 'Attitudes toward the Male Role and Their Correlates', *Sex Roles*, 13 (7–8): 413–27.

Thompson, Maxine Seaborn, Marvin Swartz, and Jeffery Swanson. 2000. 'Fighting and Acting Out: Client's Behaviors as Predictors of Caregiver's Psychological Well-Being'. Southern Sociological Society.

Thrasher, Frederick. 1927. *The Gang*. Chicago: University of Chicago Press.

Tilly, Charles. 1964. *The Vendée*. Cambridge, MA: Harvard University Press.

Tomaszewski, E. Andreas. 2003. '"Public" and "Private" Crimes against Women in Eastern Ontario Public Housing: The Role of Perceived Collective Efficacy', dissertation, *Abstracts International, A: The Humanities and Social Sciences*, 64 (5): 1857-A.

Tomsen, Stephen. 1997. 'A Top Night: Social Protest, Masculinity and the Culture of Drinking Violence', *British Journal of Criminology*, 37 (1): 90–102.

Torassa, Ulysses. 2000. 'Some with HIV Aren't Disclosing Before Sex: UCSF Researcher's 1,397-person Study Presented During AIDS Conference', *San Francisco Examiner*, 15 July.

Torres, Sam. 1999. 'Hate Crimes against African Americans: The Extent of the Problem', *Journal of Contemporary Criminal Justice*, 15 (1): 48–63.

Toulalan, Sarah. 2001. 'Private Rooms and Back Doors in Abundance: The Illusion of Privacy in Pornography in Seventeenth-Century England', *Women's History Review*, 10 (4): 701–19.

———. 2003. 'Extraordinary Satisfactions: Lesbian Visibility in Seventeenth-Century Pornography in England', *Gender & History*, 15 (1): 50–68.

Toumbourou, John W., and M. Elizabeth Gregg. 2002. 'Impact of an Empowerment-based Parent Education Program on the Reduction of Youth Suicide Risk Factors', *Journal of Adolescent Health*, 31 (3): 277–85.

Tretter, F. 1995. 'Are There Protective Factors at Consumption of Now Illegal Drugs in Industrialized Cultures?' *Curare*, 18 (2): 409–14.

Trocmé, N., B. MacLaurin, B. Fallon, J. Daciuk, D. Billingsley, M. Tourigny, M. Mayer, J. Wright, K. Barter, G. Burford, J. Hornick, R. Sullivan, and B. McKenzie. 2001. *Canadian Incidence Study of Reported Child Abuse and Neglect*. Ottawa: Public Works and Government Services.

Troth, A., and C.C. Peterson. 2000. 'Factors Predicting Safe-Sex Talk and Condom Use in Early Sexual Relationships', *Health Communication*, 12 (2): 195–218.

Tufts, J. 2000. 'Public Attitudes Toward the Criminal Justice System', *Juristat*, vol. 20, no. 12. Ottawa: Canadian Centre for Justice Statistics.

———, and Julian V. Roberts. 2002. 'Sentencing Juvenile Offenders: Comparing Public Preferences and Judicial Practice', *Criminal Justice Policy Review*, 13 (1): 46–64.

Turbin, Carole. 2002. 'Fashioning the American Man: The Arrow Collar Man, 1907–1931', *Gender & History*, 14 (3): 470–91.

Turner-Bowker, Diane M. 2001. 'How Can You Pull Yourself Up by Your Bootstraps, If You Don't Have Boots? Work-Appropriate Clothing for Poor Women', *Journal of Social Issues*, 57 (2): 311–22.

Ulmer, Jeffery T., and J. William Spencer. 1999. 'The Contributions of an Interactionist Approach to Research and Theory on Criminal Careers', *Theoretical Criminology*, 3 (1): 95–124.

Upchurch, Dawn M., Carol S. Aneshensel, Jyoti Mudgal, and Clea Sucoff McNeely. 2001. 'Sociocultural Contexts of Time to First Sex among Hispanic Adolescents', *Journal of Marriage and the Family*, 63 (4): 1158–69.

US Department of State. 2004. 'Patterns of Global Terrorism, 2003'. Released by the Office of the Coordinator for Counterterrorism, 29 April 2004. See "Overview of State-Sponsored Terrorism," also "Appendix B—Background Information on Designated Foreign Terrorist Organizations." www.state.gov/s/ct/rls/pgtrpt/2003/31711.htm.

Vail, Donald Angus. 2000. 'The Tattoos We Deserve: Producing Culture and Constructing Elitism', dissertation, *Abstracts International, A: The Humanities and Social Sciences*, 61 (3): 1172-A.

Van Gundy, Karen. 2002. 'Gender, the Assertion of Autonomy, and the Stress Process in Young Adulthood', *Social Psychology Quarterly*, 65 (4): 346–63.

Vander Ven, Thomas M. 1998. 'Fear of Victimization and the Interactional Construction of Harassment in a Latino Neighborhood', *Journal of Contemporary Ethnography*, 27 (3): 374–98.

———, and Marikay Vander Ven. 2003. 'Exploring Patterns of Mother-Blaming in Anorexia Scholarship: A Study in the Sociology of Knowledge', *Human Studies*, 26 (1): 97–119.

VanderWaal, Curtis J., Erin Ruel, Lisa Powell, Yvonne Terry-McElrath, Mark Boward, Darin Erickson, Eileen Harwood, Duane McBride, Brian Flay, and Cindy Tworek. 2003. 'The Role of School and Community Support Networks in Reducing Teen Substance Use: Variable Description and Development of a Measurement Model'. Southern Sociological Society.

Vanier Institute of the Family. March 1996. 'Communities and Families Working to Prevent Youth Crime: A Snowball's Chance', *Transition*.

———. 2000. *Families and Health*, 13 (Sept.).

Vannath, Chea. 2003. 'Khmer Rouge and National Reconciliation', *Peace Review*, 14 (3): 303–7.

Varese, Federico. 1994. 'Is Sicily the Future of Russia? Private Protection and the Rise of the Russian Mafia', *Archives Europeennes de Sociologie*, 35 (2): 224–58.

Varga, C.A. 2001. 'Coping with HIV/AIDS in Durban's Commercial Sex Industry', *AIDS Care*, 13 (3): 351–65.

Veblen, Thorstein. 1979 [1899]. *Theory of the Leisure Class*. Harmondsworth: Penguin Books.

Vergun, Pamela Bea, Sanford M. Dornbusch, and Laurence Steinberg. 1996. '"Come All of You Turn to and Help One Another": Authoritative Parenting, Community Orientation, and Deviance among High School Students', American Sociological Association.

Villarreal, Andres. 2002. 'Political Competition and Violence in Mexico: Hierarchical Social Control in Local Patronage Structures', *American Sociological Review*, 67 (4): 477–98.

Von Hirsch, A. 1990. 'The Ethics of Community-Based Sanctions', *Crime and Delinquency*, 36 (1).

von Schriltz, Karl. 1999. 'Foucault on the Prison: Torturing History to Punish Capitalism', *Critical Review*, 13 (3–4): 391–411.

Wallace, M. 2003a. 'Crime Statistics in Canada, 2002', *Juristat*, vol. 23, no. 5. Ottawa: Canadian Centre for Justice Statistics.

———. 2003b. 'Motor Vehicle Theft in Canada, 2001', *Juristat*, vol. 23, no. 1, cat. no. 85-002-XIE. Ottawa: Canadian Centre for Justice Statistics.

Walzer, Michael J. 1965. *The Revolution of the Saints: A Study in the Origins of Radical Politics*. Cambridge, MA: Harvard University Press.

Wardle, J., C. Guthrie, S. Sanderson, L. Birch, and R. Plomin. 2001. 'Food and Activity Preferences in Children of Lean and Obese Parents', *International Journal of Obesity and Related Metabolic Disorders: Journal of the International Association for the Study of Obesity*, 25 (7): 971–7.

Warner, Jessica. 1997. 'The Sanctuary of Sobriety: The Emergence of Temperance as a Feminine Virtue in Tudor and Stuart England', *Addiction*, 92 (1): 97–111.

———. 1998. 'Historical Perspectives on the Shifting Boundaries around Youth and Alcohol: The Example of Pre-Industrial England, 1350–1750', *Addiction*, 93 (5): 641–57.

Watson, John B. 1913. 'Psychology as the Behaviorist Views it', *Psychological Review*, 20: 158–77.

Watson-Franke, Maria-Barbara. 2002. 'A World in Which Women Move Freely without Fear of Men: An Anthropological Perspective on Rape', *Women's Studies International Forum*, 25 (6): 599–606.

Weber, Max. 1958. *The Protestant Ethic and the Spirit of Capitalism*. New York: Charles Scribner's Sons.

Websdale, Neil. 1991. 'Disciplining the Non-Disciplinary Spaces, the Rise of Policing as an Aspect of Governmentality in 19th Century Eugene, Oregon', *Policing and Society*, 2 (2): 89–115.

Weerasinghe, Jana, and Lorne Tepperman. 1995. 'Suicide and Happiness: Seven Tests of the Connection', *Social Indicators Research*, 32 (3): 199–233.

Weiss, Gregory L., Daniel L. Larsen, and W. Kevin Baker. 1996. 'The Development of Health Protective Behaviors among College Students', *Journal of Behavioral Medicine*, 19 (2): 143–61.

Weiss, Mitchell G., Sushrut Jadhav, R.Raguram, Penelope Vounatsou, and Roland Littlewood. 2001. 'Psychiatric Stigma across Cultures: Local Validation in Bangalore and London', *Anthropology and Medicine*, 8 (1): 71–87.

West, Candace, and Don H. Zimmerman. 1987. 'Doing Gender', *Gender & Society*, 1 (2): 125–51.

West, W. Gordon. 1978. 'Serious Theft as an Occupation', Society for the Study of Social Problems.

Westwood, L. 2001. 'A Quiet Revolution in Brighton: Dr. Helen Boyle's Pioneering Approach to Mental Health Care, 1899–1939', *Social History of Medicine*, 14 (3): 439–57.

Wheaton, Blair. 2001. 'The Role of Sociology in the Study of Mental Health . . . and the Role of Mental Health in the Study of Sociology', *Journal of Health and Social Behavior*, 42 (3): 221–34.

White, Lynn. 1994. 'Stepfamilies over the Life Course: Social Support', in *Stepfamilies: Who Benefits? Who Does Not?* ed. Alan Booth and Judy Dunn. Hillsdale, NJ: Lawrence Erlbaum.

White, Patrick. 2003. 'Sex Education; or, How the Blind Became Heterosexual', *GLQ*, 9 (1–2): 133–47.

Whitebook, Joel. 2002. 'Michel Foucault: A Marcusean in Structuralist Clothing', *Thesis Eleven*, 71: 52–70.

WHO (World Health Organization). 1996. 'Violence against Women', consultation. Geneva: World Health Organization.

———. 2000. Press release, WHO/67, 12 November 1999. www.who.int/inf-pr-1999/en/pr99-67.html. Accessed 30 April 2005.

———. 2001. 'The World Health Report 2001: Mental Disorders Affect One in Four People', press release, WHO/42, 28 September 2001. www.who.int/inf-pr-2001/en/pr2001-42.html. Accessed 30 April 2005.

———. 2004. 'World Suicide Prevention Day—10 September 2004'. www.who.int/mediacentre/news/releases/2004/pr61/en/.

Whyte, William Foote, Jr. 1993 [1943]. *Street Corner Society: The Social Structure of an Italian Slum*, 4th edn. Chicago: University of Chicago Press.

Wickrama, K.A.S., Rand D. Conger, Lora Ebert Wallace, and Glen H. Elder, Jr. 1999. 'The Intergenerational Transmission of Health-Risk Behaviors: Adolescent Lifestyles and Gender Moderating Effects', *Journal of Health and Social Behavior*, 40 (3): 258–72.

Wild, T. Cameron. 2002. 'Personal Drinking and Sociocultural Drinking Norms: A Representative Population Study', *Journal of Studies on Alcohol*, 63 (4): 469–75.

Wilkinson, R.G., I. Kawachi, and B. Kennedy. 1998. 'Mortality, the Social Environment, Crime and Violence', *Social Health and Illness*, 20: 578–97.

Williams, Linda. 1989. *Hard Core: Power, Pleasure and the Frenzy of the Visible*. Berkeley: University of California Press.

Williams, Phil, and Roy Godson. 2002. 'Anticipating Organized and Transnational Crime', *Crime, Law and Social Change*, 37: 311–55.

Williams, Robert J., and Susan P. Gloster. 1999. 'Knowledge of Fetal Alcohol Syndrome (FAS) among Natives in Northern Manitoba', *Journal of Studies on Alcohol*, 60 (6): 833–6.

Williams, S.P., P.S. Gardos, B. Ortiz-Torres, S. Tross, and A.A. Ehrhardt. 2001. 'Urban Women's Negotiation Strategies for Safer Sex with Their Male Partners', *Women & Health*, 33 (3–4): 133–48.

Williamson, Celia, and Terry Cluse-Tolar. 2002. 'Pimp-Controlled Prostitution: Still an Integral Part of Street Life', *Violence Against Women*, 8 (9): 1074–92.

Wilson, Brian S. 1998. 'Theorizing Youth Leisure Cultures, Locating Canadian Youth: The Cases of Inner City Recreation Centre Culture and "Rave" Culture' International Sociological Association.

Wilson, J.Q., and G.L. Keeling. 1982. 'Broken Windows', *The Atlantic Monthly*, 249 (3): 29–38.

Winston, Diane. 2002. 'Living in the Material World: The Changing Role of Salvation Army Women, 1880–1918', *Journal of Urban History*, 28 (4): 466–87.

Witteman, P. 1991. 'Lost in America', *Time*, 11 Feb., 76–7.

Wojcicki, Janet Maia. (002. 'Commercial Sex Work or Ukuphanda? Sex-for-Money Exchange in Soweto and Hammanskraal Area, South Africa', *Culture, Medicine and Psychiatry*, 26 (3): 339–70.

———, and Josephine Malala. 2001. 'Condom Use, Power and HIV/AIDS Risk: Sex-Workers Bargain for Survival in Hillbrow/Joubert Park/Berea, Johannesburg', *Social Science and Medicine*, 53 (1): 99–121.

Wolf, Rosalie S. 1996. 'Elder Abuse and Family Violence: Testimony Presented before the U.S. Senate Special Committee on Aging', *Journal of Elder Abuse and Neglect*, 8 (1): 81–96.

Wolfgang, Marvin. 1966. *Patterns in Criminal Homicide*. Philadelphia: University of Philadelphia Press.

———, and F. Ferracuti. 1967. *The Subculture of Violence: Towards an Integrated Theory in Criminology*, London: Tavistock.

Wolitski, R.J., C.A.M. Rietmeijer, G.M. Goldbaum, and R.M. Wilson. 1998. 'HIV Serostatus Disclosure among Gay and Bisexual Men in Four American Cities: General Patterns and Relation to Sexual Practices', *AIDS Care*, 10 (5): 599–610.

Wonderlich, Stephen A., Ross D. Crosby, James E. Mitchell, Jennifer A. Roberts, Beth Haseltine, Gail DeMuth, and Kevin M. Thompson. 2000. 'Relationship of Childhood Sexual Abuse and Eating Disturbance in Children', *Journal of the American Academy of Child & Adolescent Psychiatry*, 39 (10): 1277–83.

Wood, Robert T. 1998. 'A History of the Straightedge Youth Subculture: Towards a Theory of Subcultural Evolution'. International Sociological Association.

Woods, M. Michael. 2003. 'Deconstructing Rural Protest: The Emergence of a New Social Movement', *Journal of Rural Studies*, 19 (3): 309–25.

Wooldredge, John D. 1998. 'Inmate Lifestyles and Opportunities for Victimization', *Journal of Research in Crime and Delinquency*, 35 (4): 480–502.

Worrall, John. 2002. *Does 'Broken Windows' Law Enforcement Reduce Serious Crime?* Sacramento, CA: California Institute for County Government.

Wrangham, R., and D. Peterson. 1997. *Demonic Males: Apes and the Origins of Human Violence*. New York: Houghton Mifflin.

Wright, Eric Reaney. 1994. 'Caring for Those Who "Can't": Gender, Network Structure, and the Burden of Caring for People with Mental Illness', dissertation, *Abstracts International, A: The Humanities and Social Sciences*, 55 (2): 380-A.

———, William P. Gronfein, and Timothy J. Owens. 2000.

'Deinstitutionalization, Social Rejection, and the Self-Esteem of Former Mental Patients', *Journal of Health and Social Behavior*, 41 (1): 68–90.

Yaktin, U.S., and S. Labban. 1992. 'Traumatic War: Stress and Schizophrenia', *Journal of Psychosocial Nursing and Mental Health Services*, 30 (6): 29–33.

Yep, G.A. 2000. 'Disclosure of HIV Infection in Interpersonal Relationships: A Communication Boundary Management Approach', in *Balancing the Secrets of Private Disclosures*, ed. S. Petronio. Mahwah, NJ: Erlbaum, 83–96.

Yesilova, Katja. 2001. 'The Double Standard in Sex Education', *Sosiologia*, 38 (3): 192–204.

Yinger, J. Milton, and Mark N. Katz. 2001. 'Revolution: Refining Its Defining', *International Journal of Group Tensions*, 30 (4).

Yllo, Kersti, and Murray A. Straus. 1981. 'Interpersonal Violence among Married and Cohabiting Couples', *Family Relations*, 30 (3): 339–47.

Youth Crime Statistics Canada. 2003. http://142.206.72.67/04/04b/04b-002b-e.htm.

Zahn, Margaret A., and Patricia L. McCall. 1999. 'Homicide in the 20th-Century United States: Trends and Patterns', in *Studying and Preventing Homicide: Issues and Challenges*, ed. M. Dwayne Smith and Margaret A. Zahn. Thousand Oaks, CA: Sage, 10–30.

Zaider, Talia I., Jeffrey G. Johnson, and Sarah J. Cockell. 2002. 'Psychiatric Disorders Associated with the Onset and Persistence of Bulimia Nervosa and Binge Eating Disorder during Adolescence', *Journal of Youth and Adolescence*, 31 (5): 319–29.

Zhou, Min. 1999. 'Segmented Assimilation: Issues, Controversies and Recent Research on the New Second Generation', in *The Handbook of International Migration: The American Experience*, ed. C. Hirschman, P. Kasinitz, and J. DeWind. New York: Russell Sage, 196–211.

Zimbardo, P. 1971. 'The Pathology of Imprisonment', *Society*, 9: 4–8.

Zimmermann, E. 1983. *Political Violence, Crises and Revolutions: Theories and Research*. Cambridge, MA: Schenkman.

Zola, Irving. 1994. 'Medicine as an Institution of Social Control', in *The Sociology of Health and Illness: Critical Perspectives*, ed. Peter Conrad and Rochelle Kern. New York: St Martin's Press.

Index

Aaronson, Beatrice, 182

'ABCX family crisis model', 85

Aboriginal people: substance abuse and, 155; youth, 203

abuse: child, 220–1; dating and, 174; elder, 220; sexual, 112; youth and, 199–200; *see also* substance abuse

acceptance, 39

addiction, 137; attitudes to, 149–50; nicotine, 149; treatment for, 146–7, 162–5; *see also* substance abuse

Adler, Freda, 197

Adorno, T.W. et al., 131

advertising, 43–4, 158–9, 187

age: violent crime and, 214–15

aggressive behaviours: youth and, 173, 175

AIDS, *see* HIV/AIDS

Akpinar, Aylin, 210

alcohol, 136; abuse of, 140–1; abusers of, 150–1; age restrictions on, 143–5; gender and, 139–40, 145; harm and, 147, 149; health and, 160–1; social role of, 137–43; violence and, 139–40; youth and, 179–81, 183–4, 185; *see also* substance abuse

Alcoholics Anonymous (AA), 162–3

Alexander-Mott, D., and D.B. Lumsden, 51

Alford, C. Fred, 32

Alvarez, Gomez, 165

'anomie theory', 6, 7

anomie, 39, 52, 155–6, 237

anorexia, 40, 47–9, 56; *see also* eating disorders

antidepressants, 97

anxiety disorders, 70–1, 90

appearance issues, 38–65; communities and cultures of, 44–7; control of, 60; families and, 59–60; gendered, 40–1; health consequences of, 56–8; history of, 42–4; intended, 38, 44–7; 'norms', 39; punk, 45–7; social consequences of, 58–9; social meaning of, 40–2; stigmatization and, 54–6; theories about, 51–6, 62–3; unintended, 38, 47–51

Arens, Diana A., 82

Arrow Man, 43–4

Ashton, C.H., 154

assault: physical, 211, 212; sexual, 211, 212, 227–8, 228–9, 230, 231

asylums, lunatic, 67, 76

Atkins, Randolph Gilbert, Jr, 163

attachment, 9–10, 176–7; inadequate, 6

automobiles: crime and, 242–3; theft of, 189–90; youth and, 179–81; *see also* driving

Baba, Yoko, and D. Mark Austin, 257

Babic, Dragutin, 289

Baker, Mary Holland, et al., 258

bandit communities, 284

Baron, Stephen W., 193

bawdy-house, 108

Beal, Anne C., et al., 184

Beare, Margaret, 263

beauty: ideals of, 39, 56

Becker, Howard, 21, 139, 153

Bedlam, 67

behaviourism, 237–9

Beki, Cem, et al., 14

belief (social bond), 177

Belyea, Michael J., and Matthew T. Zingraff, 256, 257

bipolar disorder, 71

Black, Conrad, 240

blood feud, 210

Blumer, Herbert, 19, 20–1

body piercing, 44–5, 52–3; health and, 58

body standards, 39

Bolen, Rebecca M., and Leah J. Lamb, 220

Boritch, H., 123

Bornstein, Gary, and Zohar Gilula, 208

Bourdieu, Pierre, 43

Box, Steven, and Chris Hale, 197

Brent, David A., 73

Breton, Raymond, 285

bribery, 269

Britt, Chester L., 238

'broken windows theory', 252

Brookman, Fiona, 210

Brown, Marilyn, 156

'brutalization effect', 208

Buchanan, David, 283

bulimia, 40, 47–50, 57; *see also* eating disorders

Burr, Vivien, and Trevor Butt, 83

Butler, Judith, 123

caffeine, 137

Calhoun, Martin L., 290

Cambodia, 290

Canada: corruption in, 269–70, 271; populism in, 277–8; rebellions in, 277; revolutionaries in, 284–5; riots in, 273; substance abuse and, 137; terrorists in, 280

Canadian Incidence Study of Reported Child Abuse and Neglect, 220

Canadian Tobacco Use Monitoring Survey (CTUMS), 148, 149

Cancian, Francesca, and James W. Gibson, 275

career, 2–3

caregivers: burden of, 87, 89

Carlyle, Thomas, 40

Carrington, Peter, 262

Castro, Russell A., et al., 166

Chambliss, William J., 165, 253

chemicals: use of, 136–7

Cheung, Yuet W., Patricia G. Erickson, and Tammy C. Landau, 152

children: clothing and, 41–2; obesity and, 50–1, 53; patriarchy and, 199; pornography and, 116–17; sex trade and, 127, 131–2; violent crime and, 220–1; war and, 290, 292; *see also* youth

Chrétien, Jean, 269–70

cigarettes, *see* tobacco

class: appearance issues and, 42–3; delinquency and, 176, 196, 198–9

Clemente, Frank, and Michael B. Kleiman, 256, 257

Clemmer, Donald, 260

clientelism, 248

Clinard, Marshall B., and Richard Quinney, 249

clothing, 39, 40–4; gendered, 40–1; school, 62; traditional, 62

Cloward, Richard, and Lloyd Ohlin, 7

Cobain, Kurt, 74–5

cocaine, 145; abusers of, 152; health and, 162; *see also* substance abuse

Cohen, Albert, 7, 192

Cohen, Ronald, 275

Cohen, Stanley, 21

collective behaviour, 278

Collins, Alan F., 84

colonization: appearance issues and, 42; substance abuse and, 155, 156

commitment (social bond), 176–7

communities: appearance issues and, 44–7; bandit, 284; crime and, 192–3, 215–17, 246–9; delinquency and, 191–4; deviant, 23–4; guerilla, 285; mental illness and, 76–80; revolution and, 284–5; sexual deviance and, 118–19; substance abuse and, 152–4; terrorism and, 287–8; *see also* cultures; subcultures

community (three C's), 2–4

community-based treatment: mental illness and, 95–6

compulsive behaviour, 58

condom use, 181–2, 188

Conflict Tactics Scales, 221

conflict theory, 3, 10–19, 33–4; appearance issues, and, 53–4; crime and, 225; delinquency and, 195–6; mental illness and, 81; non-violent crime and, 252–3; sexual deviance and, 121–2; substance abuse and, 156; violence and, 207; war and protest and, 281–2

conformity, 7–8, 39

'conspicuous consumption', 42

consumerism, 43

'contagion', 278

control, internal *v*. external, 237–9

control theory, 176–7, 224

Cooley, Charles, 20, 173

corruption, political, 267, 269–72

Cova, Bernard, 183

Cressey, Donald, 249–50

crime, 206; amateur, 240, 242–3; business, 236, 239–40, 245–6, 255; classical sociological studies of, 249–50; corporate, 239–40, 263, 264; 'electronic', 259; fear and, 255–8; female, 197; hate, 218, 230; justifications for, 254; mental illness and, 90–1; political, 267–97; rates of, 12, 13; sexual deviance and, 102, 108–10, 131–2; statistics on, 13, 16–17; substance abuse and, 159–60; war, 257, 269, 289; white collar, 240, 241, 246, 247, 264; youth and, 191; *see also* delinquency; non-violent crime; organized crime; street crime; violent crime

criminal behaviour: internal and external controls on, 237–9

Criminal Code, 211, 212; prostitution and, 108–9

criminal justice system: violent crime and, 213–2

criminals: characteristics of, 243–6; female, 228; male and female, 28–9; violent, 213–15

Crisp, Arthur, et al., 187

culture(s), 2–4; appearance issues and, 44–7; crime and, 246–9; punk, 40, 45–7, 52, 54, 62; sexual deviance and, 118–19; strategic, 279, 281; substance abuse and, 152–4; *see also* subcultures

Dahrendorf, Ralf, 225

dating: abuse and, 174

Davidson, Julia O'Connell, 124

Davis, Kingsley, 4, 120

death(s): 'by government', 268, 294; war, 291

death penalty, 208

decriminalization: drugs and, 165–7

De Haanm, Willem, and Jaco Vos, 238

de-institutionalization, 76, 81–2, 95–6

delinquency, 172–205; communities and subcultures of, 191–4; definition, 189; 'drift' into, 173; gender and, 28–9; health and social consequences of, 200; history of, 187–9; policy and, 200–2; as term, 174; theories about, 194–200; types of, 189–91; work ethic and, 177–9; *see also* youth

D'Emilio, J., 119

De Munck, Victor C., and Andrey Korotayev, 103

depression, 68–9, 71, 89–90, 93, 97; postpartum, 92

Derrida, Jacques, 137

Dewhirst, Timothy, and Robert Sparks, 187

Differential Association Theory, 23, 196–7, 227, 253–4

disability, physical, 126

Discipline and Punish, 31–3

disease: addiction as, 163

dishonour, female, 210
disorganization, social, 6, 7
Donnelly, P.G., 257
Doob, Anthony N., and Cheryl Marie Webster, 238
'double standard', 102–5, 111
driving: impaired, 190; risky, 190; youth and, 179–81; *see also* automobiles
dropout rate, 190
drugs: attitudes to users of, 149–50; legal, 136–7; laws and, 165–7; over-the-counter (OTC), 158; prescribed, 158; punk culture and, 46; rave subculture and, 182–3; social role of, 137–43; youth and, 179, 185; *see also* substance abuse
duelling, 208–9
Duncan, Margaret Carlisle, 56
Durkheim, Emile, 4–6, 67, 71, 80, 139, 195

eating disorders, 40, 47–51, 54, 55, 62, 127; families and, 60; health and, 56–8; social consequences of, 58–9
e-crime, 259
education: sex, 186; work ethic and, 178–9
elderly people: fear and, 256; mental illness and, 86–7; violent crime and, 217–18, 220
Elshorst, Hansjorg, 270
employment: street youth and, 194; war and, 290
Erickson, Patricia G., 166–7
Ericson, Richard, and Aaron Doyle, 273
Erikson, Kai, 4
erotophobia, 186
Escobar, Pablo, 284
Ecstasy, 182–3
Evans, Angela Renee, 23
exchange theory, 237
exhibitionism, 117

facts, 'flawed', xv
'fallen woman', 123
families: alcohol and, 140–1; appearance issues and, 59–60; delinquency and, 183–7; dysfunctional, 89; mental illness and, 67, 72–3, 76, 84–9; sexual deviance and, 120–1, 132; structure v. process, 186–7; 'street', 193; suicide and, 94–5
Farley, Melissa, 126
fashion, 41; models, 47
Faulkner, Ellen, 129
fear: crime and, 255–8; violence and, 208
feminism: materialist, 24–30; radical, 24
feminist theory, 3, 24–30, 34; appearance issues and, 38; crime and, 227–8; delinquency and, 197–9; non-violent crime and, 254; pornography and, 116; sexual deviance and, 123–4; sexuality and, 104; substance abuse and, 157–9; war and protest and, 283
Ferraro, Kathleen J., and Angela M. Moe, 29
Fetal Alcohol Syndrome, 161

fetishism, 117
feuding, 210–11
Fischer, Benedikt, et al., 114
Forsyth, Alasdair J.M., 182
Forsyth, Alasdair J.M., and Marina Barnard, 140
Foucault, Michel, 31–3, 34, 38, 56, 82–3, 117, 124
France: school clothing in, 62
fraud, 240, 269
Freedman, David, and David Hemenway, 84
Freud, Sigmund, 117
Friedman, George, and Meredith Friedman, 291
Friedman, George, et al., 73
Friedman, Jonathan, 42
functionalism, 3, 4–10, 33, 62; appearance issues and, 52–3; crime and, 224; delinquency and, 195; mental illness and, 80–1; non-violent crime and, 250–2; sexual deviance and, 120–1; substance abuse and, 154–6; violence and, 207; war and protest and, 279, 281

Gable, Sarah, and Susan Lutz, 50
Gagnon, J.H., and W. Simon, 106
Gaillot, Michel, 182
'gambler's fallacy', 238
gambling: as mental illness, 84
game phase, 20
gangs, 216, 246; female, 198; youth, 191–3
Gaudette, Pamela, et al., 112
'gaze, the', 38, 56
Genain quadruplets, 71
gender, 24; crime and, 254; delinquency and, 173, 175, 179–81, 197–9; homophobia and, 130; mental illness and, 69, 70–1, 71–2; pornography and, 117; sexual assault and, 231; sexual deviance and, 102–5; unsafe sex and, 181–2; violent crime and, 212, 213–14, 220–1, 227–8; war and, 283; *see also* feminist theory; men; women
gendercide, 283
gendering, 24, 25–6, 28–30; *see also* feminist theory
gender-role: sexual deviance and, 102, 123, 125
General Anxiety Disorder, 292
genocide, 286, 289, 290
Germany: genocide in, 289, 290
Giffen, P.J., 147
globalization: crime and, 263
Goffman, Erving, 38, 40, 54–6, 76–7, 85, 260
Gordon, Robert M., 192, 193
Gorman, Elizabeth H., 179
Gottfredson, Michael R., and Travis Hirschi, 10, 224
Greaves, Lorraine, 158–9
Greenberg, David F., 189
'gross indecency', 106
guerilla communities, 285
Guidroz, Kathleen, 110
guns: crime and, 226
Gusfield, Joseph, 149, 157

Hagan, John, *xiii*, 252, 198–9
Hagan, John, and Bill McCarthy, 194
Hagan, John, Bill McCarthy, and Holly Foster, 28
'harm reduction', 164, 166–7
Hartley, Heather, and Tricia Drew, 103
Hasan, Manar, 211
hate crimes, 218, 230
Health Canada, 45, 66, 93, 160
health: appearance issues and, 56–8; delinquency and, 200;
    mental illness and, 89–90; non-violent crime and, 254–5;
    sexual deviance and, 126–7; substance abuse and, 160–2;
    terrorism and war and, 291–2
Hennen, Peter Michael, 125
heroin: abusers of, 152; health and, 162; *see also* substance
    abuse
Hier, Sean, 183
Hill, Reuben, 85
Hirschi, Travis, 6, 176–7, 179
HIV/AIDS, 113, 115, 126–7, 128, 132–3, 186, 228–9, 230
Hoffman, Martin L., 10
Homans, George, 237
Home-Based Intervention Program (HBI), 94
homelessness, 76
homicide, 140, 159–60, 161, 210, 211–12; female, 228; rates of,
    206, 207, 208, 221; risk of, 222
homophobia, 105, 129–31
homosexuality, 105, 106, 118–19; health consequences of,
    126–7; 'identity cohorts' and, 125; social consequences
    of, 127–8; theories about, 121, 122, 125–6; violent crime
    and, 218, 222
homosexual panic, 129
'homosociality', 130–1
honour, 209–10, 216
'honour killings', 210–11
Horwitz, Allan V., 83
hospitals, 76
'hot spots', 217, 218
Hudson, Valerie M., and Andrea M. den Boer, 287
Huebner, Angela J., and Sherry C. Betts, 28
Hulick, Jessica Lee, 118
Hynie, Michaela, and John E. Lydon, 104

Ianni, Francis, 250
identity: collective, 41–2; individual, 41–2
ideology, dominant, 11
Illinois Rape Myth Acceptance Scale, 27
immigrants: violent crime and, 218
incarceration: delinquency and, 201; *see also* prisons
Inglehart, R., 278
institution, 'total', 40, 76–7, 95
International Criminal Court, 289
Internet: crime and, 263–4
intoxication: location and, 138–40; social role of, 137–43
involvement (social bond), 176–7

irrationality: crime and, 237–9
Islamic tradition: clothing and, 62
Israel: military in, 273
Itzin, Catherine, 116

Janus, Mark David, et al., 199
Japan: war crimes and, 283
'johns', 114
Johnson, Mokica Kirkpatrick, and Glen H. Elder, 178–9
Junger, Marianne, Robert West, and Reinier Timman, 180
Juristat, 151, 159, 187, 200, 189, 190, 203, 213, 221, 222, 223,
    243, 256
Juvenile Delinquents Act, 189

Karp, David, 79
Katz, Stephen, and Barbara L. Marshall, 30
Kennedy, Florence, 288–9
Khmer Rouge, 285, 290
Kim, Jae Yop, and Kyu-taik Sung, 84
Kimerling, Rachel, et al., 26
Kinsey, Alfred, 104
Kite, M.E., and B.C. Whitley, Jr, 130
Klein, Jessica Sharon, 210
Klevens, Joanne, et al., 84–5
Koedt, Anne, 194
Korcybski, Alfred, 123
Kordoutis, Panos S., et al., 181, 182

labelling theory, 22–3, 24, 81–2, 122, 225, 227, 254; delin-
    quency and, 196
landmines, 290
Larsson, B., and T. Ivarsson, 73
Latin America: corruption in, 270
Lau, Thomas, 183
League for Socialist Action (LSA), 284–5
Leblanc, Lauraine, 56
Le Bon, Gustav, 278
legalization: drugs and, 165–7
Lemert, Edwin, 22
Levinson, Richard M., and Georgeann Ramsay, 91
Liberal Party, 269–70
Lloyd, Donald Arthur, 67
Lombroso, Cesar, 236, 247
loneliness: youth and, 174–5
love, romantic, 102–5
low-income cutoffs (LICOs), 251
Lowman, J., 109; and L. Fraser, 109
Luckman, Susan, 182
Lupri, Eugen, 221

McAdam, Douglas, Sidney Tarrow, and Charles Tilley, 279
McCorkel, Jill A., 33
McCreary Centre Society, 173
McCubbin, Michael, and Ronald Labonte, 199

McLorg, Penelope, and Diane Taub, 55–6
Mackenzie, William Lyon, 277
Macmillan, Ross, and Rosemary Gartner, 222
mafia, 239, 248–9; black, 250; Puerto Rican, 250
males: delinquency and, 179–81; street crime and, 243–4; *see also* masculinity; men
mania, 68–9, 89–90
Manopaiboon, C., et al., 113
marijuana: abusers of, 151–2; attitude toward, 145, 156; decriminalization of, 14, 137, 165; health and, 162; learning to use, 139, 153; medical use of, 167; mental illness and, 88; *see also* substance abuse
Martin, Paul, 270
Marx, Karl, 282
Marxism, 11, 24
Marza, David, 173
Masamura, W.T., 215
masculinity, 125–6; *see also* males; men
masochism, 117
mass behaviour, 278
Mattachines, 119
Mead, George Herbert, 20, 34
media, mass: appearance issues and, 57, 60–1; crime and, 258; drugs and, 145, 147, 152–3; sexual deviance and, 116; suicide and, 74–5; terrorism and, 293; youth and, 176
'medicalization of deviance', 157
Meisel, Joshua Sager, 19
men: alcohol and, 139–40; eating disorders and, 48, 62; feminist approach and, 24–30; media and, 61–2; sexual deviance and, 102–5; thin-ideal and, 61; violent crime and, 212, 213–14, 221–2; *see also* males; masculinity
mental illness, 66–100; characteristics of, 68–76; communities and subcultures of, 76–80; cost of, 93; diagnosis of, 93–4; fact or fiction, 83–4; health consequences of, 89–90; history of, 67–8; policy and, 93; social consequences of, 90–3; theories about, 80–4; treatment and non-compliance and, 79–80; work and, 92–3
Merton, Robert, 6–7, 12, 33, 39, 52, 155, 237, 251, 270, 279
Milgram, Stanley, 223–4
Miller, Kathleen E., et al., 186
Mills, C. Wright, *xiv*
Milosevic, Slobodan, 289
minorities, ethnic: violent crime and, 218
Money, John, 120
money-laundering, 240, 245
mood disorders, 68–71, 89–90
Moore, Barrington, 277
Moore, Wilbert, 4
morality: self-control and, 8–9
'moral panic', 21–2, 137
Morris, Albert, 249
Moser, Charles, and J.J. Madeson, 118
multiculturalism: appearance issues and, 62
Mulvey, Laura, 56

murder, mass, 210; *see also* homicide
music, techno, 182–3

Netherlands: drug use in, 152, 166
networks, social, 7–8
'neutralization', 254
'New Man', 43–4
Newman, Oscar, 252
nicotine, *see* tobacco
Nieuwbeerta, Paul, et al., 272
Nixon, Kendra, et al., 112
non-compliance: mental illness and, 79–80
non-rationality: crime and, 237–9
non-violent crime, 236–66; cultures and communities of, 246–9; enforcement and, 241; history of, 239–43; policy on, 258–62; theories about, 250–4
normality, 30–1; 'of crime', 4–5; mental illness and, 83–4
'normlessness', 6

obesity, 47–8, 50–1; childhood, 50–1, 53; families and, 60; youth, 53
O'Boyle, Timothy J., 16
opium, 145, 156
organized crime: characteristics of, 244–5; communities of, 192–3, 246–9, 250; consequences of, 254–5; history of, 239; non-violent crime and, 236
Organized Crime Impact Study, 254
Orlie, Melissa A., 125
Ost, Suzanne, 116
O'Toole, Roger, 284–5
Overstreet, Stacy, and Shawnee Braun, 222

Paetsch, Joanne J., and Lorne D. Bertrand, 172–3
'Panopticon', 31, 56, 77
paradigms, 2–3; *see also* conflict theory; feminist theory; functionalism; postmodern approach; symbolic interactionist approach
paraphilias, 101, 105, 117; *see also* sexual deviance
parenting, 9–10, 178; *see also* families
Parsons, Talcott, 5
patronage, 248, 269
Paulicelli, Eugenia, 41
Pedersen, Willy, and Kristinn Hegna, 112
pedophilia, 117–18, 119–20, 127, 128–9
peers: delinquency and, 183–7
Perrow, Charles, 30
'perversion', 105
Piaget, Jean, 8, 19
Picard, Andre, 291
Piccato, Pablo, 209
Pickett, William, et al., 180
pimps, 110, 114
Piquero, Nicole L., et al., 250
place: intoxication and, 138–40

play phase, 20
Pogarksy, Greg, and Alex Piquero, 238
police: e-mail and, 18; mental illness and, 84; powers of, 18; satisfaction with, 243; sexual deviance and, 102, 106, 114
population health perspectives, *xiv*
populism, 277–8
pornography, 115–17, 121
postmodern approach, 3, 30–3, 34; mental illness and, 82–3; sexual deviance and, 124–6
post-traumatic stress disorder (PTSD), 68, 91, 126, 230, 291–2
Poulin, Christiane, and Linda Graham, 181
poverty: crime and, 258–9; 'culture of', 176; delinquency and, 196; mental illness and, 66–7, 68, 93; prostitution and, 113, 122; substance abuse and, 160
Powers, Jane Levine, John Eckenrode, and Barbara Jaklitsch, 200
prisons, 44, 259–62; alternatives to, 262; Foucault on, 31–3; as hot spots, 218; privatized, 262
procuring, 108–9
Prohibition, 147, 149, 157
propaganda: as truth, 30
prostitution, 105, 106–15; as crime, 131–2; Criminal Code definition, 108–9; health consequences of, 126; international, 113–15; reasons for entering, 112–13; social consequences of, 127; theories about, 120–5
protest: collective, 273–4; communities and cultures of, 284–8; history of, 275–8; theories about, 278–83; violent, 276
Protestant Work Ethic, 177–9
psychology, *xiii*; appearance issues and, 51–2; delinquency and, 194; mental illness and, 80; sexual deviance and, 119–20; substance abuse and, 154; violent crime and, 223–4
punishment, 237–9, 259–62
punk appearance/culture, 40, 45–7, 52, 54, 62; females and, 56; health and, 58
Putnam, Michael Charles, 116

queer theory, 123

Rabkin, J., 93
race: drugs and, 145, 147, 152, 156; riots and, 273–4
rape, 29, 211, 212, 228, 231; war and, 283
'rape myth', 27
rape trauma syndrome, 231
rational choice, 15–19
rationality: crime and, 237–9; role of, 15–19
rave subculture, 46–7, 182–3
rebellion, 39–40, 52–3, 62, 276, 277; theories about, 278–83
Rebellion of 1837, 277
recidivism: delinquency and, 201
recreational programs: delinquency and, 201
red-light district, 107, 109

refugees: sex trade and, 114
reinforcement, 237
Reiss, Albert, 121
rejection, 39
religion: drugs and alcohol, 138–9, 145; values, 177–9
Renner, Michael, 291
reputation, 209
resistance, 272–3
revenge, 210
revolution, 276–8; communities of, 284–5; social consequences of, 288–9
rewards, 237–9
Riel, Louis, 277
riots, 273–4
risky behaviours, 172–205; multiple, 180; types of, 170–81; *see also* delinquency
ritualism, 39
robbery, 212, 218
Robin Hood, 284
Rojek, Dean G., et al., 140
Rokach, Ami, and Felix Neto, 176
Rosenfeld, Dana, 125
Ross, E.A., 249
Rotheram-Borus, Mary Jane, 94–5, 201
Rousseau, Jean-Jacques, 120
routine activities theory, 217, 251–2
Russia: corruption in, 270
Rwanda: genocide in, 286, 289

sadism, 117
sadomasochism, 117, 118
Sampson, Robert J. and John H. Laub, 8
Sato, Akihiko, 157
Scheff, Thomas, 81, 92
schizophrenia, 69–70, 71, 88, 90
Schroeder, Jonathan, 56
Schur, Edwin, 24
Schwartz, Joel, 157
'secondary deviance', 22
self, 19–20; youth and, 173
self-control, 224; morality and, 8–9
self-esteem: youth and, 174
Sennett, Richard, and Jonathan Cobb, 225
sentencing, 238, 259; delinquency and, 202
sex: abstinence from, 188; unsafe, 181–2
sex offenders, 132
sex trade, 105, 107–12
sexual behaviour: youth and, 190–1
sexual deviance, 101–35; categories of, 106; communities and cultures, 118–19; criminal, 117–18, 127; gender and, 102; history of, 105–6; health and social consequences of, 126–9; negative consequences of, 102–5; non-criminal, 117; policy and, 131–3; as term, 105–6; theories about, 119–26

sexuality: female, 103–5; postmodern approaches to, 124–6; teenage, 186

sexually transmitted diseases (STDs), 126; youth and, 186, 188, 190, 200

Shaffer, David, 71

shell shock, 67–8

Shoemaker, Robert B., 209

Silver, Eric, et al., 68

Silverstein, Martin, 32

Simmel, Georg, 21, 42, 43

Simon, Jeffrey, 287

situation: behaviour in, 20–2; definition of, 20

Skinner, B.F., 237

Skocpol, Theda, 276–7

Skog, Ole-Jorgen, 163–4

Snider, Laureen, 263

social bonds: 176–7; 'theory', 6

'social ecology', 5

socialization, 19–20

social incivilities, 257

social integration: fear and, 257–8

'social morphology', 5

social organization: fear and, 257–8

social structure, 2

social support: mental illness and, 77–9

Specialized Emergency Room Care, 94

Stack, Steven, et al., 116

stalking, 213; celebrity, 214

Statistics Canada, 212, 221

Stefani, Paolo, 289

Stein, Judith A., et al., 140–1

stigmatization, 54–6; mental illness and, 81, 91–2, 93

'strain theory', 6–7, 12, 28

strategic culture, 279, 281

Strauss, Murray A., and Denise A. Donnelly, 120

street crime: characteristics of, 243–4; communities of, 246; history of, 240; non-violent crime and, 236; prevalence of, 242–3

stress: family, 86, 87, 89; mental illness and, 84–9

structural functionalism; *see* functionalism

subcultures, 22, 216; delinquency and, 191–4; deviant, 22–4; mental illness and, 76–80; prison, 260; rave, 182–3; theory of, 215–16; violent crime and, 215–17; *see also* cultures

substance abuse, 136–69; communities and cultures of, 152–4; health and, 160–2; history of, 143–50; mental illness and, 86, 90; policy and, 162–5; social consequences of, 159–60; theories of, 154–9; violent crime and, 220; youth and, 190, 203, 200

Successful Negotiation Acting Positively (SNAP), 94–5

Sudan, 286

suicide, 71–6, 80, 89–90, 97; families and, 94–5; media and, 74–5

'suitable targets', 217

Sullivan, Thomas J., 275

sumptuary laws, 42

surgery, plastic or cosmetic, 58

Sutherland, Edwin H., 23, 196–7, 240, 249, 253

Svensson, Robert, 197–8

Swora, Maria Gabrielle, 162

Sydie, R.A., 25

Sykes, Gresham M., and David Matza, 254

symbolic interactionist (SI) approach, 3, 19–24, 34; appearance issues and, 54; crime and, 225, 227; delinquency and, 196–7; mental illness and, 81–2; non-violent crime and, 253–4; sexual deviance and, 122–3; substance abuse and, 156–7; violence and, 207; war and protest and, 282–3

Takahasi, Melanie, and Tim Olaveson, 183

Tarde, Gabriel, 236–7

tattooing, 44–5, 52–3, 58

technology, crime and, 262–3

temperance, 145, 147

terrorism, 267, 275–6; communities of, 287–8; media and, 293; state-sponsored, 287; trauma and, 292

thin-ideal image, 61

thinness, 47–8, 49

Thomas, George, et al., 186

Thombs, Dennis L., Scott Olds, and Jennifer Ray-Tomasek, 184

Thrasher, Frederick, 191, 192

'three C's', 2–4

Tilley, Charles, 278

tobacco, 141–3, 148, 149, 187; abusers of, 150; health and, 161–2; marketing of, 159; women and, 158–9; *see also* substance abuse

Tomaszewski, E. Andreas, 249

Toronto Morality Department, 106

Transparency International (TI), 270

treason, 267, 273

Tretter, F., 166

tribalism: rave subculture as, 182–3

Trocme, Nico, 220

truth-finding: problem of, 26

Turbin, Carole, 43

12-Step approach, 163

'Unibomber', 276

uniforms, 40, 41

United States: military in, 273, 281–2, 288, 290; riots in, 273–4; substance abuse and, 137, 147, 152, 157, 165

Upchurch, Dawn M., 186

Vander Ven, Thomas M. and Marikay Vander Ven, 29

Veblen, Thorstein, 42

vendetta, 210

victimization, 14–15, 26–8, 228–31; gender and, 26–8, 29–30; mental illness and, 90–1; patterns of, 217–18; problem of, 26

violence: alcohol and, 139–40; community, 222; definition, 206; family, 219–23; forms of, 207; girls and, 197; legitimate use of, 207–8; mental illness and, 84–5, 91; partner, 221–2; political, 289; rationalizations for, 227; sexual deviance and, 110, 112, 129, 130; 'subculture of', 216; substance abuse and, 159–60; youth and, 191, 200
violent crime, 206–35; communities and subcultures of, 215–17; defining, 211; health consequences of, 228–31; history of, 208–11; policy and, 231–2; predicting, 218; social consequences of, 231; theories about, 223–8; types of, 211–13
'violent predators', 215
von Schriltz, Karl, 33
voyeurism, 117
'vulnerability', 257

Walzer, Michael, 278
war(s), 267, 269; causes of, 275; concept of, 282–3; environment and, 290; history of, 275–8; social consequences of, 288–90; theories about, 278–83
'war on drugs', 147, 165
war resisters, 273
'war system', 275
Watson, John, 237
Weber, Max, 59, 177–8
Websdale, Neil, 84
'Werther Effect', 74–5
West, Candace, and Don H. Zimmerman, 102
West, W. Gordon, 193
White, Patrick, 126
Whitebrook, Joel, 124

Whyte, William Foote, 192, 195, 246
Wild, T. Cameron, 140
Williams, Linda, 115
Williams, S.P., et al., 182
Wilson, Brian S., 182
Wilson, J.Q., and G.L. Keeling, 252
Winston, Diane, 40
Witteman, P., 291
Wojcicki, Janet Maia, 113; and Josephine Malala, 125
Wolfgang, Marvin, and F. Ferracuti, 216–17
women, 24–30; body ideal and, 56; eating disorders and, 47–50, 62; fear and, 256; media and, 61; mental illness and, 92; sexual deviance and, 102–5; smoking and, 187; as soldiers, 283; substance abuse and, 145, 157–9, 161; violent crime and, 212, 213–14, 217, 221–2
work ethic, 177–9
World Health Organization, 71, 83, 93

Yatkin, U.S., and S. Labban, 292
Yep, G.A., 133
Young Offfenders Act (YOA), 187, 189, 202
youth: Aboriginal, 203; appearance issues and, 41–2, 45, 62; risky behaviours of, 172–205; runaway, 199–200; school and, 190; 'straightedge', 174; street, 193–4, 199–200; substance abuse and, 141–4, 149, 162; violent crime and, 214–15, 216, 217, 218; see also children; delinquency
Youth Criminal Justice Act (YCJA), 189, 201–2
Yugoslavia: genocide in, 289–9

Zimbardo, Philip, 223
Zimmerman, E., 276